Praise for Michael Hartl's Books and Videos on Ruby on Rails

"My former company (CD Baby) was one of the first to loudly switch to Ruby on Rails, and then even more loudly switch back to PHP (Google me to read about the drama). This book by Michael Hartl came so highly recommended that I had to try it, and the *Ruby on Rails*™ *Tutorial* is what I used to switch back to Rails again."

> —From the Foreword by Derek Sivers (sivers.org)
> Formerly: founder of CD Baby
> Currently: founder of Thoughts Ltd.

"Michael Hartl's Rails Tutorial book is the #1 (and only, in my opinion) place to start when it comes to books about learning Rails. . . . It's an amazing piece of work and, unusually, walks you through building a Rails app from start to finish with testing. If you want to read just one book and feel like a Rails master by the end of it, pick the *Ruby on Rails*™ *Tutorial*."

> —Peter Cooper, editor, Ruby Inside

"For the self-motivated reader who responds well to the 'learn by doing' method and is prepared to put in the effort, then this comes highly recommended."

> —Ian Elliot, reviewer, I Programmer

"*Ruby on Rails*™ *Tutorial* is a lot of work but if you're careful and patient, you'll learn a lot."

> —Jason Shen, tech entrepreneur, blogger at The Art of Ass-Kicking

"Michael Hartl's *Ruby on Rails*™ *Tutorial* seamlessly taught me about not only Ruby on Rails, but also the underlying Ruby language, HTML, CSS, a bit of JavaScript, and even some SQL—but most importantly it showed me how to build a web application (Twitter) in a short amount of time."

> —Mattan Griffel, co-founder & CEO of One Month

"Although I'm a Python/Django developer by trade, I can't stress enough how much this book has helped me. As an undergraduate, completely detached from industry, this book showed me how to use version control, how to write tests, and, most importantly—despite the steep learning curve for setting up and getting stuff running—how the end-result of perseverance is extremely gratifying. It made me fall in love with technology all over again. This is the book I direct all my friends to who want to start learning programming/building stuff. Thank you Michael!"

—Prakhar Srivastav, software engineer, Xcite.com, Kuwait

"It doesn't matter what you think you will be developing with in the future or what the framework *du jour* is; if you want to learn how to build something, there is no better place to start than with this tutorial. And for all the 'non-technical' people out there who want to see their ideas come to life, who are considering hiring contractors, paying for a class, or 'founder dating' in the search for a technical co-founder: stop. Take a step back. Forget about your idea for a short while and immerse yourself in this tutorial to learn what it takes to put something together. You and your software-related projects will be better for it."

—Vincent C., entrepreneur and developer

"It has to be the best-written book of its type I've ever seen, and I can't recommend it enough."

—Daniel Hollands, administrator of Birmingham.IO

"For those wanting to learn Ruby on Rails, Hartl's *Ruby on Rails*™ *Tutorial* is (in my opinion) the best way to do it."

—David Young, software developer and author at deepinthecode.com

"This is a great tutorial for a lot of reasons, because aside from just teaching Rails, Hartl is also teaching good development practices."

—Michael Denomy, full-stack web developer

"Without a doubt, the best way I learned Ruby on Rails was by building an actual working app. I used Michael Hartl's *Ruby on Rails*™ *Tutorial*, which showed me how to get a very basic Twitter-like app up and running from scratch. I cannot recommend this tutorial enough; getting something up and going fast was key; it beats memorization by a mile."

—James Fend, serial entrepreneur, JamesFend.com

"The book gives you the theory and practice, while the videos focus on showing you in person how it's done. Highly recommended combo."

—Antonio Cangiano, software engineer, IBM

"The author is clearly an expert at the Ruby language and the Rails framework, but more than that, he is a working software engineer who introduces best practices throughout the text."

—Greg Charles, senior software developer, Fairway Technologies

"Overall, [Hartl's] video tutorials should be a great resource for anyone new to Rails."

—Michael Morin, ruby.about.com

"Hands-down, I would recommend this book to anyone wanting to get into Ruby on Rails development."

—Michael Crump, Microsoft MVP

RUBY ON RAILS™ TUTORIAL

Third Edition

RUBY ON RAILS™ TUTORIAL

Learn Web Development with Rails

Third Edition

Michael Hartl

✦✦Addison-Wesley

New York • Boston • Indianapolis • San Francisco
Toronto • Montreal • London • Munich • Paris • Madrid
Capetown • Sydney • Tokyo • Singapore • Mexico City

Library of Congress Cataloging-in-Publication Data

Hartl, Michael, author.
  [Ruby on rails 3 tutorial]
  Ruby on rails tutorial : learn web development with rails / Michael Hartl.—Third edition.
    pages   cm
  Includes index.
  ISBN 978-0-13-407770-3 (pbk. : alk. paper)—ISBN 0-13-407770-9 (pbk. : alk. paper)
  1. Ruby on rails (Electronic resource) 2. Web site development.
  3. Ruby (Computer program language) I. Title.
  TK5105.8885.R83H37 2015
  006.7—dc23

                                                              2014049130

ISBN 13: 978-0-13-407770-3
ISBN 10: 0-13-407770-9
Text printed in the United States on recycled paper at Edwards Brothers Malloy in Ann Arbor, Michigan.
First printing, April 2015

Editor-in-Chief
Mark L. Taub

Acquisitions Editor
Debra Williams Cauley

Managing Editor
John Fuller

Full-Service Production Manager
Julie B. Nahil

Copy Editor
Jill E. Hobbs

Indexer
Richard Evans

Proofreader
Andrea Fox

Reviewer
Will Sommers

Assistant Editor
Kim Boedigheimer

Cover Designer
Chuti Prasertsith

Compositor
LaurelTech

Contents

Foreword to the First Edition

My former company (CD Baby) was one of the first to loudly switch to Ruby on Rails, and then even more loudly switch back to PHP (Google me to read about the drama). This book by Michael Hartl came so highly recommended that I had to try it, and the *Ruby on Rails*™ *Tutorial* is what I used to switch back to Rails again.

Though I've worked my way through many Rails books, this is the one that finally made me "get" it. Everything is done very much "the Rails way"—a way that felt very unnatural to me before, but now after doing this book finally feels natural. This is also the only Rails book that does test-driven development the entire time, an approach highly recommended by the experts but which has never been so clearly demonstrated before. Finally, by including Git, GitHub, and Heroku in the demo examples, the author really gives you a feel for what it's like to do a real-world project. The tutorial's code examples are not in isolation.

The linear narrative is such a great format. Personally, I powered through the *Rails Tutorial* in three long days,* doing all the examples and challenges at the end of each chapter. Do it from start to finish, without jumping around, and you'll get the ultimate benefit.

Enjoy!

—Derek Sivers (sivers.org)
Founder, CD Baby

---

* [Author note:] This is not typical! Getting through the entire book usually takes *much* longer than three days.

Foreword to the Third Edition

Rails is now ten years old and adoption shows no sign of slowing down. Along with the perpetual growth, we've seen a paradoxical tragedy unfolding. According to many people, Rails is now one of the hardest tech stacks for beginners to adopt. The complexity of choices to make when starting out is very high and there are ten years of blog posts and books out there, most of which are obsolete and broken to some degree or another. The supreme irony is that getting started with Rails today involves a lot of configuration, perhaps not of Rails itself, but of the myriad libraries that are recommended for use with it. In case you've forgotten, or weren't paying attention in 2005 when Rails debuted, the main goal was to achieve convention over configuration.

To some extent, we've replicated the Java web beast that we once fought hard to slay. Argh.

Don't get too depressed though, because that would be missing the point. The good news is that once you're past the daunting learning curve, Rails remains one of the most powerful and efficient stacks available for building API backends and content-driven websites.

Now maybe you're considering using this book to kick off your journey up the Rails learning curve. Trust me, it's the right choice. I've known Michael Hartl for almost ten years now and he is a highly intelligent man. Just look for his credentials elsewhere in the book and you'll see what I mean. But never mind the prestigious degrees, the approach he has adopted for this latest edition of our best-selling *Ruby on Rails*™ *Tutorial* proves just how smart he is. Instead of doubling down on the opinionated approach (like another series author I know, ahem), he's gone in the opposite direction! By getting less opinionated, he has lowered the barrier for Rails newcomers in significant ways.

First of all, he dispenses with any sort of local installation or configuration. He also eschews complex configuration options (like Spork and RubyTest), which are likely to trip up novices. All code examples run in a standardized cloud-based environment accessible via a simple web browser.

Second, he throws out tons of content from the previous edition and embraces the Rails "default stack," including its built-in MiniTest testing framework. The resulting elimination of many external dependencies (RSpec, Cucumber, Capybara, Factory Girl) makes the Rails learning curve quite a bit easier to climb, at the expense of having to rewrite big swaths of the book.

Over the years, in no small part due to his work on this book franchise, Michael has become a master of writing training materials grounded in practical, useful knowledge. And as in the past, this edition includes basics of vital tools such as Git and GitHub. Testing is front and center, which most would agree is the proper emphasis for beginners. Michael's well-polished examples always utilize small, bite-sized pieces of code—simple enough to understand and novel enough to be challenging. By the time you finish the book and are playing around with your very own little Twitter clone, you're sure to possess a deeper, more flexible knowledge of Rails. Most importantly, you'll have a foundation flexible enough to get you coding up nearly any type of web application.

Godspeed!

—Obie Fernandez,
Series Editor

Acknowledgments

The *Ruby on Rails™ Tutorial* owes a lot to my previous Rails book, *RailsSpace*, and hence to my coauthor Aurelius Prochazka. I'd like to thank Aure both for the work he did on that book and for his support of this one. I'd also like to thank Debra Williams Cauley, my editor on both *RailsSpace* and the *Ruby on Rails™ Tutorial*; as long as she keeps taking me to baseball games, I'll keep writing books for her.

I'd like to acknowledge a long list of Rubyists who have taught and inspired me over the years: David Heinemeier Hansson, Yehuda Katz, Carl Lerche, Jeremy Kemper, Xavier Noria, Ryan Bates, Geoffrey Grosenbach, Peter Cooper, Matt Aimonetti, Mark Bates, Gregg Pollack, Wayne E. Seguin, Amy Hoy, Dave Chelimsky, Pat Maddox, Tom Preston-Werner, Chris Wanstrath, Chad Fowler, Josh Susser, Obie Fernandez, Ian McFarland, Steven Bristol, Pratik Naik, Sarah Mei, Sarah Allen, Wolfram Arnold, Alex Chaffee, Giles Bowkett, Evan Dorn, Long Nguyen, James Lindenbaum, Adam Wiggins, Tikhon Bernstam, Ron Evans, Wyatt Greene, Miles Forrest, the good people at Pivotal Labs, the Heroku gang, the thoughtbot guys, and the GitHub crew. Finally, many, many readers—far too many to list—have contributed a huge number of bug reports and suggestions during the writing of this book, and I gratefully acknowledge their help in making it as good as it can be.

About the Author

Michael Hartl is the author of the *Ruby on Rails*™ *Tutorial*, one of the leading introductions to web development, and is a cofounder of the Softcover self-publishing platform. His prior experience includes writing and developing *RailsSpace*, an extremely obsolete Rails tutorial book, and developing Insoshi, a once-popular and now-obsolete social networking platform in Ruby on Rails. In 2011, Michael received a Ruby Hero Award for his contributions to the Ruby community. He is a graduate of Harvard College, has a Ph.D. in Physics from Caltech, and is an alumnus of the Y Combinator entrepreneur program.

CHAPTER 1

From Zero to Deploy

Welcome to *Ruby on Rails*™ *Tutorial: Learn Web Development with Rails*. The purpose of this book is to teach you how to develop custom web applications, and our tool of choice is the popular Ruby on Rails web framework. If you are new to the subject, the *Ruby on Rails*™ *Tutorial* will give you a thorough introduction to web application development, including a basic grounding in Ruby, Rails, HTML and CSS, databases, version control, testing, and deployment—sufficient to launch you on a career as a web developer or technology entrepreneur. On the other hand, if you already know web development, this book will quickly teach you the essentials of the Rails framework, including MVC and REST, generators, migrations, routing, and embedded Ruby. In either case, when you finish the *Ruby on Rails*™ *Tutorial* you will be in a position to benefit from the many more advanced books, blogs, and screencasts that are part of the thriving programming educational ecosystem.[1]

The *Ruby on Rails*™ *Tutorial* takes an integrated approach to web development by building three example applications of increasing sophistication, starting with a minimal *hello* app (Section 1.3), a slightly more capable *toy* app (Chapter 2), and a real *sample* app (Chapter 3 through Chapter 12). As implied by their generic names, the applications developed in the *Ruby on Rails*™ *Tutorial* are not specific to any particular kind of website; although the final sample application will bear more than a passing resemblance to a certain popular social microblogging site (a site that, coincidentally, was also originally written in Rails), the emphasis throughout the tutorial is on general principles, so you

---

1. The most up-to-date version of the *Ruby on Rails*™ *Tutorial* can be found on the book's website at http://www.railstutorial.org/. If you are reading this book offline, be sure to check the online version of the Rails Tutorial book at http://www.railstutorial.org/book for the latest updates.

will have a solid foundation no matter which kinds of web applications you want to build.

One common question is how much background is necessary to learn web development using the *Ruby on Rails*™ *Tutorial*. As discussed in more depth in Section 1.1.1, web development is a challenging subject, especially for complete beginners. Although the tutorial was originally designed for readers with some prior programming or web development experience, in fact it has found a significant audience among beginning developers. In acknowledgment of this, the third edition of the *Rails Tutorial* has taken several important steps toward lowering the barrier to getting started with Rails (Box 1.1).

Box 1.1 Lowering the Barrier

This third edition of the *Ruby on Rails*™ *Tutorial* aims to lower the barrier to getting started with Rails in a number of ways:

- Use of a standard development environment in the cloud (Section 1.2), which sidesteps many of the problems associated with installing and configuring a new system

- Use of the Rails "default stack," including the built-in MiniTest testing framework

- Elimination of many external dependencies (RSpec, Cucumber, Capybara, Factory Girl)

- A lighter-weight and more flexible approach to testing

- Deferral or elimination of more complex configuration options (Spork, RubyTest)

- Less emphasis on features specific to any given version of Rails, with greater emphasis on general principles of web development

It is my hope that these changes will make the third edition of the *Ruby on Rails*™ *Tutorial* accessible to an even broader audience than previous versions.

In this first chapter, we'll get started with Ruby on Rails by installing all the necessary software and by setting up our development environment (Section 1.2). We'll then create our first Rails application, called `hello_app`. The *Rails Tutorial* emphasizes good software development practices, so immediately after creating our fresh new Rails project we'll put it under version control with Git (Section 1.4). And, believe it or not, in this chapter we'll even put our first app on the wider web by *deploying* it to production (Section 1.5).

In Chapter 2, we'll make a second project, whose purpose is to demonstrate the basic workings of a Rails application. To get up and running quickly, we'll build this *toy app* (called `toy_app`) by using scaffolding (Box 1.2) to generate the code; because this code is both ugly and complex, Chapter 2 will focus on interacting with the toy app through its *URIs* (often called *URLs*)[2] using a web browser.

The rest of the tutorial focuses on developing a single large *real sample application* (called `sample_app`), writing all the code from scratch. We'll develop the sample app using a combination of *mockups*, *test-driven development* (TDD), and *integration tests*. We'll get started in Chapter 3 by creating static pages and then add a little dynamic content. We'll take a quick detour in Chapter 4 to learn a little about the Ruby language underlying Rails. Then, in Chapter 5 through Chapter 10, we'll complete the foundation for the sample application by making a site layout, a user data model, and a full registration and authentication system (including account activation and password resets). Finally, in Chapter 11 and Chapter 12 we'll add microblogging and social features to create a working example site.

Box 1.2 Scaffolding: Quicker, Easier, More Seductive

From the beginning, Rails has benefited from a palpable sense of excitement, starting with the famous 15-minute weblog video by Rails creator David Heinemeier Hansson. That video and its successors are a great way to get a taste of Rails' power, and I recommend watching them. But be warned: They accomplish their amazing 15-minute feats using a feature called *scaffolding*, which relies heavily on *generated code*, magically created by the Rails `generate scaffold` command.

When writing a Ruby on Rails tutorial, it is tempting to rely on the scaffolding approach—it's quicker, easier, more seductive. But the complexity and sheer amount of code in the scaffolding can be utterly overwhelming to a beginning Rails developer; you may be able to use it, but you probably won't understand it. Following the scaffolding approach risks turning you into a virtuoso script generator with little (and brittle) actual knowledge of Rails.

---

2. *URI* stands for Uniform Resource Identifier, while the slightly less general *URL* stands for Uniform Resource Locator. In practice, the URL is usually equivalent to "the thing you see in the address bar of your browser."

In the *Ruby on Rails*™ *Tutorial*, we'll take the (nearly) polar opposite approach: Although Chapter 2 will develop a small toy app using scaffolding, the core of the *Rails Tutorial* is the sample app, which we'll start writing in Chapter 3. At each stage of developing the sample application, we will write *small, bite-sized* pieces of code—simple enough to understand, yet novel enough to be challenging. The cumulative effect will be a deeper, more flexible knowledge of Rails, giving you a good background for writing nearly any type of web application.

1.1 Introduction

Ruby on Rails (or just "Rails" for short) is a web development framework written in the Ruby programming language. Since its debut in 2004, Ruby on Rails has rapidly become one of the most powerful and popular tools for building dynamic web applications. Rails is used by companies as diverse as Airbnb, Basecamp, Disney, GitHub, Hulu, Kickstarter, Shopify, Twitter, and the Yellow Pages. In addition, many web development shops specialize in Rails, such as ENTP, thoughtbot, Pivotal Labs, Hashrocket, and HappyFunCorp, plus innumerable independent consultants, trainers, and contractors.

What makes Rails so great? First, Ruby on Rails is 100% open-source, available under the permissive MIT License, and as a result it costs nothing to download or use. Rails also owes much of its success to its elegant and compact design; by exploiting the malleability of the underlying Ruby language, Rails effectively creates a domain-specific language for writing web applications. As a consequence, many common web programming tasks—such as generating HTML, making data models, and routing URLs—are easy with Rails, and the resulting application code is concise and readable.

Rails also adapts rapidly to new developments in web technology and framework design. For example, Rails was one of the first frameworks to fully digest and implement the REST architectural style for structuring web applications (which we'll learn about throughout this tutorial). And when other frameworks develop successful new techniques, Rails creator David Heinemeier Hansson and the Rails core team don't hesitate to incorporate their ideas. Perhaps the most dramatic example is the merger of Rails and Merb, a rival Ruby web framework, so that Rails now benefits from Merb's modular design, stable API, and improved performance.

Finally, Rails benefits from an unusually enthusiastic and diverse community. The results include hundreds of open-source contributors, well-attended conferences, a huge number of gems (self-contained solutions to specific problems such as pagination and image upload), a rich variety of informative blogs, and a cornucopia of discussion forums and IRC channels. The large number of Rails programmers also makes it easier to handle the inevitable application errors: The "Google the error message" algorithm nearly always produces a relevant blog post or discussion forum thread.

1.1.1   Prerequisites

There are no formal prerequisites to this book—the *Ruby on Rails*™ *Tutorial* contains integrated tutorials not only for Rails, but also for the underlying Ruby language, the default Rails testing framework (MiniTest), the Unix command line, HTML, CSS, a small amount of JavaScript, and even a little SQL. That's a lot of material to absorb, though, and I generally recommend having some HTML and programming background before starting this tutorial. That said, a surprising number of beginners have used the *Ruby on Rails*™ *Tutorial* to learn web development from scratch, so even if you have limited experience I suggest giving it a try. If you feel overwhelmed, you can always go back and start with one of the resources listed in this section. Another strategy recommended by multiple readers is simply to do the tutorial twice; you may be surprised at how much you learned the first time (and how much easier it is the second time through).

One common question when learning Rails is whether you should learn Ruby first. The answer depends on your personal learning style and how much programming experience you already have. If you prefer to learn everything systematically from the ground up, or if you have never programmed before, then learning Ruby first might work well for you. In this case I recommend *Learn to Program* by Chris Pine and *Beginning Ruby* by Peter Cooper. However, many beginning Rails developers are excited about making *web* applications and would rather not wait to finish a whole book on Ruby before ever writing a single web page. In this case, I recommend following the short interactive tutorial at Try Ruby[3] to get a general overview before starting with the *Rails Tutorial*. If you still find this tutorial too difficult, you might try starting with *Learn Ruby on Rails* by Daniel Kehoe or One Month Rails, both of which are geared more toward complete beginners than the *Ruby on Rails*™ *Tutorial*.

---

3. http://tryruby.org/

At the end of this tutorial, no matter where you started, you should be ready for the many more intermediate-to-advanced Rails resources out there. Here are some I particularly recommend:

- Code School: Good interactive, online programming courses.

- The Turing School of Software & Design: A full-time, 27-week training program in Denver, Colorado, with a $500 discount for Rails Tutorial readers using the code RAILSTUTORIAL500.

- Tealeaf Academy: A good online Rails development bootcamp (includes advanced material).

- Thinkful: An online class at about the level of this tutorial.

- Pragmatic Studio: Online Ruby and Rails courses from Mike and Nicole Clark. Along with *Programming Ruby* author Dave Thomas, Mike taught the first Rails course I took, way back in 2006.

- RailsCasts by Ryan Bates: Excellent (mostly free) Rails screencasts.

- RailsApps: A large variety of detailed topic-specific Rails projects and tutorials.

- Rails Guides: Topical and up-to-date Rails references.

1.1.2 Conventions in This Book

The conventions in this book are mostly self-explanatory. In this section, I'll mention some that may not be.

Many examples in this book use command-line commands. For simplicity, all command-line examples use a Unix-style command-line prompt (a dollar sign), as follows:

```
$ echo "hello, world"
hello, world
```

As mentioned in Section 1.2, I recommend that users of all operating systems (especially Windows) use a cloud development environment (Section 1.2.1), which comes with a built-in Unix (Linux) command line. This is particularly useful because Rails comes with many commands that can be run at the command line. For example, in Section 1.3.2 we'll run a local development web server with the `rails server` command:

```
$ rails server
```

As with the command-line prompt, the *Rails Tutorial* uses the Unix convention for directory separators (i.e., a forward slash `/`). For example, the sample application `production.rb` configuration file appears as follows:

```
config/environments/production.rb
```

This file path should be understood as being relative to the application's root directory, which will vary by system; on the cloud IDE (Section 1.2.1), it looks like this:

```
/home/ubuntu/workspace/sample_app/
```

Thus, the full path to `production.rb` is

```
/home/ubuntu/workspace/sample_app/config/environments/production.rb
```

For brevity, I will typically omit the application path and write just `config/-environments/production.rb`.

The *Rails Tutorial* often shows output from various programs (e.g., shell commands, version control status, Ruby programs). Because of the innumerable small differences between different computer systems, the output you see may not always agree exactly with what is shown in the text, but this is not cause for concern. In addition, some commands may produce errors depending on your system; rather than attempt the Sisyphean task of documenting all such errors in this tutorial, I will delegate to the "Google the error message" algorithm, which among other things is good practice for real-life software development. If you run into any problems while following the tutorial, I suggest consulting the resources listed in the Rails Tutorial help section.[4]

Because the *Rails Tutorial* covers testing of Rails applications, it is often helpful to know if a particular piece of code causes the test suite to fail (indicated by the color red)

---

4. http://www.railstutorial.org/#help

or pass (indicated by the color green). For convenience, code resulting in a failing test is thus indicated with **RED**, while code resulting in a passing test is indicated with **GREEN**.

Each chapter in the tutorial includes exercises, the completion of which is optional but recommended. To keep the main discussion independent of the exercises, the solutions are not generally incorporated into subsequent code listings. In the rare circumstance that an exercise solution is used subsequently, it is explicitly solved in the main text.

Finally, for convenience, the *Ruby on Rails*™ *Tutorial* adopts two conventions designed to make the many code samples easier to understand. First, some code listings include one or more highlighted lines, as seen below:

```
class User < ActiveRecord::Base
  validates :name,  presence: true
  validates :email, presence: true
end
```

Such highlighted lines typically indicate the most important new code in the given sample, and often (though not always) point out the difference between the present code listing and previous listings. Second, for brevity and simplicity many of the book's code listings include vertical dots, as follows:

```
class User < ActiveRecord::Base
  .
  .
  .
  has_secure_password
end
```

These dots represent omitted code and should not be copied literally.

1.2 Up and Running

Even for experienced Rails developers, installing Ruby, Rails, and all the associated supporting software can be an exercise in frustration. Compounding the problem is the multiplicity of environments: different operating systems, version numbers, preferences in text editor and integrated development environment (IDE), and so on. Users who already have a development environment installed on their local machine are welcome to use their preferred setup, but (as mentioned in Box 1.1) new users are encouraged to sidestep such installation and configuration issues by using a *cloud integrated development environment*. The cloud IDE runs inside an ordinary web browser and hence works the same across different platforms, which is especially useful for operating systems (such as Windows) on which Rails development has historically been difficult. If, despite the challenges involved, you would prefer to complete the *Ruby on Rails*™ *Tutorial* using a local development environment, I recommend following the instructions at InstallRails.com.[5]

1.2.1 Development Environment

Considering various idiosyncratic customizations, there are probably as many development environments as there are Rails programmers. To avoid this complexity, the *Ruby on Rails*™ *Tutorial* standardizes on the excellent cloud development environment Cloud9. In particular, for this third edition I am pleased to partner with Cloud9 to offer a development environment specifically tailored to the needs of this tutorial. The resulting Rails Tutorial Cloud9 workspace comes preconfigured with most of the software needed for professional-grade Rails development, including Ruby, RubyGems, and Git. [Indeed, the only big piece of software we'll install separately is Rails itself, and this is intentional (Section 1.2.2).] The cloud IDE also includes the three essential components needed to develop web applications: a text editor, a filesystem navigator, and a command-line terminal (Figure 1.1). Among other features, the cloud IDE text editor supports the "Find in Files" global search that I consider essential to navigating any large Ruby or Rails project.[6] Finally, even if you decide not to use the cloud IDE exclusively in real life (and I certainly recommend learning other tools as well), it provides an excellent introduction to the general capabilities of text editors and other development tools.

Here are the steps for getting started with the cloud development environment:

1. Sign up for a free account at Cloud9.[7]
2. Click on "Go to your Dashboard."

---

5. Even then, Windows users should be warned that the Rails installer recommended by InstallRails is often out of date, and is likely to be incompatible with the present tutorial.

6. For example, to find the definition of a function called `foo`, you can do a global search for "def foo."

7. https://c9.io/web/sign-up/free

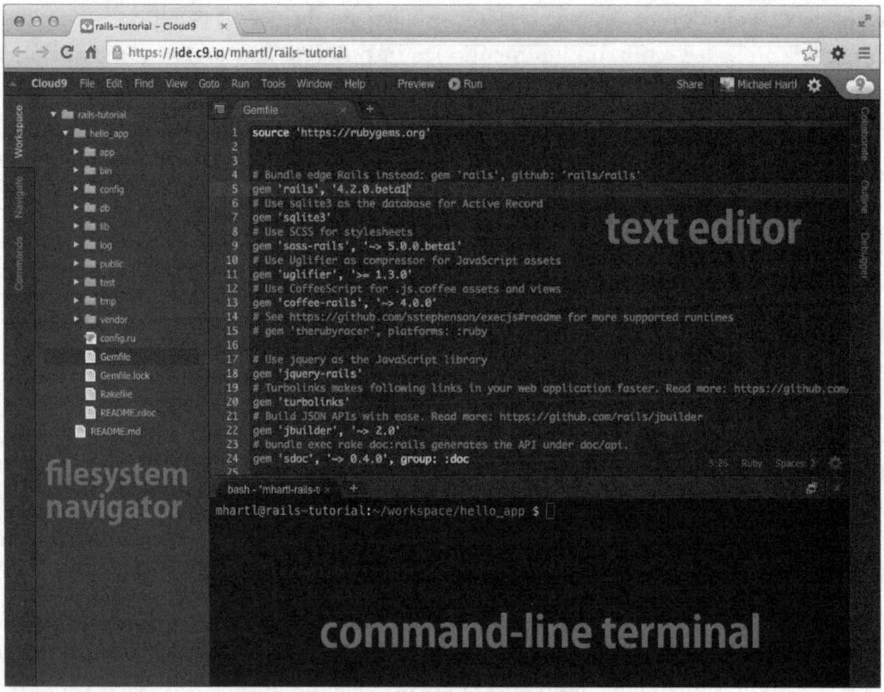

Figure 1.1 The anatomy of the cloud IDE.

3. Select "Create New Workspace."

4. As shown in Figure 1.2, create a workspace called "rails-tutorial" (*not* "rails_tutorial"), set it to "Private to the people I invite," and select the icon for the Rails Tutorial (*not* the icon for Ruby on Rails).

5. Click "Create."

6. After Cloud9 has finished provisioning the workspace, select it and click "Start editing."

Because using two spaces for indentation is a near-universal convention in Ruby, I also recommend changing the editor to use two spaces instead of the default four. As shown in Figure 1.3, you can do this by clicking the gear icon in the upper right corner and then selecting "Code Editor (Ace)" to edit the "Soft Tabs" setting. (Note that this takes effect immediately; you don't need to click a "Save" button.)

Figure 1.2   Creating a new workspace at Cloud9.

1.2.2   Installing Rails

The development environment from Section 1.2.1 includes all the software we need to get started except for Rails itself.[8] To install Rails, we'll use the **gem** command provided by the *RubyGems* package manager, which involves typing the command shown in Listing 1.1 into your command-line terminal. (If you are working on your local system, this means using a regular terminal window; if you are using the cloud IDE, it means using the command-line area shown in Figure 1.1.)

Listing 1.1   Installing Rails with a specific version number.

```
$ gem install rails -v 4.2.0
```

---

8. At present, Cloud9 includes an older version of Rails that is incompatible with the present tutorial, which is one reason why it's so important to install it ourselves.

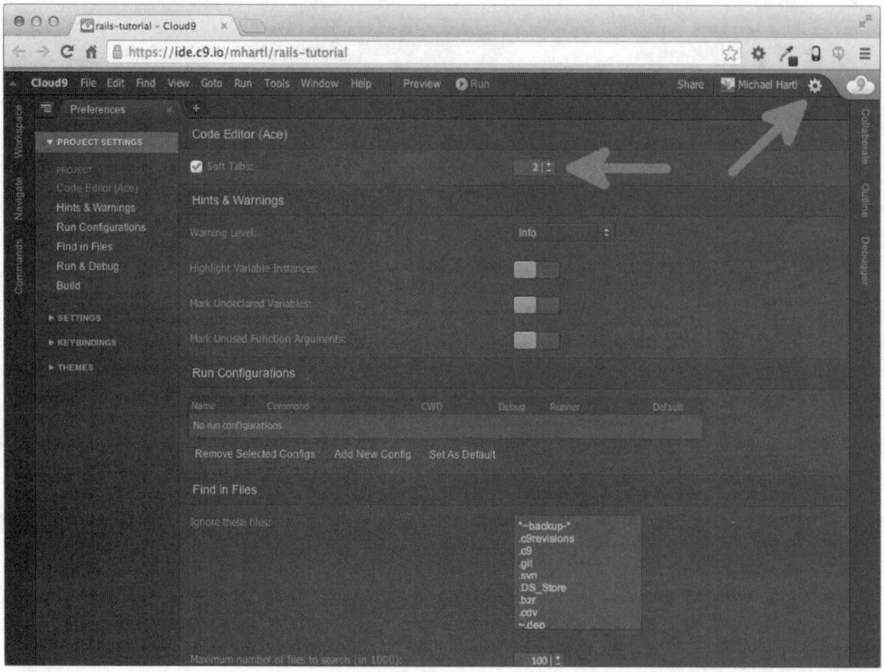

Figure 1.3 Setting Cloud9 to use two spaces for indentation.

Here the **-v** flag ensures that the specified version of Rails gets installed, which is important to get results consistent with this tutorial.

1.3 The First Application

Following a long tradition in computer programming, our goal for the first application is to write a "hello, world" program. In particular, we will create a simple application that displays the string "hello, world!" on a web page, both on our development environment (Section 1.3.4) and on the live web (Section 1.5).

Virtually all Rails applications start the same way, by running the **rails new** command. This handy command creates a skeleton Rails application in a directory of your choice. To get started, users *not* using the Cloud9 IDE recommended in Section 1.2.1 should make a **workspace** directory for their Rails projects if it doesn't already exist (Listing 1.2) and then change into the directory. (Listing 1.2 uses the

Unix commands `cd` and `mkdir`; see Box 1.3 if you are not already familiar with these commands.)

Listing 1.2 Making a **workspace** directory for Rails projects (unnecessary in the cloud).

```
$ cd                    # Change to the home directory.
$ mkdir workspace       # Make a workspace directory.
$ cd workspace/         # Change into the workspace directory.
```

Box 1.3 A Crash Course on the Unix Command Line

For readers coming from Windows or (to a lesser but still significant extent) Macintosh OS X, the Unix command line may be unfamiliar. Luckily, if you are using the recommended cloud environment, you automatically have access to a Unix (Linux) command line running a standard shell command-line interface known as Bash.

The basic idea of the command line is simple: By issuing short commands, users can perform a large number of operations, such as creating directories (`mkdir`), moving and copying files (`mv` and `cp`), and navigating the filesystem by changing directories (`cd`). Although the command line might seem primitive to users mainly familiar with graphical user interfaces (GUIs), appearances are deceiving: The command line is one of the most powerful tools in the developer's toolbox. Indeed, you will rarely see the desktop of an experienced developer without several open terminal windows running command-line shells.

The general subject is deep, but for the purposes of this tutorial we will need only a few of the most common Unix command-line commands, as summarized in Table 1.1. For a more in-depth treatment of the Unix command line, see *Conquering the Command Line* by Mark Bates (available as a free online version and as ebooks and screencasts).

The next step on both local systems and the cloud IDE is to create the first application using the command in Listing 1.3. Note that Listing 1.3 explicitly includes the Rails version number (`4.2.0`) as part of the command. This ensures that the same version of Rails we installed in Listing 1.1 is used to create the first application's file structure. (If the command in Listing 1.3 returns an error like "Could not find 'railties'," it means you don't have the right version of Rails installed, and you should double-check that you entered the command in Listing 1.1 exactly as written.)

Table 1.1 Some common Unix commands.

Description	Command	Example
list contents	ls	$ ls -l
make directory	mkdir \<dirname\>	$ mkdir workspace
change directory	cd \<dirname\>	$ cd workspace/
cd one directory up		$ cd ..
cd to home directory		$ cd ~ or just $ cd
cd to path including the home dir		$ cd ~/workspace/
move file (rename)	mv \<source\> \<target\>	$ mv README.rdoc README.md
copy file	cp \<source\> \<target\>	$ cp README.rdoc README.md
remove file	rm \<file\>	$ rm README.rdoc
remove empty directory	rmdir \<directory\>	$ rmdir workspace/
remove nonempty directory	rm -rf \<directory\>	$ rm -rf tmp/
concatenate and display file contents	cat \<file\>	$ cat ~/.ssh/id_rsa.pub

Listing 1.3 Running `rails new` (with a specific version number).

```
$ cd ~/workspace
$ rails _4.2.0_ new hello_app
    create
    create  README.rdoc
    create  Rakefile
    create  config.ru
    create  .gitignore
    create  Gemfile
    create  app
    create  app/assets/javascripts/application.js
    create  app/assets/stylesheets/application.css
    create  app/controllers/application_controller.rb
    .
    .
    .
    create  test/test_helper.rb
    create  tmp/cache
    create  tmp/cache/assets
```

```
     create  vendor/assets/javascripts
     create  vendor/assets/javascripts/.keep
     create  vendor/assets/stylesheets
     create  vendor/assets/stylesheets/.keep
        run  bundle install
Fetching gem metadata from https://rubygems.org/..........
Fetching additional metadata from https://rubygems.org/..
Resolving dependencies...
Using rake 10.3.2
Using i18n 0.6.11
.

.

Your bundle is complete!
Use `bundle show [gemname]` to see where a bundled gem is installed.
        run  bundle exec spring binstub --all
* bin/rake: spring inserted
* bin/rails: spring inserted
```

As seen at the end of Listing 1.3, running `rails new` automatically runs the `bundle install` command after the file creation is done. We'll discuss what this means in more detail starting in Section 1.3.1.

Notice how many files and directories the `rails` command creates. This standard directory and file structure (Figure 1.4) is one of the many advantages of Rails; it immediately gets you from zero to a functional (if minimal) application. Moreover, because the structure is common to all Rails apps, you can immediately get your bearings when looking at someone else's code. A summary of the default Rails files appears in Table 1.2; we'll learn about most of these files and directories throughout the rest of this book. In particular, starting in Section 5.2.1 we'll discuss the `app/assets` directory, part of the *asset pipeline* that makes it easier than ever to organize and deploy assets such as cascading style sheets and JavaScript files.

1.3.1 Bundler

After creating a new Rails application, the next step is to use *Bundler* to install and include the gems needed by the app. As noted briefly in Section 1.3, Bundler is run automatically (via `bundle install`) by the `rails` command, but in this section we'll make some changes to the default application gems and run Bundler again. This involves opening the `Gemfile` with a text editor. (With the cloud IDE, you click the arrow in the file navigator to open the sample app directory and double-click the `Gemfile` icon.)

Figure 1.4 The directory structure for a newly created Rails app.

Although the exact version numbers and details may differ slightly, the results should look something like Figure 1.5 and Listing 1.4. (The code in this file is Ruby, but don't worry at this point about the syntax; Chapter 4 will cover Ruby in more depth.) If the files and directories don't appear as shown in Figure 1.5, click on the file navigator's gear icon and select "Refresh File Tree." (As a general rule, you should refresh the file tree anytime files or directories don't appear as expected.)

Listing 1.4 The default **Gemfile** in the **hello_app** directory.

```
source 'https://rubygems.org'


# Bundle edge Rails instead: gem 'rails', github: 'rails/rails'
gem 'rails', '4.2.0'
# Use sqlite3 as the database for Active Record
```

```
gem 'sqlite3'
# Use SCSS for stylesheets
gem 'sass-rails', '~> 5.0.1'
# Use Uglifier as compressor for JavaScript assets
gem 'uglifier', '>= 1.3.0'
# Use CoffeeScript for .js.coffee assets and views
gem 'coffee-rails', '~> 4.0.0'
# See https://github.com/sstephenson/execjs#readme for more supported runtimes
# gem 'therubyracer', platforms: :ruby

# Use jquery as the JavaScript library
gem 'jquery-rails'
# Turbolinks makes following links in your web application faster. Read more:
# https://github.com/rails/turbolinks
gem 'turbolinks'
# Build JSON APIs with ease. Read more: https://github.com/rails/jbuilder
gem 'jbuilder', '~> 2.0'
# bundle exec rake doc:rails generates the API under doc/api.
gem 'sdoc', '~> 0.4.0', group: :doc

# Use ActiveModel has_secure_password
# gem 'bcrypt', '~> 3.1.7'

# Use Puma as the app server
# gem 'puma'

# Use Capistrano for deployment
# gem 'capistrano-rails', group: :development

group :development, :test do
  # Call 'debugger' anywhere in the code to stop execution and get a
  # debugger console
  gem 'byebug'

  # Access an IRB console on exceptions page and /console in development
  gem 'web-console', '~> 2.0.0.beta2'

  # Spring speeds up development by keeping your application running in the
  # background. Read more: https://github.com/rails/spring
  gem 'spring'
end
```

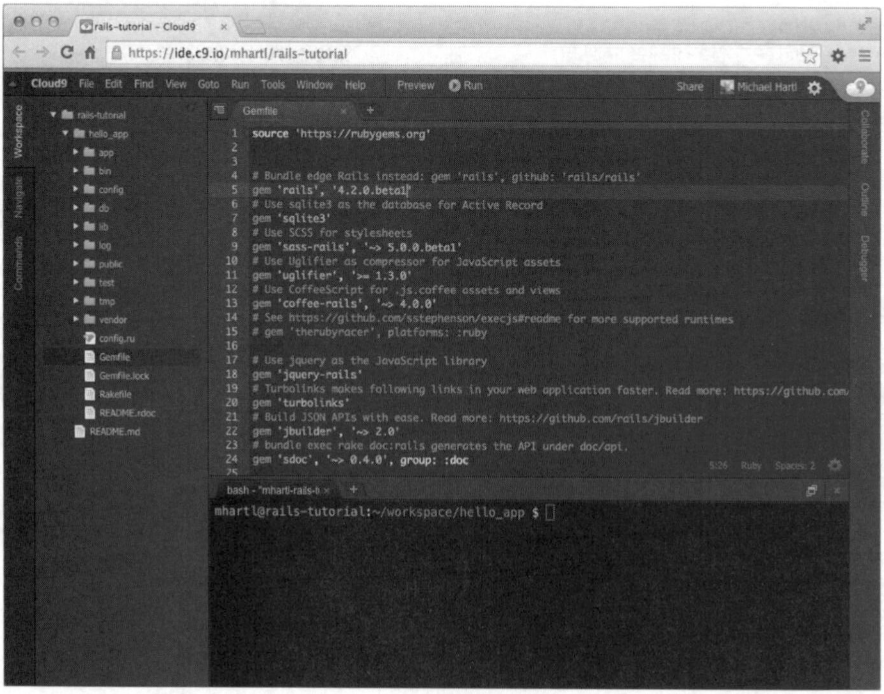

Figure 1.5 The default `Gemfile` open in a text editor.

Many of these lines are commented out with the hash symbol #; they are there to show you some commonly needed gems and to give examples of the Bundler syntax. For now, we won't need any gems other than the defaults.

Unless you specify a version number to the **gem** command, Bundler will automatically install the latest requested version of the gem. This is the case, for example, in the code

```
gem 'sqlite3'
```

There are also two common ways to specify a gem version range, which allows us to exert some control over the version used by Rails. The first looks like this:

```
gem 'uglifier', '>= 1.3.0'
```

Table 1.2 A summary of the default Rails directory structure.

File/Directory	Purpose
`app/`	Core application (app) code, including models, views, controllers, and helpers
`app/assets`	Applications assets such as cascading style sheets (CSS), JavaScript files, and images
`bin/`	Binary executable files
`config/`	Application configuration
`db/`	Database files
`doc/`	Documentation for the application
`lib/`	Library modules
`lib/assets`	Library assets such as cascading style sheets (CSS), JavaScript files, and images
`log/`	Application log files
`public/`	Data accessible to the public (e.g., via web browsers), such as error pages
`bin/rails`	A program for generating code, opening console sessions, or starting a local server
`test/`	Application tests
`tmp/`	Temporary files
`vendor/`	Third-party code such as plugins and gems
`vendor/assets`	Third-party assets such as cascading style sheets (CSS), JavaScript files, and images
`README.rdoc`	A brief description of the application
`Rakefile`	Utility tasks available via the `rake` command
`Gemfile`	Gem requirements for this app
`Gemfile.lock`	A list of gems used to ensure that all copies of the app use the same gem versions
`config.ru`	A configuration file for Rack middleware
`.gitignore`	Patterns for files that should be ignored by Git

This installs the latest version of the `uglifier` gem (which handles file compression for the asset pipeline) as long as it's greater than or equal to version `1.3.0`—even if it's, say, version `7.2`. The second method looks like this:

```
gem 'coffee-rails', '~> 4.0.0'
```

This installs the gem **coffee-rails** as long as it's newer than version **4.0.0** and *not* newer than **4.1**. In other words, the >= notation always installs the latest gem, whereas the ~> 4.0.0 notation installs only updated gems representing minor point releases (e.g., from **4.0.0** to **4.0.1**), but not major point releases (e.g., from **4.0** to **4.1**). Unfortunately, experience shows that even minor point releases can break things, so for the *Ruby on Rails*™ *Tutorial* we'll err on the side of caution by including exact version numbers for all gems. You are welcome to use the most up-to-date version of any gem, including using the ~> construction in the **Gemfile** (which I generally recommend for more advanced users), but be warned that this may cause the tutorial to act unpredictably.

Converting the **Gemfile** in Listing 1.4 to use exact gem versions results in the code shown in Listing 1.5. Note that we've also taken this opportunity to arrange for the sqlite3 gem to be included only in a development or test environment (Section 7.1.1), which prevents potential conflicts with the database used by Heroku (Section 1.5).

Listing 1.5 A **Gemfile** with an explicit version for each Ruby gem.

```
source 'https://rubygems.org'

gem 'rails',              '4.2.0'
gem 'sass-rails',         '5.0.1'
gem 'uglifier',           '2.5.3'
gem 'coffee-rails',       '4.1.0'
gem 'jquery-rails',       '4.0.3'
gem 'turbolinks',         '2.3.0'
gem 'jbuilder',           '2.2.3'
gem 'sdoc',               '0.4.0', group: :doc

group :development, :test do
  gem 'sqlite3',      '1.3.9'
  gem 'byebug',       '3.4.0'
  gem 'web-console', '2.0.0.beta3'
  gem 'spring',       '1.1.3'
end
```

Once you've placed the contents of Listing 1.5 into the application's **Gemfile**, install the gems using **bundle install**:[9]

---

9. As noted in Table 3.1, you can even leave off **install**, as the **bundle** command by itself is an alias for **bundle install**.

```
$ cd hello_app/
$ bundle install
Fetching source index for https://rubygems.org/
 .
 .
 .
```

The **bundle install** command might take a few moments to finish its work, but when it's done our application will be ready to run.

1.3.2 `rails server`

Thanks to running **rails new** in Section 1.3 and **bundle install** in Section 1.3.1, we already have an application we can run—but how? Happily, Rails comes with a command-line program, or *script*, that runs a *local* web server to assist us in developing our application. The exact command depends on the environment you're using: On a local system, you just run **rails server** (Listing 1.6), whereas on Cloud9 you need to supply an additional *IP binding address* and *port number* to tell the Rails server the address it can use to make the application visible to the outside world (Listing 1.7).[10] (Cloud9 uses the special *environment variables* **$IP** and **$PORT**, respectively, to assign the IP address and port number dynamically. If you want to see the values of these variables, type **echo $IP** or **echo $PORT** at the command line.)

Listing 1.6 Running the Rails server on a local machine.

```
$ cd ~/workspace/hello_app/
$ rails server
=> Booting WEBrick
=> Rails application starting on http://localhost:3000
=> Run `rails server -h` for more startup options
=> Ctrl-C to shutdown server
```

Listing 1.7 Running the Rails server on the cloud IDE.

```
$ cd ~/workspace/hello_app/
$ rails server -b $IP -p $PORT
```

---

10. Normally, websites run on port 80, but this usually requires special privileges, so the convention is to use a less restricted higher-numbered port for the development server.

```
=> Booting WEBrick
=> Rails application starting on http://0.0.0.0:8080
=> Run `rails server -h` for more startup options
=> Ctrl-C to shutdown server
```

Whichever option you choose, I recommend running the **rails server** command in a second terminal tab so that you can still issue commands in the first tab, as shown in Figure 1.6 and Figure 1.7. (If you already started a server in your first tab, press Ctrl-C to shut it down.)[11] On a local server, point your browser at the address http://localhost:3000/; on the cloud IDE, go to Share and click on the Application address to open it (Figure 1.8). In either case, the result should look something like Figure 1.9.

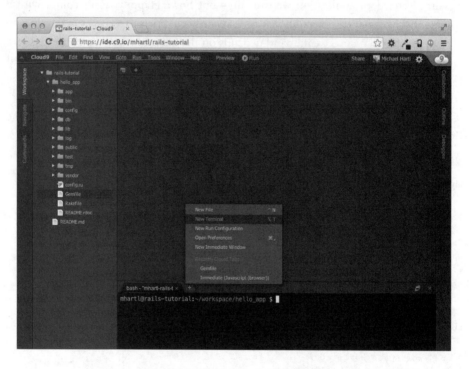

Figure 1.6 Opening a new terminal tab.

---

11. It's really "Ctrl-c"—there's no need to hold down the Shift key to get a capital "C"—but for some reason it's always written as "Ctrl-C."

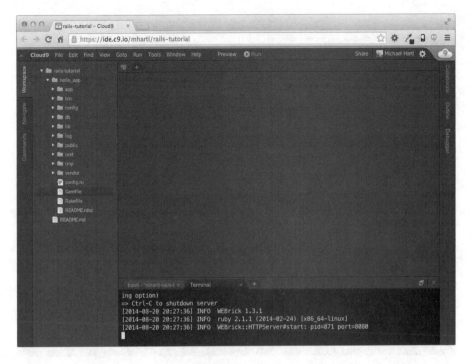

Figure 1.7 Running the Rails server in a separate tab.

To see information about the first application, click on the link "About your application's environment." Although the exact version numbers may differ, the result should look something like Figure 1.10. Of course, we don't need the default Rails page in the long run, but it's nice to see it working for now. We'll remove the default page (and replace it with a custom home page) in Section 1.3.4.

1.3.3 Model–View–Controller

Even at this early stage, it's helpful to get a high-level overview of how Rails applications work (Figure 1.11). You might have noticed that the standard Rails application structure (Figure 1.4) has an application directory called **app/** with three subdirectories: **models**, **views**, and **controllers**. This is a hint that Rails follows the Model–View–Controller (MVC) architectural pattern, which enforces a separation between "domain logic" (also called "business logic") from the input and presentation logic associated with a graphical user interface (GUI). In the case of web applications, the "domain logic" typically

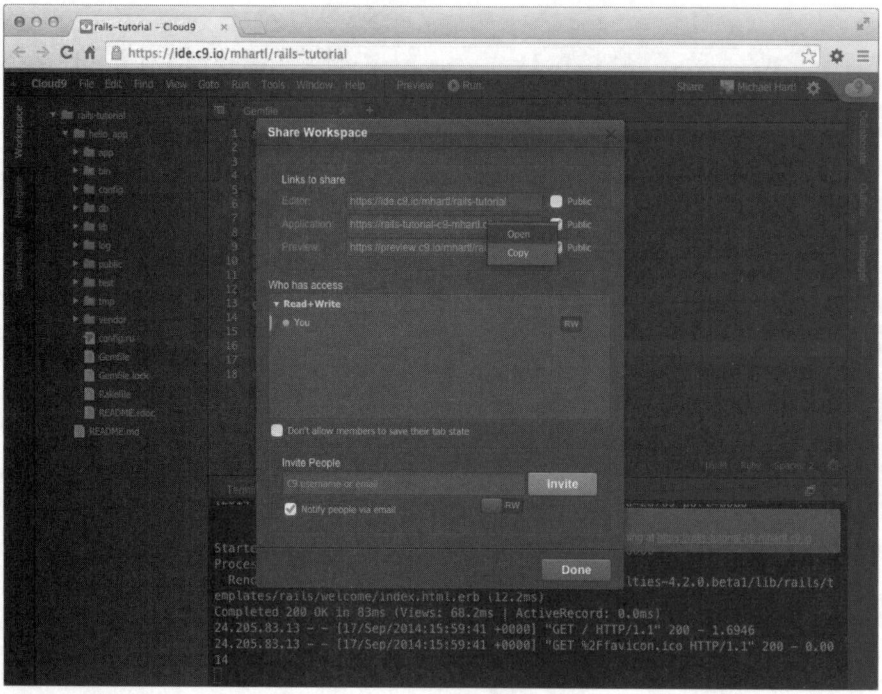

Figure 1.8 Sharing the local server running on the cloud workspace.

consists of data models for things like users, articles, and products, and the GUI is just a web page in a web browser.

When interacting with a Rails application, a browser sends a *request*, which is received by a web server and passed on to a Rails *controller*, which is in charge of what to do next. In some cases, the controller will immediately render a *view*, which is a template that gets converted to HTML and sent back to the browser. More commonly for dynamic sites, the controller interacts with a *model*, which is a Ruby object that represents an element of the site (such as a user) and is in charge of communicating with the database. After invoking the model, the controller then renders the view and returns the complete web page to the browser as HTML.

If this discussion seems a bit abstract right now, worry not; we'll refer back to this section frequently. Section 1.3.4 shows a first tentative application of MVC, while Section 2.2.2 includes a more detailed discussion of MVC in the context of the toy app. Finally, the sample app will use all aspects of MVC; we'll cover controllers and views

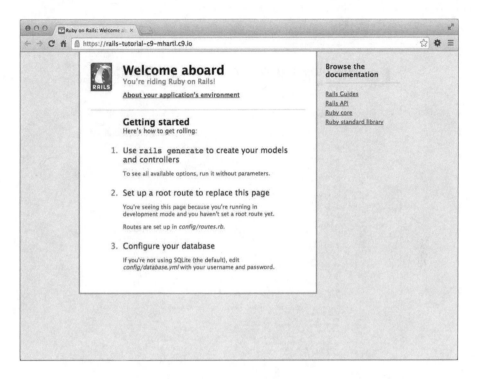

Figure 1.9   The default Rails page served by `rails server`.

starting in Section 3.2, we'll investigate models starting in Section 6.1, and we'll see all three working together in Section 7.1.2.

1.3.4 Hello, World!

As a first application of the MVC framework, we'll make a wafer-thin change to the first app by adding a *controller action* to render the string "hello, world!" (We'll learn more about controller actions starting in Section 2.2.2.) The result will be to replace the default Rails page from Figure 1.9 with the "hello, world" page that is the goal of this section.

As implied by their name, controller actions are defined inside controllers. We'll call our action `hello` and place it in the Application controller. Indeed, at this point the Application controller is the only controller we have, which you can verify by running the command

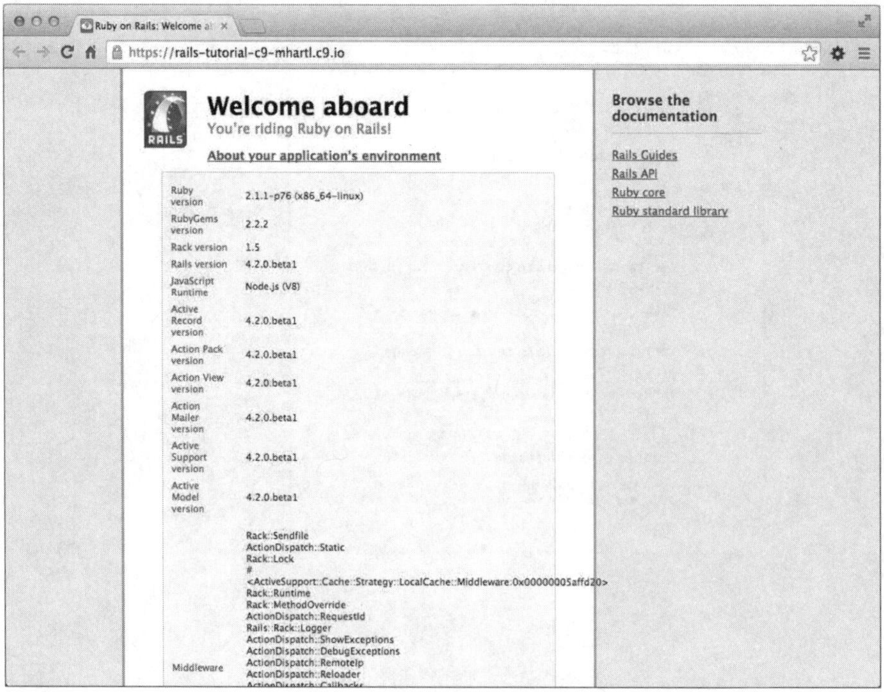

Figure 1.10 The default page with the application's environment.

```
$ ls app/controllers/*_controller.rb
```

to view the current controllers. (We'll start creating our own controllers in Chapter 2.) Listing 1.8 shows the resulting definition of **hello**, which uses the **render** function to return the text "hello, world!" (Don't worry about the Ruby syntax right now; it will be covered in more depth in Chapter 4.)

Listing 1.8 Adding a **hello** action to the Application controller.

app/controllers/application_controller.rb

```
class ApplicationController < ActionController::Base
  # Prevent CSRF attacks by raising an exception.
  # For APIs, you may want to use :null_session instead.
  protect_from_forgery with: :exception
```

```
def hello
    render text: "hello, world!"
  end
end
```

Having defined an action that returns the desired string, we need to tell Rails
to use that action instead of the default page in Figure 1.10. To do this, we'll edit
the Rails *router*, which sits in front of the controller in Figure 1.11 and determines
where to send requests that come in from the browser. (I've omitted the router from
Figure 1.11 for simplicity, but we'll discuss the router in more detail starting in Section 2.2.2.) In particular, we want to change the default page, the *root route*, which
determines the page that is served on the *root URL*. Because it's the URL for an address

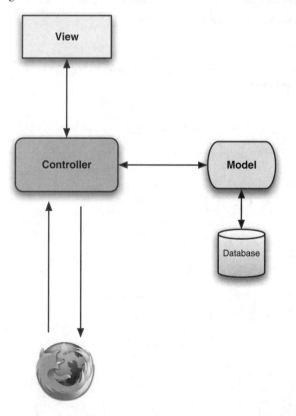

Figure 1.11 A schematic representation of the Model–View–Controller (MVC) architecture.

like http://www.example.com/ (where nothing comes after the final forward slash), the root URL is often referred to as / ("slash") for short.

As seen in Listing 1.9, the Rails routes file (`config/routes.rb`) includes a commented-out line that shows how to structure the root route. Here "welcome" is the controller name and "index" is the action within that controller. To activate the root route, uncomment this line by removing the hash character and then replace it with the code in Listing 1.10, which tells Rails to send the root route to the `hello` action in the Application controller. (As noted in Section 1.1.2, vertical dots indicate omitted code and should not be copied literally.)

Listing 1.9 The default (commented-out) root route.
config/routes.rb

```
Rails.application.routes.draw do
  .
  .
  .
  # You can have the root of your site routed with "root"
  # root 'welcome#index'
  .
  .
  .
end
```

Listing 1.10 Setting the root route.
config/routes.rb

```
Rails.application.routes.draw do
  .
  .
  .
  # You can have the root of your site routed with "root"
  root 'application#hello'
  .
  .
  .
end
```

With the code from Listing 1.8 and Listing 1.10, the root route returns "hello, world!" as required (Figure 1.12).

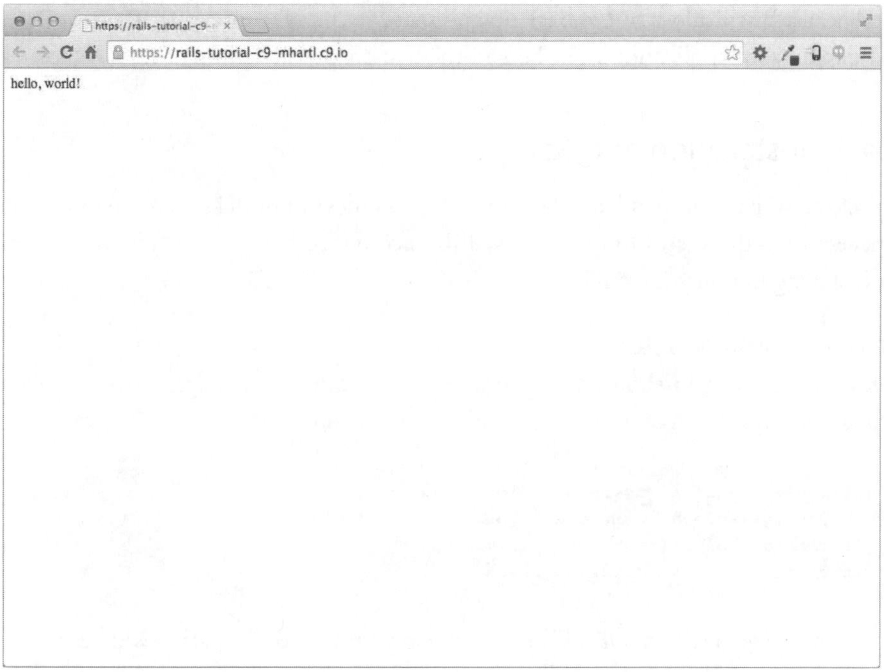

Figure 1.12 Viewing "hello, world!" in the browser.

1.4 Version Control with Git

Now that we have a fresh and working Rails application, we'll take a moment to address a step that, while technically optional, would be viewed by experienced software developers as practically essential: placing our application source code under *version control*. Version control systems allow us to track changes to our project's code, collaborate more easily, and roll back any inadvertent errors (such as accidentally deleting files). Knowing how to use a version control system is a required skill for every professional-grade software developer.

There are many options for version control, but the Rails community has largely standardized on Git, a distributed version control system originally developed by Linus Torvalds to host the Linux kernel. Git is a large subject, and we'll merely scratch the surface in this book, but there are many good free resources online; I especially recommend Bitbucket 101 for a short overview and *Pro Git* by Scott Chacon for a book-length introduction. Putting your source code under version control with Git is *strongly* recommended, not only because it's nearly a universal practice in the Rails world, but also because it will allow you to back up and share your code more easily (Section 1.4.3) and deploy your application right here in the first chapter (Section 1.5).

1.4.1 Installation and Setup

The cloud IDE recommended in Section 1.2.1 includes Git by default, so no installation is necessary in this case. Otherwise, InstallRails.com (Section 1.2) includes instructions for installing Git on your system.

First-Time System Setup

Before using Git, you should perform a set of one-time setup steps. These are *system* setups, meaning you have to do them only once per computer:

```
$ git config --global user.name "Your Name"
$ git config --global user.email your.email@example.com
$ git config --global push.default matching
$ git config --global alias.co checkout
```

Note that the name and email address you use in your Git configuration will be available in any repositories you make public. (Only the first two lines here are strictly necessary. The third line is included only to ensure forward-compatibility with an upcoming release of Git. The optional fourth line is included so that you can use `co` in place of the more verbose `checkout` command. For maximum compatibility with systems that don't have `co` configured, this tutorial will use the full `checkout` command, but in real life I nearly always use `git co`.)

First-Time Repository Setup

Now we come to some steps that are necessary each time you create a new *repository* (sometimes called a *repo* for short). First navigate to the root directory of the first app and initialize a new repository:

```
$ git init
Initialized empty Git repository in /home/ubuntu/workspace/hello_app/.git/
```

The next step is to add all the project files to the repository using `git add -A`:

```
$ git add -A
```

This command adds all the files in the current directory apart from those that match the patterns in a special file called `.gitignore`. The `rails new` command automatically generates a `.gitignore` file appropriate to a Rails project, but you can add more patterns as well.[12]

The added files are initially placed in a *staging area*, which contains pending changes to your project. You can see which files are in the staging area by using the `status` command:

```
$ git status
On branch master

Initial commit

Changes to be committed:
  (use "git rm --cached <file>..." to unstage)

  new file:   .gitignore
  new file:   Gemfile
  new file:   Gemfile.lock
  new file:   README.rdoc
  new file:   Rakefile
  .
  .
  .
```

(The results are long, so I've used vertical dots to indicate omitted output.)

To tell Git you want to keep the changes, use the `commit` command:

```
$ git commit -m "Initialize repository"
[master (root-commit) df0a62f] Initialize repository
 .
 .
 .
```

The `-m` flag lets you add a message for the commit; if you omit `-m`, Git will open the system's default editor and have you enter the message there. (All the examples in this book will use the `-m` flag.)

---

12. Although we'll never need to edit it in the main tutorial, an example of adding a rule to the `.gitignore` file appears in Section 3.7.3, which is part of the optional advanced testing setup in Section 3.7.

Git commits are *local*, meaning they are recorded only on the machine on which the commits occur. We'll see how to push the changes up to a remote repository (using `git push`) in Section 1.4.4.

By the way, you can see a list of your commit messages using the `log` command:

```
$ git log
commit df0a62f3f091e53ffa799309b3e32c27b0b38eb4
Author: Michael Hartl <michael@michaelhartl.com>
Date:   Wed August 20 19:44:43 2014 +0000

    Initialize repository
```

Depending on the length of your repository's log history, you may have to type `q` to quit.

1.4.2 What Are the Benefits of Using Git?

If you've never used version control before, it may not be entirely clear at this point what good it does you, so let me give just one example. Suppose you've made some accidental changes, such as (D'oh!) deleting the critical **app/controllers/** directory.

```
$ ls app/controllers/
application_controller.rb   concerns/
$ rm -rf app/controllers/
$ ls app/controllers/
ls: app/controllers/: No such file or directory
```

Here we're using the Unix `ls` command to list the contents of the **app/controllers/** directory and the `rm` command to remove it (Table 1.1). The `-rf` flag means "recursive force," which recursively removes all files, directories, subdirectories, and so on, without asking for explicit confirmation of each deletion.

Let's check the status to see what changed:

```
$ git status
On branch master
Changed but not updated:
  (use "git add/rm <file>..." to update what will be committed)
  (use "git checkout -- <file>..." to discard changes in working directory)

    deleted:    app/controllers/application_controller.rb

no changes added to commit (use "git add" and/or "git commit -a")
```

We see here that a file has been deleted, but the changes are only on the "working tree"; they haven't been committed yet. This means we can still undo the changes using the `checkout` command with the `-f` flag to force overwriting the current changes:

```
$ git checkout -f
$ git status
# On branch master
nothing to commit (working directory clean)
$ ls app/controllers/
application_controller.rb   concerns/
```

The missing files and directories are back. That's a relief!

1.4.3 Bitbucket

Now that we've put our project under version control with Git, it's time to push our code up to Bitbucket, a site optimized for hosting and sharing Git repositories. (Previous editions of this tutorial used GitHub instead; see Box 1.4 to learn the reasons for the switch.) Putting a copy of your Git repository at Bitbucket serves two purposes: It provides a full backup of your code (including the full history of commits), and it makes any future collaboration much easier.

Box 1.4 GitHub and Bitbucket

By far the two most popular sites for hosting Git repositories are GitHub and Bitbucket. These two services share many similarities: Both sites allow for Git repository hosting and collaboration, and both offer convenient ways to browse and search repositories. The important difference (from the perspective of this tutorial) is that GitHub offers unlimited free repositories (with collaboration) for open-source repositories while charging for private repos, whereas Bitbucket allows unlimited free private repos while charging for more than a certain number of collaborators. Which service you use for a particular repo thus depends on your specific needs.

Previous editions of this book used GitHub because of its emphasis on supporting open-source code, but growing concerns about security have led me to recommend that *all* web application repositories be private by default. The issue is that web application repositories might contain potentially sensitive information such as cryptographic keys and passwords, which could be used to compromise the security of a site running the code. It is possible, of course, to arrange for this information to be handled securely (by having Git ignore it, for example), but this technique is error-prone and requires significant expertise.

As it happens, the sample application created in this tutorial is safe for exposure on the web, but it is dangerous to rely on this fact in general. Thus, to be as secure as possible, we will err on the side of caution and use private repositories by default. Since GitHub charges for private repositories while Bitbucket offers an unlimited number for free, for our purposes Bitbucket is a better fit than GitHub.

Getting started with Bitbucket is simple:

1. Sign up for a Bitbucket account if you don't already have one.
2. Copy your *public key* to your clipboard. As indicated in Listing 1.11, users of the cloud IDE can view their public key using the `cat` command, which can then be selected and copied. If you're using your own system and see no output when running the command in Listing 1.11, follow the instructions on how to install a public key on your Bitbucket account.
3. Add your public key to Bitbucket by clicking on the avatar image in the upper right corner and selecting first "Manage account" and then "SSH keys" (Figure 1.13).

Listing 1.11 Printing the public key using `cat`.

```
$ cat ~/.ssh/id_rsa.pub
```

Once you've added your public key, click on "Create" to create a new repository, as shown in Figure 1.14. When filling in the information for the project, take care to leave the box next to "This is a private repository." checked. After clicking "Create repository," follow the instructions under "Command line > I have an existing project," which should look something like Listing 1.12. (If it doesn't look like Listing 1.12, it might be because the public key didn't get added correctly, in which case I suggest trying that step again.) When pushing up the repository, answer yes if you see the question "Are you sure you want to continue connecting (yes/no)?"

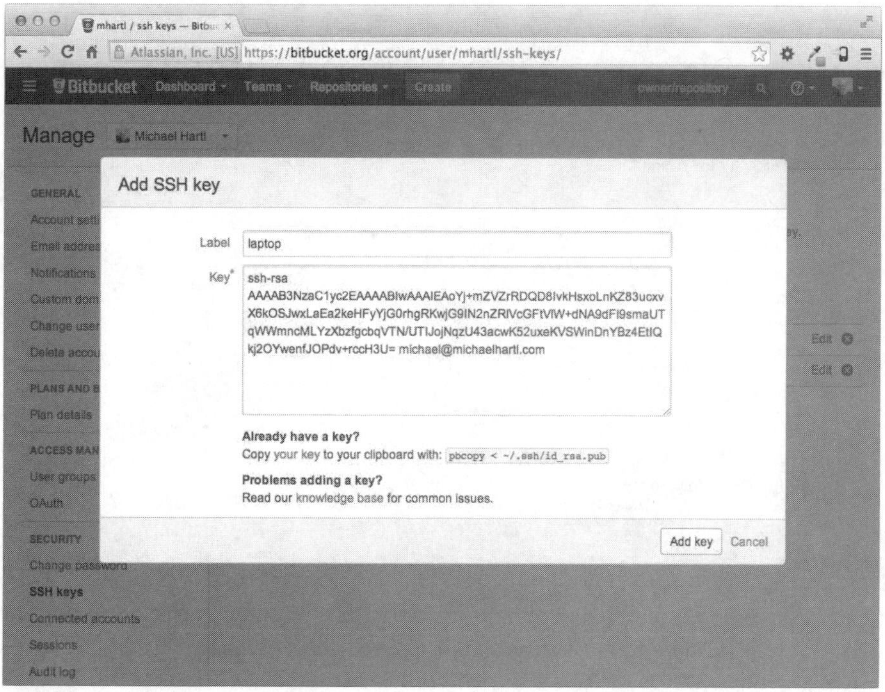

Figure 1.13 Adding the SSH public key.

Listing 1.12 Adding Bitbucket and pushing up the repository.

```
$ git remote add origin git@bitbucket.org:<username>/hello_app.git
$ git push -u origin --all # pushes up the repo and its refs for the first time
```

The commands in Listing 1.12 first tell Git that you want to add Bitbucket as the *origin* for your repository, and then push your repository up to the remote origin. (Don't worry about what the **-u** flag does; if you're curious, do a web search for "git set upstream.") Of course, you should replace <username> with your actual username. For example, the command I ran was

```
$ git remote add origin git@bitbucket.org:mhartl/hello_app.git
```

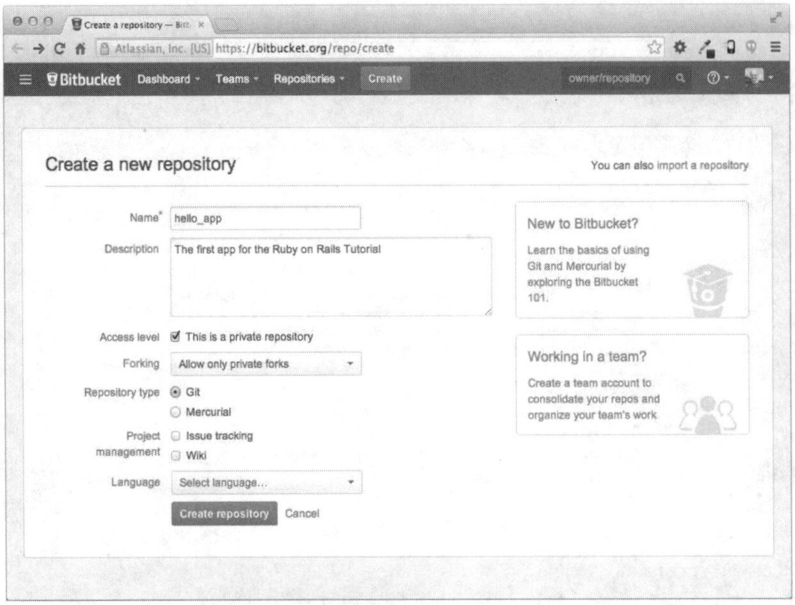

Figure 1.14 Creating the first app repository at Bitbucket.

The result is a page at Bitbucket for the hello_app repository, with file browsing, full commit history, and lots of other goodies (Figure 1.15).

1.4.4 Branch, Edit, Commit, Merge

If you've followed the steps in Section 1.4.3, you might notice that Bitbucket didn't automatically detect the **README.rdoc** file from our repository, instead complaining on the main repository page that there is no README present (Figure 1.16). This is an indication that the **rdoc** format isn't common enough for Bitbucket to support it automatically. Indeed, I and virtually every other developer I know prefer to use *Markdown* instead. In this section, we'll change the **README.rdoc** file to **README.md**, while taking the opportunity to add some Rails Tutorial–specific content to the README file. In the process, we'll see a first example of the branch, edit, commit, merge workflow that I recommend using with Git.[13]

---

13. For a convenient way to visualize Git repositories, take a look at Atlassian's SourceTree app.

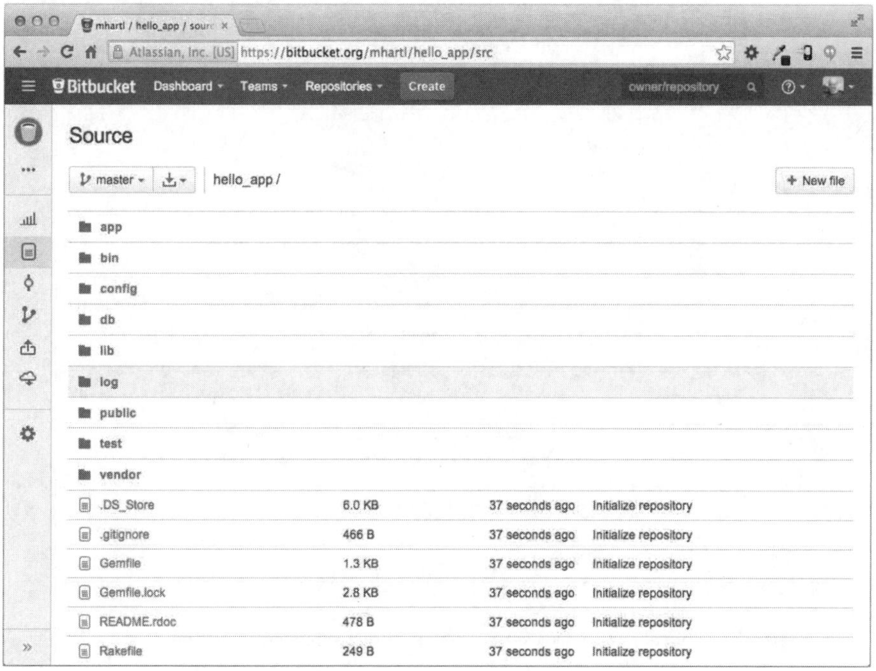

Figure 1.15 A Bitbucket repository page.

Branch

Git is incredibly good at making *branches*, which are effectively copies of a repository where we can make (possibly experimental) changes without modifying the parent files. In most cases, the parent repository is the *master* branch, and we can create a new topic branch by using **checkout** with the **-b** flag:

```
$ git checkout -b modify-README
Switched to a new branch 'modify-README'
$ git branch
  master
* modify-README
```

Here the second command, **git branch**, just lists all the local branches, and the asterisk * identifies which branch we're currently on. Note that **git checkout -b**

Figure 1.16 Bitbucket's message about a missing README.

`modify-README` both creates a new branch and switches to it, as indicated by the asterisk in front of the `modify-README` branch. (If you set up the `co` alias in Section 1.4, you can use `git co -b modify-README` instead.)

The full value of branching becomes clear only when you are working on a project with multiple developers,[14] but branches are helpful even for a single-developer tutorial such as this one. In particular, the master branch is insulated from any changes we make to the topic branch. As a consequence, even if we *really* screw things up, we can always abandon the changes by checking out the master branch and deleting the topic branch. We'll see how to do this at the end of the section.

By the way, for a change as small as this one, I wouldn't normally bother with a new branch—but in the present context it's a prime opportunity to start practicing good habits.

---

14. See the chapter Git Branching in *Pro Git* for details.

Edit

After creating the topic branch, we'll edit it to make it a little more descriptive. I prefer the Markdown markup language to the default RDoc for this purpose. If you use the file extension **.md**, then Bitbucket will automatically format it nicely for you. First we'll use Git's version of the Unix **mv** (move) command to change the name:

```
$ git mv README.rdoc README.md
```

Then we'll fill **README.md** with the contents of Listing 1.13.

Listing 1.13   The new **README** file, **README.md**.

```
# Ruby on Rails Tutorial: "hello, world!"

This is the first application for the
[*Ruby on Rails Tutorial*](http://www.railstutorial.org/)
by [Michael Hartl](http://www.michaelhartl.com/).
```

Commit

With the changes made, we can take a look at the status of our branch:

```
$ git status
On branch modify-README
Changes to be committed:
  (use "git reset HEAD <file>..." to unstage)

  renamed:    README.rdoc -> README.md

Changes not staged for commit:
  (use "git add <file>..." to update what will be committed)
  (use "git checkout -- <file>..." to discard changes in working directory)

  modified:   README.md
```

At this point, we could use **git add -A** as in Section 1.4.1, but **git commit** provides the **-a** flag as a shortcut for the (very common) case of committing all modifications to existing files (or files created using `git mv`, which don't count as new files to Git):

```
$ git commit -a -m "Improve the README file"
2 files changed, 5 insertions(+), 243 deletions(-)
delete mode 100644 README.rdoc
create mode 100644 README.md
```

Be careful about using the `-a` flag improperly; if you have added any new files to the project since the last commit, you still have to tell Git about them using `git add -A` first.

Note that we write the commit message in the *present* tense (and, technically speaking, the imperative mood). Git models commits as a series of patches, and in this context it makes sense to describe what each commit *does*, rather than what it did. Moreover, this usage matches up with the commit messages generated by Git commands themselves. See the article "Shiny new commit styles" for more information.

Merge

Now that we've finished making our changes, we're ready to *merge* the results back into our master branch:

```
$ git checkout master
Switched to branch 'master'
$ git merge modify-README
Updating 34f06b7..2c92bef
Fast forward
README.rdoc    |  243 --------------------------------------------------
README.md      |    5 +
2 files changed, 5 insertions(+), 243 deletions(-)
delete mode 100644 README.rdoc
create mode 100644 README.md
```

Note that the Git output frequently includes things like `34f06b7`, which are related to Git's internal representation of repositories. Your exact results will differ in these details, but otherwise should essentially match the output shown here.

After you've merged in the changes, you can tidy up your branches by deleting the topic branch using `git branch -d` if you're done with it:

```
$ git branch -d modify-README
Deleted branch modify-README (was 2c92bef).
```

This step is optional, and in fact it's quite common to leave the topic branch intact. This way you can switch back and forth between the topic and master branches, merging in changes every time you reach a natural stopping point.

As mentioned earlier, it's also possible to abandon your topic branch changes, in this case with `git branch -D`:

```
# For illustration only; don't do this unless you mess up a branch
$ git checkout -b topic-branch
$ <really screw up the branch>
$ git add -A
$ git commit -a -m "Major screw up"
$ git checkout master
$ git branch -D topic-branch
```

Unlike the `-d` flag, the `-D` flag will delete the branch even though we haven't merged in the changes.

Push

Now that we've updated the **README**, we can push the changes up to Bitbucket to see the result. Since we have already done one push (Section 1.4.3), on most systems we can omit **origin master** and simply run `git push`:

```
$ git push
```

As promised in Section 1.4.4, Bitbucket nicely formats the new file using Markdown (Figure 1.17).

1.5 Deploying

Even at this early stage, we're going to deploy our (nearly empty) Rails application to production. This step is optional, but deploying early and often allows us to catch any deployment problems early in our development cycle. The alternative—deploying only

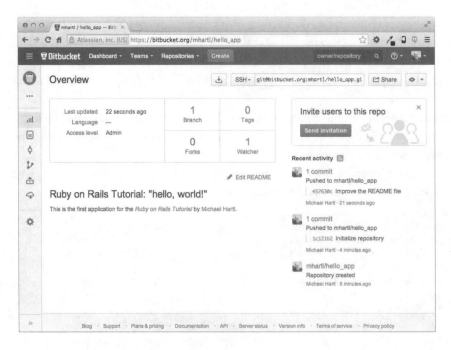

Figure 1.17 The improved `README` file formatted with Markdown.

after laborious effort sealed away in a development environment—often leads to terrible integration headaches when launch time comes.[15]

Deploying Rails applications used to be a pain, but the Rails deployment ecosystem has matured rapidly in the past few years, and now there are several great options. These include shared hosts or virtual private servers running Phusion Passenger (a module for the Apache and Nginx[16] web servers), full-service deployment companies such as Engine Yard and Rails Machine, and cloud deployment services such as Engine Yard Cloud, Ninefold, and Heroku.

My favorite Rails deployment option is Heroku, which is a hosted platform built specifically for deploying Rails and other web applications. Heroku makes deploying Rails applications ridiculously easy—as long as your source code is under version control with Git. (This is yet another reason to follow the Git setup steps in Section 1.4, if you

15. Though it shouldn't matter for the example applications in the *Rails Tutorial*, if you're worried about accidentally making your app public too soon, there are several options; see Section 1.5.4 for one.

16. Pronounced "Engine X."

haven't done so already.) The rest of this section is dedicated to deploying our first application to Heroku. Some of the ideas are fairly advanced, so don't worry about understanding all the details. What's important is that by the end of the process we'll have deployed our application to the live web.

1.5.1 Heroku Setup

Heroku uses the PostgreSQL database (pronounced "post-gres-cue-ell" and often called "Postgres" for short), which means that we need to add the pg gem in the production environment to allow Rails to talk to Postgres:[17]

```
group :production do
  gem 'pg',              '0.17.1'
  gem 'rails_12factor', '0.0.2'
end
```

Note the addition of the `rails_12factor` gem, which is used by Heroku to serve static assets such as images and style sheets. The resulting **Gemfile** appears as in Listing 1.14.

Listing 1.14 A **Gemfile** with added gems.

```
source 'https://rubygems.org'

gem 'rails',           '4.2.0'
gem 'sass-rails',      '5.0.1'
gem 'uglifier',        '2.5.3'
gem 'coffee-rails',    '4.1.0'
gem 'jquery-rails',    '4.0.3'
gem 'turbolinks',      '2.3.0'
gem 'jbuilder',        '2.2.3'
gem 'sdoc',            '0.4.0', group: :doc

group :development, :test do
  gem 'sqlite3',     '1.3.9'
  gem 'byebug',      '3.4.0'
  gem 'web-console', '2.0.0.beta3'
  gem 'spring',      '1.1.3'
end
```

---

17. Generally speaking, it's a good idea for the development and production environments to match each other as closely as possible, which includes using the same database. For the purposes of this tutorial, however, we'll always use SQLite locally and PostgreSQL in production. See Section 3.1 for more information.

```
group :production do
  gem 'pg',             '0.17.1'
  gem 'rails_12factor', '0.0.2'
end
```

To prepare the system for deployment to production, we run **bundle install** with a special flag to prevent the local installation of any production gems (which in this case consist of pg and rails_12factor):

```
$ bundle install --without production
```

Because the only gems added in Listing 1.14 are restricted to a production environment, right now this command doesn't actually install any additional local gems, but it's needed to update **Gemfile.lock** with the pg and rails_12factor gems. We can commit the resulting change as follows:

```
$ git commit -a -m "Update Gemfile.lock for Heroku"
```

Next we have to create and configure a new Heroku account. The first step is to sign up for Heroku. After you've done so, check whether your system already has the Heroku command-line client installed:

```
$ heroku version
```

Those readers using the cloud IDE should see the Heroku version number, indicating that the **heroku** command-line interface (CLI) is available. On other systems it may be necessary to install it using the Heroku Toolbelt.[18]

Once you've verified that the Heroku CLI is installed, use the **heroku** command to log in and add your SSH key:

```
$ heroku login
$ heroku keys:add
```

Finally, use the **heroku create** command to create a place on the Heroku servers for the sample app to live (Listing 1.15).

---

18. https://toolbelt.heroku.com/

Listing 1.15 Creating a new application at Heroku.

```
$ heroku create
Creating damp-fortress-5769... done, stack is cedar
http://damp-fortress-5769.herokuapp.com/ | git@heroku.com:damp-fortress-5769.git
Git remote heroku added
```

The `heroku` command creates a new subdomain just for our application, available for immediate viewing. There's nothing there yet, though, so let's get busy deploying.

1.5.2 Heroku Deployment, Step 1

To deploy the application, the first step is to use Git to push the master branch up to Heroku:

```
$ git push heroku master
```

(You may see some warning messages, which you should ignore for now. We'll discuss them in Section 7.5.)

1.5.3 Heroku Deployment, Step 2

There is no step 2! We're already done. To see your newly deployed application, visit the address that you saw when you ran `heroku create` (in Listing 1.15). (If you're working on your local machine instead of the cloud IDE, you can also use `heroku open`.) The result appears in Figure 1.18. The page is identical to Figure 1.12, but now it's running in a production environment on the live web.

1.5.4 Heroku Commands

There are many Heroku commands, and we'll barely scratch the surface of the available commands in this book. Let's take a minute to show just one of these commands by renaming the application as follows:

```
$ heroku rename rails-tutorial-hello
```

Don't use this name yourself; it's already taken by me! In fact, you probably shouldn't bother with this step right now; using the default address supplied by Heroku is fine.

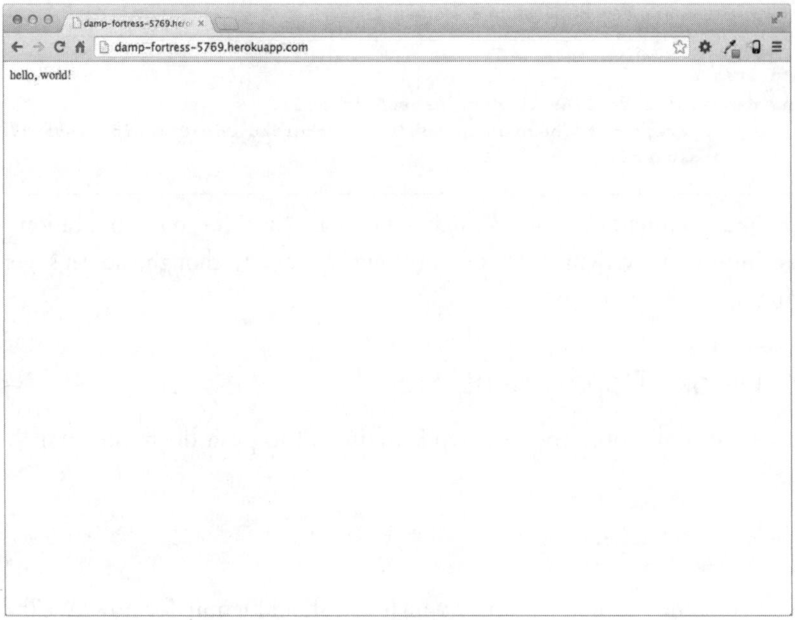

Figure 1.18 The first Rails Tutorial application running on Heroku.

But if you do want to rename your application, you can arrange for it to be reasonably secure by using a random or obscure subdomain, such as the following:

```
hwpcbmze.herokuapp.com
seyjhflo.herokuapp.com
jhyicevg.herokuapp.com
```

With a random subdomain like this, someone could visit your site only if you gave them the address. (By the way, as a preview of Ruby's compact awesomeness, here's the code I used to generate the random subdomains:

```
('a'..'z').to_a.shuffle[0..7].join
```

Pretty sweet.)

    In addition to supporting subdomains, Heroku supports custom domains. (In fact, the *Ruby on Rails*™ *Tutorial* site lives at Heroku; if you're reading this book online, you're looking at a Heroku-hosted site right now!) See the Heroku documentation for more information about custom domains and other Heroku topics.

1.6   Conclusion

We've come a long way in this chapter: installation, development environment setup, version control, and deployment. In the next chapter, we'll build on the foundation from Chapter 1 to make a database-backed *toy app*, which will give us our first real taste of what Rails can do.

If you'd like to share your progress at this point, feel free to send a tweet or Facebook status update with something like this:

I'm learning Ruby on Rails with the @railstutorial!

http://www.railstutorial.org/

I also recommend signing up for the Rails Tutorial email list,[19] which will ensure that you receive priority updates (and exclusive coupon codes) regarding the *Ruby on Rails™ Tutorial.*

1.6.1   What We Learned in This Chapter

- Ruby on Rails is a web development framework written in the Ruby programming language.

- Installing Rails, generating an application, and editing the resulting files is easy using a preconfigured cloud environment.

- Rails comes with a command-line command called `rails` that can generate new applications (`rails new`) and run local servers (`rails server`).

- We added a controller action and modified the root route to create a "hello, world" application.

- We protected against data loss while enabling collaboration by placing our application source code under version control with Git and pushing the resulting code to a private repository at Bitbucket.

- We deployed our application to a production environment using Heroku.

---

19. http://www.railstutorial.org/#email

Figure 1.19 Changing the root route to return "¡Hola, mundo!"

1.7 Exercises

Note: To receive a copy of the *Solutions Manual for Exercises*, with solutions to every exercise in the *Ruby on Rails*™ *Tutorial*, visit www.railstutorial.org/<word>, where "<word>" is the last word of the Figure 3.9 caption.

1. Change the content of the `hello` action in Listing 1.8 to read "hola, mundo!" instead of "hello, world!" *Extra credit*: Show that Rails supports non-ASCII characters by including an inverted exclamation point, as in "¡Hola, mundo!" (Figure 1.19).[20]

---

20. Your editor may display a message like "invalid multibyte character," but this is not a cause for concern. You can Google the error message if you want to learn how to make it go away.

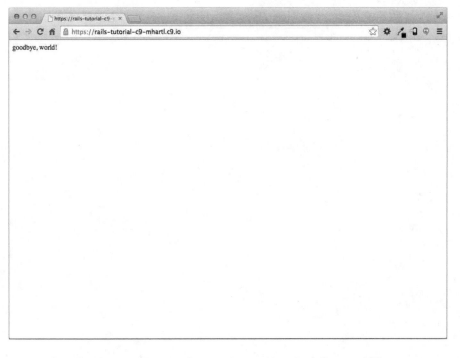

Figure 1.20   Changing the root route to return "goodbye, world!"

2. By following the example of the **hello** action in Listing 1.8, add a second action called **goodbye** that renders the text "goodbye, world!" Edit the routes file from Listing 1.10 so that the root route goes to **goodbye** instead of to **hello** (Figure 1.20).

CHAPTER 2

A Toy App

In this chapter, we'll develop a toy demo application to show off some of the power of Rails. The purpose is to get a high-level overview of Ruby on Rails programming (and web development in general) by rapidly generating an application using *scaffold generators*, which create a large amount of functionality automatically. As discussed in Box 1.2, the rest of the book will take the opposite approach, developing a full sample application incrementally and explaining each new concept as it arises. For a quick overview (and some instant gratification), though, there is no substitute for scaffolding. The resulting toy app will allow us to interact with it through its URLs, giving us insight into the structure of a Rails application, including a first example of the *REST architecture* favored by Rails.

As with the forthcoming sample application, the toy app will consist of *users* and their associated *microposts* (thus constituting a minimalist Twitter-style app). The functionality will be utterly under-developed, and many of the steps will seem like magic, but worry not: The full example will develop a similar application from the ground up starting in Chapter 3, and I will provide plentiful forward-references to later material. In the meantime, have patience and a little faith—the whole point of this tutorial is to take you *beyond* this superficial, scaffold-driven approach to achieve a deeper understanding of Rails.

2.1 Planning the Application

In this section, we'll outline our plans for the toy application. As in Section 1.3, we'll start by generating the application skeleton using the `rails new` command with a specific Rails version number:

```
$ cd ~/workspace
$ rails _4.2.0_ new toy_app
$ cd toy_app/
```

If the command above returns an error like "Could not find 'railties'," it means you don't have the right version of Rails installed, and you should double-check that you followed the command in Listing 1.1 exactly as written. (If you're using the cloud IDE as recommended in Section 1.2.1, note that this second app can be created in the same workspace as the first. It is not necessary to create a new workspace. To get the files to appear, you may need to click the gear icon in the file navigator area and select "Refresh File Tree.")

Next, we'll use a text editor to update the `Gemfile` needed by Bundler with the contents of Listing 2.1.

Listing 2.1 A `Gemfile` for the toy app.

```
source 'https://rubygems.org'

gem 'rails',              '4.2.0'
gem 'sass-rails',         '5.0.1'
gem 'uglifier',           '2.5.3'
gem 'coffee-rails',       '4.1.0'
gem 'jquery-rails',       '4.0.3'
gem 'turbolinks',         '2.3.0'
gem 'jbuilder',           '2.2.3'
gem 'sdoc',               '0.4.0', group: :doc

group :development, :test do
  gem 'sqlite3',      '1.3.9'
  gem 'byebug',       '3.4.0'
  gem 'web-console', '2.0.0.beta3'
  gem 'spring',       '1.1.3'
end

group :production do
  gem 'pg',               '0.17.1'
  gem 'rails_12factor', '0.0.2'
end
```

Note that Listing 2.1 is identical to Listing 1.14.

As in Section 1.5.1, we'll install the local gems while suppressing the installation of production gems using the `--without production` option:

```
$ bundle install --without production
```

Finally, we'll put the toy app under version control with Git:

```
$ git init
$ git add -A
$ git commit -m "Initialize repository"
```

You should also create a new repository by clicking the "Create" button at Bitbucket (Figure 2.1), and then push up to the remote repository:

```
$ git remote add origin git@bitbucket.org:<username>/toy_app.git
$ git push -u origin --all # pushes up the repo and its refs for the first time
```

Finally, it's never too early to deploy, which I suggest doing by following the same "hello, world!" steps provided in Listing 1.8 and Listing 1.9.[1] Then commit the changes and push up to Heroku:

```
$ git commit -am "Add hello"
$ heroku create
$ git push heroku master
```

(As in Section 1.5, you may see some warning messages, which you should ignore for now. We'll eliminate them in Section 7.5.) Apart from the address of the Heroku app, the result should be the same as in Figure 1.18.

Now we're ready to start making the app itself. The typical first step when making a web application is to create a *data model*, which is a representation of the structures needed by our application. In our case, the toy app will be a microblog, with only users and short (micro)posts. Thus, we'll begin with a model for *users* of the app (Section 2.1.1), and then we'll add a model for *microposts* (Section 2.1.2).

---

1. The main reason for this is that the default Rails page typically breaks at Heroku, which makes it hard to tell if the deployment was successful.

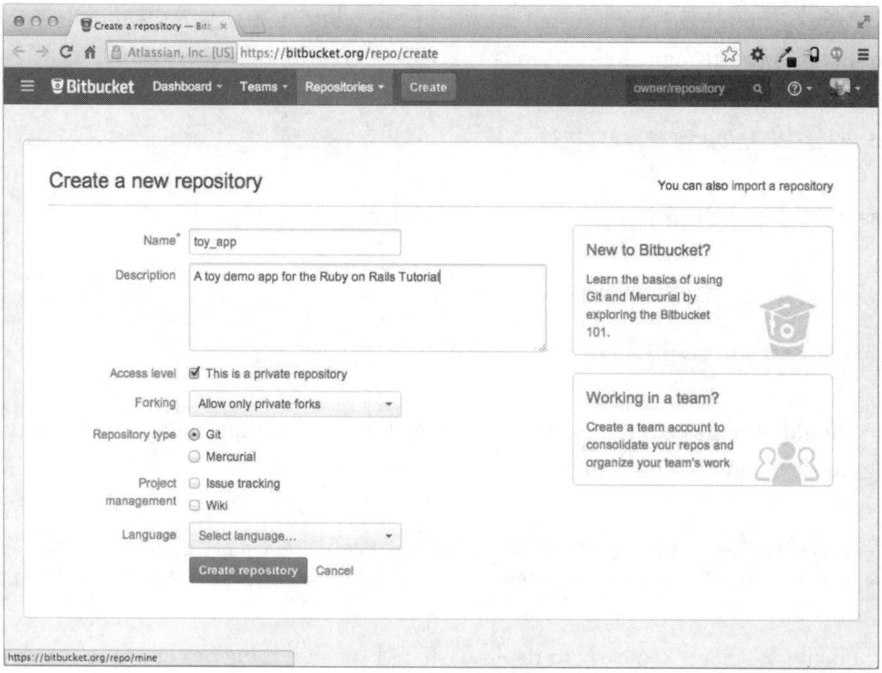

Figure 2.1 Creating the toy app repository at Bitbucket.

users	
`id`	integer
`name`	string
`email`	string

Figure 2.2 The data model for users.

2.1.1 A Toy Model for Users

There are as many choices for a user data model as there are different registration forms on the web; we'll go with a distinctly minimalist approach. Users of our toy app will have a unique **`integer`** identifier called **`id`**, a publicly viewable **`name`** (of type **`string`**), and an **`email`** address (also a **`string`**) that will double as a username. A summary of the data model for users appears in Figure 2.2.

microposts	
`id`	integer
`content`	text
`user_id`	integer

Figure 2.3 The data model for microposts.

As we'll see starting in Section 6.1.1, the label `users` in Figure 2.2 corresponds to a *table* in a database, and the `id`, `name`, and `email` attributes are *columns* in that table.

2.1.2 A Toy Model for Microposts

The core of the micropost data model is even simpler than the one for users: A micropost has only an `id` and a `content` field for the micropost's text (of type `text`).[2] There's an additional complication, though: We want to *associate* each micropost with a particular user. We'll accomplish this by recording the `user_id` of the owner of the post. The results are shown in Figure 2.3.

We'll see in Section 2.3.3 (and more fully in Chapter 11) how this `user_id` attribute allows us to succinctly express the notion that a user potentially has many associated microposts.

2.2 The Users Resource

In this section, we'll implement the users data model in Section 2.1.1, along with a web interface to that model. This combination will constitute a *Users resource*, which will allow us to think of users as objects that can be created, read, updated, and deleted through the web via the HTTP protocol. As promised in the introduction, our Users resource will be created by a scaffold generator program, which comes standard with each Rails project. I urge you not to look too closely at the generated code; at this stage, doing so will simply confuse you.

Rails scaffolding is generated by passing the `scaffold` command to the `rails generate` script. The argument of the `scaffold` command is the singular version of

---

2. Because microposts are short by design, the `string` type is actually big enough to contain them, but using `text` better expresses our intent, while also giving us greater flexibility should we ever wish to relax the length constraint.

the resource name (in this case, `User`), together with optional parameters for the data model's attributes:[3]

```
$ rails generate scaffold User name:string email:string
      invoke  active_record
      create    db/migrate/20140821011110_create_users.rb
      create    app/models/user.rb
      invoke    test_unit
      create      test/models/user_test.rb
      create      test/fixtures/users.yml
      invoke  resource_route
       route    resources :users
      invoke  scaffold_controller
      create    app/controllers/users_controller.rb
      invoke    erb
      create      app/views/users
      create      app/views/users/index.html.erb
      create      app/views/users/edit.html.erb
      create      app/views/users/show.html.erb
      create      app/views/users/new.html.erb
      create      app/views/users/_form.html.erb
      invoke    test_unit
      create      test/controllers/users_controller_test.rb
      invoke    helper
      create      app/helpers/users_helper.rb
      invoke      test_unit
      create        test/helpers/users_helper_test.rb
      invoke    jbuilder
      create      app/views/users/index.json.jbuilder
      create      app/views/users/show.json.jbuilder
      invoke  assets
      invoke    coffee
      create      app/assets/javascripts/users.js.coffee
      invoke    scss
      create      app/assets/stylesheets/users.css.scss
      invoke  scss
      create    app/assets/stylesheets/scaffolds.css.scss
```

By including `name:string` and `email:string`, we have arranged for the User model to have the form shown in Figure 2.2. (There is no need to include a parameter for `id`; it is created automatically by Rails for use as the *primary key* in the database.)

---

3. The name of the scaffold follows the convention of *models*, which are singular, rather than resources and controllers, which are plural. Thus, we have `User` instead of `Users`.

To proceed with the toy application, we first *migrate* the database using *Rake* (Box 2.1):

```
$ bundle exec rake db:migrate
==  CreateUsers: migrating ========================================================
--  create_table(:users)
    -> 0.0017s
==  CreateUsers: migrated (0.0018s) ========================================
```

This simply updates the database with our new **users** data model. (We'll learn more about database migrations starting in Section 6.1.1.) To ensure that the command uses the version of Rake corresponding to our **Gemfile**, we need to run **rake** using **bundle exec**. On many systems, including the cloud IDE, you can omit **bundle exec**, but it is necessary on some systems, so we'll include it here for completeness.

With that, we can run the local web server in a separate tab (Figure 1.7) as follows:[4]

```
$ rails server -b $IP -p $PORT    # Use only `rails server` if running locally
```

Now the toy application should be available on the local server as described in Section 1.3.2. (If you're using the cloud IDE, be sure to open the resulting development server in a new *browser* tab, not inside the IDE itself.)

Box 2.1 Rake

In the Unix tradition, the *make* utility has played an important role in building executable programs from source code. Indeed, many a computer hacker has committed to muscle memory the line

```
$ ./configure && make && sudo make install
```

commonly used to compile code on Unix systems (including Linux and Mac OS X).
    Rake is *Ruby make*, a make-like language written in Ruby. Rails uses Rake extensively, especially for the innumerable little administrative tasks that must be carried out when developing database-backed web applications. The **rake db:migrate**

---

4. The **rails** script is designed so that you don't need to use **bundle exec**.

command is probably the most widely used, but there are many others; you can see a list of database tasks using `-T db`:

```
$ bundle exec rake -T db
```

To see all the Rake tasks available, run

```
$ bundle exec rake -T
```

The list generated by this command is likely to be overwhelming, but don't worry: You don't have to know all (or even most) of these commands. By the end of the *Rails Tutorial*, you'll know all the most important ones.

2.2.1 A User Tour

If we visit the root URL at / (read "slash," as noted in Section 1.3.4), we get the same default Rails page shown in Figure 1.9. In generating the Users resource scaffolding, however, we have also created a large number of pages for manipulating users. For example, the page for listing all users is at /users, and the page for making a new user is at /users/new. The rest of this section is dedicated to taking a whirlwind tour through these user pages. As we proceed, it may help to refer to Table 2.1, which shows the correspondence between pages and URLs.

We start with the page to show all the users in our application, called index; as you might expect, initially there are no users (Figure 2.4).

To make a new user, we visit the new page, as shown in Figure 2.5. (Since the http://0.0.0.0:3000 or cloud IDE part of the address is implicit whenever we are developing locally, we'll omit it from now on.) In Chapter 7, this will become the user sign-up page.

Table 2.1 The correspondence between pages and URLs for the Users resource.

URL	Action	Purpose
/users	index	page to list all users
/users/1	show	page to show user with id 1
/users/new	new	page to make a new user
/users/1/edit	edit	page to edit user with id 1

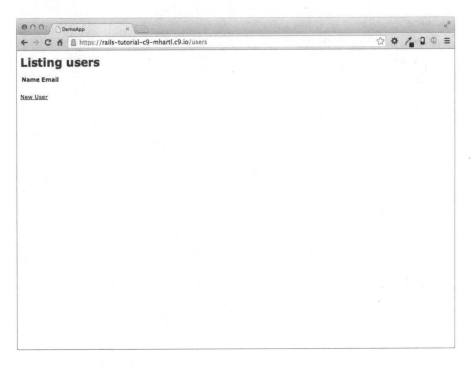

Figure 2.4 The initial index page for the Users resource (/users).

We can create a user by entering name and email values in the text fields and then clicking the Create User button. The result is the user show page, seen in Figure 2.6. (The green welcome message is accomplished using the *flash*, which we'll learn about in Section 7.4.2.) Note that the URL is /users/1; as you might suspect, the number 1 is simply the user's id attribute from Figure 2.2. In Section 7.1, this page will become the user's profile.

To change a user's information, we visit the edit page (Figure 2.11 on page 67). By modifying the user information and clicking the Update User button, we change the information for the user in the toy application (Figure 2.8). (As we'll see in detail starting in Chapter 6, this user data is stored in a database back-end.) We'll add user edit/update functionality to the sample application in Section 9.1.

Now we'll create a second user by revisiting the new page and submitting a second set of user information; the resulting user index is shown in Figure 2.9. Section 7.1 will develop the user index into a more polished page for showing all users.

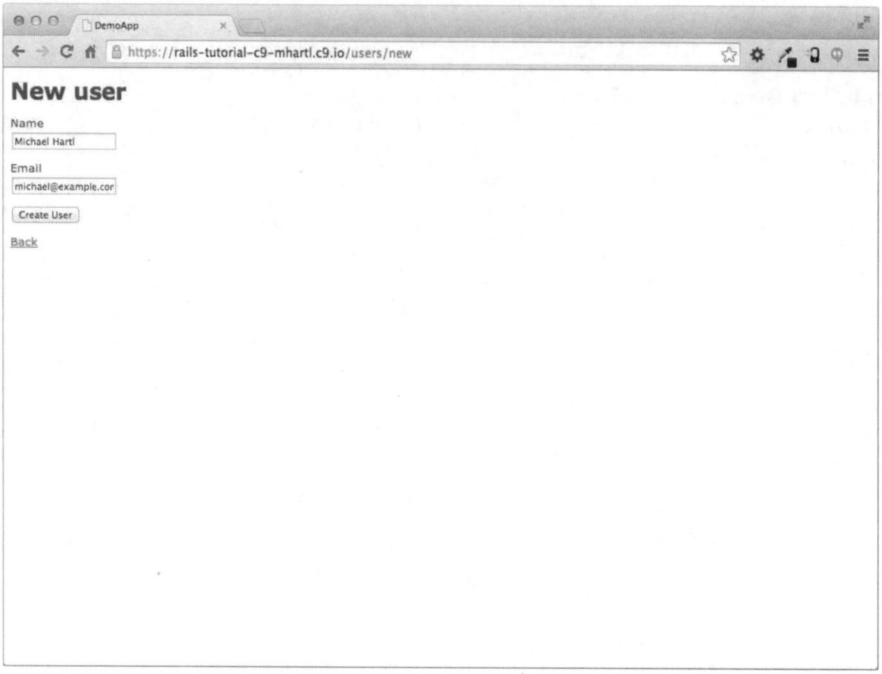

Figure 2.5 The new user page (/users/new).

Now that we know how to create, show, and edit users, we come finally to the process of destroying them (Figure 2.10). You should verify that clicking on the link in Figure 2.10 destroys the second user, yielding an index page with only one user. (If it doesn't work, make sure that JavaScript is enabled in your browser; Rails uses JavaScript to issue the request needed to destroy a user.) Section 9.4 adds user deletion to the sample app, taking care to restrict its use to a special class of administrative users.

2.2.2 MVC in Action

Now that we've completed a quick overview of the Users resource, let's examine one particular part of it in the context of the Model–View–Controller (MVC) pattern introduced in Section 1.3.3. Our strategy will be to describe the results of a typical browser hit—a visit to the user index page at /users—in terms of the MVC pattern (Figure 2.7).

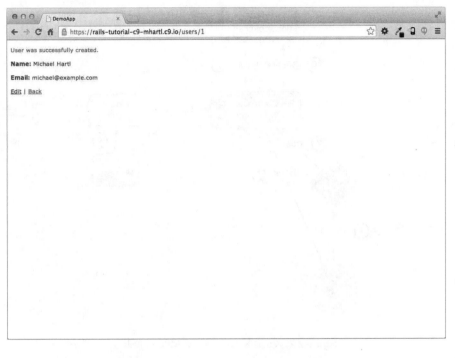

Figure 2.6 The page to show a user (/users/1).

Here is a summary of the steps shown in Figure 2.7:

1. The browser issues a request for the /users URL.

2. Rails routes /users to the **index** action in the Users controller.

3. The **index** action asks the User model to retrieve all users (**User.all**).

4. The User model pulls all the users from the database.

5. The User model returns the list of users to the controller.

6. The controller captures the users in the **@users** variable, which is passed to the **index** view.

7. The view uses embedded Ruby to render the page as HTML.

8. The controller passes the HTML back to the browser.[5]

---

5. Some references indicate that the view returns the HTML directly to the browser (via a web server such as Apache or Nginx). Regardless of the implementation details, I prefer to think of the controller as a central hub through which all the application's information flows.

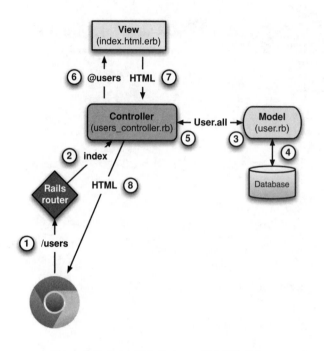

Figure 2.7 A detailed diagram of MVC in Rails.

Now let's take a look at these in more detail. We start with a request issued from the browser—that is, the result of typing a URL in the address bar or clicking on a link (Step 1 in Figure 2.7). This request is sent to the *Rails router* (Step 2), which it dispatches to the proper *controller action* based on the URL (and, as we'll see in Box 3.2, the type of request). The code to create the mapping of user URLs to controller actions for the Users resource appears in Listing 2.2; this code effectively sets up the table of URL/action pairs seen in Table 2.1. (The strange notation `:users` is a *symbol*, which we'll learn about in Section 4.3.3.)

Listing 2.2 The Rails routes, with a rule for the Users resource.
config/routes.rb

```
Rails.application.routes.draw do
  resources :users
    .
    .
    .
end
```

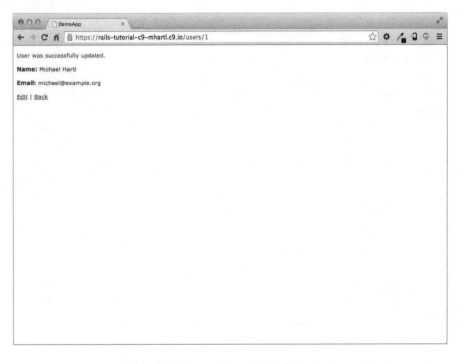

Figure 2.8 A user with updated information.

While we're looking at the routes file, let's take a moment to associate the root route with the users index, so that "slash" goes to /users. Recall from Listing 1.10 that we changed

```
# root 'welcome#index'
```

to read

```
root 'application#hello'
```

so that the root route went to the **hello** action in the Application controller. In the present case, we want to use the **index** action in the Users controller, which we can arrange using the code shown in Listing 2.3. (At this point, I also recommend removing the **hello** action from the Application controller if you added it at the beginning of this section.)

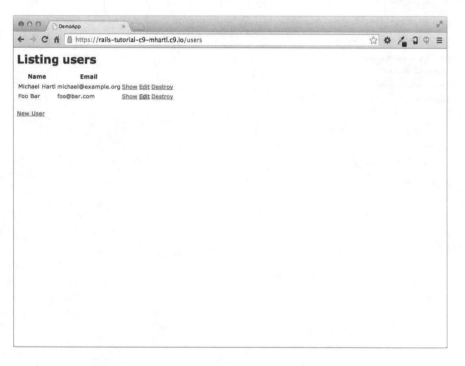

Figure 2.9 The user index page (/users) with a second user.

Listing 2.3 Adding a root route for users.
config/routes.rb

```
Rails.application.routes.draw do
  resources :users
  root 'users#index'
  .
  .
  .
end
```

The pages from the tour in Section 2.2.1 correspond to *actions* in the Users *controller*, which is a collection of related actions. The controller generated by the scaffolding is shown schematically in Listing 2.4. In this listing, the notation `class UsersController < ApplicationController`, is an example of a Ruby *class* with *inheritance*.

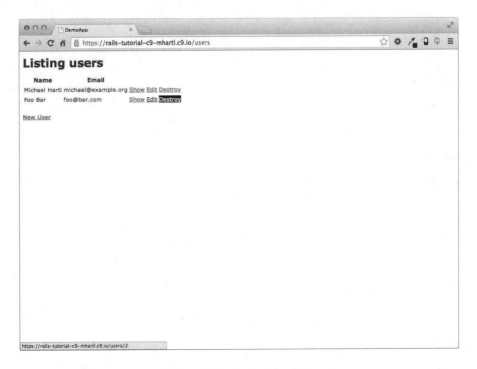

Figure 2.10 Destroying a user.

(We'll discuss inheritance briefly in Section 2.3.4 and cover both subjects in more detail in Section 4.4.)

Listing 2.4 The Users controller in schematic form.
app/controllers/users_controller.rb

```
class UsersController < ApplicationController
  .
  .
  .
  def index
    .
    .
    .
  end
```

```
def show
  .
  .
  .
end

def new
  .
  .
  .
end

def edit
  .
  .
  .
end

def create
  .
  .
  .
end

def update
  .
  .
  .
end

def destroy
  .
  .
  .
end
end
```

You may notice that there are more actions than there are pages; in this listing, `index`, `show`, `new`, and `edit` actions all correspond to pages from Section 2.2.1, but there are additional `create`, `update`, and `destroy` actions as well. These actions don't typically render pages (although they can); instead, their main purpose is to modify information about users in the database. This full suite of controller actions, summarized in Table 2.2, represents the implementation of the REST architecture in Rails (Box 2.2), which is based on the idea of *representational state transfer* identified and named by

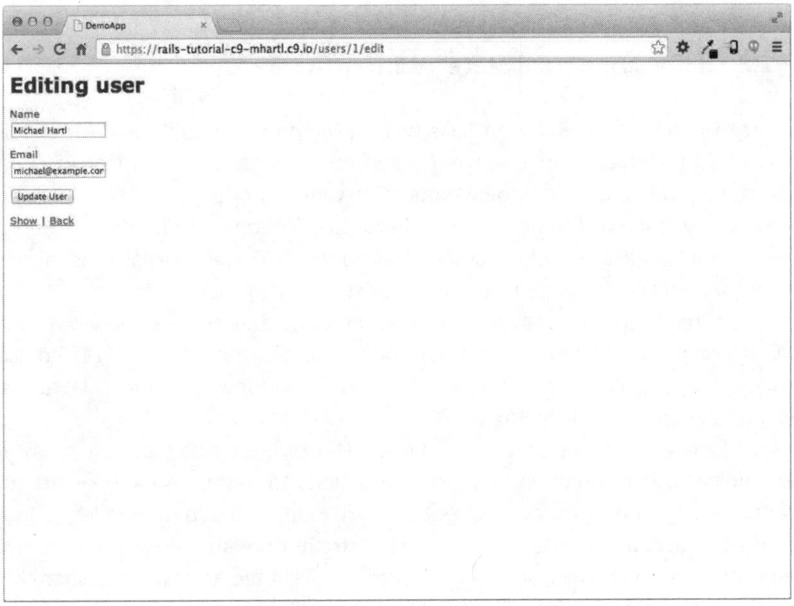

Figure 2.11   The user edit page (/users/1/edit).

Table 2.2   RESTful routes provided by the Users resource in Listing 2.2.

HTTP request	URL	Action	Purpose
GET	/users	`index`	page to list all users
GET	/users/1	`show`	page to show user with id **1**
GET	/users/new	`new`	page to make a new user
POST	/users	`create`	create a new user
GET	/users/1/edit	`edit`	page to edit user with id **1**
PATCH	/users/1	`update`	update user with id **1**
DELETE	/users/1	`destroy`	delete user with id **1**

computer scientist Roy Fielding.[6] As seen in Table 2.2, there is some overlap in the URLs; for example, both the user `show` action and the `update` action correspond to the URL /users/1. The difference between them is the HTTP request method to which they respond. We'll learn more about HTTP request methods starting in Section 3.3.

---

6. Fielding, Roy Thomas. *Architectural Styles and the Design of Network-based Software Architectures.* Doctoral dissertation, University of California, Irvine, 2000.

Box 2.2 REpresentational State Transfer (REST)

If you read much about Ruby on Rails web development, you'll see a lot of references to "REST," which is an acronym for REpresentational State Transfer. REST is an architectural style for developing distributed, networked systems and software applications such as the World Wide Web and web applications. Although this theory is rather abstract, in the context of Rails applications REST means that most application components (such as users and microposts) are modeled as *resources* that can be created, read, updated, and deleted—operations that correspond both to the CRUD operations of relational databases and to the four fundamental HTTP request methods: POST, GET, PATCH, and DELETE.[7] (We'll learn more about HTTP requests in Section 3.3 and especially Box 3.2.)

As a Rails application developer, the RESTful style of development helps you make choices about which controllers and actions to write: You simply structure the application using resources that get created, read, updated, and deleted. In the case of users and microposts, this process is straightforward, since they are naturally resources in their own right. In Chapter 12, we'll see an example where REST principles allow us to model a subtler problem, "following users," in a natural and convenient way.

To examine the relationship between the Users controller and the User model, let's focus on a simplified version of the **index** action, shown in Listing 2.5. (The scaffold code is ugly and confusing, so it's suppressed here.)

Listing 2.5 The simplified user **index** action for the toy application.
app/controllers/users_controller.rb

```
class UsersController < ApplicationController
  .
  .
  .
  def index
```

7. Earlier versions of Rails used PUT for data updates, but PATCH is the more appropriate method according to the HTTP standard.

```
      @users = User.all
  end
    .
    .
    .
end
```

This `index` action includes the line `@users = User.all` (Step 3 in Figure 2.7), which asks the User model to retrieve a list of all users from the database (Step 4), and then places them in the variable `@users` (pronounced "at-users") (Step 5). The User model itself appears in Listing 2.6; although it is rather plain, it comes equipped with a large amount of functionality because of inheritance (Section 2.3.4 and Section 4.4). In particular, by using the Rails library called *Active Record*, the code in Listing 2.6 arranges for `User.all` to return all the users in the database.

Listing 2.6   The User model for the toy application.
app/models/user.rb

```
class User < ActiveRecord::Base
end
```

Once the `@users` variable is defined, the controller calls the *view* (Step 6), shown in Listing 2.7. Variables that start with the @ sign, called *instance variables*, are automatically available in the views; in this case, the `index.html.erb` view in Listing 2.7 iterates through the `@users` list and outputs a line of HTML for each one. (Remember, you aren't supposed to understand this code right now. It is shown only for purposes of illustration.)

Listing 2.7   The view for the user index.
app/views/users/index.html.erb

```
<h1>Listing users</h1>

<table>
  <thead>
    <tr>
      <th>Name</th>
      <th>Email</th>
```

```
      <th colspan="3"></th>
    </tr>
  </thead>

<% @users.each do |user| %>
  <tr>
    <td><%= user.name %></td>
    <td><%= user.email %></td>
    <td><%= link_to 'Show', user %></td>
    <td><%= link_to 'Edit', edit_user_path(user) %></td>
    <td><%= link_to 'Destroy', user, method: :delete,
                          data: { confirm: 'Are you sure?' } %></td>
  </tr>
<% end %>
</table>

<br>

<%= link_to 'New User', new_user_path %>
```

The view converts its contents to HTML (Step 7), which is then returned by the controller to the browser for display (Step 8).

2.2.3 Weaknesses of This Users Resource

Though good for getting a general overview of Rails, the scaffold Users resource suffers from a number of severe weaknesses.

- **No data validations.** Our User model accepts data such as blank names and invalid email addresses without complaint.

- **No authentication.** We have no notion of logging in or out, and no way to prevent any user from performing any operation.

- **No tests.** This isn't technically true—the scaffolding includes rudimentary tests—but the generated tests don't test for data validation, authentication, or any other custom requirements.

- **No style or layout.** There is no consistent site styling or navigation.

- **No real understanding.** If you understand the scaffold code, you probably shouldn't be reading this book.

2.3 The Microposts Resource

Having generated and explored the Users resource, we turn now to the associated Microposts resource. Throughout this section, we recommend comparing the elements of the Microposts resource with the analogous user elements from Section 2.2; the two resources parallel each other in many ways. The RESTful structure of Rails applications is best absorbed by this sort of repetition of form—indeed, seeing the parallel structure of Users and Microposts even at this early stage is one of the prime motivations for this chapter.

2.3.1 A Micropost Microtour

As with the Users resource, we'll generate scaffold code for the Microposts resource using **rails generate scaffold**, in this case implementing the data model from Figure 2.3:[8]

```
$ rails generate scaffold Micropost content:text user_id:integer
      invoke  active_record
      create    db/migrate/20140821012832_create_microposts.rb
      create    app/models/micropost.rb
      invoke    test_unit
      create      test/models/micropost_test.rb
      create      test/fixtures/microposts.yml
      invoke  resource_route
       route    resources :microposts
      invoke  scaffold_controller
      create    app/controllers/microposts_controller.rb
      invoke    erb
      create      app/views/microposts
      create      app/views/microposts/index.html.erb
      create      app/views/microposts/edit.html.erb
      create      app/views/microposts/show.html.erb
      create      app/views/microposts/new.html.erb
      create      app/views/microposts/_form.html.erb
      invoke    test_unit
      create      test/controllers/microposts_controller_test.rb
      invoke    helper
      create      app/helpers/microposts_helper.rb
```

---

8. As with the User scaffold, the scaffold generator for microposts follows the singular convention of Rails models; thus, we have **generate Micropost**.

```
    invoke      test_unit
    create          test/helpers/microposts_helper_test.rb
    invoke      jbuilder
    create          app/views/microposts/index.json.jbuilder
    create          app/views/microposts/show.json.jbuilder
    invoke    assets
    invoke      coffee
    create          app/assets/javascripts/microposts.js.coffee
    invoke      scss
    create          app/assets/stylesheets/microposts.css.scss
    invoke    scss
 identical          app/assets/stylesheets/scaffolds.css.scss
```

(If you get an error related to Spring, just run the command again.) To update our database with the new data model, we need to run a migration as in Section 2.2:

```
$ bundle exec rake db:migrate
==  CreateMicroposts: migrating ===========================================
-- create_table(:microposts)
   -> 0.0023s
==  CreateMicroposts: migrated (0.0026s) ===================================
```

Now we are in a position to create microposts in the same way we created users in Section 2.2.1. As you might guess, the scaffold generator has updated the Rails routes file with a rule for Microposts resource, as seen in Listing 2.8.[9] As with users, the **resources :microposts** routing rule maps micropost URLs to actions in the Microposts controller, as seen in Table 2.3.

Listing 2.8 The Rails routes, with a new rule for Microposts resources.

config/routes.rb

```
Rails.application.routes.draw do
  resources :microposts
  resources :users
  .
  .
  .
end
```

---

9. The scaffold code may have extra newlines compared to Listing 2.8. This is not a cause for concern, as Ruby ignores extra newlines.

Table 2.3   RESTful routes provided by the Microposts resource in Listing 2.8.

HTTP request	URL	Action	Purpose
GET	/microposts	**index**	page to list all microposts
GET	/microposts/1	**show**	page to show micropost with id **1**
GET	/microposts/new	**new**	page to make a new micropost
POST	/microposts	**create**	create a new micropost
GET	/microposts/1/edit	**edit**	page to edit micropost with id **1**
PATCH	/microposts/1	**update**	update micropost with id **1**
DELETE	/microposts/1	**destroy**	delete micropost with id **1**

The Microposts controller itself appears in schematic form in Listing 2.9. Note that, apart from `MicropostsController` in replacing of `UsersController`, Listing 2.9 is *identical* to the code in Listing 2.4. This is a reflection of the REST architecture common to both resources.

Listing 2.9   The Microposts controller in schematic form.

app/controllers/microposts_controller.rb

```
class MicropostsController < ApplicationController
    .
    .
    .
    def index
      .
      .
      .
    end

    def show
      .
      .
    end

    def new
      .
      .
    end
```

```
    def edit
      .
      .
      .
    end

    def create
      .
      .
      .
    end

    def update
      .
      .
      .
    end

    def destroy
      .
      .
      .
    end
end
```

To make some actual microposts, we enter information at the new microposts page, /microposts/new, as seen in Figure 2.12.

At this point, go ahead and create a micropost or two, taking care to make sure that at least one has a **user_id** of **1** to match the ID of the first user created in Section 2.2.1. The result should look something like Figure 2.13.

2.3.2 Putting the *Micro* in Microposts

Any *micro*post worthy of the name should have some means of enforcing the limits on the length of the post. Implementing this constraint in Rails is easy with *validations*; to accept microposts with at most 140 characters (à la Twitter), we use a *length* validation. At this point, you should open the file **app/models/micropost.rb** in your text editor or IDE and fill it with the contents of Listing 2.10.

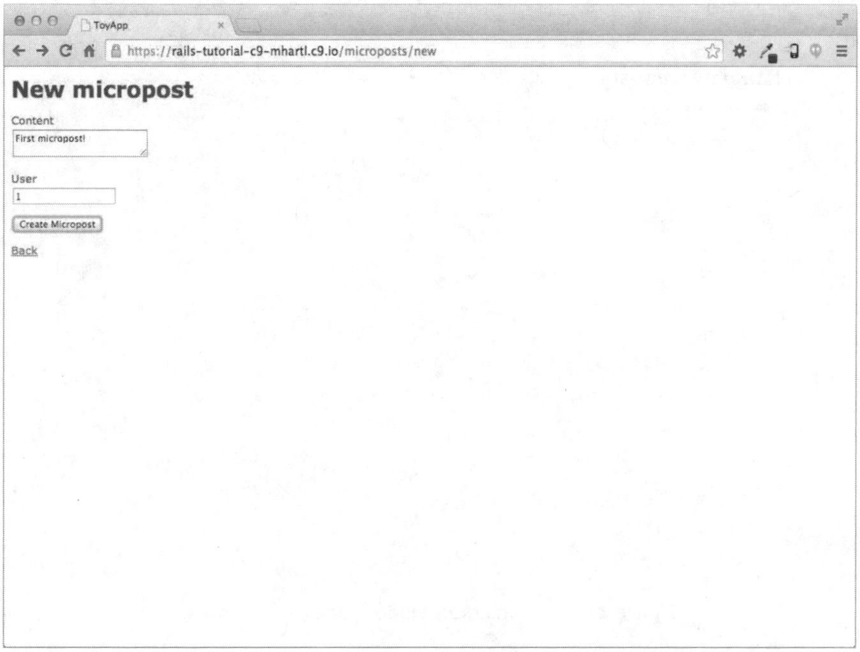

Figure 2.12 The new micropost page (/microposts/new).

Listing 2.10 Constraining microposts to be at most 140 characters.
app/models/micropost.rb

```
class Micropost < ActiveRecord::Base
  validates :content, length: { maximum: 140 }
end
```

The code in Listing 2.10 may look rather mysterious—we'll cover validations more thoroughly starting in Section 6.2—but its effects are readily apparent if we go to the new micropost page and enter more than 140 characters for the content of the post. As seen in Figure 2.14, Rails renders *error messages* indicating that the micropost's content is too long. (We'll learn more about error messages in Section 7.3.3.)

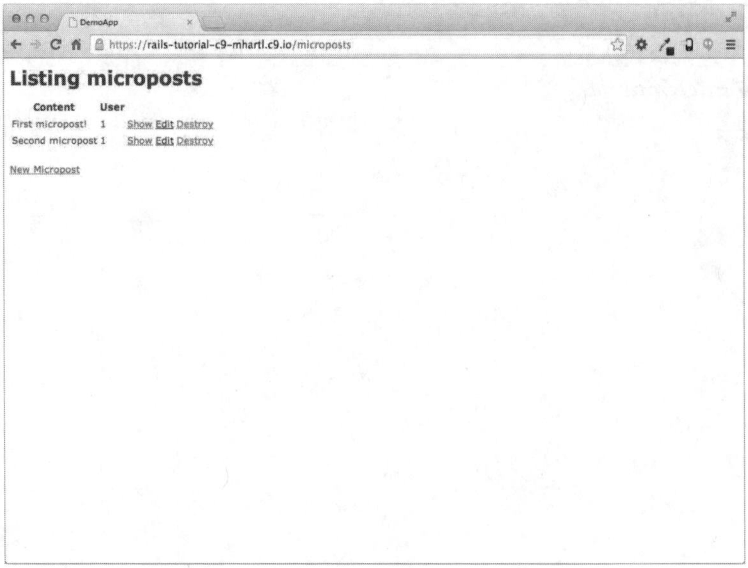

Figure 2.13 The micropost index page (/microposts).

2.3.3 A User `has_many` Microposts

One of the most powerful features of Rails is the ability to form *associations* between different data models. In the case of our User model, each user potentially has many microposts. We can express this relationship in code by updating the User and Micropost models as in Listing 2.11 and Listing 2.12, respectively.

Listing 2.11 A user has many microposts.

app/models/user.rb

```
class User < ActiveRecord::Base
  has_many :microposts
end
```

Listing 2.12 A micropost belongs to a user.

app/models/micropost.rb

```
class Micropost < ActiveRecord::Base
  belongs_to :user
```

```
  validates :content, length: { maximum: 140 }
end
```

We can visualize the result of this association in Figure 2.15. Because of the `user_id` column in the `microposts` table, Rails (using Active Record) can infer the microposts associated with each user.

In Chapter 11 and Chapter 12, we will use the association of users and microposts both to display all of a user's microposts and to construct a Twitter-like micropost feed.

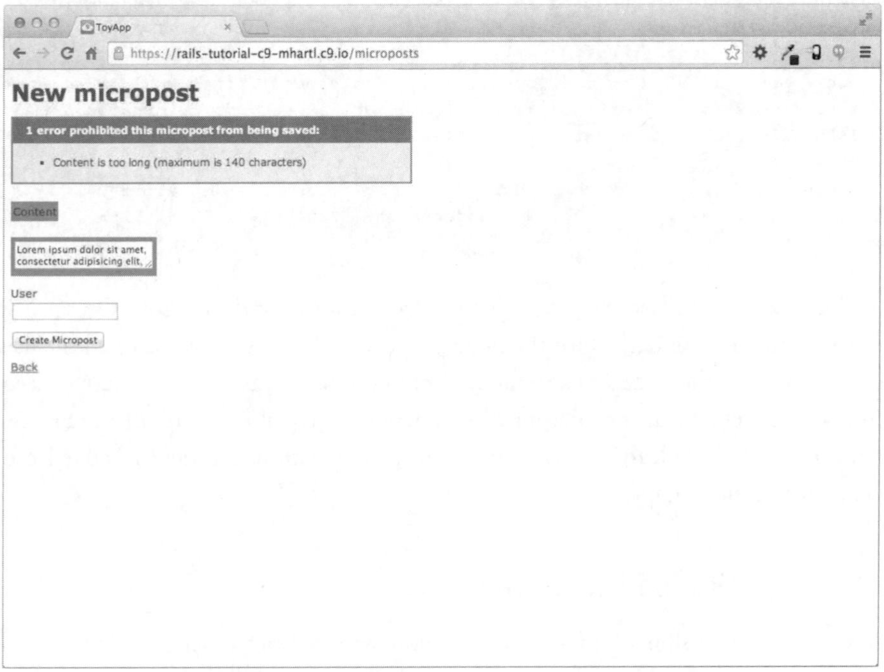

Figure 2.14 Error messages for a failed micropost creation.

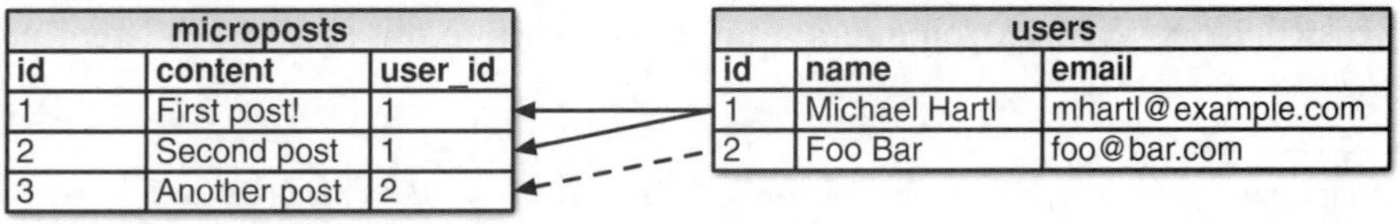

Figure 2.15 The association between microposts and users.

For now, we can examine the implications of the user—micropost association by using
the *console*, which is a useful tool for interacting with Rails applications. We first invoke
the console with **rails console** at the command line, and then retrieve the first user
from the database using **User.first** (putting the results in the variable **first_user**):[10]

```
$ rails console
>> first_user = User.first
=> #<User id: 1, name: "Michael Hartl", email: "michael@example.org",
created_at: "2014-07-21 02:01:31", updated_at: "2014-07-21 02:01:31">
>> first_user.microposts
=> [#<Micropost id: 1, content: "First micropost!", user_id: 1, created_at:
"2014-07-21 02:37:37", updated_at: "2014-07-21 02:37:37">, #<Micropost id: 2,
content: "Second micropost", user_id: 1, created_at: "2014-07-21 02:38:54",
updated_at: "2014-07-21 02:38:54">]
>> micropost = first_user.microposts.first  # Micropost.first would also work.
=> #<Micropost id: 1, content: "First micropost!", user_id: 1, created_at:
"2014-07-21 02:37:37", updated_at: "2014-07-21 02:37:37">
>> micropost.user
=> #<User id: 1, name: "Michael Hartl", email: "michael@example.org",
created_at: "2014-07-21 02:01:31", updated_at: "2014-07-21 02:01:31">
>> exit
```

(I include **exit** in the last line just to demonstrate how to exit the console. On most systems, you can also use Ctrl-D for the same purpose.[11]) Here we have accessed the user's
microposts using the code **first_user.microposts**. With this code, Active Record
automatically returns all the microposts with **user_id** equal to the ID of **first_user**
(in this case, **1**). We'll learn much more about the association facilities in Active Record
in Chapter 11 and Chapter 12.

2.3.4 Inheritance Hierarchies

We end our discussion of the toy application with a brief description of the controller and model class hierarchies in Rails. This discussion will make sense only if you
have some experience with object-oriented programming (OOP); if you haven't studied OOP, feel free to skip this section. In particular, if you are unfamiliar with *classes*
(discussed in Section 4.4), you might want to loop back to this section at a later time.

---

10. Your console prompt might be something like 2.1.1 :001 >, but the examples use >> since Ruby
versions will vary.

11. As with "Ctrl-C," the convention is to write "Ctrl-D" even though it's really "Ctrl-d."

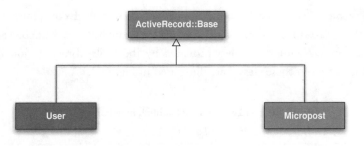

Figure 2.16 The inheritance hierarchy for the User and Micropost models.

We start with the inheritance structure for models. Comparing Listing 2.13 and Listing 2.14, we see that both the User model and the Micropost model inherit (via the left angle bracket <) from `ActiveRecord::Base`, which is the base class for models provided by Active Record; a diagram summarizing this relationship appears in Figure 2.16. It is by inheriting from `ActiveRecord::Base` that our model objects gain the ability to communicate with the database, treat the database columns as Ruby attributes, and so on.

Listing 2.13 The `User` class, highlighting inheritance.

app/models/user.rb

```
class User < ActiveRecord::Base
  .
  .
  .
end
```

Listing 2.14 The `Micropost` class, highlighting inheritance.

app/models/micropost.rb

```
class Micropost < ActiveRecord::Base
  .
  .
  .
end
```

The inheritance structure for controllers is only slightly more complicated. Comparing Listing 2.15 and Listing 2.16, we see that both the Users controller and the

Microposts controller inherit from the Application controller. Examining Listing 2.17, we see that **ApplicationController** itself inherits from **ActionController::Base**; this is the base class for controllers provided by the Rails library Action Pack. The relationships between these classes are illustrated in Figure 2.17.

Listing 2.15 The **UsersController** class, highlighting inheritance.
app/controllers/users_controller.rb

```
class UsersController < ApplicationController
  .
  .
  .
end
```

Listing 2.16 The **MicropostsController** class, highlighting inheritance.
app/controllers/microposts_controller.rb

```
class MicropostsController < ApplicationController
  .
  .
  .
end
```

Listing 2.17 The **ApplicationController** class, highlighting inheritance.
app/controllers/application_controller.rb

```
class ApplicationController < ActionController::Base
  .
  .
  .
end
```

As with model inheritance, both the Users and Microposts controllers gain a large amount of functionality by inheriting from a base class (in this case, **ActionController::Base**), including the ability to manipulate model objects, filter inbound HTTP requests, and render views as HTML. Given that all Rails controllers inherit from **ApplicationController**, rules defined in the Application controller

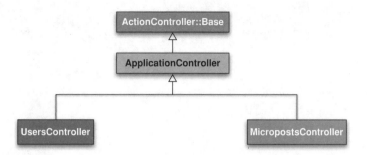

Figure 2.17 The inheritance hierarchy for the Users and Microposts controllers.

automatically apply to every action in the application. For example, in Section 8.4 we'll see how to include helpers for logging in and logging out of all of the sample application's controllers.

2.3.5 Deploying the Toy App

With the completion of the Microposts resource, now is a good time to push the repository up to Bitbucket:

```
$ git status
$ git add -A
$ git commit -m "Finish toy app"
$ git push
```

Ordinarily, you should make smaller, more frequent commits, but for the purposes of this chapter a single big commit at the end is fine.

At this point, you can also deploy the toy app to Heroku as explained in Section 1.5:

```
$ git push heroku
```

(This assumes you created the Heroku app in Section 2.1. Otherwise, you should run `heroku create` and then `git push heroku master`.)

To get the application's database to work, you'll also have to migrate the production database:

```
$ heroku run rake db:migrate
```

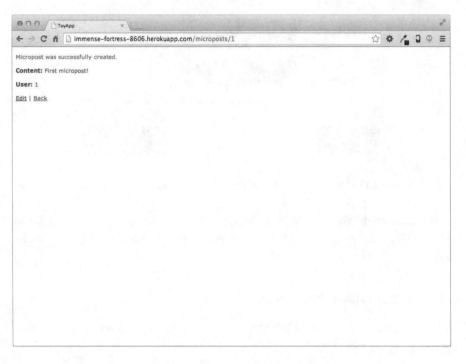

Figure 2.18 Running the toy app in production.

This updates the database at Heroku with the necessary user and micropost data models. After running the migration, you should be able to use the toy app in production, with a real PostgreSQL database back-end (Figure 2.18).

2.4 Conclusion

We've now come to the end of the high-level overview of a Rails application. The toy app developed in this chapter has several strengths and a host of weaknesses.

Strengths

- High-level overview of Rails
- Introduction to MVC
- First taste of the REST architecture

- Beginning data modeling
- A live, database-backed web application in production

Weaknesses

- No custom layout or styling
- No static pages (such as "Home" or "About")
- No user passwords
- No user images
- No logging in
- No security
- No automatic user/micropost association
- No notion of "following" or "followed"
- No micropost feed
- No meaningful tests
- **No real understanding**

The rest of this tutorial is dedicated to building on these strengths and eliminating the weaknesses.

2.4.1 What We Learned in This Chapter

- Scaffolding automatically creates code to model data and interact with it through the web.
- Scaffolding is good for getting started quickly but is bad for gaining understanding.
- Rails uses the Model–View–Controller (MVC) pattern for structuring web applications.
- As interpreted by Rails, the REST architecture includes a standard set of URLs and controller actions for interacting with data models.
- Rails supports data validations to place constraints on the values of data model attributes.

- Rails comes with built-in functions for defining associations between different data models.

- We can interact with Rails applications at the command line using the Rails console.

2.5 Exercises

Note: To receive a copy of the *Solutions Manual for Exercises*, with solutions to every exercise in the *Ruby on Rails™ Tutorial*, visit www.railstutorial.org/<word>, where "<word>" is the last word of the Figure 3.9 caption.

1. The code in Listing 2.18 shows how to add a validation for the presence of micropost content to ensure that microposts can't be blank. Verify that you get the screen shown in Figure 2.19.

2. Update Listing 2.19 by replacing `FILL_IN` with the appropriate code to validate the presence of name and email attributes in the User model (Figure 2.20).

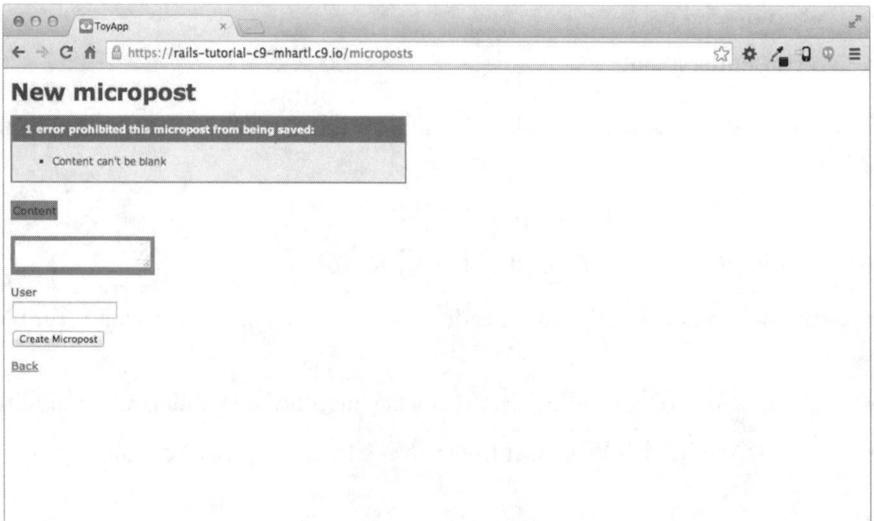

Figure 2.19 The effect of a micropost presence validation.

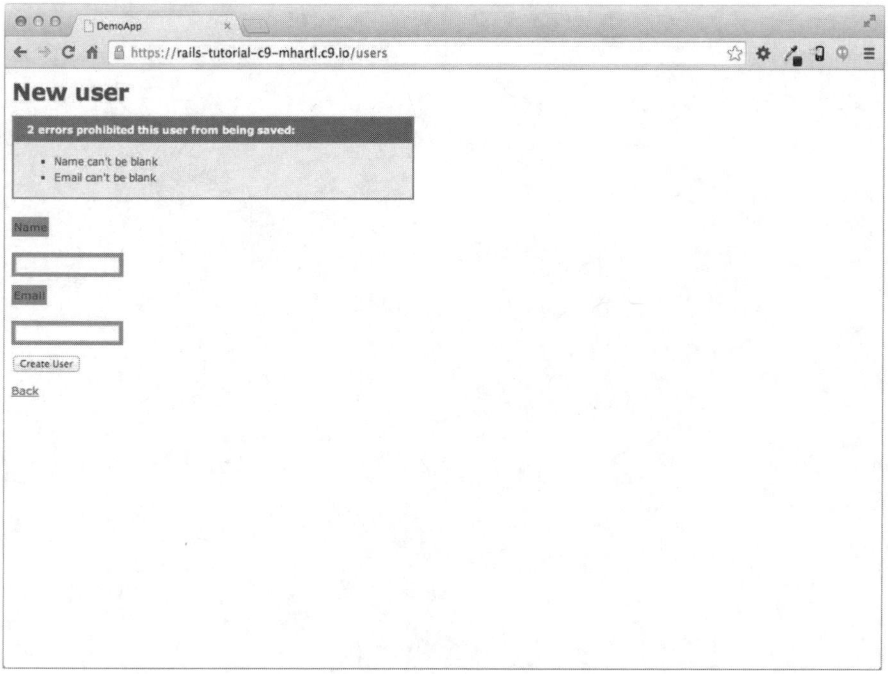

Figure 2.20   The effect of presence validations on the User model.

Listing 2.18   Code to validate the presence of micropost content.

app/models/micropost.rb

```
class Micropost < ActiveRecord::Base
  belongs_to :user
  validates :content, length: { maximum: 140 },
                      presence: true
end
```

Listing 2.19   Adding presence validations to the User model.

app/models/user.rb

```
class User < ActiveRecord::Base
  has_many :microposts
  validates FILL_IN, presence: true
  validates FILL_IN, presence: true
end
```

## CHAPTER 3

Mostly Static Pages

In this chapter, we will begin developing the professional-grade sample application that will serve as our example throughout the rest of this tutorial. Although the sample app will eventually have users, microposts, and a full login and authentication framework, we will begin with a seemingly limited topic: the creation of static pages. Despite its apparent simplicity, making static pages is a highly instructive exercise, rich in implications—a perfect start for our nascent application.

Although Rails is designed for making database-backed dynamic websites, it also excels at making the kind of static pages we might make with raw HTML files. In fact, using Rails even for static pages yields a distinct advantage: We can easily add just a *small* amount of dynamic content. In this chapter we'll learn how. Along the way, we'll get our first taste of *automated testing*, which will help us be more confident that our code is correct. Moreover, having a good test suite will allow us to *refactor* our code with confidence, changing its form without changing its function.

3.1 Sample App Setup

As in Chapter 2, before getting started we need to create a new Rails project, this time called `sample_app`, as shown in Listing 3.1.[1] If the command in Listing 3.1 returns an

---

1. If you're using the cloud IDE, it's often useful to use the "Goto Anything" command, which makes it easy to navigate the filesystem by typing in partial filenames. In this context, having the hello, toy, and sample apps present within the same project can be inconvenient due to the many common filenames. For example, when searching for a file called "Gemfile," six possibilities will show up, because each project has its own pair of files called `Gemfile` and `Gemfile.lock`. Thus, you may want to consider removing the first two apps before proceeding, which you can do by navigating to the `workspace` directory and running `rm -rf hello_app/ toy_app/` (Table 1.1). (As long as you pushed the corresponding repositories up to Bitbucket, you can always recover them later.)

error like "Could not find 'railties'," it means you don't have the right version of Rails installed, and you should double-check that you followed the command in Listing 1.1 exactly as written.

Listing 3.1 Generating a new sample app.

```
$ cd ~/workspace
$ rails _4.2.0_ new sample_app
$ cd sample_app/
```

(As in Section 2.1, note that users of the cloud IDE can create this project in the same workspace as the applications from the previous two chapters. It is not necessary to create a new workspace.)

As in Section 2.1, our next step is to use a text editor to update the `Gemfile` with the gems needed by our application. Listing 3.2 is identical to Listing 1.5 and Listing 2.1 apart from the gems in the `test` group, which are needed for the optional advanced testing setup (Section 3.7). (*Note*: If you would like to install *all* the gems needed for the sample application, you should use the code in Listing 11.67 at this time.)

Listing 3.2 A `Gemfile` for the sample app.

```
source 'https://rubygems.org'

gem 'rails',              '4.2.0'
gem 'sass-rails',         '5.0.1'
gem 'uglifier',           '2.5.3'
gem 'coffee-rails',       '4.1.0'
gem 'jquery-rails',       '4.0.3'
gem 'turbolinks',         '2.3.0'
gem 'jbuilder',           '2.2.3'
gem 'sdoc',               '0.4.0', group: :doc

group :development, :test do
  gem 'sqlite3',     '1.3.9'
  gem 'byebug',      '3.4.0'
  gem 'web-console', '2.0.0.beta3'
  gem 'spring',      '1.1.3'
end

group :test do
  gem 'minitest-reporters', '1.0.5'
  gem 'mini_backtrace',     '0.1.3'
```

```
  gem 'guard-minitest',      '2.3.1'
end

group :production do
  gem 'pg',                '0.17.1'
  gem 'rails_12factor', '0.0.2'
end
```

As in the previous two chapters, we run **bundle install** to install and include the gems specified in the **Gemfile**, while skipping the installation of production gems by using the option --without production:[2]

```
$ bundle install --without production
```

This command arranges to skip the pg gem for PostgreSQL in development and use SQLite for development and testing. Heroku recommends against using different databases in development and production, but for the sample application it won't make any difference, and SQLite is *much* easier than PostgreSQL to install and configure locally.[3] In case you've previously installed a version of a gem (such as Rails itself) other than the one specified by the **Gemfile**, it's a good idea to *update* the gems with **bundle update** to make sure the versions match:

```
$ bundle update
```

With that, all we have left is to initialize the Git repository:

```
$ git init
$ git add -A
$ git commit -m "Initialize repository"
```

---

2. It's worth noting that --without production is a "remembered option," which means it will be included automatically the next time we run **bundle install**.

3. I recommend eventually learning how to install and configure PostgreSQL in development, but the now is likely not that time. When the time comes, Google "install configure postgresql <your system>" and "rails postgresql setup" and prepare for a challenge. (On the cloud IDE, <your system> is Ubuntu.)

As with the first application, I suggest updating the **README** file (located in the root directory of the application) to be more helpful and descriptive. We start by changing the format from RDoc to Markdown:

```
$ git mv README.rdoc README.md
```

We then fill the **README** file with the contents shown in Listing 3.3.

Listing 3.3 An improved **README** file for the sample app.

```
# Ruby on Rails Tutorial: sample application

This is the sample application for the
[*Ruby on Rails Tutorial:
Learn Web Development with Rails*](http://www.railstutorial.org/)
by [Michael Hartl](http://www.michaelhartl.com/).
```

Finally, we commit the changes:

```
$ git commit -am "Improve the README"
```

You may recall from Section 1.4.4 that we used the Git command `git commit -a -m "Message"`, with flags for "all changes" (`-a`) and a message (`-m`). As shown in the second command here, Git also lets us roll the two flags into one by using `git commit -am "Message"`.

Since we'll be using this sample app throughout the rest of the book, it's a good idea to create a new repository at Bitbucket and push it up:

```
$ git remote add origin git@bitbucket.org:<username>/sample_app.git
$ git push -u origin --all # pushes up the repo and its refs for the first time
```

To avoid integration headaches later on, it's also a good idea to deploy the app to Heroku even at this early stage. To do so, you can follow the "hello, world!"

steps in Listing 1.8 and Listing 1.9.[4] Then commit the changes and push up to Heroku:

```
$ git commit -am "Add hello"
$ heroku create
$ git push heroku master
```

(As in Section 1.5, you might see some warning messages, which you should ignore for now. We'll eliminate them in Section 7.5.) Apart from the address of the Heroku app, the result should be the same as in Figure 1.18.

As you proceed through the rest of the book, you should continue pushing and deploying the application regularly, which automatically makes remote back-ups and lets you catch any production errors as soon as possible. If you run into problems at Heroku, take a look at the production logs to try to diagnose the problem:

```
$ heroku logs
```

Note: If you do end up using Heroku for a real-life application, be sure to follow the production web server configuration in Section 7.5.

3.2 Static Pages

With all the preparation from Section 3.1 finished, we're ready to get started developing the sample application. In this section, we'll take a first step toward making dynamic pages by creating a set of Rails *actions* and *views* containing only static HTML. Rails actions come bundled together inside *controllers* (the "C" in MVC, from Section 1.3.3), which contain sets of actions related by a common purpose. We got a glimpse of controllers in Chapter 2, and will come to a deeper understanding of them once we explore the REST architecture more fully (starting in Chapter 6). To get our bearings, it's helpful to recall the Rails directory structure from Section 1.3 (Figure 1.4). In this section, we'll be working mainly in the `app/controllers` and `app/views` directories.

---

4. As noted in Chapter 2, the main reason for following this approach is that the default Rails page typically breaks at Heroku, which makes it hard to tell if the deployment was successful.

Recall from Section 1.4.4 that, when using Git, it's a good practice to do our work on a separate topic branch rather than the master branch. If you're using Git for version control, you should run the following command to check out a topic branch for static pages:

```
$ git checkout master
$ git checkout -b static-pages
```

(The first line here is just to make sure that you start on the master branch, so that the **static-pages** topic branch is based on **master**. You can skip that command if you're already on the master branch.)

3.2.1 Generated Static Pages

To get started with static pages, we'll first generate a controller using the same Rails **generate** script we used in Chapter 2 to generate scaffolding. Because we'll be making a controller to handle static pages, we'll call it the Static Pages controller, designated by the CamelCase name **StaticPages**. We'll also plan to make actions for a Home page, a Help page, and an About page, designated by the lowercase action names **home**, **help**, and **about**. The **generate** script takes an optional list of actions, so we'll include actions for the Home and Help pages directly on the command line, while intentionally leaving off the action for the About page so that we can see how to add it (Section 3.3). The resulting command to generate the Static Pages controller appears in Listing 3.4.

Listing 3.4 Generating a Static Pages controller.

```
$ rails generate controller StaticPages home help
      create  app/controllers/static_pages_controller.rb
       route  get 'static_pages/help'
       route  get 'static_pages/home'
      invoke  erb
      create    app/views/static_pages
      create    app/views/static_pages/home.html.erb
      create    app/views/static_pages/help.html.erb
      invoke  test_unit
      create    test/controllers/static_pages_controller_test.rb
      invoke  helper
```

```
create    app/helpers/static_pages_helper.rb
invoke    test_unit
create        test/helpers/static_pages_helper_test.rb
invoke    assets
invoke      coffee
create        app/assets/javascripts/static_pages.js.coffee
invoke      scss
create        app/assets/stylesheets/static_pages.css.scss
```

By the way, `rails g` is a shortcut for `rails generate`, which is only one of several shortcuts supported by Rails (Table 3.1). For clarity, this tutorial always uses the full command, but in real life most Rails developers use one or more of the shortcuts shown in Table 3.1.

Before moving on, if you're using Git, it's a good idea to add the files for the Static Pages controller to the remote repository:

```
$ git status
$ git add -A
$ git commit -m "Add a Static Pages controller"
$ git push -u origin static-pages
```

The final command here arranges to push the **static-pages** topic branch up to Bitbucket. Subsequent pushes can omit the other arguments and write simply

```
$ git push
```

Table 3.1 Some Rails shortcuts.

Full command	Shortcut
$ rails server	$ rails s
$ rails console	$ rails c
$ rails generate	$ rails g
$ bundle install	$ bundle
$ rake test	$ rake

This commit and push sequence represents the kind of pattern I would ordinarily follow in real-life development, but for simplicity I'll typically omit such intermediate commits from now on.

In Listing 3.4, note that we have passed the controller name as CamelCase, which leads to the creation of a controller file written in snake case, so that a controller called StaticPages yields a file called **static_pages_controller.rb**. This is merely a convention, and in fact using snake case at the command line also works. That is, the command

```
$ rails generate controller static_pages ...
```

also generates a controller called **static_pages_controller.rb**. Because Ruby uses CamelCase for class names (Section 4.4), my preference is to refer to controllers using their CamelCase names, but this is a matter of taste. (Because Ruby filenames typically use snake case, the Rails generator converts CamelCase to snake case using the underscore method.)

If you ever make a mistake when generating code, it's useful to know how to reverse the process. Box 3.1 describes some techniques on undo things in Rails.

Box 3.1 Undoing Things

Even when you're very careful, things can sometimes go wrong when you're developing Rails applications. Happily, Rails has some facilities to help you recover.

One common scenario is wanting to undo code generation—for example, when you change your mind about the name of a controller and want to eliminate the generated files. Because Rails creates a substantial number of auxiliary files along with the controller (as seen in Listing 3.4), this isn't as easy as removing the controller file itself; undoing the generation means removing not only the principal generated file, but all the ancillary files as well. (In fact, as we saw in Section 2.2 and Section 2.3, rails generate can make automatic edits to the routes.rb file, which we also want to undo automatically.) In Rails, this can be accomplished by using the command rails destroy followed by the name of the generated element. In particular, these two commands cancel each other out:

```
$ rails generate controller StaticPages home help
$ rails destroy  controller StaticPages home help
```

Similarly, in Chapter 6 we'll generate a *model* as follows:

```
$ rails generate model User name:string email:string
```

This can be undone using

```
$ rails destroy model User
```

(In this case, it turns out we can omit the other command-line arguments. When you get to Chapter 6, see if you can figure out why.)

Another technique related to models involves undoing *migrations*, which we saw briefly in Chapter 2 and will encounter much more frequently beginning in Chapter 6. Migrations change the state of the database using the following command

```
$ bundle exec rake db:migrate
```

We can undo a single migration step with this command:

```
$ bundle exec rake db:rollback
```

To go all the way back to the beginning, we can use a third command:

```
$ bundle exec rake db:migrate VERSION=0
```

As you might guess, substituting any other number for 0 migrates to that version number, where the version numbers come from listing the migrations sequentially.

With these techniques in hand, we are well equipped to recover from the inevitable development snafus.

The Static Pages controller generation in Listing 3.4 automatically updates the routes file (**config/routes.rb**), which we saw briefly in Section 1.3.4. The routes file is responsible for implementing the router (seen in Figure 2.7) that defines the correspondence between URLs and web pages. The routes file is located in the **config** directory, where Rails collects files needed for the application configuration (Figure 3.1).

Because we included the **home** and **help** actions in Listing 3.4, the routes file already has a rule for each one, as seen in Listing 3.5.

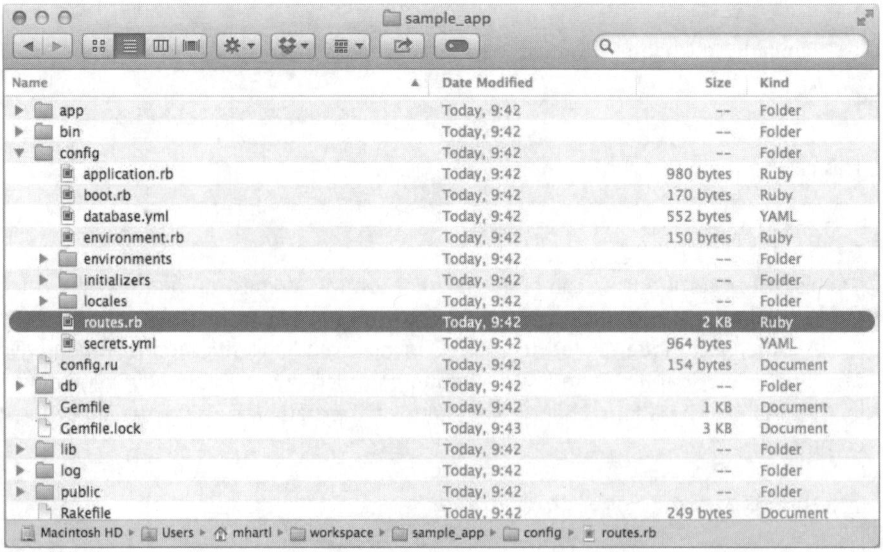

Figure 3.1 Contents of the sample app's `config` directory.

Listing 3.5 The routes for the **home** and **help** actions in the Static Pages controller.
config/routes.rb

```
Rails.application.routes.draw do
  get 'static_pages/home'
  get 'static_pages/help'
  .
  .
  .
end
```

Here the rule

```
get 'static_pages/home'
```

maps requests for the URL /static_pages/home to the **home** action in the Static Pages controller. Moreover, by using **get** we arrange for the route to respond to a GET request, which is one of the fundamental *HTTP verbs* supported by the Hypertext Transfer Protocol (Box 3.2). In our case, this means that when we generate a **home** action

Figure 3.2 The raw home view (/static_pages/home).

inside the Static Pages controller, we automatically get a page at the address /static_pages/home. To see the result, start a Rails development server as described in Section 1.3.2:

```
$ rails server -b $IP -p $PORT    # Use only `rails server` if running locally
```

Then navigate to /static_pages/home (Figure 3.2).

Box 3.2 GET, et al.

The Hypertext Transfer Protocol (HTTP) defines the basic operations GET, POST, PATCH, and DELETE. These operations occur between a *client* computer (typically running a web browser such as Chrome, Firefox, or Safari) and a *server* (typically running a web server such as Apache or Nginx). (When developing Rails applications on a local computer, the client and the server are the same physical machine, but in general they are different.) An emphasis on HTTP verbs is typical of web frameworks (including Rails) influenced by the *REST architecture*, which we saw briefly in Chapter 2 and will learn about more in Chapter 7.

GET is the most common HTTP operation, used for *reading* data on the web; it just means "get." Every time you visit a site like http://www.google.com/ or http://www.wikipedia.org/, your browser is submitting a GET request. POST is the next most common operation; it is the request sent by your browser when you submit a form. In Rails applications, POST requests are typically used for *creating* things (although HTTP also allows POST to perform updates). For example, the POST request sent when you submit a registration form creates a new user on the remote site. The other two verbs, PATCH and DELETE, are designed for *updating* and *destroying* things on the remote server. These requests are less common than GET and POST because browsers are incapable of sending them natively, but some web frameworks (including Ruby on Rails) have clever ways of making it *seem* as if browsers are issuing such requests. As a result, Rails supports all four of the request types GET, POST, PATCH, and DELETE.

To understand where this page comes from, let's look at the Static Pages controller in a text editor, which should look something like Listing 3.6. Unlike the demo Users and Microposts controllers from Chapter 2, the Static Pages controller does not use the standard REST actions. This is normal for a collection of static pages: The REST architecture isn't the best solution for every problem.

Listing 3.6 The Static Pages controller made by Listing 3.4.
app/controllers/static_pages_controller.rb

```ruby
class StaticPagesController < ApplicationController

  def home
  end

  def help
  end
end
```

As indicated by the **class** keyword in Listing 3.6, **static_pages_control-ler.rb** defines a *class*—in this case called **StaticPagesController**. Classes are simply a convenient way to organize *functions* (also called *methods*) like the **home** and **help** actions, which are defined using the **def** keyword. As discussed in Section 2.3.4, the angle bracket **<** indicates that **StaticPagesController** *inherits* from the Rails class **ApplicationController**; as we'll see momentarily, this means that our pages come equipped with a large amount of Rails-specific functionality. (We'll learn more about both classes and inheritance in Section 4.4.)

In the case of the Static Pages controller, both of its methods are initially empty:

```
def home
end

def help
end
```

In plain Ruby, these methods would simply do nothing. In Rails, the situation is different—**StaticPagesController** is a Ruby class, but because it inherits from **ApplicationController** the behavior of its methods is specific to Rails. For example, when visiting the URL /static_pages/home, Rails looks in the Static Pages controller and executes the code in the **home** action, and then renders the *view* (the "V" in MVC from Section 1.3.3) corresponding to the action. In the present case, the **home** action is empty, so all visiting /static_pages/home does is render the view. But what does a view look like, and how do we find it?

If you take another look at the output in Listing 3.4, you might be able to guess the correspondence between actions and views: An action like **home** has a corresponding view called **home.html.erb**. In Section 3.4, we'll learn what the **.erb** part means; from the **.html** part you probably won't be surprised that it basically looks like HTML (Listing 3.7).

Listing 3.7 The generated view for the Home page.

app/views/static_pages/home.html.erb

```
<h1>StaticPages#home</h1>
<p>Find me in app/views/static_pages/home.html.erb</p>
```

The view for the **help** action is analogous (Listing 3.8).

Listing 3.8 The generated view for the Help page.

app/views/static_pages/help.html.erb

```
<h1>StaticPages#help</h1>
<p>Find me in app/views/static_pages/help.html.erb</p>
```

Both of these views are just placeholders: They have a top-level heading (inside the **h1** tag) and a paragraph (**p** tag) with the full path to the corresponding file.

3.2.2 Custom Static Pages

We'll add some (very slightly) dynamic content starting in Section 3.4. As they stand, however, the views in Listing 3.7 and Listing 3.8 underscore an important point: Rails views can simply contain static HTML. This means we can begin customizing the Home and Help pages even with no knowledge of Rails, as shown in Listing 3.9 and Listing 3.10.

The results of Listing 3.9 and Listing 3.10 are shown in Figure 3.3 and Figure 3.4, respectively.

Listing 3.9 Custom HTML for the Home page.

app/views/static_pages/home.html.erb

```
<h1>Sample App</h1>
<p>
  This is the home page for the
  <a href="http://www.railstutorial.org/">Ruby on Rails Tutorial</a>
  sample application.
</p>
```

Listing 3.10 Custom HTML for the Help page.

app/views/static_pages/help.html.erb

```
<h1>Help</h1>
<p>
  Get help on the Ruby on Rails Tutorial at the
```

```
<a href="http://www.railstutorial.org/#help">Rails Tutorial help section</a>.
To get help on this sample app, see the
<a href="http://www.railstutorial.org/book"><em>Ruby on Rails Tutorial</em>
book</a>.
</p>
```

3.3 Getting Started with Testing

Having created and filled in the Home and Help pages for our sample app (Section 3.2.2), we will now add an About page as well. When making a change of this nature, it's a good practice to write an *automated test* to verify that the feature is implemented correctly. Developed over the course of building an application, the resulting

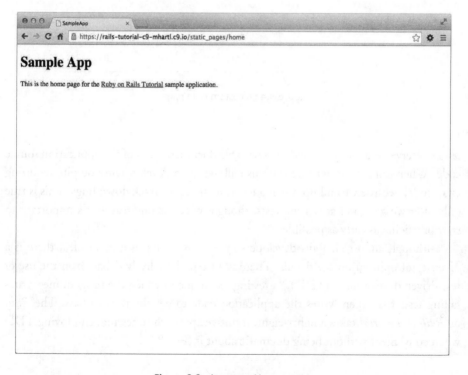

Figure 3.3 A custom Home page.

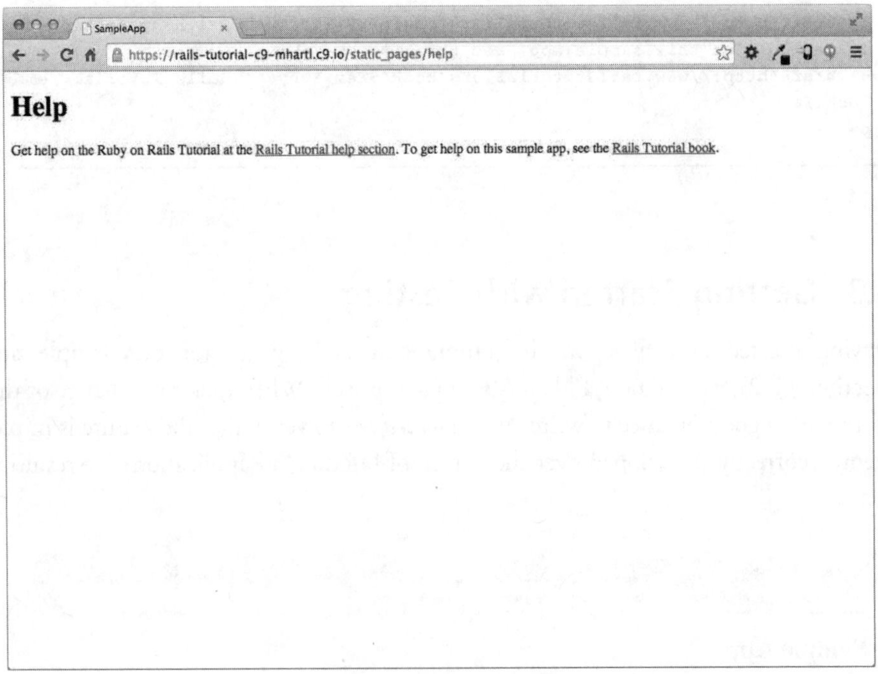

Figure 3.4 A custom Help page.

test suite serves as a safety net and as executable documentation of the application source code. When done right, writing tests also allows us to develop *faster* despite requiring extra code, because we end up wasting less time trying to track down bugs. This is true only after we get good at writing tests, though, which is one reason it's important to start practicing as early as possible.

Although almost all Rails developers agree that testing is a good idea, there is a diversity of opinion on the details. There is an especially lively debate over the use of test-driven development (TDD),[5] a testing technique in which the programmer writes failing tests first, then writes the application code to get the tests to pass. The *Ruby on Rails*™ *Tutorial* takes a lightweight, intuitive approach to testing, employing TDD when convenient without being dogmatic about it (Box 3.3).

---

5. See, e.g., "TDD is dead. Long live testing." by Rails creator David Heinemeier Hansson.

Box 3.3 When to test

When deciding when and how to test, it's helpful to understand *why* to test. Writing automated tests has three main benefits:

1. Tests protect against *regressions*, where a functioning feature stops working for some reason.
2. Tests allow code to be *refactored* (i.e., changing its form without changing its function) with greater confidence.
3. Tests act as a *client* for the application code, thereby helping determine its design and its interface with other parts of the system.

Although none of these *requires* that tests be written first, in many circumstances test-driven development (TDD) is a valuable tool to have in your kit. Deciding when and how to test depends in part on how comfortable you are writing tests; many developers find that, as they get better at writing tests, they are more inclined to write them first. It also depends on how difficult the test is relative to the application code, how precisely the desired features are known, and how likely the feature is to break in the future.

In this context, it's helpful to have a set of guidelines regarding when we should test first (or test at all). Here are some suggestions based on my own experience:

- When a test is especially short or simple compared to the application code it tests, lean toward writing the test first.
- When the desired behavior isn't crystal clear, lean toward writing the application code first, then write a test to codify the result.
- Because security is a top priority, err on the side of writing tests of the security model first.
- Whenever a bug is found, write a test to reproduce it and protect against regressions, then write the application code to fix it.
- Lean against writing tests for code (such as detailed HTML structure) likely to change in the future.
- Write tests before refactoring code, focusing on testing error-prone code that's especially likely to break.

In practice, these guidelines mean that we'll usually write controller and model tests first and integration tests (which test functionality across models, views, and

controllers) second. In contrast, when we're writing application code that isn't particularly brittle or error-prone, or is likely to change (as is often the case with views),
we'll often skip testing altogether.

Our main testing tools will be *controller tests* (starting in this section), *model tests*
(starting in Chapter 6), and *integration tests* (starting in Chapter 7). Integration tests are
especially powerful, as they allow us to simulate the actions of a user interacting with our
application using a web browser. Integration tests will eventually be our primary testing
technique, but controller tests give us an easier place to start.

3.3.1 Our First Test

Now it's time to add an About page to our application. As we'll see, this test is short and
simple, so we'll follow the guidelines from Box 3.3 and write the test first. We'll then
use the failing test to drive the writing of the application code.

Getting started with testing can be challenging, requiring extensive knowledge of
both Rails and Ruby. At this early stage, writing tests might seem hopelessly intimidat-
ing. Luckily, Rails has already done the hardest part for us, because `rails generate`
`controller` (Listing 3.4) automatically generated a test file to get us started:

```
$ ls test/controllers/
static_pages_controller_test.rb
```

Let's take a look at it (Listing 3.11).

Listing 3.11 The default tests for the StaticPages controller. **GREEN**
test/controllers/static_pages_controller_test.rb

```
require 'test_helper'

class StaticPagesControllerTest < ActionController::TestCase

  test "should get home" do
    get :home
    assert_response :success
  end
```

```
  test "should get help" do
    get :help
    assert_response :success
  end
end
```

It's not important at this point to understand the syntax in Listing 3.11 in detail, but we can see that there are two tests, one for each controller action we included on the command line in Listing 3.4. Each test simply gets an action and verifies (via an *assertion*) that the result is a success. Here the use of **get** indicates that our tests expect the Home and Help pages to be ordinary web pages, accessed using a GET request (Box 3.2). The response **:success** is an abstract representation of the underlying HTTP status code (in this case, 200 OK). In other words, a test like

```
test "should get home" do
  get :home
  assert_response :success
end
```

says, "Let's test the Home page by issuing a GET request to the **home** action and then making sure we receive a 'success' status code in response."

To begin our testing cycle, we need to run our test suite to verify that the tests currently pass. We can do this with the **rake** utility (Box 2.1) as shown in Listing 3.12:[6]

Listing 3.12   GREEN

```
$ bundle exec rake test
2 tests, 2 assertions, 0 failures, 0 errors, 0 skips
```

As required, initially our test suite is passing (**GREEN**). (You won't actually see the color green unless you add MiniTest reporters in the optional Section 3.7.1.) By the way, the tests take some time to start, which is due to two factors: (1) starting the *Spring*

---

6. As noted in Section 2.2, the use of **bundle exec** is unnecessary on some systems, including the cloud IDE recommended in Section 1.2.1, but I include it for completeness. In practice, my usual algorithm is to omit **bundle exec** unless I get an error, in which case I retry the command with **bundle exec** and see if it works.

server to preload parts of the Rails environment, which happens only the first time; and (2) overhead associated with Ruby startup time. (The second factor is ameliorated when using Guard as suggested in Section 3.7.3.)

3.3.2 Red

As noted in Box 3.3, test-driven development involves writing a failing test first, then writing the application code needed to get it to pass, and finally refactoring the code if necessary. Because many testing tools represent failing tests with the color red and passing tests with the color green, this sequence is sometimes known as the "Red–Green–Refactor" cycle. In this section, we'll complete the first step in this cycle, getting to **RED** by writing a failing test. Then we'll get to **GREEN** in Section 3.3.3, and refactor in Section 3.4.3.[7]

Our first step is to write a failing test for the About page. Following the models from Listing 3.11, you can probably guess the right test, which is shown in Listing 3.13.

Listing 3.13   A test for the About page. **RED**

test/controllers/static_pages_controller_test.rb

```ruby
require 'test_helper'

class StaticPagesControllerTest < ActionController::TestCase

  test "should get home" do
    get :home
    assert_response :success
  end

  test "should get help" do
    get :help
    assert_response :success
  end

  test "should get about" do
    get :about
    assert_response :success
  end
end
```

---

7. By default, `rake test` shows red when the tests fail, but doesn't show green when the tests pass. To arrange for a true Red–Green cycle, see Section 3.7.1.

As the highlighted lines in Listing 3.13 indicate, the test for the About page is the same as the Home and Help tests with the word "about" in place of "home" or "help."

The test initially fails, as required:

Listing 3.14 RED

```
$ bundle exec rake test
3 tests, 2 assertions, 0 failures, 1 errors, 0 skips
```

3.3.3 Green

Now that we have a failing test (**RED**), we'll use the failing test's error messages to guide us to a passing test (**GREEN**), thereby implementing a working About page.

We can get started by examining the error message output by the failing test:[8]

Listing 3.15 RED

```
$ bundle exec rake test
ActionController::UrlGenerationError:
No route matches {:action=>"about", :controller=>"static_pages"}
```

This error message says that no route matches the desired action/controller combination, which is a hint that we need to add a line to the routes file. We can accomplish this by following the pattern in Listing 3.5, as shown in Listing 3.16.

Listing 3.16 Adding the **about** route. **RED**
config/routes.rb

```
Rails.application.routes.draw do
  get 'static_pages/home'
  get 'static_pages/help'
```

---

8. On some systems, you may have to scroll past the "stack trace" or "backtrace" that traces the error's path through the source code. See Section 3.7.2 for information on how to filter this backtrace to eliminate unwanted lines.

```
  get 'static_pages/about'
    .
    .
    .
end
```

The highlighted line in Listing 3.16 tells Rails to route a GET request for the URL /static_pages/about to the **about** action in the Static Pages controller.

Running our test suite again, we see that it is still **RED**, but now the error message has changed:

Listing 3.17   RED

```
$ bundle exec rake test
AbstractController::ActionNotFound:
The action 'about' could not be found for StaticPagesController
```

This error message indicates a missing **about** action in the Static Pages controller, which we can add by following the model provided by **home** and **help** in Listing 3.6, as shown in Listing 3.18.

Listing 3.18 The Static Pages controller with added **about** action. **RED**
app/controllers/static_pages_controller.rb

```
class StaticPagesController < ApplicationController

  def home
  end

  def help
  end

  def about
  end
end
```

As before, our test suite is still **RED**, but the error message has changed again:

```
$ bundle exec rake test
ActionView::MissingTemplate: Missing template static_pages/about
```

This message indicates a template is missing, which in the context of Rails is essentially the same thing as a view. As described in Section 3.2.1, an action called **home** is associated with a view called **home.html.erb** located in the **app/views/static_pages** directory, which means that we need to create a new file called **about.html.erb** in the same directory.

The way to create a file varies depending on the system setup, but most text editors will let you control-click inside the directory where you want to create the file to bring up a menu with a "New File" menu item. Alternately you can use the File menu to create a new file and then pick the proper directory when saving it. Finally, you can use my favorite trick by applying the Unix **touch** command[9] as follows:

```
$ touch app/views/static_pages/about.html.erb
```

Although **touch** is designed to update the modification timestamp of a file or directory without otherwise affecting it, as a side effect it creates a new (blank) file if one doesn't already exist. (If you're using the cloud IDE, you may have to refresh the file tree as described in Section 1.3.1.)

Once you've created the **about.html.erb** file in the right directory, you should fill it with the content shown in Listing 3.19.

Listing 3.19 Code for the About page. **GREEN**

app/views/static_pages/about.html.erb

```
<h1>About</h1>
<p>
  The <a href="http://www.railstutorial.org/"><em>Ruby on Rails
  Tutorial</em></a> is a
  <a href="http://www.railstutorial.org/book">book</a> and
  <a href="http://screencasts.railstutorial.org/">screencast series</a>
  to teach web development with
  <a href="http://rubyonrails.org/">Ruby on Rails</a>.
  This is the sample application for the tutorial.
</p>
```

---

9. http://en.wikipedia.org/wiki/Touch_(Unix)

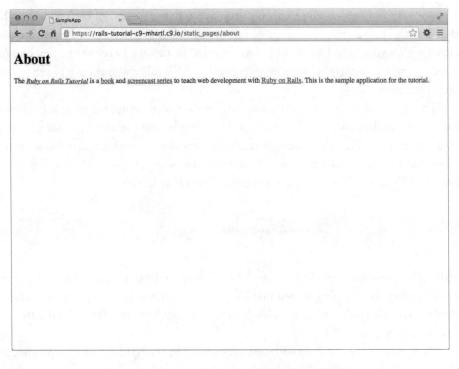

Figure 3.5 The new About page (/static_pages/about).

At this point, running `rake test` should get us back to **GREEN**:

Listing 3.20 GREEN

```
$ bundle exec rake test
3 tests, 3 assertions, 0 failures, 0 errors, 0 skips
```

Of course, it's never a bad idea to take a look at the page in a browser to make sure our tests aren't completely crazy (Figure 3.5).

3.3.4 Refactor

Now that we've gotten to **GREEN**, we are free to refactor our code with confidence. When developing an application, often code will start to "smell," meaning that it gets ugly, bloated, or filled with repetition. The computer doesn't care what the code looks like, of course, but humans do—so it is important to keep the code base clean by refactoring frequently. Although our sample app is a little too small to refactor right now, code smell seeps in at every crack, and we'll get started refactoring in Section 3.4.3.

3.4 Slightly Dynamic Pages

Now that we've created the actions and views for some static pages, we'll make them *slightly* dynamic by adding some content that changes on a per-page basis. Specifically, we'll have the title of each page change to reflect its content. Whether a changing title represents *truly* dynamic content is debatable, but in any case it lays the necessary foundation for unambiguously dynamic content in Chapter 7.

Our plan is to edit the Home, Help, and About pages to have page titles that change on each page. This will involve using the `<title>` tag in our page views. Most browsers display the contents of the title tag at the top of the browser window, and the title tag is also important for search-engine optimization. We'll be using the full "Red–Green–Refactor" cycle: first by adding simple tests for our page titles (**RED**), then by adding titles to each of our three pages (**GREEN**), and finally by using a *layout* file to eliminate duplication (Refactor). By the end of this section, all three of our static pages will have titles of the form "<page name> | Ruby on Rails Tutorial Sample App," where the first part of the title will vary depending on the page (Table 3.2).

The `rails new` command (Listing 3.1) creates a layout file by default, but it's instructive to ignore it initially, which we can do by changing its name:

```
$ mv app/views/layouts/application.html.erb layout_file   # temporary change
```

You wouldn't normally do this in a real application, but it's easier to understand the purpose of the layout file if we start by disabling it.

Table 3.2 The (mostly) static pages for the sample app.

Page	URL	Base title	Variable title
Home	/static_pages/home	`"Ruby on Rails Tutorial Sample App"`	`"Home"`
Help	/static_pages/help	`"Ruby on Rails Tutorial Sample App"`	`"Help"`
About	/static_pages/about	`"Ruby on Rails Tutorial Sample App"`	`"About"`

3.4.1 Testing Titles (Red)

To add page titles, we need to learn (or review) the structure of a typical web page, which takes the form shown in Listing 3.21.

Listing 3.21 The HTML structure of a typical web page.

```
<!DOCTYPE html>
<html>
  <head>
    <title>Greeting</title>
  </head>
  <body>
    <p>Hello, world!</p>
  </body>
</html>
```

The structure in Listing 3.21 includes a *document type*, or doctype, declaration at the top to tell browsers which version of HTML we're using (in this case, HTML5);[10] a **head** section, in this case with "Greeting" inside a **title** tag; and a **body** section, in this case with "Hello, world!" inside a **p** (paragraph) tag. (The indentation is optional—HTML is not sensitive to whitespace, and ignores both tabs and spaces—but it makes the document's structure easier to see.)

We'll write simple tests for each of the titles in Table 3.2 by combining the tests in Listing 3.13 with the **assert_select** method, which lets us test for the presence of a particular HTML tag (sometimes called a "selector"—hence the name):[11]

```
assert_select "title", "Home | Ruby on Rails Tutorial Sample App"
```

In particular, this code checks for the presence of a **<title>** tag containing the string "Home | Ruby on Rails Tutorial Sample App". Applying this idea to all three static pages gives the tests shown in Listing 3.22.

---

10. HTML changes with time; by explicitly making a doctype declaration, we increase the likelihood that browsers will render our pages properly in the future. The simple doctype `<!DOCTYPE html>` is characteristic of the latest HTML standard, HTML5.

11. For a list of common MiniTest assertions, see the table of available assertions in the Rails Guides testing article.

Listing 3.22 The Static Pages controller test with title tests. **RED**

test/controllers/static_pages_controller_test.rb

```ruby
require 'test_helper'

class StaticPagesControllerTest < ActionController::TestCase

  test "should get home" do
    get :home
    assert_response :success
    assert_select "title", "Home | Ruby on Rails Tutorial Sample App"
  end

  test "should get help" do
    get :help
    assert_response :success
    assert_select "title", "Help | Ruby on Rails Tutorial Sample App"
  end

  test "should get about" do
    get :about
    assert_response :success
    assert_select "title", "About | Ruby on Rails Tutorial Sample App"
  end
end
```

(If the repetition of the base title "Ruby on Rails Tutorial Sample App" bothers you, see the exercises in Section 3.6.)

With the tests from Listing 3.22 in place, you should verify that the test suite is currently **RED**:

Listing 3.23 RED

```
$ bundle exec rake test
3 tests, 6 assertions, 3 failures, 0 errors, 0 skips
```

3.4.2 Adding Page Titles (Green)

Now we'll add a title to each page, getting the tests from Section 3.4.1 to pass in the process. Applying the basic HTML structure from Listing 3.21 to the custom Home page from Listing 3.9 yields Listing 3.24.

Listing 3.24 The view for the Home page with full HTML structure. **RED**

app/views/static_pages/home.html.erb

```
<!DOCTYPE html>
<html>
  <head>
    <title>Home | Ruby on Rails Tutorial Sample App</title>
  </head>
  <body>
    <h1>Sample App</h1>
    <p>
      This is the home page for the
      <a href="http://www.railstutorial.org/">Ruby on Rails Tutorial</a>
      sample application.
    </p>
  </body>
</html>
```

The corresponding web page appears in Figure 3.6.[12]

Following this model for the Help page (Listing 3.10) and the About page
(Listing 3.19) yields the code in Listing 3.25 and Listing 3.26.

Listing 3.25 The view for the Help page with full HTML structure. **RED**

app/views/static_pages/help.html.erb

```
<!DOCTYPE html>
<html>
  <head>
    <title>Help | Ruby on Rails Tutorial Sample App</title>
  </head>
  <body>
    <h1>Help</h1>
    <p>
      Get help on the Ruby on Rails Tutorial at the
      <a href="http://www.railstutorial.org/#help">Rails Tutorial help
      section</a>.
      To get help on this sample app, see the
      <a href="http://www.railstutorial.org/book"><em>Ruby on Rails
      Tutorial</em> book</a>.
    </p>
```

---

12. Most of the screenshots in this book use Google Chrome, but Figure 3.6 uses Safari because Chrome doesn't
display the full page title.

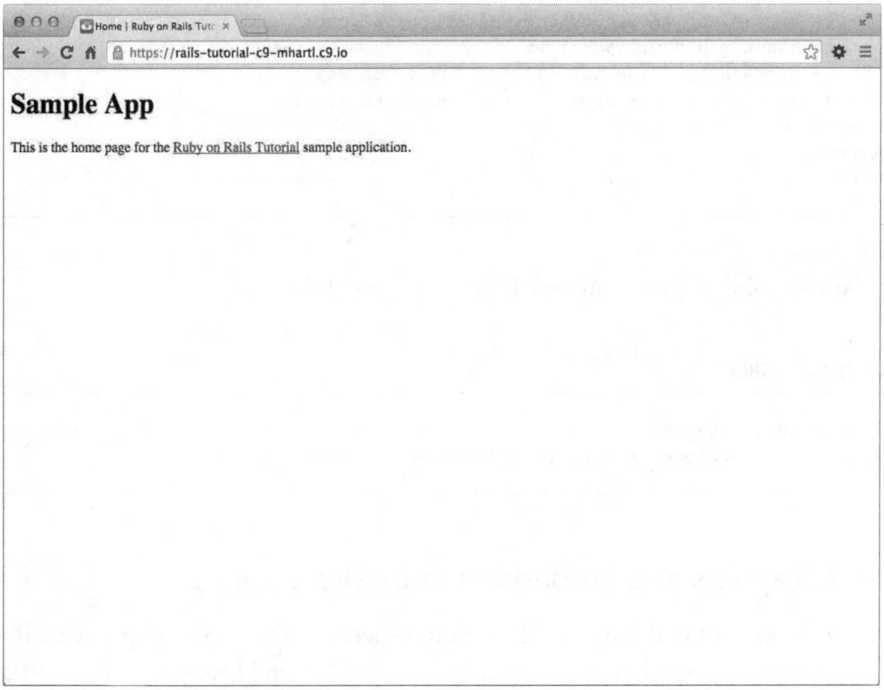

Figure 3.6   The Home page with a title.

```
  </body>
</html>
```

Listing 3.26   The view for the About page with full HTML structure. **GREEN**
app/views/static_pages/about.html.erb

```
<!DOCTYPE html>
<html>
  <head>
    <title>About | Ruby on Rails Tutorial Sample App</title>
  </head>
  <body>
    <h1>About</h1>
    <p>
      The <a href="http://www.railstutorial.org/"><em>Ruby on Rails
      Tutorial</em></a> is a
      <a href="http://www.railstutorial.org/book">book</a> and
```

```
      <a href="http://screencasts.railstutorial.org/">screencast series</a>
      to teach web development with
      <a href="http://rubyonrails.org/">Ruby on Rails</a>.
      This is the sample application for the tutorial.
    </p>
  </body>
</html>
```

At this point, the test suite should be back to **GREEN**:

Listing 3.27 GREEN

```
$ bundle exec rake test
3 tests, 6 assertions, 0 failures, 0 errors, 0 skips
```

3.4.3 Layouts and Embedded Ruby (Refactor)

We've achieved a lot already in this section, generating three valid pages using Rails controllers and actions, but they are purely static HTML and hence don't show off the power of Rails. Moreover, they suffer from terrible duplication:

- The page titles are almost (but not quite) exactly the same.

- "Ruby on Rails Tutorial Sample App" is common to all three titles.

- The entire HTML skeleton structure is repeated on each page.

This repeated code is a violation of the important "Don't Repeat Yourself" (DRY) principle; in this section we'll "DRY out our code" by removing the repetition. At the end, we'll rerun the tests from Section 3.4.2 to verify that the titles are still correct.

Paradoxically, we'll take the first step toward eliminating duplication by first adding some more: We'll make the titles of the pages, which are currently quite similar, match *exactly*. This will make it much simpler to remove all the repetition at a stroke.

The technique involves using *embedded Ruby* in our views. Since the Home, Help, and About page titles have a variable component, we'll use a special Rails function called **provide** to set a different title on each page. We can see how this works by replacing the literal title "Home" in the **home.html.erb** view with the code in Listing 3.28.

Listing 3.28 The view for the Home page with an embedded Ruby title. **GREEN**
app/views/static_pages/home.html.erb

```
<% provide(:title, "Home") %>
<!DOCTYPE html>
<html>
  <head>
    <title><%= yield(:title) %> | Ruby on Rails Tutorial Sample App</title>
  </head>
  <body>
    <h1>Sample App</h1>
    <p>
      This is the home page for the
      <a href="http://www.railstutorial.org/">Ruby on Rails Tutorial</a>
      sample application.
    </p>
  </body>
</html>
```

Listing 3.28 is our first example of embedded Ruby, also called *ERb*. (Now you know why HTML views have the file extension `.html.erb`.) ERb is the primary template system for including dynamic content in web pages.[13] The code

```
<% provide(:title, "Home") %>
```

indicates using `<% ... %>` that Rails should call the **provide** function and associate the string **"Home"** with the label **:title**.[14] Then, in the title, we use the closely related notation `<%= ... %>` to insert the title into the template using Ruby's **yield** function:[15]

```
<title><%= yield(:title) %> | Ruby on Rails Tutorial Sample App</title>
```

(The distinction between the two types of embedded Ruby is that `<% ... %>` *executes* the code inside, while `<%= ... %>` executes it *and inserts* the result into the template.)

---

13. There is a second popular template system called Haml, which I personally love, but it's not *quite* standard enough yet for use in an introductory tutorial.

14. Experienced Rails developers might have expected the use of **content_for** at this point, but it doesn't work well with the asset pipeline. The **provide** function is its replacement.

15. If you've studied Ruby before, you might suspect that Rails is *yielding* the contents to a block, and your suspicion would be correct. But you don't need to know this to develop applications with Rails.

The resulting page is exactly the same as before, only now the variable part of the title is generated dynamically by ERb.

We can verify that all this works by running the tests from Section 3.4.2 and confirming that they are still **GREEN**:

Listing 3.29   GREEN

```
$ bundle exec rake test
3 tests, 6 assertions, 0 failures, 0 errors, 0 skips
```

Then we can make the corresponding replacements for the Help and About pages (Listing 3.30 and Listing 3.31).

Listing 3.30   The view for the Help page with an embedded Ruby title. **GREEN**
app/views/static_pages/help.html.erb

```
<% provide(:title, "Help") %>
<!DOCTYPE html>
<html>
  <head>
    <title><%= yield(:title) %> | Ruby on Rails Tutorial Sample App</title>
  </head>
  <body>
    <h1>Help</h1>
    <p>
      Get help on the Ruby on Rails Tutorial at the
      <a href="http://www.railstutorial.org/#help">Rails Tutorial help
      section</a>.
      To get help on this sample app, see the
      <a href="http://www.railstutorial.org/book"><em>Ruby on Rails
      Tutorial</em> book</a>.
    </p>
  </body>
</html>
```

Listing 3.31   The view for the About page with an embedded Ruby title. **GREEN**
app/views/static_pages/about.html.erb

```
<% provide(:title, "About") %>
```

```
<!DOCTYPE html>
<html>
  <head>
    <title><%= yield(:title) %> | Ruby on Rails Tutorial Sample App</title>
  </head>
  <body>
    <h1>About</h1>
    <p>
      The <a href="http://www.railstutorial.org/"><em>Ruby on Rails
      Tutorial</em></a> is a
      <a href="http://www.railstutorial.org/book">book</a> and
      <a href="http://screencasts.railstutorial.org/">screencast series</a>
      to teach web development with
      <a href="http://rubyonrails.org/">Ruby on Rails</a>.
      This is the sample application for the tutorial.
    </p>
  </body>
</html>
```

Now that we've replaced the variable part of the page titles with ERb, each of our pages looks something like this:

```
<% provide(:title, "The Title") %>
<!DOCTYPE html>
<html>
  <head>
    <title><%= yield(:title) %> | Ruby on Rails Tutorial Sample App</title>
  </head>
  <body>
    Contents
  </body>
</html>
```

In other words, all the pages are identical in structure, including the contents of the **title** tag, with the sole exception of the material inside the **body** tag.

To factor out this common structure, Rails comes with a special *layout* file called **application.html.erb**, which we renamed in the beginning of this section (Section 3.4) and which we'll now restore:

```
$ mv layout_file app/views/layouts/application.html.erb
```

To get the layout to work, we must replace the default title with the embedded Ruby from the preceding examples:

```
<title><%= yield(:title) %> | Ruby on Rails Tutorial Sample App</title>
```

The resulting layout appears in Listing 3.32.

Listing 3.32 The sample application site layout. **GREEN**
app/views/layouts/application.html.erb

```
<!DOCTYPE html>
<html>
  <head>
    <title><%= yield(:title) %> | Ruby on Rails Tutorial Sample App</title>
    <%= stylesheet_link_tag    'application', media: 'all',
                                              'data-turbolinks-track' => true %>
    <%= javascript_include_tag 'application', 'data-turbolinks-track' => true %>
    <%= csrf_meta_tags %>
  </head>
  <body>
    <%= yield %>
  </body>
</html>
```

Note here the special line

```
<%= yield %>
```

This code is responsible for inserting the contents of each page into the layout. It's not important to know exactly how this works; what matters is that using this layout ensures that, for example, visiting the page /static_pages/home converts the contents of **home.html.erb** to HTML and then inserts it in place of <%= yield %>.

It's also worth noting that the default Rails layout includes several additional lines:

```
<%= stylesheet_link_tag ... %>
<%= javascript_include_tag "application", ... %>
<%= csrf_meta_tags %>
```

This code arranges to include the application style sheet and JavaScript, which are part of the asset pipeline (Section 5.2.1), together with the Rails method `csrf_meta_tags`, which prevents cross-site request forgery (CSRF), a type of malicious web attack.

Of course, the views in Listing 3.28, Listing 3.30, and Listing 3.31 are still filled with the HTML structure included in the layout, so we have to remove it, leaving only the interior contents. The resulting cleaned-up views appear in Listing 3.33, Listing 3.34, and Listing 3.35.

Listing 3.33 The Home page with HTML structure removed. **GREEN**
app/views/static_pages/home.html.erb

```
<% provide(:title, "Home") %>
<h1>Sample App</h1>
<p>
  This is the home page for the
  <a href="http://www.railstutorial.org/">Ruby on Rails Tutorial</a>
  sample application.
</p>
```

Listing 3.34 The Help page with HTML structure removed. **GREEN**
app/views/static_pages/help.html.erb

```
<% provide(:title, "Help") %>
<h1>Help</h1>
<p>
  Get help on the Ruby on Rails Tutorial at the
  <a href="http://www.railstutorial.org/#help">Rails Tutorial help section</a>.
  To get help on this sample app, see the
  <a href="http://www.railstutorial.org/book"><em>Ruby on Rails Tutorial</em>
  book</a>.
</p>
```

Listing 3.35 The About page with HTML structure removed. **GREEN**
app/views/static_pages/about.html.erb

```
<% provide(:title, "About") %>
<h1>About</h1>
<p>
```

```
The <a href="http://www.railstutorial.org/"><em>Ruby on Rails
Tutorial</em></a> is a
<a href="http://www.railstutorial.org/book">book</a> and
<a href="http://screencasts.railstutorial.org/">screencast series</a>
to teach web development with
<a href="http://rubyonrails.org/">Ruby on Rails</a>.
This is the sample application for the tutorial.
</p>
```

With these views defined, the Home, Help, and About pages are the same as before, but they have much less duplication.

Experience shows that even fairly simple refactoring is error-prone and can easily go awry. This is one reason why having a good test suite is so valuable. Rather than double-checking every page for correctness—a procedure that isn't especially difficult early on but rapidly becomes unwieldy as an application grows—we can simply verify that the test suite is still **GREEN**:

Listing 3.36 GREEN

```
$ bundle exec rake test
3 tests, 6 assertions, 0 failures, 0 errors, 0 skips
```

This isn't a *proof* that our code is still correct, but it greatly increases the probability, thereby providing a safety net to protect us against future bugs.

3.4.4 Setting the Root Route

Now that we've customized our site's pages and gotten a good start on the test suite, let's set the application's root route before moving on. As in Section 1.3.4 and Section 2.2.2, this involves editing the `routes.rb` file to connect / to a page of our choice, which in this case will be the Home page. (At this point, I also recommend removing the `hello` action from the Application controller if you added it in Section 3.1.) As shown in Listing 3.37, setting the root route requires replacing the generated `get` rule from Listing 3.5 with the following code:

```
root 'static_pages#home'
```

Figure 3.7 The Home page at the root route.

This changes the URL **static_pages/home** to the controller/action pair **static_pages#home**, which ensures that GET requests for / get routed to the **home** action in the Static Pages controller. The resulting routes file is shown in Figure 3.7. (Note that, with the code in Listing 3.37, the previous route **static_pages/home** will no longer work.)

Listing 3.37 Setting the root route to the Home page.
config/routes.rb

```
Rails.application.routes.draw do
  root 'static_pages#home'
  get  'static_pages/help'
  get  'static_pages/about'
end
```

3.5 Conclusion

Seen from the outside, this chapter hardly accomplished anything: We started with static pages and ended with . . . *mostly* static pages. But appearances are deceiving: By developing in terms of Rails controllers, actions, and views, we are now in a position to add arbitrary amounts of dynamic content to our site. Seeing exactly how this plays out is the task for the rest of this tutorial.

Before moving on, let's take a minute to commit the changes on our topic branch and merge them into the master branch. Back in Section 3.2 we created a Git branch for the development of static pages. If you haven't been making commits as we've been moving along, first make a commit indicating that we've reached a stopping point:

```
$ git add -A
$ git commit -m "Finish static pages"
```

Then merge the changes back into the master branch using the same technique as in Section 1.4.4:[16]

```
$ git checkout master
$ git merge static-pages
```

Once you reach a stopping point like this, it's usually a good idea to push your code up to a remote repository (which, if you followed the steps in Section 1.4.3, will be Bitbucket):

```
$ git push
```

I also recommend deploying the application to Heroku:

```
$ bundle exec rake test
$ git push heroku
```

Here we've taken care to run the test suite before deploying, which is a good habit to develop.

---

16. If you get an error message saying that the Spring process ID (pid) file would be overwritten by the merge, just remove the file using `rm -f *.pid` at the command line.

3.5.1 What We Learned in This Chapter

- For a third time, we went through the full procedure of creating a new Rails application from scratch, installing the necessary gems, pushing it up to a remote repository, and deploying it to production.

- The `rails` script generates a new controller with `rails generate controller ControllerName <optional action names>`.

- New routes are defined in the file `config/routes.rb`.

- Rails views can contain static HTML or embedded Ruby (ERb).

- Automated testing allows us to write test suites that drive the development of new features, allow for confident refactoring, and catch regressions.

- Test-driven development uses a "Red–Green–Refactor" cycle.

- Rails layouts allow the use of a common template for pages in our application, thereby eliminating duplication.

3.6 Exercises

Note: To receive a copy of the *Solutions Manual for Exercises*, with solutions to every exercise in the *Ruby on Rails™ Tutorial*, visit www.railstutorial.org/<word>, where "<word>" is the last word of the Figure 3.9 caption.

From this point until the end of the tutorial, I recommend solving the exercises on a separate topic branch:

```
$ git checkout static-pages
$ git checkout -b static-pages-exercises
```

This practice will prevent conflicts with the main tutorial.

Once you're satisfied with your solutions, you can push up the exercises branch to a remote repository (if you've set one up):

```
<solve first exercise>
$ git commit -am "Eliminate repetition (solves exercise 3.1)"
```

```
<solve second exercise>
$ git add -A
$ git commit -m "Add a Contact page (solves exercise 3.2)"
$ git push -u origin static-pages-exercises
$ git checkout master
```

(As preparation for future development, the last step here checks out the master branch, but we *don't* merge in the changes to avoid conflicts with the rest of the tutorial.) In future chapters, the branches and commit messages will differ, of course, but the basic idea is the same.

1. You may have noticed some repetition in the Static Pages controller test (Listing 3.22). In particular, the base title, "Ruby on Rails Tutorial Sample App," is the same for every title test. Using the special function **setup**, which is run automatically before every test, verify that the tests in Listing 3.38 are still **GREEN**. (Listing 3.38 uses an *instance variable*, seen briefly in Section 2.2.2 and covered further in Section 4.4.5, combined with *string interpolation*, which is covered further in Section 4.2.2.)

2. Make a Contact page for the sample app.[17] Following the model in Listing 3.13, first write a test for the existence of a page at the URL /static_pages/contact by testing for the title "Contact | Ruby on Rails Tutorial Sample App". Get your test to pass by following the same steps as when making the About page in Section 3.3.3, including filling the Contact page with the content from Listing 3.39. Note that, to keep the exercises independent, Listing 3.39 doesn't incorporate the changes made in Listing 3.38.

Listing 3.38 The Static Pages controller test with a base title. **GREEN**
test/controllers/static_pages_controller_test.rb

```
require 'test_helper'

class StaticPagesControllerTest < ActionController::TestCase
  def setup
    @base_title = "Ruby on Rails Tutorial Sample App"
  end

  test "should get home" do
    get :home
```

---

17. This exercise is solved in Section 5.3.1.

```
    assert_response :success
    assert_select "title", "Home | #{@base_title}"
  end

  test "should get help" do
    get :help
    assert_response :success
    assert_select "title", "Help | #{@base_title}"
  end

  test "should get about" do
    get :about
    assert_response :success
    assert_select "title", "About | #{@base_title}"
  end
end
```

Listing 3.39 Code for a proposed Contact page.
app/views/static_pages/contact.html.erb

```
<% provide(:title, "Contact") %>
<h1>Contact</h1>
<p>
  Contact the Ruby on Rails Tutorial about the sample app at the
  <a href="http://www.railstutorial.org/#contact">contact page</a>.
</p>
```

3.7 Advanced Testing Setup

This optional section describes the testing setup used in the *Ruby on Rails*™ *Tutorial* screencast series. There are three main elements: an enhanced pass/fail reporter (Section 3.7.1), a utility to filter the backtrace produced by failing tests (Section 3.7.2), and an automated test runner that detects file changes and automatically runs the corresponding tests (Section 3.7.3). The code in this section is advanced and is presented for convenience only; you are not expected to understand it at this time.

The changes in this section should be made on the master branch:

```
$ git checkout master
```

```
  3/3: [===========================================] 100% Time: 00:00:00, Time: 00:00:00
Finished in 0.06162s
3 tests, 2 assertions, 0 failures, 1 errors, 0 skips
mhartl@rails-tutorial:/home/ubuntu/workspace/sample_app (master) $ rake test
Started

  3/3: [===========================================] 100% Time: 00:00:00, Time: 00:00:00
Finished in 0.04396s
3 tests, 3 assertions, 0 failures, 0 errors, 0 skips
mhartl@rails-tutorial:/home/ubuntu/workspace/sample_app (master) $ ▮
```

Figure 3.8 Going from **RED** to **GREEN** in the cloud IDE.

3.7.1 MiniTest Reporters

To get the default Rails tests to show **RED** and **GREEN** at the appropriate times, I recommend adding the code in Listing 3.40 to your test helper file,[18] thereby making use of the `minitest-reporters` gem included in Listing 3.2.

Listing 3.40 Configuring the tests to show **RED** and **GREEN**.
test/test_helper.rb

```ruby
ENV['RAILS_ENV'] ||= 'test'
require File.expand_path('../../config/environment', __FILE__)
require 'rails/test_help'
require "minitest/reporters"
Minitest::Reporters.use!

class ActiveSupport::TestCase
  # Setup all fixtures in test/fixtures/*.yml for all tests in alphabetical
  # order.
  fixtures :all

  # Add more helper methods to be used by all tests here...
end
```

The resulting transition from **RED** to **GREEN** in the cloud IDE appears as in Figure 3.8.

---

18. The code in Listing 3.40 mixes single- and double-quoted strings. This is because `rails new` generates single-quoted strings, whereas the MiniTest reporters documentation uses double-quoted strings. This mixing of the two string types is common in Ruby; see Section 4.2.2 for more information.

3.7.2 Backtrace Silencer

Upon encountering an error or failing test, the test runner shows a "stack trace" or "backtrace" that traces the course of a failed test through the application. While this backtrace is usually very useful for tracking down the problem, on some systems (including the cloud IDE) it goes past the application code and into the various gem dependencies, including Rails itself. The resulting backtrace is often inconveniently long, especially given that the source of the problem is often the application and not one of its dependencies.

The solution is to filter the backtrace to eliminate unwanted lines. This requires the `mini_backtrace` gem included in Listing 3.2, combined with a *backtrace silencer*. On the cloud IDE, most unwanted lines contain the string **rvm** (referring to the Ruby Version Manager), so I recommend using the silencer shown in Listing 3.41 to filter them out.

Listing 3.41   Adding a backtrace silencer for RVM.
config/initializers/backtrace_silencers.rb

```
# Be sure to restart your server when you modify this file.

# You can add backtrace silencers for libraries that you're using but don't
# wish to see in your backtraces.
Rails.backtrace_cleaner.add_silencer { |line| line =~ /rvm/ }

# You can also remove all the silencers if you're trying to debug a problem
# that might stem from framework code.
# Rails.backtrace_cleaner.remove_silencers!
```

As noted in a comment in Listing 3.41, you should restart the local web server after adding the silencer.

3.7.3 Automated Tests with Guard

One annoyance associated with using the **rake test** command is having to switch to the command line and run the tests by hand. To avoid this inconvenience, we can use *Guard* to automate the running of the tests. Guard monitors changes in the filesystem so that, for example, when we change the **static_pages_controller_test.rb** file, only those tests are run. Even better, we can configure Guard so that when, say, the `home.html.erb` file is modified, the `static_pages_controller_test.rb` file automatically runs.

The `Gemfile` in Listing 3.2 has already included the guard gem in our application, so to get started we just need to initialize it:

```
$ bundle exec guard init
Writing new Guardfile to /home/ubuntu/workspace/sample_app/Guardfile
00:51:32 - INFO - minitest guard added to Guardfile, feel free to edit it
```

We then edit the resulting `Guardfile` so that Guard will run the right tests when the integration tests and views are updated (Listing 3.42). (Given its length and advanced nature, I recommend just copy-and-pasting the contents of Listing 3.42.)

Listing 3.42 A custom `Guardfile`.

```ruby
# Defines the matching rules for Guard.
guard :minitest, spring: true, all_on_start: false do
  watch(%r{^test/(.*)/?(.*)_test\.rb$})
  watch('test/test_helper.rb') { 'test' }
  watch('config/routes.rb')    { integration_tests }
  watch(%r{^app/models/(.*?)\.rb$}) do |matches|
    "test/models/#{matches[1]}_test.rb"
  end
  watch(%r{^app/controllers/(.*?)_controller\.rb$}) do |matches|
    resource_tests(matches[1])
  end
  watch(%r{^app/views/([^/]*?)/.*\.html\.erb$}) do |matches|
    ["test/controllers/#{matches[1]}_controller_test.rb"] +
    integration_tests(matches[1])
  end
  watch(%r{^app/helpers/(.*?)_helper\.rb$}) do |matches|
    integration_tests(matches[1])
  end
  watch('app/views/layouts/application.html.erb') do
    'test/integration/site_layout_test.rb'
  end
  watch('app/helpers/sessions_helper.rb') do
    integration_tests << 'test/helpers/sessions_helper_test.rb'
  end
  watch('app/controllers/sessions_controller.rb') do
    ['test/controllers/sessions_controller_test.rb',
     'test/integration/users_login_test.rb']
  end
```

```
  watch('app/controllers/account_activations_controller.rb') do
    'test/integration/users_signup_test.rb'
  end
  watch(%r{app/views/users/*}) do
    resource_tests('users') +
    ['test/integration/microposts_interface_test.rb']
  end
end

# Returns the integration tests corresponding to the given resource.
def integration_tests(resource = :all)
  if resource == :all
    Dir["test/integration/*"]
  else
    Dir["test/integration/#{resource}_*.rb"]
  end
end

# Returns the controller tests corresponding to the given resource.
def controller_test(resource)
  "test/controllers/#{resource}_controller_test.rb"
end

# Returns all tests for the given resource.
def resource_tests(resource)
  integration_tests(resource) << controller_test(resource)
end
```

Here the line

```
guard :minitest, spring: true, all_on_start: false do
```

causes Guard to use the Spring server supplied by Rails to speed up loading times, while also preventing Guard from running the full test suite upon starting.

To prevent conflicts between Spring and Git when using Guard, you should add the **spring/** directory to the **.gitignore** file used by Git to determine what to ignore when adding files or directories to the repository. The way to do this using the cloud IDE is as follows:

1. Click on the gear icon in the upper right part of the file navigation pane (Figure 3.9).

Figure 3.9   The (rather subtle) gear icon in the file navigator pane.

2. Select "Show hidden files" to show the `.gitignore` file in the application's root directory (Figure 3.10).

3. Double-click on the `.gitignore` file (Figure 3.11) to open it, and then fill it with the contents of Listing 3.43.

Listing 3.43   Adding Spring to the `.gitignore` file.

```
# See https://help.github.com/articles/ignoring-files for more about ignoring
# files.
#
# If you find yourself ignoring temporary files generated by your text editor
# or operating system, you probably want to add a global ignore instead:
# git config --global core.excludesfile '~/.gitignore_global'
```

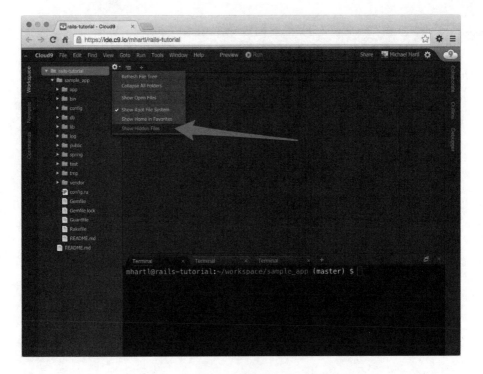

Figure 3.10 Showing hidden files in the file navigator.

```
# Ignore bundler config.
/.bundle

# Ignore the default SQLite database.
/db/*.sqlite3
/db/*.sqlite3-journal

# Ignore all logfiles and tempfiles.
/log/*.log
/tmp

# Ignore Spring files.
/spring/*.pid
```

The Spring server is still a little quirky as of this writing, and sometimes Spring *processes* will accumulate and slow performance of your tests. If your tests seem to be

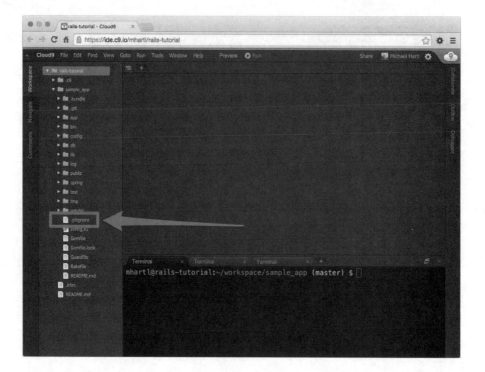

Figure 3.11 The normally hidden `.gitignore` file made visible.

getting unusually sluggish, it's a good idea to inspect the system processes and kill them if necessary (Box 3.4).

Box 3.4 Unix Processes

On Unix-like systems such as Linux and OS X, user and system tasks take place within a well-defined container called a *process*. To see all the processes on your system, you can use the `ps` command with the `aux` options:

```
$ ps aux
```

To filter the processes by type, you can run the results of `ps` through the `grep` pattern-matcher using a Unix pipe `|`:

```
$ ps aux | grep spring
ubuntu 12241 0.3 0.5 589960 178416 ? Ssl Sep20 1:46
spring app | sample_app | started 7 hours ago
```

The result shown gives some details about the process, but the most important thing is the first number, which is the *process ID* (pid). To eliminate an unwanted process, use the `kill` command to issue the Unix kill code (which happens to be 9) to the pid:

```
$ kill -9 12241
```

I recommend this technique for killing individual processes, such as a rogue Rails server (with the pid found via `ps aux | grep server`). Sometimes, however, it's convenient to kill all the processes matching a particular process name, such as when you want to kill all the `spring` processes gunking up your system. In this particular case, you should first try stopping the processes with the `spring` command itself:

```
$ spring stop
```

Sometimes this doesn't work, though, and you can kill all the processes with name `spring` using the `pkill` command as follows:

```
$ pkill -9 -f spring
```

Anytime something isn't behaving as expected or a process appears to be frozen, it's a good idea to run `ps aux` to see what's going on, and then run `kill -9 <pid>` or `pkill -9 -f <name>` to clear things up.

Once Guard is configured, you should open a new terminal and (as with the Rails server in Section 1.3.2) run it at the command line as follows:

```
$ bundle exec guard
```

The rules in Listing 3.42 are optimized for this tutorial, automatically running (for example) the integration tests when a controller is changed. To run *all* the tests, hit Return at the **guard>** prompt. (This may sometimes produce an error message indicating a failure to connect to the Spring server. To fix the problem, just hit Return again.)

To exit Guard, press Ctrl-D. To add even more matchers to Guard, refer to the examples in Listing 3.42, the Guard README, and the Guard wiki.

CHAPTER 4

Rails-Flavored Ruby

Grounded in examples from Chapter 3, this chapter explores some elements of the Ruby programming language that are important for Rails. Ruby is a big language, but fortunately the subset needed to be productive as a Rails developer is relatively small. This chapter also differs somewhat from the usual material covered in an introduction to Ruby. It is designed to give you a solid foundation in Rails-flavored Ruby, whether or not you have prior experience in the language. It covers a lot of material, and it's OK not to get it all on the first pass. I'll refer back to it frequently in future chapters.

4.1 Motivation

As we saw in the last chapter, it's possible to develop the skeleton of a Rails application, and even start testing it, with essentially no knowledge of the underlying Ruby language. We did this by relying on the test code provided by the tutorial and addressing each error message until the test suite was passing. This situation can't last forever, though, and we'll open this chapter with an addition to the site that brings us face-to-face with our Ruby limitations.

When we last saw our new application, we had just updated our mostly static pages to use Rails layouts to eliminate duplication in our views, as shown in Listing 4.1 (which is the same as Listing 3.32).

Listing 4.1 The sample application site layout.

app/views/layouts/application.html.erb

```
<!DOCTYPE html>
<html>
  <head>
    <title><%= yield(:title) %> | Ruby on Rails Tutorial Sample App</title>
    <%= stylesheet_link_tag    'application', media: 'all',
                                              'data-turbolinks-track' => true %>
    <%= javascript_include_tag 'application', 'data-turbolinks-track' => true %>
    <%= csrf_meta_tags %>
  </head>
  <body>
    <%= yield %>
  </body>
</html>
```

Let's focus on one particular line in Listing 4.1:

```
<%= stylesheet_link_tag 'application', media: 'all',
                                      'data-turbolinks-track' => true %>
```

This uses the built-in Rails function `stylesheet_link_tag` (which you can read more about at the Rails API) to include `application.css` for all media types (including computer screens and printers). To an experienced Rails developer, this line looks simple, but there are at least four potentially confusing Ruby ideas: built-in Rails methods, method invocation with missing parentheses, symbols, and hashes. We'll cover all of these ideas in this chapter.

In addition to coming equipped with a large number of built-in functions for use in the views, Rails allows the creation of new ones. Such functions are called *helpers*. To see how to make a custom helper, let's start by examining the title line from Listing 4.1:

```
<%= yield(:title) %> | Ruby on Rails Tutorial Sample App
```

This relies on the definition of a page title (using `provide`) in each view, as in this code:

```
<% provide(:title, "Home") %>
<h1>Sample App</h1>
<p>
  This is the home page for the
```

```
<a href="http://www.railstutorial.org/">Ruby on Rails Tutorial</a>
  sample application.
</p>
```

But what if we don't provide a title? It's a good convention to have a *base title* we use on every page, with an optional page title if we want to be more specific. We've *almost* achieved that with our current layout, with one wrinkle: If you delete the **provide** call in one of the views, in the absence of a page-specific title the full title appears as follows.

```
| Ruby on Rails Tutorial Sample App
```

In other words, there's a suitable base title, but there's also a leading vertical bar character | at the beginning.

To solve the problem of a missing page title, we'll define a custom helper called **full_title**. The **full_title** helper returns the base title of "Ruby on Rails Tutorial Sample App" if no page title is defined, and it adds a vertical bar preceded by the page title if one is defined (Listing 4.2).[1]

Listing 4.2 Defining a **full_title** helper.

app/helpers/application_helper.rb

```ruby
module ApplicationHelper

  # Returns the full title on a per-page basis.
  def full_title(page_title = '')
    base_title = "Ruby on Rails Tutorial Sample App"
    if page_title.empty?
      base_title
    else
      "#{page_title} | #{base_title}"
    end
  end
end
```

Now that we have a helper, we can use it to simplify our layout by replacing

---

1. If a helper is specific to a particular controller, you should put it in the corresponding helper file. For example, helpers for the Static Pages controller generally go in **app/helpers/static_pages_helper.rb**. In our case, we expect the **full_title** helper to be used on all the site's pages, and Rails has a special helper file for this case: **app/helpers/application_helper.rb**.

```
<title><%= yield(:title) %> | Ruby on Rails Tutorial Sample App</title>
```

with

```
<title><%= full_title(yield(:title)) %></title>
```

as seen in Listing 4.3.

Listing 4.3 The site layout with the `full_title` helper. GREEN
app/views/layouts/application.html.erb

```
<!DOCTYPE html>
<html>
  <head>
    <title><%=  full_title(yield(:title)) %></title>
    <%= stylesheet_link_tag    'application', media: 'all',
                                               'data-turbolinks-track' => true %>
    <%= javascript_include_tag 'application', 'data-turbolinks-track' => true %>
    <%= csrf_meta_tags %>
  </head>
  <body>
    <%= yield %>
  </body>
</html>
```

To put our helper to work, we can eliminate the unnecessary word "Home" from the Home page, allowing it to revert to the base title. We do this by first updating our test with the code in Listing 4.4, which updates the previous title test and adds a new test for the absence of the custom **"Home"** string in the title. (*Note*: If you completed the exercise corresponding to Listing 3.38, you should retain the **setup** method defining the **@base_title** variable.)

Listing 4.4 An updated test for the Home page's title. RED
test/controllers/static_pages_controller_test.rb

```
require 'test_helper'

class StaticPagesControllerTest < ActionController::TestCase
  test "should get home" do
    get :home
    assert_response :success
```

```
    assert_select "title", "Ruby on Rails Tutorial Sample App"
  end

  test "should get help" do
    get :help
    assert_response :success
    assert_select "title", "Help | Ruby on Rails Tutorial Sample App"
  end

  test "should get about" do
    get :about
    assert_response :success
    assert_select "title", "About | Ruby on Rails Tutorial Sample App"
  end
end
```

Let's run the test suite to verify that one test fails:

Listing 4.5   RED

```
$ bundle exec rake test
3 tests, 6 assertions, 1 failures, 0 errors, 0 skips
```

To get the test suite to pass, we'll remove the **provide** line from the Home page's view, as seen in Listing 4.6.

Listing 4.6   The Home page with no custom page title. **GREEN**
app/views/static_pages/home.html.erb

```
<h1>Sample App</h1>
<p>
  This is the home page for the
  <a href="http://www.railstutorial.org/">Ruby on Rails Tutorial</a>
  sample application.
</p>
```

At this point the tests should pass:

Listing 4.7   GREEN

```
$ bundle exec rake test
```

(*Note*: Previous examples have included partial output of running **rake test**, including the number of passing and failing tests, but for brevity these will usually be omitted from here on.)

As with the line to include the application style sheet, the code in Listing 4.2 may look simple to the eyes of an experienced Rails developer, but it's *full* of important Ruby ideas: modules, method definition, optional method arguments, comments, local variable assignment, booleans, control flow, string interpolation, and return values. This chapter will cover all of these ideas as well.

4.2 Strings and Methods

Our principal tool for learning Ruby will be the *Rails console*, a command-line tool for interacting with Rails applications first seen in Section 2.3.3. The console itself is built on top of interactive Ruby (**irb**), so it has access to the full power of the Ruby language. (As we'll see in Section 4.4.4, the console also has access to the Rails environment.)

If you're using the cloud IDE, there are a couple of irb configuration parameters I recommend including. Using the simple **nano** text editor, fill a file called **.irbrc** in the home directory with the contents of Listing 4.8:

```
$ nano ~/.irbrc
```

The commands in Listing 4.8 simplify the irb prompt and suppress some annoying auto-indent behavior.

Listing 4.8 Adding some irb configuration.
~/.irbrc

```
IRB.conf[:PROMPT_MODE] = :SIMPLE
IRB.conf[:AUTO_INDENT_MODE] = false
```

If you included the configuration in Listing 4.8, you can start the console at the command line as follows:

```
$ rails console
Loading development environment
>>
```

By default, the console starts in a *development environment*, which is one of three separate environments defined by Rails (the others are *test* and *production*). This distinction won't be important in this chapter, but we'll learn more about environments in Section 7.1.1.

The console is a great learning tool, and you should feel free to explore it—don't worry, you (probably) won't break anything. When using the console, type Ctrl-C if you get stuck or Ctrl-D to exit the console altogether. Throughout the rest of this chapter, you might find it helpful to consult the Ruby API. It's packed (perhaps even *too* packed) with information. For example, to learn more about Ruby strings you can look at the Ruby API entry for the **String** class.

4.2.1 Comments

Ruby *comments* start with the pound sign # (also called the "hash mark" or—more poetically—the "octothorpe") and extend to the end of the line. Ruby ignores comments, but they are useful for human readers (including the original author!). In the code

```
# Returns the full title on a per-page basis.
def full_title(page_title = '')
  .
  .
  .
end
```

the first line is a comment indicating the purpose of the subsequent function definition.

You don't ordinarily include comments in console sessions, but for instructional purposes I'll include some comments in what follows, like this:

```
$ rails console
>> 17 + 42    # Integer addition
=> 59
```

If you follow along in this section typing or copying-and-pasting commands into your own console, you can omit the comments if you like; the console will ignore them in any case.

4.2.2 Strings

Strings are probably the most important data structure for web applications, since web pages ultimately consist of strings of characters sent from the server to the browser. Let's start exploring strings with the console:

```
$ rails console
>> ""           # An empty string
=> ""
>> "foo"        # A nonempty string
=> "foo"
```

These are *string literals* (also, amusingly, called *literal strings*), created using the double quote character ". The console prints the result of evaluating each line, which in the case of a string literal is just the string itself.

We can also concatenate strings with the + operator:

```
>> "foo" + "bar"      # String concatenation
=> "foobar"
```

Here the result of evaluating **"foo"** plus **"bar"** is the string **"foobar"**.[2]

Another way to build up strings is via *interpolation* using the special syntax #{}:[3]

```
>> first_name = "Michael"      # Variable assignment
=> "Michael"
>> "#{first_name} Hartl"       # String interpolation
=> "Michael Hartl"
```

Here we've *assigned* the value **"Michael"** to the variable **first_name** and then interpolated it into the string **"#{first_name} Hartl"**. We could also assign both strings a variable name:

```
>> first_name = "Michael"
=> "Michael"
```

---

2. For more on the origins of "foo" and "bar"—and, in particular, the possible *non*-relation of "foobar" to "FUBAR"—see the Jargon File entry on "foo."

3. Programmers familiar with Perl or PHP should compare this to the automatic interpolation of dollar sign variables in expressions like **"foo $bar"**.

```
>> last_name = "Hartl"
=> "Hartl"
>> first_name + " " + last_name      # Concatenation, with a space in between
=> "Michael Hartl"
>> "#{first_name} #{last_name}"      # The equivalent interpolation
=> "Michael Hartl"
```

The final two expressions are equivalent, but I prefer the interpolated version; having to add the single space `" "` seems a bit awkward.

Printing

To *print* a string, the most commonly used Ruby function is `puts` (pronounced "put ess," for "put string"):

```
>> puts "foo"      # put string
foo
=> nil
```

The `puts` method operates as a *side effect*: the expression `puts "foo"` prints the string to the screen and then returns literally nothing: `nil` is a special Ruby value for "nothing at all." (In what follows, I'll sometimes suppress the `=> nil` part for simplicity.)

As seen in the earlier examples, using `puts` automatically appends a newline character `\n` to the output. The related `print` method does not:

```
>> print "foo"      # print string (same as puts, but without the newline)
foo=> nil
>> print "foo\n"   # Same as puts "foo"
foo
=> nil
```

Single-Quoted Strings

All the examples so far have used *double-quoted strings*, but Ruby also supports *single-quoted* strings. For many uses, the two types of strings are effectively identical:

```
>> 'foo'            # A single-quoted string
=> "foo"
>> 'foo' + 'bar'
=> "foobar"
```

There's an important difference, though. Ruby won't interpolate into single-quoted strings:

```
>> '#{foo} bar'     # Single-quoted strings don't allow interpolation
=> "\#{foo} bar"
```

Note how the console returns values using double-quoted strings, which requires a backslash to *escape* special characters such as #.

If double-quoted strings can do everything that single-quoted strings can do, and interpolate to boot, what's the point of single-quoted strings? They are often useful because they are truly literal, and contain exactly the characters you type. For example, the "backslash" character is special on most systems, as in the literal newline \n. If you want a variable to contain a literal backslash, single quotes make it easier:

```
>> '\n'         # A literal 'backslash n' combination
=> "\\n"
```

As with the # character in our previous example, Ruby needs to escape the backslash with an additional backslash; inside double-quoted strings, a literal backslash is represented with *two* backslashes. For a small example like this, there's not much savings, but if there are lots of things to escape it can be a real help:

```
>> 'Newlines (\n) and tabs (\t) both use the backslash character \.'
=> "Newlines (\\n) and tabs (\\t) both use the backslash character \\."
```

Finally, it's worth noting that, because single and double quotes are essentially interchangeable, you'll often find that the source code switches between the two without any apparent pattern. There's really nothing to be done about this, except to say, "Welcome to Ruby!"

4.2.3 Objects and Message Passing

Everything in Ruby, including strings and even **nil**, is an *object*. We'll see the technical meaning of this in Section 4.4.2, but I don't think anyone ever understood objects by reading the definition in a book; you have to build up your intuition for objects by seeing lots of examples.

It's easier to describe what objects *do*, which is respond to messages. An object such as a string, for example, can respond to the message `length`, which returns the number of characters in the string:

```
>> "foobar".length        # Passing the "length" message to a string
=> 6
```

Typically, the messages that get passed to objects are *methods*, which are functions defined on those objects.[4] Strings also respond to the `empty?` method:

```
>> "foobar".empty?
=> false
>> "".empty?
=> true
```

Note the question mark at the end of the `empty?` method. This is a Ruby convention indicating that the return value is *boolean*: `true` or `false`. Booleans are especially useful for *control flow*:

```
>> s = "foobar"
>> if s.empty?
>>    "The string is empty"
>> else
>>    "The string is nonempty"
>> end
=> "The string is nonempty"
```

To include more than one clause, we can use `elsif` (`else` + `if`):

```
>> if s.nil?
>>    "The variable is nil"
>> elsif s.empty?
>>    "The string is empty"
>> elsif s.include?("foo")
>>    "The string includes 'foo'"
>> end
=> "The string includes 'foo'"
```

---

4. Apologies in advance for switching haphazardly between *function* and *method* throughout this chapter. In Ruby, they're the same thing: All methods are functions, and all functions are methods, because everything is an object.

Booleans can also be combined using the `&&` ("and"), `||` ("or"), and `!` ("not") operators:

```
>> x = "foo"
=> "foo"
>> y = ""
=> ""
>> puts "Both strings are empty" if x.empty? && y.empty?
=> nil
>> puts "One of the strings is empty" if x.empty? || y.empty?
"One of the strings is empty"
=> nil
>> puts "x is not empty" if !x.empty?
"x is not empty"
=> nil
```

Since everything in Ruby is an object, it follows that `nil` is an object, so it can also respond to methods. One example is the `to_s` method, which can convert virtually any object to a string:

```
>> nil.to_s
=> ""
```

This certainly appears to be an empty string, as we can verify by *chaining* the messages we pass to `nil`:

```
>> nil.empty?
NoMethodError: undefined method `empty?' for nil:NilClass
>> nil.to_s.empty?      # Message chaining
=> true
```

We see here that the `nil` object doesn't itself respond to the `empty?` method, but `nil.to_s` does.

There's a special method for testing for `nil`-ness, which you might be able to guess:

```
>> "foo".nil?
=> false
>> "".nil?
=> false
>> nil.nil?
=> true
```

The code

```
puts "x is not empty" if !x.empty?
```

also shows an alternate use of the `if` keyword: Ruby allows you to write a statement that is evaluated only if the statement following `if` is true. There's a complementary `unless` keyword that works the same way:

```
>> string = "foobar"
>> puts "The string '#{string}' is nonempty." unless string.empty?
The string 'foobar' is nonempty.
=> nil
```

It's worth noting that the `nil` object is special, in that it is the *only* Ruby object that is false in a boolean context, apart from `false` itself. We can see this by using `!!` (read "bang bang"), which negates an object twice, thereby coercing it to its boolean value:

```
>> !!nil
=> false
```

In particular, all other Ruby objects are *true*, even 0:

```
>> !!0
=> true
```

4.2.4 Method Definitions

The console allows us to define methods the same way we did with the `home` action from Listing 3.6 or the `full_title` helper from Listing 4.2. (Defining methods in the console is a bit cumbersome, and ordinarily you would use a file, but it's convenient for demonstration purposes.) For example, let's define a function `string_message` that takes a single *argument* and returns a message based on whether the argument is empty:

```
>> def string_message(str = '')
>>   if str.empty?
>>     "It's an empty string!"
>>   else
```

```
>>      "The string is nonempty."
>>    end
>> end
=> :string_message
>> puts string_message("foobar")
The string is nonempty.
>> puts string_message("")
It's an empty string!
>> puts string_message
It's an empty string!
```

As seen in the final example, it's possible to leave out the argument entirely (in which case we can also omit the parentheses). This is because the code

```
def string_message(str = '')
```

contains a *default* argument, which in this case is the empty string. This makes the **str** argument optional, and if we leave it off it automatically takes the given default value.

Note that Ruby functions have an *implicit return*, meaning they return the last statement evaluated—in this case, one of the two message strings, depending on whether the method's argument **str** is empty. Ruby also has an explicit return option; the following function is equivalent to the one given earlier:

```
>> def string_message(str = '')
>>   return "It's an empty string!" if str.empty?
>>   return "The string is nonempty."
>> end
```

(The alert reader might notice at this point that the second **return** here is actually unnecessary—being the last expression in the function, the string **"The string is nonempty."** will be returned regardless of the **return** keyword, but using **return** in both places has a pleasing symmetry to it.)

It's also important to understand that the name of the function argument is irrelevant as far as the caller is concerned. In other words, the first example could replace **str** with any other valid variable name, such as **the_function_argument**, and it would work just the same:

```
>> def string_message(the_function_argument = '')
>>   if the_function_argument.empty?
>>     "It's an empty string!"
>>   else
```

```
>>      "The string is nonempty."
>>   end
>> end
=> nil
>> puts string_message("")
It's an empty string!
>> puts string_message("foobar")
The string is nonempty.
```

4.2.5 Back to the Title Helper

We are now in a position to understand the `full_title` helper from Listing 4.2,[5] which appears with commented annotations in Listing 4.9.

Listing 4.9 An annotated `title_helper`.

app/helpers/application_helper.rb

```
module ApplicationHelper

  # Returns the full title on a per-page basis.    # Documentation comment
  def full_title(page_title = '')                  # Method def, optional arg
    base_title = "Ruby on Rails Tutorial Sample App" # Variable assignment
    if page_title.empty?                           # Boolean test
      base_title                                   # Implicit return
    else
      "#{page_title} | #{base_title}"              # String interpolation
    end
  end
end
```

These elements—function definition (with an optional argument), variable assignment, boolean tests, control flow, and string interpolation—come together to make a compact helper method for use in our site layout. The final element is `module ApplicationHelper`: Modules give us a way to package together related methods, which can then be *mixed in* to Ruby classes using `include`. When writing ordinary Ruby, you often write modules and include them explicitly yourself, but in the case of a helper module Rails handles the inclusion for us. The result is that the `full_title` method is automagically available in all our views.

---

5. Well, there will still be *one* thing left that we don't understand, which is how Rails ties this all together: mapping URLs to actions, making the `full_title` helper available in views, and so on. This is an interesting subject, and I encourage you to investigate it further, but knowing exactly *how* Rails works is not necessary when *using* Rails. (For a deeper understanding, I recommend *The Rails 4 Way* by Obie Fernandez.)

4.3 Other Data Structures

Although web apps are ultimately about strings, actually *making* those strings requires using other data structures as well. In this section, we'll learn about some Ruby data structures important for writing Rails applications.

4.3.1 Arrays and Ranges

An array is just a list of elements in a particular order. We haven't discussed arrays yet in the *Rails Tutorial*, but understanding them gives a good foundation for understanding hashes (Section 4.3.3) and for appreciating aspects of Rails data modeling (such as the **has_many** association seen in Section 2.3.3 and covered in more detail in Section 11.1.3).

So far we've spent a lot of time understanding strings, and there's a natural way to get from strings to arrays using the **split** method:

```
>>  "foo bar    baz".split     # Split a string into a three-element array.
=> ["foo", "bar", "baz"]
```

The result of this operation is an array of three strings. By default, **split** divides a string into an array by splitting on whitespace, but you can split on nearly anything else as well:

```
>> "fooxbarxbazx".split('x')
=> ["foo", "bar", "baz"]
```

As is conventional in most computer languages, Ruby arrays are *zero-offset*, which means that the first element in the array has index 0, the second has index 1, and so on:

```
>> a = [42, 8, 17]
=> [42, 8, 17]
>> a[0]                 # Ruby uses square brackets for array access.
=> 42
>> a[1]
=> 8
>> a[2]
=> 17
>> a[-1]                # Indices can even be negative!
=> 17
```

We see here that Ruby uses square brackets to access array elements. In addition to this bracket notation, Ruby offers synonyms for some commonly accessed elements:[6]

```
>> a                     # Just a reminder of what 'a' is
=> [42, 8, 17]
>> a.first
=> 42
>> a.second
=> 8
>> a.last
=> 17
>> a.last == a[-1]       # Comparison using ==
=> true
```

This last line introduces the equality comparison operator `==`, which Ruby shares with many other languages, along with the associated `!=` ("not equal"), among other operators:

```
>> x = a.length          # Like strings, arrays respond to the 'length' method.
=> 3
>> x == 3
=> true
>> x == 1
=> false
>> x != 1
=> true
>> x >= 1
=> true
>> x < 1
=> false
```

In addition to `length` (seen in the first line in the preceding example), arrays respond to a wealth of other methods:

```
>> a
=> [42, 8, 17]
>> a.empty?
=> false
>> a.include?(42)
=> true
>> a.sort
=> [8, 17, 42]
>> a.reverse
```

---

6. The `second` method used here isn't currently part of Ruby itself, but rather is added by Rails. It works in this case because the Rails console automatically includes the Rails extensions to Ruby.

```
=> [17, 8, 42]
>> a.shuffle
=> [17, 42, 8]
>> a
=> [42, 8, 17]
```

Note that none of these methods changes **a** itself. To *mutate* the array, we use the corresponding "bang" methods (so called because the exclamation point is usually pronounced "bang" in this context):

```
>> a
=> [42, 8, 17]
>> a.sort!
=> [8, 17, 42]
>> a
=> [8, 17, 42]
```

You can also add to arrays with the **push** method or its equivalent operator, <<:

```
>> a.push(6)               # Pushing 6 onto an array
=> [42, 8, 17, 6]
>> a << 7                  # Pushing 7 onto an array
=> [42, 8, 17, 6, 7]
>> a << "foo" << "bar"     # Chaining array pushes
=> [42, 8, 17, 6, 7, "foo", "bar"]
```

The last example shows that you can chain pushes together, and that, unlike arrays in many other languages, Ruby arrays can contain a mixture of different types (in this case, integers and strings).

In an earlier example, we saw **split** convert a string to an array. We can also go the other way with the **join** method:

```
>> a
=> [42, 8, 17, 7, "foo", "bar"]
>> a.join                  # Join on nothing.
=> "428177foobar"
>> a.join(', ')            # Join on comma-space.
=> "42, 8, 17, 7, foo, bar"
```

Closely related to arrays are *ranges*, which can most easily be understood by converting them to arrays using the **to_a** method:

```
>> 0..9
=> 0..9
```

```
>> 0..9.to_a                # Oops, call to_a on 9.
NoMethodError: undefined method `to_a' for 9:Fixnum
>> (0..9).to_a              # Use parentheses to call to_a on the range.
=> [0, 1, 2, 3, 4, 5, 6, 7, 8, 9]
```

Although `0..9` is a valid range, the second expression shows that we need to add parentheses to call a method on it.

Ranges are useful for pulling out array elements:

```
>> a = %w[foo bar baz quux]          # Use %w to make a string array.
=> ["foo", "bar", "baz", "quux"]
>> a[0..2]
=> ["foo", "bar", "baz"]
```

A particularly useful trick is to use the index -1 at the end of the range to select every element from the starting point to the end of the array *without* explicitly having to use the array's length:

```
>> a = (0..9).to_a
=> [0, 1, 2, 3, 4, 5, 6, 7, 8, 9]
>> a[2..(a.length-1)]                # Explicitly use the array's length.
=> [2, 3, 4, 5, 6, 7, 8, 9]
>> a[2..-1]                          # Use the index -1 trick.
=> [2, 3, 4, 5, 6, 7, 8, 9]
```

Ranges also work with characters:

```
>> ('a'..'e').to_a
=> ["a", "b", "c", "d", "e"]
```

4.3.2 Blocks

Both arrays and ranges respond to a host of methods that accept *blocks*, which are simultaneously one of Ruby's most powerful and most confusing features:

```
>> (1..5).each { |i| puts 2 * i }
2
4
6
8
10
=> 1..5
```

This code calls the **each** method on the range **(1..5)** and passes it the block **{ |i| puts 2 * i }**. The vertical bars around the variable name in **|i|** are Ruby syntax for a block variable, and it's up to the method to know what to do with the block. In this case, the range's **each** method can handle a block with a single local variable, which we've called **i**, and it just executes the block for each value in the range.

Curly braces are one way to indicate a block, but there is a second way as well:

```
>> (1..5).each do |i|
?>   puts 2 * i
>> end
2
4
6
8
10
=> 1..5
```

Blocks can be more than one line, and often are. In the *Rails Tutorial* we'll follow the common convention of using curly braces only for short one-line blocks and the **do..end** syntax for longer one-liners and for multiline blocks:

```
>> (1..5).each do |number|
?>   puts 2 * number
>>   puts '--'
>> end
2
--
4
--
6
--
8
--
10
--
=> 1..5
```

Here I've used **number** in place of **i** just to emphasize that any variable name will do.

Unless you already have a substantial programming background, there is no short-cut to understanding blocks; you just have to see them a lot, and eventually you'll get used to them.[7] Luckily, humans are quite good at making generalizations from concrete

---

7. Programming experts, in contrast, might benefit from knowing that blocks are *closures*, which are one-shot anonymous functions with data attached.

examples. Here are a few more examples to help you on your way, including a couple using the **map** method:

```
>> 3.times { puts "Betelgeuse!" }    # 3.times takes a block with no variables.
"Betelgeuse!"
"Betelgeuse!"
"Betelgeuse!"
=> 3
>> (1..5).map { |i| i**2 }           # The ** notation is for 'power'.
=> [1, 4, 9, 16, 25]
>> %w[a b c]                         # Recall that %w makes string arrays.
=> ["a", "b", "c"]
>> %w[a b c].map { |char| char.upcase }
=> ["A", "B", "C"]
>> %w[A B C].map { |char| char.downcase }
=> ["a", "b", "c"]
```

As you can see, the **map** method returns the result of applying the given block to each element in the array or range. In the final two examples, the block inside **map** involves calling a particular method on the block variable, for which there's a commonly used shorthand:

```
>> %w[A B C].map { |char| char.downcase }
=> ["a", "b", "c"]
>> %w[A B C].map(&:downcase)
=> ["a", "b", "c"]
```

(This strange-looking but compact code uses a *symbol*, which we'll discuss in Section 4.3.3.) One interesting thing about this construction is that it was originally added to Ruby on Rails, and people liked it so much that it has now been incorporated into core Ruby.

As one final example of blocks, we can take a look at an individual test from the file in Listing 4.4:

```
test "should get home" do
  get :home
  assert_response :success
  assert_select "title", "Ruby on Rails Tutorial Sample App"
end
```

It's not important to understand the details (and, in fact, *I* don't know the details off-hand), but we can infer from the presence of the **do** keyword that the body of the test is a block. The `test` method takes a string argument (the description) and a block as input, and then executes the body of the block as part of running the test suite.

By the way, we're now in a position to understand the line of Ruby I threw into Section 1.5.4 to generate random subdomains:

```
('a'..'z').to_a.shuffle[0..7].join
```

Let's build it up step-by-step:

```
>> ('a'..'z').to_a                    # An alphabet array
=> ["a", "b", "c", "d", "e", "f", "g", "h", "i", "j", "k", "l", "m", "n", "o",
"p", "q", "r", "s", "t", "u", "v", "w", "x", "y", "z"]
>> ('a'..'z').to_a.shuffle            # Shuffle it.
=> ["c", "g", "l", "k", "h", "z", "s", "i", "n", "d", "y", "u", "t", "j", "q",
"b", "r", "o", "f", "e", "w", "v", "m", "a", "x", "p"]
>> ('a'..'z').to_a.shuffle[0..7]      # Pull out the first eight elements.
=> ["f", "w", "i", "a", "h", "p", "c", "x"]
>> ('a'..'z').to_a.shuffle[0..7].join # Join them together to make one string.
=> "mznpybuj"
```

4.3.3 Hashes and Symbols

Hashes are essentially arrays that aren't limited to integer indices. (In fact, some languages, especially Perl, sometimes call hashes *associative arrays* for this reason.) Instead, hash indices, or *keys*, can be almost any object. For example, we can use strings as keys:

```
>> user = {}                          # {} is an empty hash.
=> {}
>> user["first_name"] = "Michael"     # Key "first_name", value "Michael"
=> "Michael"
>> user["last_name"] = "Hartl"        # Key "last_name", value "Hartl"
=> "Hartl"
>> user["first_name"]                 # Element access is like arrays.
=> "Michael"
>> user                               # A literal representation of the hash
=> {"last_name"=>"Hartl", "first_name"=>"Michael"}
```

Hashes are indicated with curly braces containing key-value pairs; a pair of braces with no key-value pairs—that is, {}—is an empty hash. Note that the curly braces for hashes have nothing to do with the curly braces for blocks. (Yes, this can be confusing.)

Although hashes resemble arrays, one important difference is that hashes don't generally guarantee keeping their elements in a particular order.[8] If order matters, use an array.

Instead of defining hashes one item at a time using square brackets, it's easy to use a literal representation with keys and values separated by `=>`, called a "hashrocket":

```
>> user = { "first_name" => "Michael", "last_name" => "Hartl" }
=> {"last_name"=>"Hartl", "first_name"=>"Michael"}
```

Here I've used the usual Ruby convention of putting an extra space at the two ends of the hash—a convention ignored by the console output. (Don't ask me why the spaces are conventional—probably some early influential Ruby programmer liked the look of the extra spaces, and the convention stuck.)

So far we've used strings as hash keys, but in Rails it is much more common to use *symbols* instead. Symbols look somewhat like strings, but are prefixed with a colon instead of surrounded by quotes. For example, `:name` is a symbol. You can think of symbols as basically strings without all the extra baggage.[9]

```
>> "name".split('')
=> ["n", "a", "m", "e"]
>> :name.split('')
NoMethodError: undefined method 'split' for :name:Symbol
>> "foobar".reverse
=> "raboof"
>> :foobar.reverse
NoMethodError: undefined method 'reverse' for :foobar:Symbol
```

Symbols are a special Ruby data type shared with very few other languages, so they may seem weird at first. Rails uses them a lot, though, so you'll get used to them fast. Unlike strings, not all characters are valid for use in symbols:

```
>> :foo-bar
NameError: undefined local variable or method 'bar' for main:Object
```

---

8. Ruby versions 1.9 and later actually guarantee that hashes keep their elements in the same order entered, but it would be unwise ever to count on a particular ordering.

9. As a result of having less baggage, symbols are easier to compare to each other. Strings need to be compared character by character, while symbols can be compared all in one go. This makes them ideal for use as hash keys.

```
>> :2foo
SyntaxError
```

As long as you start your symbols with a letter and stick to normal word characters, you should be fine.

In terms of symbols as hash keys, we can define a **user** hash as follows:

```
>> user = { :name => "Michael Hartl", :email => "michael@example.com" }
=> {:name=>"Michael Hartl", :email=>"michael@example.com"}
>> user[:name]                # Access the value corresponding to :name.
=> "Michael Hartl"
>> user[:password]            # Access the value of an undefined key.
=> nil
```

We see here from the last example that the hash value for an undefined key is simply **nil**.

Since it's so common for hashes to use symbols as keys, as of version 1.9 Ruby supports a new syntax just for this special case:

```
>> h1 = { :name => "Michael Hartl", :email => "michael@example.com" }
=> {:name=>"Michael Hartl", :email=>"michael@example.com"}
>> h2 = { name: "Michael Hartl", email: "michael@example.com" }
=> {:name=>"Michael Hartl", :email=>"michael@example.com"}
>> h1 == h2
=> true
```

The second syntax replaces the symbol/hashrocket combination with the name of the key followed by a colon and a value:

```
{ name: "Michael Hartl", email: "michael@example.com" }
```

This construction more closely follows the hash notation in other languages (such as JavaScript) and enjoys growing popularity in the Rails community. Because both hash syntaxes are still in common use, however, it's essential to be able to recognize both of them. Unfortunately, this can be confusing, especially since **:name** is valid on its own (as a stand-alone symbol) but **name:** has no meaning by itself. The bottom line is that **:name =>** and **name:** are effectively the same *only inside literal hashes*, so that

```
{ :name => "Michael Hartl" }
```

and

```
{ name: "Michael Hartl" }
```

are equivalent. Otherwise, you need to use :**name** (with the colon coming first) to denote a symbol.

Hash values can be virtually anything, even other hashes, as seen in Listing 4.10.

Listing 4.10   Nested hashes.

```
>> params = {}            # Define a hash called 'params' (short for 'parameters').
=> {}
>> params[:user] = { name: "Michael Hartl", email: "mhartl@example.com" }
=> {:name=>"Michael Hartl", :email=>"mhartl@example.com"}
>> params
=> {:user=>{:name=>"Michael Hartl", :email=>"mhartl@example.com"}}
>>  params[:user][:email]
=> "mhartl@example.com"
```

These sorts of hashes-of-hashes, or *nested hashes*, are heavily used by Rails, as we'll see starting in Section 7.3.

As with arrays and ranges, hashes respond to the **each** method. For example, consider a hash named **flash** with keys for two conditions, :**success** and :**danger**:

```
>> flash = { success: "It worked!", danger: "It failed." }
=> {:success=>"It worked!", :danger=>"It failed."}
>> flash.each do |key, value|
?>   puts "Key #{key.inspect} has value #{value.inspect}"
>> end
Key :success has value "It worked!"
Key :danger has value "It failed."
```

While the **each** method for arrays takes a block with only one variable, **each** for hashes takes two, a *key* and a *value*. Thus, the **each** method for a hash iterates through the hash one key-value *pair* at a time.

The last example uses the useful **inspect** method, which returns a string with a literal representation of the object it's called on:

```
>> puts (1..5).to_a            # Put an array as a string.
1
2
3
4
5
>> puts (1..5).to_a.inspect    # Put a literal array.
[1, 2, 3, 4, 5]
>> puts :name, :name.inspect
name
:name
>> puts "It worked!", "It worked!".inspect
It worked!
"It worked!"
```

By the way, using **inspect** to print an object is common enough that there's a shortcut for it, the **p** function:[10]

```
>> p :name                     # Same output as 'puts :name.inspect'
:name
```

4.3.4 CSS Revisited

It's time now to revisit the line from Listing 4.1 used in the layout to include the cascading style sheets:

```
<%= stylesheet_link_tag 'application', media: 'all',
                                  'data-turbolinks-track' => true %>
```

We are now nearly in a position to understand this code. As mentioned briefly in Section 4.1, Rails defines a special function to include style sheets, and

```
stylesheet_link_tag 'application', media: 'all',
                                'data-turbolinks-track' => true
```

---

10. There's actually a subtle difference, which is that **p** returns the object being printed while **puts** always returns **nil**. Thanks to reader Katarzyna Siwek for pointing this out.

is a call to this function. But there are several mysteries. First, where are the parentheses? In Ruby, they are optional, so these two calls are equivalent:

```
# Parentheses on function calls are optional.
stylesheet_link_tag('application', media: 'all',
                                   'data-turbolinks-track' => true)
stylesheet_link_tag 'application', media: 'all',
                                   'data-turbolinks-track' => true
```

Second, the `media` argument sure looks like a hash, but where are the curly braces? When hashes are the *last* argument in a function call, the curly braces are optional, so these calls two are equivalent:

```
# Curly braces on final hash arguments are optional.
stylesheet_link_tag 'application', { media: 'all',
                                   'data-turbolinks-track' => true }
stylesheet_link_tag 'application', media: 'all',
                                   'data-turbolinks-track' => true
```

Next, why does the `data-turbolinks-track` key-value pair use the old-style hashrocket syntax? Because using the newer syntax to write

```
data-turbolinks-track: true
```

is invalid owing to the the hyphens. (Recall from Section 4.3.3 that hyphens can't be used in symbols.) This forces us to use the older syntax, yielding

```
'data-turbolinks-track' => true
```

Finally, why does Ruby correctly interpret the lines

```
stylesheet_link_tag 'application', media: 'all',
                                   'data-turbolinks-track' => true
```

even with a line break between the final elements? The answer is that Ruby doesn't distinguish between newlines and other whitespace in this context.[11] The *reason* I chose

---

11. A newline is what comes at the end of a line, thereby starting a new line. In code, it is represented by the character \n.

to break the code into pieces is that I prefer to keep lines of source code to less than 80 characters for legibility.[12]

So, we see now that the line

```
stylesheet_link_tag 'application', media: 'all',
                             'data-turbolinks-track' => true
```

calls the `stylesheet_link_tag` function with two arguments: a string, indicating the path to the style sheet, and a hash with two elements, indicating the media type and telling Rails to use the turbolinks feature added in Rails 4.0. Because of the `<%= %>` brackets, the results are inserted into the template by ERb, and if you view the source of the page in your browser you should see the HTML needed to include a style sheet (Listing 4.11). (You may see some extra things, like `?body=1`, after the CSS filenames. These are inserted by Rails to ensure that browsers reload the CSS when it changes on the server.)

Listing 4.11 The HTML source produced by the CSS includes.

```
<link data-turbolinks-track="true" href="/assets/application.css" media="all"
rel="stylesheet" />
```

If you actually view the CSS file by navigating to http://localhost:3000/assets/application.css, you'll see that (apart from some comments) it is empty. We'll set about changing this in Chapter 5.

4.4 Ruby Classes

We've said before that everything in Ruby is an object, and in this section we'll finally get to define some of our own. Ruby, like many object-oriented languages, uses *classes* to organize methods; these classes are then *instantiated* to create objects. If you're new to object-oriented programming, this may sound like gibberish, so let's look at some concrete examples.

---

12. Actually *counting* columns could drive you crazy, which is why many text editors provide a visual aid to help you. For example, if you take a look back at Figure 1.5, you'll see a small vertical line on the right to help keep code to less than 80 characters. The cloud IDE (Section 1.2.1) includes such a line by default. If you use TextMate, you can find this feature under `View > Wrap Column > 78`. In Sublime Text, you can use `View > Ruler > 78` or `View > Ruler > 80`.

4.4.1 Constructors

We've seen lots of examples of using classes to instantiate objects, but we have yet to do so explicitly. For example, we instantiated a string using the double quote characters, which is a *literal constructor* for strings:

```
>> s = "foobar"        # A literal constructor for strings using double quotes
=> "foobar"
>> s.class
=> String
```

We see here that strings respond to the method **class**, and simply return the class they belong to.

Instead of using a literal constructor, we can use the equivalent *named constructor*, which involves calling the **new** method on the class name:[13]

```
>> s = String.new("foobar")    # A named constructor for a string
=> "foobar"
>> s.class
=> String
>> s == "foobar"
=> true
```

This is equivalent to using the literal constructor, but it's more explicit about what we're doing.

Arrays work the same way as strings:

```
>> a = Array.new([1, 3, 2])
=> [1, 3, 2]
```

Hashes, in contrast, are different. While the array constructor **Array.new** takes an initial value for the array, **Hash.new** takes a *default* value for the hash, which is the value of the hash for a nonexistent key:

```
>> h = Hash.new
=> {}
>> h[:foo]             # Try to access the value for the nonexistent key :foo.
```

---

13. These results will vary based on the version of Ruby you are using. This example assumes you are using Ruby 1.9.3 or later.

```
=> nil
>> h = Hash.new(0)  # Arrange for nonexistent keys to return 0 instead of nil.
=> {}
>> h[:foo]
=> 0
```

When a method is called on the class itself, as in the case of **new**, it's known as a *class method*. The result of calling **new** on a class is an object of that class, also known as an *instance* of the class. A method called on an instance, such as **length**, is termed an *instance method*.

4.4.2 Class Inheritance

When learning about classes, it's useful to find out the *class hierarchy* using the **superclass** method:

```
>> s = String.new("foobar")
=> "foobar"
>> s.class                        # Find the class of s.
=> String
>> s.class.superclass             # Find the superclass of String.
=> Object
>> s.class.superclass.superclass  # Ruby 1.9 uses a new BasicObject base class
=> BasicObject
>> s.class.superclass.superclass.superclass
=> nil
```

A diagram of this inheritance hierarchy appears in Figure 4.1. We see here that the superclass of **String** is **Object** and the superclass of **Object** is **BasicObject**, but **BasicObject** has no superclass. This pattern is true of every Ruby object; if you trace back the class hierarchy far enough, you'll find that every class in Ruby ultimately inherits from **BasicObject**, which has no superclass itself. This is the technical meaning of "everything in Ruby is an object."

To understand classes a little more deeply, there's no substitute for making one of our own. Let's make a **Word** class with a **palindrome?** method that returns **true** if the word is the same spelled forward and backward:

```
>> class Word
>>   def palindrome?(string)
>>     string == string.reverse
```

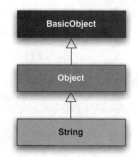

Figure 4.1 The inheritance hierarchy for the **String** class.

```
>>    end
>> end
=> :palindrome?
```

We can use it as follows:

```
>> w = Word.new              # Make a new Word object.
=> #<Word:0x22d0b20>
>> w.palindrome?("foobar")
=> false
>> w.palindrome?("level")
=> true
```

If this example strikes you as a bit contrived, good—this is by design. It's odd to create a new class just to create a method that takes a string as an argument. Since a word *is* a string, it's more natural to have our **Word** class *inherit* from **String**, as seen in Listing 4.12. (You should exit the console and reenter it to clear out the old definition of **Word**.)

Listing 4.12 Defining a **Word** class in the console.
```
>> class Word < String         # Word inherits from String.
>>   # Returns true if the string is its own reverse.
>>   def palindrome?
>>     self == self.reverse     # self is the string itself.
>>   end
>> end
=> nil
```

Here **Word** < **String** is the Ruby syntax for inheritance (discussed briefly in Section 3.2), which ensures that, in addition to the new **palindrome?** method, words also have all the same methods as strings:

```
>> s = Word.new("level")       # Make a new Word, initialized with "level".
=> "level"
>> s.palindrome?               # Words have the palindrome? method.
=> true
>> s.length                    # Words also inherit all the normal string methods.
=> 5
```

Since the **Word** class inherits from **String**, we can use the console to see the class hierarchy explicitly:

```
>> s.class
=> Word
>> s.class.superclass
=> String
>> s.class.superclass.superclass
=> Object
```

This hierarchy is illustrated in Figure 4.2.

In Listing 4.12, note that checking whether the word is its own reverse involves accessing the word inside the **Word** class. Ruby allows us to do this using the **self** keyword: Inside the **Word** class, **self** is the object itself, which means we can use

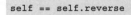

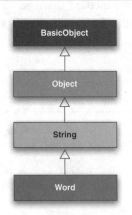

Figure 4.2 The inheritance hierarchy for the (non-built-in) **Word** class from Listing 4.12.

to check whether the word is a palindrome.[14] In fact, inside the `String` class the use of `self.` is optional on a method or attribute (unless we're making an assignment), so

```
self == reverse
```

would work as well.

4.4.3 Modifying Built-in Classes

While inheritance is a powerful idea, in the case of palindromes it might be even more natural to add the `palindrome?` method to the `String` class itself, so that (among other things) we can call `palindrome?` on a string literal, which we currently can't do:

```
>> "level".palindrome?
NoMethodError: undefined method `palindrome?' for "level":String
```

Amazingly, Ruby lets you do just this. That is, Ruby classes can be *opened* and modified, allowing ordinary mortals such as ourselves to add methods to them:

```
>> class String
>>   # Returns true if the string is its own reverse.
>>   def palindrome?
>>     self == self.reverse
>>   end
>> end
=> nil
>> "deified".palindrome?
=> true
```

(I don't know which is cooler: that Ruby lets you add methods to built-in classes or that `"deified"` is a palindrome.)

Modifying built-in classes is a powerful technique, but with great power comes great responsibility: It's considered bad form to add methods to built-in classes without having a *really* good reason for doing so. Rails does have some good reasons. For example, in web applications we often want to prevent variables from being *blank*—that is, a user's name should be something other than spaces and other whitespace—so Rails adds a `blank?`

---

14. For more on Ruby classes and the `self` keyword, see the RailsTips post "Class and Instance Variables in Ruby."

method to Ruby. Since the Rails console automatically includes the Rails extensions, we can see an example here (this won't work in plain `irb`):

```
>> "".blank?
=> true
>> "      ".empty?
=> false
>> "      ".blank?
=> true
>> nil.blank?
=> true
```

We see that a string of spaces is not *empty*, but it is *blank*. Note also that `nil` is blank; since `nil` isn't a string, this is a hint that Rails actually adds `blank?` to `String`'s base class, which (as we saw at the beginning of this section) is `Object` itself. We'll see some other examples of Rails additions to Ruby classes in Section 8.4.

4.4.4 A Controller Class

All this talk about classes and inheritance may have triggered a flash of recognition, because we have seen both before, in the Static Pages controller (Listing 3.18):

```
class StaticPagesController < ApplicationController

  def home
  end

  def help
  end

  def about
  end
end
```

You're now in a position to appreciate, at least vaguely, what this code means: `StaticPagesController` is a class that inherits from `ApplicationController`, and it comes equipped with `home`, `help`, and `about` methods. Since each Rails console session loads the local Rails environment, we can even create a controller explicitly and examine its class hierarchy:[15]

---

15. You don't have to know what each class in this hierarchy does. *I* don't know what they all do, and I've been programming in Ruby on Rails since 2005. This means either that (1) I'm grossly incompetent or (2) you can be a skilled Rails developer without knowing all its innards. I hope for both our sakes that it's the latter.

```
>> controller = StaticPagesController.new
=> #<StaticPagesController:0x22855d0>
>> controller.class
=> StaticPagesController
>> controller.class.superclass
=> ApplicationController
>> controller.class.superclass.superclass
=> ActionController::Base
>> controller.class.superclass.superclass.superclass
=> ActionController::Metal
>> controller.class.superclass.superclass.superclass.superclass
=> AbstractController::Base
>> controller.class.superclass.superclass.superclass.superclass.superclass
=> Object
```

A diagram of this hierarchy appears in Figure 4.3.

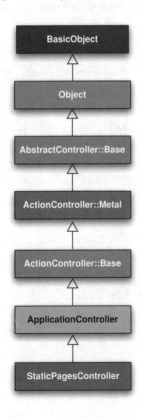

Figure 4.3   The inheritance hierarchy for the Static Pages.

We can even call the controller actions—which are just methods—inside the console:

```
>> controller.home
=> nil
```

Here the return value is `nil` because the `home` action is blank.

But wait—actions don't have return values, at least not ones that matter. The point of the `home` action, as we saw in Chapter 3, is to render a web page, not to return a value. And I sure don't remember ever calling `StaticPagesController.new` anywhere. What's going on?

What's going on is that Rails is *written in* Ruby, but Rails isn't Ruby. Some Rails classes are used like ordinary Ruby objects, but some are just grist for Rails' magic mill. Rails is *sui generis*, and should be studied and understood separately from Ruby.

4.4.5 A User Class

We end our tour of Ruby with a complete class of our own, a `User` class that anticipates the User model coming up in Chapter 6.

So far we've entered class definitions at the console, but this quickly becomes tiresome. Instead, create the file `example_user.rb` in your application root directory and fill it with the contents of Listing 4.13.

Listing 4.13 Code for an example user.

example_user.rb

```ruby
class User
  attr_accessor :name, :email

  def initialize(attributes = {})
    @name  = attributes[:name]
    @email = attributes[:email]
  end

  def formatted_email
    "#{@name} <#{@email}>"
  end
end
```

There's quite a bit going on here, so let's take it step by step. The first line

```
attr_accessor :name, :email
```

creates *attribute accessors* corresponding to a user's name and email address. This creates "getter" and "setter" methods that allow us to retrieve (get) and assign (set) **@name** and **@email** *instance variables* (instance variables were mentioned briefly in Section 2.2.2 and Section 3.6). In Rails, the principal importance of instance variables is that they are automatically available in the views, but in general they are used for variables that need to be available throughout a Ruby class. (We'll have more to say about this in a moment.) Instance variables always begin with an **@** sign, and are **nil** when undefined.

The first method, **initialize**, is special in Ruby: It's the method called when we execute **User.new**. This particular **initialize** method takes one argument, **attributes**:

```
def initialize(attributes = {})
  @name  = attributes[:name]
  @email = attributes[:email]
end
```

Here the **attributes** variable has a *default value* equal to the empty hash, so that we can define a user with no name or email address. (Recall from Section 4.3.3 that hashes return **nil** for nonexistent keys, so **attributes[:name]** will be **nil** if there is no **:name** key, and similarly for **attributes[:email]**.)

Finally, our class defines a method called **formatted_email** that uses the values of the assigned **@name** and **@email** variables to build up a nicely formatted version of the user's email address using string interpolation (Section 4.2.2):

```
def formatted_email
  "#{@name} <#{@email}>"
end
```

Because **@name** and **@email** are both instance variables (as indicated by the **@** sign), they are automatically available in the **formatted_email** method.

Let's fire up the console, **require** the example user code, and take our User class out for a spin:

```
>> require './example_user'       # This is how you load the example_user code.
=> true
>> example = User.new
=> #<User:0x224ceec @email=nil, @name=nil>
>> example.name                   # nil since attributes[:name] is nil
=> nil
>> example.name = "Example User"           # Assign a non-nil name
=> "Example User"
>> example.email = "user@example.com"      # and a non-nil email address
=> "user@example.com"
>> example.formatted_email
=> "Example User <user@example.com>"
```

Here the `'.'` is Unix for "current directory," and `'./example_user'` tells Ruby to look for an example user file relative to that location. The subsequent code creates an empty example user and then fills in the name and email address by assigning directly to the corresponding attributes (assignments made possible by the **attr_accessor** line in Listing 4.13). When we write

```
example.name = "Example User"
```

Ruby sets the **@name** variable to **"Example User"** (and similarly for the **email** attribute), which we then use in the **formatted_email** method.

Recall from Section 4.3.4 that we can omit the curly braces for final hash arguments. Thus we can create another user by passing a hash to the **initialize** method to create a user with predefined attributes:

```
>> user = User.new(name: "Michael Hartl", email: "mhartl@example.com")
=> #<User:0x225167c @email="mhartl@example.com", @name="Michael Hartl">
>> user.formatted_email
=> "Michael Hartl <mhartl@example.com>"
```

We will see starting in Chapter 7 that initializing objects using a hash argument, a technique known as *mass assignment*, is common in Rails applications.

4.5 Conclusion

This concludes our overview of the Ruby language. In Chapter 5, we'll start putting it to good use in developing the sample application.

We won't be using the `example_user.rb` file from Section 4.4.5, so I suggest removing it:

```
$ rm example_user.rb
```

Then commit the other changes to the main source code repository, push up to Bitbucket, and deploy to Heroku:

```
$ git status
$ git commit -am "Add a full_title helper"
$ git push
$ bundle exec rake test
$ git push heroku
```

4.5.1 What We Learned in This Chapter

- Ruby has a large number of methods for manipulating strings of characters.
- Everything in Ruby is an object.
- Ruby supports method definition via the `def` keyword.
- Ruby supports class definition via the `class` keyword.
- Rails views can contain static HTML or embedded Ruby (ERb).
- Built-in Ruby data structures include arrays, ranges, and hashes.
- Ruby blocks are a flexible construct that (among other things) allow natural iteration over enumerable data structures.
- Symbols are labels, similar to strings but without any additional structure.
- Ruby supports object inheritance.

- It is possible to open up and modify built-in Ruby classes.
- The word "deified" is a palindrome.

4.6 Exercises

Note: To receive a copy of the *Solutions Manual for Exercises*, with solutions to every exercise in the *Ruby on Rails™ Tutorial*, visit www.railstutorial.org/<word>, where "<word>" is the last word of the Figure 3.9 caption.

1. By replacing the question marks in Listing 4.14 with the appropriate methods, combine **split**, **shuffle**, and **join** to write a function that shuffles the letters in a given string.

2. Using Listing 4.15 as a guide, add a **shuffle** method to the **String** class.

3. Create three hashes called **person1**, **person2**, and **person3**, with first and last names under the keys **:first** and **:last**. Then create a **params** hash so that **params[:father]** is **person1**, **params[:mother]** is **person2**, and **params[:child]** is **person3**. Verify that, for example, **params[:father] :first** has the right value.

4. Find an online version of the Ruby API and read about the **Hash** method **merge**. What is the value of the following expression?

```
{ "a" => 100, "b" => 200 }.merge({ "b" => 300 })
```

Listing 4.14 Skeleton for a string shuffle function.

```
>> def string_shuffle(s)
>>    s.?('').?.?
>> end
>> string_shuffle("foobar")
=> "oobfra"
```

Listing 4.15 Skeleton for a **shuffle** method attached to the **String** class.

```
>> class String
>>   def shuffle
>>     self.?('').?.?
>>   end
>> end
>> "foobar".shuffle
=> "borafo"
```

CHAPTER 5

Filling in the Layout

In the process of taking a brief tour of Ruby in Chapter 4, we learned about including the application style sheet in the sample application (Section 4.1), but (as noted in Section 4.3.4) the style sheet doesn't yet contain any CSS. In this chapter, we'll start filling in the custom style sheet by incorporating a CSS framework into our application, and then we'll add some custom styles of our own.[1] We'll also start filling in the layout with links to the pages (such as Home and About) that we've created so far (Section 5.1). Along the way, we'll learn about partials, Rails routes, and the asset pipeline, including an introduction to Sass (Section 5.2). We'll end by taking a first important step toward letting users sign up to our site (Section 5.4).

Most of the changes in this chapter involve adding and editing markup in the sample application's site layout, which (based on the guidelines in Box 3.3) is exactly the kind of work that we wouldn't ordinarily test-drive, or even test at all. As a result, we'll spend most of our time in our text editor and browser, using TDD only to add a Contact page (Section 5.3.1). We will add an important new test, though; that is, we'll write our first *integration test* to check that the links on the final layout are correct (Section 5.3.4).

5.1 Adding Some Structure

Ruby on Rails™ Tutorial is a book on web development, not web design, but it would be depressing to work on an application that looks like *complete* crap, so in

---

1. Thanks to reader Colm Tuite for his excellent work in helping to convert the sample application to the Bootstrap CSS framework.

this section we'll add some structure to the layout and give it some minimal styling with CSS. In addition to using some custom CSS rules, we'll make use of *Bootstrap*, an open-source web design framework from Twitter. We'll also give our *code* some styling, so to speak, using *partials* to tidy up the layout once it gets a little cluttered.

When building web applications, it is often useful to get a high-level overview of the user interface as early as possible. Throughout the rest of this book, I will thus often include *mockups* (in a web context often called *wireframes*), which are rough sketches of what the eventual application will look like.[2] In this chapter, we will principally be developing the static pages introduced in Section 3.2, including a site logo, a navigation header, and a site footer. A mockup for the most important of these pages, the Home page, appears in Figure 5.1. You can see the final result in Figure 5.7. You'll note that it differs in some details—for example, we'll end up adding a Rails logo on the page—but that's fine, since a mockup need not be exact.

As usual, if you're using Git for version control, now would be a good time to make a new branch:

```
$ git checkout master
$ git checkout -b filling-in-layout
```

5.1.1 Site Navigation

As a first step toward adding links and styles to the sample application, we'll update the site layout file `application.html.erb` (last seen in Listing 4.3) with additional HTML structure. This includes some additional divisions, some CSS classes, and the start of our site navigation. The full file is in Listing 5.1; explanations for the various pieces follow immediately thereafter. If you'd rather not delay gratification, you can see the results in Figure 5.2. [*Note*: It's not (yet) very gratifying.]

---

2. The mockups in *Ruby on Rails*[TM] *Tutorial* are made with an excellent online mockup application called Mockingbird.

Figure 5.1 A mockup of the sample application's Home page.

Listing 5.1 The site layout with added structure.

app/views/layouts/application.html.erb

```
<!DOCTYPE html>
<html>
  <head>
    <title><%= full_title(yield(:title)) %></title>
    <%= stylesheet_link_tag 'application', media: 'all',
                                           'data-turbolinks-track' => true %>
    <%= javascript_include_tag 'application', 'data-turbolinks-track' => true %>
    <%= csrf_meta_tags %>
    <!--[if lt IE 9]>
      <script src="//cdnjs.cloudflare.com/ajax/libs/html5shiv/r29/html5.min.js">
      </script>
    <![endif]-->
  </head>
  <body>
    <header class="navbar navbar-fixed-top navbar-inverse">
      <div class="container">
```

```
      <%= link_to "sample app", "#", id: "logo" %>
      <nav>
        <ul class="nav navbar-nav navbar-right">
          <li><%= link_to "Home",   "#" %></li>
          <li><%= link_to "Help",   "#" %></li>
          <li><%= link_to "Log in", "#" %></li>
        </ul>
      </nav>
    </div>
  </header>
  <div class="container">
    <%= yield %>
  </div>
  </body>
</html>
```

Let's look at the new elements in Listing 5.1 from top to bottom. As alluded to briefly in Section 3.4.1, Rails uses HTML5 by default (as indicated by the doctype `<!DOCTYPE html>`); since the HTML5 standard is relatively new, some browsers

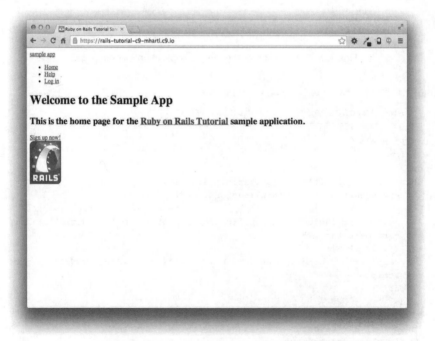

Figure 5.2 The Home page with no custom CSS.

(especially older versions of Internet Explorer) don't fully support it, so we include some
JavaScript code (known as an "HTML5 shim [or shiv]")[3] to work around the issue:

```
<!--[if lt IE 9]>
  <script src="//cdnjs.cloudflare.com/ajax/libs/html5shiv/r29/html5.min.js">
  </script>
<![endif]-->
```

The somewhat odd syntax

```
<!--[if lt IE 9]>
```

includes the enclosed line only if the version of Microsoft Internet Explorer (IE) is less
than 9 (**if lt IE 9**). The weird **[if lt IE 9]** syntax is *not* part of Rails; it's actually
a conditional comment supported by Internet Explorer browsers for just this sort of
situation. It's a good thing, too, because it means we can include the HTML5 shim *only*
for IE browsers less than version 9, leaving other browsers such as Firefox, Chrome, and
Safari unaffected.

The next section includes a **header** for the site's (plain-text) logo, a couple of
divisions (using the **div** tag), and a list of elements with navigation links:

```
<header class="navbar navbar-fixed-top navbar-inverse">
  <div class="container">
    <%= link_to "sample app", "#", id: "logo" %>
    <nav>
      <ul class="nav navbar-nav navbar-right">
        <li><%= link_to "Home",   "#" %></li>
        <li><%= link_to "Help",   "#" %></li>
        <li><%= link_to "Log in", "#" %></li>
      </ul>
    </nav>
  </div>
</header>
```

---

3. The words *shim* and *shiv* are used interchangeably in this context; the former is the proper term, based on
the English word whose meaning is "a washer or thin strip of material used to align parts, make them fit, or
reduce wear," while the latter (meaning "a knife or razor used as a weapon") is apparently a play on the name
of the HTML5 shim's original author, Sjoerd Visscher.

Here the **header** tag indicates elements that should go at the top of the page. We've given the **header** tag three *CSS classes*,[4] called **navbar**, **navbar-fixed-top**, and **navbar-inverse**, separated by spaces:

```
<header class="navbar navbar-fixed-top navbar-inverse">
```

All HTML elements can be assigned both classes and *IDs*; these are merely labels, and are useful for styling with CSS (Section 5.1.2). The main difference between classes and IDs is that classes can be used multiple times on a page, but IDs can be used only once. In the present case, all the navbar classes have special meaning to the Bootstrap framework, which we'll install and use in Section 5.1.2.

Inside the **header** tag, we see a **div** tag:

```
<div class="container">
```

The **div** tag is a generic division; it doesn't do anything apart from divide the document into distinct parts. In older-style HTML, **div** tags are used for nearly all site divisions, but HTML5 adds the **header**, **nav**, and **section** elements for divisions common to many applications. In this case, the **div** has a CSS class as well (**container**). As with the **header** tag's classes, this class has special meaning to Bootstrap.

After the div, we encounter some embedded Ruby:

```
<%= link_to "sample app", "#", id: "logo" %>
<nav>
  <ul class="nav navbar-nav navbar-right">
    <li><%= link_to "Home",   "#" %></li>
    <li><%= link_to "Help",   "#" %></li>
    <li><%= link_to "Log in", "#" %></li>
  </ul>
</nav>
```

This code uses the Rails helper **link_to** to create links (which we created directly with the anchor tag **a** in Section 3.2.2); the first argument to **link_to** is the link text, while the second is the URL. We'll fill in the URLs with *named routes* in Section 5.3.3, but for now we use the stub URL **"#"** commonly used in web design. The third argument is an options hash, in this case adding the CSS ID **logo** to the sample app link. (The other three links have no options hash, which is fine since it's optional.) Rails helpers

---

4. These are completely unrelated to Ruby classes.

often take options hashes in this way, giving us the flexibility to add arbitrary HTML options without ever leaving Rails.

The second element inside the divs is a list of navigation links, made using the *unordered list* tag `ul`, together with the *list item* tag `li`:

```
<nav>
  <ul class="nav navbar-nav navbar-right">
    <li><%= link_to "Home",    "#" %></li>
    <li><%= link_to "Help",    "#" %></li>
    <li><%= link_to "Log in", "#" %></li>
  </ul>
</nav>
```

The `<nav>` tag, though formally unnecessary here, is used to more clearly communicate the purpose of the navigation links. Meanwhile, the `nav`, `navbar-nav`, and `navbar-right` classes on the `ul` tag have special meaning to Bootstrap and will be styled automatically when we include the Bootstrap CSS in Section 5.1.2. As you can verify by inspecting the navigation in your browser, once Rails has processed the layout and evaluated the embedded Ruby, the list looks like this:[5]

```
<nav>
  <ul class="nav navbar-nav navbar-right">
    <li><a href="#">Home</a></li>
    <li><a href="#">Help</a></li>
    <li><a href="#">Log in</a></li>
  </ul>
</nav>
```

This is the text that will be returned to the browser.

The final part of the layout is a `div` for the main content:

```
<div class="container">
  <%= yield %>
</div>
```

As before, the `container` class has special meaning to Bootstrap. As we learned in Section 3.4.3, the `yield` method inserts the contents of each page into the site layout.

---

5. The spacing might look slightly different, which is fine because (as noted in Section 3.4.1) HTML is insensitive to whitespace.

Apart from the site footer, which we'll add in Section 5.1.3, our layout is now complete, and we can look at the results by visiting the Home page. To take advantage of the upcoming style elements, we'll add some extra elements to the **home.html.erb** view (Listing 5.2).

Listing 5.2 The Home page with a link to the sign-up page.

app/views/static_pages/home.html.erb

```
<div class="center jumbotron">
  <h1>Welcome to the Sample App</h1>

  <h2>
    This is the home page for the
    <a href="http://www.railstutorial.org/">Ruby on Rails Tutorial</a>
    sample application.
  </h2>

  <%= link_to "Sign up now!", "#", class: "btn btn-lg btn-primary" %>
</div>

<%= link_to image_tag("rails.png", alt: "Rails logo"),
            'http://rubyonrails.org/' %>
```

In preparation for adding users to our site in Chapter 7, the first **link_to** creates a stub link of the form

```
<a href="#" class="btn btn-lg btn-primary">Sign up now!</a>
```

In the **div** tag, the **jumbotron** CSS class has a special meaning to Bootstrap, as do the **btn**, **btn-lg**, and **btn-primary** classes in the sign-up button.

The second **link_to** shows off the **image_tag** helper, which takes as arguments the path to an image and an optional options hash—in this case, setting the **alt** attribute of the image tag using symbols. For this approach to work, we need an image called **rails.png**, which you should download from the main Ruby on Rails page at http://rubyonrails.org/images/rails.png and place in the **app/assets/images/** directory. If you're using the cloud IDE or another Unix-like system, you can accomplish this with the **curl** utility as follows:[6]

---

6. If you have Homebrew on OS X, you can install **curl** using **brew install curl**.

```
$ curl -O http://rubyonrails.org/images/rails.png
$ mv rails.png app/assets/images/
```

(For more on **curl**, see Chapter 3 of *Conquering the Command Line*.) Because we used the **image_tag** helper in Listing 5.2, Rails will automatically find any images in the **app/assets/images/** directory using the asset pipeline (Section 5.2).

To make the effects of **image_tag** clearer, let's look at the HTML it produces:[7]

```
<img alt="Rails logo"
src="/assets/rails-9308b8f92fea4c19a3a0d8385b494526.png" />
```

Here the string **9308b8f92fea4c19a3a0d8385b494526** (which will differ on your system) is added by Rails to ensure that the filename is unique, which causes browsers to load images properly when they have been updated (instead of retrieving them from the browser cache). Note that the **src** attribute *doesn't* include **images**, instead using an **assets** directory common to all assets (e.g., images, JavaScript, CSS). On the server, Rails associates images in the **assets** directory with the proper **app/assets/images** directory, but as far as the browser is concerned all the assets look like they are in the same directory, which allows them to be served faster. Meanwhile, the **alt** attribute is what will be displayed if the page is accessed by a program that can't display images (such as screen readers for the visually impaired).

Now we're finally ready to see the fruits of our labors, as shown in Figure 5.2. Pretty underwhelming, you say? Perhaps so. Happily, though, we've done a good job of giving our HTML elements sensible classes, which puts us in a great position to add style to the site with CSS.

5.1.2 Bootstrap and Custom CSS

In Section 5.1.1, we associated many of the HTML elements with CSS classes, which gives us considerable flexibility in constructing a layout based on CSS. As noted in Section 5.1.1, many of these classes are specific to Bootstrap, a framework from Twitter that makes it easy to add nice web design and user interface elements to an HTML5 application. In this section, we'll combine Bootstrap with some custom CSS rules to start adding some style to the sample application. It's worth noting that using Bootstrap

---

7. You might notice that the **img** tag, rather than looking like <img>...</img>, instead looks like <img ... />. Tags that follow this form are known as *self-closing* tags.

automatically makes our application's design responsive, ensuring that it looks sensible across a wide range of devices.

Our first step is to add Bootstrap, which in Rails applications can be accomplished with the `bootstrap-sass` gem, as shown in Listing 5.3. The Bootstrap framework natively uses the Less CSS language for making dynamic style sheets, but the Rails asset pipeline supports the (very similar) Sass language by default (Section 5.2), so `bootstrap-sass` converts Less to Sass and makes all the necessary Bootstrap files available to the current application.[8]

Listing 5.3 Adding the `bootstrap-sass` gem to the **Gemfile**.

```
source 'https://rubygems.org'

gem 'rails',             '4.2.0'
gem 'bootstrap-sass',    '3.2.0.0'
  .
  .
  .
```

To install Bootstrap, we run **bundle install** as usual:

```
$ bundle install
```

Although **rails generate** automatically creates a separate CSS file for each controller, it's surprisingly hard to include all of these files properly and in the right order, so for simplicity we'll put all of the CSS needed for this tutorial in a single file. The first step toward getting custom CSS to work is to create such a custom CSS file:

```
$ touch app/assets/stylesheets/custom.css.scss
```

(This command uses the **touch** trick from Section 3.3.3 en route, but you can create the file however you like.) Here both the directory name and filename extension are important. The directory

```
app/assets/stylesheets/
```

---

8. It is also possible to use Less with the asset pipeline; see the `less-rails-bootstrap` gem for details.

is part of the asset pipeline (Section 5.2), and any style sheets in this directory will automatically be included as part of the **application.css** file included in the site layout. Furthermore, the filename **custom.css.scss** includes the **.css** extension, which indicates a CSS file, and the **.scss** extension, which indicates a "Sassy CSS" file and arranges for the asset pipeline to process the file using Sass. (We won't be using Sass until Section 5.2.2, but it's needed now for the bootstrap-sass gem to work its magic.)

Inside the file for the custom CSS, we can use the **@import** function to include Bootstrap (together with the associated Sprockets utility), as shown in Listing 5.4.[9]

Listing 5.4 Adding Bootstrap CSS.

app/assets/stylesheets/custom.css.scss

```
@import "bootstrap-sprockets";
@import "bootstrap";
```

The two lines in Listing 5.4 include the entire Bootstrap CSS framework. After restarting the web server to incorporate the changes into the development application (by pressing Ctrl-C and then running **rails server** as in Section 1.3.2), the results appear as in Figure 5.3. The placement of the text isn't good and the logo doesn't have any style, but the colors and sign-up button look promising.

Next we'll add some CSS that will be used site-wide for styling the layout and each individual page, as shown in Listing 5.5. The result is shown in Figure 5.4. (There are quite a few rules in Listing 5.5; to get a sense of what a CSS rule does, it's often helpful to comment it out using CSS comments—that is, by putting it inside /* . . . */, and seeing what changes.)

Listing 5.5 Adding CSS for some universal styling applying to all pages.

app/assets/stylesheets/custom.css.scss

```
@import "bootstrap-sprockets";
@import "bootstrap";

/* universal */

body {
  padding-top: 60px;
}
```

---

9. If these steps seem mysterious, take heart: I'm just following the instructions from the bootstrap-sass README file.

```
section {
  overflow: auto;
}

textarea {
  resize: vertical;
}

.center {
  text-align: center;
}

.center h1 {
  margin-bottom: 10px;
}
```

Figure 5.3 The sample application with Bootstrap CSS.

Figure 5.4 Adding some spacing and other universal styling.

Note that the CSS in Listing 5.5 has a consistent form. In general, CSS rules refer to either a class, an ID, an HTML tag, or some combination thereof, followed by a list of styling commands. For example,

```
body {
  padding-top: 60px;
}
```

puts 60 pixels of padding at the top of the page. Because of the `navbar-fixed-top` class in the `header` tag, Bootstrap affixes the navigation bar to the top of the page, so the padding serves to separate the main text from the navigation. (Because the default navbar color changed after Bootstrap 2.0, we need the `navbar-inverse` class to make it dark instead of light.) Meanwhile, the CSS in the rule

```
.center {
  text-align: center;
}
```

associates the **center** class with the **text-align: center** property. In other words, the dot **.** in **.center** indicates that the rule styles a class. (As we'll see in Listing 5.7, the pound sign **#** identifies a rule to style a CSS *ID*.) This means that elements inside any tag (such as a **div**) with class **center** will be centered on the page. (We saw an example of this class in Listing 5.2.)

Although Bootstrap comes with CSS rules for nice typography, we'll also add some custom rules for the appearance of the text on our site, as shown in Listing 5.6. (Not all of these rules apply to the Home page, but each rule here will be used at some point in the sample application.) The result of Listing 5.6 is shown in Figure 5.5.

Listing 5.6 Adding CSS for nice typography.
app/assets/stylesheets/custom.css.scss

```scss
@import "bootstrap-sprockets";
@import "bootstrap";
.
.
.
/* typography */

h1, h2, h3, h4, h5, h6 {
  line-height: 1;
}

h1 {
  font-size: 3em;
  letter-spacing: -2px;
  margin-bottom: 30px;
  text-align: center;
}

h2 {
  font-size: 1.2em;
  letter-spacing: -1px;
  margin-bottom: 30px;
  text-align: center;
  font-weight: normal;
  color: #777;
```

```
}

p {
  font-size: 1.1em;
  line-height: 1.7em;
}
```

Finally, we'll add some rules to style the site's logo, which simply consists of the text "sample app." The CSS in Listing 5.7 converts the text to uppercase and modifies its size, color, and placement. (We've used a CSS ID because we expect the site logo to appear on the page only once, but you could use a class instead.)

Figure 5.5 Adding some typographic styling.

Listing 5.7 Adding CSS for the site logo.

`app/assets/stylesheets/custom.css.scss`

```
@import "bootstrap-sprockets";
@import "bootstrap";
.
.
.
/* header */

#logo {
  float: left;
  margin-right: 10px;
  font-size: 1.7em;
  color: #fff;
  text-transform: uppercase;
  letter-spacing: -1px;
  padding-top: 9px;
  font-weight: bold;
}

#logo:hover {
  color: #fff;
  text-decoration: none;
}
```

Here `color: #fff` changes the color of the logo to white. HTML colors can be coded with three pairs of base-16 (hexadecimal) numbers—one each for the primary colors red, green, and blue (in that order). The code `#ffffff` maxes out all three colors, yielding pure white, and `#fff` is a shorthand for the full `#ffffff`. The CSS standard also defines a large number of synonyms for common HTML colors, including `white` for `#fff`. The result of the CSS in Listing 5.7 is shown in Figure 5.6.

5.1.3 Partials

Although the layout in Listing 5.1 serves its purpose, it's getting a little cluttered. The HTML shim takes up three lines and uses weird Internet Explorer-specific syntax, so it would be nice to tuck it away somewhere on its own. In addition, the header HTML forms a logical unit, so it should be packaged up in one place. The way to achieve this in Rails is to use a facility called *partials*. Let's first take a look at what the layout looks like after the partials are defined (Listing 5.8).

Figure 5.6 The sample app with a nicely styled logo.

Listing 5.8 The site layout with partials for the style sheets and header.

app/views/layouts/application.html.erb

```
<!DOCTYPE html>
<html>
  <head>
    <title><%= full_title(yield(:title)) %></title>
    <%= stylesheet_link_tag 'application', media: 'all',
                                           'data-turbolinks-track' => true %>
    <%= javascript_include_tag 'application', 'data-turbolinks-track' => true %>
    <%= csrf_meta_tags %>
    <%= render 'layouts/shim' %>
  </head>
  <body>
    <%= render 'layouts/header' %>
    <div class="container">
      <%= yield %>
    </div>
  </body>
</html>
```

In Listing 5.8, we've replaced the HTML shim stylesheet lines with a single call to a Rails helper called **render**:

```
<%= render 'layouts/shim' %>
```

The effect of this line is to look for a file called **app/views/layouts/_shim. html.erb**, evaluate its contents, and insert the results into the view.[10] (Recall that `<%= ... %>` is the embedded Ruby syntax needed to evaluate a Ruby expression and then insert the results into the template.) Note the leading underscore on the filename **_shim.html.erb**; this underscore is the universal convention for naming partials, and among other things it permits us to identify all the partials in a directory at a glance.

Of course, to get the partial to work, we have to create the corresponding file and fill it with some content. In the case of the shim partial, this is just the three lines of shim code from Listing 5.1. The result appears in Listing 5.9.

Listing 5.9 A partial for the HTML shim.
app/views/layouts/_shim.html.erb

```
<!--[if lt IE 9]>
  <script src="//cdnjs.cloudflare.com/ajax/libs/html5shiv/r29/html5.min.js">
  </script>
<![endif]-->
```

Similarly, we can move the header material into the partial shown in Listing 5.10 and insert it into the layout with another call to **render**. (As usual with partials, you will have to create the file by hand using your text editor.)

Listing 5.10 A partial for the site header.
app/views/layouts/_header.html.erb

```
<header class="navbar navbar-fixed-top navbar-inverse">
  <div class="container">
    <%= link_to "sample app", "#", id: "logo" %>
```

---

10. Many Rails developers use a **shared** directory for partials shared across different views. I prefer to use the **shared** folder for utility partials that are useful on multiple views, while putting partials that are literally on every page (as part of the site layout) in the **layouts** directory. (We'll create the **shared** directory starting in Chapter 7.) That seems to me a logical division, but putting all of the partials in the **shared** folder certainly works too.

```
    <nav>
      <ul class="nav navbar-nav navbar-right">
        <li><%= link_to "Home",    "#" %></li>
        <li><%= link_to "Help",    "#" %></li>
        <li><%= link_to "Log in", "#" %></li>
      </ul>
    </nav>
  </div>
</header>
```

Now that we know how to make partials, let's add a site footer to go along with the header. By now you can probably guess that we'll call it `_footer.html.erb` and put it in the layouts directory (Listing 5.11).[11]

Listing 5.11 A partial for the site footer.

app/views/layouts/_footer.html.erb

```
<footer class="footer">
  <small>
    The <a href="http://www.railstutorial.org/">Ruby on Rails Tutorial</a>
    by <a href="http://www.michaelhartl.com/">Michael Hartl</a>
  </small>
  <nav>
    <ul>
      <li><%= link_to "About",   "#" %></li>
      <li><%= link_to "Contact", "#" %></li>
      <li><a href="http://news.railstutorial.org/">News</a></li>
    </ul>
  </nav>
</footer>
```

As with the header, in the footer we've used `link_to` for the internal links to the About and Contact pages and stubbed out the URLs with `"#"` for now. (As as is true of `header`, the `footer` tag is new in HTML5.)

We can render the footer partial in the layout by following the same pattern as the style sheets and header partials (Listing 5.12).

---

11. You might wonder why we use both the `footer` tag and the `.footer` class. The answer is that the tag has a clear meaning to human readers, and the class is used by Bootstrap. Using a `div` tag in place of `footer` would work as well.

Listing 5.12 The site layout with a footer partial.

app/views/layouts/application.html.erb

```
<!DOCTYPE html>
<html>
  <head>
    <title><%= full_title(yield(:title)) %></title>
    <%= stylesheet_link_tag "application", media: "all",
                                           "data-turbolinks-track" => true %>
    <%= javascript_include_tag "application", "data-turbolinks-track" => true %>
    <%= csrf_meta_tags %>
    <%= render 'layouts/shim' %>
  </head>
  <body>
    <%= render 'layouts/header' %>
    <div class="container">
      <%= yield %>
      <%= render 'layouts/footer' %>
    </div>
  </body>
</html>
```

Of course, the footer will be ugly without some styling (Listing 5.13). The results appear in Figure 5.7.

Listing 5.13 Adding the CSS for the site footer.

app/assets/stylesheets/custom.css.scss

```
.
.
.
/* footer */

footer {
  margin-top: 45px;
  padding-top: 5px;
  border-top: 1px solid #eaeaea;
  color: #777;
}

footer a {
  color: #555;
}

footer a:hover {
```

```
  color: #222;
}

footer small {
  float: left;
}

footer ul {
  float: right;
  list-style: none;
}

footer ul li {
  float: left;
  margin-left: 15px;
}
```

Figure 5.7 The Home page with an added footer.

5.2 Sass and the Asset Pipeline

One of the most notable additions in recent versions of Rails is the *asset pipeline*, which significantly improves the production and management of static assets such as CSS, JavaScript, and images. This section first gives a high-level overview of the asset pipeline, and then shows how to use *Sass*, a powerful tool for writing CSS.

5.2.1 The Asset Pipeline

The asset pipeline involves lots of changes under Rails' hood, but from the perspective of a typical Rails developer there are three principal features to understand: asset directories, manifest files, and preprocessor engines.[12] Let's consider each in turn.

Asset Directories

In Rails version 3.0 and earlier, static assets lived in the **public/** directory, as follows:

- **public/stylesheets**
- **public/javascripts**
- **public/images**

Files in these directories are (even post-3.0) automatically served up via requests to http://www.example.com/stylesheets of another site.

The latest version of Rails includes *three* canonical directories for static assets, each with its own purpose:

- **app/assets**: assets specific to the present application
- **lib/assets**: assets for libraries written by your dev team
- **vendor/assets**: assets from third-party vendors

As you might guess, each of these directories has a subdirectory for each asset class. For example,

```
$ ls app/assets/
images/  javascripts/  stylesheets/
```

---

12. The structure of this section is based on the excellent blog post "The Rails 3 Asset Pipeline in (about) 5 Minutes" by Michael Erasmus. For more details, see Rails Guide on the Asset Pipeline.

At this point, we're in a position to understand the motivation behind the location of the custom CSS file in Section 5.1.2: **custom.css.scss** is specific to the sample application, so it goes in **app/assets/stylesheets**.

Manifest Files

Once you've placed your assets in their logical locations, you can use *manifest files* to tell Rails (via the Sprockets gem) how to combine them to form single files. (This applies to CSS and JavaScript, but not to images.) As an example, let's take a look at the default manifest file for app style sheets (Listing 5.14).

Listing 5.14 The manifest file for app-specific CSS.

app/assets/stylesheets/application.css

```
/*
 * This is a manifest file that'll be compiled into application.css, which
 * will include all the files listed below.
 *
 * Any CSS and SCSS file within this directory, lib/assets/stylesheets,
 * vendor/assets/stylesheets, or vendor/assets/stylesheets of plugins, if any,
 * can be referenced here using a relative path.
 *
 * You're free to add application-wide styles to this file and they'll appear
 * at the bottom of the compiled file so the styles you add here take
 * precedence over styles defined in any styles defined in the other CSS/SCSS
 * files in this directory. It is generally better to create a new file per
 * style scope.
 *
 *= require_tree .
 *= require_self
 */
```

The key lines here are actually CSS comments, but they are used by Sprockets to include the proper files:

```
/*
 .
 .
 .
 *= require_tree .
 *= require_self
 */
```

Here

```
*= require_tree .
```

ensures that all CSS files in the **app/assets/stylesheets** directory (including the tree subdirectories) are included in the application CSS. The line

```
*= require_self
```

specifies where in the loading sequence the CSS in **application.css** itself gets included.

Rails comes with sensible default manifest files, and in the *Rails Tutorial* we won't need to make any changes. Nevertheless, the Rails Guides entry on the asset pipeline has more details if you need them.

Preprocessor Engines

After you've assembled your assets, Rails prepares them for the site template by running them through several preprocessing engines and using the manifest files to combine them for delivery to the browser. We tell Rails which processor to use using filename extensions; the three most common cases are **.scss** for Sass, **.coffee** for CoffeeScript, and **.erb** for embedded Ruby (ERb). We first covered ERb in Section 3.4.3, and we cover Sass in Section 5.2.2. We won't be needing CoffeeScript in this tutorial, but it's an elegant little language that compiles to JavaScript. (The RailsCast on CoffeeScript basics is a good place to start.)

The preprocessor engines can be chained, so that

foobar.js.coffee

gets run through the CoffeeScript processor, and

foobar.js.erb.coffee

gets run through both CoffeeScript and ERb (with the code running from right to left—in other words, so that CoffeeScript is processed first).

Efficiency in Production

One of the best things about the asset pipeline is that it automatically results in assets that are optimized to be efficient in a production application. Traditional methods for organizing CSS and JavaScript involve splitting functionality into separate files and using nice formatting (with lots of indentation). While convenient for the programmer, this is inefficient in production. In particular, including multiple full-sized files can significantly slow page-load times, which is one of the most important factors affecting the quality of the user experience. With the asset pipeline, we don't have to choose between speed and convenience: We can work with multiple nicely formatted files in development, and then use the asset pipeline to make efficient files in production. In particular, the asset pipeline combines all the application style sheets into one CSS file (`application.css`), combines all the application JavaScript into one JavaScript file (`application.js`), and then *minifies* them to remove the unnecessary spacing and indentation that bloats file size. The result is the best of both worlds: convenience in development and efficiency in production.

5.2.2 Syntactically Awesome Style Sheets

Sass is a language for writing style sheets that improves on CSS in many ways. In this section, we cover two of the most important improvements: *nesting* and *variables*. (A third technique, *mixins*, is introduced in Section 7.1.1.)

As noted briefly in Section 5.1.2, Sass supports a format called SCSS (indicated with a `.scss` filename extension), which is a strict superset of CSS itself; that is, SCSS only *adds* features to CSS, rather than defining an entirely new syntax.[13] As a consequence, every valid CSS file is also a valid SCSS file, which is convenient for projects with existing style rules. In our case, we used SCSS from the start to take advantage of Bootstrap. Since the Rails asset pipeline automatically uses Sass to process files with the `.scss` extension, the `custom.css.scss` file will be run through the Sass preprocessor before being packaged up for delivery to the browser.

Nesting

A common pattern in style sheets is having rules that apply to nested elements. For example, in Listing 5.5 we have rules both for `.center` and for `.center h1`:

```
.center {
  text-align: center;
}
```

---

13. The older `.sass` format, also supported by Sass, defines a new language that is less verbose (and has fewer curly braces) but is less convenient for existing projects and is harder to learn for those already familiar with CSS.

```
.center h1 {
  margin-bottom: 10px;
}
```

We can replace this in Sass with

```
.center {
  text-align: center;
  h1 {
    margin-bottom: 10px;
  }
}
```

Here the nested **h1** rule automatically inherits the **.center** context.

There's a second candidate for nesting that requires a slightly different syntax. In Listing 5.7, we have the code

```
#logo {
  float: left;
  margin-right: 10px;
  font-size: 1.7em;
  color: #fff;
  text-transform: uppercase;
  letter-spacing: -1px;
  padding-top: 9px;
  font-weight: bold;
}

#logo:hover {
  color: #fff;
  text-decoration: none;
}
```

Here the logo id **#logo** appears twice—once by itself and once with the **hover** attribute (which controls its appearance when the mouse pointer hovers over the element in question). To nest the second rule, we need to reference the parent element **#logo**. In SCSS, this is accomplished with the ampersand character **&** as follows:

```
#logo {
  float: left;
  margin-right: 10px;
```

```
    font-size: 1.7em;
    color: #fff;
    text-transform: uppercase;
    letter-spacing: -1px;
    padding-top: 9px;
    font-weight: bold;
    &:hover {
      color: #fff;
      text-decoration: none;
    }
}
```

Sass changes `&:hover` into `#logo:hover` as part of converting from SCSS to CSS.

Both of these nesting techniques apply to the footer CSS in Listing 5.13, which can be transformed into the following:

```
footer {
  margin-top: 45px;
  padding-top: 5px;
  border-top: 1px solid #eaeaea;
  color: #777;
  a {
    color: #555;
    &:hover {
      color: #222;
    }
  }
  small {
    float: left;
  }
  ul {
    float: right;
    list-style: none;
    li {
      float: left;
      margin-left: 15px;
    }
  }
}
```

Converting Listing 5.13 by hand is a good exercise, and you should verify that the CSS still works properly after the conversion.

Variables

Sass allows us to define *variables* to eliminate duplication and write more expressive code. For example, looking at Listing 5.6 and Listing 5.13, we see that there are repeated references to the same color:

```
h2 {
  .
  .
  .
  color: #777;
}
  .
  .
  .
footer {
  .
  .
  .
  color: #777;
}
```

In this case, **#777** is a light gray, and we can give it a name by defining a variable as follows:

```
$light-gray: #777;
```

This allows us to rewrite our SCSS like this:

```
$light-gray: #777;
  .
  .
  .
h2 {
  .
  .
  .
  color: $light-gray;
}
  .
  .
  .
footer {
  .
```

```
  .
  .
  color: $light-gray;
}
```

Because variable names such as `$light-gray` are more descriptive than `#777`, it's often useful to define variables even for values that aren't repeated. Indeed, the Bootstrap framework defines a large number of variables for colors, available online on the Bootstrap page of Less variables. That page defines variables using Less, not Sass, but the `bootstrap-sass` gem provides the Sass equivalents. It is not difficult to guess the correspondence: Where Less uses an "at" sign `@`, Sass uses a dollar sign `$`. Looking at the Bootstrap variable page, we see that there is a variable for light gray:

```
@gray-light: #777;
```

This means that, via the `bootstrap-sass` gem, there should be a corresponding SCSS variable `$gray-light`. We can use this to replace our custom variable, `$light-gray`, which gives

```
h2 {
  .
  .
  color: $gray-light;
}
  .
  .
footer {
  .
  .
  color: $gray-light;
}
```

Applying the Sass nesting and variable definition features to the full SCSS file gives the file in Listing 5.15. It uses both Sass variables (as inferred from the Bootstrap Less variable page) and built-in named colors (i.e., `white` for `#fff`). Note in particular the dramatic improvement in the rules for the `footer` tag.

Listing 5.15 The initial SCSS file converted to use nesting and variables.

app/assets/stylesheets/custom.css.scss

```scss
@import "bootstrap-sprockets";
@import "bootstrap";

/* mixins, variables, etc. */

$gray-medium-light: #eaeaea;

/* universal */

body {
  padding-top: 60px;
}

section {
  overflow: auto;
}

textarea {
  resize: vertical;
}

.center {
  text-align: center;
  h1 {
    margin-bottom: 10px;
  }
}

/* typography */

h1, h2, h3, h4, h5, h6 {
  line-height: 1;
}

h1 {
  font-size: 3em;
  letter-spacing: -2px;

  margin-bottom: 30px;
  text-align: center;
}

h2 {
  font-size: 1.2em;
  letter-spacing: -1px;
```

```scss
  margin-bottom: 30px;
  text-align: center;
  font-weight: normal;
  color: $gray-light;
}

p {
  font-size: 1.1em;
  line-height: 1.7em;
}


/* header */

#logo {
  float: left;
  margin-right: 10px;
  font-size: 1.7em;
  color: white;
  text-transform: uppercase;
  letter-spacing: -1px;
  padding-top: 9px;
  font-weight: bold;
  &:hover {
    color: white;
    text-decoration: none;
  }
}

/* footer */

footer {
  margin-top: 45px;
  padding-top: 5px;
  border-top: 1px solid $gray-medium-light;
  color: $gray-light;
  a {
    color: $gray;
    &:hover {
      color: $gray-darker;
    }
  }
  small {
    float: left;
  }
  ul {
    float: right;
    list-style: none;
```

```
li {
  float: left;
  margin-left: 15px;
}
}
}
```

Sass offers us even more ways to simplify our style sheets, but the code in Listing 5.15 uses the most important features and gives us a great start. See the Sass website for more details.

5.3 Layout Links

Now that we've developed a site layout with decent styling, it's time to start filling in the links we've stubbed out with `"#"`. Of course, we could hard-code links like

```
<a href="/static_pages/about">About</a>
```

but that isn't the Rails Way. For one thing, it would be nice if the URL for the About page were /about rather than /static_pages/about. Moreover, Rails conventionally uses *named routes*, which involves code like

```
<%= link_to "About", about_path %>
```

This way the code has a more transparent meaning, and it's also more flexible because we can change the definition of **about_path** and have the URL change everywhere **about_path** is used.

The full list of our planned links appears in Table 5.1, along with their mapping to URLs and routes. We took care of the first route in Section 3.4.4, and we'll have implemented all but the last one by the end of this chapter. (We'll make the last one in Chapter 8.)

Table 5.1 Route and URL mapping for site links.

Page	URL	Named route
Home	/	root_path
About	/about	about_path
Help	/help	help_path
Contact	/contact	contact_path
Sign up	/signup	signup_path
Log in	/login	login_path

5.3.1 Contact Page

For completeness, we'll add the Contact page, which was left as an exercise in Chapter 3. The test appears in Listing 5.16, which simply follows the model last seen in Listing 3.22.

Listing 5.16   A test for the Contact page. **RED**

test/controllers/static_pages_controller_test.rb

```
require 'test_helper'

class StaticPagesControllerTest < ActionController::TestCase

  test "should get home" do
    get :home
    assert_response :success
    assert_select "title", "Ruby on Rails Tutorial Sample App"
  end

  test "should get help" do
    get :help
    assert_response :success
    assert_select "title", "Help | Ruby on Rails Tutorial Sample App"
  end

  test "should get about" do
    get :about
    assert_response :success
    assert_select "title", "About | Ruby on Rails Tutorial Sample App"
  end
```

```
  test "should get contact" do
    get :contact
    assert_response :success
    assert_select "title", "Contact | Ruby on Rails Tutorial Sample App"
  end
end
```

At this point, the tests in Listing 5.16 should be **RED**:

Listing 5.17 RED

```
$ bundle exec rake test
```

The application code parallels the addition of the About page in Section 3.3: First we update the routes (Listing 5.18), then we add a **contact** action to the Static Pages controller (Listing 5.19), and finally we create a Contact view (Listing 5.20).

Listing 5.18 Adding a route for the Contact page. **RED**
config/routes.rb

```
Rails.application.routes.draw do
  root 'static_pages#home'
  get  'static_pages/help'
  get  'static_pages/about'
  get  'static_pages/contact'
end
```

Listing 5.19 Adding an action for the Contact page. **RED**
app/controllers/static_pages_controller.rb

```
class StaticPagesController < ApplicationController
  .
  .
  .
  def contact
  end
end
```

Listing 5.20 The view for the Contact page. **GREEN**
app/views/static_pages/contact.html.erb

```
<% provide(:title, 'Contact') %>
<h1>Contact</h1>
<p>
  Contact the Ruby on Rails Tutorial about the sample app at the
  <a href="http://www.railstutorial.org/#contact">contact page</a>.
</p>
```

Now make sure that the tests are **GREEN**:

Listing 5.21 GREEN

```
$ bundle exec rake test
```

5.3.2 Rails Routes

To add the named routes for the sample app's static pages, we'll edit the routes file, `config/routes.rb`, that Rails uses to define URL mappings. We'll begin by reviewing the route for the Home page (defined in Section 3.4.4), which is a special case, and then define a set of routes for the remaining static pages.

So far, we've seen three examples of how to define a root route, starting with the code

```
root 'application#hello'
```

in the hello app (Listing 1.10), the code

```
root 'users#index'
```

in the toy app (Listing 2.3), and the code

```
root 'static_pages#home'
```

in the sample app (Listing 3.37). In each case, the **root** method arranges for the root path / to be routed to a controller and action of our choice. Defining the root route in this way has a second important effect, which is to create named routes that allow us to refer to routes by a name rather than by the raw URL. In this case, these routes are **root_path** and **root_url**, with the only difference being that the latter includes the full URL:

```
root_path -> '/'
root_url  -> 'http://www.example.com/'
```

In the *Rails Tutorial*, we'll follow the common convention of using the **_path** form except when doing redirects, where we'll use the **_url** form. (The HTTP standard technically requires a full URL after redirects, though in most browsers it will work either way.)

To define the named routes for the Help, About, and Contact pages, we need to make changes to the **get** rules from Listing 5.18, transforming lines like

```
get 'static_pages/help'
```

to

```
get 'help' => 'static_pages#help'
```

The second of these patterns routes a GET request for the URL /help to the **help** action in the Static Pages controller. Thus we can use the URL /help in place of the more verbose /static_pages/help. As with the rule for the root route, this creates two named routes, **help_path** and **help_url**:

```
help_path -> '/help'
help_url  -> 'http://www.example.com/help'
```

Applying this rule change to the remaining static page routes from Listing 5.18 gives Listing 5.22.

Listing 5.22 Routes for static pages.
config/routes.rb

```
Rails.application.routes.draw do
  root             'static_pages#home'
  get 'help'    => 'static_pages#help'
  get 'about'   => 'static_pages#about'
```

```
  get 'contact' => 'static_pages#contact'
end
```

5.3.3 Using Named Routes

With the routes defined in Listing 5.22, we're now in a position to use the resulting named routes in the site layout. This simply involves filling in the second arguments of the `link_to` functions with the proper named routes. For example, we'll convert

```
<%= link_to "About", "#" %>
```

to

```
<%= link_to "About", about_path %>
```

and so on.

We'll start in the header partial, `_header.html.erb` (Listing 5.23), which has links to the Home and Help pages. While we're at it, we'll follow a common web convention and link the logo to the Home page.

Listing 5.23 Header partial with links.
app/views/layouts/_header.html.erb

```
<header class="navbar navbar-fixed-top navbar-inverse">
  <div class="container">
    <%= link_to "sample app", root_path, id: "logo" %>
    <nav>
      <ul class="nav navbar-nav navbar-right">
        <li><%= link_to "Home",    root_path %></li>
        <li><%= link_to "Help",    help_path %></li>
        <li><%= link_to "Log in", "#" %></li>
      </ul>
    </nav>
  </div>
</header>
```

We won't have a named route for the "Log in" link until Chapter 8, so we've left it as `"#"` for now.

The other place with links is the footer partial, **_footer.html.erb**, which has links for the About and Contact pages (Listing 5.24).

Listing 5.24 Footer partial with links.
app/views/layouts/_footer.html.erb

```
<footer class="footer">
  <small>
    The <a href="http://www.railstutorial.org/">Ruby on Rails Tutorial</a>
    by <a href="http://www.michaelhartl.com/">Michael Hartl</a>
  </small>
  <nav>
    <ul>
      <li><%= link_to "About",   about_path %></li>
      <li><%= link_to "Contact", contact_path %></li>
      <li><a href="http://news.railstutorial.org/">News</a></li>
    </ul>
  </nav>
</footer>
```

With that, our layout has links to all the static pages created in Chapter 3, so that, for example, /about goes to the About page (Figure 5.8).

5.3.4 Layout Link Tests

Now that we've filled in several of the layout links, it's a good idea to test them to make sure they're working correctly. We could do this by hand with a browser—that is, by first visiting the root path and then checking the links by hand—but this quickly becomes cumbersome. Instead, we'll simulate the same series of steps using an *integration test*, which allows us to write an end-to-end test of our application's behavior. We can get started by generating a template test, which we'll call **site_layout**:

```
$ rails generate integration_test site_layout
      invoke  test_unit
      create    test/integration/site_layout_test.rb
```

Note that the Rails generator automatically appends **_test** to the name of the test file.

Our plan for testing the layout links involves checking the HTML structure of our site:

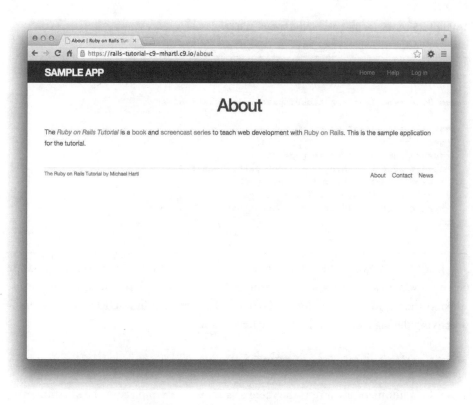

Figure 5.8 The About page at /about.

1. Get the root path (Home page).
2. Verify that the right page template is rendered.
3. Check for the correct links to the Home, Help, About, and Contact pages.

Listing 5.25 shows how we can use Rails integration tests to translate these steps into code, beginning with the **assert_template** method to verify that the Home page is rendered using the correct view.[14]

---

14. Some developers insist that a single test shouldn't contain multiple assertions. I find this practice to be unnecessarily complicated, while also incurring extra overhead if common setup tasks are needed before each test. In addition, a well-written test tells a coherent story, and breaking it up into individual pieces disrupts the narrative. Thus I have a strong preference for including multiple assertions in a test, relying on Ruby (via MiniTest) to tell me the exact lines of any failed assertions.

Listing 5.25 A test for the links on the layout. **GREEN**
test/integration/site_layout_test.rb

```
require 'test_helper'

class SiteLayoutTest < ActionDispatch::IntegrationTest

  test "layout links" do
    get root_path
    assert_template 'static_pages/home'
    assert_select "a[href=?]", root_path, count: 2
    assert_select "a[href=?]", help_path
    assert_select "a[href=?]", about_path
    assert_select "a[href=?]", contact_path
  end
end
```

Listing 5.25 uses some of the more advanced options of the `assert_select` method, which we saw earlier in Listing 3.22 and Listing 5.16. In this case, we use a syntax that allows us to test for the presence of a particular link–URL combination by specifying the tag name **a** and attribute **href**, as in

```
assert_select "a[href=?]", about_path
```

Here Rails automatically inserts the value of **about_path** in place of the question mark (escaping any special characters if necessary), thereby checking for an HTML tag of the form

```
<a href="/about">...</a>
```

Note that the assertion for the root path verifies that there are *two* such links (one each for the logo and navigation menu element):

```
assert_select "a[href=?]", root_path, count: 2
```

This ensures that both links to the Home page defined in Listing 5.23 are present.

Other uses of `assert_select` appear in Table 5.2. While `assert_select` is flexible and powerful (having many more options than the ones shown here), experience suggests that it's wise to take a lightweight approach by testing only HTML elements (such as site layout links) that are unlikely to change much over time.

Table 5.2 Some uses of `assert_select`.

Code	Matching HTML
`assert_select "div"`	`<div>foobar</div>`
`assert_select "div", "foobar"`	`<div>foobar</div>`
`assert_select "div.nav"`	`<div class="nav">foobar</div>`
`assert_select "div#profile"`	`<div id="profile">foobar</div>`
`assert_select "div[name=yo]"`	`<div name="yo">hey</div>`
`assert_select "a[href=?]",` `  '/', count: 1`	`<a href="/">foo</a>`
`assert_select "a[href=?]",` `  '/', text: "foo"`	`<a href="/">foo</a>`

To check that the new test in Listing 5.25 passes, we can run just the integration tests using the following Rake task:

Listing 5.26   GREEN

```
$ bundle exec rake test:integration
```

If all went well, you should run the full test suite to verify that all the tests are **GREEN**:

Listing 5.27   GREEN

```
$ bundle exec rake test
```

With the added integration test for layout links, we are now in a good position to catch regressions quickly using our test suite.

5.4 User Sign-up: A First Step

As a capstone to our work on the layout and routing, in this section we'll make a route for the sign-up page, which will mean creating a second controller along the way. This is an important first step toward allowing users to register for our site; we'll take the next step, modeling users, in Chapter 6, and we'll finish the job in Chapter 7.

5.4.1 Users Controller

We created our first controller, the Static Pages controller, in Section 3.2. It's now time to create a second one, the Users controller. As before, we'll use **generate** to make the simplest controller that meets our present needs—namely, one with a stub sign-up page for new users. Following the conventional REST architecture favored by Rails, we'll call the action for new users **new**, which we can arrange to create automatically by passing **new** as an argument to **generate**. The result is shown in Listing 5.28.

Listing 5.28 Generating a Users controller (with a **new** action).

```
$ rails generate controller Users new
      create  app/controllers/users_controller.rb
       route  get 'users/new'
      invoke  erb
      create    app/views/users
      create    app/views/users/new.html.erb
      invoke  test_unit
      create    test/controllers/users_controller_test.rb
      invoke  helper
      create    app/helpers/users_helper.rb
      invoke    test_unit
      create      test/helpers/users_helper_test.rb
      invoke  assets
      invoke    coffee
      create      app/assets/javascripts/users.js.coffee
      invoke    scss
      create      app/assets/stylesheets/users.css.scss
```

As required, Listing 5.28 creates a Users controller with a **new** action (Listing 5.30) and a stub user view (Listing 5.31). It also creates a minimal test for the new user page (Listing 5.32), which should currently pass:

Listing 5.29 GREEN

```
$ bundle exec rake test
```

Listing 5.30 The initial Users controller, with a **new** action.
app/controllers/users_controller.rb

```
class UsersController < ApplicationController
```

```
    def new
    end
end
```

Listing 5.31   The initial **new** view for Users.

app/views/users/new.html.erb

```
<h1>Users#new</h1>
<p>Find me in app/views/users/new.html.erb</p>
```

Listing 5.32   A test for the new user page. **GREEN**

test/controllers/users_controller_test.rb

```
require 'test_helper'

class UsersControllerTest < ActionController::TestCase

  test "should get new" do
    get :new
    assert_response :success
  end
end
```

5.4.2 Sign-up URL

With the code from Section 5.4.1, we already have a working page for new users at /users/new, but recall from Table 5.1 that we want the URL to be /signup instead. We'll follow the examples from Listing 5.22 and add a **get '/signup'** rule for the sign-up URL, as shown in Listing 5.33.

Listing 5.33   A route for the sign-up page.

config/routes.rb

```
Rails.application.routes.draw do
  root             'static_pages#home'
  get 'help'    => 'static_pages#help'
  get 'about'   => 'static_pages#about'
  get 'contact' => 'static_pages#contact'
```

```
  get 'signup'  => 'users#new'
end
```

Next, we'll use the newly defined named route to add the proper link to the button on the Home page. As with the other routes, `get 'signup'` automatically gives us the named route `signup_path`, which we put to use in Listing 5.34. Adding a test for the sign-up page is left as an exercise (Section 5.6.)

Listing 5.34 Linking the button to the sign-up page.
app/views/static_pages/home.html.erb

```
<div class="center jumbotron">
  <h1>Welcome to the Sample App</h1>

  <h2>
    This is the home page for the
    <a href="http://www.railstutorial.org/">Ruby on Rails Tutorial</a>
    sample application.
  </h2>

  <%= link_to "Sign up now!", signup_path, class: "btn btn-lg btn-primary" %>
</div>

<%= link_to image_tag("rails.png", alt: "Rails logo"),
           'http://rubyonrails.org/' %>
```

Finally, we'll add a custom stub view for the sign-up page (Listing 5.35).

Listing 5.35 The initial (stub) sign-up page.
app/views/users/new.html.erb

```
<% provide(:title, 'Sign up') %>
<h1>Sign up</h1>
<p>This will be a sign-up page for new users.</p>
```

With that, we're done with the links and named routes, at least until we add a route for logging in (Chapter 8). The resulting new user page (at the URL /signup) appears in Figure 5.9.

Figure 5.9 The new sign-up page at /signup.

5.5 Conclusion

In this chapter, we hammered our application layout into shape and polished up the routes. The rest of the book is dedicated to fleshing out the sample application: first, by adding users who can sign up, log in, and log out; next, by adding user microposts; and, finally, by adding the ability to follow other users.

At this point, if you are using Git, you should merge your changes back into the master branch:

```
$ bundle exec rake test
$ git add -A
$ git commit -m "Finish layout and routes"
$ git checkout master
$ git merge filling-in-layout
```

Figure 5.10 The sample application in production.

Then push up to Bitbucket:

```
$ git push
```

Finally, deploy to Heroku:

```
$ git push heroku
```

The result of the deployment should be a working sample application on the production server (Figure 5.10).

5.5.1 What We Learned in This Chapter

- Using HTML5, we can define a site layout with logo, header, footer, and main body content.
- Rails partials are used to place markup in a separate file for convenience.
- CSS allows us to style the site layout based on CSS classes and IDs.

- The Bootstrap framework makes it easy to make a nicely designed site quickly.

- Sass and the asset pipeline allow us to eliminate duplication in our CSS while packaging up the results efficiently for production.

- Rails allows us to define custom routing rules, thereby providing named routes.

- Integration tests effectively simulate a browser clicking from page to page.

5.6 Exercises

Note: To receive a copy of the *Solutions Manual for Exercises*, with solutions to every exercise in the *Ruby on Rails*™ *Tutorial*, visit www.railstutorial.org/<word>, where "<word>" is the last word of the Figure 3.9 caption.

For a suggestion on how to avoid conflicts between exercises and the main tutorial, see the note on exercise topic branches in Section 3.6.

1. As suggested in Section 5.2.2, go through the steps to convert the footer CSS from Listing 5.13 to Listing 5.15 to SCSS by hand.

2. In the integration test from Listing 5.25, add code to visit the sign-up page using the `get` method and verify that the resulting page title is correct.

3. It's convenient to use the `full_title` helper in the tests by including the Application helper in the test helper, as shown in Listing 5.36. We can then test for the correct title using code like Listing 5.37 (which extends the solution from the previous exercise). This is brittle, though, because now any typo in the base title (such as "Ruby on Rails Tutoial") won't be caught by the test suite. Fix this problem by writing a direct test of the `full_title` helper, which involves creating a file to test the application helper and then filling in the code indicated with `FILL_IN` in Listing 5.38. (Listing 5.38 uses the `assert_equal` method, which verifies that its two arguments are the same when compared with the `==` operator.)

Listing 5.36 Including the Application helper in tests.

`test/test_helper.rb`

```
ENV['RAILS_ENV'] ||= 'test'
  .
  .
  .
class ActiveSupport::TestCase
  fixtures :all
```

```
    include ApplicationHelper
    .
    .
    .
end
```

Listing 5.37 Using the `full_title` helper in a test. **GREEN**

test/integration/site_layout_test.rb

```
require 'test_helper'

class SiteLayoutTest < ActionDispatch::IntegrationTest

  test "layout links" do
    get root_path
    assert_template 'static_pages/home'
    assert_select "a[href=?]", root_path, count: 2
    assert_select "a[href=?]", help_path
    assert_select "a[href=?]", about_path
    assert_select "a[href=?]", contact_path
    get signup_path
    assert_select "title", full_title("Sign up")
  end
end
```

Listing 5.38 A direct test the `full_title` helper.

test/helpers/application_helper_test.rb

```
require 'test_helper'

class ApplicationHelperTest < ActionView::TestCase
  test "full title helper" do
    assert_equal full_title,         FILL_IN
    assert_equal full_title("Help"), FILL_IN
  end
end
```

CHAPTER 6

Modeling Users

In Chapter 5, we ended with a stub page for creating new users (Section 5.4). Over the course of the next five chapters, we'll fulfill the promise implicit in this incipient sign-up page. In this chapter, we'll take the first critical step by creating a *data model* for users of our site, together with a way to store that data. In Chapter 7, we'll give users the ability to sign up for our site and create a user profile page. Once users can sign up, we'll let them log in and log out as well (Chapter 8), and in Chapter 9 (Section 9.2.1) we'll learn how to protect pages from improper access. Finally, in Chapter 10 we'll add account activation (thereby confirming a valid email address) and password resets. Taken together, the material in Chapter 6 through Chapter 10 develops a full Rails login and authentication system. As you may know, there are various prebuilt authentication solutions for Rails; Box 6.1 explains why, at least at first, it's probably a better idea to roll your own.

Box 6.1 Roll Your Own Authentication System

Virtually all web applications require a login and authentication system of some sort. As a result, most web frameworks have a plethora of options for implementing such systems, and Rails is no exception. Examples of authentication and authorization systems include Clearance, Authlogic, Devise, and CanCan (as well as non-Rails-specific solutions built on top of OpenID or OAuth). It's reasonable to ask why we should reinvent the wheel. Why not just use an off-the-shelf solution instead of rolling our own?

For one, practical experience shows that authentication on most sites requires extensive customization, and modifying a third-party product is often more work than writing the system from scratch. In addition, off-the-shelf systems can be "black boxes," with potentially mysterious innards; when you write your own system, you are far more likely to understand it. Moreover, recent additions to Rails (Section 6.3) make it easy to write a custom authentication system. Finally, if you *do* end up using a third-party system later on, you'll be in a much better position to understand and modify it if you've first built one yourself.

6.1 User Model

Although the ultimate goal of the next three chapters is to make a sign-up page for our site (as mocked up in Figure 6.1), it would do little good now to accept information for new users: We don't currently have any place to put it. Thus, the first step in signing up users is to make a data structure to capture and store their information.

In Rails, the default data structure for a data model is called, naturally enough, a *model* (the "M" in MVC from Section 1.3.3). The default Rails solution to the problem of persistence is to use a *database* for long-term data storage, and the default library for interacting with the database is called *Active Record*.[1] Active Record comes with a host of methods for creating, saving, and finding data objects, all without having to use the Structured Query Language (SQL)[2] used by relational databases. Moreover, Rails has a feature called *migrations* to allow data definitions to be written in pure Ruby, without having to learn an SQL data definition language (DDL). The effect is that Rails insulates you almost entirely from the details of the data store. In this book, by using SQLite for development and PostgreSQL (via Heroku) for deployment (Section 1.5), we have developed this theme even further, to the point where we barely ever have to think about how Rails stores data, even for production applications.

---

1. The name comes from the "active record pattern," identified and named in *Patterns of Enterprise Application Architecture* by Martin Fowler.

2. Pronounced "ess-cue-ell," though the alternate pronunciation "sequel" is also common.

Figure 6.1 A mockup of the user sign-up page.

As usual, if you're following along using Git for version control, now would be a good time to make a topic branch for modeling users:

```
$ git checkout master
$ git checkout -b modeling-users
```

6.1.1 Database Migrations

You may recall from Section 4.4.5 that we have already encountered, via a custom-built **User** class, user objects with **name** and **email** attributes. That class served as a useful example, but it lacked the critical property of *persistence*: When we created a User object at the Rails console, it disappeared as soon as we exited. Our goal in this section is to create a model for users that won't disappear quite so easily.

As with the User class in Section 4.4.5, we'll start by modeling a user with two attributes, a `name` and an `email` address, the latter of which we'll use as a unique username.[3] (We'll add an attribute for passwords in Section 6.3.) In Listing 4.13, we did this with Ruby's `attr_accessor` method:

```
class User
  attr_accessor :name, :email
  .
  .
  .
end
```

In contrast, when using Rails to model users, we don't need to identify the attributes explicitly. To store data, Rails uses a relational database by default, which consists of *tables* composed of data *rows*, where each row has *columns* of data attributes. For example, to store users with names and email addresses, we'll create a `users` table with `name` and `email` columns (with each row corresponding to one user). An example of such a table appears in Figure 6.2, corresponding to the data model shown in Figure 6.3. (Figure 6.3 is just a sketch; the full data model appears in Figure 6.4.) By naming the columns `name` and `email`, we'll let Active Record figure out the User object attributes for us.

You may recall from Listing 5.28 that we created a Users controller (along with a `new` action) by using the command

```
$ rails generate controller Users new
```

users		
id	name	email
1	Michael Hartl	mhartl@example.com
2	Sterling Archer	archer@example.gov
3	Lana Kane	lana@example.gov
4	Mallory Archer	boss@example.gov

Figure 6.2 A diagram of sample data in a `users` table.

---

3. By using an email address as the username, we open the possibility of communicating with our users at a future date (Chapter 10).

users	
id	integer
name	string
email	string

Figure 6.3 A sketch of the User data model.

The analogous command for making a model is `generate model`, which we can use to generate a User model with `name` and `email` attributes, as shown in Listing 6.1.

Listing 6.1 Generating a User model.

```
$ rails generate model User name:string email:string
      invoke  active_record
      create    db/migrate/20140724010738_create_users.rb
      create    app/models/user.rb
      invoke    test_unit
      create      test/models/user_test.rb
      create      test/fixtures/users.yml
```

(Note that, in contrast to the plural convention for controller names, model names are singular: a *Users* controller, but a *User* model.) By passing the optional parameters `name:string` and `email:string`, we tell Rails about the two attributes we want, along with which types those attributes should be (in this case, `string`). Compare this with including the action names in Listing 3.4 and Listing 5.28.

One of the results of the `generate` command in Listing 6.1 is a new file called a *migration*. Migrations provide a way to alter the structure of the database incrementally, so that our data model can adapt to changing requirements. In the case of the User model, the migration is created automatically by the model generation script; it creates a `users` table with two columns, `name` and `email`, as shown in Listing 6.2. (We'll see starting in Section 6.2.5 how to make a migration from scratch.)

Listing 6.2 Migration for the User model (to create a `users` table).
db/migrate/[timestamp]_create_users.rb

```
class CreateUsers < ActiveRecord::Migration
  def change
```

```
    create_table :users do |t|
      t.string :name
      t.string :email

      t.timestamps null: false
    end
  end
end
```

The name of the migration file is prefixed by a *timestamp* based on when the migration was generated. In the early days of migrations, the filenames were prefixed with incrementing integers, which caused conflicts for collaborating teams if multiple programmers had migrations with the same number. Barring the improbable scenario of migrations generated the same second, using timestamps conveniently avoids such collisions.

The migration itself consists of a **change** method that determines the change to be made to the database. In the case of Listing 6.2, **change** uses a Rails method called **create_table** to create a table in the database for storing users. The **create_table** method accepts a block (Section 4.3.2) with one block variable, in this case called **t** (for "table"). Inside the block, the **create_table** method uses the **t** object to create **name** and **email** columns in the database, both of type **string**.[4] Here the table name is plural (**users**) even though the model name is singular (User), which reflects a linguistic convention followed by Rails: A model represents a single user, whereas a database table consists of many users. The final line in the block, **t.timestamps null: false**, is a special command that creates two *magic columns* called **created_at** and **updated_at**, which are timestamps that automatically record when a given user is created and updated. (We'll see concrete examples of the magic columns starting in Section 6.1.3.) The full data model represented by the migration in Listing 6.2 is shown in Figure 6.4. (Note the addition of the magic columns, which weren't present in the sketch shown in Figure 6.3.)

We can run the migration, known as "migrating up," using the **rake** command (Box 2.1) as follows:

```
$ bundle exec rake db:migrate
```

---

4. Don't worry about exactly how the **t** object manages to do this; the beauty of *abstraction layers* is that we don't have to know. We can just trust the **t** object to do its job.

users	
`id`	integer
`name`	string
`email`	string
`created_at`	datetime
`updated_at`	datetime

Figure 6.4 The User data model produced by Listing 6.2.

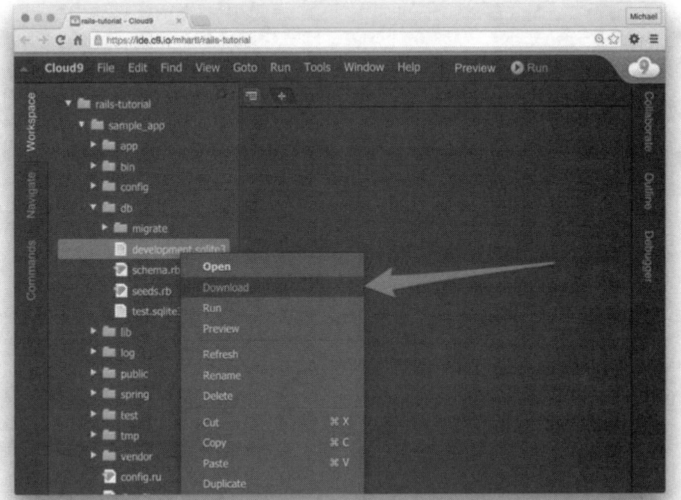

Figure 6.5 Downloading a file from the cloud IDE.

(You may recall that we ran this command in a similar context in Section 2.2.) The first time `db:migrate` is run, it creates a file called `db/development.sqlite3`, which is an SQLite[5] database. We can see the structure of the database by opening `development.sqlite3` with DB Browser for SQLite. (If you're using the cloud IDE, you should first download the database file to the local disk, as shown in Figure 6.5.) The result appears in Figure 6.6; compare with the diagram in Figure 6.4. You might note that there's one column in Figure 6.6 not accounted for in the migration: the `id`

---

5. Officially pronounced "ess-cue-ell-ite," although the (mis)pronunciation "sequel-ite" is also common.

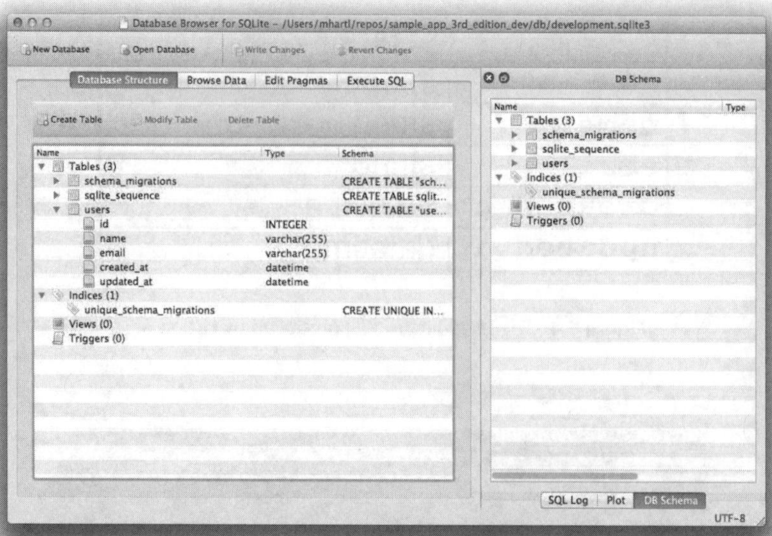

Figure 6.6 The DB Browser for SQLite with our new **users** table.

column. As noted briefly in Section 2.2, this column is created automatically, and is used by Rails to identify each row uniquely.

Most migrations (including all the ones in this tutorial) are *reversible*, which means we can "migrate down" and undo them with a single Rake task, called **db:rollback**:

```
$ bundle exec rake db:rollback
```

(See Box 3.1 for another technique useful for reversing migrations.) Under the hood, this command executes the **drop_table** command to remove the users table from the database. The reason this works is that the **change** method knows **drop_table** is the inverse of **create_table**, which means that the rollback migration can be easily inferred. In the case of an irreversible migration, such as one to remove a database column, it is necessary to define separate **up** and **down** methods in place of the single **change** method. Read about migrations in the Rails Guides for more information.

If you rolled back the database, migrate up again before proceeding:

```
$ bundle exec rake db:migrate
```

6.1.2 The Model File

We've seen how the User model generation in Listing 6.1 generated a migration file (Listing 6.2), and we saw in Figure 6.6 the results of running this migration: It updated a file called **development.sqlite3** by creating a table **users** with columns **id**, **name**, **email**, **created_at**, and **updated_at**. Listing 6.1 also created the model itself. The rest of this section is dedicated to understanding it.

We begin by looking at the code for the User model, which lives in the file **user.rb** inside the **app/models/** directory. It is, to put it mildly, very compact (Listing 6.3).

Listing 6.3 The brand-new User model.

app/models/user.rb

```
class User < ActiveRecord::Base
end
```

Recall from Section 4.4.2 that the syntax **class User < ActiveRecord::Base** means that the **User** class *inherits* from **ActiveRecord::Base**, so that the User model automatically has all the functionality of the **ActiveRecord::Base** class. Of course, this knowledge doesn't do us any good unless we know what **ActiveRecord::Base** contains, so let's get started with some concrete examples.

6.1.3 Creating User Objects

As in Chapter 4, our tool of choice for exploring data models is the Rails console. Since we don't (yet) want to make any changes to our database, we'll start the console in a *sandbox*:

```
$ rails console --sandbox
Loading development environment in sandbox
Any modifications you make will be rolled back on exit
>>
```

As indicated by the helpful message "Any modifications you make will be rolled back on exit," when started in a sandbox the console will "roll back" (i.e., undo) any database changes introduced during the session.

In the console session in Section 4.4.5, we created a new user object with **User.new**, which we could access only after requiring the example user file in Listing 4.13. With models, the situation is different; as you may recall from Section 4.4.4, the Rails console

automatically loads the Rails environment, which includes the models. This means that
we can make a new user object without any further work:

```
>> User.new
=> #<User id: nil, name: nil, email: nil, created_at: nil, updated_at: nil>
```

We see here the default console representation of a user object.

When called with no arguments, `User.new` returns an object with all `nil` attributes.
In Section 4.4.5, we designed the example User class to take an *initialization hash* to set
the object attributes; that design choice was motivated by Active Record, which allows
objects to be initialized in the same way:

```
>> user = User.new(name: "Michael Hartl", email: "mhartl@example.com")
=> #<User id: nil, name: "Michael Hartl", email: "mhartl@example.com",
created_at: nil, updated_at: nil>
```

Here we see that the name and email attributes have been set as expected.

The notion of *validity* is important for understanding Active Record model objects.
We'll explore this subject in more depth in Section 6.2, but for now it's worth noting
that our initial `user` object is valid, which we can verify by calling the boolean `valid?`
method on it:

```
>> user.valid?
true
```

So far, we haven't touched the database: `User.new` only creates an object *in memory*,
while `user.valid?` merely checks to see whether the object is valid. To save the User
object to the database, we need to call the `save` method on the `user` variable:

```
>> user.save
   (0.2ms)  begin transaction
 User Exists (0.2ms)  SELECT  1 AS one FROM "users"  WHERE LOWER("users".
 "email") = LOWER('mhartl@example.com') LIMIT 1
 SQL (0.5ms)  INSERT INTO "users" ("created_at", "email", "name", "updated_at)
   VALUES (?, ?, ?, ?)  [["created_at", "2014-09-11 14:32:14.199519"],
   ["email", "mhartl@example.com"], ["name", "Michael Hartl"], ["updated_at",
   "2014-09-11 14:32:14.199519"]]
   (0.9ms)  commit transaction
=> true
```

The **save** method returns **true** if it succeeds and **false** otherwise. (Currently, all saves should succeed because there are as yet no validations; we'll see cases in Section 6.2 when some will fail.) For reference, the Rails console also shows the SQL command corresponding to **user.save** (namely, **INSERT INTO "users"**...). We'll hardly ever need raw SQL in this book,[6] and I'll omit discussion of the SQL commands from now on, but you can learn a lot by reading the SQL corresponding to Active Record commands.

You may have noticed that the new user object had **nil** values for the **id** and the magic columns **created_at** and **updated_at** attributes. Let's see if our **save** changed anything:

```
>> user
=> #<User id: 1, name: "Michael Hartl", email: "mhartl@example.com",
created_at: "2014-07-24 00:57:46", updated_at: "2014-07-24 00:57:46">
```

We see that the **id** has been assigned a value of **1**, while the magic columns have been assigned the current time and date.[7] Currently, the created and updated timestamps are identical; we'll see them differ in Section 6.1.5.

As with the User class in Section 4.4.5, instances of the User model allow access to their attributes using a dot notation:

```
>> user.name
=> "Michael Hartl"
>> user.email
=> "mhartl@example.com"
>> user.updated_at
=> Thu, 24 Jul 2014 00:57:46 UTC +00:00
```

As we'll see in Chapter 7, it's often convenient to make and save a model in two steps as we have here, but Active Record also lets you combine them into one step with **User.create:**

---

6. The only exception is in Section 12.3.3.

7. In case you're curious about **"2014-07-24 00:57:46"**, I'm not writing this after midnight; the timestamps are recorded in Coordinated Universal Time (UTC), which for most practical purposes is the same as Greenwich Mean Time. From the NIST Time and Frequency FAQ: **Q:** Why is UTC used as the acronym for Coordinated Universal Time instead of CUT? **A:** In 1970 the Coordinated Universal Time system was devised by an international advisory group of technical experts within the International Telecommunication Union (ITU). The ITU felt it was best to designate a single abbreviation for use in all languages in order to minimize confusion. Since unanimous agreement could not be achieved on using either the English word order, CUT, or the French word order, TUC, the acronym UTC was chosen as a compromise.

```
>> User.create(name: "A Nother", email: "another@example.org")
#<User id: 2, name: "A Nother", email: "another@example.org", created_at:
"2014-07-24 01:05:24", updated_at: "2014-07-24 01:05:24">
>> foo = User.create(name: "Foo", email: "foo@bar.com")
#<User id: 3, name: "Foo", email: "foo@bar.com", created_at: "2014-07-24
01:05:42", updated_at: "2014-07-24 01:05:42">
```

Note that `User.create`, rather than returning `true` or `false`, returns the User object itself, which we can optionally assign to a variable (such as `foo` in the second command above).

The inverse of `create` is `destroy`:

```
>> foo.destroy
=> #<User id: 3, name: "Foo", email: "foo@bar.com", created_at: "2014-07-24
01:05:42", updated_at: "2014-07-24 01:05:42">
```

Like `create`, `destroy` returns the object in question, though I can't recall ever having used the return value of `destroy`. In addition, the destroyed object still exists in memory:

```
>> foo
=> #<User id: 3, name: "Foo", email: "foo@bar.com", created_at: "2014-07-24
01:05:42", updated_at: "2014-07-24 01:05:42">
```

So how do we know if we really destroyed an object? And for saved and non-destroyed objects, how can we retrieve users from the database? To answer these questions, we need to learn how to use Active Record to find user objects.

6.1.4 Finding User Objects

Active Record provides several options for finding objects. Let's use them to find the first user we created while verifying that the third user (`foo`) has been destroyed. We'll start with the existing user:

```
>> User.find(1)
=> #<User id: 1, name: "Michael Hartl", email: "mhartl@example.com",
created_at: "2014-07-24 00:57:46", updated_at: "2014-07-24 00:57:46">
```

Here we've passed the ID of the user to `User.find`; Active Record returns the user with that ID.

Let's see if the user with an `id` of `3` still exists in the database:

```
>> User.find(3)
ActiveRecord::RecordNotFound: Couldn't find User with ID=3
```

Since we destroyed our third user in Section 6.1.3, Active Record can't find it in the database. Instead, `find` raises an *exception*, which is a way of indicating an exceptional event in the execution of a program—in this case, a nonexistent Active Record ID, which causes `find` to raise an `ActiveRecord::RecordNotFound` exception.[8]

In addition to the generic `find`, Active Record allows us to find users by specific attributes:

```
>> User.find_by(email: "mhartl@example.com")
=> #<User id: 1, name: "Michael Hartl", email: "mhartl@example.com",
created_at: "2014-07-24 00:57:46", updated_at: "2014-07-24 00:57:46">
```

Since we will be using email addresses as usernames, this sort of `find` will be useful when we learn how to let users log in to our site (Chapter 7). If you're worried that `find_by` will be inefficient if there are a large number of users, you're ahead of the game; we'll cover this issue, and its solution via database indices, in Section 6.2.5.

We'll end with a couple of more general ways of finding users. First, there's `first`:

```
>> User.first
=> #<User id: 1, name: "Michael Hartl", email: "mhartl@example.com",
created_at: "2014-07-24 00:57:46", updated_at: "2014-07-24 00:57:46">
```

Naturally, `first` just returns the first user in the database. There's also `all`:

```
>> User.all
=> #<ActiveRecord::Relation [#<User id: 1, name: "Michael Hartl",
email: "mhartl@example.com", created_at: "2014-07-24 00:57:46",
```

---

8. Exceptions and exception handling are somewhat advanced Ruby subjects, and we won't need them much in this book. They are important, though, and I suggest learning about them using one of the Ruby books recommended in Section 12.4.1.

```
updated_at: "2014-07-24 00:57:46">, #<User id: 2, name: "A Nother",
email: "another@example.org", created_at: "2014-07-24 01:05:24",
updated_at: "2014-07-24 01:05:24">]>
```

As you can see from the console output, `User.all` returns all the users in the
database as an object of class `ActiveRecord::Relation`, which is effectively an array
(Section 4.3.1).

6.1.5 Updating User Objects

Once we've created objects, we often want to update them. There are two basic ways to
do this. First, we can assign attributes individually, as we did in Section 4.4.5:

```
>> user              # Just a reminder about our user's attributes
=> #<User id: 1, name: "Michael Hartl", email: "mhartl@example.com",
created_at: "2014-07-24 00:57:46", updated_at: "2014-07-24 00:57:46">
>> user.email = "mhartl@example.net"
=> "mhartl@example.net"
>> user.save
=> true
```

Note that the final step is necessary to write the changes to the database. We can see
what happens without a save by using `reload`, which reloads the object based on the
database information:

```
>> user.email
=> "mhartl@example.net"
>> user.email = "foo@bar.com"
=> "foo@bar.com"
>> user.reload.email
=> "mhartl@example.net"
```

Now that we've updated the user by running `user.save`, the magic columns differ,
as promised in Section 6.1.3:

```
>> user.created_at
=> "2014-07-24 00:57:46"
>> user.updated_at
=> "2014-07-24 01:37:32"
```

The second way to update multiple attributes is to use **update_attributes**:[9]

```
>> user.update_attributes(name: "The Dude", email: "dude@abides.org")
=> true
>> user.name
=> "The Dude"
>> user.email
=> "dude@abides.org"
```

The **update_attributes** method accepts a hash of attributes, and on success performs both the update and the save in one step (returning **true** to indicate that the save went through). Note that if any of the validations fail, such as when a password is required to save a record (as implemented in Section 6.3), the call to **update_attributes** will fail. If we need to update only a single attribute, using the singular **update_attribute** bypasses this restriction:

```
>> user.update_attribute(:name, "The Dude")
=> true
>> user.name
=> "The Dude"
```

6.2   User Validations

The User model we created in Section 6.1 now has working **name** and **email** attributes, but they are completely generic: Any string (including an empty one) is currently valid in either case. Of course, names and email addresses are actually more specific than this. For example, **name** should be non-blank, and **email** should match the specific format characteristic of email addresses. Moreover, since we'll be using email addresses as unique usernames when users log in, we shouldn't allow email duplicates in the database.

In short, we shouldn't allow **name** and **email** to be just any strings; we should enforce certain constraints on their values. Active Record allows us to impose such constraints using *validations* (seen before in Section 2.3.2). In this section, we'll cover several

---

9. The **update_attributes** method is an alias for the shorter **update** method, but I prefer the longer version because of its similarity to the singular version of the method, **update_attribute**.

of the most common cases, validating *presence*, *length*, *format*, and *uniqueness*. In Section 6.3.2, we'll add a final common validation, *confirmation*. In addition, we'll see in Section 7.3 how validations give us convenient error messages when users provide inputs that violate them.

6.2.1 A Validity Test

As noted in Box 3.3, test-driven development isn't always the right tool for the job, but model validations are exactly the kind of features for which TDD is a perfect fit. It's difficult to be confident that a given validation is doing exactly what we expect it to without writing a failing test and then getting it to pass.

Our method will be to start with a *valid* model object, set one of its attributes to something we want to be invalid, and then test that it is, in fact, invalid. As a safety net, we'll first write a test to make sure the initial model object is valid. This way, when the validation tests fail, we'll know it's for the right reason (and not because the initial object was invalid in the first place).

To get us started, the command in Listing 6.1 produced an initial test for testing users, though in this case it's practically blank (Listing 6.4).

Listing 6.4 The practically blank default User test.
`test/models/user_test.rb`

```
require 'test_helper'

class UserTest < ActiveSupport::TestCase
  # test "the truth" do
  #   assert true
  # end
end
```

To write a test for a valid object, we'll create an initially valid User model object `@user` using the special **setup** method (discussed briefly in the Chapter 3 exercises), which automatically gets run before each test. Because `@user` is an instance variable, it's automatically available in all the tests, and we can test its validity using the **valid?** method (Section 6.1.3). The result appears in Listing 6.5.

Listing 6.5 A test for an initially valid user. **GREEN**

test/models/user_test.rb

```
require 'test_helper'

class UserTest < ActiveSupport::TestCase

  def setup
    @user = User.new(name: "Example User", email: "user@example.com")
  end

  test "should be valid" do
    assert @user.valid?
  end
end
```

Listing 6.5 uses the plain **assert** method, which in this case succeeds if **@user.valid?** returns **true** and fails if it returns **false**.

Because our User model doesn't currently have any validations, the initial test should pass:

Listing 6.6   GREEN

```
$ bundle exec rake test:models
```

Here we've used **rake test:models** to run just the model tests (compare to **rake test:integration** from Section 5.3.4).

6.2.2 Validating Presence

Perhaps the most elementary validation is *presence*, which simply verifies that a given attribute is present. For example, in this section we'll ensure that both the name and the email fields are present before a user gets saved to the database. In Section 7.3.3, we'll see how to propagate this requirement to the sign-up form for creating new users.

We'll start with a test for the presence of a **name** attribute by building on the test in Listing 6.5. As seen in Listing 6.7, all we need to do is set the **@user** variable's **name** attribute to a blank string (in this case, a string of spaces) and then check (using the **assert_not** method) that the resulting User object is not valid.

Listing 6.7 A test for validation of the **name** attribute. **RED**

test/models/user_test.rb

```
require 'test_helper'

class UserTest < ActiveSupport::TestCase

  def setup
    @user = User.new(name: "Example User", email: "user@example.com")
  end

  test "should be valid" do
    assert @user.valid?
  end

  test "name should be present" do
    @user.name = "      "
    assert_not @user.valid?
  end
end
```

At this point, the model tests should be **RED**:

Listing 6.8 RED

```
$ bundle exec rake test:models
```

As we saw briefly in the Chapter 2 exercises, the way to validate the presence of the name attribute is to use the **validates** method with the argument **presence: true**, as shown in Listing 6.9. The **presence: true** argument is a one-element *options hash*; recall from Section 4.3.4 that curly braces are optional when passing hashes as the final argument in a method. (As noted in Section 5.1.1, the use of options hashes is a recurring theme in Rails.)

Listing 6.9 Validating the presence of a **name** attribute. **GREEN**

app/models/user.rb

```
class User < ActiveRecord::Base
  validates :name, presence: true
end
```

Listing 6.9 may look like magic, but `validates` is just a method. An equivalent formulation of Listing 6.9 using parentheses is as follows:

```
class User < ActiveRecord::Base
  validates(:name, presence: true)
end
```

Let's drop into the console to see the effects of adding a validation to our User model:[10]

```
$ rails console --sandbox
>> user = User.new(name: "", email: "mhartl@example.com")
>> user.valid?
=> false
```

Here we check the validity of the `user` variable using the `valid?` method, which returns `false` when the object fails one or more validations, and `true` when all validations pass. In this case, we have only one validation, so we know which one failed, but it can still be helpful to check using the `errors` object generated on failure:

```
>> user.errors.full_messages
=> ["Name can't be blank"]
```

(The error message is a hint that Rails validates the presence of an attribute using the `blank?` method, which we saw at the end of Section 4.4.3.)

Because the user isn't valid, an attempt to save the user to the database automatically fails:

```
>> user.save
=> false
```

As a result, the test in Listing 6.7 should now be **GREEN**:

Listing 6.10 GREEN

```
$ bundle exec rake test:models
```

---

10. I'll omit the output of console commands when they are not particularly instructive—for example, the results of `User.new`.

Following the model in Listing 6.7, writing a test for **email** attribute presence is easy (Listing 6.11), as is the application code to get it to pass (Listing 6.12).

Listing 6.11 A test for validation of the **email** attribute. **RED**
test/models/user_test.rb

```
require 'test_helper'

class UserTest < ActiveSupport::TestCase

  def setup
    @user = User.new(name: "Example User", email: "user@example.com")
  end

  test "should be valid" do
    assert @user.valid?
  end

  test "name should be present" do
    @user.name = ""
    assert_not @user.valid?
  end

  test "email should be present" do
    @user.email = "       "
    assert_not @user.valid?
  end
end
```

Listing 6.12 Validating the presence of an **email** attribute. **GREEN**
app/models/user.rb

```
class User < ActiveRecord::Base
  validates :name,  presence: true
  validates :email, presence: true
end
```

At this point, the presence validations are complete, and the test suite should be **GREEN**:

Listing 6.13   GREEN

```
$ bundle exec rake test
```

6.2.3 Length Validation

We've constrained our User model to require a name for each user, but we should go further: The user's names will be displayed on the sample site, so we should enforce some limit on their length. With all the work we did in Section 6.2.2, this step is easy.

There's no science to picking a maximum length; we'll just pull **50** out of thin air as a reasonable upper bound, which means verifying that names of **51** characters are too long. In addition, although it's unlikely ever to be a problem, a user's email address could potentially overrun the maximum length of strings, which for many databases is 255. Because the format validation in Section 6.2.4 won't enforce such a constraint, we'll add one in this section for completeness. Listing 6.14 shows the resulting tests.

Listing 6.14   A test for **name** length validation. **RED**

test/models/user_test.rb

```
require 'test_helper'

class UserTest < ActiveSupport::TestCase

  def setup
    @user = User.new(name: "Example User", email: "user@example.com")
  end
  .
  .
  .
  test "name should not be too long" do
    @user.name = "a" * 51
    assert_not @user.valid?
  end

  test "email should not be too long" do
    @user.email = "a" * 244 + "@example.com"
    assert_not @user.valid?
  end
end
```

For convenience, we've used "string multiplication" in Listing 6.14 to make a string 51 characters long. We can see how this works using the console:

```
>> "a" * 51
=> "aaaaaaaaaaaaaaaaaaaaaaaaaaaaaaaaaaaaaaaaaaaaaaaaaaa"
>> ("a" * 51).length
=> 51
```

The email length validation arranges to make a valid email address that's one character too long:

```
>> "a" * 244 + "@example.com"
=> "aaaaaaaaaaaaaaaaaaaaaaaaaaaaaaaaaaaaaaaaaaaaaaaaaaaaaaaaaaaaaaaaaaaaaaaa
aaaaaaaaaaaaaaaaaaaaaaaaaaaaaaaaaaaaaaaaaaaaaaaaaaaaaaaaaaaaaaaaaaaaaaaaaaaaaaa
aaaaaaaaaaaaaaaaaaaaaaaaaaaaaaaaaaaaaaaaaaaaaaaaaaaaaaaaaaaaaaaaaaaaaaaaaaaaaaa
aaaaaaaaaaa@example.com"
>> ("a" * 244 + "@example.com").length
=> 256
```

At this point, the tests in Listing 6.14 should be **RED**:

Listing 6.15 RED

```
$ bundle exec rake test
```

To get them to pass, we need to use the validation argument to constrain length, which is just `length`, along with the `maximum` parameter to enforce the upper bound (Listing 6.16).

Listing 6.16 Adding a length validation for the **name** attribute. **GREEN**
app/models/user.rb

```
class User < ActiveRecord::Base
  validates :name,  presence: true, length: { maximum: 50 }
  validates :email, presence: true, length: { maximum: 255 }
end
```

Now the tests should be **GREEN**:

Listing 6.17   GREEN

```
$ bundle exec rake test
```

With our test suite passing again, we can move on to a more challenging validation: email format.

6.2.4   Format Validation

Our validations for the `name` attribute enforce only minimal constraints—any nonblank name under 51 characters will do—but, of course, the `email` attribute must satisfy the more stringent requirement of being a valid email address. So far we've rejected only blank email addresses; in this section, we'll require email addresses to conform to the familiar pattern `user@example.com`.

Neither the tests nor the validation will be exhaustive, but rather just good enough to accept most valid email addresses and reject most invalid ones. We'll start with a couple of tests involving collections of valid and invalid addresses. To make these collections, it's worth knowing about the useful `%w[]` technique for making arrays of strings, as seen in this console session:

```
>> %w[foo bar baz]
=> ["foo", "bar", "baz"]
>> addresses = %w[USER@foo.COM THE_US-ER@foo.bar.org first.last@foo.jp]
=> ["USER@foo.COM", "THE_US-ER@foo.bar.org", "first.last@foo.jp"]
>> addresses.each do |address|
?>   puts address
>> end
USER@foo.COM
THE_US-ER@foo.bar.org
first.last@foo.jp
```

Here we've iterated over the elements of the `addresses` array using the `each` method (Section 4.3.2). With this technique in hand, we're ready to write some basic email format validation tests.

Because email format validation is tricky and error-prone, we'll start with some passing tests for *valid* email addresses to catch any errors in the validation. In other words, we want to make sure not just that invalid email addresses like *user@example,com* are rejected, but also that valid addresses like *user@example.com* are accepted, even after we impose the validation constraint. (Right now, they'll be accepted because all nonblank email addresses are currently valid.) The result for a representative sample of valid email addresses appears in Listing 6.18.

Listing 6.18 Tests for valid email formats. **GREEN**
test/models/user_test.rb

```
require 'test_helper'

class UserTest < ActiveSupport::TestCase

  def setup
    @user = User.new(name: "Example User", email: "user@example.com")
  end
  .
  .
  .
  test "email validation should accept valid addresses" do
    valid_addresses = %w[user@example.com USER@foo.COM A_US-ER@foo.bar.org
                         first.last@foo.jp alice+bob@baz.cn]
    valid_addresses.each do |valid_address|
      @user.email = valid_address
      assert @user.valid?, "#{valid_address.inspect} should be valid"
    end
  end
end
```

Note that we've included an optional second argument to the assertion with a custom error message, which in this case identifies the address causing the test to fail:

```
assert @user.valid?, "#{valid_address.inspect} should be valid"
```

(This line uses the interpolated **inspect** method mentioned in Section 4.3.3.) Including the specific address that causes any failure is especially useful in a test with an **each** loop like Listing 6.18; otherwise, any failure would merely identify the line number, which is the same for all the email addresses, and which wouldn't be sufficient to identify the source of the problem.

Next we'll add tests for the *invalidity* of a variety of invalid email addresses, such as *user@example,com* (comma in place of dot) and *user_at_foo.org* (missing the "@" sign).

As in Listing 6.18, Listing 6.19 includes a custom error message to identify the exact address causing any failure.

Listing 6.19 Tests for email format validation. **RED**

test/models/user_test.rb

```
require 'test_helper'

class UserTest < ActiveSupport::TestCase

  def setup
    @user = User.new(name: "Example User", email: "user@example.com")
  end
  .
  .
  .
  test "email validation should reject invalid addresses" do
    invalid_addresses = %w[user@example,com user_at_foo.org user.name@example.
                           foo@bar_baz.com foo@bar+baz.com]
    invalid_addresses.each do |invalid_address|
      @user.email = invalid_address
      assert_not @user.valid?, "#{invalid_address.inspect} should be invalid"
    end
  end
end
```

At this point, the tests should be **RED**:

Listing 6.20 RED

```
$ bundle exec rake test
```

The application code for email format validation uses the **format** validation, which works like this:

```
validates :email, format: { with: /<regular expression>/ }
```

This validates the attribute with the given *regular expression* (or *regex*), which is a powerful (and often cryptic) language for matching patterns in strings. This means we need to construct a regular expression to match valid email addresses while *not* matching invalid ones.

There actually exists a full regex for matching email addresses according to the official email standard, but it's enormous, obscure, and quite possibly counterproductive.[11] In this tutorial, we'll adopt a more pragmatic regex that has proven to be robust in practice. Here's what it looks like:

```
VALID_EMAIL_REGEX = /\A[\w+\-.]+@[a-z\d\-.]+\.[a-z]+\z/i
```

To help understand where this comes from, Table 6.1 breaks it into bite-sized pieces.[12]

Although you can learn a lot by studying Table 6.1, to really understand regular expressions I consider using an interactive regular expression matcher like Rubular to be essential (Figure 6.7).[13] The Rubular website has a beautiful interactive interface for making regular expressions, along with a handy regex quick reference. I encourage you to study Table 6.1 with a browser window open to Rubular—no amount of reading about regular expressions can replace playing with them interactively. (*Note*: If you use

Table 6.1 Breaking down the valid email regex.

Expression	Meaning
`/\A[\w+\-.]+@[a-z\d\-.]+\.[a-z]+\z/i`	full regex
`/`	start of regex
`\A`	match start of a string
`[\w+\-.]+`	at least one word character, plus, hyphen, or dot
`@`	literal "at sign"
`[a-z\d\-.]+`	at least one letter, digit, hyphen, or dot
`\.`	literal dot
`[a-z]+`	at least one letter
`\z`	match end of a string
`/`	end of regex
`i`	case-insensitive

---

11. For example, did you know that `"Michael Hartl"@example.com`, with quotation marks and a space in the middle, is a valid email address according to the standard? Incredibly, it is—but it's absurd.

12. Note that, in Table 6.1, "letter" really means "lowercase letter," but the **i** at the end of the regex enforces case-insensitive matching.

13. If you find it as useful as I do, I encourage you to donate to Rubular to reward developer Michael Lovitt for his wonderful work.

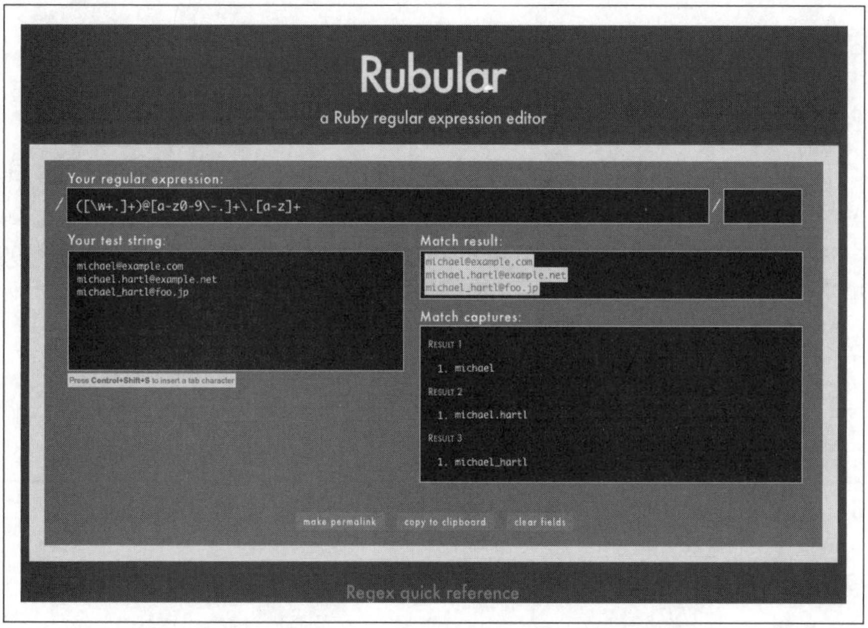

Figure 6.7 The awesome Rubular regular expression editor.

the regex from Table 6.1 in Rubular, you should leave off the \A and \z characters because Rubular doesn't have a well-defined notion of the beginning or end of an input string.)

Applying the regular expression from Table 6.1 to the **email** format validation yields the code in Listing 6.21.

Listing 6.21 Validating the email format with a regular expression. **GREEN**
app/models/user.rb

```
class User < ActiveRecord::Base
  validates :name,  presence: true, length: { maximum: 50 }
  VALID_EMAIL_REGEX = /\A[\w+\-.]+@[a-z\d\-.]+\.[a-z]+\z/i
  validates :email, presence: true, length: { maximum: 255 },
                    format: { with: VALID_EMAIL_REGEX }
end
```

Here the regex **VALID_EMAIL_REGEX** is a *constant*, indicated in Ruby by a name starting with a capital letter. The code

```
VALID_EMAIL_REGEX = /\A[\w+\-.]+@[a-z\d\-.]+\.[a-z]+\z/i
validates :email, presence: true, length: { maximum: 255 },
                  format: { with: VALID_EMAIL_REGEX }
```

ensures that only email addresses that match the pattern are considered valid. [The expression above has one notable weakness: it allows invalid addresses that contain consecutive dots, such as **foo@bar..com**. Fixing this blemish requires a significantly more complicated regular expression and is left as an exercise (Section 6.5).]

At this point, the tests should be **GREEN**:

Listing 6.22 GREEN

```
$ bundle exec rake test:models
```

This means that there's only one constraint left: enforcing email uniqueness.

6.2.5 Uniqueness Validation

To enforce uniqueness of email addresses (so that we can use them as usernames), we'll be using the **:unique** option to the **validates** method. But be warned: There's a *major* caveat, so don't just skim this section—read it carefully.

We'll start with some short tests. In our previous model tests, we've mainly used **User.new**, which just creates a Ruby object in memory. For uniqueness tests, however, we actually need to put a record into the database.[14] The initial duplicate email test appears in Listing 6.23.

Listing 6.23 A test for the rejection of duplicate email addresses. **RED**
test/models/user_test.rb

```
require 'test_helper'

class UserTest < ActiveSupport::TestCase

  def setup
    @user = User.new(name: "Example User", email: "user@example.com")
  end
```

---

14. As noted briefly in the introduction to this section, there is a dedicated test database, **db/test.sqlite3**, for this purpose.

```
        .
        .
        .
  test "email addresses should be unique" do
    duplicate_user = @user.dup
    @user.save
    assert_not duplicate_user.valid?
  end
end
```

The method here is to make a user with the same email address as **@user** using **@user.dup**, which creates a duplicate user with the same attributes. Since we then save **@user**, the duplicate user has an email address that already exists in the database, therefore, should not be valid.

We can get the new test in Listing 6.23 to pass by adding **uniqueness: true** to the **email** validation, as shown in Listing 6.24.

Listing 6.24   Validating the uniqueness of email addresses. **GREEN**
app/models/user.rb

```
class User < ActiveRecord::Base
  validates :name,  presence: true, length: { maximum: 50 }
  VALID_EMAIL_REGEX = /\A[\w+\-.]+@[a-z\d\-.]+\.[a-z]+\z/i
  validates :email, presence: true, length: { maximum: 255 },
                    format: { with: VALID_EMAIL_REGEX },
                    uniqueness: true
end
```

We're not quite done, though. Email addresses are typically processed as if they were case-insensitive—that is, **foo@bar.com** is treated the same as **FOO@BAR.COM** or **FoO@BAr.coM**—so our validation should incorporate this as well.[15] For this reason, it's important to test for case insensitivity, which we do with the code in Listing 6.25.

---

15. Technically, only the domain part of the email address is case-insensitive: *foo@bar.com* is actually different from *Foo@bar.com*. In practice, though, it is a bad idea to rely on this fact; as noted at about.com, "Since the case sensitivity of email addresses can create a lot of confusion, interoperability problems and widespread headaches, it would be foolish to require email addresses to be typed with the correct case. Hardly any email service or ISP does enforce case sensitive email addresses, returning messages whose recipient's email address was not typed correctly (in all uppercase, for example)." Thanks to reader Riley Moses for pointing this out.

Listing 6.25 Testing case-insensitive email uniqueness. **RED**

test/models/user_test.rb

```ruby
require 'test_helper'

class UserTest < ActiveSupport::TestCase

  def setup
    @user = User.new(name: "Example User", email: "user@example.com")
  end
  .
  .
  .
  test "email addresses should be unique" do
    duplicate_user = @user.dup
    duplicate_user.email = @user.email.upcase
    @user.save
    assert_not duplicate_user.valid?
  end
end
```

In Listing 6.25 we are using the **upcase** method on strings (seen briefly in Section 4.3.2). This test does the same thing as the initial duplicate email test, but with an uppercase email address instead. If this test feels a little abstract, go ahead and fire up the console:

```
$ rails console --sandbox
>> user = User.create(name: "Example User", email: "user@example.com")
>> user.email.upcase
=> "USER@EXAMPLE.COM"
>> duplicate_user = user.dup
>> duplicate_user.email = user.email.upcase
>> duplicate_user.valid?
=> true
```

Of course, **duplicate_user.valid?** is currently **true** because the uniqueness validation is case-sensitive, but we want it to be **false**. Fortunately, **:uniqueness** accepts an option, **:case_sensitive**, for just this purpose (Listing 6.26).

Listing 6.26 Validating the uniqueness of email addresses, ignoring case. **GREEN**

app/models/user.rb

```ruby
class User < ActiveRecord::Base
  validates :name,  presence: true, length: { maximum: 50 }
  VALID_EMAIL_REGEX = /\A[\w+\-.]+@[a-z\d\-.]+\.[a-z]+\z/i
```

```
validates :email, presence: true, length: { maximum: 255 },
                  format: { with: VALID_EMAIL_REGEX },
                  uniqueness: case_sensitive: false
end
```

Note that we have simply replaced **true** in Listing 6.24 with **case_sensitive: false** in Listing 6.26. (Rails infers that **uniqueness** should be **true** as well.)

At this point, our application—with an important caveat—enforces email uniqueness, and our test suite should pass:

Listing 6.27 GREEN

```
$ bundle exec rake test
```

There's just one small problem: The *the Active Record uniqueness validation does not guarantee uniqueness at the database level*. Here's a scenario that explains why:

1. Alice signs up for the sample app, with address alice@wonderland.com.
2. Alice accidentally clicks on "Submit" *twice*, sending two requests in quick succession.
3. The following sequence occurs: Request 1 creates a user in memory that passes validation, request 2 does the same, request 1's user gets saved, request 2's user gets saved.
4. Result: Two user records with the exact same email address exist, despite the uniqueness validation.

If this sequence seems implausible, believe me, it isn't: It can happen on any Rails website with significant traffic (which I once learned the hard way). Luckily, the solution is straightforward to implement: We just need to enforce uniqueness at the database level as well as at the model level. Our method is to create a database *index* on the email column (Box 6.2), and then require that the index be unique.

Box 6.2 Database Indices

When creating a column in a database, it is important to consider whether we will need to *find* records by that column. Consider, for example, the email attribute created by the migration in Listing 6.2. When we allow users to log in to the sample app starting in Chapter 7, we will need to find the user record corresponding to the submitted email address. Unfortunately, based on the naïve data model, the only way to find a user by email address is to look through *each* user row in the database and compare its email attribute to the given email—which means we might have to examine *every* row (because the user could be the last one in the database). This is known in the database business as a *full-table scan*, and for a real site with thousands of users it is a Bad Thing.

Putting an index on the email column fixes the problem. To understand a database index, it's helpful to consider the analogy of a book index. In a book, to find all the occurrences of a given string—say "foobar"—you would have to scan each page for "foobar"; this is the paper version of a full-table scan. With a book index, however, you can just look up "foobar" in the index to see all the pages containing "foobar". A database index works essentially the same way.

The email index represents an update to our data modeling requirements, which (as discussed in Section 6.1.1) is handled in Rails using migrations. We saw in Section 6.1.1 that generating the User model automatically created a new migration (Listing 6.2); in the present case, we are adding structure to an existing model, so we need to create a migration directly using the **migration** generator:

```
$ rails generate migration add_index_to_users_email
```

Unlike the migration for users, the email uniqueness migration is not predefined, so we need to fill in its contents with Listing 6.28.[16]

Listing 6.28 The migration for enforcing email uniqueness.
db/migrate/[timestamp]_add_index_to_users_email.rb

```
class AddIndexToUsersEmail < ActiveRecord::Migration
  def change
    add_index :users, :email, unique: true
  end
end
```

16. Of course, we could just edit the migration file for the **users** table in Listing 6.2, but that would require rolling back and then migrating back up. The Rails Way is to use migrations every time we discover that our data model needs to change.

This code uses a Rails method called **add_index** to add an index on the **email** column of the **users** table. The index by itself doesn't enforce uniqueness, but the option **unique: true** does.

The final step is to migrate the database:

```
$ bundle exec rake db:migrate
```

(If this fails, try exiting any running sandbox console sessions, which can lock the database and prevent migrations.)

At this point, the test suite should be **RED** due to a violation of the uniqueness constraint in the *fixtures*, which contain sample data for the test database. User fixtures were generated automatically in Listing 6.1, and as shown in Listing 6.29 the email addresses are not unique. (They're not *valid* either, but fixture data doesn't get run through the validations.)

Listing 6.29   The default user fixtures. **RED**

test/fixtures/users.yml

```
# Read about fixtures at http://api.rubyonrails.org/classes/ActiveRecord/
# FixtureSet.html

one:
  name: MyString
  email: MyString

two:
  name: MyString
  email: MyString
```

Because we won't need fixtures until Chapter 8, for now we'll just remove them, leaving an empty fixtures file (Listing 6.30).

Listing 6.30   An empty fixtures file. **GREEN**

test/fixtures/users.yml

```
# empty
```

Having addressed the uniqueness caveat, there's one more change we need to make to be assured of email uniqueness. Some database adapters use case-sensitive indices, considering the strings "Foo@ExAMPle.CoM" and "foo@example.com" to be distinct, but our application treats those addresses as the same. To avoid this incompatibility, we'll standardize on all-lowercase addresses, converting "Foo@ExAMPle.CoM" to "foo@example.com" before saving it to the database. The way to do this is with a *callback*, which is a method that gets invoked at a particular point in the life cycle of an Active Record object. In the present case, that point is before the object is saved, so we'll use a `before_save` callback to downcase the email attribute before saving the user.[17] The result appears in Listing 6.31. (This is just a first implementation; we'll discuss this subject again in Section 8.4, where we'll use the preferred *method reference* convention for defining callbacks.)

Listing 6.31 Ensuring email uniqueness by downcasing the email attribute. **GREEN**

app/models/user.rb

```
class User < ActiveRecord::Base
  before_save { self.email = email.downcase }
  validates :name,  presence: true, length: { maximum: 50 }
  VALID_EMAIL_REGEX = /\A[\w+\-.]+@[a-z\d\-.]+\.[a-z]+\z/i
  validates :email, presence: true, length: { maximum: 255 },
                    format: { with: VALID_EMAIL_REGEX },
                    uniqueness: { case_sensitive: false }
end
```

The code in Listing 6.31 passes a block to the `before_save` callback and sets the user's email address to a lowercase version of its current value using the `downcase` string method. Writing a test for email downcasing is left as an exercise (Section 6.5).

In Listing 6.31, we could have written the assignment as

```
self.email = self.email.downcase
```

(where `self` refers to the current user), but inside the User model the `self` keyword is optional on the right-hand side:

```
self.email = email.downcase
```

We encountered this idea briefly in the context of `reverse` in the `palindrome` method (Section 4.4.2), which also noted that `self` is *not* optional in an assignment, so

---

17. See the Rails API entry on callbacks for more information on which callbacks Rails supports.

```
email = email.downcase
```

wouldn't work. (We'll discuss this subject in more depth in Section 8.4.)

At this point, the Alice scenario presented earlier will work fine: The database will save a user record based on the first request, and it will reject the second save for violating the uniqueness constraint. (An error will appear in the Rails log, but that doesn't do any harm.) Moreover, adding this index on the email attribute accomplishes a second goal, alluded to briefly in Section 6.1.4: As noted in Box 6.2, the index on the `email` attribute fixes a potential efficiency problem by preventing a full-table scan when finding users by email address.

6.3 Adding a Secure Password

Now that we've defined validations for the name and email fields, we're ready to add the last of the basic User attributes: a secure password. The method is to require each user to have a password (with a password confirmation), and then store a *hashed* version of the password in the database. (There is some potential for confusion here. In the present context, a *hash* refers not to the Ruby data structure from Section 4.3.3 but rather to the result of applying an irreversible hash function to input data.) We'll also add a way to *authenticate* a user based on a given password, a method we'll use in Chapter 8 to allow users to log in to the site.

The method for authenticating users will be to take a submitted password, hash it, and compare the result to the hashed value stored in the database. If the two match, then the submitted password is correct and the user is authenticated. By comparing hashed values instead of raw passwords, we will be able to authenticate users without storing the passwords themselves. This means that, even if our database is compromised, our users' passwords will still be secure.

6.3.1 A Hashed Password

Most of the secure password machinery will be implemented using a single Rails method called `has_secure_password`, which we'll include in the User model as follows:

```
class User < ActiveRecord::Base
  .
  .
  .
```

```
    has_secure_password
end
```

When included in a model, this one method adds the following functionality:

- The ability to save a securely hashed **password_digest** attribute to the database
- A pair of virtual attributes[18] (**password** and **password_confirmation**), including presence validations upon object creation and a validation requiring that they match
- An **authenticate** method that returns the user when the password is correct (and **false** otherwise)

The only requirement for **has_secure_password** to work its magic is for the corresponding model to have an attribute called **password_digest**. (The name *digest* comes from the terminology of cryptographic hash functions. In this context, *hashed password* and *password digest* are synonyms.)[19] In the case of the User model, this leads to the data model shown in Figure 6.8.

To implement the data model in Figure 6.8, we first generate an appropriate migration for the **password_digest** column. We can choose any migration name we want, but it's convenient to end the name with **to_users**, since in this case Rails automatically constructs a migration to add columns to the **users** table. The result, with migration name **add_password_digest_to_users**, appears as follows:

```
$ rails generate migration add_password_digest_to_users password_digest:string
```

Here we've also supplied the argument **password_digest:string** with the name and type of attribute we want to create. (Compare this to the original generation of the **users** table in Listing 6.1, which included the arguments **name:string** and **email:string**.)

---

18. In this context, *virtual* means that the attributes exist on the model object but do not correspond to columns in the database.

19. Hashed password digests are often erroneously referred to as *encrypted passwords*. For example, the source code of **has_secure_password** makes this mistake, as did the first two editions of this tutorial. This terminology is wrong because by design encryption is *reversible*—the ability to encrypt implies the ability to *decrypt* as well. In contrast, the whole point of calculating a password's hash digest is to be *irreversible*, so that it is computationally intractable to infer the original password from the digest. (Thanks to reader Andy Philips for pointing out this issue and for encouraging me to fix the broken terminology.)

users	
id	integer
name	string
email	string
created_at	datetime
updated_at	datetime
password_digest	string

Figure 6.8 The User data model with an added **password_digest** attribute.

By including **password_digest:string**, we've given Rails enough information to construct the entire migration for us, as seen in Listing 6.32.

Listing 6.32 The migration to add a **password_digest** column to the **users** table.
db/migrate/[timestamp]_add_password_digest_to_users.rb

```
class AddPasswordDigestToUsers < ActiveRecord::Migration
  def change
    add_column :users, :password_digest, :string
  end
end
```

Listing 6.32 uses the **add_column** method to add a **password_digest** column to the **users** table. To apply it, we just migrate the database:

```
$ bundle exec rake db:migrate
```

To make the password digest, **has_secure_password** uses a state-of-the-art hash function called bcrypt. By hashing the password with bcrypt, we ensure that an attacker won't be able to log in to the site even if he or she manages to obtain a copy of the database. To use bcrypt in the sample application, we need to add the **bcrypt** gem to our **Gemfile** (Listing 6.33).

Listing 6.33 Adding **bcrypt** to the **Gemfile**.

```
source 'https://rubygems.org'

gem 'rails',              '4.2.0'
gem 'bcrypt',             '3.1.7'
  .
  .
  .
```

We then run **bundle install** as usual:

```
$ bundle install
```

6.3.2 User Has Secure Password

Now that we've supplied the User model with the required **password_digest** attribute and installed bcrypt, we're ready to add **has_secure_password** to the User model, as shown in Listing 6.34.

Listing 6.34 Adding **has_secure_password** to the User model. **RED**
app/models/user.rb

```
class User < ActiveRecord::Base
  before_save { self.email = email.downcase }
  validates :name, presence: true, length: { maximum: 50 }
  VALID_EMAIL_REGEX = /\A[\w+\-.]+@[a-z\d\-.]+\.[a-z]+\z/i
  validates :email, presence: true, length: { maximum: 255 },
                    format: { with: VALID_EMAIL_REGEX },
                    uniqueness: { case_sensitive: false }
  has_secure_password
end
```

As indicated by the **RED** indicator in Listing 6.34, the tests are now failing, as you can confirm at the command line:

Listing 6.35 RED

```
$ bundle exec rake test
```

The reason for the failure is that, as noted in Section 6.3.1, `has_secure_password` enforces validations on the virtual `password` and `password_confirmation` attributes, but the tests in Listing 6.25 create an `@user` variable without these attributes:

```
def setup
  @user = User.new(name: "Example User", email: "user@example.com")
end
```

To ensure that the test suite passes, we just need to add a password and its confirmation, as shown in Listing 6.36.

Listing 6.36 Adding a password and its confirmation. **GREEN**
test/models/user_test.rb

```
require 'test_helper'

class UserTest < ActiveSupport::TestCase

  def setup
    @user = User.new(name: "Example User", email: "user@example.com",
                     password: "foobar", password_confirmation: "foobar")
  end
  .
  .
  .
end
```

Now the tests should be **GREEN**:

Listing 6.37   GREEN

```
$ bundle exec rake test
```

We'll see in a moment the benefits of adding `has_secure_password` to the User model (Section 6.3.4), but first we'll add a minimal requirement on password security.

6.3.3 Minimum Password Length

It's good practice in general to enforce some minimum standards on passwords to make them harder to guess. There are many options for enforcing password strength in Rails, but for simplicity we'll just enforce a minimum length. Picking a length of 6 as a reasonable minimum leads to the validation test shown in Listing 6.38.

Listing 6.38 Testing for a minimum password length. **RED**
test/models/user_test.rb

```
require 'test_helper'

class UserTest < ActiveSupport::TestCase

  def setup
    @user = User.new(name: "Example User", email: "user@example.com",
                     password: "foobar", password_confirmation: "foobar")
  end
  .
  .
  .
  test "password should have a minimum length" do
    @user.password = @user.password_confirmation = "a" * 5
    assert_not @user.valid?
  end
end
```

Note the use of the compact multiple assignment

```
@user.password = @user.password_confirmation = "a" * 5
```

in Listing 6.38. This arranges to assign a particular value to the password and its confirmation at the same time (in this case, a string of length 5, constructed using string multiplication as in Listing 6.14).

You may be able to guess the code for enforcing a **minimum** length constraint by referring to the corresponding **maximum** validation for the user's name (Listing 6.16):

```
validates :password, length: { minimum: 6 }
```

This leads to the User model shown in Listing 6.39.

Listing 6.39 The complete implementation for secure passwords. **GREEN**
app/models/user.rb

```
class User < ActiveRecord::Base
  before_save { self.email = email.downcase }
  validates :name, presence: true, length: { maximum: 50 }
```

```
VALID_EMAIL_REGEX = /\A[\w+\-.]+@[a-z\d\-.]+\.[a-z]+\z/i
validates :email, presence: true, length: { maximum: 255 },
                  format: { with: VALID_EMAIL_REGEX },
                  uniqueness: { case_sensitive: false }
has_secure_password
validates :password, length: { minimum: 6 }
end
```

At this point, the tests should be **GREEN**:

Listing 6.40 GREEN

```
$ bundle exec rake test:models
```

6.3.4 Creating and Authenticating a User

Now that the basic User model is complete, we'll create a user in the database as preparation for making a page to show the user's information in Section 7.1. We'll also take a more concrete look at the effects of adding `has_secure_password` to the User model, including an examination of the important `authenticate` method.

Since users can't yet sign up for the sample application through the web—that's the goal of Chapter 7—we'll use the Rails console to create a new user by hand. For convenience, we'll use the `create` method discussed in Section 6.1.3, but in the present case we'll take care *not* to start in a sandbox so that the resulting user will be saved to the database. This means starting an ordinary `rails console` session and then creating a user with a valid name and email address together with a valid password and matching confirmation:

```
$ rails console
>> User.create(name: "Michael Hartl", email: "mhartl@example.com",
?>             password: "foobar", password_confirmation: "foobar")
=> #<User id: 1, name: "Michael Hartl", email: "mhartl@example.com",
created_at: "2014-09-11 14:26:42", updated_at: "2014-09-11 14:26:42",
password_digest: "$2a$10$sLcMI2f8VglgirzjSJOln.Fv9NdLMbqmR4rdTWIXY1G...">
```

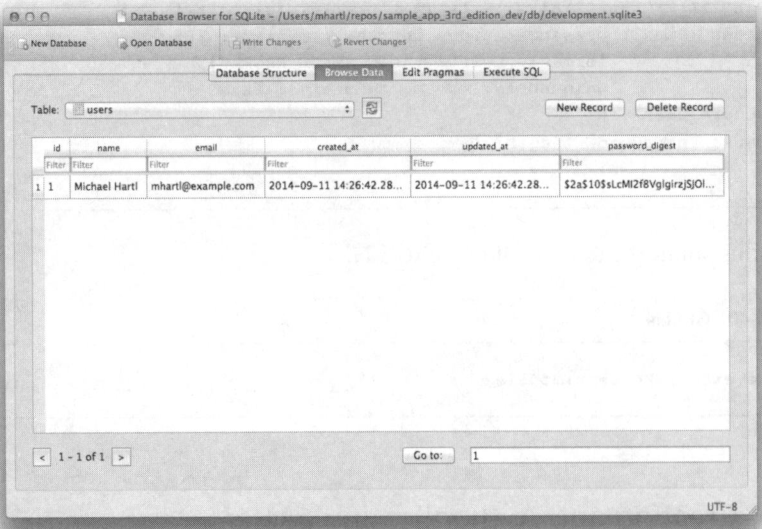

Figure 6.9 A user row in the SQLite database `db/development.sqlite3`.

To check that this process worked, let's look at the resulting **users** table in the development database using DB Browser for SQLite as shown in Figure 6.9.[20] (If you're using the cloud IDE, you should download the database file as in Figure 6.5.) Note that the columns correspond to the attributes of the data model defined in Figure 6.8.

Returning to the console, we can see the effect of **has_secure_password** from Listing 6.39 by looking at the **password_digest** attribute:

```
>> user = User.find_by(email: "mhartl@example.com")
>> user.password_digest
=> "$2a$10$YmQTuuDNOszvu5yi7auOC.F4G//FGhyQSWCpghqRWQWITUYlG3XVy"
```

---

20. If for any reason something went wrong, you can always reset the database as follows:

1. Quit the console.

2. Run `$ rm -f development.sqlite3` at the command line to remove the database. (We'll learn a more elegant method for doing this in Chapter 7.)

3. Rerun the migrations using `$ bundle exec rake db:migrate`.

4. Restart the console.

This is the hashed version of the password (`"foobar"`) used to initialize the user object. Because it's constructed using bcrypt, it is computationally impractical to use the digest to discover the original password.[21]

As noted in Section 6.3.1, `has_secure_password` automatically adds an `authenticate` method to the corresponding model objects. This method determines if a given password is valid for a particular user by computing its digest and comparing the result to `password_digest` in the database. In the case of the user we just created, we can try a couple of invalid passwords:

```
>> user.authenticate("not_the_right_password")
false
>> user.authenticate("foobaz")
false
```

Here `user.authenticate` returns `false`, indicating an invalid password. If we instead authenticate with the correct password, `authenticate` returns the corresponding user itself:

```
>> user.authenticate("foobar")
=> #<User id: 1, name: "Michael Hartl", email: "mhartl@example.com",
created_at: "2014-07-25 02:58:28", updated_at: "2014-07-25 02:58:28",
password_digest: "$2a$10$YmQTuuDNOszvu5yi7auOC.F4G//FGhyQSWCpghqRWQW...">
```

In Chapter 8, we'll use the `authenticate` method to sign registered users into our site. In fact, it will turn out not to be important that `authenticate` returns the user itself; all that will matter is that it returns a value that is `true` in a boolean context. Since a user object is neither `nil` nor `false`, it does the job nicely:[22]

```
>> !!user.authenticate("foobar")
=> true
```

6.4 Conclusion

Starting from scratch, in this chapter we created a working User model with name, email, and password attributes, together with validations enforcing several important constraints on their values. In addition, we have the ability to securely authenticate users

---

21. By design, the bcrypt algorithm produces a salted hash, which protects against two important classes of attacks: dictionary attacks and rainbow table attacks.

22. Recall from Section 4.2.3 that `!!` converts an object to its corresponding boolean value.

using a given password. This is a remarkable amount of functionality for only 12 lines of code.

In Chapter 7, we'll make a working sign-up form to create new users, together with a page to display each user's information. In Chapter 8, we'll use the authentication machinery from Section 6.3 to let users log in to the site.

If you're using Git, now would be a good time to commit if you haven't done so in a while:

```
$ bundle exec rake test
$ git add -A
$ git commit -m "Make a basic User model (including secure passwords)"
```

Then merge back into the master branch and push to the remote repository:

```
$ git checkout master
$ git merge modeling-users
$ git push
```

To get the User model working in production, we need to run the migrations at Heroku, which we can do with `heroku run`:

```
$ bundle exec rake test
$ git push heroku
$ heroku run rake db:migrate
```

We can verify that this process worked by running a console in production:

```
$ heroku run console --sandbox
>> User.create(name: "Michael Hartl", email: "michael@example.com",
?>            password: "foobar", password_confirmation: "foobar")
=> #<User id: 1, name: "Michael Hartl", email: "michael@example.com",
created_at: "2014-08-29 03:27:50", updated_at: "2014-08-29 03:27:50",
password_digest: "$2a$10$IViF0Q5j3hsEVgHgrrKH3uDou86Ka21EPz8zkwQopwj...">
```

6.4.1 What We Learned in This Chapter

- Migrations allow us to modify our application's data model.

- Active Record comes with a large number of methods for creating and manipulating data models.

- Active Record validations allow us to place constraints on the data in our models.

- Common validations include presence, length, and format.

- Regular expressions are cryptic but powerful.

- Defining a database index improves lookup efficiency while allowing enforcement of uniqueness at the database level.

- We can add a secure password to a model using the built-in `has_secure_password` method.

6.5 Exercises

Note: To receive a copy of the *Solutions Manual for Exercises*, with solutions to every exercise in the *Ruby on Rails™ Tutorial*, visit www.railstutorial.org/<word>, where "<word>" is the last word of the Figure 3.9 caption.

For a suggestion on how to avoid conflicts between exercises and the main tutorial, see the note on exercise topic branches in Section 3.6.

1. Add a test for the email downcasing from Listing 6.31, as shown in Listing 6.41. This test uses the `reload` method for reloading a value from the database and the `assert_equal` method for testing equality. To verify that Listing 6.41 tests the right thing, comment out the `before_save` line to get to **RED**, then uncomment it to get to **GREEN**.

2. By running the test suite, verify that the `before_save` callback can be written using the "bang" method `email.downcase!` to modify the `email` attribute directly, as shown in Listing 6.42.

3. As noted in Section 6.2.4, the email regex in Listing 6.21 allows invalid email addresses with consecutive dots in the domain name—addresses of the form *foo@bar..com*. Add this address to the list of invalid addresses in Listing 6.19 to get a failing test, and then use the more complicated regex shown in Listing 6.43 to get the test to pass.

Listing 6.41 A test for the email downcasing from Listing 6.31.
test/models/user_test.rb

```
require 'test_helper'

class UserTest < ActiveSupport::TestCase
```

```
  def setup
    @user = User.new(name: "Example User", email: "user@example.com",
                     password: "foobar", password_confirmation: "foobar")
  end
  .
  .
  .
  test "email addresses should be unique" do
    duplicate_user = @user.dup
    duplicate_user.email = @user.email.upcase
    @user.save
    assert_not duplicate_user.valid?
  end

  test "email addresses should be saved as lowercase" do
    mixed_case_email = "Foo@ExAMPle.CoM"
    @user.email = mixed_case_email
    @user.save
    assert_equal mixed_case_email.downcase, @user.reload.email
  end

  test "password should have a minimum length" do
    @user.password = @user.password_confirmation = "a" * 5
    assert_not @user.valid?
  end
end
```

Listing 6.42 An alternate implementation of the `before_save` callback. **GREEN**

app/models/user.rb

```
class User < ActiveRecord::Base
  before_save { email.downcase! }
  validates :name, presence: true, length: { maximum: 50 }
  VALID_EMAIL_REGEX = /\A[\w+\-.]+@[a-z\d\-.]+\.[a-z]+\z/i
  validates :email, presence: true, length: { maximum: 255 },
                    format: { with: VALID_EMAIL_REGEX },
                    uniqueness: { case_sensitive: false }
  has_secure_password
  validates :password, length: { minimum: 6 }
end
```

Listing 6.43   Disallowing double dots in email domain names. **GREEN**
app/models/user.rb

```ruby
class User < ActiveRecord::Base
  before_save { email.downcase! }
  validates :name, presence: true, length: { maximum: 50 }
  VALID_EMAIL_REGEX = /\A[\w+\-.]+@[a-z\d\-]+(\.[a-z\d\-]+)*\.[a-z]+\z/i
  validates :email, presence:   true,
                    format:     { with: VALID_EMAIL_REGEX },
                    uniqueness: { case_sensitive: false }
  has_secure_password
  validates :password, length: { minimum: 6 }
end
```

## CHAPTER 7

Sign Up

Now that we have a working User model, it's time to add an ability few websites can live without: letting users sign up. We'll use an HTML *form* to submit user sign-up information to our application (Section 7.2), which will then be used to create a new user and save its attributes to the database (Section 7.4). At the end of the sign-up process, it's important to render a profile page with the newly created user's information, so we'll begin by making a page for *showing* users, which will serve as the first step toward implementing the REST architecture for users (Section 2.2.2). Along the way, we'll build on our work in Section 5.3.4 to write succinct and expressive integration tests.

In this chapter, we'll rely on the User model validations from Chapter 6 to increase the odds of new users having valid email addresses. In Chapter 10, we'll make *sure* of email validity by adding a separate *account activation* step to user sign-up.

7.1 Showing Users

In this section, we'll take the first steps toward the final profile by making a page to display a user's name and profile photo, as indicated by the mockup in Figure 7.1.[1] Our eventual goal for the user profile pages is to show the user's profile image, basic user data, and a list of microposts, as mocked up in Figure 7.2.[2] (Figure 7.2 has our first

---

1. Mockingbird doesn't support custom images like the profile photo in Figure 7.1; I put that in by hand using GIMP.

2. The hippopotamus here is from http://www.flickr.com/photos/43803060@N00/24308857/.

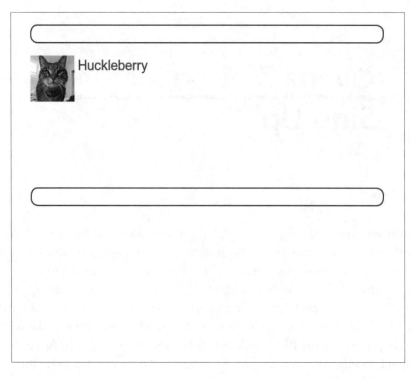

Huckleberry

Figure 7.1 A mockup of the user profile made in this section.

example of *lorem ipsum* text, which has a fascinating story that you should definitely read about some time.) We'll complete this task, and with it the sample application, in Chapter 12.

If you're following along with version control, make a topic branch as usual:

```
$ git checkout master
$ git checkout -b sign-up
```

7.1.1 Debug and Rails Environments

The profiles in this section will be the first truly dynamic pages in our application. Although the view will exist as a single page of code, each profile will be customized using information retrieved from the application's database. As preparation for adding dynamic pages to our sample application, now is a good time to add some debug

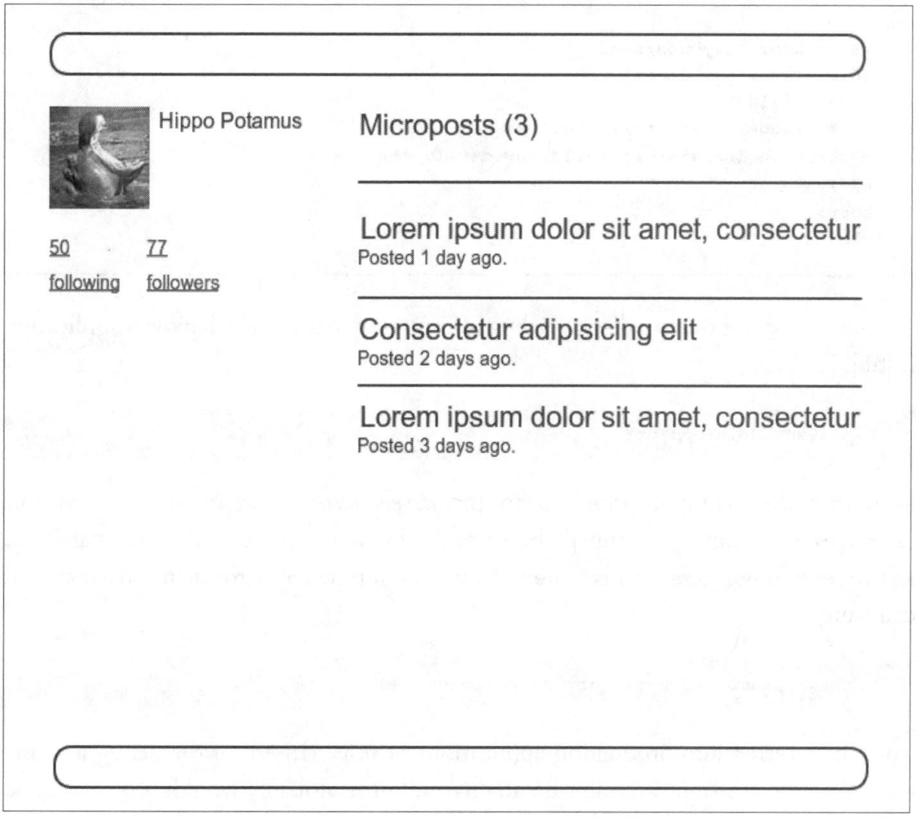

Figure 7.2   A mockup of our best guess at the final profile page.

information to our site layout (Listing 7.1). This displays some useful information about each page using the built-in `debug` method and `params` variable (which we'll learn more about in Section 7.1.2).

Listing 7.1   Adding some debug information to the site layout.

app/views/layouts/application.html.erb

```
<!DOCTYPE html>
<html>
    .
    .
    .
```

```
<body>
  <%= render 'layouts/header' %>
  <div class="container">
    <%= yield %>
    <%= render 'layouts/footer' %>
    <%= debug(params) if Rails.env.development? %>
  </div>
</body>
</html>
```

Since we don't want to display debug information to users of a deployed application, Listing 7.1 uses

```
if Rails.env.development?
```

to restrict the debug information to the *development environment*, which is one of three environments defined by default in Rails (Box 7.1).[3] In particular, `Rails.env.development?` is `true` only in a development environment, so the embedded Ruby

```
<%= debug(params) if Rails.env.development? %>
```

won't be inserted into production applications or tests. (Inserting the debug information into tests probably wouldn't do any harm, but it probably wouldn't do any good, either—so it's best to restrict the debug display to development only.)

Box 7.1 Rails Environments

Rails comes equipped with three environments: `test`, `development`, and `production`. The default environment for the Rails console is `development`:

```
$ rails console
Loading development environment
>> Rails.env
```

---

3. You can define your own custom environments as well; see the RailsCast on adding an environment for details.

```
=> "development"
>> Rails.env.development?
=> true
>> Rails.env.test?
=> false
```

As you can see, Rails provides a `Rails` object with an `env` attribute and associated environment boolean methods, so that, for example, `Rails.env.test?` returns `true` in a test environment and `false` otherwise.

If you ever need to run a console in a different environment (to debug a test, for example), you can pass the environment as a parameter to the `console` script:

```
$ rails console test
Loading test environment
>> Rails.env
=> "test"
>> Rails.env.test?
=> true
```

As with the console, `development` is the default environment for the Rails server, but you can also run it in a different environment:

```
$ rails server --environment production
```

If you view your app running in production, it won't work without a production database, which we can create by running `rake db:migrate` in production:

```
$ bundle exec rake db:migrate RAILS_ENV=production
```

(I find it confusing that the console, server, and migrate commands specify non-default environments in three mutually incompatible ways, which is why I bothered showing all three.)

By the way, if you have deployed your sample app to Heroku, you can see its environment using the command `heroku run console`:

```
$ heroku run console
>> Rails.env
=> "production"
>> Rails.env.production?
=> true
```

Naturally, since Heroku is a platform for production sites, it runs each application in a production environment.

To make the debug output look nice, we'll add some rules to the custom style sheet created in Chapter 5, as shown in Listing 7.2.

Listing 7.2 Adding code for a pretty debug box, including a Sass mixin.
app/assets/stylesheets/custom.css.scss

```
@import "bootstrap-sprockets";
@import "bootstrap";

/* mixins, variables, etc. */

$gray-medium-light: #eaeaea;

@mixin box_sizing {
  -moz-box-sizing:    border-box;
  -webkit-box-sizing: border-box;
  box-sizing:         border-box;
}
.
.
.
/* miscellaneous */

.debug_dump {
  clear: both;
  float: left;
  width: 100%;
  margin-top: 45px;
  @include box_sizing;
}
```

This introduces the Sass *mixin* facility, in this case called **box_sizing**. A mixin allows a group of CSS rules to be packaged up and used for multiple elements, converting

```
.debug_dump {
  .
  .
  .
  @include box_sizing;
}
```

to

```
.debug_dump {
  .
  .
  .
  -moz-box-sizing:      border-box;
  -webkit-box-sizing:   border-box;
  box-sizing:           border-box;
}
```

We'll put this mixin to use again in Section 7.2.1. The result in the case of the debug
box is shown in Figure 7.3.

The debug output in Figure 7.3 gives potentially useful information about the page
being rendered:

```
---
controller: static_pages
action: home
```

Figure 7.3   The sample application Home page with debug information.

This is a YAML[4] representation of **params**, which is basically a hash, and in this case identifies the controller and the action for the page. We'll see another example in Section 7.1.2.

7.1.2   A Users Resource

To make a user profile page, we need to have a user in the database, which introduces a chicken-and-egg problem: How can the site have a user before there is a working sign-up page? Happily, this problem has already been solved. In Section 6.3.4, we created a User record by hand using the Rails console, so there should be one user in the database:

```
$ rails console
>> User.count
=> 1
>> User.first
=> #<User id: 1, name: "Michael Hartl", email: "mhartl@example.com",
created_at: "2014-08-29 02:58:28", updated_at: "2014-08-29 02:58:28",
password_digest: "$2a$10$YmQTuuDNOszvu5yi7auOC.F4G//FGhyQSWCpghqRWQW...">
```

(If you don't currently have a user in your database, you should visit Section 6.3.4 now and complete the steps there before proceeding.) We see from the console output that the user has **id 1**, and our goal now is to make a page to display this user's information. We'll follow the conventions of the REST architecture favored in Rails applications (Box 2.2), which means representing data as *resources* that can be created, shown, updated, or destroyed—four actions corresponding to the four fundamental operations POST, GET, PATCH, and DELETE defined by the HTTP standard (Box 3.2).

When following REST principles, resources are typically referenced using the resource name and a unique identifier. What this means in the context of users—which we're now thinking of as a Users *resource*—is that we should view the user with id **1** by issuing a GET request to the URL /users/1. Here the **show** action is *implicit* in the type of request—when Rails' REST features are activated, GET requests are automatically handled by the **show** action.

We saw in Section 2.2.1 that the page for a user with id **1** has URL /users/1. Unfortunately, visiting that URL right now just gives an error, as seen in the server log (Figure 7.4).

---

4. The Rails **debug** information is shown as YAML (a recursive acronym standing for "YAML Ain't Markup Language"), which is a friendly data format designed to be both machine- *and* human-readable.

```
ActionController::RoutingError (No route matches [GET] "/users/1"):
  web-console (2.0.0.beta3) lib/action_dispatch/debug_exceptions.rb:22:in `middleware_call'
  web-console (2.0.0.beta3) lib/action_dispatch/debug_exceptions.rb:13:in `call'
  actionpack (4.2.0.beta1) lib/action_dispatch/middleware/show_exceptions.rb:30:in `call'
  railties (4.2.0.beta1) lib/rails/rack/logger.rb:38:in `call_app'
  railties (4.2.0.beta1) lib/rails/rack/logger.rb:20:in `block in call'
  activesupport (4.2.0.beta1) lib/active_support/tagged_logging.rb:68:in `block in tagged'
  activesupport (4.2.0.beta1) lib/active_support/tagged_logging.rb:26:in `tagged'
  activesupport (4.2.0.beta1) lib/active_support/tagged_logging.rb:68:in `tagged'
  railties (4.2.0.beta1) lib/rails/rack/logger.rb:20:in `call'
  actionpack (4.2.0.beta1) lib/action_dispatch/middleware/request_id.rb:21:in `call'
  rack (1.6.0.beta) lib/rack/methodoverride.rb:22:in `call'
  rack (1.6.0.beta) lib/rack/runtime.rb:17:in `call'
```

Figure 7.4 The server log error for /users/1.

We can get the routing for /users/1 to work by adding a single line to our routes file (`config/routes.rb`):

```
resources :users
```

The result appears in Listing 7.3.

Listing 7.3 Adding a Users resource to the routes file.
config/routes.rb

```
Rails.application.routes.draw do
  root             'static_pages#home'
  get 'help'    => 'static_pages#help'
  get 'about'   => 'static_pages#about'
  get 'contact' => 'static_pages#contact'
  get 'signup'  => 'users#new'
  resources :users
end
```

Although our immediate motivation is making a page to show users, the single line `resources :users` doesn't just add a working /users/1 URL; it endows our sample application with *all* the actions needed for a RESTful Users resource,[5] along with a large number of named routes (Section 5.3.3) for generating user URLs. The resulting correspondence of URLs, actions, and named routes is shown in Table 7.1. (Compare

---

5. This means that the *routing* works, but the corresponding pages don't necessarily work at this point. For example, /users/1/edit gets routed properly to the `edit` action of the Users controller, but since the `edit` action doesn't exist yet, actually hitting that URL will return an error.

Table 7.1 RESTful routes provided by the Users resource in Listing 7.3.

HTTP request	URL	Action	Named route	Purpose
GET	/users	**index**	**users_path**	page to list all users
GET	/users/1	**show**	**user_path(user)**	page to show user
GET	/users/new	**new**	**new_user_path**	page to make a new user (signup)
POST	/users	**create**	**users_path**	create a new user
GET	/users/1/edit	**edit**	**edit_user_path(user)**	page to edit user with id **1**
PATCH	/users/1	**update**	**user_path(user)**	update user
DELETE	/users/1	**destroy**	**user_path(user)**	delete user

to Table 2.2.) Over the course of the next three chapters, we'll cover all of the other entries in Table 7.1 as we fill in all the actions necessary to make Users a fully RESTful resource.

With the code in Listing 7.3, the routing works, but there's still no page there (Figure 7.5). To fix this, we'll begin with a minimalist version of the profile page, which we'll flesh out in Section 7.1.4.

We'll use the standard Rails location for showing a user, which is **app/views/-users/show.html.erb**. Unlike the **new.html.erb** view, which we created with the generator in Listing 5.28, the **show.html.erb** file doesn't currently exist, so you'll have to create it by hand, and then fill it with the content shown in Listing 7.4.

Listing 7.4 A stub view for showing user information.
app/views/users/show.html.erb

```
<%= @user.name %>, <%= @user.email %>
```

This view uses embedded Ruby to display the user's name and email address, assuming the existence of an instance variable called **@user**. Of course, eventually the real user show page will look very different (and won't display the email address publicly).

To get the user show view to work, we need to define an **@user** variable in the corresponding **show** action in the Users controller. As you might expect, we use the **find** method on the User model (Section 6.1.4) to retrieve the user from the database, as shown in Listing 7.5.

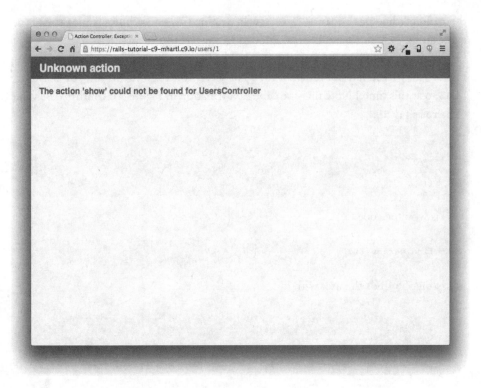

Figure 7.5 The URL /users/1 with routing but no page.

Listing 7.5 The Users controller with a **show** action.
app/controllers/users_controller.rb

```ruby
class UsersController < ApplicationController

  def show
    @user = User.find(params[:id])
  end

  def new
  end
end
```

Here we've used **params** to retrieve the user id. When we make the appropriate request
to the Users controller, **params[:id]** will be the user id 1, so the effect is the same as

the `find` method `User.find(1)` we saw in Section 6.1.4. (Technically, `params[:id]` is the string `"1"`, but `find` is smart enough to convert this to an integer.)

With the user view and action defined, the URL /users/1 works perfectly, as seen in Figure 7.6. (If you haven't restarted the Rails server since adding bcrypt, you may have to do so at this time.) Note that the debug information in Figure 7.6 confirms the value of `params[:id]`:

```
---
action: show
controller: users
id: '1'
```

This is why the code

```
User.find(params[:id])
```

in Listing 7.5 finds the user with id 1.

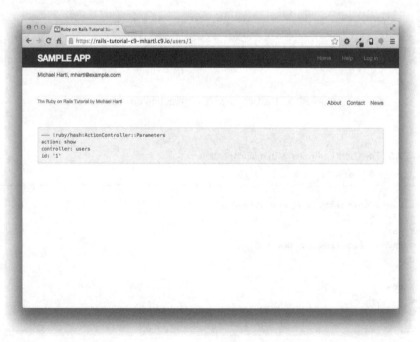

Figure 7.6 The user show page after adding a Users resource.

7.1.3 Debugger

We saw in Section 7.1.2 how the information in the **debug** section of the page could help us understand what's going on in our application. As of Rails 4.2, there's an even more direct way to get debugging information using the byebug gem (Listing 3.2). To see how it works, we just need to add a line consisting of **debugger** to our application, as shown in Listing 7.6.

Listing 7.6 The Users controller with a debugger.
app/controllers/users_controller.rb

```ruby
class UsersController < ApplicationController

  def show
    @user = User.find(params[:id])
    debugger
  end

  def new
  end
end
```

Now, when we visit /users/1, the Rails server shows a **byebug** prompt:

```
(byebug)
```

We can treat this like a Rails console, issuing commands to figure out the state of the application:

```
(byebug) @user.name
"Example User"
(byebug) @user.email
"example@railstutorial.org"
(byebug) params[:id]
"1"
```

To release the prompt and continue execution of the application, press Ctrl-D, then remove the **debugger** line from the **show** action (Listing 7.7).

Listing 7.7 The Users controller with the debugger line removed.
app/controllers/users_controller.rb

```
class UsersController < ApplicationController

  def show
    @user = User.find(params[:id])
  end

  def new
  end
end
```

Whenever you're confused about something in a Rails application, it's a good practice to put **debugger** close to the code you think might be causing the trouble. Inspecting the state of the system using byebug is a powerful method for tracking down application errors and interactively debugging your application.

7.1.4 A Gravatar Image and a Sidebar

Having defined a basic user page in the previous section, we'll now flesh it out a little with a profile image for each user and the first cut of the user sidebar. We'll start by adding a "globally recognized avatar," or Gravatar, to the user profile.[6] Gravatar is a free service that allows users to upload images and associate them with email addresses they control. As a result, Gravatars are a convenient way to include user profile images without going through the trouble of managing image upload, cropping, and storage; all we need to do is construct the proper Gravatar image URL using the user's email address and the corresponding Gravatar image will automatically appear. (We'll learn how to handle custom image upload in Section 11.4.)

Our plan is to define a **gravatar_for** helper function to return a Gravatar image for a given user, as shown in Listing 7.8.

---

6. In Hinduism, an avatar is the manifestation of a deity in human or animal form. By extension, the term *avatar* is commonly used to mean some kind of personal representation, especially in a virtual environment.

Listing 7.8 The user show view with name and Gravatar.
app/views/users/show.html.erb

```erb
<% provide(:title, @user.name) %>
<h1>
  <%= gravatar_for @user %>
  <%= @user.name %>
</h1>
```

By default, methods defined in any helper file are automatically available in any view, but for convenience we'll put the `gravatar_for` method in the file for helpers associated with the Users controller. As noted in the Gravatar documentation, Gravatar URLs are based on an MD5 hash of the user's email address. In Ruby, the MD5 hashing algorithm is implemented using the `hexdigest` method, which is part of the `Digest` library:

```
>> email = "MHARTL@example.COM".
>> Digest::MD5::hexdigest(email.downcase)
=> "1fda4469bcbec3badf5418269ffc5968"
```

Since email addresses are case-insensitive (Section 6.2.4) but MD5 hashes are not, we've used the `downcase` method to ensure that the argument to `hexdigest` is all lowercase. (Because of the email downcasing callback in Listing 6.31, this will never make a difference in this tutorial, but it's a good practice in case the `gravatar_for` ever gets used on email addresses from other sources.) The resulting `gravatar_for` helper appears in Listing 7.9.

Listing 7.9 Defining a `gravatar_for` helper method.
app/helpers/users_helper.rb

```ruby
module UsersHelper

  # Returns the Gravatar for the given user.
  def gravatar_for(user)
    gravatar_id = Digest::MD5::hexdigest(user.email.downcase)
    gravatar_url = "https://secure.gravatar.com/avatar/#{gravatar_id}"
    image_tag(gravatar_url, alt: user.name, class: "gravatar")
  end
end
```

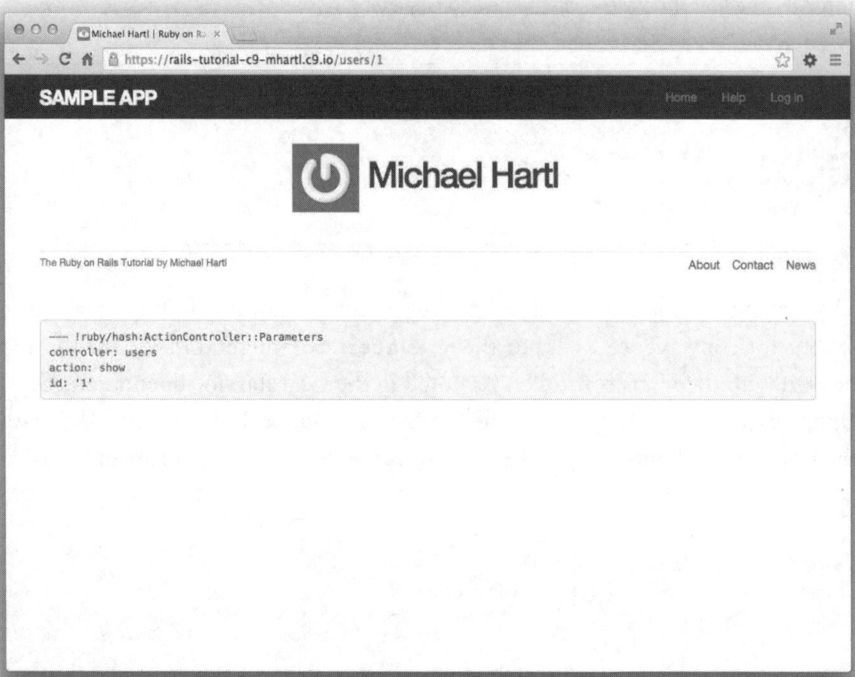

Figure 7.7 The user profile page with the default Gravatar.

The code in Listing 7.9 returns an image tag for the Gravatar with a `gravatar` CSS class and `alt` text equal to the user's name (which is especially convenient for sight-impaired users using a screen reader).

The profile page appears as in Figure 7.7, which shows the default Gravatar image, which appears because `user@example.com` isn't a real email address. (In fact, as you can see by visiting it, the example.com domain is reserved for examples like this one.)

To get our application to display a custom Gravatar, we'll use `update_attributes` (Section 6.1.5) to change the user's email to something I control:

```
$ rails console
>> user = User.first
>> user.update_attributes(name: "Example User",
```

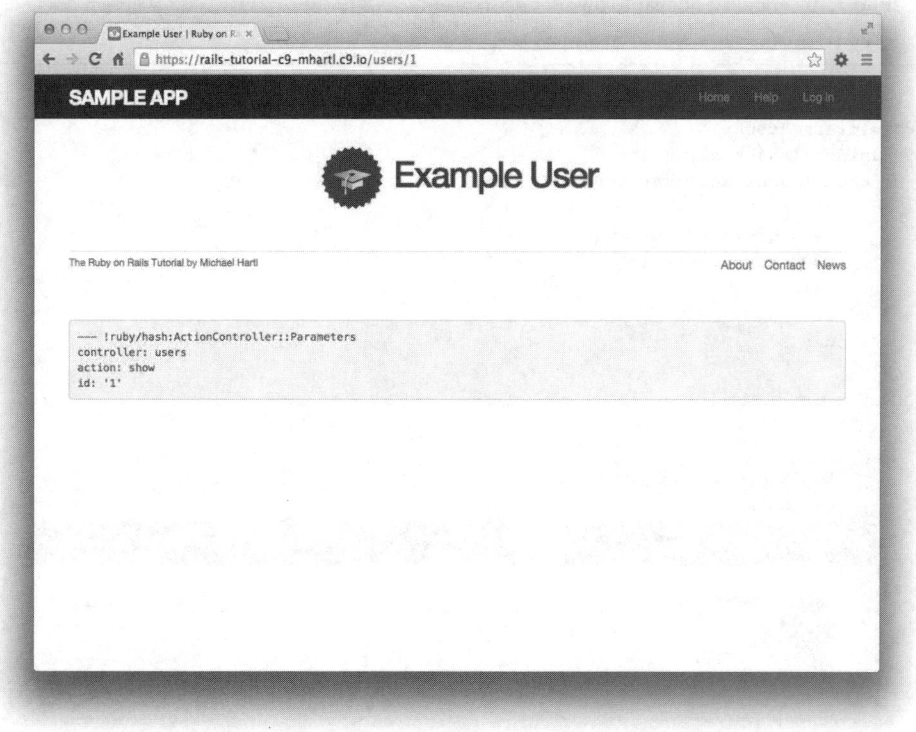

Figure 7.8 The user show page with a custom Gravatar.

```
?>                          email: "example@railstutorial.org",
?>                          password: "foobar",
?>                          password_confirmation: "foobar")
=> true
```

Here we've assigned the user the email address **example@railstutorial.org**, which I've associated with the Rails Tutorial logo, as seen in Figure 7.8.

The last element needed to complete the mockup from Figure 7.1 is the initial version of the user sidebar. We'll implement it using the **aside** tag, which is used for content (such as sidebars) that complements the rest of the page but can also stand alone. We include **row** and **col-md-4** classes, which are both part of Bootstrap. The code for the modified user show page appears in Listing 7.10.

Listing 7.10 Adding a sidebar to the user **show** view.

app/views/users/show.html.erb

```
<% provide(:title, @user.name) %>
<div class="row">
  <aside class="col-md-4">
    <section class="user_info">
      <h1>
        <%= gravatar_for @user %>
        <%= @user.name %>
      </h1>
    </section>
  </aside>
</div>
```

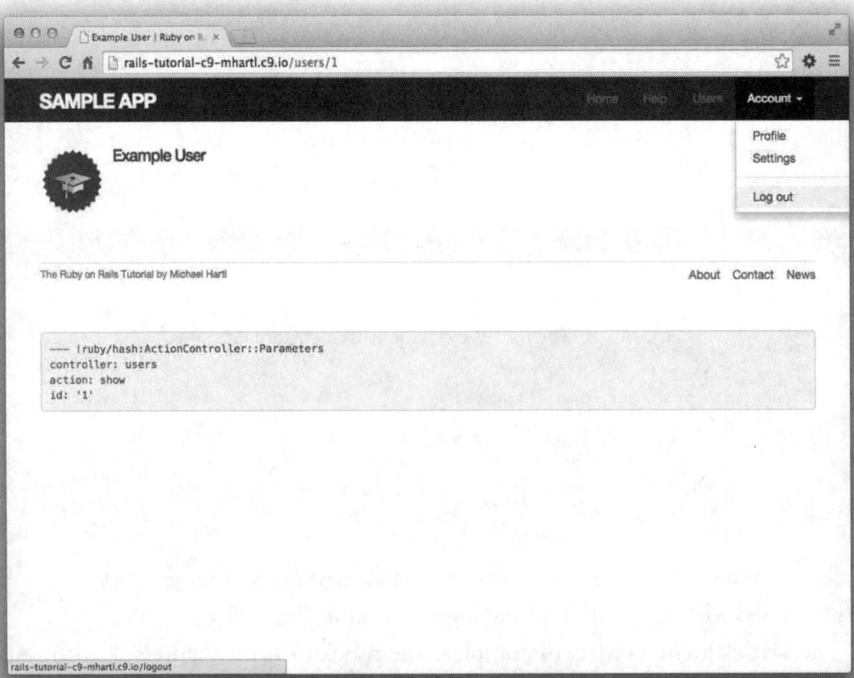

Figure 7.9 The user show page with a sidebar and CSS.

With the HTML elements and CSS classes in place, we can style the profile page (including the sidebar and the Gravatar) with the SCSS shown in Listing 7.11.[7] (Note the nesting of the table CSS rules, which works only because of the Sass engine used by the asset pipeline.) The resulting page is shown in Figure 7.9.

Listing 7.11 SCSS for styling the user show page, including the sidebar.
app/assets/stylesheets/custom.css.scss

```
  .
  .
  .
/* sidebar */

aside {
  section.user_info {
    margin-top: 20px;
  }
  section {
    padding: 10px 0;
    margin-top: 20px;
    &:first-child {
      border: 0;
      padding-top: 0;
    }
    span {
      display: block;
      margin-bottom: 3px;
      line-height: 1;
    }
    h1 {
      font-size: 1.4em;
      text-align: left;
      letter-spacing: -1px;
      margin-bottom: 3px;
      margin-top: 0px;
    }
  }
}

.gravatar {
  float: left;
  margin-right: 10px;
}
```

---

7. Listing 7.11 includes the `.gravatar_edit` class, which we'll put to work in Chapter 9.

```
.gravatar_edit {
  margin-top: 15px;
}
```

7.2 Sign-up Form

Now that we have a working (though not yet complete) user profile page, we're ready
to make a sign-up form for our site. We saw in Figure 5.9 (shown again in Figure 7.10)
that the sign-up page is currently blank: It's useless for signing up new users. The goal
of this section is to start changing this sad state of affairs by producing the sign-up form
mocked up in Figure 7.11.

Since we're about to add the ability to create new users through the web, let's remove
the user created at the console in Section 6.3.4. The cleanest way to do this is to reset
the database with the **db:migrate:reset** Rake task:

```
$ bundle exec rake db:migrate:reset
```

On some systems you might have to restart the web server (using Ctrl-C) for the changes
to take effect.

7.2.1 Using `form_for`

The heart of the sign-up page is a *form* for submitting the relevant sign-up information (name, email, password, confirmation). We can create this form in Rails with the
form_for helper method, which takes in an Active Record object and constructs a form
using the object's attributes.

Recall that the sign-up page /signup is routed to the **new** action in the Users
controller (Listing 5.33). Thus our first step is to create the User object required
as an argument to **form_for**. The resulting **@user** variable definition appears in
Listing 7.12.

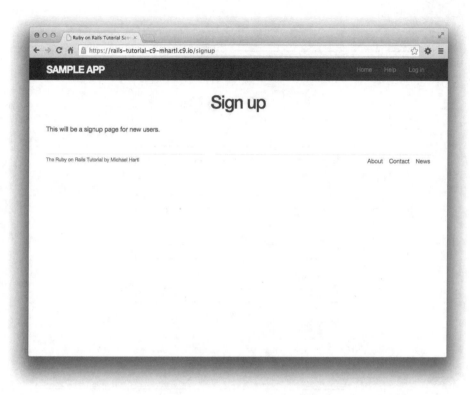

Figure 7.10 The current state of the sign-up page /signup.

Listing 7.12 Adding an **@user** variable to the **new** action.
app/controllers/users_controller.rb

```ruby
class UsersController < ApplicationController

  def show
    @user = User.find(params[:id])
  end

  def new
    @user = User.new
  end
end
```

Figure 7.11 A mockup of the user sign-up page.

The form itself appears as in Listing 7.13. We'll discuss it in detail in Section 7.2.2, but first let's style it a little with the SCSS in Listing 7.14. (Note the reuse of the **box_sizing** mixin from Listing 7.2.) Once these CSS rules have been applied, the sign-up page appears as in Figure 7.12.

Listing 7.13 A form to sign up new users.
app/views/users/new.html.erb

```
<% provide(:title, 'Sign up') %>
<h1>Sign up</h1>

<div class="row">
  <div class="col-md-6 col-md-offset-3">
```

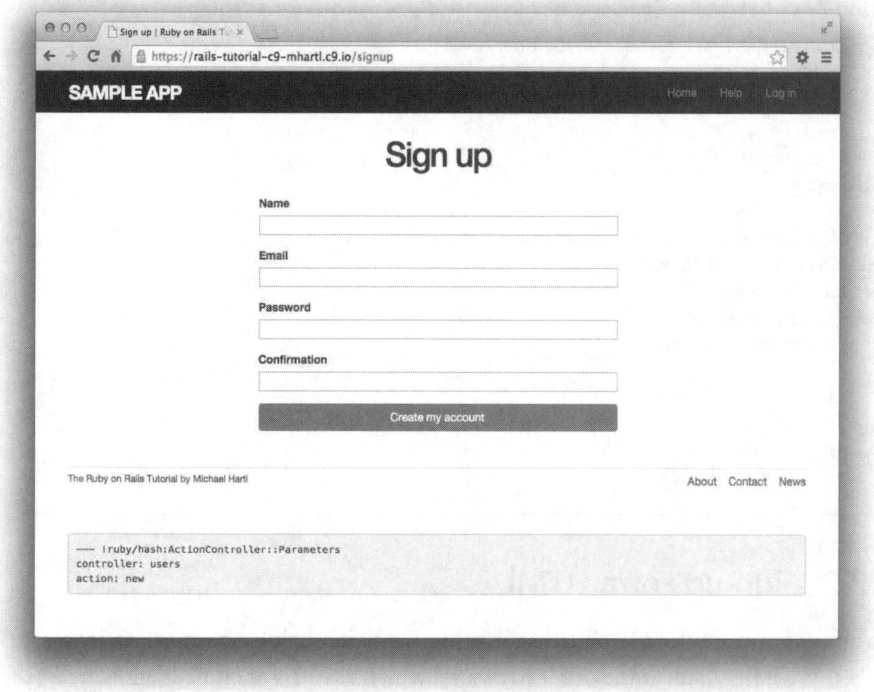

Figure 7.12 The user sign-up form.

```erb
<%= form_for(@user) do |f| %>
  <%= f.label :name %>
  <%= f.text_field :name %>

  <%= f.label :email %>
  <%= f.email_field :email %>

  <%= f.label :password %>
  <%= f.password_field :password %>

  <%= f.label :password_confirmation, "Confirmation" %>
  <%= f.password_field :password_confirmation %>

  <%= f.submit "Create my account", class: "btn btn-primary" %>
<% end %>
  </div>
</div>
```

Listing 7.14 CSS for the sign-up form.
app/assets/stylesheets/custom.css.scss

```
.
.
.
/* forms */

input, textarea, select, .uneditable-input {
  border: 1px solid #bbb;
  width: 100%;
  margin-bottom: 15px;
  @include box_sizing;
}

input {
  height: auto !important;
}
```

7.2.2 Sign-up Form HTML

To understand the form defined in Listing 7.13, it's helpful to break it into smaller pieces. We'll first look at the outer structure, which consists of embedded Ruby opening with a call to **form_for** and closing with **end**:

```
<%= form_for(@user) do |f| %>
  .
  .
  .
<% end %>
```

The presence of the **do** keyword indicates that **form_for** takes a block with one variable, which we've called **f** (for "form").

As is usually the case with Rails helpers, we don't need to know any details about the implementation. However, we *do* need to know what the **f** object does: When called with a method corresponding to an HTML form element—such as a text field, radio button, or password field—**f** returns code for that element specifically designed to set an attribute of the **@user** object. In other words,

```
<%= f.label :name %>
<%= f.text_field :name %>
```

creates the HTML needed to make a labeled text field element appropriate for setting the **name** attribute of a User model.

If you look at the HTML for the generated form by Ctrl-clicking and using the "inspect element" function of your browser, the page's source should look something like Listing 7.15. Let's take a moment to discuss its structure.

Listing 7.15   The HTML for the form in Figure 7.12.

```
<form accept-charset="UTF-8" action="/users" class="new_user"
    id="new_user" method="post">
  <input name="utf8" type="hidden" value="&#x2713;" />
  <input name="authenticity_token" type="hidden"
        value="NNb6+J/j46LcrgYUC60wQ2titMuJQ51LqyAbnbAUkdo=" />

  <label for="user_name">Name</label>
  <input id="user_name" name="user[name]" type="text" />

  <label for="user_email">Email</label>
  <input id="user_email" name="user[email]" type="email" />

  <label for="user_password">Password</label>
  <input id="user_password" name="user[password]"
        type="password" />

  <label for="user_password_confirmation">Confirmation</label>
  <input id="user_password_confirmation"
        name="user[password_confirmation]" type="password" />

  <input class="btn btn-primary" name="commit" type="submit"
        value="Create my account" />
</form>
```

We'll start with the internal structure of the document. Comparing Listing 7.13 with Listing 7.15, we see that the embedded Ruby

```
<%= f.label :name %>
<%= f.text_field :name %>
```

produces the HTML

```
<label for="user_name">Name</label>
<input id="user_name" name="user[name]" type="text" />
```

while

```
<%= f.label :email %>
<%= f.email_field :email %>
```

produces the HTML

```
<label for="user_email">Email</label>
<input id="user_email" name="user[email]" type="email" />
```

and

```
<%= f.label :password %>
<%= f.password_field :password %>
```

produces the HTML

```
<label for="user_password">Password</label>
<input id="user_password" name="user[password]" type="password" />
```

As seen in Figure 7.13, text and email fields (`type="text"` and `type="email"`) simply display their contents, whereas password fields (`type="password"`) obscure the input for security purposes.

As we'll see in Section 7.4, the key to creating a user is the special `name` attribute in each `input`:

```
<input id="user_name" name="user[name]" - - - />
  .
  .
  .
<input id="user_password" name="user[password]" - - - />
```

These `name` values allow Rails to construct an initialization hash (via the `params` variable) for creating users using the values entered by the user, as we'll see in Section 7.3.

The second important element is the `form` tag itself. Rails creates the `form` tag using the `@user` object. Because every Ruby object knows its own class (Section 4.4.1), Rails figures out that `@user` is of class `User`. Moreover, because `@user` is a *new* user, Rails knows to construct a form with the `post` method, which is the proper verb for creating a new object (Box 3.2):

```
<form action="/users" class="new_user" id="new_user" method="post">
```

Here the **class** and **id** attributes are largely irrelevant; what's important is **act-ion="/users"** and **method="post"**. Together, these constitute instructions to issue an HTTP POST request to the /users URL. In the next two sections, we'll see the effects of these instructions.

You may also have noticed the code that appears just inside the **form** tag:

```
<div style="display:none">
  <input name="utf8" type="hidden" value="&#x2713;" />
  <input name="authenticity_token" type="hidden"
         value="NNb6+J/j46LcrgYUC60wQ2titMuJQ5lLqyAbnbAUkdo=" />
</div>
```

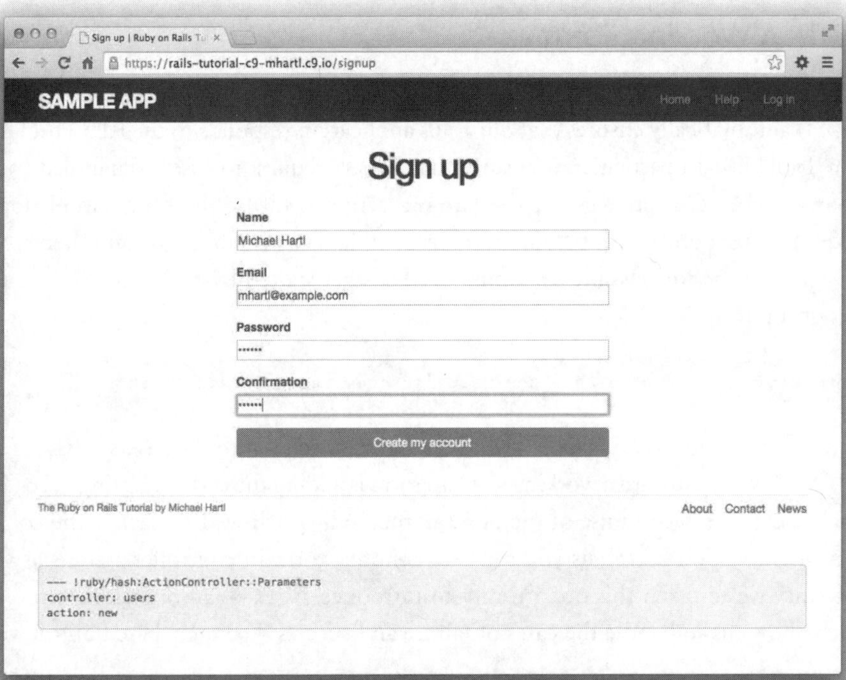

Figure 7.13 A filled-in form with **text** and **password** fields.

This code, which isn't displayed in the browser, is used internally by Rails, so it's not important for us to understand what it does. Briefly, it uses the Unicode character `&#x2713;` (a checkmark ✓) to force browsers to submit data using the right character encoding, and then it includes an *authenticity token*, which Rails uses to thwart a type of attack called a *cross-site request forgery* (CSRF).[8]

7.3 Unsuccessful Sign-ups

Although we've briefly examined the HTML for the form in Figure 7.12 (shown in Listing 7.15), we haven't yet covered any details, and the form is best understood in the context of *sign-up failure*. In this section, we'll create a sign-up form that accepts an invalid submission and re-renders the sign-up page with a list of errors, as mocked up in Figure 7.14.

7.3.1 A Working Form

Recall from Section 7.1.2 that adding `resources :users` to the `routes.rb` file (Listing 7.3) automatically ensures that our Rails application responds to the RESTful URLs from Table 7.1. In particular, it ensures that a POST request to /users is handled by the `create` action. Our strategy for the `create` action is to use the form submission to make a new user object using `User.new`, try (and fail) to save that user, and then render the sign-up page for possible resubmission. Let's get started by reviewing the code for the sign-up form:

```
<form action="/users" class="new_user" id="new_user" method="post">
```

As noted in Section 7.2.2, this HTML issues a POST request to the /users URL.

Our first step toward a working sign-up form is adding the code in Listing 7.16. This listing includes a second use of the `render` method, which we first saw in the context of partials (Section 5.1.3); as you can see, `render` works in controller actions as well. Note that we've taken this opportunity to introduce an `if-else` branching structure, which allows us to handle the cases of failure and success separately based on the value

---

8. See the Stack Overflow entry on the Rails authenticity token if you're interested in the details of how this works.

Figure 7.14 A mockup of the sign-up failure page.

of `@user.save`, which (as we saw in Section 6.1.3) is either `true` or `false` depending on whether the save succeeds.

Listing 7.16 A `create` action that can handle sign-up failure.
app/controllers/users_controller.rb

```ruby
class UsersController < ApplicationController

  def show
    @user = User.find(params[:id])
  end
```

```
  def new
    @user = User.new
  end

  def create
    @user = User.new(params[:user])        # Not the final implementation!
    if @user.save
      # Handle a successful save.
    else
      render 'new'
    end
  end
end
```

Note the comment includes in Listing 7.16; this is not the final implementation. Nevertheless, it's enough to get us started, and we'll finish the implementation in Section 7.3.2.

The best way to understand how the code in Listing 7.16 works is to *submit* the form with some invalid sign-up data. The result appears in Figure 7.15, and the full debug information (with an increased font size) appears in Figure 7.16. (Figure 7.15 also shows the *web console*, which opens a Rails console in the browser to assist in debugging. It's useful for examining the User model, for example, but in this case we need to inspect **params**, which is not available in the web console as far as I can tell.)

To get a better picture of how Rails handles the submission, let's take a closer look at the **user** part of the parameters hash from the debug information (Figure 7.16):

```
"user" => { "name" => "Foo Bar",
            "email" => "foo@invalid",
            "password" => "[FILTERED]",
            "password_confirmation" => "[FILTERED]"
          }
```

This hash gets passed to the Users controller as part of **params**, and we saw starting in Section 7.1.2 that the **params** hash contains information about each request. In the case of a URL like /users/1, the value of **params[:id]** is the **id** of the corresponding user (**1** in this example). In the case of posting to the sign-up form, **params** instead contains a hash of hashes—a construction we first saw in Section 4.3.3, which introduced the strategically named **params** variable in a console session.

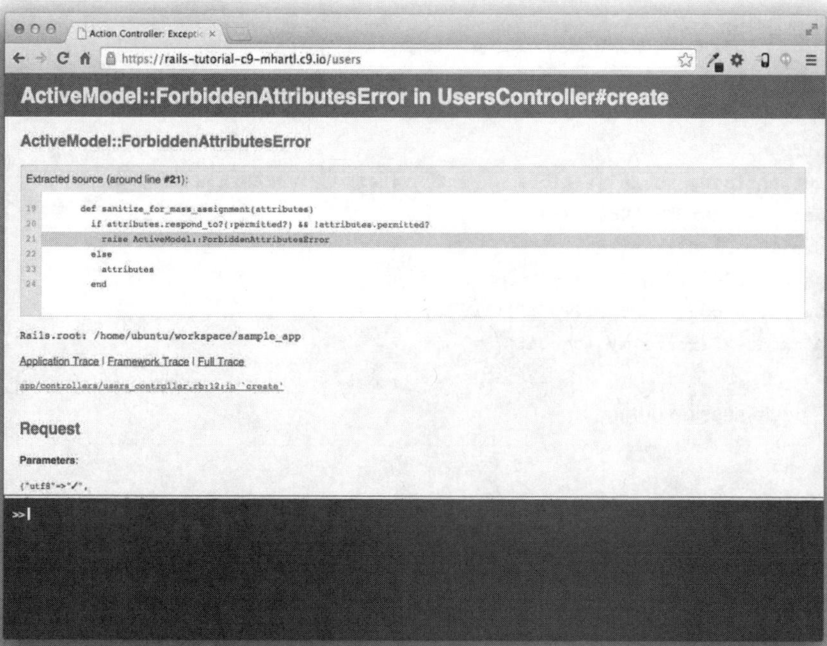

Figure 7.15 Sign-up failure.

The debug information shows that submitting the form results in a **user** hash with attributes corresponding to the submitted values, where the keys come from the **name** attributes of the **input** tags seen in Listing 7.13. For example, the value of

```
<input id="user_email" name="user[email]" type="email" />
```

with name **"user[email]"** is precisely the **email** attribute of the **user** hash.

Although the hash keys appear as strings in the debug output, we can access them in the Users controller as symbols, so that **params[:user]** is the hash of user attributes—in fact, exactly the attributes needed as an argument to **User.new**, as first seen in Section 4.4.5 and appearing in Listing 7.16. This means that the line

```
@user = User.new(params[:user])
```

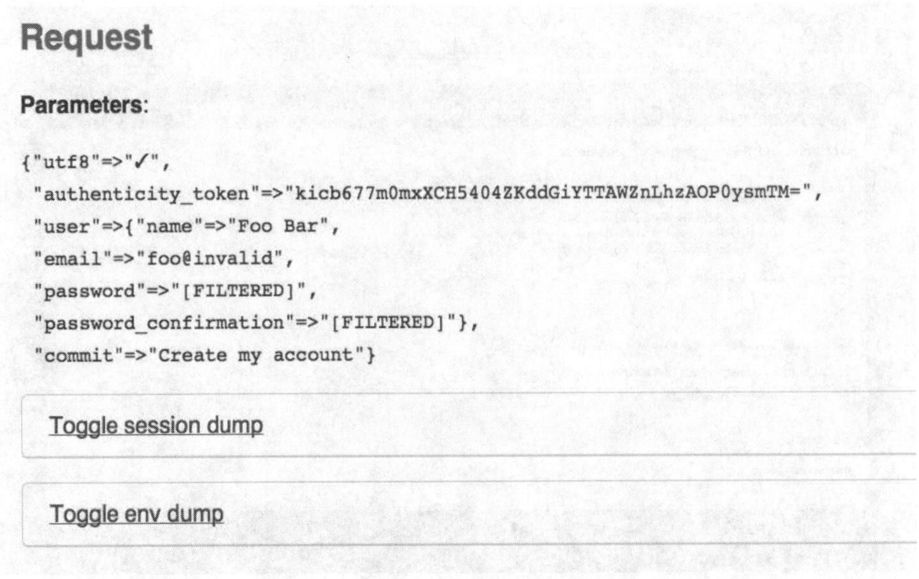

Request

Parameters:

```
{"utf8"=>"✓",
 "authenticity_token"=>"kicb677m0mxXCH5404ZKddGiYTTAWZnLhzAOP0ysmTM=",
 "user"=>{"name"=>"Foo Bar",
 "email"=>"foo@invalid",
 "password"=>"[FILTERED]",
 "password_confirmation"=>"[FILTERED]"},
 "commit"=>"Create my account"}
```

Toggle session dump

Toggle env dump

Figure 7.16 Sign-up failure debug information.

is mostly equivalent to

```
@user = User.new(name: "Foo Bar", email: "foo@invalid",
                 password: "foo", password_confirmation: "bar")
```

In previous versions of Rails, using

```
@user = User.new(params[:user])
```

actually worked, but it was insecure by default and required a careful and error-prone procedure to prevent malicious users from potentially modifying the application database. In Rails versions later than 4.0, this code raises an error (as seen in Figure 7.15 and Figure 7.16), which means it is secure by default.

7.3.2 Strong Parameters

In Section 4.4.5 we briefly mentioned the idea of *mass assignment*, which involves initializing a Ruby variable using a hash of values. For example,

```
@user = User.new(params[:user])     # Not the final implementation!
```

The comment included in Listing 7.16 and reproduced here indicates that this is not the final implementation. The reason is that initializing the entire **params** hash is *extremely dangerous*—it arranges to pass to **User.new** *all* data submitted by a user. Suppose that, in addition to the current attributes, the User model included an **admin** attribute used to identify administrative users of the site. (We will implement just such an attribute in Section 9.4.1.) The way to set such an attribute to **true** is to pass the value **admin='1'** as part of **params[:user]**, a task that is easy to accomplish using a command-line HTTP client such as curl. The result would be that, by passing in the entire **params** hash to **User.new**, we would allow any user of the site to gain administrative access by including **admin='1'** in the web request.

Previous versions of Rails used a method called **attr_accessible** in the *model* layer to solve this problem, and you may still see that method in legacy Rails applications. As of Rails 4.0, however, the preferred technique is to use so-called *strong parameters* in the controller layer. This allows us to specify which parameters are *required* and which ones are *permitted*. In addition, passing in a raw **params** hash will cause an error to be raised, so that Rails applications are now immune to mass assignment vulnerabilities by default.

In the present instance, we want to require the **params** hash to have a **:user** attribute, and we want to permit the name, email, password, and password confirmation attributes (but no others). We can accomplish this as follows:

```
params.require(:user).permit(:name, :email, :password, :password_confirmation)
```

This code returns a version of the **params** hash with only the permitted attributes (while raising an error if the **:user** attribute is missing).

To facilitate the use of these parameters, it's conventional to introduce an auxiliary method called **user_params** (which returns an appropriate initialization hash) and use it in place of **params[:user]**:

```
@user = User.new(user_params)
```

Since **user_params** will be used only internally by the Users controller and need not be exposed to external users via the web, we'll make it *private* using Ruby's **private** keyword, as shown in Listing 7.17. (We'll discuss **private** in more detail in Section 8.4.)

Listing 7.17 Using strong parameters in the **create** action.
app/controllers/users_controller.rb

```ruby
class UsersController < ApplicationController
  .
  .
  .
  def create
    @user = User.new(user_params)
    if @user.save
      # Handle a successful save.
    else
      render 'new'
    end
  end

  private

    def user_params
      params.require(:user).permit(:name, :email, :password,
                                   :password_confirmation)
    end
end
```

By the way, the extra level of indentation for the **user_params** method is designed to make it visually apparent which methods are defined after **private**. (Experience shows that this is a wise practice; in classes with a large number of methods, it is easy to define a private method accidentally, which leads to considerable confusion when that method isn't available to call on the corresponding object.)

At this point, the sign-up form is working, at least in the sense that it no longer produces an error upon submission. Nevertheless, as seen in Figure 7.17, it doesn't display any feedback on invalid submissions (apart from the development-only debug area), which is potentially confusing. It also doesn't actually create a new user. We'll fix the first issue in Section 7.3.3 and the second in Section 7.4.

7.3.3   Sign-up Error Messages

As a final step in handling failed user creation, we'll add helpful error messages to indicate the problems that prevented successful sign-up. Conveniently, Rails automatically

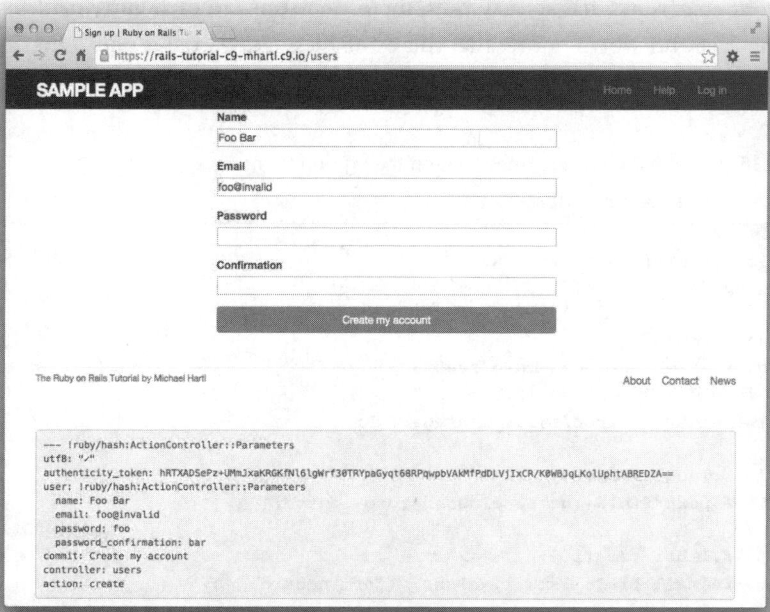

Figure 7.17 The sign-up form submitted with invalid information.

provides such messages based on the User model validations. For example, consider trying to save a user with an invalid email address and with a password that's too short:

```
$ rails console
>> user = User.new(name: "Foo Bar", email: "foo@invalid",
?>                 password: "dude", password_confirmation: "dude")
>> user.save
=> false
>> user.errors.full_messages
=> ["Email is invalid", "Password is too short (minimum is 6 characters)"]
```

Here the **errors.full_messages** object (which we saw briefly before in Section 6.2.2) contains an array of error messages.

As in the earlier console session, the failed save in Listing 7.16 generates a list of error messages associated with the **@user** object. To display the messages in the browser, we'll render an error-messages partial on the user **new** page while adding the CSS class `form-control` (which has special meaning to Bootstrap) to each entry field, as shown in Listing 7.18. It's worth noting that this error-messages partial is only a first attempt; the final version appears in Section 11.3.2.

Listing 7.18 Code to display error messages on the sign-up form.

app/views/users/new.html.erb

```erb
<% provide(:title, 'Sign up') %>
<h1>Sign up</h1>

<div class="row">
  <div class="col-md-6 col-md-offset-3">
    <%= form_for(@user) do |f| %>
      <%= render 'shared/error_messages' %>

      <%= f.label :name %>
      <%= f.text_field :name, class: 'form-control' %>

      <%= f.label :email %>
      <%= f.email_field :email, class: 'form-control' %>

      <%= f.label :password %>
      <%= f.password_field :password, class: 'form-control' %>

      <%= f.label :password_confirmation, "Confirmation" %>
      <%= f.password_field :password_confirmation, class: 'form-control' %>

      <%= f.submit "Create my account", class: "btn btn-primary" %>
    <% end %>
  </div>
</div>
```

Notice that we **render** a partial called `'shared/error_messages'`; this reflects the common Rails convention of using a dedicated **shared/** directory for partials expected to be used in views across multiple controllers. (We'll see this expectation fulfilled in Section 9.1.1.) As a consequence, we have to create a new **app/views/shared** directory using **mkdir** (Table 1.1):

```
$ mkdir app/views/shared
```

We then need to create the **_error_messages.html.erb** partial file using our text editor as usual. The contents of the partial appear in Listing 7.19.

Listing 7.19   A partial for displaying form submission error messages.
app/views/shared/_error_messages.html.erb

```erb
<% if @user.errors.any? %>
  <div id="error_explanation">
    <div class="alert alert-danger">
      The form contains <%= pluralize(@user.errors.count, "error") %>.
    </div>
    <ul>
    <% @user.errors.full_messages.each do |msg| %>
      <li><%= msg %></li>
    <% end %>
    </ul>
  </div>
<% end %>
```

This partial introduces several new Rails and Ruby constructs, including two methods for Rails error objects. The first method is **count**, which simply returns the number of errors:

```
>> user.errors.count
=> 2
```

The other new method is **any?**, which (together with **empty?**) is one of a pair of complementary methods:

```
>> user.errors.empty?
=> false
>> user.errors.any?
=> true
```

The **empty?** method, which we first saw in Section 4.2.3 in the context of strings, also works on Rails error objects, returning **true** for an empty object and **false** otherwise. The **any?** method is just the opposite of **empty?**, returning **true** if there are any elements present and **false** otherwise. (All of these methods—**count**, **empty?**, and **any?**—work on Ruby arrays as well. We'll put this fact to good use starting in Section 11.2.)

The other new idea is the **pluralize** text helper. It isn't available in the console by default, but we can include it explicitly through the **ActionView::Helpers::Text-Helper** module:[9]

---

9. I figured this out by looking up **pluralize** in the Rails API.

```
>> include ActionView::Helpers::TextHelper
>> pluralize(1, "error")
=> "1 error"
>> pluralize(5, "error")
=> "5 errors"
```

We see here that **pluralize** takes an integer argument and then returns the number with a properly pluralized version of its second argument. Underlying this method is a powerful *inflector* that knows how to pluralize a large number of words, including many with irregular plurals:

```
>> pluralize(2, "woman")
=> "2 women"
>> pluralize(3, "erratum")
=> "3 errata"
```

As a result of its use of **pluralize**, the code

```
<%= pluralize(@user.errors.count, "error") %>
```

returns **"0 errors"**, **"1 error"**, **"2 errors"**, and so on, depending on how many errors there are, thereby avoiding ungrammatical phrases such as **"1 errors"** (a distressingly common mistake in apps and on the web).

Note that Listing 7.19 includes the CSS id **error_explanation** for use in styling the error messages. (Recall from Section 5.1.2 that CSS uses the pound sign # to style IDs.) In addition, after an invalid submission Rails automatically wraps the fields with errors in **divs** with the CSS class **field_with_errors**. These labels then allow us to style the error messages with the SCSS shown in Listing 7.20, which makes use of Sass's **@extend** function to include the functionality of the Bootstrap class **has-error**.

Listing 7.20 CSS for styling error messages.
app/assets/stylesheets/custom.css.scss

```
.
.
.
/* forms */
.
.
.
```

```scss
#error_explanation {
  color: red;
  ul {
    color: red;
    margin: 0 0 30px 0;
  }
}

.field_with_errors {
  @extend .has-error;
  .form-control {
    color: $state-danger-text;
  }
}
```

With the code in Listing 7.18 and Listing 7.19 and the SCSS from Listing 7.20, helpful error messages now appear when users submit invalid sign-up information to our app, as seen in Figure 7.18. Because the messages are generated by the model validations, they will automatically change if you ever change your mind about, say, the format of email addresses, or the minimum length of passwords.

7.3.4 A Test for Invalid Submission

In the days before powerful web frameworks with full testing capabilities were available, developers had to test forms by hand. For example, to test a sign-up page manually, we would have to visit the page in a browser and then submit both invalid and valid data, verifying in each case that the application's behavior was correct. Moreover, we would have to remember to repeat the process anytime the application changed. This process was painful and error-prone.

Happily, with Rails we can write tests to automate the testing of forms. In this section, we'll write one such test to verify the correct behavior upon invalid form submission; in Section 7.4.4, we'll write the corresponding test for valid submission.

To get started, we first generate an integration test file for signing up users, which we'll call **users_signup** (adopting the controller convention of a plural resource name):

```
$ rails generate integration_test users_signup
      invoke  test_unit
      create    test/integration/users_signup_test.rb
```

(We'll use this same file in Section 7.4.4 to test a valid sign-up.)

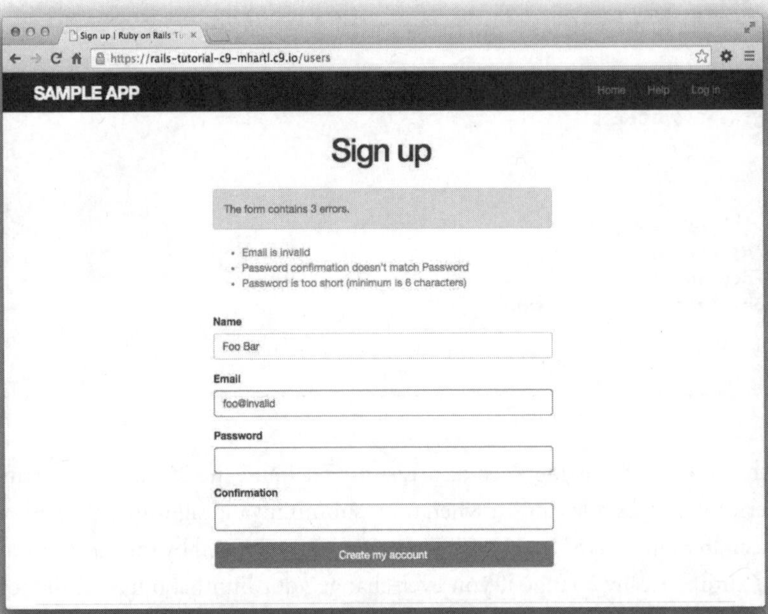

Figure 7.18 Failed sign-up with error messages.

The main purpose of our test is to verify that clicking the sign-up button results in *not* creating a new user when the submitted information is invalid. [Writing a test for the error messages is left as an exercise (Section 7.7).] The way to do this is to check the *count* of users. Under the hood, therefore, our tests will use the `count` method available on every Active Record class, including `User`:

```
$ rails console
>> User.count
=> 0
```

Here `User.count` is `0` because we reset the database at the beginning of Section 7.2. As in Section 5.3.4, we'll use `assert_select` to test HTML elements of the relevant pages, taking care to check only elements unlikely to change in the future.

We'll start by visiting the sign-up path using `get`:

```
get signup_path
```

To test the form submission, we need to issue a POST request to the **users_path** (Table 7.1), which we can do with the **post** function:

```
assert_no_difference 'User.count' do
  post users_path, user: { name:   "",
                           email: "user@invalid",
                           password:              "foo",
                           password_confirmation: "bar" }
end
```

Here we've included the **params[:user]** hash expected by **User.new** in the **create** action (Listing 7.24). By wrapping the **post** in the **assert_no_difference** method with the string argument **'User.count'**, we arrange for a comparison between **User.count** before and after the contents of the **assert_no_difference** block. This is equivalent to recording the user count, posting the data, and verifying that the count is the same:

```
before_count = User.count
post users_path, ...
after_count  = User.count
assert_equal before_count, after_count
```

Although the two are equivalent, using **assert_no_difference** is cleaner and is more idiomatically correct Ruby.

It's worth noting that the **get** and **post** steps above are technically unrelated, and it's actually not necessary to get the sign-up path before posting to the users path. I prefer to include both steps, though, both for conceptual clarity and to double-check that the sign-up form renders without error.

Putting these above ideas together leads to the test in Listing 7.21. We've also included a call to **assert_template** to check that a failed submission re-renders the **new** action. Adding lines to check for the appearance of error messages is left as an exercise (Section 7.7).

Listing 7.21 A test for an invalid sign-up. GREEN

test/integration/users_signup_test.rb

```
require 'test_helper'

class UsersSignupTest < ActionDispatch::IntegrationTest

  test "invalid signup information" do
```

```
    get signup_path
    assert_no_difference 'User.count' do
      post users_path, user: { name:  "",
                               email: "user@invalid",
                               password:              "foo",
                               password_confirmation: "bar" }
    end
    assert_template 'users/new'
  end
end
```

Because we wrote the application code before the integration test, the test suite should
be **GREEN**:

Listing 7.22 GREEN

```
$ bundle exec rake test
```

7.4 Successful Sign-ups

Having handled invalid form submissions, now it's time to complete the sign-up form
by actually saving a new user (if valid) to the database. First, we try to save the user; if the
save succeeds, the user's information gets written to the database automatically, and we
then *redirect* the browser to show the user's profile (together with a friendly greeting),
as mocked up in Figure 7.19. If it fails, we simply fall back on the behavior developed
in Section 7.3.

7.4.1 The Finished Sign-up Form

To complete a working sign-up form, we need to fill in the commented-out section in
Listing 7.16 with the appropriate behavior. Currently, the form fails on valid submission. As indicated in Figure 7.20, this is because the default behavior for a Rails action
is to render the corresponding view, and there isn't a view template corresponding to
the `create` action.

Rather than render a page on successful user creation, we'll instead *redirect* the user
to a different page. We'll follow the common convention of redirecting to the newly

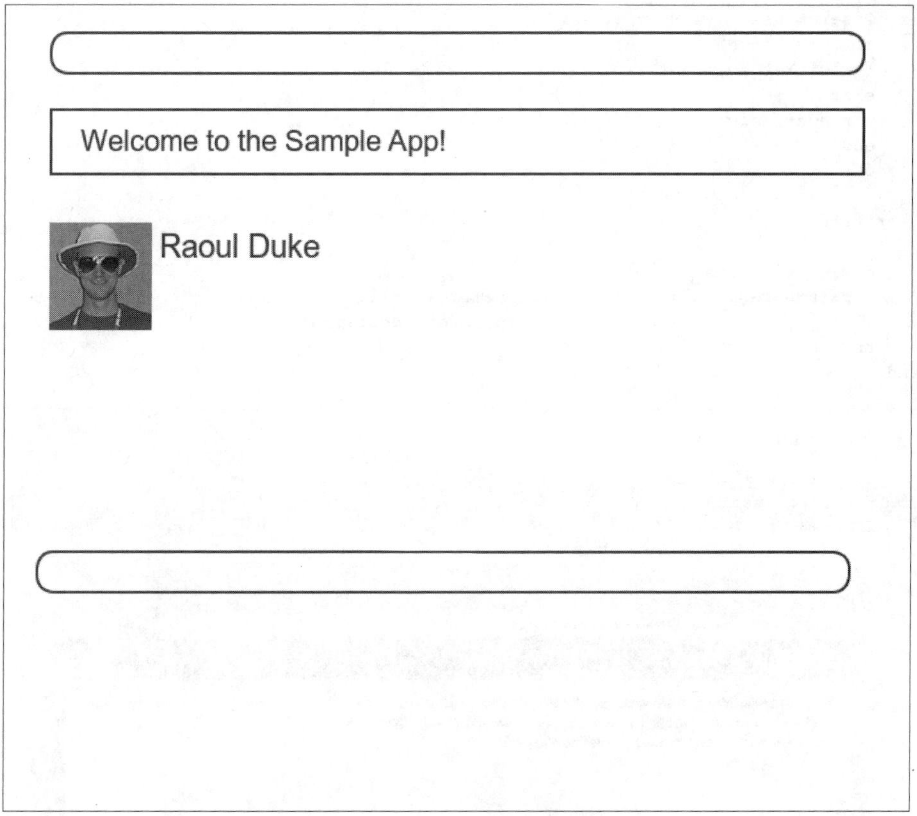

Figure 7.19 A mockup of successful sign-up.

created user's profile, although the root path would also work. The application code, which introduces the **redirect_to** method, appears in Listing 7.23.

Listing 7.23 The user **create** action with a save and a redirect.
app/controllers/users_controller.rb

```
class UsersController < ApplicationController
  .
  .
  .
  def create
```

```ruby
  @user = User.new(user_params)
  if @user.save
    redirect_to @user
  else
    render 'new'
  end
end

private

  def user_params
    params.require(:user).permit(:name, :email, :password,
                                 :password_confirmation)
  end
end
```

Note that we've written

```ruby
redirect_to @user
```

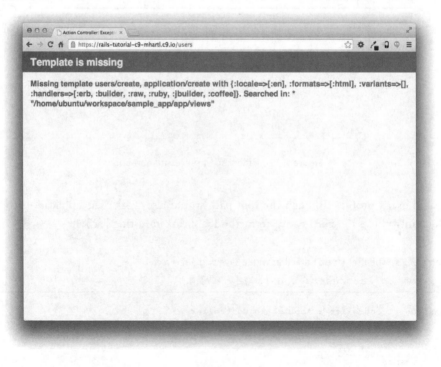

Figure 7.20 The error page for a valid signup submission.

where we could have used the equivalent

```
redirect_to user_url(@user)
```

Rails automatically infers from **redirect_to @user** that we want to redirect to **user_url(@user)**.

7.4.2 The Flash

With the code in Listing 7.23, our sign-up form is actually working. Before submitting a valid registration in a browser, however, let's add a bit of polish common in web applications: a message that appears on the subsequent page (in this case, welcoming our new user to the application) and then disappears upon visiting a second page or on page reload.

The Rails way to display a temporary message is to use a special method called the *flash*, which we can treat like a hash. Rails adopts the convention of a **:success** key for a message indicating a successful result (Listing 7.24).

Listing 7.24 Adding a flash message to user sign-up.

app/controllers/users_controller.rb

```
class UsersController < ApplicationController
  .
  .
  .
  def create
    @user = User.new(user_params)
    if @user.save
      flash[:success] = "Welcome to the Sample App!"
      redirect_to @user
    else
      render 'new'
    end
  end

  private

    def user_params
      params.require(:user).permit(:name, :email, :password,
                                   :password_confirmation)
    end
end
```

By assigning a message to **flash**, we are now in a position to display the message on the first page after the redirect. Our method is to iterate through **flash** and insert all relevant messages into the site layout. You might recall the console example in Section 4.3.3, where we saw how to iterate through a hash using the strategically named **flash** variable:

```
$ rails console
>> flash = { success: "It worked!", danger: "It failed." }
=> {:success=>"It worked!", danger: "It failed."}
>> flash.each do |key, value|
?>   puts "#{key}"
?>   puts "#{value}"
>> end
success
It worked!
danger
It failed.
```

By following this pattern, we can arrange to display the contents of the flash site-wide using code like this:

```
<% flash.each do |message_type, message| %>
  <div class="alert alert-<%= message_type %>"><%= message %></div>
<% end %>
```

This code is a particularly ugly combination of HTML and ERb; making it prettier is left as an exercise (Section 7.7). Notice, however, that the embedded Ruby

```
alert-<%= message_type %>
```

makes a CSS class corresponding to the type of message, so that for a **:success** message the class is

```
alert-success
```

The key **:success** is a symbol, but embedded Ruby automatically converts it to the string **"success"** before inserting it into the template.

Using a different class for each key allows us to apply different styles to different kinds of messages. For example, in Section 8.1.4 we'll use **flash[:danger]** to indicate a failed login attempt.[10] (In fact, we've already used **alert-danger** once, to style the error message div in Listing 7.19.) Bootstrap CSS supports styling for four such flash classes (**success**, **info**, **warning**, and **danger**), and we'll find occasion to use all of them in the course of developing the sample application.

Because the message is also inserted into the template, the full HTML result for

```
flash[:success] = "Welcome to the Sample App!"
```

appears as follows:

```
<div class="alert alert-success">Welcome to the Sample App!</div>
```

Putting the embedded Ruby into the site layout leads to the code in Listing 7.25.

Listing 7.25 Adding the contents of the **flash** variable to the site layout.
app/views/layouts/application.html.erb

```
<!DOCTYPE html>
<html>
  .
  .
  .
  <body>
    <%= render 'layouts/header' %>
    <div class="container">
      <% flash.each do |message_type, message| %>
        <div class="alert alert-<%= message_type %>"><%= message %></div>
      <% end %>
      <%= yield %>
      <%= render 'layouts/footer' %>
      <%= debug(params) if Rails.env.development? %>
    </div>
    .
    .
    .
  </body>
</html>
```

---

10. Actually, we'll use the closely related **flash.now**, but we'll defer that subtlety until we need it.

7.4.3 The First Sign-up

We can see the result of all this work by signing up our first user under the name "Rails Tutorial" and email address "example@railstutorial.org" (Figure 7.21).

The resulting page (Figure 7.22) shows a friendly message upon successful sign-up, including nice green styling for the **success** class, which comes included with the Bootstrap CSS framework from Section 5.1.2. (If you get an error message indicating that the email address has already been taken, be sure to run the **db:migrate:reset** Rake task as indicated in Section 7.2 and restart the development web server.) Then, upon reloading the user show page, the flash message disappears as promised (Figure 7.23).

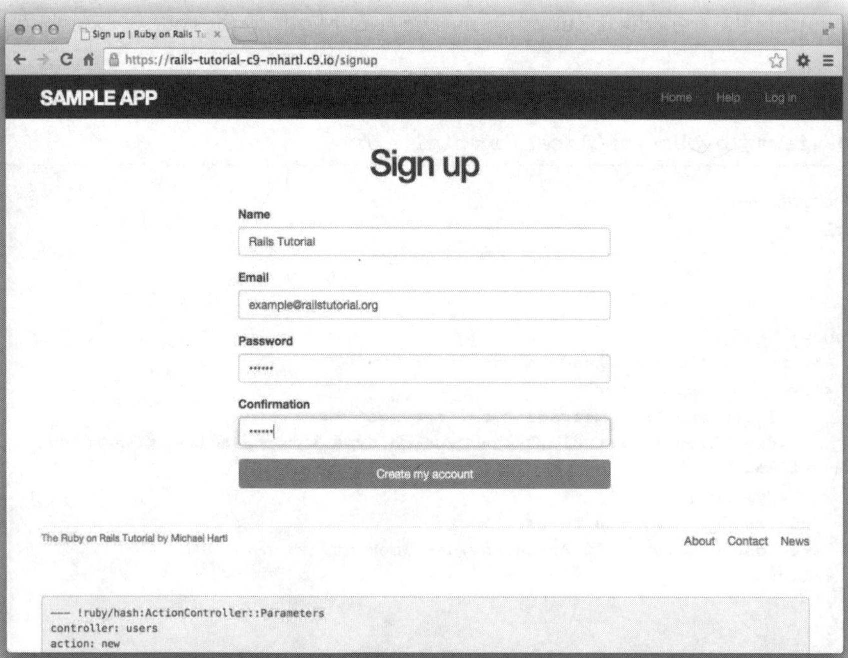

Figure 7.21 Filling in the information for the first sign-up.

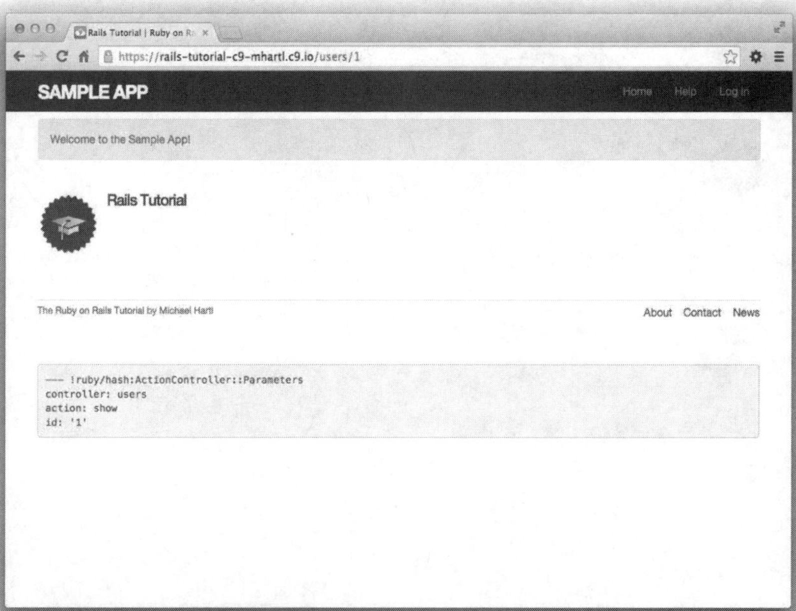

Figure 7.22   The results of a successful user sign-up, with flash message.

We can now check our database just to double-check that the new user was actually created:

```
$ rails console
>> User.find_by(email: "example@railstutorial.org")
=> #<User id: 1, name: "Rails Tutorial", email: "example@railstutorial.org",
created_at: "2014-08-29 19:53:17", updated_at: "2014-08-29 19:53:17",
password_digest: "$2a$10$zthScEx9x6EkuLa4NolGye6OOZgrkp1B6LQ12pTHlNB...">
```

7.4.4   A Test for Valid Submission

Before moving on, we'll write a test for valid submission to verify our application's behavior and catch regressions. As with the test for invalid submission in Section 7.3.4, our main purpose is to verify the contents of the database. In this case, we want to submit

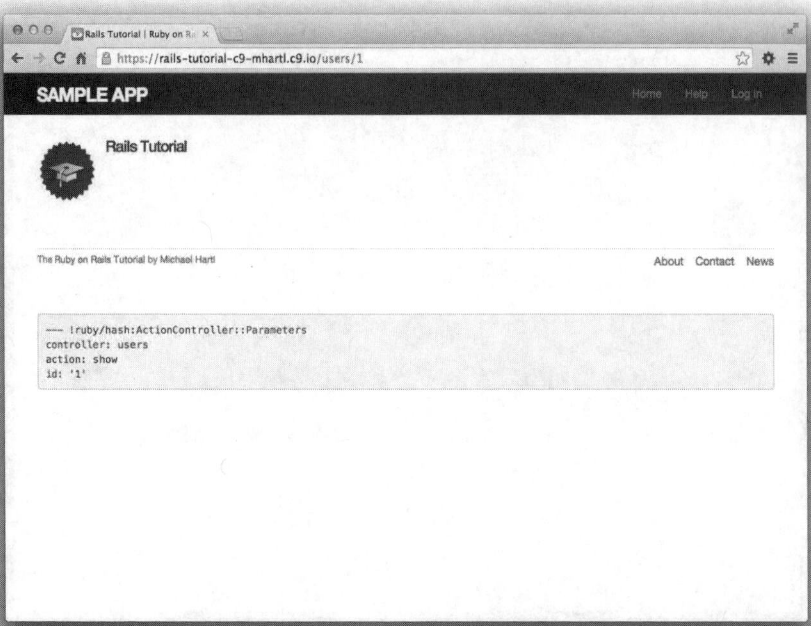

Figure 7.23 The flash-less profile page after a browser reload.

valid information and then confirm that a user *was* created. In analogy with Listing 7.21, which used

```
assert_no_difference 'User.count' do
  post users_path, ...
end
```

here we'll use the corresponding `assert_difference` method:

```
assert_difference 'User.count', 1 do
  post_via_redirect users_path, ...
end
```

As with `assert_no_difference`, the first argument is the string `'User.count'`, which arranges for a comparison between `User.count` before and after the contents of the `assert_difference` block. The second (optional) argument specifies the size of the difference (in this case, 1).

Incorporating `assert_difference` into the file from Listing 7.21 yields the test shown in Listing 7.26. Note that we've used the `post_via_redirect` variant to post to the users path. This simply arranges to follow the redirect after submission, resulting in a rendering of the `'users/show'` template. It's probably a good idea to write a test for the flash as well, but that task is left as an exercise (Section 7.7).

Listing 7.26   A test for a valid sign-up. **GREEN**
test/integration/users_signup_test.rb

```
require 'test_helper'

class UsersSignupTest < ActionDispatch::IntegrationTest
  .
  .
  .
  test "valid signup information" do
    get signup_path
    assert_difference 'User.count', 1 do
      post_via_redirect users_path, user: { name:  "Example User",
                                            email: "user@example.com",
                                            password:              "password",
                                            password_confirmation: "password" }
    end
    assert_template 'users/show'
  end
end
```

Note that Listing 7.26 also verifies that the user show template renders the correct output following successful sign-up. For this test to work, it's necessary for the Users routes (Listing 7.3), the Users `show` action (Listing 7.5), and the `show.html.erb` view (Listing 7.8) to work correctly. As a result, the one line

```
assert_template 'users/show'
```

is a sensitive test for almost everything related to a user's profile page. This sort of end-to-end coverage of important application features illustrates one reason why integration tests are so useful.

7.5 Professional-Grade Deployment

Now that we have a working sign-up page, it's time to deploy our application and get it working in production. Although we started deploying our application in Chapter 3, this is the first time it will actually *do* something, so we'll take this opportunity to make the deployment professional-grade. In particular, we'll add an important feature to the production application to make sign-up secure, and we'll replace the default web server with one suitable for real-world use.

As preparation for the deployment, you should merge your changes into the **master** branch at this point:

```
$ git add -A
$ git commit -m "Finish user sign-up"
$ git checkout master
$ git merge sign-up
```

7.5.1 SSL in Production

When submitting the sign-up form developed in this chapter, the name, email address, and password get sent over the network, which means they are vulnerable to intercept. This is a potentially serious security flaw in our application, and the way to fix it is to use Secure Sockets Layer (SSL)[11] to encrypt all relevant information before it leaves the local browser. Although we could use SSL on just the signup page, it's actually easier to implement it site-wide, which has the additional benefits of securing user login (Chapter 8) and making our application immune to a critical *session hijacking* vulnerability discussed in Section 8.4.

Enabling SSL is as easy as uncommenting a single line in **production.rb**, the configuration file for production applications. As shown in Listing 7.27, all we need to do is set the **config** variable to force the use of SSL in production.

Listing 7.27 Configuring the application to use SSL in production.

config/environments/production.rb

```
Rails.application.configure do
  .
  .
  .
```

---

11. Technically, SSL is now TLS, for Transport Layer Security, but everyone I know still says "SSL."

```
# Force all access to the app over SSL, use Strict-Transport-Security,
# and use secure cookies.
config.force_ssl = true
  .
  .
  .
end
```

At this stage, we need to set up SSL on the remote server. Setting up a production site to use SSL involves purchasing and configuring an *SSL certificate* for your domain. That's a lot of work, though, and luckily we won't need it here. For an application running on a Heroku domain (such as the sample application), we can piggyback on Heroku's SSL certificate. As a result, when we deploy the application in Section 7.5.2, SSL will automatically be enabled. (If you want to run SSL on a custom domain, such as **www.example.com**, refer to Heroku's page on SSL.)

7.5.2 Production Web Server

Having added SSL, we now need to configure our application to use a web server suitable for production applications. By default, Heroku uses a pure-Ruby web server called WEBrick, which is easy to set up and run but isn't good at handling significant traffic. As a result, WEBrick isn't suitable for production use, so we'll replace WEBrick with Puma, an HTTP server that is capable of handling a large number of incoming requests.

To add the new web server, we simply follow the Heroku Puma documentation. The first step is to include the puma gem in our **Gemfile**, as shown in Listing 7.28. Because we don't need the Puma gem locally, Listing 7.28 puts it in the **:production** group.

Listing 7.28 Adding Puma to the **Gemfile**.

```
source 'https://rubygems.org'
  .
  .
  .
group :production do
  gem 'pg',              '0.17.1'
  gem 'rails_12factor', '0.0.2'
  gem 'puma',            '2.11.1'
end
```

Because we configured Bundler not to install production gems (Section 3.1), Listing 7.28 won't add any gems to the development environment, but we still need to run Bundler to update `Gemfile.lock`:

```
$ bundle install
```

The next step is to create a file called `config/puma.rb` and fill it with the contents of Listing 7.29. The code in Listing 7.29 comes straight from the Heroku documentation,[12] and there is no need to understand it.

Listing 7.29 The configuration file for the production web server.
config/puma.rb

```
workers Integer(ENV['WEB_CONCURRENCY'] || 2)
threads_count = Integer(ENV['MAX_THREADS'] || 5)
threads threads_count, threads_count

preload_app!

rackup      DefaultRackup
port        ENV['PORT'] || 3000
environment ENV['RACK_ENV'] || 'development'

on_worker_boot do
  # Worker specific setup for Rails 4.1+
  # See: https://devcenter.heroku.com/articles/
  # deploying-rails-applications-with-the-puma-web-server#on-worker-boot
  ActiveRecord::Base.establish_connection
end
```

Finally, we need to make a so-called `Procfile` to tell Heroku to run a Puma process in production, as shown in Listing 7.30. The `Procfile` should be created in your application's root directory (i.e., in the same location as the `Gemfile`).

Listing 7.30 Defining a `Procfile` for Puma.
./Procfile

```
web: bundle exec puma -C config/puma.rb
```

---

12. Listing 7.29 changes the formatting slightly so that the code fits in the standard 80 columns.

With the production web server configuration completed, we're ready to commit and deploy:[13]

```
$ bundle exec rake test
$ git add -A
$ git commit -m "Use SSL and the Puma web server in production"
$ git push
$ git push heroku
$ heroku run rake db:migrate
```

The sign-up form is now live, and the result of a successful sign-up is shown in Figure 7.24. Note the presence of `https://` and a lock icon in the address bar of Figure 7.24, which indicate that SSL is working.

7.5.3 Ruby Version Number

When deploying to Heroku, you may get a warning message like this one:

```
###### WARNING:
       You have not declared a Ruby version in your Gemfile.
       To set your Ruby version add this line to your Gemfile:
       ruby '2.1.5'
```

Experience shows that, at the level of this tutorial, the costs associated with including such an explicit Ruby version number outweigh the (negligible) benefits, so you should ignore this warning for now. The main issue is that keeping your sample app and system in sync with the latest Ruby version can be a huge inconvenience,[14] and yet it almost never makes a difference which exact Ruby version number you use. Nevertheless, you should bear in mind that, should you ever end up running a mission-critical app on Heroku, specifying an exact Ruby version in the **Gemfile** is recommended to ensure maximum compatibility between development and production environments.

---

13. We haven't changed the data model in this chapter, so running the migration at Heroku shouldn't be necessary, but only if you followed the steps in Section 6.4. Because several readers reported having trouble, I've added **heroku run rake db:migrate** as a final step just to be safe.

14. For example, after spending several hours unsuccessfully trying to install Ruby 2.1.4 on my local machine, I discovered that Ruby 2.1.5 had been released the day before. Attempts to install 2.1.5 also failed.

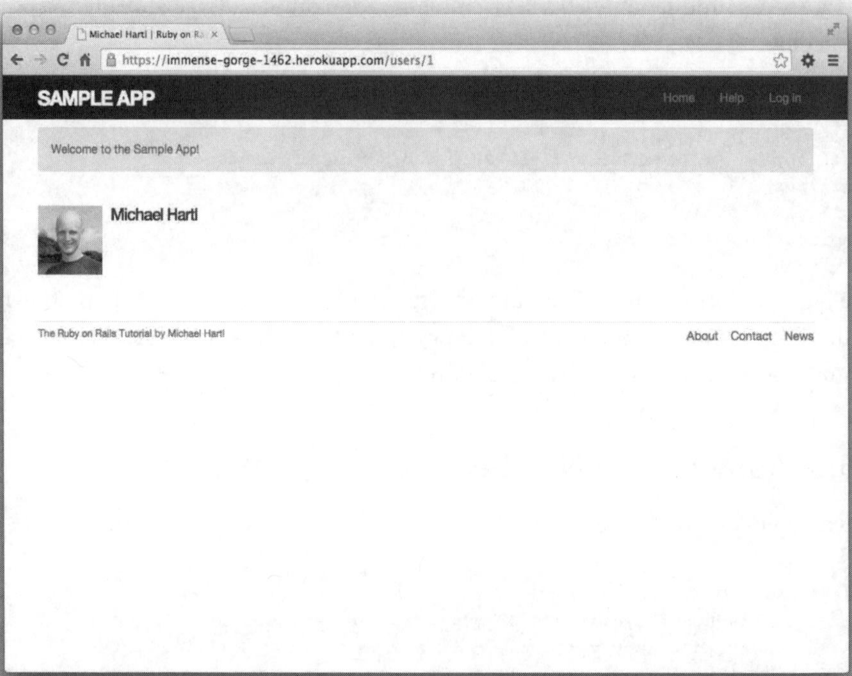

Figure 7.24 Signing up on the live web.

7.6 Conclusion

Being able to sign up users is a major milestone for our application. Although the sample app has yet to accomplish anything useful, we have laid an essential foundation for all future development. In Chapter 8, we will complete our authentication machinery by allowing users to log in and out of the application. In Chapter 9, we will allow all users to update their account information, and we will allow site administrators to delete users, thereby completing the full suite of Users resource REST actions from Table 7.1.

7.6.1 What We Learned in This Chapter

- Rails displays useful debug information via the `debug` method.
- Sass mixins allow a group of CSS rules to be bundled and reused in multiple places.

- Rails comes with three standard environments: `development`, `test`, and `production`.

- We can interact with users as a *resource* through a standard set of REST URLs.

- Gravatars provide a convenient way of displaying images to represent users.

- The `form_for` helper is used to make forms for interacting with Active Record objects.

- Sign-up failure renders the new user page and displays error messages automatically as determined by Active Record.

- Rails provides `flash` as a standard way to display temporary messages.

- Sign-up success creates a user in the database, redirects to the user show page, and displays a welcome message.

- We can use integration tests to verify form submission behavior and catch regressions.

- We can configure our production application to use SSL for secure communications and Puma for high performance.

7.7 Exercises

Note: To receive a copy of the *Solutions Manual for Exercises*, with solutions to every exercise in the *Ruby on Rails™ Tutorial*, visit www.railstutorial.org/<word>, where "<word>" is the last word of the Figure 3.9 caption.

For a suggestion on how to avoid conflicts between exercises and the main tutorial, see the note on exercise topic branches in Section 3.6.

1. Verify that the code in Listing 7.31 allows the `gravatar_for` helper defined in Section 7.1.4 to take an optional `size` parameter, allowing code like `gravatar_for user, size: 50` in the view. (We'll put this improved helper to use in Section 9.3.1.)

2. Write a test for the error messages implemented in Listing 7.18. How detailed you want to make your tests is up to you; a suggested template appears in Listing 7.32.

3. Write a test for the flash implemented in Section 7.4.2. How detailed you want to make your tests is up to you; a suggested ultra-minimalist template appears in

Listing 7.33, which you should complete by replacing **FILL_IN** with the
appropriate code. (Even testing for the right key, much less the text, is likely to be
brittle, so I prefer to test only that the flash isn't **nil**.)

4. As noted in Section 7.4.2, the flash HTML in Listing 7.25 is ugly. Verify by
running the test suite that the cleaner code in Listing 7.34, which uses the Rails
content_tag helper, also works.

Listing 7.31 Adding an options hash in the **gravatar_for** helper.

app/helpers/users_helper.rb

```
module UsersHelper

  # Returns the Gravatar for the given user.
  def gravatar_for(user, options = { size: 80 })
    gravatar_id = Digest::MD5::hexdigest(user.email.downcase)
    size = options[:size]
    gravatar_url = "https://secure.gravatar.com/avatar/#{gravatar_id}?s=#{size}"
    image_tag(gravatar_url, alt: user.name, class: "gravatar")
  end
end
```

Listing 7.32 A template for tests of the error messages.

test/integration/users_signup_test.rb

```
require 'test_helper'

class UsersSignupTest < ActionDispatch::IntegrationTest

  test "invalid signup information" do
    get signup_path
    assert_no_difference 'User.count' do
      post users_path, user: { name:    "",
                               email: "user@invalid",
                               password:               "foo",
                               password_confirmation: "bar" }
    end
    assert_template 'users/new'
    assert_select 'div#<CSS id for error explanation>'
    assert_select 'div.<CSS class for field with error>'
  end
  .
```

> .
> .
> .
```
end
```

___

Listing 7.33   A template for a test of the flash.

test/integration/users_signup_test.rb

___

```ruby
require 'test_helper'
  .
  .
  .
  test "valid signup information" do
    get signup_path
    assert_difference 'User.count', 1 do
      post_via_redirect users_path, user: { name:  "Example User",
                                            email: "user@example.com",
                                            password:              "password",
                                            password_confirmation: "password" }
    end
    assert_template 'users/show'
    assert_not flash.FILL_IN
  end
end
```

___

Listing 7.34   The `flash` ERb in the site layout using `content_tag`.

app/views/layouts/application.html.erb

___

```erb
<!DOCTYPE html>
<html>
    .
    .
    .
    <% flash.each do |message_type, message| %>
      <%= content_tag(:div, message, class: "alert alert-#{message_type}") %>
    <% end %>
    .
    .
    .
</html>
```

___

CHAPTER 8
Log In, Log Out

Now that new users can sign up for our site (Chapter 7), it's time to give them the ability to log in and log out. We'll be implementing all three of the most common models for login/logout behavior on the web: "forgetting" users on browser close (Section 8.1 and Section 8.2), *automatically* remembering users (Section 8.4), and *optionally* remembering users based on the value of a "remember me" check box (Section 8.4.5).[1]

The authentication system we develop in this chapter will allow us to customize the site and implement an authorization model based on login status and identity of the current user. For example, in this chapter we'll update the site header with login/logout links and a profile link. In Chapter 9, we'll impose a security model in which only logged-in users can visit the user index page, only the correct user can access the page for editing his or her own information, and only administrative users can delete other users from the database. Finally, in Chapter 11, we'll use the identity of a logged-in user to create microposts associated with that user, and in Chapter 12, we'll allow the current user to follow other users of the application (thereby receiving a feed of their microposts).

---

1. Another common model is to expire the session after a certain amount of time. This is especially appropriate on sites containing sensitive information, such as banking and financial trading accounts.

8.1 Sessions

HTTP is a *stateless protocol*, treating each request as an independent transaction that is unable to use information from any previous requests. This means there is no way within the Hypertext Transfer Protocol to remember a user's identity from page to page; instead, web applications requiring user login must use a *session*, which is a semi-permanent connection between two computers (such as a client computer running a web browser and a server running Rails).

The most common techniques for implementing sessions in Rails involve using *cookies*, which are small pieces of text placed on the user's browser. Because cookies persist from one page to the next, they can store information (such as a user ID) that can be used by the application to retrieve the logged-in user from the database. In this section and Section 8.2, we'll use the Rails method called `session` to make temporary sessions that expire automatically on browser close,[2] and then in Section 8.4 we'll add longer-lived sessions using another Rails method called `cookies`.

It's convenient to model sessions as a RESTful resource: Visiting the login page will render a form for *new* sessions, logging in will *create* a session, and logging out will *destroy* it. Unlike the Users resource, which uses a database back-end (via the User model) to persist data, the Sessions resource will use cookies, and much of the work involved in login comes from building this cookie-based authentication machinery. In this section and the next, we'll prepare for this work by constructing a Sessions controller, a login form, and the relevant controller actions. We'll then complete user login in Section 8.2 by adding the necessary session-manipulation code.

As in previous chapters, we'll do our work on a topic branch and merge in the changes at the end:

```
$ git checkout master
$ git checkout -b log-in-log-out
```

8.1.1 Sessions Controller

The elements of logging in and out correspond to particular REST actions of the Sessions controller: The login form is handled by the `new` action (covered in this

---

2. Some browsers offer an option to restore such sessions via a "continue where you left off" feature, but Rails has no control over this behavior.

section), actually logging in is handled by sending a POST request to the **create** action (Section 8.2), and logging out is handled by sending a DELETE request to the **destroy** action (Section 8.3). (Recall the association of HTTP verbs with REST actions from Table 7.1.)

To get started, we'll generate a Sessions controller with a **new** action:

```
$ rails generate controller Sessions new
```

(Including **new** generates *views* as well, which is why we don't include actions like **create** and **delete** that don't correspond to views.) Following the model from Section 7.2 for the sign-up page, our plan is to create a login form for creating new sessions, as mocked up in Figure 8.1.

Unlike the Users resource, which used the special **resources** method to obtain a full suite of RESTful routes automatically (Listing 7.3), the Sessions resource will use only named routes, handling GET and POST requests with the **login** route and DELETE requests with the **logout** route. The result appears in Listing 8.1 (which also deletes the unneeded routes generated by **rails generate controller**).

Listing 8.1 Adding a resource to get the standard RESTful actions for sessions.
config/routes.rb

```
Rails.application.routes.draw do
  root                  'static_pages#home'
  get    'help'    => 'static_pages#help'
  get    'about'   => 'static_pages#about'
  get    'contact' => 'static_pages#contact'
  get    'signup'  => 'users#new'
  get    'login'   => 'sessions#new'
  post   'login'   => 'sessions#create'
  delete 'logout'  => 'sessions#destroy'
  resources :users
end
```

The routes defined in Listing 8.1 correspond to URLs and actions similar to those for users (Table 7.1), as shown in Table 8.1.

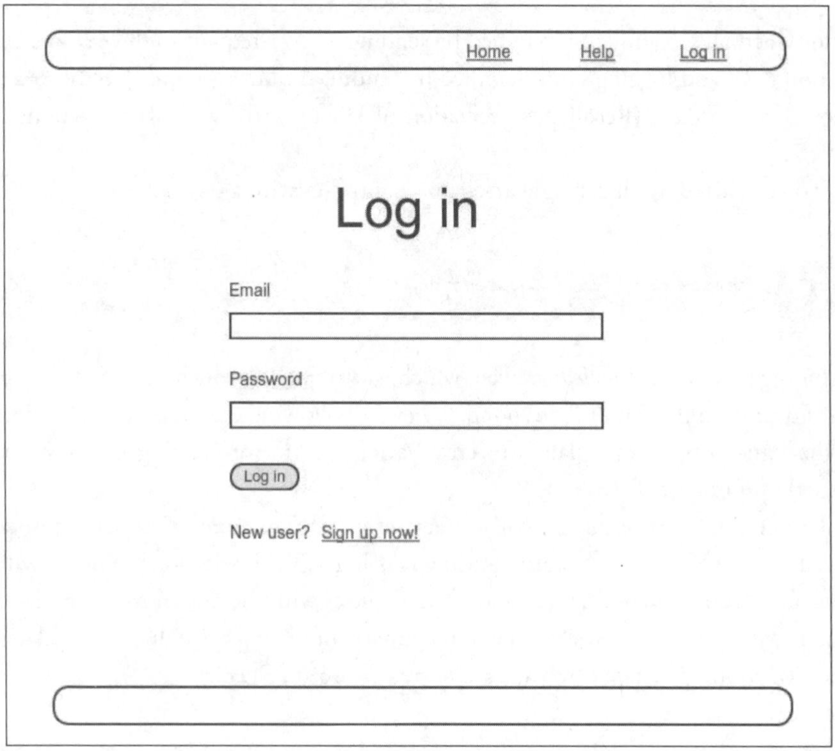

Figure 8.1   A mockup of the login form.

Table 8.1   Routes provided by the sessions rules in Listing 8.1.

HTTP request	URL	Named route	Action	Purpose
GET	/login	`login_path`	`new`	page for a new session (login)
POST	/login	`login_path`	`create`	create a new session (login)
DELETE	/logout	`logout_path`	`destroy`	delete a session (log out)

Since we've now added several custom named routes, it's useful to look at the complete list of the routes for our application, which we can generate using **rake routes**:

```
$ bundle exec rake routes
 Prefix Verb   URI Pattern                Controller#Action
   root GET    /                          static_pages#home
   help GET    /help(.:format)            static_pages#help
```

```
     about GET     /about(.:format)          static_pages#about
   contact GET     /contact(.:format)        static_pages#contact
    signup GET     /signup(.:format)         users#new
     login GET     /login(.:format)          sessions#new
           POST    /login(.:format)          sessions#create
    logout DELETE  /logout(.:format)         sessions#destroy
     users GET     /users(.:format)          users#index
           POST    /users(.:format)          users#create
  new_user GET     /users/new(.:format)      users#new
 edit_user GET     /users/:id/edit(.:format) users#edit
      user GET     /users/:id(.:format)      users#show
           PATCH   /users/:id(.:format)      users#update
           PUT     /users/:id(.:format)      users#update
           DELETE  /users/:id(.:format)      users#destroy
```

It's not necessary to understand these results in detail, but viewing the routes in this manner gives us a high-level overview of the actions supported by our application.

8.1.2 Login Form

Having defined the relevant controller and route, now we'll fill in the view for new sessions—that is, the login form. Comparing Figure 8.1 with Figure 7.11, we see that the login form is similar in appearance to the sign-up form, except with two fields (email and password) in place of four.

As seen in Figure 8.2, when the login information is invalid we want to re-render the login page and display an error message. In Section 7.3.3, we used an error-messages partial to display error messages, but we saw in that section that those messages are provided automatically by Active Record. This approach won't work for session creation errors because the session isn't an Active Record object, so we'll render the error as a flash message instead.

Recall from Listing 7.13 that the sign-up form uses the `form_for` helper, taking as an argument the user instance variable `@user`:

```erb
<%= form_for(@user) do |f| %>
  .
  .
  .
<% end %>
```

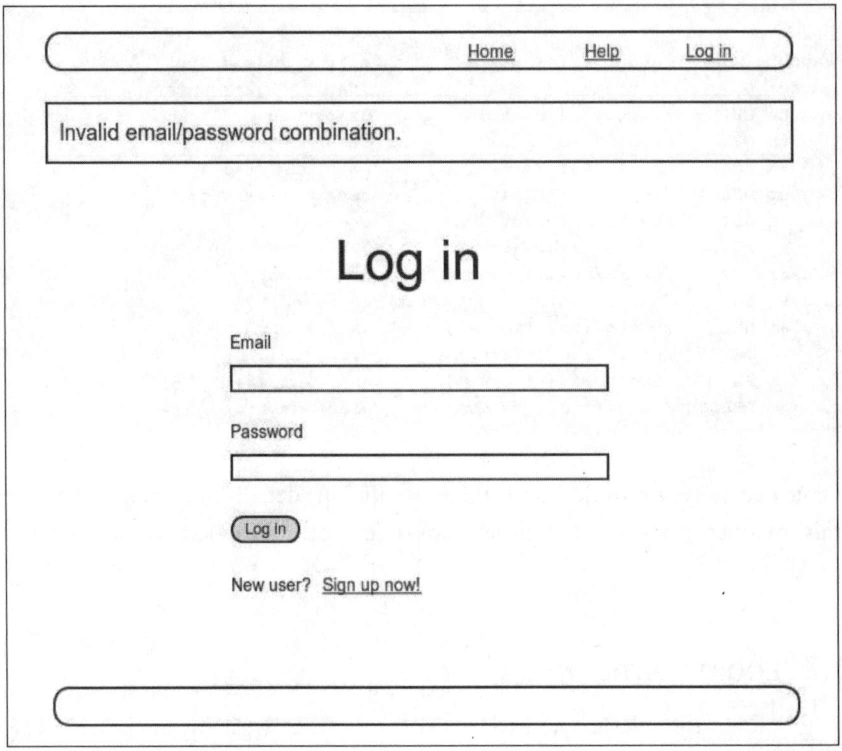

Figure 8.2 A mockup of login failure.

The main difference between the session form and the sign-up form is that we have no Session model, and hence no analogue for the `@user` variable. This means that, in constructing the new session form, we have to give `form_for` slightly more information. In particular, whereas

```
form_for(@user)
```

allows Rails to infer that the `action` of the form should be to POST to the URL /users, in the case of sessions we need to indicate the *name* of the resource and the corresponding URL:[3]

---

[3]. A second option is to use `form_tag` in place of `form_for`, which might be even more idiomatically correct Rails. It has less in common with the sign-up form, however, and at this stage I want to emphasize the parallel structure.

```
form_for(:session, url: login_path)
```

With the proper **form_for** in hand, it's easy to make a login form to match the mockup in Figure 8.1 using the sign-up form (Listing 7.13) as a model, as shown in Listing 8.2.

Listing 8.2 Code for the login form.
app/views/sessions/new.html.erb

```erb
<% provide(:title, "Log in") %>
<h1>Log in</h1>

<div class="row">
  <div class="col-md-6 col-md-offset-3">
    <%= form_for(:session, url: login_path) do |f| %>

      <%= f.label :email %>
      <%= f.email_field :email, class: 'form-control' %>

      <%= f.label :password %>
      <%= f.password_field :password, class: 'form-control' %>

      <%= f.submit "Log in", class: "btn btn-primary" %>
    <% end %>

    <p>New user? <%= link_to "Sign up now!", signup_path %></p>
  </div>
</div>
```

Note that we've added a link to the sign-up page for convenience. With the code in Listing 8.2, the login form appears as in Figure 8.3. (Because the "Log in" navigation link hasn't yet been filled in, you'll have to type the /login URL directly into your address bar. We'll fix this blemish in Section 8.2.3.)

The generated form HTML appears in Listing 8.3.

Listing 8.3 HTML for the login form produced by Listing 8.2.

```html
<form accept-charset="UTF-8" action="/login" method="post">
  <input name="utf8" type="hidden" value="&#x2713;" />
  <input name="authenticity_token" type="hidden"
         value="NNb6+J/j46LcrgYUC60wQ2titMuJQ5lLqyAbnbAUkdo=" />
```

```
<label for="session_email">Email</label>
<input class="form-control" id="session_email"
       name="session[email]" type="text" />
<label for="session_password">Password</label>
<input id="session_password" name="session[password]"
       type="password" />
<input class="btn btn-primary" name="commit" type="submit"
      value="Log in" />
</form>
```

Comparing Listing 8.3 with Listing 7.15, you might be able to guess that submitting this form will result in a `params` hash, where `params[:session][:email]` and `params[:session][:password]` correspond to the email and password fields.

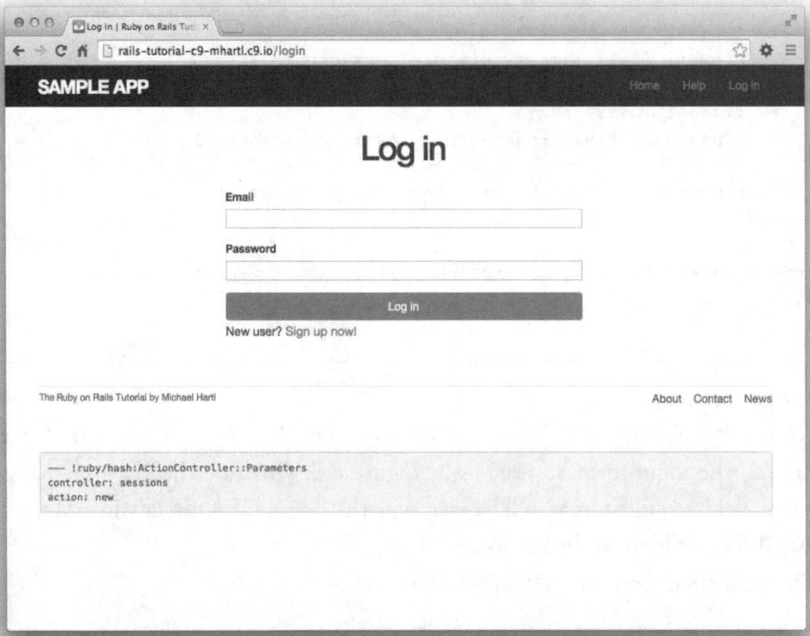

Figure 8.3 The login form.

8.1.3 Finding and Authenticating a User

As in the case of creating users (signing up), the first step in creating sessions (logging in) is to handle *invalid* input. We'll start by reviewing what happens when a form gets submitted, and then arrange for helpful error messages to appear in the case of login failure (as mocked up in Figure 8.2.) Then we'll lay the foundation for successful login (Section 8.2) by evaluating each login submission based on the validity of its email/password combination.

Let's start by defining a minimalist **create** action for the Sessions controller, along with empty **new** and **destroy** actions (Listing 8.4). The **create** action in Listing 8.4 does nothing but render the **new** view, but it's enough to get us started. Submitting the /sessions/new form then yields the result shown in Figure 8.4.

Listing 8.4 A preliminary version of the Sessions **create** action.
`app/controllers/sessions_controller.rb`

```ruby
class SessionsController < ApplicationController

  def new
  end

  def create
    render 'new'
  end

  def destroy
  end
end
```

Carefully inspecting the debug information in Figure 8.4 shows that, as hinted at the end of Section 8.1.2, the submission results in a **params** hash containing the email and password under the key **session**, which (omitting some irrelevant details used internally by Rails) appears as follows:

```yaml
---
session:
  email: 'user@example.com'
  password: 'foobar'
```

```
commit: Log in
action: create
controller: sessions
```

As with the case of user sign-up (Figure 7.15), these parameters form a *nested* hash like the one we saw in Listing 4.10. In particular, `params` contains a nested hash of the form

```
{ session: { password: "foobar", email: "user@example.com" } }
```

This means that

```
params[:session]
```

is itself a hash:

```
{ password: "foobar", email: "user@example.com" }
```

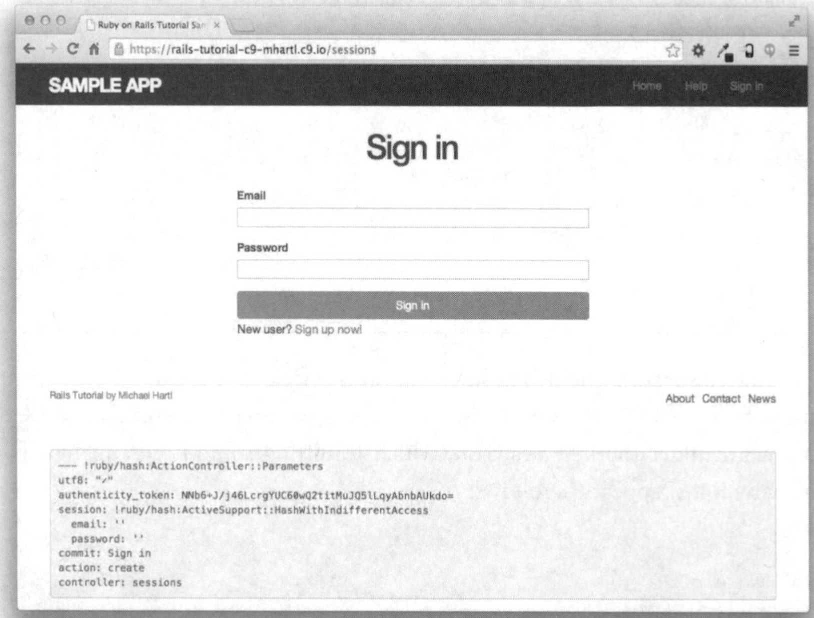

Figure 8.4 The initial failed login, with `create` as in Listing 8.4.

As a result,

```
params[:session][:email]
```

is the submitted email address and

```
params[:session][:password]
```

is the submitted password.

In other words, inside the **create** action the **params** hash has all the information needed to authenticate users by email and password. Not coincidentally, we already have exactly the methods we need: the **User.find_by** method provided by Active Record (Section 6.1.4) and the **authenticate** method provided by **has_secure_password** (Section 6.3.4). Recalling that **authenticate** returns **false** for an invalid authentication (Section 6.3.4), our strategy for user login can be summarized as shown in Listing 8.5.

Listing 8.5 Finding and authenticating a user.
app/controllers/sessions_controller.rb

```ruby
class SessionsController < ApplicationController

  def new
  end

  def create
    user = User.find_by(email: params[:session][:email].downcase)
    if user && user.authenticate(params[:session][:password])
      # Log the user in and redirect to the user's show page.
    else
      # Create an error message.
      render 'new'
    end
  end

  def destroy
  end
end
```

The first highlighted line in Listing 8.5 pulls the user out of the database using the submitted email address. (Recall from Section 6.2.5 that email addresses are saved as all

Table 8.2 Possible results of `user && user.authenticate(...)`.

User	Password	a && b
nonexistent	*anything*	`(nil && [anything]) == false`
valid user	wrong password	`(true && false) == false`
valid user	right password	`(true && true) == true`

lowercase, so here we use the `downcase` method to ensure a match when the submitted address is valid.) The next line can be a bit confusing but is fairly common in idiomatic Rails programming:

```
user && user.authenticate(params[:session][:password])
```

This uses `&&` (logical *and*) to determine if the resulting user is valid. Taking into account that any object other than `nil` and `false` itself is `true` in a boolean context (Section 4.2.3), the possibilities appear as in Table 8.2. We see from Table 8.2 that the `if` statement is `true` only if a user with the given email both exists in the database and has the given password, exactly as required.

8.1.4 Rendering with a Flash Message

Recall from Section 7.3.3 that we displayed sign-up errors using the User model error messages. These errors are associated with a particular Active Record object, but this strategy won't work here because the session isn't an Active Record model. Instead, we'll put a message in the flash to be displayed upon failed login. A first, slightly incorrect, attempt appears in Listing 8.6.

Listing 8.6 An (unsuccessful) attempt at handling failed login.
app/controllers/sessions_controller.rb

```
class SessionsController < ApplicationController

  def new
  end

  def create
    user = User.find_by(email: params[:session][:email].downcase)
```

```
  if user && user.authenticate(params[:session][:password])
    # Log the user in and redirect to the user's show page.
  else
    flash[:danger] = 'Invalid email/password combination' # Not quite right!
    render 'new'
  end
 end

 def destroy
 end
end
```

Because of the flash message display in the site layout (Listing 7.25), the `flash-[:danger]` message automatically gets displayed; because of the Bootstrap CSS, it automatically gets nice styling (Figure 8.5).

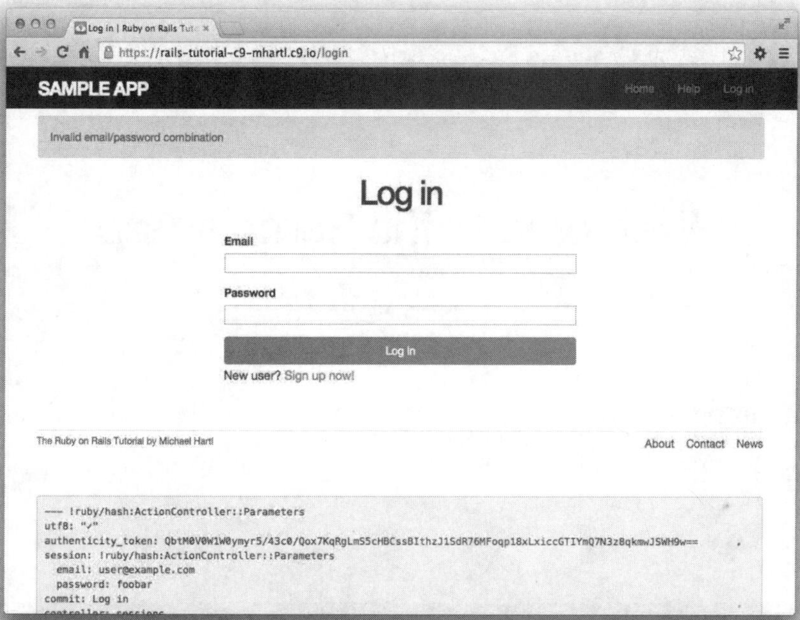

Figure 8.5 The flash message for a failed login.

Unfortunately, as noted in the text and in the comment in Listing 8.6, this code isn't quite right. The page looks fine, though, so what's the problem? The issue is that the contents of the flash persist for one *request*, but—unlike a redirect, which we used in Listing 7.24—re-rendering a template with `render` doesn't count as a request. As a consequence, the flash message persists one request longer than we want. For example, if we submit invalid login information and then click on the Home page, the flash gets displayed a second time (Figure 8.6). Fixing this blemish is the task of Section 8.1.5.

8.1.5 A Flash Test

The incorrect flash behavior is a minor bug in our application. According to the testing guidelines from Box 3.3, this is exactly the sort of situation where we should write a test to catch the error so that it doesn't recur. Thus we'll write a short integration test for

Figure 8.6 An example of flash persistence.

the login form submission before proceeding. In addition to documenting the bug and preventing a regression, this will give us a good foundation for further integration tests of login and logout.

We start by generating an integration test for our application's login behavior:

```
$ rails generate integration_test users_login
      invoke  test_unit
      create    test/integration/users_login_test.rb
```

Next, we need a test to capture the sequence shown in Figure 8.5 and Figure 8.6. The basic steps appear as follows:

1. Visit the login path.
2. Verify that the new sessions form renders properly.
3. Post to the sessions path with an invalid **params** hash.
4. Verify that the new sessions form gets re-rendered and that a flash message appears.
5. Visit another page (such as the Home page).
6. Verify that the flash message *doesn't* appear on the new page.

A test implementing these steps appears in Listing 8.7.

Listing 8.7 A test to catch unwanted flash persistence. **RED**
test/integration/users_login_test.rb

```
require 'test_helper'

class UsersLoginTest < ActionDispatch::IntegrationTest

  test "login with invalid information" do
    get login_path
    assert_template 'sessions/new'
    post login_path, session: { email: "", password: "" }
    assert_template 'sessions/new'
    assert_not flash.empty?
    get root_path
    assert flash.empty?
  end
end
```

After adding the test in Listing 8.7, the login test should be **RED**:

Listing 8.8 RED

```
$ bundle exec rake test TEST=test/integration/users_login_test.rb
```

This shows how to run one (and only one) test file using the argument **TEST** and the full path to the file.

The way to get the failing test in Listing 8.7 to pass is to replace **flash** with the special variant **flash.now**, which is specifically designed for displaying flash messages on rendered pages. Unlike the contents of **flash**, the contents of **flash.now** disappear when an additional request is made, which is exactly the behavior we've tested in Listing 8.7. With this substitution, the corrected application code appears as in Listing 8.9.

Listing 8.9 Correct code for failed login. **GREEN**
app/controllers/sessions_controller.rb

```
class SessionsController < ApplicationController

  def new
  end

  def create
    user = User.find_by(email: params[:session][:email].downcase)
    if user && user.authenticate(params[:session][:password])
      # Log the user in and redirect to the user's show page.
    else
      flash.now[:danger] = 'Invalid email/password combination'
      render 'new'
    end
  end

  def destroy
  end
end
```

We can then verify that both the login integration test and the full test suite are **GREEN**:

Listing 8.10 GREEN

```
$ bundle exec rake test TEST=test/integration/users_login_test.rb
$ bundle exec rake test
```

8.2 Logging In

Now that our login form can handle invalid submissions, the next step is to handle valid submissions correctly by actually logging a user in. In this section, we'll log the user in with a temporary session cookie that expires automatically upon browser close. In Section 8.4, we'll add sessions that persist even after closing the browser.

Implementing sessions will involve defining a large number of related functions for use across multiple controllers and views. Recall from Section 4.2.5 that Ruby provides a *module* facility for packaging such functions in one place. Conveniently, a Sessions helper module is generated automatically when generating the Sessions controller (Section 8.1.1). Moreover, such helpers are automatically included in Rails views; by including the module into the base class of all controllers (the Application controller), we arrange to make them available in our controllers as well (Listing 8.11).

Listing 8.11 Including the Sessions helper module into the Application controller.
app/controllers/application_controller.rb

```
class ApplicationController < ActionController::Base
  protect_from_forgery with: :exception
  include SessionsHelper
end
```

With this configuration complete, we're now ready to write the code to log users in.

8.2.1 The `log_in` Method

Logging a user in is a simple matter with the help of the **session** method defined by Rails. (This method is separate and distinct from the Sessions controller generated in Section 8.1.1.) We can treat **session** as if it were a hash, and assign to it as follows:

```
session[:user_id] = user.id
```

This places a temporary cookie on the user's browser containing an encrypted version of the user's ID, which allows us to retrieve the ID on subsequent pages using **session[:user_id]**. In contrast to the persistent cookie created by the **cookies** method (Section 8.4), the temporary cookie created by the **session** method expires immediately when the browser is closed.

Because we'll want to use the same login technique in several different places, we'll define a method called **log_in** in the Sessions helper, as shown in Listing 8.12.

Listing 8.12 The **log_in** function.
app/helpers/sessions_helper.rb

```
module SessionsHelper

  # Logs in the given user.
  def log_in(user)
    session[:user_id] = user.id
  end
end
```

Because temporary cookies created using the **session** method are automatically encrypted, the code in Listing 8.12 is secure, and there is no way for an attacker to use the session information to log in as the user. This applies only to temporary sessions initiated with the **session** method, though, and is *not* the case for persistent sessions created using the **cookies** method. Permanent cookies are vulnerable to a *session hijacking* attack, so in Section 8.4 we'll have to be much more careful about the information we place on the user's browser.

With the **log_in** method defined in Listing 8.12, we're now ready to complete the session **create** action by logging the user in and redirecting to the user's profile page. The result appears in Listing 8.13.[4]

Listing 8.13 Logging in a user.
app/controllers/sessions_controller.rb

```
class SessionsController < ApplicationController

  def new
  end

  def create
    user = User.find_by(email: params[:session][:email].downcase)
    if user && user.authenticate(params[:session][:password])
```

_____

4. The **log_in** method is available in the Sessions controller because of the module inclusion in Listing 8.11.

```
      log_in user
      redirect_to user
    else
      flash.now[:danger] = 'Invalid email/password combination'
      render 'new'
    end
  end

  def destroy
  end
end
```

Note the compact redirect

```
redirect_to user
```

which we saw earlier, in Section 7.4.1. Rails automatically converts this to the route for the user's profile page:

```
user_url(user)
```

With the `create` action defined in Listing 8.13, the login form defined in Listing 8.2 should now be working. It doesn't have any effects on the application display, though, so short of inspecting the browser session directly there's no way to tell that you're logged in. As a first step toward enabling more visible changes, in Section 8.2.2 we'll retrieve the current user from the database using the ID in the session. In Section 8.2.3, we'll change the links on the application layout, including a URL to the current user's profile.

8.2.2 Current User

Having placed the user's ID securely in the temporary session, we are now in a position to retrieve it on subsequent pages, which we'll do by defining a `current_user` method to find the user in the database corresponding to the session ID. The purpose of `current_user` is to allow constructions such as

```
<%= current_user.name %>
```

and

```
redirect_to current_user
```

To find the current user, one possibility is to use the **find** method, as on the user profile page (Listing 7.5):

```
User.find(session[:user_id])
```

But recall from Section 6.1.4 that **find** raises an exception if the user ID doesn't exist. This behavior is appropriate on the user profile page because it will happen only if the ID is invalid, but in the present case **session[:user_id]** will often be **nil** (i.e., for non-logged-in users). To handle this possibility, we'll use the same **find_by** method used to find users by email address in the **create** method, with **id** in place of **email**:

```
User.find_by(id: session[:user_id])
```

Rather than raising an exception, this method returns **nil** (indicating no such user) if the ID is invalid.

We could now define the **current_user** method as follows:

```
def current_user
  User.find_by(id: session[:user_id])
end
```

This approach would work, but it would hit the database multiple times if, for example, **current_user** appeared multiple times on a page. Instead, we'll follow a common Ruby convention by storing the result of **User.find_by** in an instance variable, which hits the database the first time but returns the instance variable immediately on subsequent invocations:[5]

```
if @current_user.nil?
  @current_user = User.find_by(id: session[:user_id])
else
  @current_user
end
```

---

5. This practice of remembering variable assignments from one method invocation to the next is known as *memoization*. (Note that this is a technical term; in particular, it's *not* a misspelling of "memorization.")

Recalling the *or* operator || seen in Section 4.2.3, we can rewrite this as follows:

```
@current_user = @current_user || User.find_by(id: session[:user_id])
```

Because a User object is true in a boolean context, the call to **find_by** gets executed only if **@current_user** hasn't yet been assigned.

Although the preceding code would work, it's not idiomatically correct Ruby. Instead, the proper way to write the assignment to **@current_user** is like this:

```
@current_user ||= User.find_by(id: session[:user_id])
```

This uses the potentially confusing but frequently used ||= ("or equals") operator (Box 8.1).

Box 8.1 What the *$@! Is ||= ?

The ||= ("or equals") assignment operator is a common Ruby idiom and, therefore, is important for aspiring Rails developers to recognize. Although at first it may seem mysterious, *or equals* is easy to understand by analogy.

We start by noting the common pattern of incrementing a variable:

```
x = x + 1
```

Many languages provide a syntactic shortcut for this operation. In Ruby (and in C, C++, Perl, Python, Java, and some other languages), it can also appear as follows:

```
x += 1
```

Analogous constructs exist for other operators as well:

```
$ rails console
>> x = 1
=> 1
>> x += 1
=> 2
>> x *= 3
=> 6
```

```
>> x -= 8
=> -2
>> x /= 2
=> -1
```

In each case, the pattern is that x = x O y and x O= y are equivalent for any operator O.

Another common Ruby pattern is assigning to a variable if it's nil but otherwise leaving it alone. Recalling the *or* operator || seen in Section 4.2.3, we can write this as follows:

```
>> @foo
=> nil
>> @foo = @foo || "bar"
=> "bar"
>> @foo = @foo || "baz"
=> "bar"
```

Since nil is false in a boolean context, the first assignment to @foo is nil || "bar", which evaluates to "bar". Similarly, the second assignment is @foo || "baz"—that is, "bar" || "baz", which also evaluates to "bar". This outcome occurs because anything other than nil or false is true in a boolean context, and the series of || expressions terminates after the first true expression is evaluated. (This practice of evaluating || expressions from left to right and stopping on the first true value is known as *short-circuit evaluation*. The same principle applies to && statements, except in this case evaluation stops on the first *false* value.)

Comparing the console sessions for the various operators, we see that @foo = @foo || "bar" follows the x = x O y pattern with || in the place of O:

```
x    =   x   +   1       ->    x       +=    1
x    =   x   *   3       ->    x       *=    3
x    =   x   -   8       ->    x       -=    8
x    =   x   /   2       ->    x       /=    2
@foo = @foo || "bar"     ->    @foo   ||=  "bar"
```

Thus @foo = @foo || "bar" and @foo ||= "bar" are equivalent. In the context of the current user, this suggests the following construction:

```
@current_user ||= User.find_by(id: session[:user_id])
```

Voilà!

Applying the results of this discussion yields the succinct `current_user` method shown in Listing 8.14.

Listing 8.14 Finding the current user in the session.
app/helpers/sessions_helper.rb

```ruby
module SessionsHelper

  # Logs in the given user.
  def log_in(user)
    session[:user_id] = user.id
  end

  # Returns the current logged-in user (if any).
  def current_user
    @current_user ||= User.find_by(id: session[:user_id])
  end
end
```

With the working `current_user` method in Listing 8.14, we're now in a position to make changes to our application based on user login status.

8.2.3 Changing the Layout Links

The first practical application of logging in involves changing the layout links based on login status. In particular, as seen in the Figure 8.7 mockup,[6] we'll add links for logging out, for user settings, for listing all users, and for the current user's profile page. Note in Figure 8.7 that the logout and profile links appear in a drop-down "Account" menu; we'll see in Listing 8.16 how to make such a menu with Bootstrap.

At this point, in real life I would consider writing an integration test to capture the behavior described here. As noted in Box 3.3, as you become more familiar with the testing tools in Rails, you may find yourself more inclined to write tests first. In this case, though, such a test involves several new ideas, so for now it's best deferred to its own section (Section 8.2.4).

---

6. Image from http://www.flickr.com/photos/hermanusbackpackers/3343254977/.

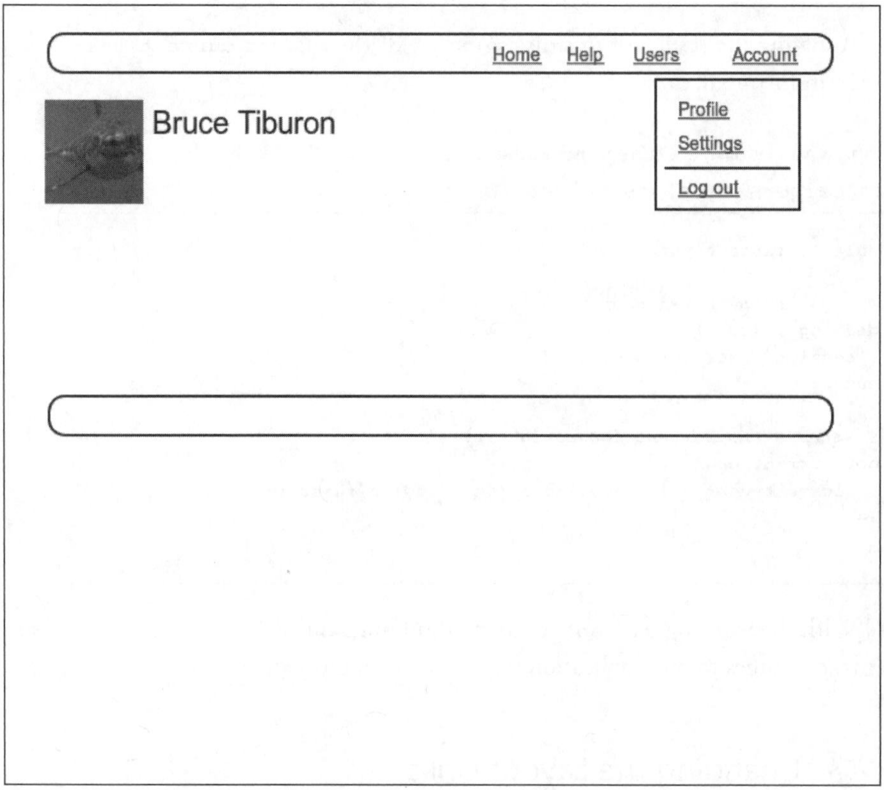

Figure 8.7 A mockup of the user profile after a successful login.

The way to change the links in the site layout involves using an `if-else` statement inside embedded Ruby to show one set of links if the user is logged in and another set of links otherwise:

```
<% if logged_in? %>
  # Links for logged-in users
<% else %>
  # Links for non-logged-in-users
<% end %>
```

This kind of code requires the existence of a `logged_in?` boolean method, which we'll now define.

A user is logged in if there is a current user in the session, i.e., if `current_user` is not `nil`. Checking for this requires the use of the "not" operator (Section 4.2.3), written using an exclamation point ! and usually read as "bang." The resulting `logged_in?` method appears in Listing 8.15.

Listing 8.15 The `logged_in?` helper method.
app/helpers/sessions_helper.rb

```ruby
module SessionsHelper

  # Logs in the given user.
  def log_in(user)
    session[:user_id] = user.id
  end

  # Returns the current logged-in user (if any).
  def current_user
    @current_user ||= User.find_by(id: session[:user_id])
  end

  # Returns true if the user is logged in, false otherwise.
  def logged_in?
    !current_user.nil?
  end
end
```

With addition in Listing 8.15, we're now ready to change the layout links if a user is logged in. There are four new links, two of which are stubbed out (to be completed in Chapter 9):

```erb
<%= link_to "Users",    "#" %>
<%= link_to "Settings", "#" %>
```

The logout link, meanwhile, uses the logout path defined in Listing 8.1:

```erb
<%= link_to "Log out", logout_path, method: :delete %>
```

Notice that the logout link passes a hash argument indicating that it should submit an HTTP DELETE request.[7] We'll also add a profile link as follows:

```erb
<%= link_to "Profile", current_user %>
```

---

7. Web browsers can't actually issue DELETE requests; Rails fakes it with JavaScript.

Here we could write

```
<%= link_to "Profile", user_path(current_user) %>
```

but as usual Rails allows us to link directly to the user by automatically converting `current_user` into `user_path(current_user)` in this context. Finally, when users *aren't* logged in, we'll use the login path defined in Listing 8.1 to make a link to the login form:

```
<%= link_to "Log in", login_path %>
```

Putting everything together gives the updated header partial shown in Listing 8.16.

Listing 8.16   Changing the layout links for logged-in users.
app/views/layouts/_header.html.erb

```erb
<header class="navbar navbar-fixed-top navbar-inverse">
  <div class="container">
    <%= link_to "sample app", root_path, id: "logo" %>
    <nav>
      <ul class="nav navbar-nav navbar-right">
        <li><%= link_to "Home", root_path %></li>
        <li><%= link_to "Help", help_path %></li>
        <% if logged_in? %>
          <li><%= link_to "Users", "#" %></li>
          <li class="dropdown">
            <a href="#" class="dropdown-toggle" data-toggle="dropdown">
              Account <b class="caret"></b>
            </a>
            <ul class="dropdown-menu">
              <li><%= link_to "Profile", current_user %></li>
              <li><%= link_to "Settings", "#" %></li>
              <li class="divider"></li>
              <li>
                <%= link_to "Log out", logout_path, method: "delete" %>
              </li>
            </ul>
          </li>
        <% else %>
          <li><%= link_to "Log in", login_path %></li>
        <% end %>
      </ul>
    </nav>
  </div>
</header>
```

As part of including the new links in the layout, Listing 8.16 takes advantage of Bootstrap's ability to make drop-down menus.[8] Note in particular the inclusion of the special Bootstrap CSS classes such as **dropdown**, **dropdown-menu**, and so on. To activate the drop-down menu, we need to include Bootstrap's custom JavaScript library in the Rails asset pipeline's **application.js** file, as shown in Listing 8.17.

Listing 8.17 Adding the Bootstrap JavaScript library to **application.js**.
app/assets/javascripts/application.js

```
//= require jquery
//= require jquery_ujs
//= require bootstrap
//= require turbolinks
//= require_tree .
```

At this point, you should visit the login path and log in as a valid user, which effectively tests the code in the previous three sections.[9] With the code in Listing 8.16 and Listing 8.17, you should see the drop-down menu and links for logged-in users, as shown in Figure 8.8. If you quit your browser completely, you should be able to verify that the application forgets your login status, requiring you to log in again to see the changes described previously.

8.2.4 Testing Layout Changes

Having verified by hand that the application is behaving properly upon successful login, before moving on we'll write an integration test to capture that behavior and catch regressions. We'll build on the test from Listing 8.7 and write a series of steps to verify the following sequence of actions:

1. Visit the login path.
2. Post valid information to the sessions path.
3. Verify that the login link disappears.

---

8. See the Bootstrap components page for more information.

9. If you're using the cloud IDE, I recommend using a different browser to test the login behavior so that you don't have to close down the browser running the IDE.

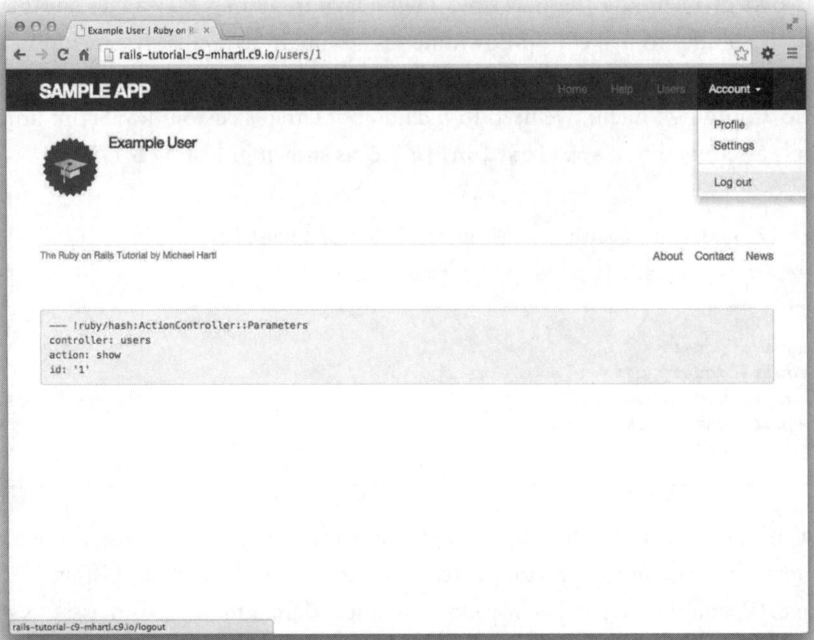

Figure 8.8 A logged-in user with new links and a drop-down menu.

4. Verify that a logout link appears
5. Verify that a profile link appears.

To see these changes, our test needs to log in as a previously registered user, which means that such a user must already exist in the database. The default Rails way to do this is to use *fixtures*, which are a way of organizing data to be loaded into the test database. We discovered in Section 6.2.5 that we needed to delete the default fixtures so that our email uniqueness tests would pass (Listing 6.30). Now we're ready to start filling in that empty file with custom fixtures of our own.

In the present case, we need only one user, whose information should consist of a valid name and email address. Because we'll need to log the user in, we also have to include a valid password to compare with the password submitted to the Sessions controller's `create` action. Referring to the data model in Figure 6.8, we see that this means creating a **password_digest** attribute for the user fixture, which we'll accomplish by defining a **digest** method of our own.

As discussed in Section 6.3.1, the password digest is created using bcrypt (via **has_secure_password**), so we'll need to create the fixture password using the same method. By inspecting the secure password source code, we find that this method is

```
BCrypt::Password.create(string, cost: cost)
```

where **string** is the string to be hashed and **cost** is the *cost parameter* that determines the computational cost to calculate the hash. Using a high cost makes it computationally intractable to use the hash to determine the original password, which is an important security precaution in a production environment, but in tests we want the **digest** method to be as fast as possible. The secure password source code has a line for this as well:

```
cost = ActiveModel::SecurePassword.min_cost ? BCrypt::Engine::MIN_COST :
                                               BCrypt::Engine.cost
```

This rather obscure code, which you don't need to understand in detail, arranges for precisely the behavior described previously: It uses the minimum cost parameter in tests and a normal (high) cost parameter in production. (We'll learn more about the strange **?-:** notation in Section 8.4.5.)

We could put the resulting **digest** method in any of several, but we'll have an opportunity in Section 8.4.1 to reuse **digest** in the User model. This suggests placing the method in **user.rb**. Because we won't necessarily have access to a user object when calculating the digest (as will be the case in the fixtures file), we'll attach the **digest** method to the User class itself, which (as we saw briefly in Section 4.4.1) makes it a *class method*. The result appears in Listing 8.18.

Listing 8.18   Adding a digest method for use in fixtures.
app/models/user.rb

```
class User < ActiveRecord::Base
  before_save { self.email = email.downcase }
  validates :name,  presence: true, length: { maximum: 50 }
  VALID_EMAIL_REGEX = /\A[\w+\-.]+@[a-z\d\-.]+\.[a-z]+\z/i
  validates :email, presence: true, length: { maximum: 255 },
```

```
                   format: { with: VALID_EMAIL_REGEX },
                   uniqueness: { case_sensitive: false }
  has_secure_password
  validates :password, length: { minimum: 6 }

  # Returns the hash digest of the given string.
  def User.digest(string)
    cost = ActiveModel::SecurePassword.min_cost ? BCrypt::Engine::MIN_COST :
                                                  BCrypt::Engine.cost
    BCrypt::Password.create(string, cost: cost)
  end
end
```

With the `digest` method from Listing 8.18, we are now ready to create a user
fixture for a valid user, as shown in Listing 8.19.

Listing 8.19   A fixture for testing user login.
test/fixtures/users.yml

```
michael:
  name: Michael Example
  email: michael@example.com
  password_digest: <%= User.digest('password') %>
```

Note in particular that fixtures support embedded Ruby, which allows us to use

```
<%= User.digest('password') %>
```

to create the valid password digest for the test user.

Although we've defined the `password_digest` attribute required by `has_`
`secure_password`, sometimes it's convenient to refer to the plain (virtual) password
as well. Unfortunately, this is impossible to arrange with fixtures, and adding a `pass-`
`word` attribute to Listing 8.19 causes Rails to complain that no such column exists in
the database (which is true). We'll make do by adopting the convention that all fixture
users have the same password (`'password'`).

Having created a fixture with a valid user, we can retrieve it inside a test as follows:

```
user = users(:michael)
```

Here `users` corresponds to the fixture filename `users.yml`, while the symbol
`:michael` references the user with the key shown in Listing 8.19.

With the fixture user established, we can now write a test for the layout links by converting the sequence enumerated at the beginning of this section into code, as shown in Listing 8.20.

Listing 8.20 A test for user logging in with valid information. **GREEN**
test/integration/users_login_test.rb

```
require 'test_helper'

class UsersLoginTest < ActionDispatch::IntegrationTest

  def setup
    @user = users(:michael)
  end
  .
  .
  .
  test "login with valid information" do
    get login_path
    post login_path, session: { email: @user.email, password: 'password' }
    assert_redirected_to @user
    follow_redirect!
    assert_template 'users/show'
    assert_select "a[href=?]", login_path, count: 0
    assert_select "a[href=?]", logout_path
    assert_select "a[href=?]", user_path(@user)
  end
end
```

Here we've used

```
assert_redirected_to @user
```

to check for the correct redirect target and

```
follow_redirect!
```

to actually visit the target page. Listing 8.20 also verifies that the login link disappears by verifying that there are *zero* login path links on the page:

```
assert_select "a[href=?]", login_path, count: 0
```

By including the extra `count: 0` option, we tell `assert_select` that we expect there to be zero links matching the given pattern. (Compare this to `count: 2` in Listing 5.25, which checks for exactly two matching links.)

Because the application code was already working, this test should be **GREEN**:

Listing 8.21 GREEN

```
$ bundle exec rake test TEST=test/integration/users_login_test.rb \
>                       TESTOPTS="--name test_login_with_valid_information"
```

This shows how to run a specific test within a test file by passing the option

```
TESTOPTS="--name test_login_with_valid_information"
```

containing the name of the test. (A test's name is just the word "test" and the words in the test description joined using underscores.)

8.2.5 Login upon Sign-up

Although our authentication system is now working, newly registered users might be confused, as they are not logged in by default. Because it would be strange to force users to log in immediately after signing up, we'll log in new users automatically as part of the sign-up process. To arrange this behavior, all we need to do is add a call to `log_in` in the Users controller `create` action, as shown in Listing 8.22.[10]

Listing 8.22 Logging in the user upon sign-up.
app/controllers/users_controller.rb

```
class UsersController < ApplicationController

  def show
    @user = User.find(params[:id])
  end

  def new
    @user = User.new
  end
```

---

10. As with the Sessions controller, the `log_in` method is available in the Users controller because of the module inclusion in Listing 8.11.

```
  def create
    @user = User.new(user_params)
    if @user.save
      log_in @user
      flash[:success] = "Welcome to the Sample App!"
      redirect_to @user
    else
      render 'new'
    end
  end

  private

    def user_params
      params.require(:user).permit(:name, :email, :password,
                                   :password_confirmation)
    end
end
```

To test the behavior from Listing 8.22, we can add a line to the test from Listing 7.26 to check that the user is logged in. It's helpful in this context to define an
is_logged_in? helper method to parallel the **logged_in?** helper defined in Listing 8.15, which returns **true** if there's a user ID in the (test) session and false otherwise
(Listing 8.23). (Because helper methods aren't available in tests, we can't use the **cur-
rent_user** method as in Listing 8.15, but the **session** method is available, so we
use that instead.) Here we use **is_logged_in?** instead of **logged_in?** so that the test
helper and Sessions helper methods have different names, which prevents them from
being mistaken for each other.[11]

Listing 8.23   A boolean method for checking login status inside tests.

test/test_helper.rb

```
ENV['RAILS_ENV'] ||= 'test'
.
.
.
class ActiveSupport::TestCase
  fixtures :all

  # Returns true if a test user is logged in.
```

---

11. For example, I once had a test suite that was **GREEN** even after I accidentally deleted the main **log_in**
method in the Sessions helper. The reason is that the tests were happily using a test helper with the same name,
thereby passing even though the application was completely broken. As with **is_logged_in?**, we'll avoid this
issue by defining the test helper **log_in_as** in Listing 8.50.

```
  def is_logged_in?
      !session[:user_id].nil?
  end
end
```

With the code in Listing 8.23, we can assert that the user is logged in after sign-up using the line shown in Listing 8.24.

Listing 8.24 A test of login after sign-up. **GREEN**

test/integration/users_signup_test.rb

```
require 'test_helper'

class UsersSignupTest < ActionDispatch::IntegrationTest
  .
  .
  .
  test "valid sign-up information" do
    get signup_path
    assert_difference 'User.count', 1 do
      post_via_redirect users_path, user: { name:  "Example User",
                                            email: "user@example.com",
                                            password:             "password",
                                            password_confirmation: "password" }
    end
    assert_template 'users/show'
    assert is_logged_in?
  end
end
```

At this point, the test suite should still be **GREEN**:

Listing 8.25 **GREEN**

```
$ bundle exec rake test
```

8.3 Logging Out

As discussed in Section 8.1, our authentication model expects to keep users logged in until they log out explicitly. In this section, we'll add this necessary logout capability. Because the "Log out" link has already been defined (Listing 8.16), all we need is to write a valid controller action to destroy user sessions.

So far, the Sessions controller actions have followed the RESTful convention of using **new** for a login page and **create** to complete the login. We'll continue this theme by using a **destroy** action to delete sessions—that is, to log out. Unlike with the login functionality, which we use in both Listing 8.13 and Listing 8.22, we'll log out in only one place, so we'll put the relevant code directly in the **destroy** action. As we'll see in Section 8.4.6, this design (with a little refactoring) will make the authentication machinery easier to test.

Logging out involves undoing the effects of the **log_in** method from Listing 8.12, which involves deleting the user ID from the session.[12] To do this, we use the **delete** method as follows:

```
session.delete(:user_id)
```

We'll also set the current user to **nil**, although in the present case this won't matter because of an immediate redirect to the root URL.[13] As with **log_in** and associated methods, we'll put the resulting **log_out** method in the Sessions helper module, as shown in Listing 8.26.

Listing 8.26 The **log_out** method.
app/helpers/sessions_helper.rb

```
module SessionsHelper

  # Logs in the given user.
  def log_in(user)
    session[:user_id] = user.id
  end
  .
  .
  .
  # Logs out the current user.
  def log_out
    session.delete(:user_id)
    @current_user = nil
  end
end
```

---

12. Some browsers offer a "remember where I left off" feature, which restores the session automatically, so be sure to disable any such feature before trying to log out.

13. Setting **@current_user** to **nil** would matter only if **@current_user** were created before the **destroy** action (which it isn't) *and* if we didn't issue an immediate redirect (which we do). This is an unlikely combination of events, and with the application as presently constructed it isn't necessary. Nevertheless, because it's a security-related issue, I include it for completeness.

We can put the `log_out` method to use in the Sessions controller's `destroy` action, as shown in Listing 8.27.

Listing 8.27 Destroying a session (user logout).

app/controllers/sessions_controller.rb

```ruby
class SessionsController < ApplicationController

  def new
  end

  def create
    user = User.find_by(email: params[:session][:email].downcase)
    if user && user.authenticate(params[:session][:password])
      log_in user
      redirect_to user
    else
      flash.now[:danger] = 'Invalid email/password combination'
      render 'new'
    end
  end

  def destroy
    log_out
    redirect_to root_url
  end
end
```

To test the logout machinery, we can add some steps to the user login test from Listing 8.20. After logging in, we use `delete` to issue a DELETE request to the logout path (Table 8.1) and verify that the user is logged out and redirected to the root URL. We also check that the login link reappears and that the logout and profile links disappear. The new steps appear in Listing 8.28.

Listing 8.28 A test for user logout. **GREEN**

test/integration/users_login_test.rb

```ruby
require 'test_helper'

class UsersLoginTest < ActionDispatch::IntegrationTest
  .
  .
  .
  test "login with valid information followed by logout" do
    get login_path
```

```
    post login_path, session: { email: @user.email, password: 'password' }
    assert is_logged_in?
    assert_redirected_to @user
    follow_redirect!
    assert_template 'users/show'
    assert_select "a[href=?]", login_path, count: 0
    assert_select "a[href=?]", logout_path
    assert_select "a[href=?]", user_path(@user)
    delete logout_path
    assert_not is_logged_in?
    assert_redirected_to root_url
    follow_redirect!
    assert_select "a[href=?]", login_path
    assert_select "a[href=?]", logout_path,       count: 0
    assert_select "a[href=?]", user_path(@user), count: 0
  end
end
```

Now that we have **is_logged_in?** available in tests, we've also thrown in a bonus **assert is_logged_in?** immediately after posting valid information to the sessions path.

With the session **destroy** action now defined and tested, the initial signup/log-in/logout triumvirate is complete, and the test suite should be **GREEN**:

Listing 8.29 GREEN

```
$ bundle exec rake test
```

8.4 Remember Me

The login system we finished in Section 8.2 is self-contained and fully functional, but most websites have the additional capability of remembering users' sessions even after they close their browsers. In this section, we'll start by remembering user logins by default, expiring sessions only when users explicitly log out. In Section 8.4.5, we'll enable a common alternative model, a "remember me" check box that allows users to opt out of being remembered. Both of these models are professional-grade approaches, with the first being used by sites such as GitHub and Bitbucket, and the second being used by sites such as Facebook and Twitter.

8.4.1 Remember Token and Digest

In Section 8.2, we used the Rails `session` method to store the user's ID, but this information disappears when the user closes the browser. In this section, we'll take the first step toward persistent sessions by generating a *remember token* appropriate for creating permanent cookies using the `cookies` method, together with a secure *remember digest* for authenticating those tokens.

As noted in Section 8.2.1, information stored using `session` is automatically secure, but this is not the case with information stored using `cookies`. In particular, persistent cookies are vulnerable to session hijacking, in which an attacker uses a stolen remember token to log in as a particular user. There are four main ways to steal cookies: (1) using a packet sniffer to detect cookies being passed over insecure networks,[14] (2) compromising a database containing remember tokens, (3) using cross-site scripting (XSS), and (4) gaining physical access to a machine with a logged-in user. We prevented the first problem in Section 7.5 by using Secure Sockets Layer (SSL) on a site-wide basis, which protects network data from packet sniffers. We'll prevent the second problem by storing a hash digest of the remember token instead of the token itself, in much the same way that we stored password digests instead of raw passwords in Section 6.3. Rails automatically prevents the third problem by escaping any content inserted into view templates. Finally, although there's no iron-clad way to stop attackers who have physical access to a logged-in computer, we'll minimize the fourth problem by changing tokens every time a user logs out and by taking care to *cryptographically sign* any potentially sensitive information we place on the browser.

With these design and security considerations in mind, our plan for creating persistent sessions appears as follows:

1. Create a random string of digits for use as a remember token.

2. Place the token in the browser cookies with an expiration date far in the future.

3. Save the hash digest of the token to the database.

4. Place an encrypted version of the user's ID in the browser cookies.

5. When presented with a cookie containing a persistent user ID, find the user in the database using the given ID, and verify that the remember token cookie matches the associated hash digest from the database.

---

14. Session hijacking was widely publicized by the Firesheep application, which showed that remember tokens at many high-profile sites were visible when connected to public Wi-Fi networks.

users	
id	integer
name	string
email	string
created_at	datetime
updated_at	datetime
password_digest	string
remember_digest	string

Figure 8.9 The User model with an added **remember_digest** attribute.

Note how similar the final step is to logging a user in, where we retrieve the user by email address and then verify (using the **authenticate** method) that the submitted password matches the password digest (Listing 8.5). As a result, our implementation will parallel aspects of **has_secure_password**.

We'll start by adding the required **remember_digest** attribute to the User model, as shown in Figure 8.9. To add the data model from Figure 8.9 to our application, we'll generate a migration:

```
$ rails generate migration add_remember_digest_to_users remember_digest:string
```

(Compare to the password digest migration in Section 6.3.1.) As in previous migrations, we've used a migration name that ends in **_to_users** to tell Rails that the migration is designed to alter the **users** table in the database. Because we also included the attribute (**remember_digest**) and type (**string**), Rails generates a default migration for us, as shown in Listing 8.30.

Listing 8.30 The generated migration for the remember digest.
db/migrate/[timestamp]_add_remember_digest_to_users.rb

```
class AddRememberDigestToUsers < ActiveRecord::Migration
  def change
    add_column :users, :remember_digest, :string
  end
end
```

Because we don't expect to retrieve users by remember digest, there's no need to put an index on the `remember_digest` column, and we can use the default migration as generated earlier:

```
$ bundle exec rake db:migrate
```

Now we have to decide what to use as a remember token. Many mostly equivalent possibilities exist—essentially, any long random string will do. The `urlsafe_base64` method from the `SecureRandom` module in the Ruby standard library fits the bill:[15] It returns a random string of length 16 composed of the characters A–Z, a–z, 0–9, "-", and "_" (for a total of 64 possibilities, explaining the "base64"). A typical base64 string appears as follows:

```
$ rails console
>> SecureRandom.urlsafe_base64
=> "q5lt38hQDc_959PVoo6b7A"
```

Just as it's perfectly fine if two users have the same password,[16] there's no need for remember tokens to be unique—but the system is more secure if they are.[17] In the case of the base64 string, each of the 22 characters has 64 possibilities, so the probability of two remember tokens colliding is a negligibly small $1/64^{22} = 2^{-132} \approx 10^{-40}$. As a bonus, by using base64 strings specifically designed to be safe in URLs (as indicated by the name `urlsafe_base64`), we'll be able to use the same token generator to make account activation and password reset links in Chapter 10.

Remembering users involves creating a remember token and saving the digest of the token to the database. We've already defined a `digest` method for use in the test fixtures (Listing 8.18), and we can use the results of the earlier discussion to create a `new_token` method to create a new token. As with `digest`, the new token method doesn't need a user object, so we'll make it a class method.[18] The result is the User model shown in Listing 8.31.

---

15. This choice is based on the RailsCast on remember me.

16. Indeed, it had better be OK, because with bcrypt's salted hashes there's no way for us to tell if two users' passwords match.

17. With unique remember tokens, an attacker always needs *both* the user ID and the remember token cookies to hijack the session.

18. As a general rule, if a method doesn't need an instance of an object, it should be a class method. Indeed, this decision will prove important in Section 10.1.2.

Listing 8.31 Adding a method for generating tokens.
app/models/user.rb

```
class User < ActiveRecord::Base
  before_save { self.email = email.downcase }
  validates :name, presence: true, length: { maximum: 50 }
  VALID_EMAIL_REGEX = /\A[\w+\-.]+@[a-z\d\-.]+\.[a-z]+\z/i
  validates :email, presence: true, length: { maximum: 255 },
                    format: { with: VALID_EMAIL_REGEX },
                    uniqueness: { case_sensitive: false }
  has_secure_password
  validates :password, length: { minimum: 6 }

  # Returns the hash digest of the given string.
  def User.digest(string)
    cost = ActiveModel::SecurePassword.min_cost ? BCrypt::Engine::MIN_COST :
                                                  BCrypt::Engine.cost
    BCrypt::Password.create(string, cost: cost)
  end

  # Returns a random token.
  def User.new_token
    SecureRandom.urlsafe_base64
  end
end
```

Our plan for the implementation is to make a `user.remember` method that associates a remember token with the user and saves the corresponding remember digest to the database. Because of the migration in Listing 8.30, the User model already has a `remember_digest` attribute, but it doesn't yet have a `remember_token` attribute. We need a way to make a token available via `user.remember_token` (for storage in the cookies) *without* storing it in the database. We solved a similar problem with secure passwords in Section 6.3, by pairing a virtual `password` attribute with a secure `password_digest` attribute in the database. In that case, the virtual `password` attribute was created automatically by `has_secure_password`, but we'll have to write the code for a `remember_token` ourselves. To do so, we use `attr_accessor` to create an accessible attribute, like the one we saw in Section 4.4.5:

```
class User < ActiveRecord::Base
  attr_accessor :remember_token
  .
  .
  .
  def remember
```

```
    self.remember_token = ...
    update_attribute(:remember_digest, ...)
  end
end
```

Note the form of the assignment in the first line of the **remember** method. Because of the way Ruby handles assignments inside objects, without **self** the assignment would create a *local* variable called **remember_token**, which isn't what we want. Using **self** ensures that the assignment sets the user's **remember_token** attribute. (Now you know why the **before_save** callback from Listing 6.31 uses **self.email** instead of just **email**.) Meanwhile, the second line of **remember** uses the **update_attribute** method to update the remember digest. (As noted in Section 6.1.5, this method bypasses the validations, which is necessary in this case because we don't have access to the user's password or confirmation.)

With these considerations in mind, we can create a valid token and associated digest by first making a new remember token using **User.new_token**, and then updating the remember digest with the result of applying **User.digest**. This procedure gives the **remember** method shown in Listing 8.32.

Listing 8.32 Adding a **remember** method to the User model. **GREEN**
app/models/user.rb

```
class User < ActiveRecord::Base
  attr_accessor :remember_token
  before_save { self.email = email.downcase }
  validates :name,  presence: true, length: { maximum: 50 }
  VALID_EMAIL_REGEX = /\A[\w+\-.]+@[a-z\d\-.]+\.[a-z]+\z/i
  validates :email, presence: true, length: { maximum: 255 },
                    format: { with: VALID_EMAIL_REGEX },
                    uniqueness: { case_sensitive: false }
  has_secure_password
  validates :password, length: { minimum: 6 }

  # Returns the hash digest of the given string.
  def User.digest(string)
    cost = ActiveModel::SecurePassword.min_cost ? BCrypt::Engine::MIN_COST :
                                                  BCrypt::Engine.cost
    BCrypt::Password.create(string, cost: cost)
  end

  # Returns a random token.
  def User.new_token
```

```
    SecureRandom.urlsafe_base64
  end

  # Remembers a user in the database for use in persistent sessions.
  def remember
    self.remember_token = User.new_token
    update_attribute(:remember_digest, User.digest(remember_token))
  end
end
```

8.4.2 Login with Remembering

Having created a working **user.remember** method, we're now in a position to create a persistent session by storing a user's (encrypted) ID and remember token as permanent cookies on the browser. The way to do this is with the **cookies** method, which (like **session**) we can treat as a hash. A cookie consists of two pieces of information: a **value** and an optional **expires** date. For example, we could make a persistent session by creating a cookie with a value equal to the remember token that expires 20 years from now:

```
cookies[:remember_token] = { value:   remember_token,
                             expires: 20.years.from_now.utc }
```

(This uses one of the convenient Rails time helpers, as discussed in Box 8.2.) This pattern of setting a cookie that expires 20 years in the future is so common that Rails has a special **permanent** method to implement it. Thus we can simply write

```
cookies.permanent[:remember_token] = remember_token
```

This causes Rails to set the expiration to **20.years.from_now** automatically.

> **Box 8.2 Cookies Expire** 20.years.from_now
>
> Recall from Section 4.4.2 that Ruby lets you add methods to *any* class, even built-in ones. In that section, we added a palindrome? method to the String class (and discovered as a result that "deified" is a palindrome), and we also saw how Rails adds a blank? method to class Object (so that "".blank?, " ".blank?,

and `nil.blank?` are all `true`). The `cookies.permanent` method, which creates "permanent" cookies with an expiration `20.years.from_now`, gives yet another example of this practice through one of Rails' *time helpers*, which are methods added to `Fixnum` (the base class for integers):

```
$ rails console
>> 1.year.from_now
=> Sun, 09 Aug 2015 16:48:17 UTC +00:00
>> 10.weeks.ago
=> Sat, 31 May 2014 16:48:45 UTC +00:00
```

Rails adds other helpers, too:

```
>> 1.kilobyte
=> 1024
>> 5.megabytes
=> 5242880
```

These are useful for upload validations, making it easy to restrict, say, image uploads to `5.megabytes`.

Although the time helpers should be used with caution, the flexibility to add methods to built-in classes allows for extraordinarily natural additions to plain Ruby. Indeed, much of the elegance of Rails ultimately derives from the malleability of the underlying Ruby language.

To store the user's ID in the cookies, we could follow the pattern used with the **session** method (Listing 8.12) by using something like this:

```
cookies[:user_id] = user.id
```

Because it presents the ID as plain text, this method exposes the form of the application's cookies and makes it easier for an attacker to compromise user accounts. To avoid this problem, we'll use a *signed* cookie, which securely encrypts the cookie before placing it on the browser:

```
cookies.signed[:user_id] = user.id
```

Because we want the user ID to be paired with the permanent remember token, we should make it permanent as well, which we can do by chaining the `signed` and `permanent` methods:

```
cookies.permanent.signed[:user_id] = user.id
```

After the cookies are set, on subsequent page views we can retrieve the user with code like

```
User.find_by(id: cookies.signed[:user_id])
```

where `cookies.signed[:user_id]` automatically decrypts the user ID cookie. We can then use bcrypt to verify that `cookies[:remember_token]` matches the `remember_digest` generated in Listing 8.32. (In case you're wondering why we don't just use the signed user ID, without the remember token, this would allow an attacker with possession of the encrypted ID to log in as the user in perpetuity. In the present design, an attacker with both cookies can log in as the user only until the user logs out.)

The final piece of the puzzle is to verify that a given remember token matches the user's remember digest, and in this context there are a couple of equivalent ways to use bcrypt to verify a match. If you look at the secure password source code, you'll find a comparison like this:[19]

```
BCrypt::Password.new(password_digest) == unencrypted_password
```

In our case, the analogous code would look like this:

```
BCrypt::Password.new(remember_digest) == remember_token
```

If you think about it, this code is really strange: It appears to be comparing a bcrypt password digest directly with a token, which would imply *decrypting* the digest to compare it using `==`. But the whole point of using bcrypt is for hashing to be irreversible, so this can't be right. Indeed, digging into the source code of the bcrypt gem verifies

---

19. As noted in Section 6.3.1, "unencrypted password" is a misnomer, as the secure password is *hashed*, not encrypted.

•

that the comparison operator `==` is being *redefined*, and under the hood the preceding comparison is equivalent to the following:

```
BCrypt::Password.new(remember_digest).is_password?(remember_token)
```

Instead of `==`, this line uses the boolean method **is_password?** to perform the comparison. Because its meaning is a little clearer, we'll prefer this second comparison form in the application code.

The previous discussion suggests putting the digest–token comparison into an **authenticated?** method in the User model, which plays a similar role to the **authenticate** method provided by **has_secure_password** for authenticating a user (Listing 8.13). The implementation appears in Listing 8.33.

Listing 8.33 Adding an **authenticated?** method to the User model.

app/models/user.rb

```
class User < ActiveRecord::Base
  attr_accessor :remember_token
  before_save { self.email = email.downcase }
  validates :name,  presence: true, length: { maximum: 50 }
  VALID_EMAIL_REGEX = /\A[\w+\-.]+@[a-z\d\-.]+\.[a-z]+\z/i
  validates :email, presence: true, length: { maximum: 255 },
                    format: { with: VALID_EMAIL_REGEX },
                    uniqueness: { case_sensitive: false }
  has_secure_password
  validates :password, length: { minimum: 6 }

  # Returns the hash digest of the given string.
  def User.digest(string)
    cost = ActiveModel::SecurePassword.min_cost ? BCrypt::Engine::MIN_COST :
                                                  BCrypt::Engine.cost
    BCrypt::Password.create(string, cost: cost)
  end

  # Returns a random token.
  def User.new_token
    SecureRandom.urlsafe_base64
  end

  # Remembers a user in the database for use in persistent sessions.
  def remember
    self.remember_token = User.new_token
    update_attribute(:remember_digest, User.digest(remember_token))
  end

  # Returns true if the given token matches the digest.
```

```
    def authenticated?(remember_token)
      BCrypt::Password.new(remember_digest).is_password?(remember_token)
    end
end
```

Although the **authenticated?** method in Listing 8.33 is tied specifically to the remember token, it will turn out to be useful in other contexts as well. In fact, we'll generalize it in Chapter 10.

We're now in a position to remember a logged-in user, which we'll do by adding a **remember** helper to go along with **log_in**, as shown in Listing 8.34.

Listing 8.34 Logging in and remembering a user.
app/controllers/sessions_controller.rb

```
class SessionsController < ApplicationController

  def new
  end

  def create
    user = User.find_by(email: params[:session][:email].downcase)
    if user && user.authenticate(params[:session][:password])
      log_in user
      remember user
      redirect_to user
    else
      flash.now[:danger] = 'Invalid email/password combination'
      render 'new'
    end
  end

  def destroy
    log_out
    redirect_to root_url
  end
end
```

As with **log_in**, Listing 8.34 defers the real work to the Sessions helper, where we define a **remember** method that calls **user.remember**, thereby generating a remember token and saving its digest to the database. It then uses **cookies** to create permanent cookies for the user ID and remember token as described earlier. The result appears in Listing 8.35.

Listing 8.35 Remembering the user.

app/helpers/sessions_helper.rb

```
module SessionsHelper

  # Logs in the given user.
  def log_in(user)
    session[:user_id] = user.id
  end

  # Remembers a user in a persistent session.
  def remember(user)
    user.remember
    cookies.permanent.signed[:user_id] = user.id
    cookies.permanent[:remember_token] = user.remember_token
  end

  # Returns the current logged-in user (if any).
  def current_user
    @current_user ||= User.find_by(id: session[:user_id])
  end

  # Returns true if the user is logged in, false otherwise.
  def logged_in?
    !current_user.nil?
  end

  # Logs out the current user.
  def log_out
    session.delete(:user_id)
    @current_user = nil
  end
end
```

With the code in Listing 8.35, a user logging in will be remembered in the sense that the browser gets a valid remember token, but it doesn't yet do us any good because the **current_user** method defined in Listing 8.14 knows only about the temporary session:

```
@current_user ||= User.find_by(id: session[:user_id])
```

In the case of persistent sessions, we want to retrieve the user from the temporary session if **session[:user_id]** exists, but otherwise we should look for **cookies[:user_id]** to retrieve (and log in) the user corresponding to the persistent session. We can accomplish this as follows:

```
if session[:user_id]
  @current_user ||= User.find_by(id: session[:user_id])
elsif cookies.signed[:user_id]
  user = User.find_by(id: cookies.signed[:user_id])
  if user && user.authenticated?(cookies[:remember_token])
    log_in user
    @current_user = user
  end
end
```

(This follows the same `user && user.authenticated` pattern we saw in Listing 8.5.) This code will work, but note the repeated use of both `session` and `cookies`. We can eliminate this duplication as follows:

```
if (user_id = session[:user_id])
  @current_user ||= User.find_by(id: user_id)
elsif (user_id = cookies.signed[:user_id])
  user = User.find_by(id: user_id)
  if user && user.authenticated?(cookies[:remember_token])
    log_in user
    @current_user = user
  end
end
```

This version uses the common but potentially confusing construction

```
if (user_id = session[:user_id])
```

Despite appearances, this statement is *not* a comparison (which would use double-equals `==`), but rather an *assignment*. If you were to read it in words, you wouldn't say, "If user ID equals session of user ID…," but rather something like "If session of user ID exists (while setting user ID to session of user ID)…."[20]

Defining the `current_user` helper as discussed previously leads to the implementation shown in Listing 8.36.

---

20. I generally use the convention of putting such assignments in parentheses, which is a visual reminder that the statement is not a comparison.

Listing 8.36   Updating `current_user` for persistent sessions. **RED**

app/helpers/sessions_helper.rb

```ruby
module SessionsHelper

  # Logs in the given user.
  def log_in(user)
    session[:user_id] = user.id
  end

  # Remembers a user in a persistent session.
  def remember(user)
    user.remember
    cookies.permanent.signed[:user_id] = user.id
    cookies.permanent[:remember_token] = user.remember_token
  end

  # Returns the user corresponding to the remember token cookie.
  def current_user
    if (user_id = session[:user_id])
      @current_user ||= User.find_by(id: user_id)
    elsif (user_id = cookies.signed[:user_id])
      user = User.find_by(id: user_id)
      if user && user.authenticated?(cookies[:remember_token])
        log_in user
        @current_user = user
      end
    end
  end

  # Returns true if the user is logged in, false otherwise.
  def logged_in?
    !current_user.nil?
  end

  # Logs out the current user.
  def log_out
    session.delete(:user_id)
    @current_user = nil
  end
end
```

With the code as in Listing 8.36, newly logged-in users are correctly remembered, as you can verify by logging in, closing the browser, and checking that you're still logged in when you restart the sample application and revisit the sample application. If you want, you can even inspect the browser cookies to see the result directly (Figure 8.10).[21]

---

21. Google "<your browser name> inspect cookies" to learn how to inspect the cookies on your system.

Name	remember_token
Value	vb4iQ7Oy3dCLv2R2TEdQ0g
Host	rails-tutorial-c9-mhartl.c9.io
Path	/
Expires	Sun, 30 Jul 2034 00:18:56 GMT
Secure	No
HttpOnly	No

Figure 8.10 The remember token cookie in the local browser.

There's only one problem with our application as it stands: Short of clearing their browser cookies (or waiting 20 years), there's no way for users to log out. This is exactly the sort of thing our test suite should catch, and indeed the test should currently be **RED**:

Listing 8.37 RED

```
$ bundle exec rake test
```

8.4.3 Forgetting Users

To allow users to log out, we'll define methods to forget users in analogy with the ones to remember them. The resulting **user.forget** method just undoes **user.remember** by updating the remember digest with **nil**, as shown in Listing 8.38.

Listing 8.38 Adding a **forget** method to the User model.
app/models/user.rb

```
class User < ActiveRecord::Base
  attr_accessor :remember_token
  before_save { self.email = email.downcase }
  validates :name,  presence: true, length: { maximum: 50 }
  VALID_EMAIL_REGEX = /\A[\w+\-.]+@[a-z\d\-.]+\.[a-z]+\z/i
  validates :email, presence: true, length: { maximum: 255 },
```

```
                    format: { with: VALID_EMAIL_REGEX },
                    uniqueness: { case_sensitive: false }
  has_secure_password
  validates :password, length: { minimum: 6 }

  # Returns the hash digest of the given string.
  def User.digest(string)
    cost = ActiveModel::SecurePassword.min_cost ? BCrypt::Engine::MIN_COST :
                                                  BCrypt::Engine.cost
    BCrypt::Password.create(string, cost: cost)
  end

  # Returns a random token.
  def User.new_token
    SecureRandom.urlsafe_base64
  end

  # Remembers a user in the database for use in persistent sessions.
  def remember
    self.remember_token = User.new_token
    update_attribute(:remember_digest, User.digest(remember_token))
  end

  # Returns true if the given token matches the digest.
  def authenticated?(remember_token)
    BCrypt::Password.new(remember_digest).is_password?(remember_token)
  end

  # Forgets a user.
  def forget
    update_attribute(:remember_digest, nil)
  end
end
```

With the code in Listing 8.38, we're now ready to forget a permanent session by adding a **forget** helper and calling it from the **log_out** helper (Listing 8.39). As seen in Listing 8.39, the **forget** helper calls **user.forget** and then deletes the **user_id** and **remember_token** cookies.

Listing 8.39 Logging out from a persistent session.
app/helpers/sessions_helper.rb

```
module SessionsHelper

  # Logs in the given user.
  def log_in(user)
    session[:user_id] = user.id
  end
    .
```

```
     .
     .
  # Forgets a persistent session.
  def forget(user)
    user.forget
    cookies.delete(:user_id)
    cookies.delete(:remember_token)
  end

  # Logs out the current user.
  def log_out
    forget(current_user)
    session.delete(:user_id)
    @current_user = nil
  end
end
```

8.4.4 Two Subtle Bugs

There are two closely related subtleties left to address. The first subtlety is that, even though the "Log out" link appears only when the user is logged-in, a user could potentially have multiple browser windows open to the site. If the user then logged out in one window, clicking the "Log out" link in a second window would result in an error due to the use of **current_user** in Listing 8.39.[22] We can avoid this by logging out only if the user is logged in.

The second subtlety is that a user could be logged in (and remembered) in multiple browsers, such as Chrome and Firefox, which causes a problem if the user logs out in one browser but not the other.[23] For example, suppose that the user logs out in Firefox, thereby setting the remember digest to **nil** (via **user.forget** in Listing 8.38). The application will still work in Firefox; because the **log_out** method in Listing 8.39 deletes the user's ID, both highlighted conditionals are **false**:

```
# Returns the user corresponding to the remember token cookie.
def current_user
  if (user_id = session[:user_id])
    @current_user ||= User.find_by(id: user_id)
  elsif (user_id = cookies.signed[:user_id])
```

---

22. Thanks to reader Paulo Célio Júnior for pointing this out.

23. Thanks to reader Niels de Ron for pointing this out.

```
    user = User.find_by(id: user_id)
    if user && user.authenticated?(cookies[:remember_token])
      log_in user
      @current_user = user
    end
  end
end
```

As a result, evaluation falls off the end of the `current_user` method, thereby returning `nil` as required.

In contrast, inside Chrome the `user_id` cookie hasn't been deleted, so `user_id` will be `true` in a boolean context and the corresponding user will be found in the database:

```
# Returns the user corresponding to the remember token cookie.
def current_user
  if (user_id = session[:user_id])
    @current_user ||= User.find_by(id: user_id)
  elsif (user_id = cookies.signed[:user_id])
    user = User.find_by(id: user_id)
    if user && user.authenticated?(cookies[:remember_token])
      log_in user
      @current_user = user
    end
  end
end
```

Consequently, the inner `if` conditional will be evaluated:

```
user && user.authenticated?(cookies[:remember_token])
```

In particular, because `user` isn't `nil`, the *second* expression will be evaluated, which raises an error. This is because the user's remember digest was deleted as part of logging out (Listing 8.38) in Firefox, so when we access the application in Chrome we end up calling

```
BCrypt::Password.new(remember_digest).is_password?(remember_token)
```

with a `nil` remember digest, thereby raising an exception inside the bcrypt library. To fix this, we want `authenticated?` to return `false` instead.

These are exactly the sorts of subtleties that can benefit from test-driven development, so we'll write tests to catch the two errors before correcting them. We first get the integration test from Listing 8.28 to **RED**, as shown in Listing 8.40.

Listing 8.40   A test for user logout. **RED**
test/integration/users_login_test.rb

```
require 'test_helper'

class UsersLoginTest < ActionDispatch::IntegrationTest
  .
  .
  .
  test "login with valid information followed by logout" do
    get login_path
    post login_path, session: { email: @user.email, password: 'password' }
    assert is_logged_in?
    assert_redirected_to @user
    follow_redirect!
    assert_template 'users/show'
    assert_select "a[href=?]", login_path, count: 0
    assert_select "a[href=?]", logout_path
    assert_select "a[href=?]", user_path(@user)
    delete logout_path
    assert_not is_logged_in?
    assert_redirected_to root_url
    # Simulate a user clicking logout in a second window.
    delete logout_path
    follow_redirect!
    assert_select "a[href=?]", login_path
    assert_select "a[href=?]", logout_path,      count: 0
    assert_select "a[href=?]", user_path(@user), count: 0
  end
end
```

The second call to `delete logout_path` in Listing 8.40 should raise an error due to the missing `current_user`, leading to a **RED** test suite:

Listing 8.41 **RED**

```
$ bundle exec rake test
```

The application code simply involves calling `log_out` only if `logged_in?` is true, as shown in Listing 8.42.

Listing 8.42 Logging out only if logged in. **GREEN**
app/controllers/sessions_controller.rb

```ruby
class SessionsController < ApplicationController
  .
  .
  .
  def destroy
    log_out if logged_in?
    redirect_to root_url
  end
end
```

The second case, involving a scenario with two different browsers, is more challenging to simulate with an integration test, but it's easy to check in the User model test directly. All we need is to start with a user that has no remember digest (which is true for the **@user** variable defined in the **setup** method) and then call **authenticated?**, as shown in Listing 8.43. (Note that we've just left the remember token blank; it doesn't matter what its value is, because the error occurs before it ever gets used.)

Listing 8.43 A test of **authenticated?** with a nonexistent digest. **RED**
test/models/user_test.rb

```ruby
require 'test_helper'

class UserTest < ActiveSupport::TestCase

  def setup
    @user = User.new(name: "Example User", email: "user@example.com",
                     password: "foobar", password_confirmation: "foobar")
  end
  .
  .
  .
  test "authenticated? should return false for a user with nil digest" do
    assert_not @user.authenticated?('')
  end
end
```

Because **BCrypt::Password.new(nil)** raises an error, the test suite should now be **RED**:

Listing 8.44 RED

```
$ bundle exec rake test
```

To fix the error and get to **GREEN**, all we need to do is return `false` if the remember digest is `nil`, as shown in Listing 8.45.

Listing 8.45 Updating `authenticated?` to handle a nonexistent digest. **GREEN**
app/models/user.rb

```
class User < ActiveRecord::Base
  .
  .
  .
  # Returns true if the given token matches the digest.
  def authenticated?(remember_token)
    return false if remember_digest.nil?
    BCrypt::Password.new(remember_digest).is_password?(remember_token)
  end
end
```

This uses the `return` keyword to return immediately if the remember digest is `nil`, which is a common way to emphasize that the rest of the method gets ignored in that case. The equivalent code

```
if remember_digest.nil?
  false
else
  BCrypt::Password.new(remember_digest).is_password?(remember_token)
end
```

would also work fine, but I prefer the explicitness of the version in Listing 8.45 (which also happens to be slightly shorter).

With the code in Listing 8.45, our full test suite should be **GREEN**, and both subtleties should now be addressed:

Listing 8.46 GREEN

```
$ bundle exec rake test
```

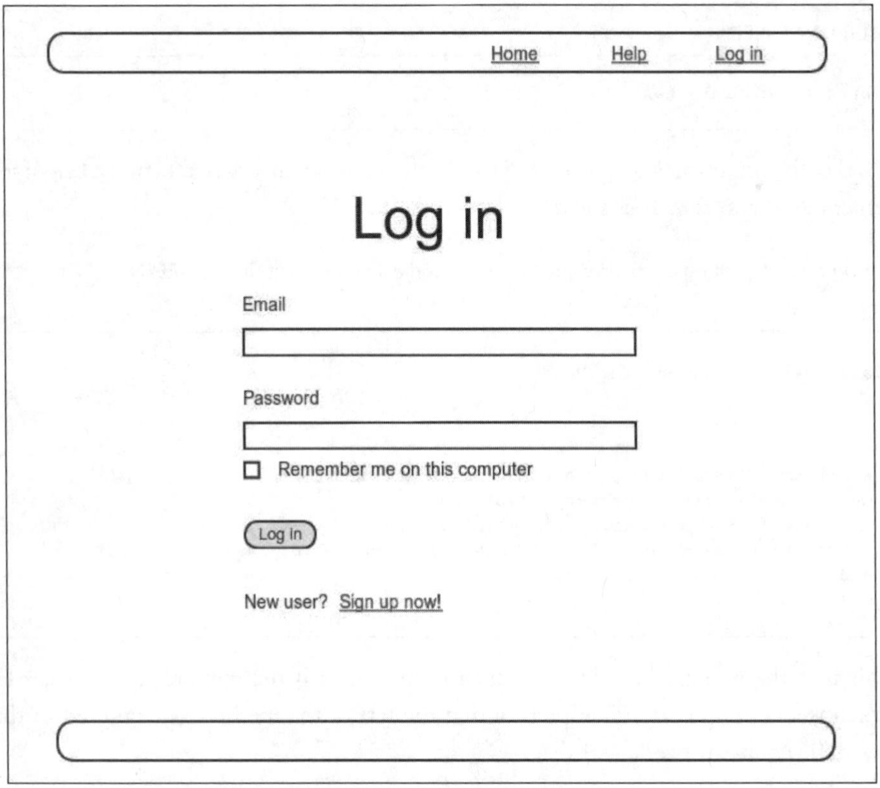

Figure 8.11 A mockup of a "remember me" check box.

8.4.5 "Remember Me" Check Box

With the code in Section 8.4.3, our application has a complete, professional-grade authentication system. As a final step, we'll see how to make staying logged in optional using a "remember me" check box. A mockup of the login form with such a check box appears in Figure 8.11.

To write the implementation, we start by adding a check box to the login form from Listing 8.2. As with labels, text fields, password fields, and submit buttons, check boxes can be created with a Rails helper method. To get the styling right, though, we have to *nest* the check box inside the label, as follows:

```
<%= f.label :remember_me, class: "checkbox inline" do %>
  <%= f.check_box :remember_me %>
  <span>Remember me on this computer</span>
<% end %>
```

Putting this into the login form gives the code shown in Listing 8.47.

Listing 8.47 Adding a "remember me" check box to the login form.
app/views/sessions/new.html.erb

```
<% provide(:title, "Log in") %>
<h1>Log in</h1>

<div class="row">
  <div class="col-md-6 col-md-offset-3">
    <%= form_for(:session, url: login_path) do |f| %>

      <%= f.label :email %>
      <%= f.email_field :email, class: 'form-control' %>

      <%= f.label :password %>
      <%= f.password_field :password, class: 'form-control' %>

      <%= f.label :remember_me, class: "checkbox inline" do %>
        <%= f.check_box :remember_me %>
        <span>Remember me on this computer</span>
      <% end %>

      <%= f.submit "Log in", class: "btn btn-primary" %>
    <% end %>

    <p>New user? <%= link_to "Sign up now!", signup_path %></p>
  </div>
</div>
```

In Listing 8.47, we've included the CSS classes **checkbox** and **inline**, which Bootstrap uses to put the check box and the text ("Remember me on this computer") in the same line. To complete the styling, we need just a few more CSS rules, as shown in Listing 8.48. The resulting login form appears in Figure 8.12.

Listing 8.48 CSS for the "remember me" check box.
app/assets/stylesheets/custom.css.scss

.
.
.

```
/* forms */
.
.
.
.checkbox {
  margin-top: -10px;
  margin-bottom: 10px;
  span {
    margin-left: 20px;
    font-weight: normal;
  }
}

#session_remember_me {
  width: auto;
  margin-left: 0;
}
```

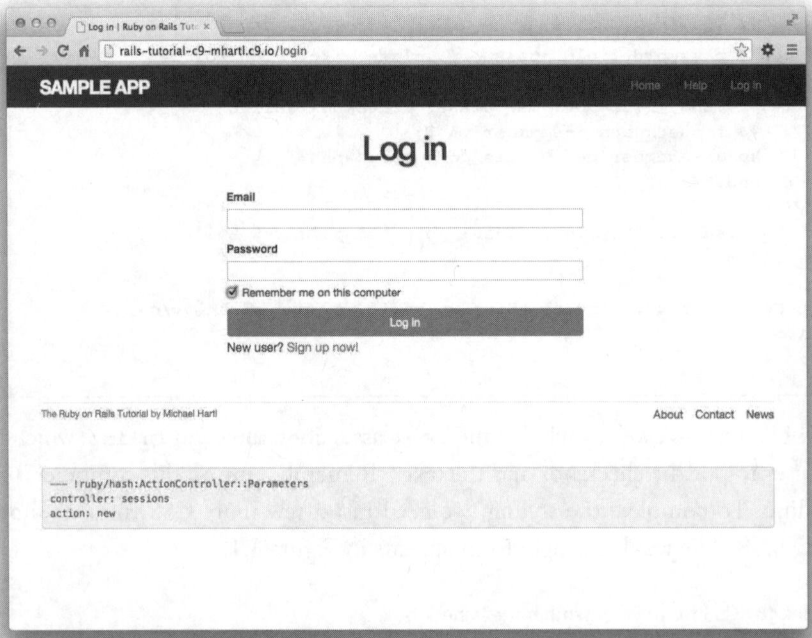

Figure 8.12 The login form with an added "remember me" checkbox.

Having edited the login form, we're now ready to remember users if they check the check box and forget them otherwise. Incredibly, because of all our work in the previous sections, the implementation can be reduced to one line. We start by noting that the `params` hash for submitted login forms now includes a value based on the check box (as you can verify by submitting the form in Listing 8.47 with invalid information and inspecting the values in the debug section of the page). In particular, the value of

```
params[:session][:remember_me]
```

is `'1'` if the box is checked and `'0'` if it isn't.

By testing the relevant value of the `params` hash, we can now remember or forget the user based on the value of the submission:

```
if params[:session][:remember_me] == '1'
  remember(user)
else
  forget(user)
end
```

As explained in Box 8.3, this sort of `if-then` branching structure can be converted to one line using the *ternary operator*:[24]

```
params[:session][:remember_me] == '1' ? remember(user) : forget(user)
```

Adding this to the Sessions controller's `create` method leads to the incredibly compact code shown in Listing 8.49. (Now you're in a position to understand the code in Listing 8.18, which uses the ternary operator to define the bcrypt `cost` variable.)

Listing 8.49 Handling the submission of the "remember me" check box.
app/controllers/sessions_controller.rb

```
class SessionsController < ApplicationController

  def new
  end

  def create
```

---

24. Before we wrote `remember user` without parentheses, but with the ternary operator omitting the parentheses results in a syntax error.

```ruby
    user = User.find_by(email: params[:session][:email].downcase)
    if user && user.authenticate(params[:session][:password])
      log_in user
      params[:session][:remember_me] == '1' ? remember(user) : forget(user)
      redirect_to user
    else
      flash.now[:danger] = 'Invalid email/password combination'
      render 'new'
    end
  end

  def destroy
    log_out if logged_in?
    redirect_to root_url
  end
end
```

With the implementation in Listing 8.49, our login system is complete, as you can verify by checking or unchecking the box in your browser.

Box 8.3 10 Types of People

There's an old joke that there are 10 kinds of people in the world: those who understand binary and those who don't (10, of course, being 2 in binary). In this spirit, we can say that there are 10 kinds of people in the world: those who like the ternary operator, those who don't, and those who don't yet know about it. (If you happen to be in the third category, soon you won't be any longer.)

When you do a lot of programming, you quickly learn that one of the most common bits of control flow goes something like this:

```ruby
if boolean?
  do_one_thing
else
  do_something_else
end
```

Ruby, like many other languages (including C/C++, Perl, PHP, and Java), allows you to replace this with a much more compact expression using the *ternary operator* (so called because it consists of three parts):

```ruby
boolean? ? do_one_thing : do_something_else
```

You can also use the ternary operator to replace assignment, so that

```
if boolean?
  var = foo
else
  var = bar
end
```

becomes

```
var = boolean? ? foo : bar
```

Finally, it's often convenient to use the ternary operator in a function's return value:

```
def foo
  do_stuff
  boolean? ? "bar" : "baz"
end
```

Because Ruby implicitly returns the value of the last expression in a function, here the foo method returns "bar" or "baz" depending on whether boolean? is true or false.

8.4.6 Remember Tests

Although our "remember me" functionality is now working, it's important to write some tests to verify its behavior. One reason is to catch implementation errors, as discussed momentarily. Even more important, though, is that the core user persistence code is, in fact, completely untested at present. Fixing these issues will require some trickery, but the result will be a far more powerful test suite.

Testing the "Remember Me" Check Box

When I originally implemented the check box handling in Listing 8.49, instead of the correct

```
params[:session][:remember_me] == '1' ? remember(user) : forget(user)
```

I actually used

```
params[:session][:remember_me] ? remember(user) : forget(user)
```

In this context, `params[:session][:remember_me]` is either `'0'` or `'1'`, both of which are `true` in a boolean context, so the resulting expression is *always true*, and the application acts as if the check box is always checked. This is easily missed and is exactly the kind of error a test can catch.

Because remembering users requires that they be logged in, our first step is to define a helper to log users in inside tests. In Listing 8.20, we logged a user in using the `post` method and a valid `session` hash, but it's cumbersome to do this every time. To avoid needless repetition, we'll write a helper method called `log_in_as` to log in for us.

Our method for logging a user in depends on the type of test. Inside integration tests, we can post to the sessions path as in Listing 8.20, but in other tests (such as controller and model tests) this approach won't work, and we need to manipulate the `session` method directly. As a result, `log_in_as` should detect the kind of test being used and adjust accordingly. We can tell the difference between integration tests and other kinds of tests using Ruby's convenient `defined?` method, which returns true if its argument is defined and false otherwise. In the present case, the `post_via_redirect` method (seen before in Listing 7.26) is available only in integration tests, so the code

```
defined?(post_via_redirect) ...
```

will return `true` inside an integration test and `false` otherwise. This suggests defining an `integration_test?` boolean method and writing an `if-else` statement schematically as follows:

```
if integration_test?
  # Log in by posting to the sessions path
else
  # Log in using the session
end
```

Filling in the comments with code leads to the `log_in_as` helper method shown in Listing 8.50. (This is a fairly advanced method, so you are doing well if you can read it with full comprehension.)

Listing 8.50   Adding a `log_in_as` helper.
test/test_helper.rb

```
ENV['RAILS_ENV'] ||= 'test'
 .
 .
 .
class ActiveSupport::TestCase
  fixtures :all

  # Returns true if a test user is logged in.
  def is_logged_in?
    !session[:user_id].nil?
  end

  # Logs in a test user.
  def log_in_as(user, options = {})
    password    = options[:password]    || 'password'
    remember_me = options[:remember_me] || '1'
    if integration_test?
      post login_path, session: { email:       user.email,
                                  password:    password,
                                  remember_me: remember_me }
    else
      session[:user_id] = user.id
    end
  end

  private

    # Returns true inside an integration test.
    def integration_test?
      defined?(post_via_redirect)
    end
end
```

For maximum flexibility, the `log_in_as` method in Listing 8.50 accepts an **options** hash (as in Listing 7.31), with default options for the password and for the "remember me" check box set to `'password'` and `'1'`, respectively. In particular, because hashes return **nil** for nonexistent keys, code like

```
remember_me = options[:remember_me] || '1'
```

evaluates to the given option if present and to the default otherwise (an application of the short-circuit evaluation described in Box 8.1).

To verify the behavior of the "remember me" check box, we'll write two tests, one each for submitting a user with and without the check box checked. This is easy using the login helper defined in Listing 8.50, with the two cases appearing as

```
log_in_as(@user, remember_me: '1')
```

and

```
log_in_as(@user, remember_me: '0')
```

(Because `'1'` is the default value of `remember_me`, we could omit the corresponding option in the first case, but I've included it to make the parallel structure more apparent.)

After logging in, we can check whether the user has been remembered by looking for the `remember_token` key in the `cookies`. Ideally, we would check that the cookie's value is equal to the user's remember token, but as currently designed there's no way for the test to get access to it: The `user` variable in the controller has a remember token attribute, but (because `remember_token` is virtual) the `@user` variable in the test doesn't. Fixing this minor blemish is left as an exercise (Section 8.6), but for now we can just test whether the relevant cookie is `nil`.

There's one more subtlety, which is that for some reason the `cookies` method doesn't work inside tests with symbols as keys, so that

```
cookies[:remember_token]
```

is always `nil`. Luckily, `cookies` *does* work with string keys, so that

```
cookies['remember_token']
```

has the value we need. The resulting tests appear in Listing 8.51. (Recall from Listing 8.20 that `users(:michael)` references the fixture user from Listing 8.19.)

Listing 8.51 A test of the "remember me" check box. **GREEN**
test/integration/users_login_test.rb

```
require 'test_helper'

class UsersLoginTest < ActionDispatch::IntegrationTest

  def setup
```

```
  @user = users(:michael)
end
  .
  .
  .
test "login with remembering" do
  log_in_as(@user, remember_me: '1')
  assert_not_nil cookies['remember_token']
end

test "login without remembering" do
  log_in_as(@user, remember_me: '0')
  assert_nil cookies['remember_token']
end
end
```

Assuming you didn't make the same implementation mistake I did, the tests should be **GREEN**:

Listing 8.52   GREEN

```
$ bundle exec rake test
```

Testing the Remember Branch

In Section 8.4.2, we verified by hand that the persistent session implemented in the preceding sections is working, but in fact the relevant branch in the `current_user` method is currently completely untested. My favorite way to handle this kind of situation is to raise an exception in the suspected untested block of code: If the code isn't covered, the tests will still pass; if it is covered, the resulting error will identify the relevant test. The result in the present case appears in Listing 8.53.

Listing 8.53   Raising an exception in an untested branch. **GREEN**
app/helpers/sessions_helper.rb

```
module SessionsHelper
  .
  .
  .
  # Returns the user corresponding to the remember token cookie.
  def current_user
    if (user_id = session[:user_id])
      @current_user ||= User.find_by(id: user_id)
    elsif (user_id = cookies.signed[:user_id])
```

```
    raise        # The tests still pass, so this branch is currently untested.
  user = User.find_by(id: user_id)
  if user && user.authenticated?(cookies[:remember_token])
    log_in user
    @current_user = user
  end
 end
end
 .
 .
 .
end
```

At this point, the tests are **GREEN**:

Listing 8.54 GREEN

```
$ bundle exec rake test
```

This is a problem, of course, because the code in Listing 8.53 is broken. Moreover, persistent sessions are cumbersome to check by hand, so if we ever want to refactor the `current_user` method (as we will in Chapter 10) it's important to test it.

Because the `log_in_as` helper method defined in Listing 8.50 automatically sets `session[:user_id]`, testing the "remember" branch of the `current_user` method is difficult in an integration test. Luckily, we can bypass this restriction by testing the `current_user` method directly in a Sessions helper test, whose file we have to create:

```
$ touch test/helpers/sessions_helper_test.rb
```

The test sequence is simple:

1. Define a `user` variable using the fixtures.
2. Call the `remember` method to remember the given user.
3. Verify that `current_user` is equal to the given user.

Because the `remember` method doesn't set `session[:user_id]`, this procedure will test the desired "remember" branch. The result appears in Listing 8.55.

Listing 8.55   A test for persistent sessions.

`test/helpers/sessions_helper_test.rb`

```
require 'test_helper'

class SessionsHelperTest < ActionView::TestCase

  def setup
    @user = users(:michael)
    remember(@user)
  end

  test "current_user returns right user when session is nil" do
    assert_equal @user, current_user
    assert is_logged_in?
  end

  test "current_user returns nil when remember digest is wrong" do
    @user.update_attribute(:remember_digest, User.digest(User.new_token))
    assert_nil current_user
  end
end
```

Note that we've added a second test, which checks that the current user is **nil** if the user's remember digest doesn't correspond correctly to the remember token, thereby testing the **authenticated?** expression in the nested **if** statement:

```
if user && user.authenticated?(cookies[:remember_token])
```

The test in Listing 8.55 is **RED** as required:

Listing 8.56   RED

```
$ bundle exec rake test TEST=test/helpers/sessions_helper_test.rb
```

We can get the tests in Listing 8.55 to pass by removing the **raise** method and restoring the original **current_user** method, as shown in Listing 8.57. (You can also remove the **authenticated?** expression in Listing 8.57 so that the second test in Listing 8.55 fails, which confirms that it tests the right thing.)

Listing 8.57   Removing the raised exception. **GREEN**
app/helpers/sessions_helper.rb

```
module SessionsHelper
    .
    .
    .
  # Returns the user corresponding to the remember token cookie.
  def current_user
    if (user_id = session[:user_id])
      @current_user ||= User.find_by(id: user_id)
    elsif (user_id = cookies.signed[:user_id])
      user = User.find_by(id: user_id)
      if user && user.authenticated?(cookies[:remember_token])
        log_in user
        @current_user = user
      end
    end
  end
    .
    .
    .
end
```

At this point, the test suite should be **GREEN**:

Listing 8.58   GREEN

```
$ bundle exec rake test
```

Now that the "remember" branch of `current_user` is tested, we can be confident of catching regressions without having to check by hand.

8.5   Conclusion

We've covered a lot of ground in the last two chapters, transforming our promising but unformed application into a site capable of the full suite of signup and login behaviors. All that is needed to complete the authentication functionality is to restrict access to pages based on login status and user identity. We'll accomplish this task en route to giving users the ability to edit their information, which is the main goal of Chapter 9.

Before moving on, merge your changes back into the master branch:

```
$ bundle exec rake test
$ git add -A
$ git commit -m "Finish log in/log out"
$ git checkout master
$ git merge log-in-log-out
```

Then push up the remote repository and the production server:

```
$ bundle exec rake test
$ git push
$ git push heroku
$ heroku run rake db:migrate
```

Note that the application will briefly be in an invalid state after pushing but before the migration is finished. On a production site with significant traffic, it is a good idea to turn on *maintenance mode* before making the changes:

```
$ heroku maintenance:on
$ git push heroku
$ heroku run rake db:migrate
$ heroku maintenance:off
```

This arranges to show a standard error page during the deployment and migration. (We won't bother with this step again, but it's good to see it at least once.) For more information, see the Heroku documentation on error pages.

8.5.1 What We Learned in This Chapter

- Rails can maintain state from one page to the next using both temporary and persistent cookies.
- The login form is designed to create a new session to log a user in.
- The `flash.now` method is used for flash messages on rendered pages.
- Test-driven development is useful when debugging by reproducing the bug in a test.
- Using the `session` method, we can securely place a user ID in the browser to create a temporary session.
- We can change features such as links on the layouts based on login status.

- Integration tests can verify correct routes, database updates, and proper changes to the layout.

- We associate to each user a remember token and a corresponding remember digest for use in persistent sessions.

- Using the `cookies` method, we create a persistent session by placing a permanent remember token cookie on the browser.

- Login status is determined by the presence of a current user based on the temporary session's user ID or the permanent session's unique remember token.

- The application signs users out by deleting the session's user ID and removing the permanent cookie from the browser.

- The ternary operator is a compact way to write simple `if-then` statements.

8.6 Exercises

Note: To receive a copy of the *Solutions Manual for Exercises*, with solutions to every exercise in the *Ruby on Rails*™ *Tutorial*, visit www.railstutorial.org/<word>, where "<word>" is the last word of the Figure 3.9 caption.

For a suggestion on how to avoid conflicts between exercises and the main tutorial, see the note on exercise topic branches in Section 3.6.

1. In Listing 8.32, we defined the new token and digest class methods by explicitly prefixing them with `User`. This works fine and, because they are actually *called* using `User.new_token` and `User.digest`, it is probably the clearest way to define them. But there are two perhaps more idiomatically correct ways to define class methods—one slightly confusing and one extremely confusing. By running the test suite, verify that the implementations in Listing 8.59 (slightly confusing) and Listing 8.60 (extremely confusing) are correct. (Note that, in the context of Listing 8.59 and Listing 8.60, `self` is the `User` class, whereas the other uses of `self` in the User model refer to a user object *instance*. This is part of what makes them confusing.)

2. As indicated in Section 8.4.6, as the application is currently designed, there's no way to access the virtual `remember_token` attribute in the integration test in Listing 8.51. It is possible, though, using a special test method called `assigns`.

Inside a test, you can access *instance* variables defined in the controller by using **assigns** with the corresponding symbol. For example, if the **create** action defines an **@user** variable, we can access it in the test using **assigns(:user)**. Right now, the Sessions controller **create** action defines a normal (non-instance) variable called **user**, but if we change it to an instance variable we can test that **cookies** correctly contains the user's remember token. By filling in the missing elements in Listing 8.61 and Listing 8.62 (indicated with question marks **?** and **FILL_IN**), complete this improved test of the "remember me" check box.

Listing 8.59 Defining the new token and digest methods using **self**. GREEN
app/models/user.rb

```
class User < ActiveRecord::Base
  .
  .
  .
  # Returns the hash digest of the given string.
  def self.digest(string)
    cost = ActiveModel::SecurePassword.min_cost ? BCrypt::Engine::MIN_COST :
                                                  BCrypt::Engine.cost
    BCrypt::Password.create(string, cost: cost)
  end

  # Returns a random token.
  def self.new_token
    SecureRandom.urlsafe_base64
  end
  .
  .
  .
end
```

Listing 8.60 Defining the new token and digest methods using **class << self**. GREEN
app/models/user.rb

```
class User < ActiveRecord::Base
  .
  .
  .
  class << self
    # Returns the hash digest of the given string.
```

```
    def digest(string)
      cost = ActiveModel::SecurePassword.min_cost ? BCrypt::Engine::MIN_COST :
                                                     BCrypt::Engine.cost
      BCrypt::Password.create(string, cost: cost)
    end

    # Returns a random token.
    def new_token
      SecureRandom.urlsafe_base64
    end
  end
  .
  .
  .
```

Listing 8.61 A template for using an instance variable in the **create** action.
app/controllers/sessions_controller.rb

```
class SessionsController < ApplicationController

  def new
  end

  def create
    ?user = User.find_by(email: params[:session][:email].downcase)
    if ?user && ?user.authenticate(params[:session][:password])
      log_in ?user
      params[:session][:remember_me] == '1' ? remember(?user) : forget(?user)
      redirect_to ?user
    else
      flash.now[:danger] = 'Invalid email/password combination'
      render 'new'
    end
  end

  def destroy
    log_out if logged_in?
    redirect_to root_url
  end
end
```

Listing 8.62 A template for an improved "remember me" test. **GREEN**
test/integration/users_login_test.rb

```ruby
require 'test_helper'

class UsersLoginTest < ActionDispatch::IntegrationTest

  def setup
    @user = users(:michael)
  end
  .
  .
  .
  test "login with remembering" do
    log_in_as(@user, remember_me: '1')
    assert_equal assigns(:user).FILL_IN, FILL_IN
  end

  test "login without remembering" do
    log_in_as(@user, remember_me: '0')
    assert_nil cookies['remember_token']
  end
  .
  .
  .
end
```

CHAPTER 9

Updating, Showing, and Deleting Users

In this chapter, we will complete the REST actions for the Users resource (Table 7.1) by adding **edit**, **update**, **index**, and **destroy** actions. We'll start by giving users the ability to update their profiles, which will also provide a natural opportunity to enforce an authorization model (made possible by the authentication code in Chapter 8). Then we'll make a listing of all users (also requiring authentication), which will motivate the introduction of sample data and pagination. Finally, we'll add the ability to destroy users, wiping them clear from the database. Since we can't allow just any user to have such dangerous powers, we'll take care to create a privileged class of administrative users authorized to delete other users.

9.1 Updating Users

The pattern for editing user information closely parallels that for creating new users (Chapter 7). Instead of a **new** action rendering a view for new users, we have an **edit** action rendering a view to edit users; instead of **create** responding to a POST request, we have an **update** action responding to a PATCH request (Box 3.2). The biggest difference is that, while anyone can sign up, only the current user should be able to update his or her own information. The authentication machinery from Chapter 8 will allow us to use a *before filter* to ensure that this is the case.

411

To get started, let's start work on an **updating-users** topic branch:

```
$ git checkout master
$ git checkout -b updating-users
```

9.1.1 Edit Form

We start with the edit form, whose mockup appears in Figure 9.1.[1] To turn the mockup in Figure 9.1 into a working page, we need to fill in both the Users controller **edit** action and the user edit view. We start with the **edit** action, which requires pulling the relevant user out of the database. Note from Table 7.1 that the proper URL for a user's edit page is /users/1/edit (assuming the user's ID is 1). Recall that the ID of the user is available in the **params[:id]** variable, which means that we can find the user with the code in Listing 9.1.

Listing 9.1   The user **edit** action.
app/controllers/users_controller.rb

```
class UsersController < ApplicationController

  def show
    @user = User.find(params[:id])
  end

  def new
    @user = User.new
  end

  def create
    @user = User.new(user_params)
    if @user.save
      log_in @user
      flash[:success] = "Welcome to the Sample App!"
      redirect_to @user
    else
      render 'new'
    end
  end
```

---

1. Image from http://www.flickr.com/photos/sashawolff/4598355045/.

```
def edit
  @user = User.find(params[:id])
end

private

  def user_params
    params.require(:user).permit(:name, :email, :password,
                                 :password_confirmation)
  end
end
```

Figure 9.1   A mockup of the user edit page.

The corresponding user edit view (which you will have to create by hand) is shown in Listing 9.2. Note how closely it resembles the new user view from Listing 7.13; the large overlap suggests factoring the repeated code into a partial, which is left as an exercise (Section 9.6).

Listing 9.2 The user edit view.
app/views/users/edit.html.erb

```erb
<% provide(:title, "Edit user") %>
<h1>Update your profile</h1>

<div class="row">
  <div class="col-md-6 col-md-offset-3">
    <%= form_for(@user) do |f| %>
      <%= render 'shared/error_messages' %>

      <%= f.label :name %>
      <%= f.text_field :name, class: 'form-control' %>

      <%= f.label :email %>
      <%= f.email_field :email, class: 'form-control' %>

      <%= f.label :password %>
      <%= f.password_field :password, class: 'form-control' %>

      <%= f.label :password_confirmation, "Confirmation" %>
      <%= f.password_field :password_confirmation, class: 'form-control' %>

      <%= f.submit "Save changes", class: "btn btn-primary" %>
    <% end %>

    <div class="gravatar_edit">
      <%= gravatar_for @user %>
      <a href="http://gravatar.com/emails" target=_blank>change</a>
    </div>
  </div>
</div>
```

Here we have reused the shared **error_messages** partial introduced in Section 7.3.3. By the way, the use of **target=_blank** in the Gravatar link is a neat trick to get the browser to open the page in a new window or tab, which is convenient behavior when linking to a third-party site.

With the **@user** instance variable from Listing 9.1, the edit page should render properly, as shown in Figure 9.2. The "Name" and "Email" fields in Figure 9.2 also

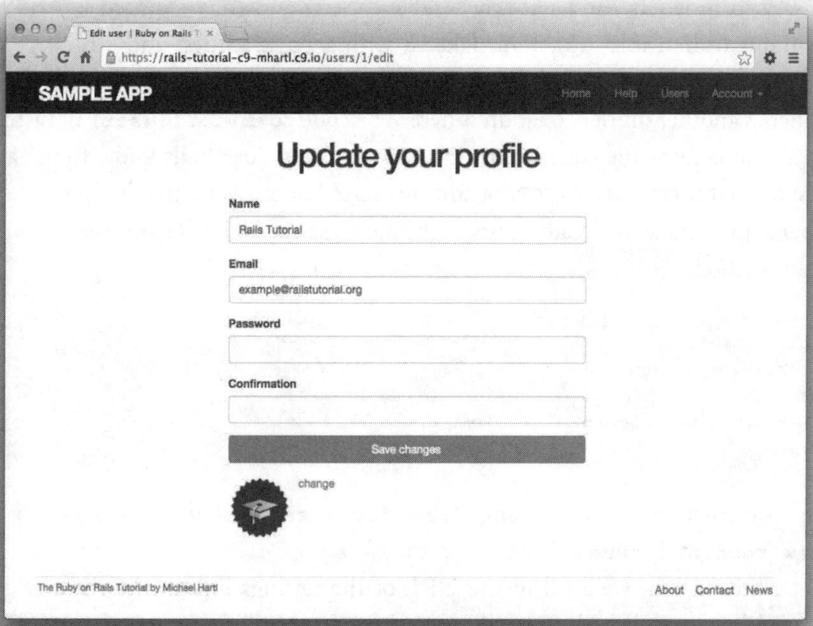

Figure 9.2 The initial user edit page with prefilled name and email fields.

show how Rails automatically prefills the Name and Email fields using the attributes of the existing `@user` variable.

Looking at the HTML source for Figure 9.2, we see a form tag as expected, as in Listing 9.3 (slight details may differ).

Listing 9.3 HTML for the edit form defined in Listing 9.2 and shown in Figure 9.2.

```
<form accept-charset="UTF-8" action="/users/1" class="edit_user"
    id="edit_user_1" method="post">
  <input name="_method" type="hidden" value="patch" />
  .
  .
  .
</form>
```

Note here the hidden input field

```
<input name="_method" type="hidden" value="patch" />
```

Because web browsers can't natively send PATCH requests (as required by the REST conventions from Table 7.1), Rails fakes it with a POST request and a hidden **input** field.[2]

There's another subtlety to address here: The code **form_for(@user)** in Listing 9.2 is *exactly* the same as the code in Listing 7.13—so how does Rails know to use a POST request for new users and a PATCH for editing users? The answer is that it is possible to tell whether a user is new or already exists in the database via Active Record's **new_record?** boolean method:

```
$ rails console
>> User.new.new_record?
=> true
>> User.first.new_record?
=> false
```

When constructing a form using **form_for(@user)**, Rails uses POST if **@user.new_record?** is **true** and PATCH if it is **false**.

As a final touch, we'll fill in the URL of the settings link in the site navigation. This is easily accomplished using the named route **edit_user_path** from Table 7.1, together with the handy **current_user** helper method defined in Listing 8.36:

```
<%= link_to "Settings", edit_user_path(current_user) %>
```

The full application code appears in Listing 9.4.

Listing 9.4 Adding a URL to the "Settings" link in the site layout.
app/views/layouts/_header.html.erb

```
<header class="navbar navbar-fixed-top navbar-inverse">
  <div class="container">
    <%= link_to "sample app", root_path, id: "logo" %>
    <nav>
      <ul class="nav navbar-nav navbar-right">
        <li><%= link_to "Home", root_path %></li>
```

---

2. Don't worry about how this works; the details are of interest to developers of the Rails framework itself, and by design are not important for Rails application developers.

```
        <li><%= link_to "Help", help_path %></li>
        <% if logged_in? %>
          <li><%= link_to "Users", '#' %></li>
          <li class="dropdown">
            <a href="#" class="dropdown-toggle" data-toggle="dropdown">
              Account <b class="caret"></b>
            </a>
            <ul class="dropdown-menu">
              <li><%= link_to "Profile", current_user %></li>
              <li><%= link_to "Settings",
                      edit_user_path(current_user) %></li>
              <li class="divider"></li>
              <li>
                <%= link_to "Log out", logout_path, method: "delete" %>
              </li>
            </ul>
          </li>
        <% else %>
          <li><%= link_to "Log in", login_path %></li>
        <% end %>
      </ul>
    </nav>
  </div>
</header>
```

9.1.2 Unsuccessful Edits

In this section we'll handle unsuccessful edits, following similar ideas to how we handled unsuccessful sign-ups (Section 7.3). We start by creating an **update** action, which uses **update_attributes** (Section 6.1.5) to update the user based on the submitted **params** hash, as shown in Listing 9.5. With invalid information, the update attempt returns **false**, so the **else** branch renders the edit page. We've seen this pattern before; the structure closely parallels the first version of the **create** action (Listing 7.16).

Listing 9.5 The initial user **update** action.
app/controllers/users_controller.rb

```
class UsersController < ApplicationController

  def show
    @user = User.find(params[:id])
```

```
  end

  def new
    @user = User.new
  end

  def create
    @user = User.new(user_params)
    if @user.save
      log_in @user
      flash[:success] = "Welcome to the Sample App!"
      redirect_to @user
    else
      render 'new'
    end
  end

  def edit
    @user = User.find(params[:id])
  end

  def update
    @user = User.find(params[:id])
    if @user.update_attributes(user_params)
      # Handle a successful update.
    else
      render 'edit'
    end
  end

  private

    def user_params
      params.require(:user).permit(:name, :email, :password,
                                   :password_confirmation)
    end
end
```

Note the use of **user_params** in the call to **update_attributes**, which uses strong parameters to prevent mass assignment vulnerability (as described in Section 7.3.2).

Because of the existing User model validations and the error-messages partial in Listing 9.2, submission of invalid information results in helpful error messages (Figure 9.3).

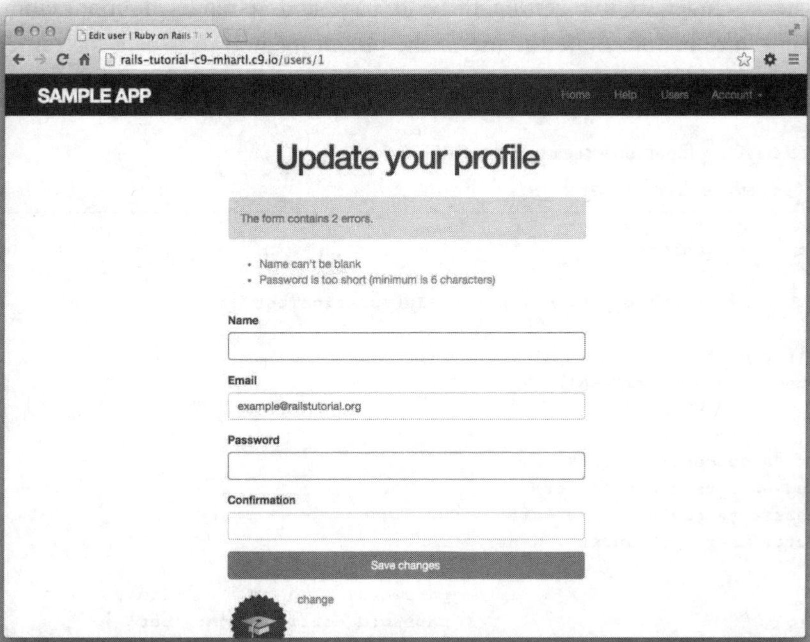

Figure 9.3 Error message from submitting the update form.

9.1.3 Testing Unsuccessful Edits

We left Section 9.1.2 with a working edit form. Following the testing guidelines from Box 3.3, we'll now write an integration test to catch any regressions. Our first step is to generate an integration test as usual:

```
$ rails generate integration_test users_edit
    invoke  test_unit
    create    test/integration/users_edit_test.rb
```

Then we'll write a simple test of an unsuccessful edit, as shown in Listing 9.6. The test in Listing 9.6 checks for the correct behavior by verifying that the edit template is rendered after getting the edit page and re-rendered upon submission of invalid information. Note the use of the **patch** method to issue a PATCH request, which follows the same pattern as **get**, **post**, and **delete**.

Listing 9.6 A test for an unsuccessful edit. **GREEN**

test/integration/users_edit_test.rb

```
require 'test_helper'

class UsersEditTest < ActionDispatch::IntegrationTest

  def setup
    @user = users(:michael)
  end

  test "unsuccessful edit" do
    get edit_user_path(@user)
    assert_template 'users/edit'
    patch user_path(@user), user: { name:  '',
                                    email: 'foo@invalid',
                                    password:              'foo',
                                    password_confirmation: 'bar' }
    assert_template 'users/edit'
  end
end
```

At this point, the test suite should still be **GREEN**:

Listing 9.7 GREEN

```
$ bundle exec rake test
```

9.1.4 Successful Edits (with TDD)

Now it's time to get the edit form to work. The ability to edit the profile images is already functional because we've outsourced image upload to the Gravatar website; we can edit Gravatars by clicking on the "change" link from Figure 9.2, as shown in Figure 9.4. Let's get the rest of the user edit functionality working as well.

As you get more comfortable with testing, you might find that it's useful to write integration tests before you write the application code, instead of after. In this context,

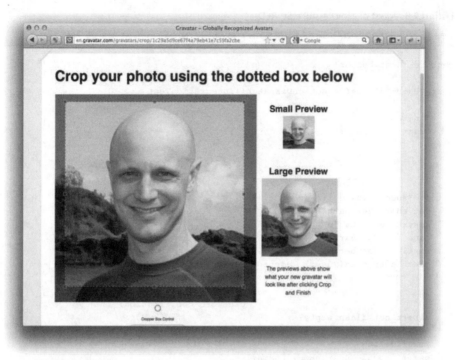

Figure 9.4   The Gravatar image-cropping interface, with a picture of some dude.

the tests are sometimes known as *acceptance tests*, because they determine when a particular feature should be accepted as complete. To see how this works, we'll complete the user edit feature using test-driven development.

We'll test for the correct behavior of updating users by writing a test similar to the one shown in Listing 9.6, except that this time we'll submit valid information. Then we'll check for a nonempty flash message and a successful redirect to the profile page, while also verifying that the user's information was correctly changed in the database. The result appears in Listing 9.8. Note that the password and confirmation in Listing 9.8 are blank, which is convenient for users who don't want to update their passwords every time they update their names or email addresses. Note also the use of `@user.reload` (first seen in Section 6.1.5) to reload the user's values from the database and confirm that the use profile was successfully updated. (This is the kind of detail you could easily forget initially, which is why acceptance testing—and TDD generally—require a certain level of experience to be effective.)

Listing 9.8 A test of a successful edit. **RED**

test/integration/users_edit_test.rb

```ruby
require 'test_helper'

class UsersEditTest < ActionDispatch::IntegrationTest

  def setup
    @user = users(:michael)
  end
  .
  .
  .
  test "successful edit" do
    get edit_user_path(@user)
    assert_template 'users/edit'
    name  = "Foo Bar"
    email = "foo@bar.com"
    patch user_path(@user), user: { name:  name,
                                    email: email,
                                    password:             "",
                                    password_confirmation: "" }
    assert_not flash.empty?
    assert_redirected_to @user
    @user.reload
    assert_equal @user.name,  name
    assert_equal @user.email, email
  end
end
```

The **update** action needed to get the tests in Listing 9.8 to pass is similar to the final form of the **create** action (Listing 8.22), as seen in Listing 9.9.

Listing 9.9 The user **update** action. **RED**

app/controllers/users_controller.rb

```ruby
class UsersController < ApplicationController
  .
  .
  .
  def update
    @user = User.find(params[:id])
    if @user.update_attributes(user_params)
      flash[:success] = "Profile updated"
      redirect_to @user
    else
      render 'edit'
```

```
      end
    end
    .
    .
    .
end
```

As indicated in the Listing 9.9 caption, the test suite is still **RED**, which is the result of the password length validation (Listing 6.39) failing due to the blank password and confirmation in Listing 9.8. To get the tests to become **GREEN**, we need to make an exception to the minimum length validation if the password is blank. We can do this by passing the `allow_blank: true` option to `validates`, as seen in Listing 9.10.

Listing 9.10 Allowing blank passwords on update. **GREEN**
app/models/user.rb

```
class User < ActiveRecord::Base
  before_save { self.email = email.downcase }
  validates :name, presence: true, length: { maximum: 50 }
  VALID_EMAIL_REGEX = /\A[\w+\-.]+@[a-z\d\-.]+\.[a-z]+\z/i
  validates :email, presence: true, length: { maximum: 255 }
                    format: { with: VALID_EMAIL_REGEX },
                    uniqueness: { case_sensitive: false }
  has_secure_password
  validates :password, length: {minimum: 6}, allow_blank: true
  .
  .
  .
end
```

In case you're worried that Listing 9.10 might allow new users to sign up with blank passwords, recall from Section 6.3 that `has_secure_password` enforces presence validations upon object creation.

With the code in this section, the user edit page should be working (Figure 9.5), as you can double-check by rerunning the test suite, which should now be **GREEN**:

Listing 9.11 **GREEN**

```
$ bundle exec rake test
```

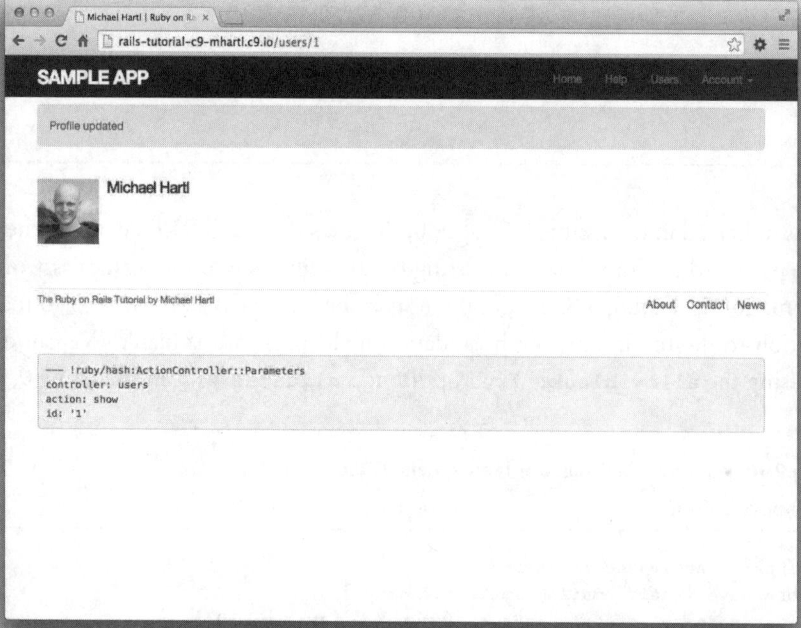

Figure 9.5 The result of a successful edit.

9.2 Authorization

In the context of web applications, *authentication* allows us to identify users of our site, and *authorization* lets us control what they can do. One nice effect of building the authentication machinery in Chapter 8 is that we are now in a position to implement authorization as well.

Although the edit and update actions from Section 9.1 are functionally complete, they suffer from a ridiculous security flaw: they allow anyone (even non-logged-in users) to access either action, and any logged-in user can update the information for any other user. In this section, we'll implement a security model that requires users to be logged in and prevents them from updating any information other than their own.

In Section 9.2.1, we'll handle the case of non-logged-in users who try to access a protected page to which they might normally have access. Because this could easily happen in the normal course of using the application, such users will be forwarded to the login page with a helpful message, as mocked up in Figure 9.6. In contrast, users who try to access a page for which they would never be authorized (such as a logged-in user trying to access a different user's edit page) will be redirected to the root URL (Section 9.2.2).

9.2.1 Requiring Logged-in Users

To implement the forwarding behavior shown in Figure 9.6, we'll use a *before filter* in the Users controller. Before filters use the `before_action` command to arrange

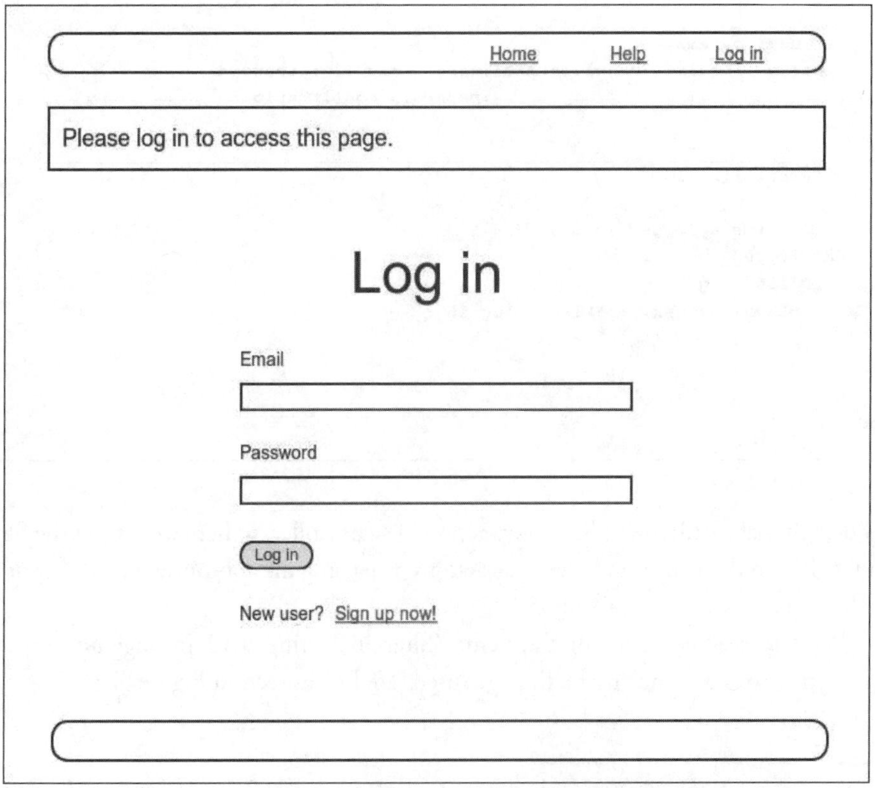

Figure 9.6 A mockup of the result of visiting a protected page.

for a particular method to be called before the given actions.[3] To require users to be logged in, we define a `logged_in_user` method and invoke it using **before_action** **:logged_in_user**, as shown in Listing 9.12.

Listing 9.12 Adding a `logged_in_user` before filter. **RED**
app/controllers/users_controller.rb

```
class UsersController < ApplicationController
  before_action :logged_in_user, only: [:edit, :update]
    .
    .
    .
  private

    def user_params
      params.require(:user).permit(:name, :email, :password,
                                   :password_confirmation)
    end

    # Before filters

    # Confirms a logged-in user.
    def logged_in_user
      unless logged_in?
        flash[:danger] = "Please log in."
        redirect_to login_url
      end
    end
end
```

By default, before filters apply to *every* action in a controller, so here we restrict the filter to act only on the `:edit` and `:update` actions by passing the appropriate `:only` options hash.

We can see the result of the before filter in Listing 9.12 by logging out and attempting to access the "user edit page /users/1/edit," as seen in Figure 9.7.

---

3. The command for before filters used to be called **before_filter**, but the Rails core team decided to rename it to emphasize that the filter is executed before particular controller actions.

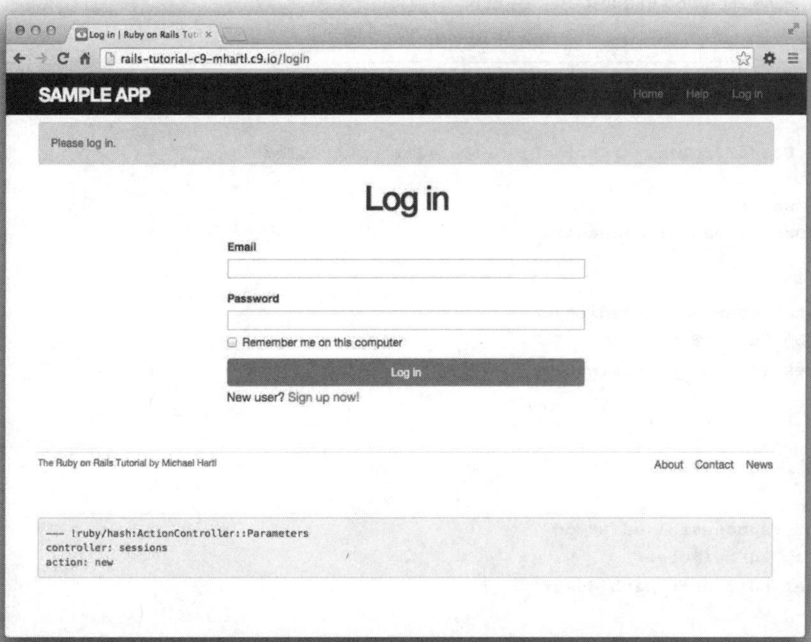

Figure 9.7 The login form after trying to access a protected page.

As indicated in the Listing 9.12 caption, our test suite is currently **RED**:

Listing 9.13 RED

```
$ bundle exec rake test
```

The reason is that the edit and update actions now require a logged-in user, but no user is logged in inside the corresponding tests.

We'll fix our test suite by logging the user in before carrying out the edit or update actions. This is easily accomplished using the `log_in_as` helper developed in Section 8.4.6 (Listing 8.50), as shown in Listing 9.14.

Listing 9.14 Logging in a test user. **GREEN**

test/integration/users_edit_test.rb

```ruby
require 'test_helper'

class UsersEditTest < ActionDispatch::IntegrationTest

  def setup
    @user = users(:michael)
  end

  test "unsuccessful edit" do
    log_in_as(@user)
    get edit_user_path(@user)
    .
    .
    .
  end

  test "successful edit" do
    log_in_as(@user)
    get edit_user_path(@user)
    .
    .
    .
  end
end
```

We could eliminate some duplication by putting the test login in the `setup` method
of Listing 9.14, but in Section 9.2.3 we'll change one of the tests to visit the edit page
before logging in, which isn't possible if the login step happens during the test setup.

At this point, our test suite should be green:

Listing 9.15 GREEN

```
$ bundle exec rake test
```

Even though our test suite is now passing, we're not finished with the before filter,
because the suite is still **GREEN** even if we remove our security model, as you can verify
by commenting it out (Listing 9.16). This is a Bad Thing—of all the regressions we'd

like our test suite to catch, a massive security hole is probably number 1, so the code in Listing 9.16 should definitely be **RED**. Let's write tests to arrange that.

Listing 9.16 Commenting out the before filter to test our security model. **GREEN**
app/controllers/users_controller.rb

```
class UsersController < ApplicationController
  # before_action :logged_in_user, only: [:edit, :update]
  .
  .
  .
end
```

Because the before filter operates on a per-action basis, we'll put the corresponding tests in the Users controller test. The plan is to hit the `edit` and `update` action with the right kinds of requests and verify that the flash is set and that the user is redirected to the login path. From Table 7.1, we see that the proper requests are GET and PATCH, respectively, which means using the `get` and `patch` methods inside the tests. The results appear in Listing 9.17.

Listing 9.17 Testing that `edit` and `update` are protected. **RED**
test/controllers/users_controller_test.rb

```
require 'test_helper'

class UsersControllerTest < ActionController::TestCase

  def setup
    @user = users(:michael)
  end

  test "should get new" do
    get :new
    assert_response :success
  end

  test "should redirect edit when not logged in" do
    get :edit, id: @user
    assert_not flash.empty?
    assert_redirected_to login_url
```

```
   end

   test "should redirect update when not logged in" do
     patch :update, id: @user, user: { name: @user.name, email: @user.email }
     assert_not flash.empty?
     assert_redirected_to login_url
   end
end
```

Note the arguments to `get` and `patch` involve code like

```
get :edit, id: @user
```

and

```
patch :update, id: @user, user: { name: @user.name, email: @user.email }
```

This uses the Rails convention of `id: @user`, which (as in controller redirects) automatically uses `@user.id`. In the second case, we need to supply an additional `user` hash for the routes to work properly. (If you look at the generated Users controller tests from the toy app in Chapter 2, you'll see the preceding code.)

The test suite should now be **RED**, as required. To get it to become **GREEN**, just uncomment the before filter (Listing 9.18).

Listing 9.18 Uncommenting the before filter. **GREEN**
app/controllers/users_controller.rb

```
class UsersController < ApplicationController
  before_action :logged_in_user, only: [:edit, :update]
  .
  .
  .
end
```

With that, our test suite should be **GREEN**:

Listing 9.19 GREEN

```
$ bundle exec rake test
```

Any accidental exposure of the edit methods to unauthorized users will now be caught immediately by our test suite.

9.2.2 Requiring the Right User

Of course, requiring users to log in isn't quite enough; users should be allowed to edit only their *own* information. As we saw in Section 9.2.1, it's easy to have a test suite that misses an essential security flaw, so we'll proceed using test-driven development to ensure that our code implements the security model correctly. To do this, we'll add tests to the Users controller test to complement the ones shown in Listing 9.17.

To make sure users can't edit other users' information, we need to be able to log in as a second user. This means adding a second user to our users fixture file, as shown in Listing 9.20.

Listing 9.20 Adding a second user to the fixture file.
test/fixtures/users.yml

```
michael:
  name: Michael Example
  email: michael@example.com
  password_digest: <%= User.digest('password') %>

archer:
  name: Sterling Archer
  email: duchess@example.gov
  password_digest: <%= User.digest('password') %>
```

By using the `log_in_as` method defined in Listing 8.50, we can test the `edit` and `update` actions as in Listing 9.21. Note that we expect to redirect users to the root path instead of the login path because a user trying to edit a different user would already be logged in.

Listing 9.21 Tests for trying to edit as the wrong user. **RED**
test/controllers/users_controller_test.rb

```ruby
require 'test_helper'

class UsersControllerTest < ActionController::TestCase

  def setup
    @user       = users(:michael)
    @other_user = users(:archer)
  end

  test "should get new" do
    get :new
    assert_response :success
  end

  test "should redirect edit when not logged in" do
    get :edit, id: @user
    assert_not flash.empty?
    assert_redirected_to login_url
  end

  test "should redirect update when not logged in" do
    patch :update, id: @user, user: { name: @user.name, email: @user.email }
    assert_not flash.empty?
    assert_redirected_to login_url
  end

  test "should redirect edit when logged in as wrong user" do
    log_in_as(@other_user)
    get :edit, id: @user
    assert flash.empty?
    assert_redirected_to root_url
  end

  test "should redirect update when logged in as wrong user" do
    log_in_as(@other_user)
    patch :update, id: @user, user: { name: @user.name, email: @user.email }
    assert flash.empty?
    assert_redirected_to root_url
  end
end
```

To redirect users trying to edit another user's profile, we'll add a second method called **correct_user**, together with a before filter to call it (Listing 9.22). Note that the **correct_user** before filter defines the **@user** variable, so Listing 9.22 also shows that we can eliminate the **@user** assignments in the **edit** and **update** actions.

Listing 9.22 A **correct_user** before filter to protect the edit/update pages. **GREEN**
app/controllers/users_controller.rb

```ruby
class UsersController < ApplicationController
  before_action :logged_in_user, only: [:edit, :update]
  before_action :correct_user,   only: [:edit, :update]
  .
  .
  .
  def edit
  end

  def update
    if @user.update_attributes(user_params)
      flash[:success] = "Profile updated"
      redirect_to @user
    else
      render 'edit'
    end
  end
  .
  .
  .
  private

    def user_params
      params.require(:user).permit(:name, :email, :password,
                                   :password_confirmation)
    end

    # Before filters

    # Confirms a logged-in user.
    def logged_in_user
      unless logged_in?
        flash[:danger] = "Please log in."
        redirect_to login_url
      end
    end

    # Confirms the correct user.
    def correct_user
```

```
      @user = User.find(params[:id])
      redirect_to(root_url) unless @user == current_user
    end
end
```

At this point, our test suite should be **GREEN**:

Listing 9.23   GREEN

```
$ bundle exec rake test
```

As a final refactoring, we'll adopt a common convention and define a `current_user?` boolean method for use in the `correct_user` before filter, which we define in the Sessions helper (Listing 9.24). We'll use this method to replace code like

```
unless @user == current_user
```

with the (slightly) more expressive

```
unless current_user?(@user)
```

Listing 9.24   The `current_user?` method.
app/helpers/sessions_helper.rb

```
module SessionsHelper

  # Logs in the given user.
  def log_in(user)
    session[:user_id] = user.id
  end

  # Remembers a user in a persistent session.
  def remember(user)
    user.remember
    cookies.permanent.signed[:user_id] = user.id
    cookies.permanent[:remember_token] = user.remember_token
  end
```

```
  # Returns true if the given user is the current user.
  def current_user?(user)
    user == current_user
  end
  .
  .
  .
end
```

Replacing the direct comparison with the boolean method gives the code shown in Listing 9.25.

Listing 9.25 The final `correct_user` before filter. **GREEN**
app/controllers/users_controller.rb

```
class UsersController < ApplicationController
  before_action :logged_in_user, only: [:edit, :update]
  before_action :correct_user,   only: [:edit, :update]
  .
  .
  .
  def edit
  end

  def update
    if @user.update_attributes(user_params)
      flash[:success] = "Profile updated"
      redirect_to @user
    else
      render 'edit'
    end
  end
  .
  .
  .
  private

    def user_params
      params.require(:user).permit(:name, :email, :password,
                                   :password_confirmation)
    end

    # Before filters
```

```ruby
  # Confirms a logged-in user.
  def logged_in_user
    unless logged_in?
      flash[:danger] = "Please log in."
      redirect_to login_url
    end
  end

  # Confirms the correct user.
  def correct_user
    @user = User.find(params[:id])
    redirect_to(root_url) unless current_user?(@user)
  end
end
```

9.2.3 Friendly Forwarding

Our site authorization is complete as written, but there is one minor blemish: When users try to access a protected page, they are currently redirected to their profile pages regardless of where they were trying to go. In other words, if a non-logged-in user tries to visit the edit page, after logging in the user will be redirected to /users/1 instead of /users/1/edit. It would be much friendlier to redirect users to their intended destination instead.

The application code will turn out to be relatively complicated, but we can write a ridiculously simple test for friendly forwarding just by reversing the order of logging in and visiting the edit page in Listing 9.14. As seen in Listing 9.26, the resulting test tries to visit the edit page, then logs in, and then checks that the user is redirected to the *edit* page instead of the default profile page. (Listing 9.26 also removes the test for rendering the edit template since that's no longer the expected behavior.)

Listing 9.26 A test for friendly forwarding. **RED**

test/integration/users_edit_test.rb

```ruby
require 'test_helper'

class UsersEditTest < ActionDispatch::IntegrationTest

  def setup
    @user = users(:michael)
  end
```

```
        .
        .
        .
  test "successful edit with friendly forwarding" do
    get edit_user_path(@user)
    log_in_as(@user)
    assert_redirected_to edit_user_path(@user)
    name  = "Foo Bar"
    email = "foo@bar.com"
    patch user_path(@user), user: { name:  name,
                                    email: email,
                                    password:              "foobar",
                                    password_confirmation: "foobar" }
    assert_not flash.empty?
    assert_redirected_to @user
    @user.reload
    assert_equal @user.name,  name
    assert_equal @user.email, email
  end
end
```

Now that we have a failing test, we're ready to implement friendly forwarding.[4] To forward users to their intended destination, we need to store the location of the requested page somewhere, and then redirect the user to that location instead of to the default. We accomplish this with a pair of methods, `store_location` and `redirect_back_or`, both of which are defined in the Sessions helper (Listing 9.27).

Listing 9.27 Code to implement friendly forwarding.

app/helpers/sessions_helper.rb

```
module SessionsHelper
  .
  .
  .
  # Redirects to stored location (or to the default).
  def redirect_back_or(default)
    redirect_to(session[:forwarding_url] || default)
    session.delete(:forwarding_url)
  end
```

---

4. The code in this section is adapted from the Clearance gem by thoughtbot.

```
# Stores the URL trying to be accessed.
def store_location
  session[:forwarding_url] = request.url if request.get?
end
end
```

Here the storage mechanism for the forwarding URL is the same **session** facility we used in Section 8.2.1 to log the user in. Listing 9.27 also uses the **request** object (via **request.url**) to get the URL of the requested page.

The **store_location** method in Listing 9.27 puts the requested URL in the **session** variable under the key **:forwarding_url**, but only for a **GET** request. This prevents storing the forwarding URL if a user, say, submits a form when not logged in (which is an edge case but could happen if, for example, a user deleted the session cookies by hand before submitting the form). In such a case, the resulting redirect would issue a **GET** request to a URL expecting **POST**, **PATCH**, or **DELETE**, thereby causing an error. Including **if request.get?** prevents this from happening.[5]

To make use of **store_location**, we need to add it to the **logged_in_user** before filter, as shown in Listing 9.28.

Listing 9.28 Adding **store_location** to the logged-in user before filter.

app/controllers/users_controller.rb

```
class UsersController < ApplicationController
  before_action :logged_in_user, only: [:edit, :update]
  before_action :correct_user,   only: [:edit, :update]
  .
  .
  .
  def edit
  end
  .
  .
  .
  private

    def user_params
      params.require(:user).permit(:name, :email, :password,
                                   :password_confirmation)
    end
```

---

5. Thanks to reader Yoel Adler for pointing out this subtle issue, and for discovering the solution.

```
    # Before filters

    # Confirms a logged-in user.

    def logged_in_user
      unless logged_in?
        store_location
        flash[:danger] = "Please log in."
        redirect_to login_url
      end
    end

    # Confirms the correct user.
    def correct_user
      @user = User.find(params[:id])
      redirect_to(root_url) unless current_user?(@user)
    end
end
```

To implement the forwarding itself, we use the **redirect_back_or** method to redirect to the requested URL if it exists, or some default URL otherwise, which we add to the Sessions controller **create** action to redirect after successful login (Listing 9.29). The **redirect_back_or** method uses the or operator || through

```
session[:forwarding_url] || default
```

This evaluates to **session[:forwarding_url]** unless it's **nil**, in which case it evaluates to the given default URL. Note that Listing 9.27 is careful to remove the forwarding URL; otherwise, subsequent login attempts would forward to the protected page until the user closed the browser. [Testing for this is left as an exercise (Section 9.6).] Also note that the session deletion occurs even though the line with the redirect appears first; redirects don't happen until an explicit **return** or the end of the method, so any code appearing after the redirect is still executed.

Listing 9.29   The Sessions **create** action with friendly forwarding.
app/controllers/sessions_controller.rb

```
class SessionsController < ApplicationController
    .
    .
    .
```

```
  def create
    user = User.find_by(email: params[:session][:email].downcase)
    if user && user.authenticate(params[:session][:password])
      log_in user
      params[:session][:remember_me] == '1' ? remember(user) : forget(user)
      redirect_back_or user
    else
      flash.now[:danger] = 'Invalid email/password combination'
      render 'new'
    end
  end
  .
  .
  .
end
```

With that, the friendly forwarding integration test in Listing 9.26 should pass, and the basic user authentication and page protection implementation is complete. As usual, it's a good idea to verify that the test suite is **GREEN** before proceeding:

Listing 9.30 GREEN

```
$ bundle exec rake test
```

9.3 Showing All Users

In this section, we'll add the penultimate user action, the `index` action, which is designed to display *all* the users instead of just one. Along the way, we'll learn how to seed the database with sample users and how to *paginate* the user output so that the index page can scale up to display a potentially large number of users. A mockup of the result—users, pagination links, and a "Users" navigation link—appears in Figure 9.8.[6] In Section 9.4, we'll add an administrative interface to the users index so that users can also be destroyed.

---

6. Baby photo from http://www.flickr.com/photos/glasgows/338937124/.

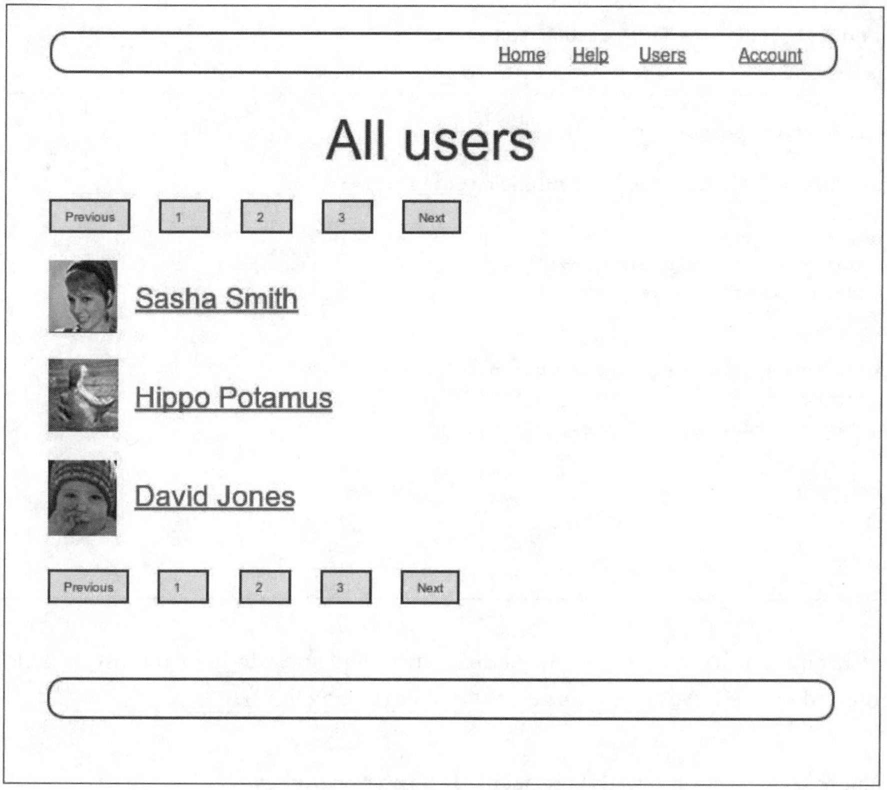

Figure 9.8 A mockup of the users index page.

9.3.1 Users Index

To get started with the users index, we'll first implement a security model. Although we'll keep individual user **show** pages visible to all site visitors, the user **index** will be restricted to logged-in users so that there's a limit to how much unregistered users can see by default.[7]

To protect the **index** page from unauthorized access, we'll first add a short test to verify that the **index** action is redirected properly (Listing 9.31).

---

7. This is the same authorization model used by Twitter.

Listing 9.31 Testing the **index** action redirect. **RED**

test/controllers/users_controller_test.rb

```
require 'test_helper'

class UsersControllerTest < ActionController::TestCase

  def setup
    @user       = users(:michael)
    @other_user = users(:archer)
  end

  test "should redirect index when not logged in" do
    get :index
    assert_redirected_to login_url
  end
  .
  .
  .
end
```

Then we just need to add an **index** action and include it in the list of actions protected by the **logged_in_user** before filter (Listing 9.32).

Listing 9.32 Requiring a logged-in user for the **index** action. **GREEN**

app/controllers/users_controller.rb

```
class UsersController < ApplicationController
  before_action :logged_in_user, only: [:index, :edit, :update]
  before_action :correct_user,   only: [:edit, :update]

  def index
  end

  def show
    @user = User.find(params[:id])
  end
  .
  .
  .
end
```

To display the users themselves, we need to make a variable containing all the site's users and then render each one by iterating through them in the index view. As you may recall from the corresponding action in the toy app (Listing 2.5), we can use **User.all** to pull all the users out of the database, assigning them to an **@users** instance variable for use in the view, as seen in Listing 9.33. (If displaying all the users at once seems like a bad idea, you're right, and we'll remove this blemish in Section 9.3.3.)

Listing 9.33   The user **index** action.
app/controllers/users_controller.rb

```
class UsersController < ApplicationController
  before_action :logged_in_user, only: [:index, :edit, :update]
    .
    .
    .
  def index
    @users = User.all
  end
    .
    .
    .
end
```

To make the actual index page, we'll make a view (whose file you'll have to create) that iterates through the users and wraps each one in an **li** tag. We do this with the **each** method, displaying each user's Gravatar and name, while wrapping the whole thing in a **ul** tag (Listing 9.34).

Listing 9.34   The users index view.
app/views/users/index.html.erb

```
<% provide(:title, 'All users') %>
<h1>All users</h1>

<ul class="users">
  <% @users.each do |user| %>
    <li>
      <%= gravatar_for user, size: 50 %>
      <%= link_to user.name, user %>
    </li>
```

```
  <% end %>
</ul>
```

The code in Listing 9.34 uses the result of Listing 7.31 from Section 7.7, which allows us to pass an option to the Gravatar helper specifying a size other than the default. If you didn't do that exercise, update your Users helper file with the contents of Listing 7.31 before proceeding.

Let's also add a little CSS (or, rather, SCSS) for style (Listing 9.35).

Listing 9.35 CSS for the users index.

app/assets/stylesheets/custom.css.scss

```
. . . /* Users index */

.users {
  list-style: none;
  margin: 0;
  li {
    overflow: auto;
    padding: 10px 0;
    border-bottom: 1px solid $gray-lighter;
  }
}
```

Finally, we'll add the URL to the users link in the site's navigation header using **users_path**, thereby using the last of the unused named routes in Table 7.1. The result appears in Listing 9.36.

Listing 9.36 Adding the URL to the users link.

app/views/layouts/_header.html.erb

```
<header class="navbar navbar-fixed-top navbar-inverse">
  <div class="container">
    <%= link_to "sample app", root_path, id: "logo" %>
    <nav>
      <ul class="nav navbar-nav navbar-right">
        <li><%= link_to "Home", root_path %></li>
        <li><%= link_to "Help", help_path %></li>
        <% if logged_in? %>
          <li><%= link_to "Users", users_path %></li>
          <li class="dropdown">
            <a href="#" class="dropdown-toggle" data-toggle="dropdown">
              Account <b class="caret"></b>
```

```
          </a>
          <ul class="dropdown-menu">
            <li><%= link_to "Profile", current_user %></li>
            <li><%= link_to "Settings", edit_user_path(current_user) %></li>
            <li class="divider"></li>
            <li>
              <%= link_to "Log out", logout_path, method: "delete" %>
            </li>
          </ul>
        </li>
      <% else %>
        <li><%= link_to "Log in", login_path %></li>
      <% end %>
    </ul>
  </nav>
</div>
</header>
```

With that, the users index is fully functional, with all tests **GREEN**:

Listing 9.37   GREEN

```
$ bundle exec rake test
```

Of course, as seen in Figure 9.9, it is a bit … lonely. Let's remedy this sad situation.

9.3.2   Sample Users

In this section, we'll give our lonely sample user some company. Of course, to create enough users to make a decent users index, we *could* use our web browser to visit the sign-up page and make the new users one by one, but a far better solution is to use Ruby (and Rake) to make the users for us.

First, we'll add the *Faker* gem to the `Gemfile`, which will allow us to make sample users with semi-realistic names and email addresses (Listing 9.38).

Listing 9.38   Adding the Faker gem to the `Gemfile`.

```
source 'https://rubygems.org'

gem 'rails',          '4.2.0'
gem 'bcrypt',         '3.1.7'
```

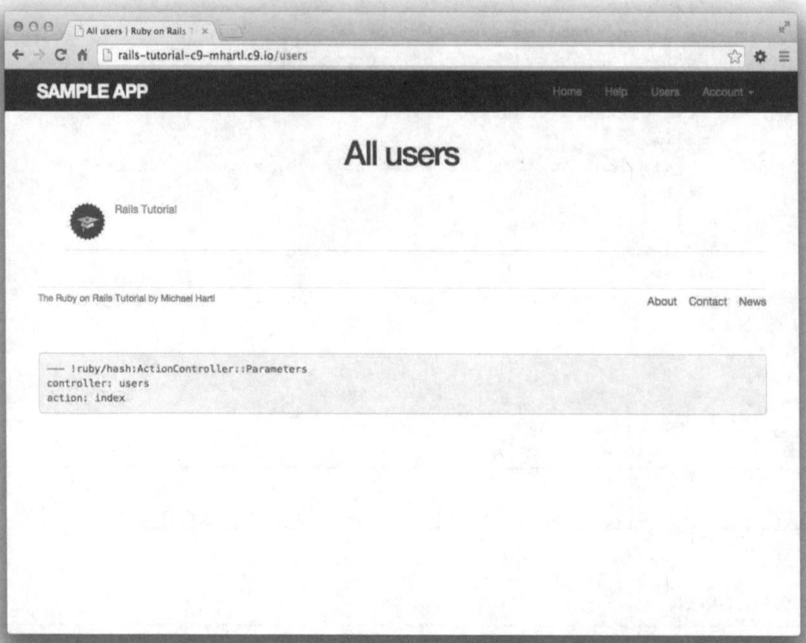

Figure 9.9 The users index page with only one user.

```
gem 'faker',                           '1.4.2'
   .
   .
   .
```

Then install the gem as usual:

```
$ bundle install
```

Next, we'll add a Rake task to seed the database with sample users, for which Rails uses the standard location **db/seeds.rb**. The result appears in Listing 9.39. (The code in Listing 9.39 is a bit advanced, so don't worry too much about the details.)

Listing 9.39 A Rake task for seeding the database with sample users.
db/seeds.rb

```
User.create!(name:  "Example User",
             email: "example@railstutorial.org",
             password:               "foobar",
             password_confirmation: "foobar")

99.times do |n|
  name  = Faker::Name.name
  email = "example-#{n+1}@railstutorial.org"
  password = "password"
  User.create!(name:  name,
               email: email,
               password:               password,
               password_confirmation: password)
end
```

The code in Listing 9.39 creates an example user with a name and email address replicating our previous one, and then makes 99 more. The `create!` method is just like the `create` method, except it raises an exception (Section 6.1.4) for an invalid user rather than returning `false`. This behavior makes debugging easier by avoiding silent errors.

With the code as in Listing 9.39, we can reset the database and then invoke the Rake task using `db:seed`:[8]

```
$ bundle exec rake db:migrate:reset
$ bundle exec rake db:seed
```

Seeding the database can be slow, and on some systems it could take a few minutes.

After running the `db:seed` Rake task, our application has 100 sample users. As seen in Figure 9.10, I've taken the liberty of associating the first few sample addresses with Gravatars so that they're not all the default Gravatar image. (You may have to restart the web server at this point.)

---

8. In principle, these two tasks can be combined in `rake db:reset`, but as of this writing this command doesn't work with the latest version of Rails.

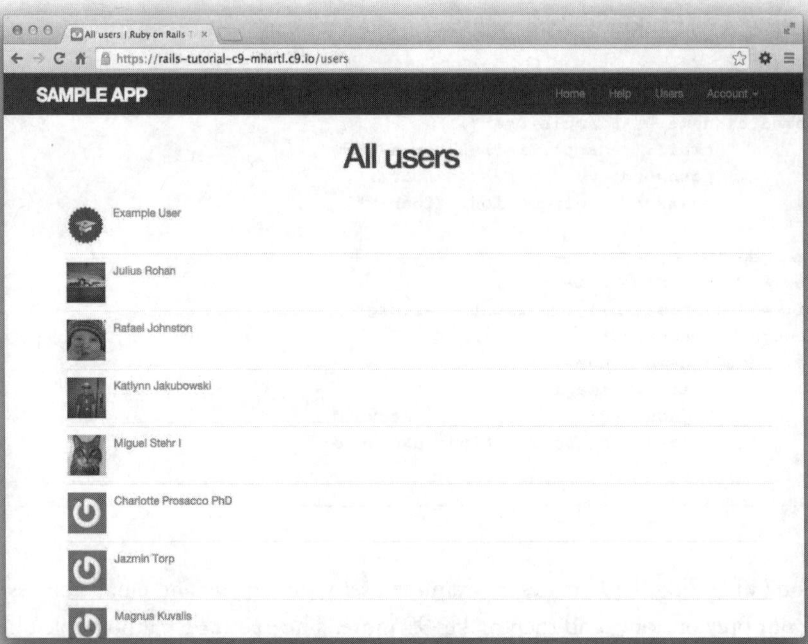

Figure 9.10 The users index page with 100 sample users.

9.3.3 Pagination

Our original user doesn't suffer from loneliness any more, but now we have the opposite problem: Our user has *too many* companions, and they all appear on the same page. Right now there are a hundred, which is already a reasonably large number, and on a real site it could be thousands. The solution is to *paginate* the users, so that (for example) only 30 show up on a page at any one time.

Rails offers are several pagination methods; we'll use one of the simplest and most robust, called will_paginate. To use it, we need to include both the `will_paginate` and `bootstrap-will_paginate` gems; the latter of which configures `will_paginate` to use Bootstrap's pagination styles. The updated **Gemfile** appears in Listing 9.40.

Listing 9.40 Including `will_paginate` in the **Gemfile**.

```
source 'https://rubygems.org'

gem 'rails',                    '4.2.0'
gem 'bcrypt',                   '3.1.7'
gem 'faker',                    '1.4.2'
gem 'will_paginate',            '3.0.7'
gem 'bootstrap-will_paginate', '0.0.10'
    .
    .
    .
```

Then run **bundle install**:

```
$ bundle install
```

You should also restart the web server to ensure that the new gems are loaded properly.

To get pagination working, we need to add some code to the index view telling Rails to paginate the users, and we need to replace **User.all** in the **index** action with an object that knows about pagination. We'll start by adding the special **will_paginate** method in the view (Listing 9.41); we'll see in a moment why the code appears both above and below the user list.

Listing 9.41 The users index with pagination.
app/views/users/index.html.erb

```erb
<% provide(:title, 'All users') %>
<h1>All users</h1>

<%= will_paginate %>

<ul class="users">
  <% @users.each do |user| %>
    <li>
      <%= gravatar_for user, size: 50 %>
      <%= link_to user.name, user %>
    </li>
```

```
  <% end %>
</ul>

<%= will_paginate %>
```

The **will_paginate** method is a little magical; inside a **users** view, it automatically looks for an **@users** object, and then displays pagination links to access other pages. The view in Listing 9.41 doesn't work yet, though, because currently **@users** contains the results of **User.all** (Listing 9.33), whereas **will_paginate** requires that we paginate the results explicitly using the **paginate** method:

```
$ rails console
>> User.paginate(page: 1)
  User Load (1.5ms)  SELECT "users".* FROM "users" LIMIT 30 OFFSET 0
    (1.7ms)   SELECT COUNT(*) FROM "users"
=> #<ActiveRecord::Relation [#<User id: 1,...
```

Note that **paginate** takes a hash argument with a key **:page** and a value equal to the page requested. **User.paginate** pulls the users out of the database one chunk at a time (30 by default), based on the **:page** parameter. So, for example, page 1 is users 1–30, page 2 is users 31–60, and so on. If **page** is **nil**, **paginate** simply returns the first page.

Using the **paginate** method, we can paginate the users in the sample application by using **paginate** in place of **all** in the **index** action (Listing 9.42). Here the **page** parameter comes from **params[:page]**, which is generated automatically by **will_paginate**.

Listing 9.42 Paginating the users in the **index** action.

app/controllers/users_controller.rb

```
class UsersController < ApplicationController
  before_action :logged_in_user, only: [:index, :edit, :update]
  .
  .
  .
  def index
    @users = User.paginate(page: params[:page])
  end
```

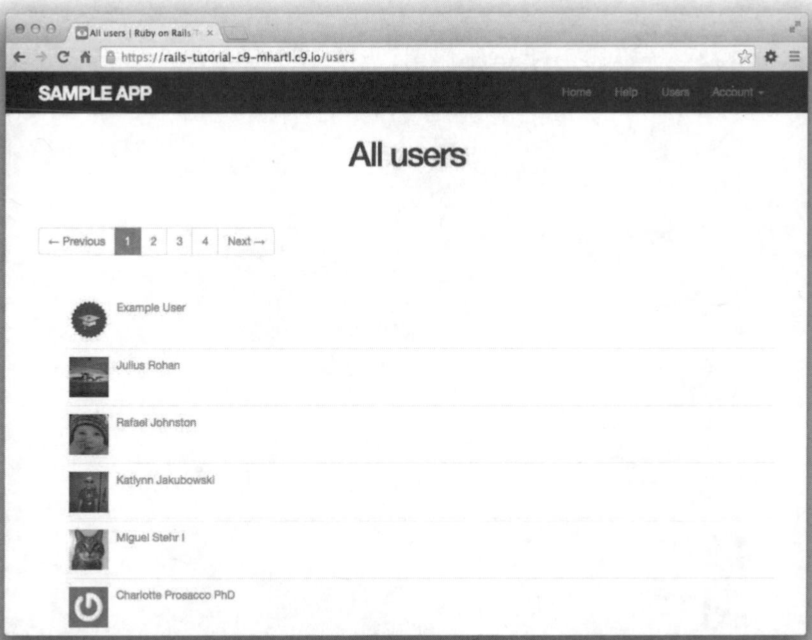

Figure 9.11 The users index page with pagination.

.
.
.

end

The users index page should now be working, appearing as in Figure 9.11. (On some systems, you may have to restart the Rails server at this point.) Because we included **will_paginate** both above and below the user list, the pagination links appear in both places.

If you now click on either the "2" link or the "Next" link, you'll get the second page of results, as shown in Figure 9.12.

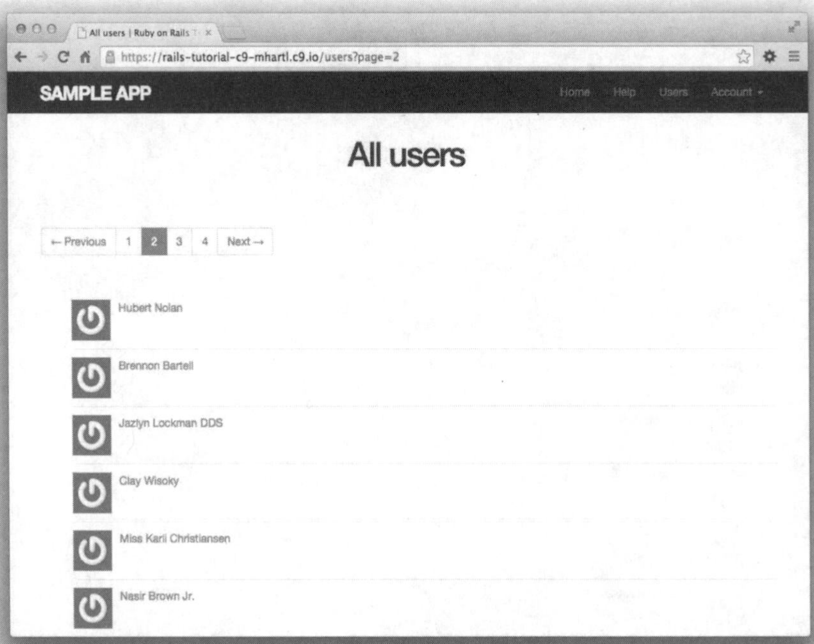

Figure 9.12 Page 2 of the users index.

9.3.4   Users Index Test

Now that our users index page is working, we'll write a lightweight test for it, including a minimal test for the pagination from Section 9.3.3. The idea is to log in, visit the index path, verify the first page of users is present, and then confirm that pagination is present on the page. For these last two steps to work, we need to have enough users in the test database to invoke pagination—that is, we need more than 30.

We created a second user in the fixtures in Listing 9.20, but 30 or so more users is a lot to create by hand. Luckily, as we've seen with the user fixture's `password_digest` attribute, fixture files support embedded Ruby, which means we can create 30 additional users as shown in Listing 9.43. (Listing 9.43 also creates a couple of other named users for future reference.)

Listing 9.43   Adding 30 extra users to the fixture.

test/fixtures/users.yml

```
michael:
  name: Michael Example
  email: michael@example.com
  password_digest: <%= User.digest('password') %>

archer:
  name: Sterling Archer
  email: duchess@example.gov
  password_digest: <%= User.digest('password') %>

lana:
  name: Lana Kane
  email: hands@example.gov
  password_digest: <%= User.digest('password') %>

mallory:
  name: Mallory Archer
  email: boss@example.gov
  password_digest: <%= User.digest('password') %>

<% 30.times do |n| %>
user_<%= n %>:
  name:  <%= "User #{n}" %>
  email: <%= "user-#{n}@example.com" %>
  password_digest: <%= User.digest('password') %>
<% end %>
```

With the fixtures defined in Listing 9.43, we're ready to write a test of the users index. First we generate the relevant test:

```
$ rails generate integration_test users_index
     invoke  test_unit
     create    test/integration/users_index_test.rb
```

The test itself involves checking for a `div` with the required **pagination** class and verifying that the first page of users is present. The result appears in Listing 9.44.

Listing 9.44 A test of the users index, including pagination. **GREEN**

test/integration/users_index_test.rb

```ruby
require 'test_helper'

class UsersIndexTest < ActionDispatch::IntegrationTest

  def setup
    @user = users(:michael)
  end

  test "index including pagination" do
    log_in_as(@user)
    get users_path
    assert_template 'users/index'
    assert_select 'div.pagination'
    User.paginate(page: 1).each do |user|
      assert_select 'a[href=?]', user_path(user), text: user.name
    end
  end
end
```

The result should be a **GREEN** test suite:

Listing 9.45 GREEN

```
$ bundle exec rake test
```

9.3.5 Partial Refactoring

The paginated users index is now complete, but there's one improvement I can't resist including: Rails has some incredibly slick tools for making compact views, and in this section we'll refactor the index page to use them. Because our code is well tested, we can refactor with confidence, resting assured that we are unlikely to break our site's functionality.

The first step in our refactoring is to replace the user **li** from Listing 9.41 with a **render** call (Listing 9.46).

Listing 9.46 The first refactoring attempt in the index view.

app/views/users/index.html.erb

```erb
<% provide(:title, 'All users') %>
<h1>All users</h1>
```

```
<%= will_paginate %>

<ul class="users">
  <% @users.each do |user| %>
    <%= render user %>
  <% end %>
</ul>

<%= will_paginate %>
```

Here we call **render** not on a string with the name of a partial, but rather on a **user** variable of class **User**.[9] In this context, Rails automatically looks for a partial called **_user.html.erb**, which we must create (Listing 9.47).

Listing 9.47 A partial to render a single user.

app/views/users/_user.html.erb

```
<li>
  <%= gravatar_for user, size: 50 %>
  <%= link_to user.name, user %>
</li>
```

This is a definite improvement, but we can do even better: We can call **render** *directly* on the **@users** variable (Listing 9.48).

Listing 9.48 The fully refactored users index. **GREEN**

app/views/users/index.html.erb

```
<% provide(:title, 'All users') %>
<h1>All users</h1>

<%= will_paginate %>

<ul class="users">
  <%= render @users %>
</ul>

<%= will_paginate %>
```

---

9. The name **user** is immaterial—we could have written **@users.each do |foobar|** and then used **render foobar**. The key is the *class* of the object—in this case, **User**.

Here Rails infers that `@users` is a list of `User` objects. Moreover, when called with a collection of users, Rails automatically iterates through them and renders each one with the `_user.html.erb` partial. The result is the impressively compact code in Listing 9.48.

As with any refactoring, you should verify that the test suite is still **GREEN** after changing the application code:

Listing 9.49   GREEN

```
$ bundle exec rake test
```

9.4 Deleting Users

Now that the users index is complete, there's only one canonical REST action left: `destroy`. In this section, we'll add links to delete users, as mocked up in Figure 9.13, and define the `destroy` action necessary to accomplish the deletion. But first, we'll create the class of administrative users, or *admins*, authorized to do so.

9.4.1 Administrative Users

We will identify privileged administrative users with a boolean `admin` attribute in the User model, which will lead automatically to an `admin?` boolean method to test for admin status. The resulting data model appears in Figure 9.14.

As usual, we add the `admin` attribute with a migration, indicating the `boolean` type on the command line:

```
$ rails generate migration add_admin_to_users admin:boolean
```

The migration adds the `admin` column to the `users` table, as shown in Listing 9.50. Note that we've added the argument `default: false` to `add_column` in Listing 9.50, which means that users will *not* be administrators by default. (Without the `default: false` argument, `admin` will be `nil` by default, which is still `false`, so this step is not strictly necessary. It is more explicit, though, and communicates our intentions more clearly both to Rails and to readers of our code.)

Listing 9.50   The migration to add a boolean `admin` attribute to users.
db/migrate/[timestamp]_add_admin_to_users.rb

```
class AddAdminToUsers < ActiveRecord::Migration
  def change
```

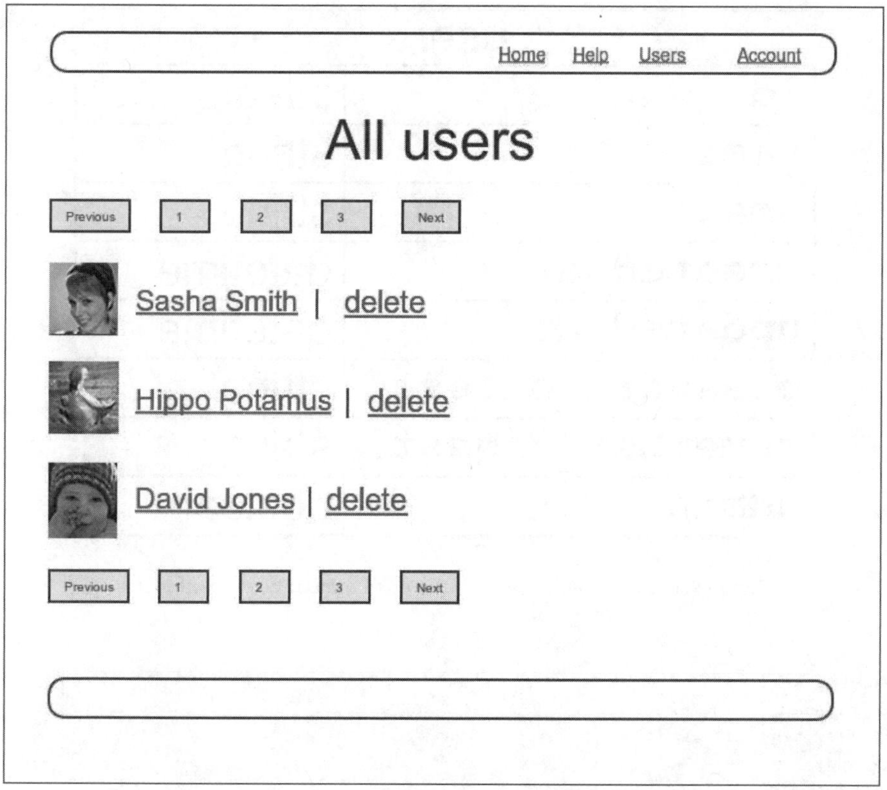

Figure 9.13 A mockup of the users index with delete links.

```
      add_column :users, :admin, :boolean, default: false
   end
end
```

Next, we migrate as usual:

```
$ bundle exec rake db:migrate
```

As expected, Rails figures out the boolean nature of the **admin** attribute and automatically adds the question-mark method **admin?**:

```
$ rails console --sandbox
>> user = User.first
```

users	
`id`	integer
`name`	string
`email`	string
`created_at`	datetime
`updated_at`	datetime
`password_digest`	string
`remember_digest`	string
`admin`	boolean

Figure 9.14 The User model with an added `admin` boolean attribute.

```
>> user.admin?
=> false
>> user.toggle!(:admin)
=> true
>> user.admin?
=> true
```

Here we've used the `toggle!` method to flip the `admin` attribute from `false` to `true`.

As a final step, let's update our seed data to make the first user an admin by default (Listing 9.51).

Listing 9.51 The seed data code with an admin user.

db/seeds.rb

```
User.create!(name:  "Example User",
             email: "example@railstutorial.org",
             password:              "foobar",
             password_confirmation: "foobar",
             admin: true)

99.times do |n|
  name  = Faker::Name.name
```

```
email = "example-#{n+1}@railstutorial.org"
password = "password"
User.create!(name:  name,
             email: email,
             password:              password,
             password_confirmation: password)
end
```

Then reset the database:

```
$ bundle exec rake db:migrate:reset
$ bundle exec rake db:seed
```

Revisiting Strong Parameters

You might have noticed that Listing 9.51 makes the user an admin by including `admin: true` in the initialization hash. This underscores the danger of exposing our objects to the wild web. That is, if we simply passed an initialization hash in from an arbitrary web request, a malicious user could send a PATCH request as follows:[10]

```
patch /users/17?admin=1
```

This request would make user 17 an admin, which would be a potentially serious security breach.

Because of this danger, it is essential that we update only those attributes that are safe to edit through the web. As noted in Section 7.3.2, this is accomplished using *strong parameters* by calling `require` and `permit` on the `params` hash:

```
def user_params
  params.require(:user).permit(:name, :email, :password,
                               :password_confirmation)
end
```

Note that `admin` is *not* in the list of permitted attributes. This approach prevents arbitrary users from granting themselves administrative access to our application. Because of its importance, it's a good idea to write a test for any attribute that isn't editable, and writing such a test for the `admin` attribute is left as an exercise (Section 9.6).

---

10. Command-line tools such as `curl` can issue PATCH requests of this form.

9.4.2 The `destroy` Action

The final step needed to complete the Users resource is to add delete links and a **destroy** action. We'll start by adding a delete link for each user on the users index page, restricting access to administrative users. The resulting **"delete"** links will be displayed only if the current user is an admin (Listing 9.52).

Listing 9.52 User delete links (viewable only by admins).
app/views/users/_user.html.erb

```
<li>
  <%= gravatar_for user, size: 50 %>
  <%= link_to user.name, user %>
  <% if current_user.admin? && !current_user?(user) %>
    | <%= link_to "delete", user, method: :delete,
                            data: { confirm: "You sure?" } %>
  <% end %>
</li>
```

The **method: :delete** argument arranges for the link to issue the necessary DELETE request. We've also wrapped each link inside an **if** statement so that only admins can see them. The result for our admin user appears in Figure 9.15.

Web browsers can't send DELETE requests natively, so Rails fakes them with Java-Script. As a consequence, the delete links won't work if the user has JavaScript disabled. If you must support non-JavaScript-enabled browsers, you can fake a DELETE request using a form and a POST request, which works even without JavaScript.[11]

To get the delete links to work, we need to add a **destroy** action (Table 7.1), which finds the corresponding user and destroys it with the Active Record **destroy** method, finally redirecting to the users index, as seen in Listing 9.53. Because users have to be logged in to delete users, Listing 9.53 also adds **:destroy** to the **logged_in_user** before filter.

Listing 9.53 Adding a working **destroy** action.
app/controllers/users_controller.rb

```
class UsersController < ApplicationController
  before_action :logged_in_user, only: [:index, :edit, :update, :destroy]
  before_action :correct_user,   only: [:edit, :update]
```

---

11. See the RailsCast on "Destroy Without JavaScript" for details.

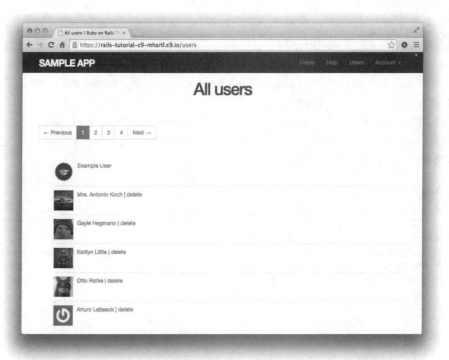

Figure 9.15 The users index with delete links.

```
   .
   .
   .
   def destroy
     User.find(params[:id]).destroy
     flash[:success] = "User deleted"
     redirect_to users_url
   end
   .
   .
   .
end
```

Note that the **destroy** action uses method chaining to combine the **find** and **destroy** operations into one line:

```
User.find(params[:id]).destroy
```

Now only admins can destroy users through the web since only they can see the delete links, but there's still a terrible security hole: Any sufficiently sophisticated attacker could simply issue a DELETE request directly from the command line to delete any user on the site. To secure the site properly, we need access control on the **destroy** action, so that *only* admins can delete users.

As in Section 9.2.1 and Section 9.2.2, we'll enforce access control using a before filter, this time to restrict access to the **destroy** action to admins. The resulting **admin_user** before filter appears in Listing 9.54.

Listing 9.54 A before filter restricting the **destroy** action to admins.

app/controllers/users_controller.rb

```ruby
class UsersController < ApplicationController
  before_action :logged_in_user, only: [:index, :edit, :update, :destroy]
  before_action :correct_user,   only: [:edit, :update]
  before_action :admin_user,     only: :destroy
  .
  .
  .
  private
    .
    .
    .
    # Confirms an admin user.
    def admin_user
      redirect_to(root_url) unless current_user.admin?
    end
end
```

9.4.3 User Destroy Tests

With something as dangerous as destroying users, it's important to have good tests for the expected behavior. We start by arranging for one of our fixture users to be an admin, as shown in Listing 9.55.

Listing 9.55 Making one of the fixture users an admin.

test/fixtures/users.yml

```yaml
michael:
  name: Michael Example
```

```
  email: michael@example.com
  password_digest: <%= User.digest('password') %>
  admin: true

archer:
  name: Sterling Archer
  email: duchess@example.gov
  password_digest: <%= User.digest('password') %>

lana:
  name: Lana Kane
  email: hands@example.gov
  password_digest: <%= User.digest('password') %>

mallory:
  name: Mallory Archer
  email: boss@example.gov
  password_digest: <%= User.digest('password') %>

<% 30.times do |n| %>
user_<%= n %>:
  name:  <%= "User #{n}" %>
  email: <%= "user-#{n}@example.com" %>
  password_digest: <%= User.digest('password') %>
<% end %>
```

Following the practice from Section 9.2.1, we'll put action-level tests of access control in the Users controller test file. As with the logout test in Listing 8.28, we'll use **delete** to issue a DELETE request directly to the **destroy** action. We need to check two cases: (1) Users who aren't logged in should be redirected to the login page and (2) users who are logged in but who aren't admins should be redirected to the Home page. The result appears in Listing 9.56.

Listing 9.56 Action-level tests for admin access control. **GREEN**
test/controllers/users_controller_test.rb

```
require 'test_helper'

class UsersControllerTest < ActionController::TestCase

  def setup
    @user       = users(:michael)
    @other_user = users(:archer)
  end
```

```
      .
      .
      .
  test "should redirect destroy when not logged in" do
    assert_no_difference 'User.count' do
      delete :destroy, id: @user
    end
    assert_redirected_to login_url
  end

  test "should redirect destroy when logged in as a non-admin" do
    log_in_as(@other_user)
    assert_no_difference 'User.count' do
      delete :destroy, id: @user
    end
    assert_redirected_to root_url
  end
end
```

Listing 9.56 also makes sure that the user count doesn't change using the **assert_no_difference** method (seen before in Listing 7.21).

The tests in Listing 9.56 verify the behavior in the case of an unauthorized (non-admin) user, but we also want to check that an admin can use a delete link to successfully destroy a user. Given that the delete links appear on the users index, we'll add these tests to the users index test from Listing 9.44. The only really tricky part is verifying that a user gets deleted when an admin clicks on a delete link, which we'll accomplish as follows:

```
assert_difference 'User.count', -1 do
  delete user_path(@other_user)
end
```

This code uses the **assert_difference** method that we saw earlier in Listing 7.26 when creating a user, but this time it verifies that a user is *destroyed* by checking that **User.count** changes by -1 when issuing a **delete** request to the corresponding user path.

Putting everything together gives the pagination and delete test in Listing 9.57, which includes tests for both admins and non-admins.

Listing 9.57 An integration test for delete links and destroying users. **GREEN**
test/integration/users_index_test.rb

```ruby
require 'test_helper'

class UsersIndexTest < ActionDispatch::IntegrationTest

  def setup
    @admin     = users(:michael)
    @non_admin = users(:archer)
  end

  test "index as admin including pagination and delete links" do
    log_in_as(@admin)
    get users_path
    assert_template 'users/index'
    assert_select 'div.pagination'
    first_page_of_users = User.paginate(page: 1)
    first_page_of_users.each do |user|
      assert_select 'a[href=?]', user_path(user), text: user.name
      unless user == @admin
        assert_select 'a[href=?]', user_path(user), text: 'delete',
                                                    method: :delete
      end
    end
    assert_difference 'User.count', -1 do
      delete user_path(@non_admin)
    end
  end

  test "index as non-admin" do
    log_in_as(@non_admin)
    get users_path
    assert_select 'a', text: 'delete', count: 0
  end
end
```

Note that Listing 9.57 checks for the right delete links, including skipping the test if the user happens to be the admin (which lacks a delete link due to Listing 9.52).

At this point, our deletion code is well tested, and the test suite should be **GREEN**:

Listing 9.58 GREEN

```
$ bundle exec rake test
```

9.5 Conclusion

We've come a long way since introducing the Users controller way back in Section 5.4. Those users couldn't even sign up; now users can sign up, log in, log out, view their profiles, edit their settings, and see an index of all users—and some can even destroy other users.

As it presently stands, the sample application forms a solid foundation for any website requiring users with authentication and authorization. In Chapter 10, we'll add two additional refinements: an account activation link for newly registered users (verifying a valid email address in the process) and password resets to help users who forget their passwords.

Before moving on, be sure to merge all the changes into the master branch:

```
$ git add -A
$ git commit -m "Finish user edit, update, index, and destroy actions"
$ git checkout master
$ git merge updating-users
$ git push
```

You can also deploy the application and even populate the production database with sample users (using the `pg:reset` task to reset the production database):

```
$ bundle exec rake test
$ git push heroku
$ heroku pg:reset DATABASE
$ heroku run rake db:migrate
$ heroku run rake db:seed
$ heroku restart
```

Of course, on a real site you probably wouldn't want to seed the database with sample data, but I include this step here for purposes of illustration (Figure 9.16). Incidentally, the order of the sample users in Figure 9.16 may vary, and on my system it doesn't match the local version from Figure 9.11; this is because we haven't specified a default ordering for users when retrieved from the database, so the current order is database dependent. This doesn't matter much for users, but it will for microposts, and we'll address this issue further in Section 11.1.4.

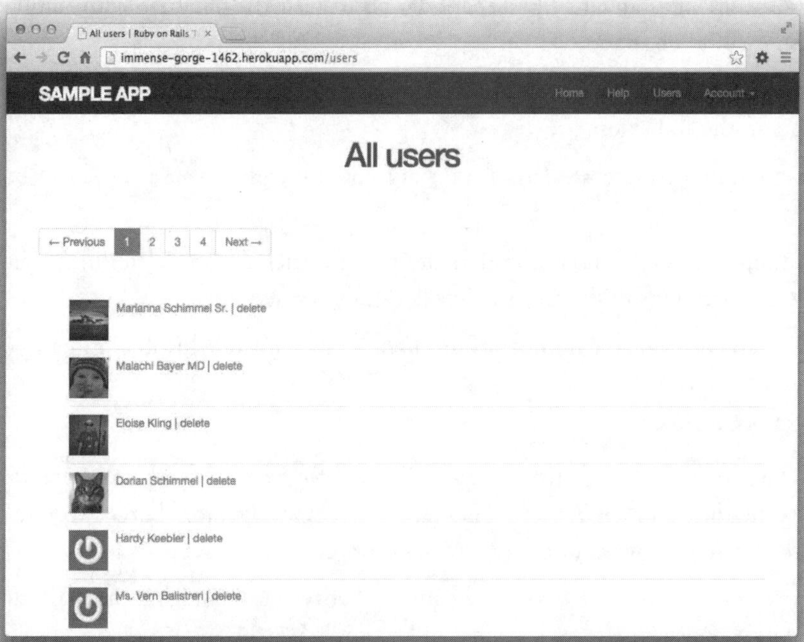

Figure 9.16 The sample users in production.

9.5.1 What We Learned in This Chapter

- Users can be updated using an edit form, which sends a PATCH request to the **update** action.

- Safe updating through the web is enforced using strong parameters.

- Before filters give a standard way to run methods before particular controller actions.

- We can implement an authorization using before filters.

- Authorization tests use both low-level commands to submit particular HTTP requests directly to controller actions and high-level integration tests.

- Friendly forwarding redirects users where they wanted to go after logging in.

- The users index page shows all users, one page at a time.

- Rails uses the standard file `db/seeds.rb` to seed the database with sample data using `rake db:seed`.

- Running `render @users` automatically calls the `_user.html.erb` partial on each user in the collection.

- A boolean attribute `admin` on users automatically gives a `user.admin?` boolean method.

- Admins can delete users through the web by clicking on delete links that issue DELETE requests to the Users controller `destroy` action.

- We can create a large number of test users using embedded Ruby inside fixtures.

9.6 Exercises

Note: To receive a copy of the *Solutions Manual for Exercises*, with solutions to every exercise in the *Ruby on Rails*™ *Tutorial*, visit www.railstutorial.org/<word>, where "<word>" is the last word of the Figure 3.9 caption.

For a suggestion on how to avoid conflicts between exercises and the main tutorial, see the note on exercise topic branches in Section 3.6.

1. Write a test to make sure that friendly forwarding forwards to the given URL only the first time. On subsequent login attempts, the forwarding URL should revert to the default (i.e., the profile page). *Hint*: Add to the test in Listing 9.26 by checking for the right value of `session[:forwarding_url]`.

2. Write an integration test for all the layout links, including the proper behavior for logged-in and non-logged-in users. *Hint*: Add to the test in Listing 5.25 using the `log_in_as` helper.

3. By issuing a PATCH request directly to the `update` method as shown in Listing 9.59, verify that the `admin` attribute isn't editable through the web. To be sure your test is covering the right thing, your first step should be to *add* `admin` to the list of permitted parameters in `user_params` so that the initial test is **RED**.

4. Remove the duplicated form code by refactoring the `new.html.erb` and `edit.html.erb` views to use the partial in Listing 9.60. Note that you will have to pass the form variable `f` explicitly as a local variable, as shown in Listing 9.61.

Listing 9.59 Testing that the **admin** attribute is forbidden.

test/controllers/users_controller_test.rb

```ruby
require 'test_helper'

class UsersControllerTest < ActionController::TestCase

  def setup
    @user       = users(:michael)
    @other_user = users(:archer)
  end
  .
  .
  .
  test "should redirect update when logged in as wrong user" do
    log_in_as(@other_user)
    patch :update, id: @user, user: { name: @user.name, email: @user.email }
    assert_redirected_to root_url
  end

  test "should not allow the admin attribute to be edited via the web" do
    log_in_as(@other_user)
    assert_not @other_user.admin?
    patch :update, id: @other_user, user: { password:                FILL_IN,
                                            password_confirmation: FILL_IN,
                                            admin: FILL_IN }
    assert_not @other_user.FILL_IN.admin?
  end
  .
  .
  .
end
```

Listing 9.60 A partial for the **new** and **edit** form fields.

app/views/users/_fields.html.erb

```erb
<%= render 'shared/error_messages' %>

<%= f.label :name %>
<%= f.text_field :name, class: 'form-control' %>

<%= f.label :email %>
<%= f.email_field :email, class: 'form-control' %>

<%= f.label :password %>
<%= f.password_field :password, class: 'form-control' %>
```

```
<%= f.label :password_confirmation, "Confirmation" %>
<%= f.password_field :password_confirmation, class: 'form-control' %>
```

Listing 9.61 The sign-up view with a partial.

app/views/users/new.html.erb

```
<% provide(:title, 'Sign up') %>
<h1>Sign up</h1>

<div class="row">
  <div class="col-md-6 col-md-offset-3">
    <%= form_for(@user) do |f| %>
      <%= render 'fields', f: f %>
      <%= f.submit "Create my account", class: "btn btn-primary" %>
    <% end %>
  </div>
</div>
```

CHAPTER 10

Account Activation and Password Reset

In Chapter 9, we finished making a basic Users resource (filling in all the standard REST actions from Table 7.1), together with a flexible authentication and authorization system. In this chapter, we'll put the finishing touches on this system by adding two closely related features: account activation (which verifies a new user's email address) and password reset (for users who forget their passwords). Each of these two features will involve creating a new resource, thereby giving us a chance to see further examples of controllers, routing, and database migrations. In the process, we'll also have a chance to learn how to send email in Rails, both in development and in production. Finally, the two features complement each other nicely, because password resets involve sending a reset link to a user's email address, the validity of which is confirmed by the initial account activation.[1]

10.1 Account Activation

At present, newly registered users immediately have full access to their accounts (Chapter 7). In this section, we'll implement an account activation step to verify that the user controls the email address he or she used to sign up. This will involve associating an

---

1. Technically, users could update their account with an erroneous email address using the account settings update feature from Section 9.1, but the current implementation gets us most of the benefit of email verification without too much work.

activation token and digest with a user, sending the user an email with a link including the token, and activating the user upon clicking the link.

Our strategy for handling account activation parallels user login (Section 8.2) and especially remembering users (Section 8.4). The basic sequence appears as follows:

1. Start users in an "unactivated" state.

2. When a user signs up, generate an activation token and the corresponding activation digest.

3. Save the activation digest to the database, and then send an email to the user with a link containing the activation token and user's email address.[2]

4. When the user clicks the link, find the user by email address, and then authenticate the token by comparing with the activation digest.

5. If the user is authenticated, change the status from "unactivated" to "activated."

Because of the similarity with passwords and remember tokens, we will be able to reuse many of the same ideas for account activation (as well as password reset), including the `User.digest` and `User.new_token` methods and a modified version of the `user.authenticated?` method. Table 10.1 illustrates the analogy (including the password reset from Section 10.2). We'll define the generalized version of the `authenticated?` method from Table 10.1 in Section 10.1.3.

As usual, we'll make a topic branch for the new feature. As we'll see in Section 10.3, account activation and password reset include some common email configuration, which we'll want to apply to both features before merging to master. As a result, it's convenient to use a common topic branch:

```
$ git checkout master
$ git checkout -b account-activation-password-reset
```

---

2. We could use the user's ID instead, since it's already exposed in the URLs of our application, but using email addresses is more future-proof in case we want to obfuscate user IDs for any reason (e.g., to prevent competitors from knowing how many users your application has).

Table 10.1 The analogy between login, remembering, account activation, and password reset.

find by	string	digest	authentication
`email`	`password`	`password_digest`	`authenticate (password)`
`id`	`remember_token`	`remember_digest`	`authenticated? (:remember, token)`
`email`	`activation_token`	`activation_digest`	`authenticated? (:activation, token)`
`email`	`reset_token`	`reset_digest`	`authenticated? (:reset, token)`

10.1.1 Account Activations Resource

As with sessions (Section 8.1), we'll model account activations as a resource even though they won't be associated with an Active Record model. Instead, we'll include the relevant data (including the activation token and activation status) in the User model. Nevertheless, we'll interact with account activations via a standard REST URL; because the activation link will be modifying the user's activation status, we'll plan to use the `edit` action.[3] This requires an Account Activations controller, which we can generate as follows:[4]

```
$ rails generate controller AccountActivations
```

The activation email will involve a URL of the form

```
edit_account_activation_url(activation_token, ...)
```

---

3. It might make even more sense to use an `update` action, but the activation link needs to be sent in an email and hence should involve a regular browser click, which issues a GET request instead of the PATCH request required by the `update` action.

4. Because we'll be using an `edit` action, we could include `edit` on the command line, but this would also generate both an edit view and a test, neither of which we'll turn out to need.

which means we'll need a named route for the **edit** action. We can arrange this with the **resources** line shown in Listing 10.1.

Listing 10.1 Adding a resource for account activations.
config/routes.rb

```
Rails.application.routes.draw do
  root                   'static_pages#home'
  get     'help'    => 'static_pages#help'
  get     'about'   => 'static_pages#about'
  get     'contact' => 'static_pages#contact'
  get     'signup'  => 'users#new'
  get     'login'   => 'sessions#new'
  post    'login'   => 'sessions#create'
  delete 'logout'   => 'sessions#destroy'
  resources :users
  resources :account_activations, only: [:edit]
end
```

Next, we need a unique activation token to activate users. Security is less of a concern with account activations than it is with passwords, remember tokens, or (as we'll see in Section 10.2) password resets—all of which could give an attacker full control over an account—but there are still some scenarios in which an unhashed activation token could compromise an account.[5] Thus, following the example of the remember token in Section 8.4, we'll pair a publicly exposed virtual token with a hash digest in the database. This way we can access the activation token using

```
user.activation_token
```

and authenticate the user with code like

```
user.authenticated?(:activation, token)
```

(This will require a modification of the **authenticated?** method defined in Listing 8.33.) We'll also add a boolean attribute **activated**, which will allow us to test

---

5. For example, an attacker with access to the database could immediately activate a newly created account, thereby logging in as the user, and could then change the password to gain control.

users	
id	integer
name	string
email	string
created_at	datetime
updated_at	datetime
password_digest	string
remember_digest	string
admin	boolean
activation_digest	string
activated	boolean
activated_at	datetime

Figure 10.1   The User model with added account activation attributes.

whether a user is activated using the same kind of auto-generated boolean method we saw in Section 9.4.1:

```
if user.activated? ...
```

Finally, although we won't use it in this tutorial, we'll record the time and date of the activation in case we want it for future reference. The full data model appears in Figure 10.1.

The migration to add the data model from Figure 10.1 adds all three attributes at the command line:

```
$ rails generate migration add_activation_to_users \
> activation_digest:string activated:Boolean activated_at:datetime
```

As with the **admin** attribute (Listing 9.50), we'll add a default boolean value of **false** to the **activated** attribute, as shown in in Listing 10.2.

Listing 10.2   A migration for account activation (with added index).
db/migrate/[timestamp]_add_activation_to_users.rb

```
class AddActivationToUsers < ActiveRecord::Migration
  def change
    add_column :users, :activation_digest, :string
    add_column :users, :activated, :Boolean, default: false
    add_column :users, :activated_at, :datetime
  end
end
```

We then apply the migration as usual:

```
$ bundle exec rake db:migrate
```

Because every newly signed-up user will require activation, we should assign an activation token and digest to each user object before it's created. We saw a similar idea in Section 6.2.5, where we needed to convert an email address to lowercase before saving a user to the database. In that case, we used a **before_save** callback combined with the **downcase** method (Listing 6.31). A **before_save** callback is automatically called before the object is saved, which happens with both object creation and updates, but in the case of the activation digest we want the callback to fire only when the user is created. This requires a **before_create** callback, which we'll define as follows:

```
before_create :create_activation_digest
```

This code, called a *method reference*, arranges for Rails to look for a method called **create_activation_digest** and run it before creating the user. (In Listing 6.31, we passed **before_save** an explicit block, but the method reference technique is generally preferred.) Because the **create_activation_digest** method itself is only used internally by the User model, there's no need to expose it to outside users. As we saw in Section 7.3.2, the Ruby way to accomplish this is to use the **private** keyword:

```
private

  def create_activation_digest
    # Create the token and digest.
  end
```

All methods defined in a class after **private** are automatically hidden, as seen in this console session:

```
$ rails console
>> User.first.create_activation_digest
NoMethodError: private method `create_activation_digest' called for #<User>
```

The purpose of the **before_create** callback is to assign the token and corresponding digest, which we can accomplish as follows:

```
self.activation_token  = User.new_token
self.activation_digest = User.digest(activation_token)
```

This code simply reuses the token and digest methods used for the remember token, as we can see by comparing with the **remember** method from Listing 8.32:

```
# Remembers a user in the database for use in persistent sessions.
def remember
  self.remember_token = User.new_token
  update_attribute(:remember_digest, User.digest(remember_token))
end
```

The main difference is the use of **update_attribute** in the latter case. The difference occurs because remember tokens and digests are created for users who already exist in the database, whereas the **before_create** callback happens *before* the user has been created. As a result of the callback, when a new user is defined with **User.new** (as in user sign-up, Listing 7.17), that user will automatically get both **activation_token** and **activation_digest** attributes; because the latter is associated with a column in the database (Figure 10.1), it will be written automatically when the user is saved.

The result of this discussion yields the User model shown in Listing 10.3. As required by the virtual nature of the activation token, we've added a second **attr_accessor** to our model. Note that we've taken the opportunity to use a method reference for email downcasing as well.

Listing 10.3 Adding account activation code to the User model. **GREEN**
app/models/user.rb

```
class User < ActiveRecord::Base
  attr_accessor :remember_token, :activation_token
  before_save   :downcase_email
  before_create :create_activation_digest
  validates :name,  presence: true, length: { maximum: 50 }
  .
  .
  .
```

```
  private

    # Converts email to all lower-case.
    def downcase_email
      self.email = email.downcase
    end

    # Creates and assigns the activation token and digest.
    def create_activation_digest
      self.activation_token  = User.new_token
      self.activation_digest = User.digest(activation_token)
    end
end
```

Before moving on, we should also update our seed data and fixtures so that our sample and test users are initially activated, as shown in Listing 10.4 and Listing 10.5. (The **Time.zone.now** method is a built-in Rails helper that returns the current timestamp, taking into account the time zone on the server.)

Listing 10.4 Activating seed users by default.
db/seeds.rb

```
User.create!(name:  "Example User",
             email: "example@railstutorial.org",
             password:               "foobar",
             password_confirmation: "foobar",
             admin:        true,
             activated: true,
             activated_at: Time.zone.now)

99.times do |n|
  name  = Faker::Name.name
  email = "example-#{n+1}@railstutorial.org"
  password = "password"
  User.create!(name:  name,
               email: email,
               password:               password,
               password_confirmation: password,
               activated: true,
               activated_at: Time.zone.now)
end
```

Listing 10.5 Activating fixture users.

test/fixtures/users.yml

```
michael:
  name: Michael Example
  email: michael@example.com
  password_digest: <%= User.digest('password') %>
  admin: true
  activated: true
  activated_at: <%= Time.zone.now %>

archer:
  name: Sterling Archer
  email: duchess@example.gov
  password_digest: <%= User.digest('password') %>
  activated: true
  activated_at: <%= Time.zone.now %>

lana:
  name: Lana Kane
  email: hands@example.gov
  password_digest: <%= User.digest('password') %>
  activated: true
  activated_at: <%= Time.zone.now %>

mallory:
  name: Mallory Archer
  email: boss@example.gov
  password_digest: <%= User.digest('password') %>
  activated: true
  activated_at: <%= Time.zone.now %>

<% 30.times do |n| %>
user_<%= n %>:
  name:  <%= "User #{n}" %>
  email: <%= "user-#{n}@example.com" %>
  password_digest: <%= User.digest('password') %>
  activated: true
  activated_at: <%= Time.zone.now %>
<% end %>
```

To apply the changes in Listing 10.4, we reset the database to reseed the data as usual:

```
$ bundle exec rake db:migrate:reset
$ bundle exec rake db:seed
```

10.1.2 Account Activation Mailer Method

With the data modeling complete, we're now ready to add the code needed to send an account activation email. The method is to add a User *mailer* using the Action Mailer library, which we'll use in the Users controller `create` action to send an email with an activation link. Mailers are structured much like controller actions, with email templates defined as views. Our task in this section is to define the mailers and views with links containing the activation token and the email address associated with the account to be activated.

As with models and controllers, we can generate a mailer using `rails generate`:

```
$ rails generate mailer UserMailer account_activation password_reset
```

Here we've generated the necessary `account_activation` method as well as the `password_reset` method we'll need in Section 10.2.

As part of generating the mailer, Rails also generates two view templates for each mailer, one for plain-text email and one for HTML email. For the account activation mailer method, they appear as in Listing 10.6 and Listing 10.7.

Listing 10.6 The generated account activation text view.
app/views/user_mailer/account_activation.text.erb

```
UserMailer#account_activation

<%= @greeting %>, find me in app/views/user_mailer/account_activation.text.erb
```

Listing 10.7 The generated account activation HTML view.
app/views/user_mailer/account_activation.html.erb

```
<h1>UserMailer#account_activation</h1>

<p>
  <%= @greeting %>, find me in app/views/user_mailer/account_activation.html.erb
</p>
```

Let's take a look at the generated mailers to get a sense of how they work (Listing 10.8 and Listing 10.9). We see in Listing 10.8 that there is a default `from` address common to all mailers in the application, and each method in Listing 10.10 has a recipient's address as well. (Listing 10.9 also uses a mailer layout corresponding to the email format; although it won't ever matter in this tutorial, the resulting HTML and plain-text mailer layouts can be found in **app/views/layouts**.) The generated code also includes an instance variable (**@greeting**), which is available in the mailer views in much the same way that instance variables in controllers are available in ordinary views.

Listing 10.8   The generated application mailer.

app/mailers/application_mailer.rb

```ruby
class ApplicationMailer < ActionMailer::Base
  default from: "from@example.com"
  layout 'mailer'
end
```

Listing 10.9   The generated User mailer.

app/mailers/user_mailer.rb

```ruby
class UserMailer < ApplicationMailer

  # Subject can be set in your I18n file at config/locales/en.yml
  # with the following lookup:
  #
  #   en.user_mailer.account_activation.subject
  #
  def account_activation
    @greeting = "Hi"

    mail to: "to@example.org"
  end

  # Subject can be set in your I18n file at config/locales/en.yml
  # with the following lookup:
  #
  #   en.user_mailer.password_reset.subject
  #
  def password_reset
    @greeting = "Hi"

    mail to: "to@example.org"
  end
end
```

To make a working activation email, we'll create an instance variable containing the user (for use in the view) and then mail the result to **user.email**. As seen in

Listing 10.10, the `mail` method also takes a `subject` key, whose value is used as the email's subject line.

Listing 10.10 Mailing the account activation link.
app/mailers/user_mailer.rb

```ruby
class UserMailer < ApplicationMailer

  def account_activation(user)
    @user = user
    mail to: user.email, subject: "Account activation"
  end

  def password_reset
    @greeting = "Hi"

    mail to: "to@example.org"
  end
end
```

As with ordinary views, we can use embedded Ruby to customize the template views—in this case, greeting the user by name and including a link to a custom activation link. Our plan is to find the user by email address and then authenticate the activation token, so the link needs to include both the email and the token. Because we're modeling activations using an Account Activations resource, the token itself can appear as the argument of the named route defined in Listing 10.1:

```ruby
edit_account_activation_url(@user.activation_token, ...)
```

Recalling that

```ruby
edit_user_url(user)
```

produces a URL of the form

```
http://www.example.com/users/1/edit
```

the corresponding account activation link's base URL will look like this:

```
http://www.example.com/account_activations/q5lt38hQDc_959PVoo6b7A/edit
```

Here `q5lt38hQDc_959PVoo6b7A` is a URL-safe base64 string generated by the `new_token` method (Listing 8.31). It plays the same role as the user id in /users/1/edit. In particular, in the Activations controller `edit` action, the token will be available in the `params` hash as `params[:id]`.

To include the email as well, we need to use a *query parameter*, which in a URL appears as a key-value pair located after a question mark:[6]

```
account_activations/q5lt38hQDc_959PVoo6b7A/edit?email=foo%40example.com
```

Notice that the '@' in the email address appears as `%40`; in other words, it's "escaped out" to guarantee a valid URL. The way to set a query parameter in Rails is to include a hash in the named route:

```
edit_account_activation_url(@user.activation_token, email: @user.email)
```

When using named routes in this way to define query parameters, Rails automatically escapes out any special characters. The resulting email address will also be unescaped automatically in the controller, and will be available via `params[:email]`.

With the `@user` instance variable as defined in Listing 10.10, we can create the necessary links using the named edit route and embedded Ruby, as shown in Listing 10.11 and Listing 10.12. Note that the HTML template in Listing 10.12 uses the `link_to` method to construct a valid link.

Listing 10.11 The account activation text view.
app/views/user_mailer/account_activation.text.erb

```
Hi <%= @user.name %>,

Welcome to the Sample App! Click on the link below to activate your account:

<%= edit_account_activation_url(@user.activation_token, email: @user.email) %>
```

---

6. URLs can contain multiple query parameters, consisting of multiple key-value pairs separated by the ampersand character `&`, as in `/edit?name=Foo%20Bar&email=foo%40example.com`.

Listing 10.12 The account activation HTML view.

app/views/user_mailer/account_activation.html.erb

```
<h1>Sample App</h1>

<p>Hi <%= @user.name %>,</p>

<p>
Welcome to the Sample App! Click on the link below to activate your account:
</p>

<%= link_to "Activate", edit_account_activation_url(@user.activation_token,
                                                    email: @user.email) %>
```

To see the results of the templates defined in Listing 10.11 and Listing 10.12, we can use *email previews*, which are special URLs exposed by Rails that shows us what our email messages look like. First, we need to add some configuration to our application's development environment, as shown in Listing 10.13.

Listing 10.13 Email settings in development.

config/environments/development.rb

```
Rails.application.configure do
  .
  .
  .
  config.action_mailer.raise_delivery_errors = true
  config.action_mailer.delivery_method = :test
  host = 'example.com'
  config.action_mailer.default_url_options = { host: host }
  .
  .
  .
end
```

Listing 10.13 uses a hostname of `'example.com'`, but you should use the actual host of your development environment. For example, on my system either of the following works (depending on whether I'm using the cloud IDE or the local server):

```
host = 'rails-tutorial-c9-mhartl.c9.io'       # Cloud IDE
```

or

```
host = 'localhost:3000'                          # Local server
```

After restarting the development server to activate the configuration in Listing 10.13, we next need to update the User mailer *preview file*. This file was automatically
generated in Section 10.1.2, as shown in Listing 10.14.

Listing 10.14   The generated User mailer previews.
test/mailers/previews/user_mailer_preview.rb

```
# Preview all emails at http://localhost:3000/rails/mailers/user_mailer
class UserMailerPreview < ActionMailer::Preview

  # Preview this email at
  # http://localhost:3000/rails/mailers/user_mailer/account_activation
  def account_activation
    UserMailer.account_activation
  end

  # Preview this email at
  # http://localhost:3000/rails/mailers/user_mailer/password_reset
  def password_reset
    UserMailer.password_reset
  end

end
```

Because the `account_activation` method defined in Listing 10.10 requires a
valid user object as an argument, the code in Listing 10.14 won't work as written. To
fix it, we define a `user` variable equal to the first user in the development database, and
then pass it as an argument to `UserMailer.account_activation` (Listing 10.15).
Note that Listing 10.15 also assigns a value to `user.activation_token`, which is
necessary because the account activation templates in Listing 10.11 and Listing 10.12
need an account activation token. [Because `activation_token` is a virtual attribute
(Section 10.1.1), the user from the database doesn't have one.]

Listing 10.15 A working preview method for account activation.

test/mailers/previews/user_mailer_preview.rb

```ruby
# Preview all emails at http://localhost:3000/rails/mailers/user_mailer
class UserMailerPreview < ActionMailer::Preview

  # Preview this email at
  # http://localhost:3000/rails/mailers/user_mailer/account_activation
  def account_activation
    user = User.first
    user.activation_token = User.new_token
    UserMailer.account_activation(user)
  end

  # Preview this email at
  # http://localhost:3000/rails/mailers/user_mailer/password_reset
  def password_reset
    UserMailer.password_reset
  end
end
```

With the preview code as in Listing 10.15, we can visit the suggested URLs to preview the account activation emails. (If you are using the cloud IDE, you should replace **localhost:3000** with the corresponding base URL.) The resulting HTML and text emails appear as in Figure 10.2 and Figure 10.3.

As a final step, we'll write a couple of tests to double-check the results shown in the email previews. This isn't as hard as it sounds, because Rails has generated useful example tests for us (Listing 10.16).

Listing 10.16 The User mailer test generated by Rails.

test/mailers/user_mailer_test.rb

```ruby
require 'test_helper'

class UserMailerTest < ActionMailer::TestCase

  test "account_activation" do
    mail = UserMailer.account_activation
    assert_equal "Account activation", mail.subject
    assert_equal ["to@example.org"], mail.to
    assert_equal ["from@example.com"], mail.from
```

```
    assert_match "Hi", mail.body.encoded
  end

  test "password_reset" do
    mail = UserMailer.password_reset
    assert_equal "Password reset", mail.subject
    assert_equal ["to@example.org"], mail.to
    assert_equal ["from@example.com"], mail.from
    assert_match "Hi", mail.body.encoded
  end
end
```

The tests in Listing 10.16 use the powerful **assert_match** method, which can be used with either a string or a regular expression:

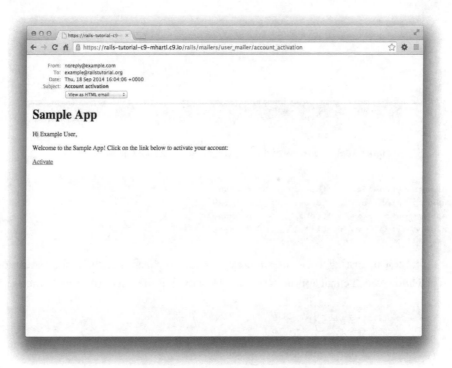

Figure 10.2 A preview of the HTML version of the account activation email.

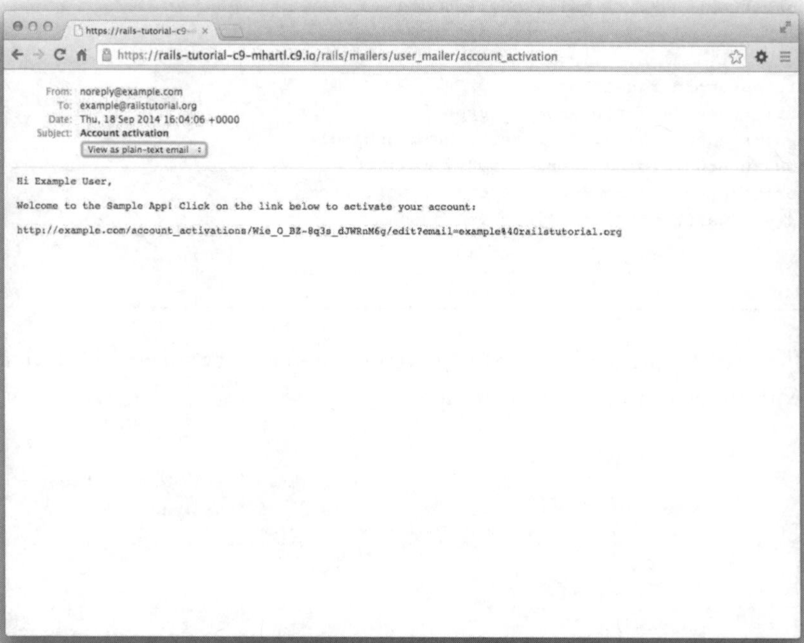

Figure 10.3 A preview of the text version of the account activation email.

```
assert_match 'foo', 'foobar'       # true
assert_match 'baz', 'foobar'       # false
assert_match /\w+/, 'foobar'       # true
assert_match /\w+/, '$#!*+@'       # false
```

The test in Listing 10.17 uses `assert_match` to check that the name, activation token, and escaped email appear in the email's body. For the last of these, note the use of

```
CGI::escape(user.email)
```

to escape the test user's email.[7]

---

7. To learn how to do something like this, Google "ruby rails escape url." You will find two main possibilities: `URI::encode(str)` and `CGI.escape(str)`. Trying them both reveals that the latter works. (Actually, there's a third possibility as well: the `ERB::Util` library supplies a url_encode method that has the same effect.)

Listing 10.17   A test of the current email implementation. **RED**

test/mailers/user_mailer_test.rb

```
require 'test_helper'

class UserMailerTest < ActionMailer::TestCase

  test "account_activation" do
    user = users(:michael)
    user.activation_token = User.new_token
    mail = UserMailer.account_activation(user)
    assert_equal "Account activation", mail.subject
    assert_equal [user.email], mail.to
    assert_equal ["noreply@example.com"], mail.from
    assert_match user.name,              mail.body.encoded
    assert_match user.activation_token,  mail.body.encoded
    assert_match CGI::escape(user.email), mail.body.encoded
  end
end
```

Note that Listing 10.18 takes care to add an activation token to the fixture user, which would otherwise be blank.

To get the test to pass, we have to configure our test file with the proper domain host, as shown in Listing 10.18.

Listing 10.18   Setting the test domain host.

config/environments/test.rb

```
Rails.application.configure do
  .
  .
  .
  config.action_mailer.delivery_method = :test
  config.action_mailer.default_url_options = { host: 'example.com' }
  .
  .
  .
end
```

With this code in place, the mailer test should be **GREEN**:

Listing 10.19 GREEN

```
$ bundle exec rake test:mailers
```

To use the mailer in our application, we just need to add a couple of lines to the **create** action used to sign users up, as shown in Listing 10.20. Note that Listing 10.20 has changed the redirect behavior upon signing up. In the past, we redirected the user to the user's profile page (Section 7.4), but that doesn't make sense now that we're requiring account activation. Instead, we now redirect the user to the root URL.

Listing 10.20 Adding account activation to user sign-up. **RED**
app/controllers/users_controller.rb

```
class UsersController < ApplicationController
  .
  .
  .
  def create
    @user = User.new(user_params)
    if @user.save
      UserMailer.account_activation(@user).deliver_now
      flash[:info] = "Please check your email to activate your account."
      redirect_to root_url
    else
      render 'new'
    end
  end
  .
  .
  .
end
```

Because Listing 10.20 redirects the user to the root URL instead of to the profile page and doesn't log the user in as before, the test suite is currently **RED**, even though the application is working as designed. We'll fix this by temporarily commenting out the failing lines, as shown in Listing 10.21. We'll uncomment those lines and write passing tests for account activation in Section 10.1.4.

Listing 10.21 Temporarily commenting out failing tests. **GREEN**
test/integration/users_signup_test.rb

```ruby
require 'test_helper'

class UsersSignupTest < ActionDispatch::IntegrationTest

  test "invalid sign-up information" do
    get signup_path
    assert_no_difference 'User.count' do
      post users_path, user: { name:  "",
                               email: "user@invalid",
                               password:            "foo",
                               password_confirmation: "bar" }
    end
    assert_template 'users/new'
    assert_select 'div#error_explanation'
    assert_select 'div.field_with_errors'
  end

  test "valid sign-up information" do
    get signup_path
    assert_difference 'User.count', 1 do
      post_via_redirect users_path, user: { name:  "Example User",
                                            email: "user@example.com",
                                            password:            "password",
                                            password_confirmation: "password" }
    end
    # assert_template 'users/show'
    # assert is_logged_in?
  end
end
```

If you now try signing up as a new user, you should be redirected as shown in Figure 10.4, and an email like the one shown in Listing 10.22 should be generated. Note that you will *not* receive an actual email in a development environment, but it will show up in your server logs. (You may have to scroll up a bit to see it.) Section 10.3 discusses how to send email for real in a production environment.

Listing 10.22 A sample account activation email from the server log.

```
Sent mail to michael@michaelhartl.com (931.6ms)
Date: Wed, 03 Sep 2014 19:47:18 +0000
```

Figure 10.4   The Home page with an activation message after sign-up.

```
From: noreply@example.com
To: michael@michaelhartl.com
Message-ID: <540770474e16_61d3fd1914f4cd0300a0@mhartl-rails-tutorial-953753.mail>
Subject: Account activation
Mime-Version: 1.0
Content-Type: multipart/alternative;
 boundary="--==_mimepart_5407704656b50_61d3fd1914f4cd02996a";
 charset=UTF-8
Content-Transfer-Encoding: 7bit


----==_mimepart_5407704656b50_61d3fd1914f4cd02996a
Content-Type: text/plain;
 charset=UTF-8
Content-Transfer-Encoding: 7bit

Hi Michael Hartl,
```

```
Welcome to the Sample App! Click on the link below to activate your account:

http://rails-tutorial-c9-mhartl.c9.io/account_activations/
fFb_F94mgQtmlSvRFGsITw/edit?email=michael%40michaelhartl.com
----==_mimepart_5407704656b50_61d3fd1914f4cd02996a
Content-Type: text/html;
 charset=UTF-8
Content-Transfer-Encoding: 7bit

<h1>Sample App</h1>

<p>Hi Michael Hartl,</p>

<p>
Welcome to the Sample App! Click on the link below to activate your account:
</p>

<a href="http://rails-tutorial-c9-mhartl.c9.io/account_activations/
fFb_F94mgQtmlSvRFGsITw/edit?email=michael%40michaelhartl.com">Activate</a>
----==_mimepart_5407704656b50_61d3fd1914f4cd02996a--
```

10.1.3 Activating the Account

Now that we have a correctly generated email as in Listing 10.22, we need to write an **edit** action in the Account Activations controller to activate the user. Recall from the discussion in Section 10.1.2 that the activation token and email are available as **params[:id]** and **params[:email]**, respectively. Following the model of passwords (Listing 8.5) and remember tokens (Listing 8.36), we plan to find and authenticate the user with code something like this:

```
user = User.find_by(email: params[:email])
if user && user.authenticated?(:activation, params[:id])
```

As we'll see momentarily, there will be one extra boolean in this expression. See if you can guess what it will be.

   The preceding code uses the **authenticated?** method to test whether the account activation digest matches the given token, but at present this won't work because that method is specialized to the remember token (Listing 8.33):

```ruby
# Returns true if the given token matches the digest.
def authenticated?(remember_token)
  return false if remember_digest.nil?
  BCrypt::Password.new(remember_digest).is_password?(remember_token)
end
```

Here **remember_digest** is an attribute on the User model, and inside the model we can rewrite it as follows:

```ruby
self.remember_digest
```

Somehow, we want to be able to make this *variable*, so we can call

```ruby
self.activation_token
```

instead by passing in the appropriate parameter to **authenticated?**.

The solution involves our first example of *metaprogramming*, which is essentially a program that writes a program. (Metaprogramming is one of Ruby's strongest suits, and many of the "magic" features of Rails are due to its use of Ruby metaprogramming.) The key in this case is the powerful **send** method, which lets us call a method with a name of our choice by "sending a message" to a given object. For example, in this console session we use **send** on a native Ruby object to find the length of an array:

```
$ rails console
>> a = [1, 2, 3]
>> a.length
=> 3
>> a.send(:length)
=> 3
>> a.send('length')
=> 3
```

Here we see that passing the symbol **:length** or string **'length'** to **send** is equivalent to calling the **length** method on the given object. As a second example, we'll access the **activation_digest** attribute of the first user in the database:

```
>> user = User.first
>> user.activation_digest
=> "$2a$10$4e6TFzEJAVNyjLv8Q5u22ensMt28qEkx0roaZvtRcp6UZKRM6N9Ae"
```

```
>> user.send(:activation_digest)
=> "$2a$10$4e6TFzEJAVNyjLv8Q5u22ensMt28qEkx0roaZvtRcp6UZKRM6N9Ae"
>> user.send('activation_digest')
=> "$2a$10$4e6TFzEJAVNyjLv8Q5u22ensMt28qEkx0roaZvtRcp6UZKRM6N9Ae"
>> attribute = :activation
>> user.send("#{attribute}_digest")
=> "$2a$10$4e6TFzEJAVNyjLv8Q5u22ensMt28qEkx0roaZvtRcp6UZKRM6N9Ae"
```

Note in the last example that we've defined an **attribute** variable equal to the symbol **:activation** and used string interpolation to build up the proper argument to **send**. This would work also with the string **'activation'**, but using a symbol is more conventional. In either case,

```
"#{attribute}_digest"
```

becomes

```
"activation_digest"
```

once the string is interpolated. (We saw how symbols are interpolated as strings in Section 7.4.2.)

Based on this discussion of **send**, we can rewrite the current **authenticated?** method as follows:

```
def authenticated?(remember_token)
  digest = self.send('remember_digest')
  return false if digest.nil?
  BCrypt::Password.new(digest).is_password?(remember_token)
end
```

With this template in place, we can generalize the method by adding a function argument with the name of the digest, and then use string interpolation as shown earlier:

```
def authenticated?(attribute, token)
  digest = self.send("#{attribute}_digest")
  return false if digest.nil?
  BCrypt::Password.new(digest).is_password?(token)
end
```

(Here we have renamed the second argument `token` to emphasize that it's now generic.) Because we're inside the user model, we can also omit `self`, yielding the most idiomatically correct version:

```
def authenticated?(attribute, token)
  digest = send("#{attribute}_digest")
  return false if digest.nil?
  BCrypt::Password.new(digest).is_password?(token)
end
```

We can now reproduce the previous behavior of `authenticated?` by invoking it like this:

```
user.authenticated?(:remember, remember_token)
```

Applying this discussion to the User model yields the generalized `authenticated?` method shown in Listing 10.23.

Listing 10.23 A generalized `authenticated?` method. **RED**

app/models/user.rb

```
class User < ActiveRecord::Base
  .
  .
  .
  # Returns true if the given token matches the digest.
  def authenticated?(attribute, token)
    digest = send("#{attribute}_digest")
    return false if digest.nil?
    BCrypt::Password.new(digest).is_password?(token)
  end
  .
  .
  .
end
```

The Listing 10.23 caption indicates we have a **RED** test suite:

Listing 10.24 RED

```
$ bundle exec rake test
```

The failure occurs because the **current_user** method (Listing 8.36) and the test for **nil** digests (Listing 8.43) both use the old version of **authenticated?**, which expects one argument instead of two. To fix this, we simply update the two cases to use the generalized method, as shown in Listing 10.25 and Listing 10.26.

Listing 10.25 Using the generalized **authenticated?** method in **current_user**.
app/helpers/sessions_helper.rb

```
module SessionsHelper
  .
  .
  .
  # Returns the current logged-in user (if any).
  def current_user
    if (user_id = session[:user_id])
      @current_user ||= User.find_by(id: user_id)
    elsif (user_id = cookies.signed[:user_id])
      user = User.find_by(id: user_id)
      if user && user.authenticated?(:remember, cookies[:remember_token])
        log_in user
        @current_user = user
      end
    end
  end
  .
  .
  .
end
```

Listing 10.26 Using the generalized **authenticated?** method in the User test. **GREEN**
test/models/user_test.rb

```
require 'test_helper'

class UserTest < ActiveSupport::TestCase

  def setup
    @user = User.new(name: "Example User", email: "user@example.com",
                     password: "foobar", password_confirmation: "foobar")
  end
  .
  .
  .
```

```
test "authenticated? should return false for a user with nil digest" do
  assert_not @user.authenticated?(:remember, '')
end
end
```

At this point, the tests should be **GREEN**:

Listing 10.27 GREEN

```
$ bundle exec rake test
```

Refactoring the code as shown here is incredibly more error-prone without a solid test suite. That risk explains why we went to such trouble to write good tests in Section 8.4.2 and Section 8.4.6.

With the `authenticated?` method as in Listing 10.23, we're now ready to write an `edit` action that authenticates the user corresponding to the email address in the `params` hash. Our test for validity will look like this:

```
if user && !user.activated? && user.authenticated?(:activation, params[:id])
```

Note the presence of `!user.activated?`, which is the extra boolean mentioned earlier. It prevents our code from activating users who have already been activated, which is important because we'll be logging in users upon confirmation, and we don't want to allow attackers who manage to obtain the activation link to log in as the user.

If the user is successfully authenticated according to the booleans above, we need to activate the user and update the `activated_at` timestamp:

```
user.update_attribute(:activated,    true)
user.update_attribute(:activated_at, Time.zone.now)
```

This leads to the `edit` action shown in Listing 10.28. Note that Listing 10.28 also handles the case of an invalid activation token. Such a case should rarely happen, but it's easy enough to redirect the user in this case to the root URL.

Listing 10.28 An `edit` action to activate accounts.

app/controllers/account_activations_controller.rb

```ruby
class AccountActivationsController < ApplicationController

  def edit
    user = User.find_by(email: params[:email])
    if user && !user.activated? && user.authenticated?(:activation, params[:id])
      user.update_attribute(:activated,    true)
      user.update_attribute(:activated_at, Time.zone.now)
      log_in user
      flash[:success] = "Account activated!"
      redirect_to user
    else
      flash[:danger] = "Invalid activation link"
      redirect_to root_url
    end
  end
end
```

With the code in Listing 10.28, you should now be able to paste in the URL from Listing 10.22 to activate the relevant user. For example, on my system I visited the URL

```
http://rails-tutorial-c9-mhartl.c9.io/account_activations/
fFb_F94mgQtmlSvRFGsITw/edit?email=michael%40michaelhartl.com
```

and got the result shown in Figure 10.5.

Of course, currently user activation doesn't actually *do* anything, because we haven't changed how users log in. To have account activation mean something, we need to allow users to log in only if they are activated. As shown in Listing 10.29, the way to do this is to log the user in as usual if **`user.activated?`** is true; otherwise, we redirect the user to the root URL with a **warning** message (Figure 10.6).

Listing 10.29 Preventing unactivated users from logging in.

app/controllers/sessions_controller.rb

```ruby
class SessionsController < ApplicationController

  def new
  end
```

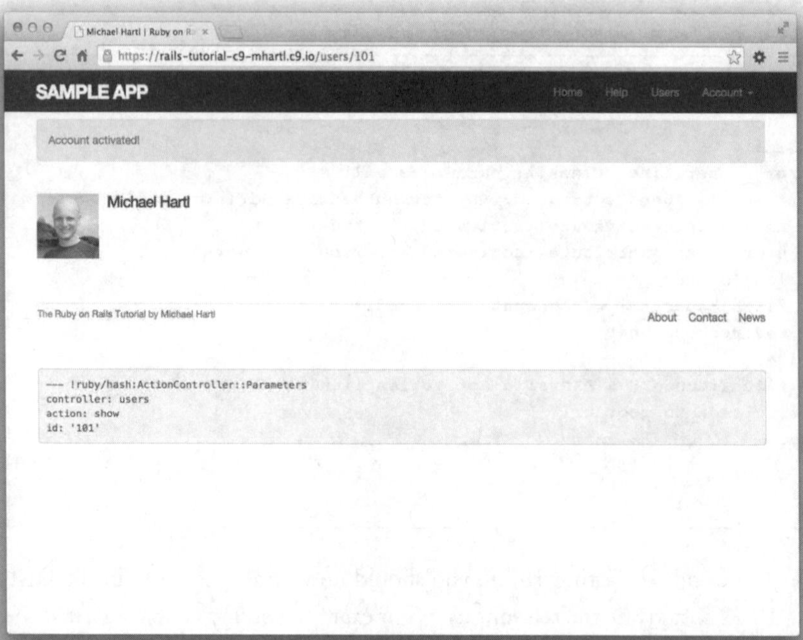

Figure 10.5 The profile page after a successful activation.

```
def create
  user = User.find_by(email: params[:session][:email].downcase)
  if user && user.authenticate(params[:session][:password])
    if user.activated?
      log_in user
      params[:session][:remember_me] == '1' ? remember(user) : forget(user)
      redirect_back_or user
    else
      message  = "Account not activated. "
      message += "Check your email for the activation link."
      flash[:warning] = message
      redirect_to root_url
    end
  else
    flash.now[:danger] = 'Invalid email/password combination'
    render 'new'
  end
```

```
    end

    def destroy
      log_out if logged_in?
      redirect_to root_url
    end
  end
```

With that, apart from one refinement, the basic functionality of user activation is finished. That refinement is preventing unactivated users from being displayed, which is left as an exercise (Section 10.5). In Section 10.1.4, we'll complete the process by adding some tests and then doing a little refactoring.

Figure 10.6   The warning message for a not-yet-activated user.

10.1.4 Activation Test and Refactoring

In this section, we'll add an integration test for account activation. Because we already have a test for signing up with valid information, we'll add the steps to the test developed in Section 7.4.4 (Listing 7.26). There are quite a few steps, but they are mostly straightforward; see if you can follow along in Listing 10.30.

Listing 10.30 Adding account activation to the user sign-up test. **GREEN**
test/integration/users_signup_test.rb

```ruby
require 'test_helper'

class UsersSignupTest < ActionDispatch::IntegrationTest

  def setup
    ActionMailer::Base.deliveries.clear
  end

  test "invalid signup information" do
    get signup_path
    assert_no_difference 'User.count' do
      post users_path, user: { name:  "",
                               email: "user@invalid",
                               password:              "foo",
                               password_confirmation: "bar" }
    end
    assert_template 'users/new'
    assert_select 'div#error_explanation'
    assert_select 'div.field_with_errors'
  end

  test "valid signup information with account activation" do
    get signup_path
    assert_difference 'User.count', 1 do
      post users_path, user: { name:  "Example User",
                               email: "user@example.com",
                               password:              "password",
                               password_confirmation: "password" }
    end
    assert_equal 1, ActionMailer::Base.deliveries.size
    user = assigns(:user)
    assert_not user.activated?
    # Try to log in before activation.
    log_in_as(user)
    assert_not is_logged_in?
    # Invalid activation token
```

```
      get edit_account_activation_path("invalid token")
      assert_not is_logged_in?
      # Valid token, wrong email
      get edit_account_activation_path(user.activation_token, email: 'wrong')
      assert_not is_logged_in?
      # Valid activation token
      get edit_account_activation_path(user.activation_token, email: user.email)
      assert user.reload.activated?
      follow_redirect!
      assert_template 'users/show'
      assert is_logged_in?
    end
end
```

There's a lot of code in Listing 10.30, but the only completely novel line is

```
assert_equal 1, ActionMailer::Base.deliveries.size
```

This code verifies that exactly one message was delivered. Because the **deliveries** array is global, we have to reset it in the **setup** method to prevent our code from breaking if any other tests deliver email (as will be the case in Section 10.2.5). Listing 10.30 also uses the **assigns** method for the first time in the main tutorial; as explained in the Chapter 8 exercise (Section 8.6), **assigns** lets us access instance variables in the corresponding action. For example, the Users controller's **create** action defines an **@user** variable (Listing 10.20), so we can access it in the test using **assigns(:user)**. Finally, note that Listing 10.30 restores the lines we commented out in Listing 10.21.

At this point, the test suite should be **GREEN**:

Listing 10.31 GREEN

```
$ bundle exec rake test
```

With the test in Listing 10.30, we're ready to refactor a little by moving some of the user manipulation out of the controller and into the model. In particular,

we'll develop an **activate** method to update the user's activation attributes and a
send_activation_email to send the activation email. The extra methods appear
in Listing 10.32, and the refactored application code appears in Listing 10.33 and
Listing 10.34.

Listing 10.32 Adding user activation methods to the User model.
app/models/user.rb

```
class User < ActiveRecord::Base
  .
  .
  .
  # Activates an account.
  def activate
    update_attribute(:activated,    true)
    update_attribute(:activated_at, Time.zone.now)
  end

  # Sends activation email.
  def send_activation_email
    UserMailer.account_activation(self).deliver_now
  end

  private
    .
    .
    .
end
```

Listing 10.33 Sending email via the user model object.
app/controllers/users_controller.rb

```
class UsersController < ApplicationController
  .
  .
  .
  def create
    @user = User.new(user_params)
    if @user.save
      @user.send_activation_email
      flash[:info] = "Please check your email to activate your account."
```

```
      redirect_to root_url
    else
      render 'new'
    end
  end
  .
  .
  .
end
```

Listing 10.34   Account activation via the user model object.

app/controllers/account_activations_controller.rb

```
class AccountActivationsController < ApplicationController

  def edit
    user = User.find_by(email: params[:email])
    if user && !user.activated? && user.authenticated?(:activation, params[:id])
      user.activate
      log_in user
      flash[:success] = "Account activated!"
      redirect_to user
    else
      flash[:danger] = "Invalid activation link"
      redirect_to root_url
    end
  end
end
```

Note that Listing 10.32 eliminates the use of **user.**, which would break inside the User model because there is no such variable:

```
-user.update_attribute(:activated,    true)
-user.update_attribute(:activated_at, Time.zone.now)
+update_attribute(:activated,    true)
+update_attribute(:activated_at, Time.zone.now)
```

(We could have switched from **user** to **self**, but recall from Section 6.2.5 that **self** is optional inside the model.) Listing 10.32 also changes **@user** to **self** in the call to the User mailer:

```
-UserMailer.account_activation(@user).deliver_now
+UserMailer.account_activation(self).deliver_now
```

These are *exactly* the kinds of details that are easy to miss during even a simple refactoring but will be caught by a good test suite. Speaking of which, the test suite should still be **GREEN**:

Listing 10.35 GREEN

```
$ bundle exec rake test
```

Account activation is now completed, which is a milestone worthy of a commit:

```
$ git add -A
$ git commit -m "Add account activations"
```

10.2 Password Reset

Having completed account activation (and thereby verified the user's email address), we're now in a good position to handle the common case of users forgetting their passwords. As we'll see, many of the steps are similar, and we will have several opportunities to apply the lessons learned in Section 10.1. The beginning is different, though: Unlike account activation, implementing password resets requires both a change to one of our views and two new forms (to handle email and new password submission).

Before writing any code, let's mock up the expected sequence for resetting passwords. We'll start by adding a "forgot password" link to the sample application's login form (Figure 10.7). The "forgot password" link will go to a page with a form that takes in an email address and sends an email containing a password reset link (Figure 10.8). The reset link will go to a form for resetting the user's password (with confirmation, as shown in Figure 10.9).

In analogy with account activations, our general plan is to make a Password Resets resource, with each password reset consisting of a reset token and the corresponding reset digest. The primary sequence goes like this:

1. When a user requests a password reset, find the user by the submitted email address.

2. If the email address exists in the database, generate a reset token and the corresponding reset digest.

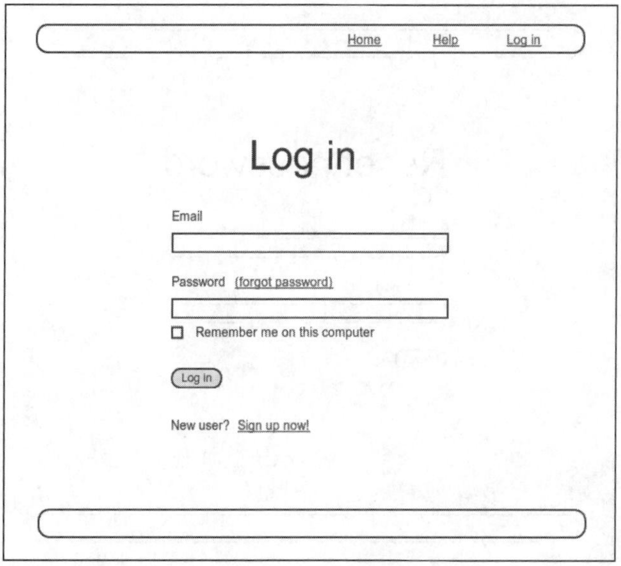

Figure 10.7 A mockup of a "forgot password" link.

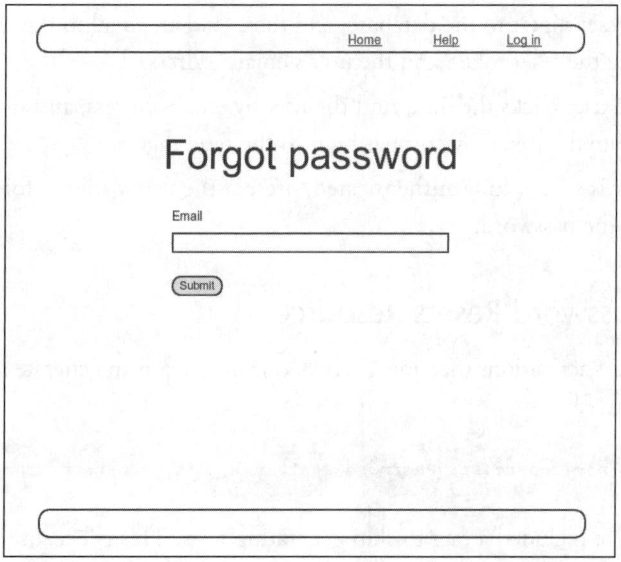

Figure 10.8 A mockup of the "forgot password" form.

Figure 10.9 A mockup of the reset password form.

3. Save the reset digest to the database, and then send an email to the user with a link containing the reset token and the user's email address.

4. When the user clicks the link, find the user by email address, and then authenticate the token by comparing it to the reset digest.

5. If the user is successfully authenticated, present the user with the form for changing the password.

10.2.1 Password Resets Resource

As with account activations (Section 10.1.1), our first step is to generate a controller for our new resource:

```
$ rails generate controller PasswordResets new edit --no-test-framework
```

Note that we've included a flag to skip generating tests. This is because we don't need the controller tests (preferring instead to use the integration test in Section 10.1.4), so it's convenient to omit them.

Because we'll need forms both for creating new password resets (Figure 10.8) and for updating them by changing the password in the User model (Figure 10.9), we need routes for **new**, **create**, **edit**, and **update**. We can arrange this with the **resources** line shown in Listing 10.36.

Listing 10.36 Adding a resource for password resets.

config/routes.rb

```
Rails.application.routes.draw do
  root                    'static_pages#home'
  get     'help'    => 'static_pages#help'
  get     'about'   => 'static_pages#about'
  get     'contact' => 'static_pages#contact'
  get     'signup'  => 'users#new'
  get     'login'   => 'sessions#new'
  post    'login'   => 'sessions#create'
  delete  'logout'  => 'sessions#destroy'
  resources :users
  resources :account_activations, only: [:edit]
  resources :password_resets,     only: [:new, :create, :edit, :update]
end
```

The code in Listing 10.36 arranges for the RESTful routes shown in Table 10.2. In particular, the first route in Table 10.2 gives a link to the "forgot password" form via

```
new_password_reset_path
```

as seen in Listing 10.37 and Figure 10.10.

Table 10.2 RESTful routes provided by the Password Resets resource in Listing 10.36.

HTTP request	URL	Action	Named route
GET	/password_resets/new	new	`new_password_reset_path`
POST	/password_resets	create	`password_resets_path`
GET	/password_resets/<token>/edit	edit	`edit_password_reset_path(token)`
PATCH	/password_resets/<token>	update	`password_reset_path(token)`

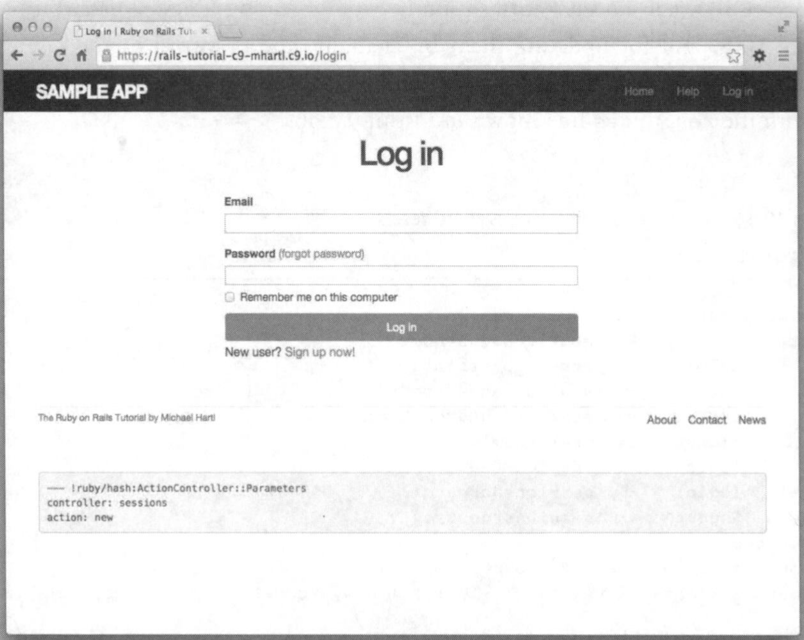

Figure 10.10 The login page with a "forgot password" link.

Listing 10.37 Adding a link to password resets.

app/views/sessions/new.html.erb

```
<% provide(:title, "Log in") %>
<h1>Log in</h1>

<div class="row">
  <div class="col-md-6 col-md-offset-3">
    <%= form_for(:session, url: login_path) do |f| %>

      <%= f.label :email %>
      <%= f.email_field :email, class: 'form-control' %>
```

```
    <%= f.label :password %>
    <%= link_to "(forgot password)", new_password_reset_path %>
    <%= f.password_field :password, class: 'form-control' %>

    <%= f.label :remember_me, class: "checkbox inline" do %>
      <%= f.check_box :remember_me %>
      <span>Remember me on this computer</span>
    <% end %>

    <%= f.submit "Log in", class: "btn btn-primary" %>
  <% end %>

  <p>New user? <%= link_to "Sign up now!", signup_path %></p>
  </div>
</div>
```

The data model for password resets is similar to the one used for account activation (Figure 10.7). Following the pattern established by remember tokens (Section 8.4) and account activation tokens (Section 10.1), password resets will pair a virtual reset token for use in the reset email with a corresponding reset digest for retrieving the user. If we instead stored an unhashed token, an attacker with access to the database could send a reset request to the user's email address and then use the token and email to visit the corresponding password reset link, thereby gaining control of the account. Using a digest for password resets is thus essential. As an additional security precaution, we'll plan to *expire* the reset link after a couple of hours, which requires recording the time when the reset is sent. The resulting **reset_digest** and **reset_sent_at** attributes appear in Figure 10.11.

The migration to add the attributes from Figure 10.11 appears as follows:

```
$ rails generate migration add_reset_to_users reset_digest:string \
> reset_sent_at:datetime
```

We then migrate as usual:

```
$ bundle exec rake db:migrate
```

users	
id	integer
name	string
email	string
created_at	datetime
updated_at	datetime
password_digest	string
remember_digest	string
admin	boolean
activation_digest	string
activated	boolean
activated_at	datetime
reset_digest	string
reset_sent_at	datetime

Figure 10.11 The User model with added password reset attributes.

10.2.2 Password Resets Controller and Form

To make the view for new password resets, we'll work in analogy with the previous form for making a new non–Active Record resource—namely, the login form (Listing 8.2) for creating a new session, shown again in Listing 10.38 for reference.

Listing 10.38 Reviewing the code for the login form.
app/views/sessions/new.html.erb

```erb
<% provide(:title, "Log in") %>
<h1>Log in</h1>

<div class="row">
  <div class="col-md-6 col-md-offset-3">
    <%= form_for(:session, url: login_path) do |f| %>

      <%= f.label :email %>
      <%= f.email_field :email, class: 'form-control' %>

      <%= f.label :password %>
      <%= f.password_field :password, class: 'form-control' %>

      <%= f.submit "Log in", class: "btn btn-primary" %>
    <% end %>

    <p>New user? <%= link_to "Sign up now!", signup_path %></p>
```

```
  </div>
</div>
```

The new password resets form has a lot in common with Listing 10.38. The most important differences are the use of a different resource and URL in the call to **form_for** and the omission of the password attribute. The result appears in Listing 10.39 and Figure 10.12.

Listing 10.39 A new password reset view.
app/views/password_resets/new.html.erb

```
<% provide(:title, "Forgot password") %>
<h1>Forgot password</h1>

<div class="row">
  <div class="col-md-6 col-md-offset-3">
    <%= form_for(:password_reset, url: password_resets_path) do |f| %>
      <%= f.label :email %>
      <%= f.email_field :email, class: 'form-control' %>

      <%= f.submit "Submit", class: "btn btn-primary" %>
    <% end %>
  </div>
</div>
```

Upon submitting the form in Figure 10.12, we need to find the user by email address and update the user's attributes with the password reset token and sent-at timestamp. We then redirect the user to the root URL with an informative flash message. As with login (Listing 8.9), in the case of an invalid submission, we re-render the **new** page with a **flash.now** message. The results appear in Listing 10.40.

Listing 10.40 A **create** action for password resets.
app/controllers/password_resets_controller.rb

```
class PasswordResetsController < ApplicationController

  def new
  end

  def create
```

```
    @user = User.find_by(email: params[:password_reset][:email].downcase)
    if @user
      @user.create_reset_digest
      @user.send_password_reset_email
      flash[:info] = "Email sent with password reset instructions"
      redirect_to root_url
    else
      flash.now[:danger] = "Email address not found"
      render 'new'
    end
  end

  def edit
  end
end
```

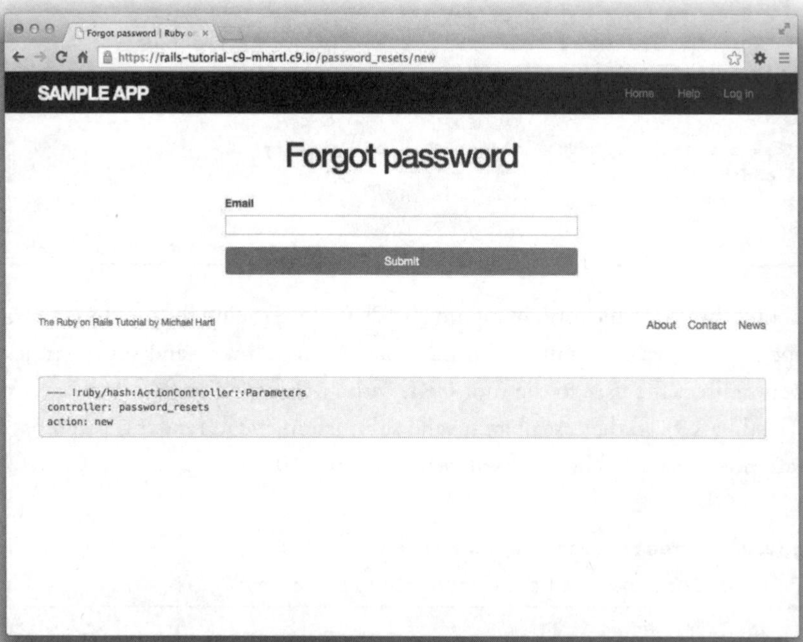

Figure 10.12 The "forgot password" form.

The code in the User model parallels the `create_activation_digest` method used in the `before_create` callback (Listing 10.3), as seen in Listing 10.41.

Listing 10.41   Adding password reset methods to the User model.

app/models/user.rb

```ruby
class User < ActiveRecord::Base
  attr_accessor :remember_token, :activation_token, :reset_token
  before_save    :downcase_email
  before_create :create_activation_digest
  .
  .
  .
  # Activates an account.
  def activate
    update_attribute(:activated,    true)
    update_attribute(:activated_at, Time.zone.now)
  end

  # Sends activation email.
  def send_activation_email
    UserMailer.account_activation(self).deliver_now
  end

  # Sets the password reset attributes.
  def create_reset_digest
    self.reset_token = User.new_token
    update_attribute(:reset_digest,  User.digest(reset_token))
    update_attribute(:reset_sent_at, Time.zone.now)
  end

  # Sends password reset email.
  def send_password_reset_email
    UserMailer.password_reset(self).deliver_now
  end

  private

    # Converts email to all lowercase.
    def downcase_email
      self.email = email.downcase
    end

    # Creates and assigns the activation token and digest.
    def create_activation_digest
      self.activation_token  = User.new_token
```

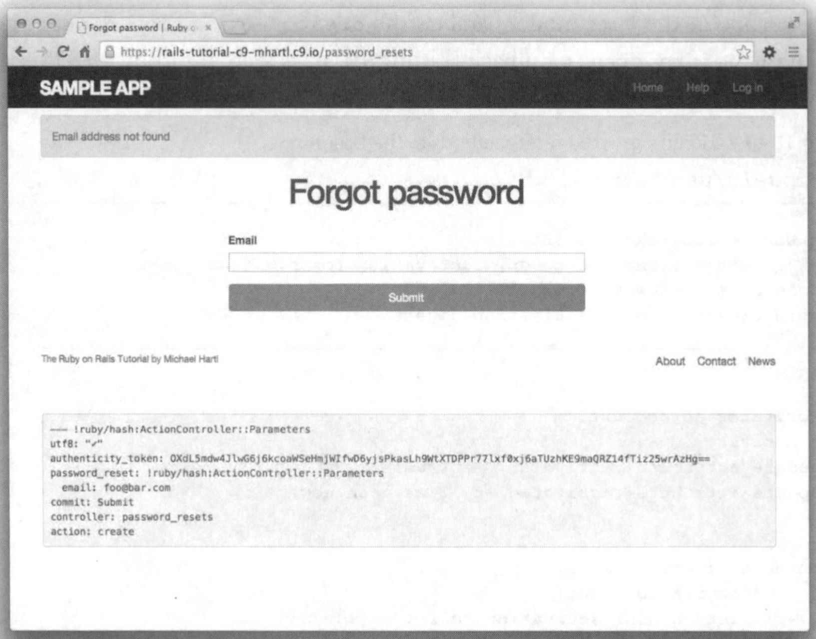

Figure 10.13 The "forgot password" form for an invalid email address.

```
      self.activation_digest = User.digest(activation_token)
    end
end
```

As shown in Figure 10.13, at this point the application's behavior for invalid email addresses is already working. To get the application working upon submission of a valid email address as well, we need to define a password reset mailer method.

10.2.3 Password Reset Mailer Method

The code to send the password reset email appears in Listing 10.41 as follows:

```
UserMailer.password_reset(self).deliver_now
```

The password reset mailer method needed to get this operation working is nearly identical to the mailer for account activation developed in Section 10.1.2. We first create a **password_reset** method in the user mailer (Listing 10.42), and then define view templates for plain-text email (Listing 10.43) and HTML email (Listing 10.44).

Listing 10.42   Mailing the password reset link.
app/mailers/user_mailer.rb

```ruby
class UserMailer < ApplicationMailer

  def account_activation(user)
    @user = user
    mail to: user.email, subject: "Account activation"
  end

  def password_reset(user)
    @user = user
    mail to: user.email, subject: "Password reset"
  end
end
```

Listing 10.43   The password reset plain-text email template.
app/views/user_mailer/password_reset.text.erb

```erb
To reset your password click the link below:

<%= edit_password_reset_url(@user.reset_token, email: @user.email) %>

This link will expire in two hours.

If you did not request your password to be reset, please ignore this email and
your password will stay as it is.
```

Listing 10.44   The password reset HTML email template.
app/views/user_mailer/password_reset.html.erb

```erb
<h1>Password reset</h1>

<p>To reset your password click the link below:</p>
```

```
<%= link_to "Reset password",
            edit_password_reset_url(@user.reset_token,
                                    email: @user.email) %>

<p>This link will expire in two hours.</p>

<p>
If you did not request your password to be reset, please ignore this email and
your password will stay as it is.
</p>
```

As with account activation emails (Section 10.1.2), we can preview password reset emails using the Rails email previewer. The code is exactly analogous to Listing 10.15, as shown in Listing 10.45.

Listing 10.45   A working preview method for password reset.

test/mailers/previews/user_mailer_preview.rb

```
# Preview all emails at http://localhost:3000/rails/mailers/user_mailer
class UserMailerPreview < ActionMailer::Preview

  # Preview this email at
  # http://localhost:3000/rails/mailers/user_mailer/account_activation
  def account_activation
    user = User.first
    user.activation_token = User.new_token
    UserMailer.account_activation(user)
  end

  # Preview this email at
  # http://localhost:3000/rails/mailers/user_mailer/password_reset
  def password_reset
    user = User.first
    user.reset_token = User.new_token
    UserMailer.password_reset(user)
  end
end
```

With the code in Listing 10.45, the HTML and text email previews appear as in Figure 10.14 and Figure 10.15.

In analogy with the account activation mailer method test (Listing 10.17), we'll write a short test of the password reset mailer method, as shown in Listing 10.46. Note that we need to create a password reset token for use in the views; unlike the activation token, which is created for every user by a **before_create** callback (Listing 10.3),

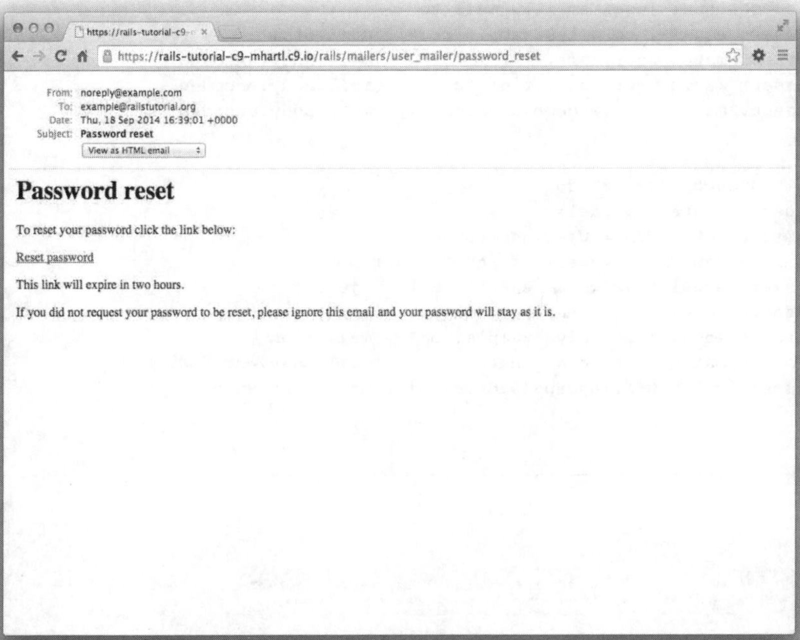

Figure 10.14 A preview of the HTML version of the password reset email.

the password reset token is created only when a user successfully submits the "forgot password" form. This step will occur naturally in an integration test (Listing 10.53), but in the present context we need to create one by hand.

Listing 10.46 Adding a test of the password reset mailer method. **GREEN**

test/mailers/user_mailer_test.rb

```
require 'test_helper'

class UserMailerTest < ActionMailer::TestCase

  test "account_activation" do
    user = users(:michael)
    user.activation_token = User.new_token
    mail = UserMailer.account_activation(user)
    assert_equal "Account activation", mail.subject
```

```
    assert_equal [user.email], mail.to
    assert_equal ["noreply@example.com"], mail.from
    assert_match user.name,                mail.body.encoded
    assert_match user.activation_token,    mail.body.encoded
    assert_match CGI::escape(user.email), mail.body.encoded
  end

  test "password_reset" do
    user = users(:michael)
    user.reset_token = User.new_token
    mail = UserMailer.password_reset(user)
    assert_equal "Password reset", mail.subject
    assert_equal [user.email], mail.to
    assert_equal ["noreply@example.com"], mail.from
    assert_match user.reset_token,         mail.body.encoded
    assert_match CGI::escape(user.email), mail.body.encoded
  end
end
```

Figure 10.15 A preview of the text version of the password reset email.

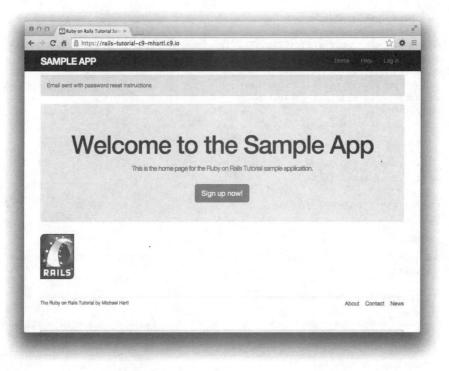

Figure 10.16 The result of submitting a valid email address.

At this point, the test suite should be **GREEN**:

Listing 10.47 GREEN

```
$ bundle exec rake test
```

With the code in Listing 10.42, Listing 10.43, and Listing 10.44, submission of a valid email address appears as shown in Figure 10.16. The corresponding email appears in the server log and should look something like Listing 10.48.

Listing 10.48 A sample password reset email from the server log.

```
Sent mail to michael@michaelhartl.com (66.8ms)
Date: Thu, 04 Sep 2014 01:04:59 +0000
```

```
From: noreply@example.com
To: michael@michaelhartl.com
Message-ID: <5407babbee139_8722b257d04576a@mhartl-rails-tutorial-953753.mail>
Subject: Password reset
Mime-Version: 1.0
Content-Type: multipart/alternative;
 boundary="--==_mimepart_5407babbe3505_8722b257d045617";
 charset=UTF-8
Content-Transfer-Encoding: 7bit


----==_mimepart_5407babbe3505_8722b257d045617
Content-Type: text/plain;
 charset=UTF-8
Content-Transfer-Encoding: 7bit

To reset your password click the link below:

http://rails-tutorial-c9-mhartl.c9.io/password_resets/3BdBrXeQZSWqFIDRN8cxHA/
edit?email=michael%40michaelhartl.com

This link will expire in two hours.

If you did not request your password to be reset, please ignore this email and
your password will stay as it is.
----==_mimepart_5407babbe3505_8722b257d045617
Content-Type: text/html;
 charset=UTF-8
Content-Transfer-Encoding: 7bit

<h1>Password reset</h1>

<p>To reset your password click the link below:</p>

<a href="http://rails-tutorial-c9-mhartl.c9.io/
password_resets/3BdBrXeQZSWqFIDRN8cxHA/
edit?email=michael%40michaelhartl.com">Reset password</a>

<p>This link will expire in two hours.</p>

<p>
If you did not request your password to be reset, please ignore this email and
your password will stay as it is.
</p>
----==_mimepart_5407babbe3505_8722b257d045617--
```

10.2.4 Resetting the Password

To get links formatted like

```
http://example.com/password_resets/
3BdBrXeQZSWqFIDRN8cxHA/edit?email=foo%40bar.com
```

to work, we need a form for resetting passwords. This task is similar to updating users via the user edit view (Listing 9.2), but in this case only password and confirmation fields are needed. There's an additional complication, though: We expect to find the user by email address, which means we need this value in both the **edit** and **update** actions. The email will automatically be available in the **edit** action because of its presence in the link, but after we submit the form its value will be lost. The solution is to use a *hidden field* to place (but not display) the email on the page, and then submit it along with the rest of the form's information. The result appears in Listing 10.49.

Listing 10.49 The form to reset a password.

app/views/password_resets/edit.html.erb

```erb
<% provide(:title, 'Reset password') %>
<h1>Reset password</h1>

<div class="row">
  <div class="col-md-6 col-md-offset-3">
    <%= form_for(@user, url: password_reset_path(params[:id])) do |f| %>
      <%= render 'shared/error_messages' %>

      <%= hidden_field_tag :email, @user.email %>

      <%= f.label :password %>
      <%= f.password_field :password, class: 'form-control' %>

      <%= f.label :password_confirmation, "Confirmation" %>
      <%= f.password_field :password_confirmation, class: 'form-control' %>

      <%= f.submit "Update password", class: "btn btn-primary" %>
    <% end %>
  </div>
</div>
```

Note that Listing 10.49 uses the form tag helper

```
hidden_field_tag :email, @user.email
```

instead of

```
f.hidden_field :email, @user.email
```

because the reset link puts the email in `params[:email]`, whereas the latter helper would put it in `params[:user][:email]`.

   To get the form to render, we need to define an `@user` variable in the Password Resets controller's `edit` action. As with account activation (Listing 10.28), this involves finding the user corresponding to the email address in `params[:email]`. We then need to verify that the user is valid (i.e., that it exists, is activated, and is authenticated according to the reset token from `params[:id]` using the generalized `authenticated?` method defined in Listing 10.23). Because the existence of a valid `@user` is needed in both the `edit` and `update` actions, we'll put the code to find and validate it in a couple of filters, as shown in Listing 10.50.

Listing 10.50   The `edit` action for password reset.
app/controllers/password_resets_controller.rb

```
class PasswordResetsController < ApplicationController
  before_action :get_user,    only: [:edit, :update]
  before_action :valid_user, only: [:edit, :update]
  .
  .
  .
  def edit
  end

  private

    def get_user
      @user = User.find_by(email: params[:email])
    end

    # Confirms a valid user.
    def valid_user
      unless (@user && @user.activated? &&
              @user.authenticated?(:reset, params[:id]))
```

```
      redirect_to root_url
    end
  end
end
```

In Listing 10.50, compare the use of

```
authenticated?(:reset, params[:id])
```

to

```
authenticated?(:remember, cookies[:remember_token])
```

in Listing 10.25 and to

```
authenticated?(:activation, params[:id])
```

in Listing 10.28. Together, these three uses complete the authentication methods shown in Table 10.1.

Following the link from Listing 10.48 should now render a password reset form. The result appears in Figure 10.17.

To define the **update** action corresponding to the **edit** action in Listing 10.50, we need to consider four cases: an expired password reset, a successful update, a failed update (due to an invalid password), and a failed update (which initially looks "successful") due to a blank password and confirmation. The first case applies to both the **edit** and **update** actions, and so logically belongs in a before filter (Listing 10.51). The next two cases correspond to the two branches in the main **if** statement shown in Listing 10.51. Because the edit form is modifying an Active Record model object (i.e., a user), we can rely on the shared partial from Listing 10.49 to render error messages. The only exception is the case where the password is blank, which is currently allowed by our User model (Listing 9.10) and so needs to be caught explicitly and handled with a flash message.[8]

---

8. We need only handle the case where the password is blank because if the confirmation is blank, the confirmation validation (which is skipped if the password is blank) will catch the problem and supply a relevant error message.

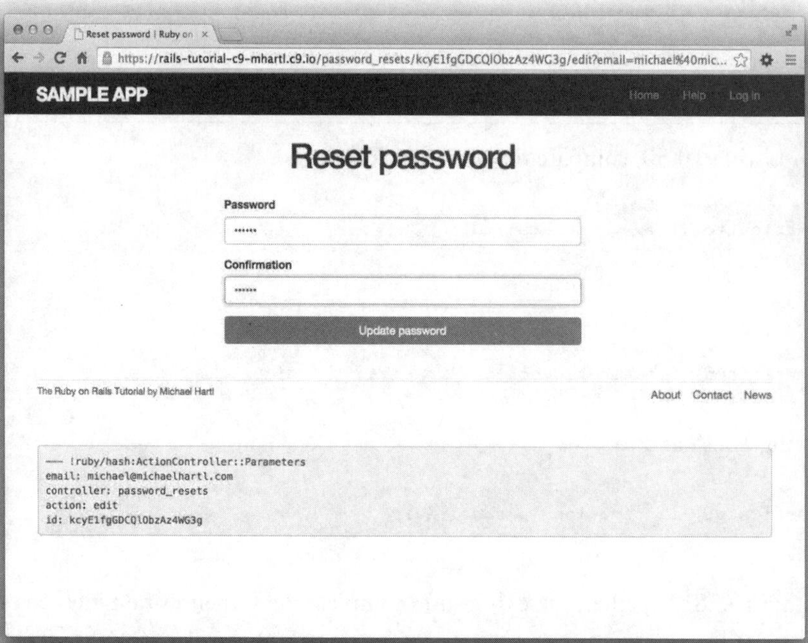

Figure 10.17 The password reset form.

Listing 10.51 The **update** action for password reset.

app/controllers/password_resets_controller.rb

```
class PasswordResetsController < ApplicationController
  before_action :get_user,         only: [:edit, :update]
  before_action :valid_user,       only: [:edit, :update]
  before_action :check_expiration, only: [:edit, :update]

  def new
  end

  def create
    @user = User.find_by(email: params[:password_reset][:email].downcase)
    if @user
      @user.create_reset_digest
```

```
    @user.send_password_reset_email
    flash[:info] = "Email sent with password reset instructions"
    redirect_to root_url
  else
    flash.now[:danger] = "Email address not found"
    render 'new'
  end
end

def edit
end

def update
  if password_blank?
    flash.now[:danger] = "Password can't be blank"
    render 'edit'
  elsif @user.update_attributes(user_params)
    log_in @user
    flash[:success] = "Password has been reset."
    redirect_to @user
  else
    render 'edit'
  end
end

private

  def user_params
    params.require(:user).permit(:password, :password_confirmation)
  end

  # Returns true if password is blank.
  def password_blank?
    params[:user][:password].blank?
  end

  # Before filters

  def get_user
    @user = User.find_by(email: params[:email])
  end

  # Confirms a valid user.
  def valid_user
    unless (@user && @user.activated? &&
            @user.authenticated?(:reset, params[:id]))
      redirect_to root_url
    end
```

```
      end

      # Checks expiration of reset token.
      def check_expiration
        if @user.password_reset_expired?
          flash[:danger] = "Password reset has expired."
          redirect_to new_password_reset_url
        end
      end
end
```

The implementation in Listing 10.53 delegates the boolean test for password reset expiration to the User model via the code

```
@user.password_reset_expired?
```

To get this to work, we need to define the **password_reset_expired?** method. As indicated in the email templates from Section 10.2.3, we'll consider a password reset to be expired if it was sent more than two hours ago, which we can express in Ruby as follows:

```
reset_sent_at < 2.hours.ago
```

This line can be confusing if you read < as "less than," because then it sounds like "Password reset sent less than two hours ago," which is the opposite of what we want. In this context, it's better to read < as "earlier than," which gives something like "Password reset sent earlier than two hours ago." That *is* what we want, and it leads to the **password_reset_expired?** method in Listing 10.52. (For a formal demonstration that the comparison is correct, see the proof in Section 10.6.)

Listing 10.52 Adding password reset methods to the User model.
app/models/user.rb

```
class User < ActiveRecord::Base
  .
  .
  .
  # Returns true if a password reset has expired.
  def password_reset_expired?
    reset_sent_at < 2.hours.ago
  end
```

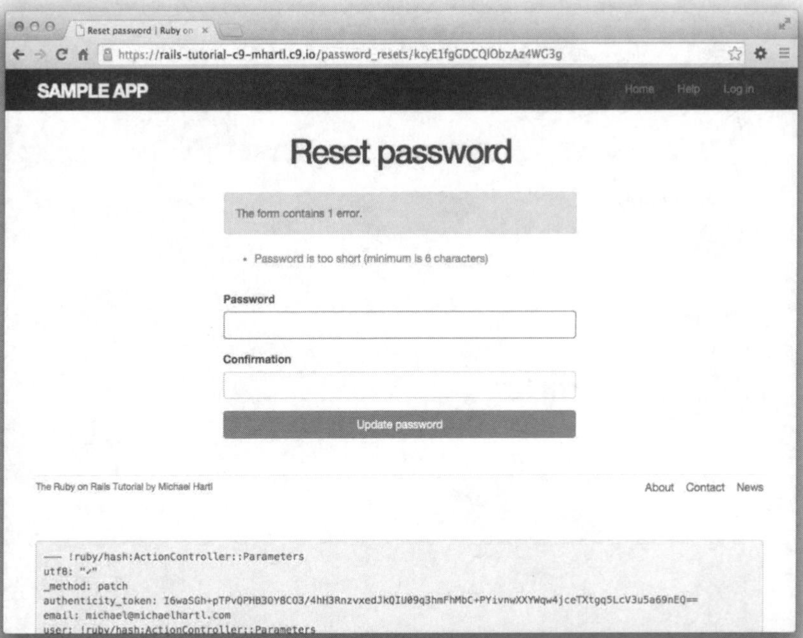

Figure 10.18 A failed password reset.

```
    private
        .
        .
        .
end
```

With the code in Listing 10.52, the `update` action in Listing 10.53 should be working. The results for invalid and valid submissions are shown in Figure 10.18 and Figure 10.19, respectively. Lacking the patience to wait two hours, we'll cover the third branch in a test, which is left as an exercise (Section 10.5).

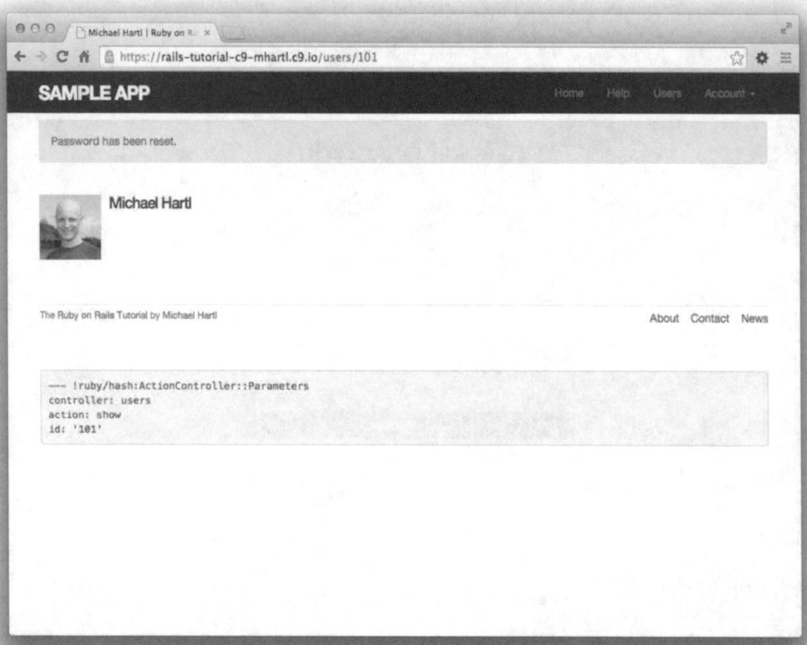

Figure 10.19 A successful password reset.

10.2.5 Password Reset Test

In this section, we'll write an integration test covering two of the three branches in Listing 10.53, invalid and valid submission. (As noted earlier, testing the third branch is left as an exercise.) We'll get started by generating a test file for password resets:

```
$ rails generate integration_test password_resets
    invoke  test_unit
    create    test/integration/password_resets_test.rb
```

The steps to test password resets broadly parallel the test for account activation from Listing 10.30, though there is a difference at the outset: We visit the "forgot password" form and submit first invalid and then valid email addresses, the latter of which creates a password reset token and sends the reset email. We next visit the link from the email and again submit invalid and valid information, verifying the correct behavior in each case. The resulting test, shown in Listing 10.53, is an excellent exercise in reading code.

Listing 10.53 An integration test for password resets.

test/integration/password_resets_test.rb

```ruby
require 'test_helper'

class PasswordResetsTest < ActionDispatch::IntegrationTest
  def setup
    ActionMailer::Base.deliveries.clear
    @user = users(:michael)
  end

  test "password resets" do
    get new_password_reset_path
    assert_template 'password_resets/new'
    # Invalid email
    post password_resets_path, password_reset: { email: "" }
    assert_not flash.empty?
    assert_template 'password_resets/new'
    # Valid email
    post password_resets_path, password_reset: { email: @user.email }
    assert_not_equal @user.reset_digest, @user.reload.reset_digest
    assert_equal 1, ActionMailer::Base.deliveries.size
    assert_not flash.empty?
    assert_redirected_to root_url
    # Password reset form
    user = assigns(:user)
    # Wrong email
    get edit_password_reset_path(user.reset_token, email: "")
    assert_redirected_to root_url
    # Inactive user
    user.toggle!(:activated)
    get edit_password_reset_path(user.reset_token, email: user.email)
    assert_redirected_to root_url
    user.toggle!(:activated)
    # Right email, wrong token
    get edit_password_reset_path('wrong token', email: user.email)
    assert_redirected_to root_url
    # Right email, right token
    get edit_password_reset_path(user.reset_token, email: user.email)
    assert_template 'password_resets/edit'
    assert_select "input[name=email][type=hidden][value=?]", user.email
    # Invalid password & confirmation
    patch password_reset_path(user.reset_token),
          email: user.email,
          user: { password:              "foobaz",
                  password_confirmation: "barquux" }
```

```
    assert_select 'div#error_explanation'
    # Blank password
    patch password_reset_path(user.reset_token),
          email: user.email,
          user: { password:              " ",
                  password_confirmation: "foobar" }
    assert_not flash.empty?
    assert_template 'password_resets/edit'
    # Valid password & confirmation
    patch password_reset_path(user.reset_token),
          email: user.email,
          user: { password:              "foobaz",
                  password_confirmation: "foobaz" }
    assert is_logged_in?
    assert_not flash.empty?
    assert_redirected_to user
  end
end
```

Most of the ideas in Listing 10.53 have appeared previously in this tutorial; the only really novel element is the test of the **input** tag:

```
assert_select "input[name=email][type=hidden][value=?]", user.email
```

This line makes sure that there is an **input** tag with the right name, (hidden) type, and email address:

```
<input id="email" name="email" type="hidden" value="michael@example.com" />
```

With the code as in Listing 10.53, our test suite should be **GREEN**:

Listing 10.54 GREEN

```
$ bundle exec rake test
```

10.3 Email in Production

As a capstone to our work on account activation and password reminders, in this section we'll configure our application so that it can actually send email in production. We'll first get set up with a free service to send email, and then we'll configure and deploy our application.

To send email in production, we'll use SendGrid, which is available as an add-on at Heroku for verified accounts. (This requires adding credit card information to your Heroku account, but there is no charge when verifying an account.) For our purposes, the "starter" tier (which is limited to 200 emails per day but costs nothing) is the best fit. We can add it to our app as follows:

```
$ heroku addons:add sendgrid:starter
```

To configure our application to use SendGrid, we need to fill out the SMTP settings for our production environment. As shown in Listing 10.55, you will also have to define a **host** variable with the address of your production website.

Listing 10.55 Configuring Rails to use SendGrid in production.
config/environments/production.rb

```
Rails.application.configure do
  .
  .
  .
  config.action_mailer.raise_delivery_errors = true
  config.action_mailer.delivery_method = :smtp
  host = '<your heroku app>.herokuapp.com'
  config.action_mailer.default_url_options = { host: host }
  ActionMailer::Base.smtp_settings = {
    :address            => 'smtp.sendgrid.net',
    :port               => '587',
    :authentication     => :plain,
    :user_name          => ENV['SENDGRID_USERNAME'],
    :password           => ENV['SENDGRID_PASSWORD'],
    :domain             => 'heroku.com',
    :enable_starttls_auto => true
  }
  .
  .
  .
end
```

The email configuration in Listing 10.55 includes the **user_name** and **password** of the SendGrid account, but note that they are accessed via the **ENV** environment variable instead of being hard-coded. This is a best practice for production applications, which for security reasons should never expose sensitive information such as raw passwords in source code. In the present case, these variables are configured automatically via the SendGrid add-on, but we'll see an example in Section 11.4.4 where we'll have to define them ourselves. In case you're curious, you can view the environment variables used in Listing 10.55 as follows:

```
$ heroku config:get SENDGRID_USERNAME
$ heroku config:get SENDGRID_PASSWORD
```

At this point, you should merge the topic branch into **master**:

```
$ bundle exec rake test
$ git add -A
$ git commit -m "Add password resets & email configuration"
$ git checkout master
$ git merge account-activation-password-reset
```

Then push up to the remote repository and deploy to Heroku:

```
$ bundle exec rake test
$ git push
$ git push heroku
$ heroku run rake db:migrate
```

Once the Heroku deploy has finished, try signing up for the sample application in production using an email address that you control. You should get an activation email as implemented in Section 10.1.1 (Figure 10.20). If you then forget (or pretend to forget) your password, you can reset it as developed in Section 10.2 (Figure 10.21).

10.4 Conclusion

With the added account activation and password resets, our sample application's sign-up, login, and logout machinery is complete and professional grade. The rest of the *Ruby on Rails™ Tutorial* builds on this foundation to make a site with Twitter-like microposts (Chapter 11) and a status feed consisting of posts from followed users (Chapter 12). In the process, we'll learn about some of the most powerful features of Rails, including

Figure 10.20 An account activation email sent in production.

Figure 10.21 A password reset email sent in production.

image upload, custom database queries, and advanced data modeling with `has_many` and `has_many :through`.

10.4.1 What We Learned in This Chapter

- Like sessions, account activations can be modeled as a resource despite not being Active Record objects.

- Rails can generate Active Mailer actions and views to send email.

- Action Mailer supports both plain-text and HTML mail.

- As with ordinary actions and views, instance variables defined in mailer actions are available in mailer views.

- Like sessions and account activations, password resets can be modeled as a resource despite not being Active Record objects.

- Account activations and password resets use a generated token to create a unique URL for activating users or resetting passwords, respectively.

- Both mailer tests and integration tests are useful for verifying the behavior of the User mailer.

- We can send email in production using SendGrid.

10.5 Exercises

Note: To receive a copy of the *Solutions Manual for Exercises*, with solutions to every exercise in the *Ruby on Rails™ Tutorial*, visit www.railstutorial.org/<word>, where "<word>" is the last word of the Figure 3.9 caption.

For a suggestion on how to avoid conflicts between exercises and the main tutorial, see the note on exercise topic branches in Section 3.6.

1. Write an integration test for the expired password reset branch in Listing 10.53 by filling in the template shown in Listing 10.56. (This code introduces `response.body`, which returns the full HTML body of the page.) There are many ways to test for the result of an expiration, but the method suggested by Listing 10.56 is to (case-insensitively) check that the response body includes the word "expired".

2. Right now *all* users are displayed on the user index page at /users and are visible via the URL /users/:id, but it makes sense to show only activated users. Arrange for this behavior by filling in the template shown in Listing 10.57.[9] (This code uses the Active Record **where** method, which we'll learn more about in Section 11.3.3.) *Extra credit*: Write integration tests for both /users and /users/:id.

3. In Listing 10.41, both the **activate** and **create_reset_digest** methods make two calls to **update_attribute**, each of which requires a separate database transaction. By filling in the template shown in Listing 10.58, replace each pair of **update_attribute** calls with a single call to **update_columns**, which hits the database only once. After making the changes, verify that the test suite is still **GREEN**.

Listing 10.56   A test for an expired password reset. **GREEN**

test/integration/password_resets_test.rb

```
require 'test_helper'

class PasswordResetsTest < ActionDispatch::IntegrationTest

  def setup
    ActionMailer::Base.deliveries.clear
    @user = users(:michael)
  end
  .
  .
  .
  test "expired token" do
    get new_password_reset_path
    post password_resets_path, password_reset: { email: @user.email }

    @user = assigns(:user)
    @user.update_attribute(:reset_sent_at, 3.hours.ago)
    patch password_reset_path(@user.reset_token),
          email: @user.email,
          user: { password:              "foobar",
                  password_confirmation: "foobar" }
    assert_response :redirect
    follow_redirect!
    assert_match /FILL_IN/i, response.body
```

---

9. Note that Listing 10.57 uses **and** instead of **&&**. The two are nearly identical, but the latter operator has a higher *precedence*, which binds too tightly to **root_url** in this case. We could fix the problem by putting **root_url** in parentheses, but the idiomatically correct way to write it is to use **and** instead.

```
      end
end
```

Listing 10.57   A template for code to show only activated users.

app/controllers/users_controller.rb

```
class UsersController < ApplicationController
  .
  .
  .
  def index
    @users = User.where(activated: FILL_IN).paginate(page: params[:page])
  end

  def show
    @user = User.find(params[:id])
    redirect_to root_url and return unless FILL_IN
  end
  .
  .
  .
end
```

Listing 10.58   A template for using **update_columns**.

app/models/user.rb

```
class User < ActiveRecord::Base
  attr_accessor :remember_token, :activation_token, :reset_token
  before_save    :downcase_email
  before_create  :create_activation_digest
  .
  .
  .
  # Activates an account.
  def activate
    update_columns(activated: FILL_IN, activated_at: FILL_IN)
  end

  # Sends activation email.
  def send_activation_email
    UserMailer.account_activation(self).deliver_now
  end

  # Sets the password reset attributes.
```

```
def create_reset_digest
  self.reset_token = User.new_token
  update_columns(reset_digest:  FILL_IN,
                 reset_sent_at: FILL_IN)
end

# Sends password reset email.
def send_password_reset_email
  UserMailer.password_reset(self).deliver_now
end

private

  # Converts email to all lowercase.
  def downcase_email
    self.email = email.downcase
  end

  # Creates and assigns the activation token and digest.
  def create_activation_digest
    self.activation_token  = User.new_token
    self.activation_digest = User.digest(activation_token)
  end
end
```

10.6 Proof of Expiration Comparison

In this section, we'll prove that the comparison for password expiration in Section 10.2.4 is correct. We start by defining two time intervals. Let Δt_r be the time interval since sending the password reset and let Δt_e be the expiration time limit (e.g., two hours). A password reset has expired if the time interval since the reset was sent is greater than the expiration limit:

$$\Delta t_r > \Delta t_e. \tag{10.1}$$

If we write the time now as t_N, the password reset sending time as t_r, and the expiration time as t_e (e.g., two hours ago), then we have

$$\Delta t_r = t_N - t_r \tag{10.2}$$

and

$$\Delta t_e = t_N - t_e. \tag{10.3}$$

Plugging Eq. (10.2) and Eq. (10.3) into Eq. (10.1) then gives

$$\Delta t_r \quad > \quad \Delta t_e$$
$$t_N - t_r \quad > \quad t_N - t_e$$
$$-t_r \quad > \quad -t_e,$$

which upon multiplying through by -1 yields

$$t_r < t_e. \tag{10.4}$$

Converting Eq. (10.4) to code with the value $t_e = 2$ hours ago gives the `password_reset_expired?` method shown in Listing 10.52:

```
def password_reset_expired?
  reset_sent_at < 2.hours.ago
end
```

As noted in Section 10.2.4, if we read `<` as "earlier than" instead of "less than," this code makes sense as the English sentence "The password reset was sent earlier than two hours ago."

Chapter 11

User Microposts

In the course of developing the core sample application, we've now encountered four resources—users, sessions, account activations, and password resets—but only the first of these is backed by an Active Record model with a table in the database. The time has finally come to add a second such resource: user *microposts*, which are short messages associated with a particular user.[1] We first saw microposts in larval form in Chapter 2, and in this chapter we will make a full-strength version of the sketch from Section 2.3 by constructing the Micropost data model, associating it with the User model using the `has_many` and `belongs_to` methods, and then making the forms and partials needed to manipulate and display the results (including, in Section 11.4, uploaded images). In Chapter 12, we'll complete our tiny Twitter clone by adding the notion of *following* users to receive a *feed* of their microposts.

11.1 A Micropost Model

We begin the Microposts resource by creating a Micropost model, which captures the essential characteristics of microposts. What follows builds on the work from Section 2.3; as with the model in that section, our new Micropost model will include data validations and an association with the User model. Unlike that model, the present Micropost model will be fully tested, and will also have a default *ordering* and automatic *destruction* if its parent user is destroyed.

---

1. The name is motivated by the common description of Twitter as a *microblog*; since blogs have posts, microblogs should have microposts.

If you're using Git for version control, I suggest making a topic branch at this time:

```
$ git checkout master
$ git checkout -b user-microposts
```

11.1.1 The Basic Model

The Micropost model needs only two attributes: a `content` attribute to hold the micropost's content and a `user_id` to associate a micropost with a particular user. The result is a Micropost model with the structure shown in Figure 11.1.

Notice that the model in Figure 11.1 uses the `text` data type for micropost content (instead of `string`), which is capable of storing an arbitrary amount of text. Even though the content will be restricted to fewer than 140 characters and hence would fit inside the 255-character `string` type, using `text` better expresses the nature of microposts, which are more naturally thought of as blocks of text. Indeed, in Section 11.3.2 we'll use a text *area* instead of a text field for submitting microposts. In addition, using `text` gives us greater flexibility should we wish to increase the length limit at a future date (as part of internationalization, for example). Finally, using the `text` type results in no performance difference in production,[2] so it costs us nothing to use it here.

As with the User model (Listing 6.1), we generate the Micropost model using `generate model`:

```
$ rails generate model Micropost content:text user:references
```

microposts	
id	integer
content	text
user_id	integer
created_at	datetime
updated_at	datetime

Figure 11.1 The Micropost data model.

---

2. http://www.postgresql.org/docs/9.1/static/datatype-character.html

The **generate** command produces a migration to create a **microposts** table in the database (Listing 11.1); compare it to the analogous migration for the **users** table from Listing 6.2. The biggest difference is the use of **references**, which automatically adds a **user_id** column (along with an index and a foreign key reference)[3] for use in the user/micropost association. As with the User model, the Micropost model migration automatically includes the **t.timestamps** line, which (as mentioned in Section 6.1.1) adds the magic **created_at** and **updated_at** columns shown in Figure 11.1. (We'll put the **created_at** column to work in Section 11.1.4 and Section 11.2.1.)

Listing 11.1   The Micropost migration with added index.
db/migrate/[timestamp]_create_microposts.rb

```
class CreateMicroposts < ActiveRecord::Migration
  def change
    create_table :microposts do |t|
      t.text :content
      t.references :user, index: true

      t.timestamps null: false
    end
    add_foreign_key :microposts, :users
    add_index :microposts, [:user_id, :created_at]
  end
end
```

Because we expect to retrieve all the microposts associated with a given user ID in reverse order of creation, Listing 11.1 adds an index (Box 6.2) on the **user_id** and **created_at** columns:

```
add_index :microposts, [:user_id, :created_at]
```

By including both the **user_id** and **created_at** columns as an array, we arrange for Rails to create a *multiple key index*, which means that Active Record uses *both* keys at the same time.

---

3. The foreign key reference is a database-level constraint indicating that the user ID in the microposts table refers to the id column in the users table. This detail will never be important in this tutorial, and the foreign key constraint isn't even supported by all databases. (It's supported by PostgreSQL, which we use in production, but not by the development SQLite database adapter.) We'll learn more about foreign keys in Section 12.1.2.

With the migration in Listing 11.1, we can update the database as usual:

```
$ bundle exec rake db:migrate
```

11.1.2 Micropost Validations

Now that we've created the basic model, we'll add some validations to enforce the desired design constraints. One of the necessary aspects of the Micropost model is the presence of a user ID to indicate which user made the micropost. The idiomatically correct way to do this is to use Active Record *associations*, which we'll implement in Section 11.1.3, but for now we'll work with the `Micropost` model directly.

The initial micropost tests parallel those for the User model (Listing 6.7). In the `setup` step, we create a new micropost while associating it with a valid user from the fixtures; we then check that the result is valid. Because every micropost should have a user ID, we'll add a test for a `user_id` presence validation. Putting these elements together yields the test in Listing 11.2.

Listing 11.2 Tests for the validity of a new micropost. **RED**

test/models/micropost_test.rb

```
require 'test_helper'

class MicropostTest < ActiveSupport::TestCase

  def setup
    @user = users(:michael)
    # This code is not idiomatically correct.
    @micropost = Micropost.new(content: "Lorem ipsum", user_id: @user.id)
  end

  test "should be valid" do
    assert @micropost.valid?
  end

  test "user ID should be present" do
    @micropost.user_id = nil
    assert_not @micropost.valid?
  end
end
```

As indicated by the comment in the **setup** method, the code to create the micropost is not idiomatically correct—a problem that we'll fix in Section 11.1.3.

The validity test is already **GREEN**, but the user ID presence test should be **RED** because there are not currently any validations on the Micropost model:

Listing 11.3 RED

```
$ bundle exec rake test:models
```

To fix this, we just need to add the user ID presence validation shown in Listing 11.4. (Note the **belongs_to** line in Listing 11.4, which is generated automatically by the migration in Listing 11.1. Section 11.1.3 discusses the effects of this line in more depth.)

Listing 11.4 A validation for the micropost's **user_id**. GREEN

app/models/micropost.rb

```
class Micropost < ActiveRecord::Base
   belongs_to :user
   validates :user_id, presence: true
end
```

The model tests should now be **GREEN**:

Listing 11.5 GREEN

```
$ bundle exec rake test :models
```

Next, we'll add validations for the micropost's **content** attribute (following the example from Section 2.3.2). As with the **user_id**, the **content** attribute must be present, and it is further constrained to be no longer than 140 characters, making it an honest *micro*post. We'll first write some simple tests, which generally follow the examples from the User model validation tests in Section 6.2, as shown in Listing 11.6.

Listing 11.6   Tests for the Micropost model validations. **RED**

test/models/micropost_test.rb

```ruby
require 'test_helper'

class MicropostTest < ActiveSupport::TestCase

  def setup
    @user = users(:michael)
    @micropost = Micropost.new(content: "Lorem ipsum", user_id: @user.id)
  end

  test "should be valid" do
    assert @micropost.valid?
  end

  test "user id should be present" do
    @micropost.user_id = nil
    assert_not @micropost.valid?
  end

  test "content should be present" do
    @micropost.content = " "
    assert_not @micropost.valid?
  end

  test "content should be at most 140 characters" do
    @micropost.content = "a" * 141
    assert_not @micropost.valid?
  end
end
```

As in Section 6.2, the code in Listing 11.6 uses string multiplication to test the micropost length validation:

```
$ rails console
>> "a" * 10
=> "aaaaaaaaaa"
>> "a" * 141
=> "aaaaaaaaaaaaaaaaaaaaaaaaaaaaaaaaaaaaaaaaaaaaaaaaaaaaaaaaaaaaaaaaaaaaaaaaa
aaaaaaaaaaaaaaaaaaaaaaaaaaaaaaaaaaaaaaaaaaaaaaaaaaaaaaaaaaaaaaaaaaaaaaa"
```

The corresponding application code is virtually identical to the **name** validation for users (Listing 6.16), as shown in Listing 11.7.

Listing 11.7   The Micropost model validations. **GREEN**

app/models/micropost.rb

```
class Micropost < ActiveRecord::Base
  belongs_to :user
  validates :user_id, presence: true
  validates :content, presence: true, length: { maximum: 140 }
end
```

At this point, the full test suite should be **GREEN**:

Listing 11.8   GREEN

```
$ bundle exec rake test models
```

11.1.3 User/Micropost Associations

When constructing data models for web applications, it is essential to be able to make *associations* between individual models. In the present case, each micropost is associated with one user, and each user is associated with (potentially) many microposts—a relationship mentioned briefly in Section 2.3.3 and shown schematically in Figure 11.2 and Figure 11.3. As part of implementing these associations, we'll write tests for the Micropost model and add a couple of tests to the User model.

Using the **belongs_to/has_many** association defined in this section, Rails constructs the methods shown in Table 11.1. Note from Table 11.1 that instead of

```
Micropost.create
Micropost.create!
Micropost.new
```

we have

```
user.microposts.create
user.microposts.create!
user.microposts.build
```

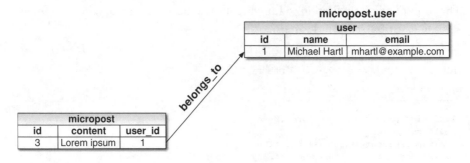

Figure 11.2 The `belongs_to` relationship between a micropost and its associated user.

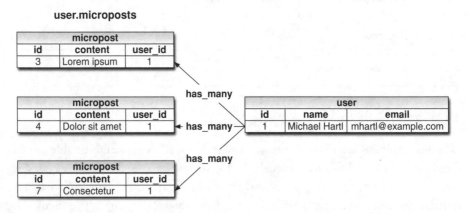

Figure 11.3 The `has_many` relationship between a user and the user's microposts.

These latter methods constitute the idiomatically correct way to make a micropost—namely, *through* its association with a user. When a new micropost is made in this way, its `user_id` is automatically set to the right value. In particular, we can replace the code

```
@user = users(:michael)
# This code is not idiomatically correct.
@micropost = Micropost.new(content: "Lorem ipsum", user_id: @user.id)
```

from Listing 11.2 with this:

Table 11.1 A summary of user/micropost association methods.

Method	Purpose
`micropost.user`	returns the User object associated with the micropost
`user.microposts`	returns a collection of the user's microposts
`user.microposts.create(arg)`	creates a micropost associated with `user`
`user.microposts.create!(arg)`	creates a micropost associated with `user` (exception on failure)
`user.microposts.build(arg)`	returns a new Micropost object associated with `user`
`user.microposts.find_by(id: 1)`	finds the micropost with ID `1` and `user_id` equal to `user.id`

```
@user = users(:michael)
@micropost = @user.microposts.build(content: "Lorem ipsum")
```

(As with **new**, **build** returns an object in memory but doesn't modify the database.) Once we define the proper associations, the resulting **@micropost** variable will automatically have a **user_id** attribute equal to its associated user's ID.

To get code like **@user.microposts.build** to work, we need to update the User and Micropost models with code to associate them. The first of these was included automatically by the migration in Listing 11.1 via **belongs_to :user**, as shown in Listing 11.9. The second half of the association, **has_many :microposts**, needs to be added by hand, as shown in Listing 11.10.

Listing 11.9 A micropost **belongs_to** a user. **GREEN**
app/models/micropost.rb

```
class Micropost < ActiveRecord::Base
  belongs_to :user
  validates :user_id, presence: true
  validates :content, presence: true, length: { maximum: 140 }
end
```

Listing 11.10 A user **has_many** microposts. **GREEN**
app/models/user.rb

```
class User < ActiveRecord::Base
  has_many :microposts
```

.
.
.
```
end
```

With the association made in this way, we can update the **setup** method in
Listing 11.2 with the idiomatically correct way to build a new micropost, as shown
in Listing 11.11.

Listing 11.11 Using idiomatically correct code to build a micropost. **GREEN**
test/models/micropost_test.rb

```ruby
require 'test_helper'

class MicropostTest < ActiveSupport::TestCase

  def setup
    @user = users(:michael)
    @micropost = @user.microposts.build(content: "Lorem ipsum")
  end

  test "should be valid" do
    assert @micropost.valid?
  end

  test "user ID should be present" do
    @micropost.user_id = nil
    assert_not @micropost.valid?
  end
  .
  .
  .
end
```

Of course, after this minor refactoring the test suite should still be **GREEN**:

Listing 11.12 GREEN

```
$ bundle exec rake test
```

11.1.4 Micropost Refinements

In this section, we'll add a couple of refinements to the user/micropost association. In
particular, we'll arrange for a user's microposts to be retrieved in a specific *order*, and

we'll make microposts *dependent* on users so that they will be automatically destroyed if their associated user is destroyed.

Default Scope

By default, the **user.microposts** method makes no guarantees about the order of the posts, but (following the convention of blogs and Twitter) we want the microposts to come out in reverse order of when they were created so that the most recent post appears first.[4] We'll arrange for this to happen using a *default scope*.

This is exactly the sort of feature that could easily lead to a spurious passing test (i.e., a test that would pass even if the application code were wrong), so we'll proceed using test-driven development to be sure we're testing the right thing. In particular, let's write a test to ensure the first micropost in the database is the same as a fixture micropost we'll call **most_recent**, as shown in Listing 11.13.

Listing 11.13   Testing the micropost order. RED
test/models/micropost_test.rb

```
require 'test_helper'

class MicropostTest < ActiveSupport::TestCase
  .
  .
  .
  test "order should be most recent first" do
    assert_equal Micropost.first, microposts(:most_recent)
  end
end
```

Listing 11.13 relies on having some micropost fixtures, which we define in Listing 11.14.

Listing 11.14   Micropost fixtures.
test/fixtures/microposts.yml

```
orange:
  content: "I just ate an orange!"
  created_at: <%= 10.minutes.ago %>
```

---

4. We briefly encountered a similar issue in Section 9.5 in the context of the users index.

```
tau_manifesto:
  content: "Check out the @tauday site by @mhartl: http://tauday.com"
  created_at: <%= 3.years.ago %>

cat_video:
  content: "Sad cats are sad: http://youtu.be/PKffm2uI4dk"
  created_at: <%= 2.hours.ago %>

most_recent:
  content: "Writing a short test"
  created_at: <%= Time.zone.now %>
```

Note that we have explicitly set the `created_at` column using embedded Ruby. Because it's a "magic" column automatically updated by Rails, setting it by hand isn't ordinarily possible, but it is possible in fixtures. In practice this might not be necessary, and in fact on many systems the fixtures are created in order. In this case, the final fixture in the file is created last (and hence is most recent), but it would be foolish to rely on this behavior, which is brittle and probably system dependent.

With the code in Listing 11.13 and Listing 11.14, the test suite should be **RED**:

Listing 11.15 RED

```
$ bundle exec rake test TEST=test/models/micropost_test.rb \
>                       TESTOPTS="--name test_order_should_be_most_recent_first"
```

We'll get the test to pass using a Rails method called `default_scope`, which among other things can be used to set the default order in which elements are retrieved from the database. To enforce a particular order, we'll include the `order` argument in `default_scope`, which lets us order by the `created_at` column as follows:

```
order(:created_at)
```

Unfortunately, this orders the results in *ascending* order from smallest to biggest, which means that the oldest microposts come out first. To pull them out in reverse order, we can push down one level deeper and include a string with some raw SQL:

```
order('created_at DESC')
```

Here **DESC** is SQL for "descending," meaning in descending order from newest to oldest.[5] In older versions of Rails, using this raw SQL used to be the only option to get the desired behavior, but as of Rails 4.0 we can use a more natural pure-Ruby syntax as well:

```
order(created_at: :desc)
```

Adding this in a default scope for the Micropost model gives Listing 11.16.

Listing 11.16 Ordering the microposts with **default_scope**. GREEN
app/models/micropost.rb

```
class Micropost < ActiveRecord::Base
  belongs_to :user
  default_scope -> { order(created_at: :desc) }
  validates :user_id, presence: true
  validates :content, presence: true, length: { maximum: 140 }
end
```

Listing 11.16 introduces the "stabby lambda" syntax for an object called a *Proc* (procedure) or *lambda*, which is an *anonymous function* (a function created without a name). The stabby lambda -> takes in a block (Section 4.3.2) and returns a Proc, which can then be evaulated with the **call** method. We can see how it works at the console:

```
>> -> { puts "foo" }
=> #<Proc:0x007fab938d0108@(irb):1 (lambda)>
>> -> { puts "foo" }.call
foo
=> nil
```

This is a somewhat advanced Ruby topic, so don't worry if it doesn't make sense right away.

With the code in Listing 11.16, the tests should be **GREEN**:

Listing 11.17 GREEN

```
$ bundle exec rake test
```

---

5. SQL is case-insensitive, but it is conventional to write SQL keywords (such as **DESC**) in all-caps.

Dependent: Destroy

Apart from proper ordering, there is a second refinement we'd like to add to microposts. Recall from Section 9.4 that site administrators have the power to *destroy* users. It stands to reason that, if a user is destroyed, the user's microposts should be destroyed as well.

We can arrange for this behavior by passing an option to the `has_many` association method, as shown in Listing 11.18.

Listing 11.18 Ensuring that a user's microposts are destroyed along with the user.
app/models/user.rb

```
class User < ActiveRecord::Base
  has_many :microposts, dependent: :destroy
  .
  .
  .
end
```

Here the option `dependent: :destroy` arranges for the dependent microposts to be destroyed when the user itself is destroyed. This prevents userless microposts from being stranded in the database when admins choose to remove users from the system.

We can verify that Listing 11.18 is working with a test for the User model. All we need to do is save the user (so it gets an ID) and create an associated micropost. Then we check that destroying the user reduces the micropost count by 1. The result appears in Listing 11.19. (Compare it to the integration test for "delete" links in Listing 9.57.)

Listing 11.19 A test of `dependent: :destroy`. GREEN
test/models/user_test.rb

```
require 'test_helper'

class UserTest < ActiveSupport::TestCase

  def setup
    @user = User.new(name: "Example User", email: "user@example.com",
                     password: "foobar", password_confirmation: "foobar")
  end
  .
  .
  .
```

```
test "associated microposts should be destroyed" do
  @user.save
  @user.microposts.create!(content: "Lorem ipsum")
  assert_difference 'Micropost.count', -1 do
    @user.destroy
  end
end
end
```

If the code in Listing 11.18 is working correctly, the test suite should still be **GREEN**:

Listing 11.20 GREEN

```
$ bundle exec rake test
```

11.2 Showing Microposts

Although we don't yet have a way to create microposts through the web—that comes in Section 11.3.2—this won't stop us from displaying them (and testing that display). Following Twitter's lead, we'll plan to display a user's microposts not on a separate microposts `index` page, but rather directly on the user `show` page itself, as mocked up in Figure 11.4. We'll start with fairly simple ERb templates for adding a micropost display to the user profile, and then we'll add microposts to the seed data from Section 9.3.2 so that we have something to display.

11.2.1 Rendering Microposts

Our plan is to display the microposts for each user on his or her respective profile page (`show.html.erb`), together with a running count of how many microposts the user has made. As we'll see, many of the ideas are similar to our work in Section 9.3 on showing all users.

Although we won't need the Microposts controller until Section 11.3, we will need the views directory in just a moment, so let's generate the controller now:

```
$ rails generate controller Microposts
```

Figure 11.4 A mockup of a profile page with microposts.

Our primary purpose in this section is to render all the microposts for each user. We saw in Section 9.3.5 that the code

```
<ul class="users">
  <%= render @users %>
</ul>
```

automatically renders each of the users in the **@users** variable using the **_user.-html.erb** partial. We'll define an analogous **_micropost.html.erb** partial so that we can use the same technique on a collection of microposts:

```
<ol class="microposts">
  <%= render @microposts %>
</ol>
```

Note that we've used the *ordered list* tag `ol` (as opposed to an unordered list `ul`) because microposts are listed in a particular order (reverse-chronological). The corresponding partial appears in Listing 11.21.

Listing 11.21   A partial for showing a single micropost.
`app/views/microposts/_micropost.html.erb`

```erb
<li id="micropost-<%= micropost.id %>">
  <%= link_to gravatar_for(micropost.user, size: 50), micropost.user %>
  <span class="user"><%= link_to micropost.user.name, micropost.user %></span>
  <span class="content"><%= micropost.content %></span>
  <span class="timestamp">
    Posted <%= time_ago_in_words(micropost.created_at) %> ago.
  </span>
</li>
```

This uses the awesome `time_ago_in_words` helper method, whose meaning is probably clear and whose effect we will see in Section 11.2.2. Listing 11.21 also adds a CSS ID for each micropost using:

```erb
<li id="micropost-<%= micropost.id %>">
```

This is a generally good practice, as it opens up the possibility of manipulating individual microposts at a future date (using JavaScript, for example).

The next step is to address the difficulty of displaying a potentially large number of microposts. We'll solve this problem the same way we solved it for users in Section 9.3.3—namely, by using pagination. As before, we'll use the `will_paginate` method:

```erb
<%= will_paginate @microposts %>
```

If you compare this with the analogous line on the user index page (Listing 9.41), you'll see that before we had just

```erb
<%= will_paginate %>
```

This worked because, in the context of the Users controller, `will_paginate` *assumes* the existence of an instance variable called `@users` (which, as we saw in Section 9.3.3, should be of class **ActiveRecord::Relation**). In the present case, because we are still in the Users controller but want to paginate *microposts* instead, we'll pass an explicit **@microposts** variable to **will_paginate**. Of course, this means that we will have to define such a variable in the user **show** action (Listing 11.22).

Listing 11.22 Adding an **@microposts** instance variable to the user **show** action.
app/controllers/users_controller.rb

```
class UsersController < ApplicationController
  .
  .
  .
  def show
    @user = User.find(params[:id])
    @microposts = @user.microposts.paginate(page: params[:page])
  end
  .
  .
  .
end
```

Notice here how clever **paginate** is: It even works *through* the microposts association, reaching into the **microposts** table and pulling out the desired page of microposts.

Our final task is to display the number of microposts for each user, which we can do with the **count** method:

```
user.microposts.count
```

As with **paginate**, we can use the **count** method through the association. In particular, **count** does *not* pull all the microposts out of the database and then call **length** on the resulting array, as this would become inefficient as the number of microposts grew. Instead, it performs the calculation directly in the database, asking the database to count the microposts with the given **user_id** (an operation for which all databases are highly optimized). In the unlikely event that finding the count is still a bottleneck in your application, you can make it even faster using a *counter cache*.

Putting all the elements together, we are now in a position to add microposts to the profile page, as shown in Listing 11.23. Note the use of **if @user.microposts.any?** (a construction we saw in Listing 7.19), which ensures that an empty list won't be displayed when the user has no microposts.

Listing 11.23 Adding microposts to the user **show** page.

app/views/users/show.html.erb

```erb
<% provide(:title, @user.name) %>
<div class="row">
  <aside class="col-md-4">
    <section class="user_info">
      <h1>
        <%= gravatar_for @user %>
        <%= @user.name %>
      </h1>
    </section>
  </aside>
  <div class="col-md-8">
    <% if @user.microposts.any? %>
      <h3>Microposts (<%= @user.microposts.count %>)</h3>
      <ol class="microposts">
        <%= render @microposts %>
      </ol>
      <%= will_paginate @microposts %>
    <% end %>
  </div>
</div>
```

At this point, we can get a look at our updated user profile page in Figure 11.5. It's rather... disappointing. Of course, there are not currently any microposts. It's time to change that.

11.2.2 Sample Microposts

Given all the work we did in making templates for user microposts in Section 11.2.1, the ending was rather anticlimactic. We can rectify this sad situation by adding microposts to the seed data from Section 9.3.2.

Adding sample microposts for *all* the users actually takes a rather long time, so first we'll select just the first six users (i.e., the five users with custom Gravatars, and one with the default Gravatar) using the **take** method:

```
User.order(:created_at).take(6)
```

The call to **order** ensures that we find the first six users that were created.

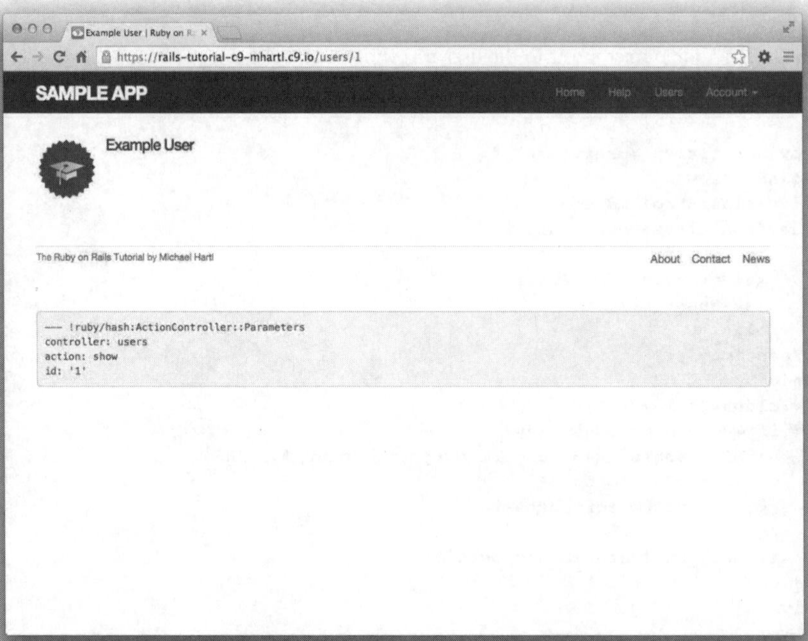

Figure 11.5 The user profile page with code for microposts—but no microposts.

For each of the selected users, we'll make 50 microposts (plenty to overflow the pagination limit of 30). To generate sample content for each micropost, we'll use the Faker gem's handy `Lorem.sentence` method.[6] The result is the new seed data method shown in Listing 11.24. [The reason for the order of the loops in Listing 11.24 is to intermix the microposts for use in the status feed (Section 12.3). Looping over the users first gives feeds with big runs of microposts from the same user, which is visually unappealing.]

Listing 11.24 Adding microposts to the sample data.
db/seeds.rb

.
.
.

6. `Faker::Lorem.sentence` returns *lorem ipsum* text; as noted in Chapter 6, *lorem ipsum* has a fascinating back story.

```
users = User.order(:created_at).take(6)
50.times do
  content = Faker::Lorem.sentence(5)
  users.each { |user| user.microposts.create!(content: content) }
end
```

At this point, we can reseed the development database as usual:

```
$ bundle exec rake db:migrate:reset
$ bundle exec rake db:seed
```

You should also quit and restart the Rails development server.

With that, we are in a position to enjoy the fruits of our Section 11.2.1 labors by displaying information for each micropost.[7] The preliminary results appear in Figure 11.6.

The page shown in Figure 11.6 has no micropost-specific styling, so let's add some (Listing 11.25) and take a look at the resulting pages.[8]

Listing 11.25   The CSS for microposts (including all the CSS for this chapter).

app/assets/stylesheets/custom.css.scss

```
.
.
.
/* microposts */

.microposts {
  list-style: none;
  padding: 0;
  li {
    padding: 10px 0;
    border-top: 1px solid #e8e8e8;
  }
  .user {
    margin-top: 5em;
    padding-top: 0;
  }
```

---

7. By design, the Faker gem's *lorem ipsum* text is randomized, so the contents of your sample microposts will differ.

8. For convenience, Listing 11.25 actually has *all* the CSS needed for this chapter.

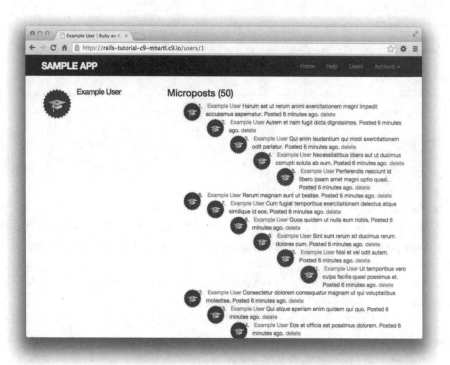

Figure 11.6 The user profile with unstyled microposts.

```
.content {
  display: block;
  margin-left: 60px;
  img {
    display: block;
    padding: 5px 0;
  }
}
.timestamp {
  color: $gray-light;
  display: block;
  margin-left: 60px;
}
.gravatar {
  float: left;
  margin-right: 10px;
  margin-top: 5px;
}
```

```
}

aside {
  textarea {
    height: 100px;
    margin-bottom: 5px;
  }
}

span.picture {
  margin-top: 10px;
  input {
    border: 0;
  }
}
```

Figure 11.7 shows the user profile page for the first user, while Figure 11.8 shows the profile for a second user. Finally, Figure 11.9 shows the *second* page of microposts for the first user, along with the pagination links at the bottom of the display. In all three cases, observe that each micropost display indicates the time since it was created (e.g., "Posted 1 minute ago."); this is the work of the `time_ago_in_words` method from Listing 11.21. If you wait a few minutes and then reload the pages, you'll see that the text is automatically updated based on the new time.

11.2.3 Profile Micropost Tests

Because newly activated users are redirected to their profile pages, we already have a test that the profile page renders correctly (Listing 10.30). In this section, we'll write a short integration test for some of the other elements on the profile page, including the work from this section. We'll start by generating an integration test for the profiles of our site's users:

```
$ rails generate integration_test users_profile
      invoke  test_unit
      create    test/integration/users_profile_test.rb
```

To test the micropost display on the profile, we need to associate the fixture microposts with a user. Rails includes a convenient way to build associations in fixtures:

```
orange:
  content: "I just ate an orange!"
  created_at: <%= 10.minutes.ago %>
  user: michael
```

By identifying the `user` as `michael`, we tell Rails to associate this micropost with the corresponding user in the users fixture:

```
michael:
  name: Michael Example
  email: michael@example.com
  .
  .
  .
```

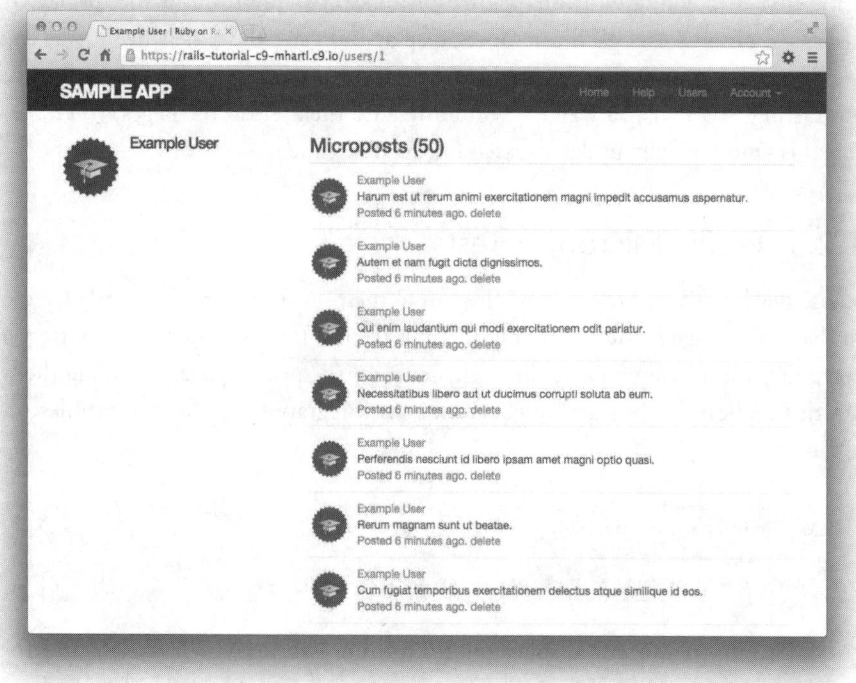

Figure 11.7 The user profile with microposts (/users/1).

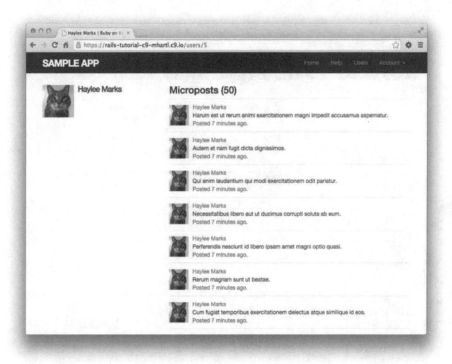

Figure 11.8 The profile of a different user, also with microposts (/users/5).

To test micropost pagination, we'll generate some additional micropost fixtures using the same embedded Ruby technique we used to make additional users in Listing 9.43:

```
<% 30.times do |n| %>
micropost_<%= n %>:
  content: <%= Faker::Lorem.sentence(5) %>
  created_at: <%= 42.days.ago %>
  user: michael
<% end %>
```

Putting all this together gives the updated micropost fixtures in Listing 11.26.

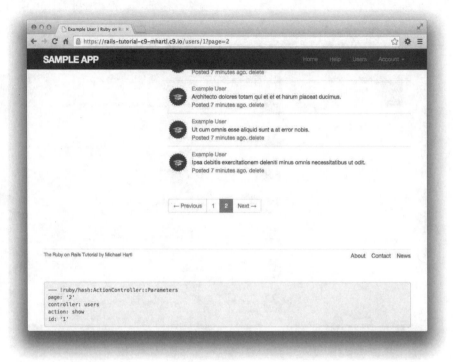

Figure 11.9 Micropost pagination links (/users/1?page=2).

Listing 11.26 Micropost fixtures with user associations.

`test/fixtures/microposts.yml`

```
orange:
  content: "I just ate an orange!"
  created_at: <%= 10.minutes.ago %>
  user: michael

tau_manifesto:
  content: "Check out the @tauday site by @mhartl: http://tauday.com"
  created_at: <%= 3.years.ago %>
  user: michael

cat_video:
  content: "Sad cats are sad: http://youtu.be/PKffm2uI4dk"
  created_at: <%= 2.hours.ago %>
  user: michael

most_recent:
```

```
  content: "Writing a short test"
  created_at: <%= Time.zone.now %>
  user: michael

<% 30.times do |n| %>
micropost_<%= n %>:
  content: <%= Faker::Lorem.sentence(5) %>
  created_at: <%= 42.days.ago %>
  user: michael
<% end %>
```

With the test data thus prepared, the test itself is fairly straightforward: We visit the user profile page and check for the page title and the user's name, Gravatar, micropost count, and paginated microposts. The result appears in Listing 11.27. Note the use of the `full_title` helper from Listing 4.2 to test the page's title, to which we gain access by including the Application Helper module in the test.[9]

Listing 11.27 A test for the user profile. **GREEN**
test/integration/users_profile_test.rb

```
require 'test_helper'

class UsersProfileTest < ActionDispatch::IntegrationTest
  include ApplicationHelper

  def setup
    @user = users(:michael)
  end

  test "profile display" do
    get user_path(@user)
    assert_template 'users/show'
    assert_select 'title', full_title(@user.name)
    assert_select 'h1', text: @user.name
    assert_select 'h1>img.gravatar'
    assert_match @user.microposts.count.to_s, response.body
    assert_select 'div.pagination'
    @user.microposts.paginate(page: 1).each do |micropost|
      assert_match micropost.content, response.body
    end
  end
end
```

---

9. If you'd like to refactor other tests to use `full_title` (such as those in Listing 3.38), you should include the Application Helper in `test_helper.rb` instead.

The micropost count assertion in Listing 11.27 uses **response.body**, which we saw briefly in the Chapter 10 exercises (Section 10.5). Despite its name, **response.body** contains the full HTML source of the page (and not just the page's body). As a consequence, if all we care about is that the number of microposts appears *somewhere* on the page, we can look for a match as follows:

```
assert_match @user.microposts.count.to_s, response.body
```

This is a much less specific assertion than **assert_select**. In particular, unlike **assert_select**, using **assert_match** in this context doesn't require us to indicate which HTML tag we're looking for.

Listing 11.27 also introduces the nesting syntax for **assert_select**:

```
assert_select 'h1>img.gravatar'
```

This checks for an **img** tag with class **gravatar** *inside* a top-level heading tag (**h1**).

Because the application code was working, the test suite should be **GREEN**:

Listing 11.28 GREEN

```
$ bundle exec rake test
```

11.3 Manipulating Microposts

Having finished both the data modeling and display templates for microposts, we now turn our attention to the interface for creating them through the web. In this section, we'll also see the first hint of a *status feed*—a notion brought to full fruition in Chapter 12. Finally, as with users, we'll make it possible to destroy microposts through the web.

There is one break with past convention worth noting: The interface to the Microposts resource will run principally through the Profile and Home pages, so we won't need actions like **new** or **edit** in the Microposts controller. Instead, we'll need only **create** and **destroy**. This leads to the routes for the Microposts resource shown in

Table 11.2 RESTful routes provided by the Microposts resource in Listing 11.29.

HTTP request	URL	Action	Purpose
POST	/microposts	`create`	create a new micropost
DELETE	/microposts/1	`destroy`	delete micropost with ID **1**

Listing 11.29. The code in Listing 11.29 leads in turn to the RESTful routes shown in Table 11.2, which is a small subset of the full set of routes seen in Table 2.3. Of course, this simplicity is a sign of being *more* advanced, not less—we've come a long way since our reliance on scaffolding in Chapter 2, and we no longer need most of its complexity.

Listing 11.29 Routes for the Microposts resource.

config/routes.rb

```
Rails.application.routes.draw do
  root            'static_pages#home'
  get     'help'    => 'static_pages#help'
  get     'about'   => 'static_pages#about'
  get     'contact' => 'static_pages#contact'
  get     'signup'  => 'users#new'
  get     'login'   => 'sessions#new'
  post    'login'   => 'sessions#create'
  delete  'logout'  => 'sessions#destroy'
  resources :users
  resources :account_activations, only: [:edit]
  resources :password_resets,      only: [:new, :create, :edit, :update]
  resources :microposts,           only: [:create, :destroy]
end
```

11.3.1 Micropost Access Control

We begin our development of the Microposts resource with some access control in the Microposts controller. In particular, because we access microposts through their associated users, both the **create** and the **destroy** actions must require users to be logged in.

Tests to enforce logged-in status mirror those for the Users controller (Listing 9.17 and Listing 9.56). We simply issue the correct request to each action and confirm that the micropost count is unchanged and the result is redirected to the login URL, as seen in Listing 11.30.

Listing 11.30 Authorization tests for the Microposts controller. **RED**
test/controllers/microposts_controller_test.rb

```ruby
require 'test_helper'

class MicropostsControllerTest < ActionController::TestCase

  def setup
    @micropost = microposts(:orange)
  end

  test "should redirect create when not logged in" do
    assert_no_difference 'Micropost.count' do
      post :create, micropost: { content: "Lorem ipsum" }
    end
    assert_redirected_to login_url
  end

  test "should redirect destroy when not logged in" do
    assert_no_difference 'Micropost.count' do
      delete :destroy, id: @micropost
    end
    assert_redirected_to login_url
  end
end
```

Writing the application code needed to get the tests in Listing 11.30 to pass requires a little refactoring first. Recall from Section 9.2.1 that we enforced the login requirement using a before filter that called the **logged_in_user** method (Listing 9.12). At the time, we needed that method only in the Users controller, but now we find that we need it in the Microposts controller as well. To meet this need, we'll move the **logged_in_user** method into the Application controller, which is the base class of all controllers (Section 4.4.4). The result appears in Listing 11.31.

Listing 11.31 Moving the **logged_in_user** method into the Application controller.
app/controllers/application_controller.rb

```ruby
class ApplicationController < ActionController::Base
  protect_from_forgery with: :exception
  include SessionsHelper
```

```
  private

    # Confirms a logged-in user.
    def logged_in_user
      unless logged_in?
        store_location
        flash[:danger] = "Please log in."
        redirect_to login_url
      end
    end
end
```

To avoid code repetition, you should also remove `logged_in_user` from the Users controller at this time.

With the code in Listing 11.31, the `logged_in_user` method is now available in the Microposts controller, which means that we can add `create` and `destroy` actions and then restrict access to them using a before filter, as shown in Listing 11.32.

Listing 11.32 Adding authorization to the Microposts controller actions. **GREEN**
app/controllers/microposts_controller.rb

```
class MicropostsController < ApplicationController
  before_action :logged_in_user, only: [:create, :destroy]

  def create
  end

  def destroy
  end
end
```

At this point, the tests should pass:

Listing 11.33 GREEN

```
$ bundle exec rake test
```

11.3.2 Creating Microposts

In Chapter 7, we implemented user sign-up by making an HTML form that issued an HTTP POST request to the **create** action in the Users controller. The implementation of micropost creation is similar; the main difference is that, rather than using a separate page at /microposts/new, we will put the form on the Home page itself (i.e., the root path /), as mocked up in Figure 11.10.

When we last left the Home page, it appeared as in Figure 5.6—that is, it had a "Sign up now!" button in the middle. Since a micropost creation form makes sense only in the context of a particular logged-in user, one goal of this section will be to serve different versions of the Home page depending on a visitor's login status. We'll implement this in Listing 11.35.

We'll start with the **create** action for microposts, which is similar to its user analogue (Listing 7.23); the principal difference lies in using the user/micropost association

Figure 11.10 A mockup of the Home page with a form for creating microposts.

to **build** the new micropost, as seen in Listing 11.34. Note the use of strong parameters via **micropost_params**, which permits only the micropost's **content** attribute to be modified through the web.

Listing 11.34   The Microposts controller **create** action.
app/controllers/microposts_controller.rb

```ruby
class MicropostsController < ApplicationController
  before_action :logged_in_user, only: [:create, :destroy]

  def create
    @micropost = current_user.microposts.build(micropost_params)
    if @micropost.save
      flash[:success] = "Micropost created!"
      redirect_to root_url
    else
      render 'static_pages/home'
    end
  end

  def destroy
  end

  private

    def micropost_params
      params.require(:micropost).permit(:content)
    end
end
```

To build a form for creating microposts, we use the code in Listing 11.35, which serves up different HTML based on whether the site visitor is logged in.

Listing 11.35   Adding microposts creation to the Home page (/).
app/views/static_pages/home.html.erb

```erb
<% if logged_in? %>
  <div class="row">
    <aside class="col-md-4">
      <section class="user_info">
        <%= render 'shared/user_info' %>
      </section>
      <section class="micropost_form">
```

```erb
          <%= render 'shared/micropost_form' %>
        </section>
    </aside>
  </div>
<% else %>
  <div class="center jumbotron">
    <h1>Welcome to the Sample App</h1>

    <h2>
      This is the home page for the
      <a href="http://www.railstutorial.org/">Ruby on Rails Tutorial</a>
      sample application.
    </h2>

    <%= link_to "Sign up now!", signup_path, class: "btn btn-lg btn-primary" %>
  </div>

  <%= link_to image_tag("rails.png", alt: "Rails logo"),
              'http://rubyonrails.org/' %>
<% end %>
```

Having so much code in each branch of the **if-else** conditional is a bit messy, and cleaning it up using partials is left as an exercise (Section 11.6).

To get the page defined in Listing 11.35 working, we need to create and fill in a couple of partials. The first is the new Home page sidebar, as shown in Listing 11.36.

Listing 11.36 The partial for the user info sidebar.

app/views/shared/_user_info.html.erb

```erb
<%= link_to gravatar_for(current_user, size: 50), current_user %>
<h1><%= current_user.name %></h1>
<span><%= link_to "view my profile", current_user %></span>
<span><%= pluralize(current_user.microposts.count, "micropost") %></span>
```

As in the profile sidebar (Listing 11.23), the user info in Listing 11.36 displays the total number of microposts for the user. There's a slight difference in the display, though; in the profile sidebar, "Microposts" is a label, so showing "Microposts (1)" makes sense. In the present case, though, saying "1 microposts" is ungrammatical, so we arrange to display "1 micropost" and "2 microposts" using the **pluralize** method we saw in Section 7.3.3.

We next define the form for creating microposts (Listing 11.37), which is similar to the sign-up form in Listing 7.13.

Listing 11.37   The form partial for creating microposts.
app/views/shared/_micropost_form.html.erb

```erb
<%= form_for(@micropost) do |f| %>
  <%= render 'shared/error_messages', object: f.object %>
  <div class="field">
    <%= f.text_area :content, placeholder: "Compose new micropost..." %>
  </div>
  <%= f.submit "Post", class: "btn btn-primary" %>
<% end %>
```

We need to make two changes before the form in Listing 11.37 will work. First, we need to define **@micropost**, which (as before) we do through the association:

```ruby
@micropost = current_user.microposts.build
```

The result appears in Listing 11.38.

Listing 11.38   Adding a micropost instance variable to the **home** action.
app/controllers/static_pages_controller.rb

```ruby
class StaticPagesController < ApplicationController

  def home
    @micropost = current_user.microposts.build if logged_in?
  end

  def help
  end

  def about
  end

  def contact
  end
end
```

Of course, `current_user` exists only if the user is logged in, so the `@micropost` variable should be defined only in this case.

The second change needed to get Listing 11.37 to work is to redefine the error-messages partial so the following code from Listing 11.37 works:

```
<%= render 'shared/error_messages', object: f.object %>
```

Recall from Listing 7.18 that the error-messages partial references the `@user` variable explicitly. In the present case, however, we have an `@micropost` variable instead. To unify these cases, we can pass the form variable `f` to the partial and access the associated object through `f.object`, so that in

```
form_for(@user) do |f|
```

`f.object` is `@user`; in

```
form_for(@micropost) do |f|
```

`f.object` is `@micropost`, and so on.

To pass the object to the partial, we use a hash with a value equal to the object and a key equal to the desired name of the variable in the partial, which is what the second line in Listing 11.37 accomplishes. In other words, `object: f.object` creates a variable called `object` in the `error_messages` partial, which we can use to construct a customized error message, as shown in Listing 11.39.

Listing 11.39   Error messages that work with other objects. **RED**
app/views/shared/_error_messages.html.erb

```
<% if object.errors.any? %>
  <div id="error_explanation">
    <div class="alert alert-danger">
      The form contains <%= pluralize(object.errors.count, "error") %>.
    </div>
    <ul>
    <% object.errors.full_messages.each do |msg| %>
      <li><%= msg %></li>
    <% end %>
    </ul>
```

```
  </div>
<% end %>
```

At this point, you should verify that the test suite is **RED**:

Listing 11.40 RED

```
$ bundle exec rake test
```

This is a hint that we need to update the other occurrences of the error-messages partial, which we used when signing up users (Listing 7.18), editing users (Listing 9.2), and resetting passwords (Listing 10.49). The updated versions are shown in Listing 11.41, Listing 11.43, and Listing 11.42, respectively.

Listing 11.41 Updating the rendering of user sign-up errors.
app/views/users/new.html.erb

```
<% provide(:title, 'Sign up') %>
<h1>Sign up</h1>

<div class="row">
  <div class="col-md-6 col-md-offset-3">
    <%= form_for(@user) do |f| %>
      <%= render 'shared/error_messages', object: f.object %>
      <%= f.label :name %>
      <%= f.text_field :name, class: 'form-control' %>

      <%= f.label :email %>
      <%= f.email_field :email, class: 'form-control' %>

      <%= f.label :password %>
      <%= f.password_field :password, class: 'form-control' %>

      <%= f.label :password_confirmation, "Confirmation" %>
      <%= f.password_field :password_confirmation, class: 'form-control' %>

      <%= f.submit "Create my account", class: "btn btn-primary" %>
    <% end %>
  </div>
</div>
```

Listing 11.42 Updating the errors for editing users.

app/views/users/edit.html.erb

```
<% provide(:title, "Edit user") %>
<h1>Update your profile</h1>

<div class="row">
  <div class="col-md-6 col-md-offset-3">
    <%= form_for(@user) do |f| %>
      <%= render 'shared/error_messages', object: f.object %>

      <%= f.label :name %>
      <%= f.text_field :name, class: 'form-control' %>

      <%= f.label :email %>
      <%= f.email_field :email, class: 'form-control' %>

      <%= f.label :password %>
      <%= f.password_field :password, class: 'form-control' %>

      <%= f.label :password_confirmation, "Confirmation" %>
      <%= f.password_field :password_confirmation, class: 'form-control' %>

      <%= f.submit "Save changes", class: "btn btn-primary" %>
    <% end %>

    <div class="gravatar_edit">
      <%= gravatar_for @user %>
      <a href="http://gravatar.com/emails">change</a>
    </div>
  </div>
</div>
```

Listing 11.43 Updating the errors for password resets.

app/views/password_resets/edit.html.erb

```
<% provide(:title, 'Reset password') %>
<h1>Password reset</h1>

<div class="row">
  <div class="col-md-6 col-md-offset-3">
    <%= form_for(@user, url: password_reset_path(params[:id])) do |f| %>
      <%= render 'shared/error_messages', object: f.object %>

      <%= hidden_field_tag :email, @user.email %>
```

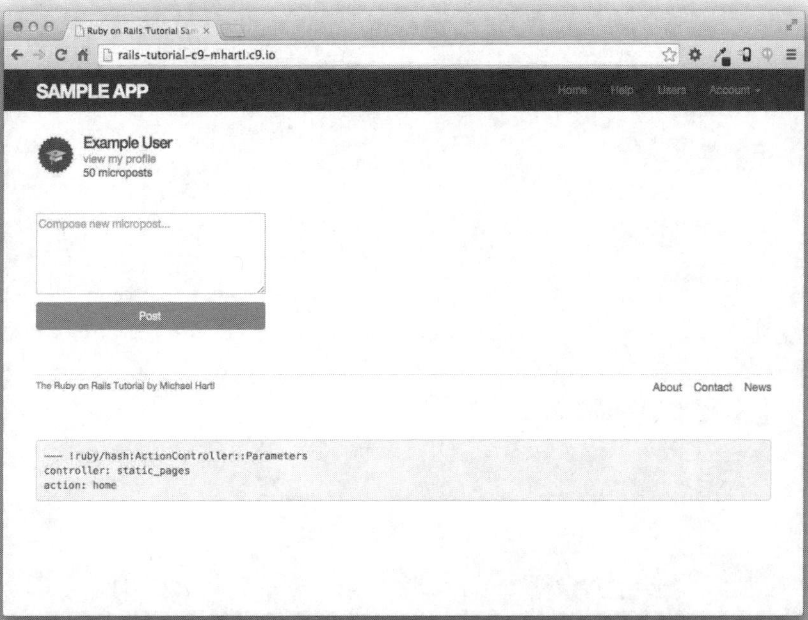

Figure 11.11 The Home page with a new micropost form.

```
    <%= f.label :password %>
    <%= f.password_field :password, class: 'form-control' %>

    <%= f.label :password_confirmation, "Confirmation" %>
    <%= f.password_field :password_confirmation, class: 'form-control' %>

    <%= f.submit "Update password", class: "btn btn-primary" %>
  <% end %>
  </div>
</div>
```

At this point, all the tests should be **GREEN**:

```
$ bundle exec rake test
```

Additionally, all the HTML in this section should render properly, showing the form as in Figure 11.11, and a form with a submission error as in Figure 11.12.

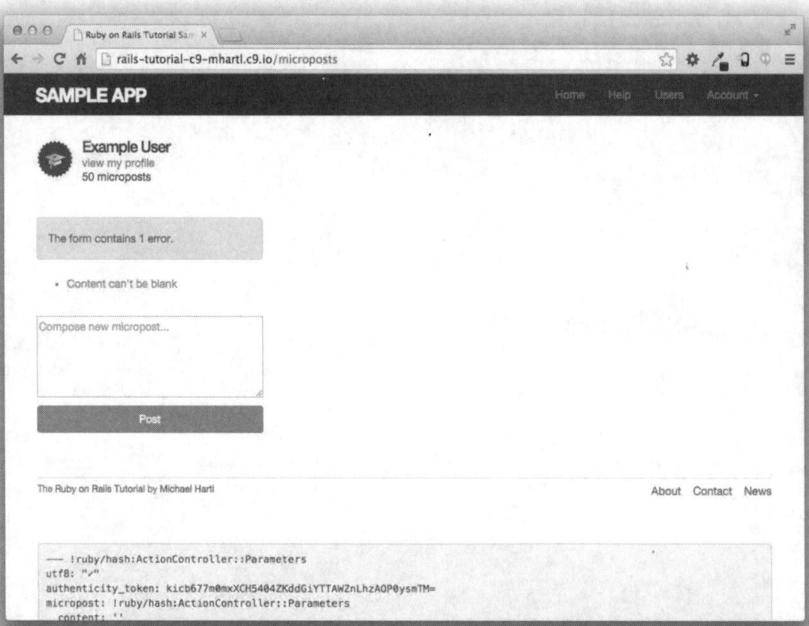

Figure 11.12 The Home page with a form error.

11.3.3 A Proto-feed

Although the micropost form is actually now working, users can't immediately see the results of a successful submission because the current Home page doesn't display any microposts. If you like, you can verify that the form shown in Figure 11.11 is working by submitting a valid entry and then navigating to the profile page to see the post, but that's rather cumbersome. It would be far better to have a *feed* of microposts that includes the user's own posts, as mocked up in Figure 11.13. (In Chapter 12, we'll generalize this feed to include the microposts of users being *followed* by the current user.)

Given that each user should have a feed, we are led naturally to a `feed` method in the User model, which will initially just select all the microposts belonging to the

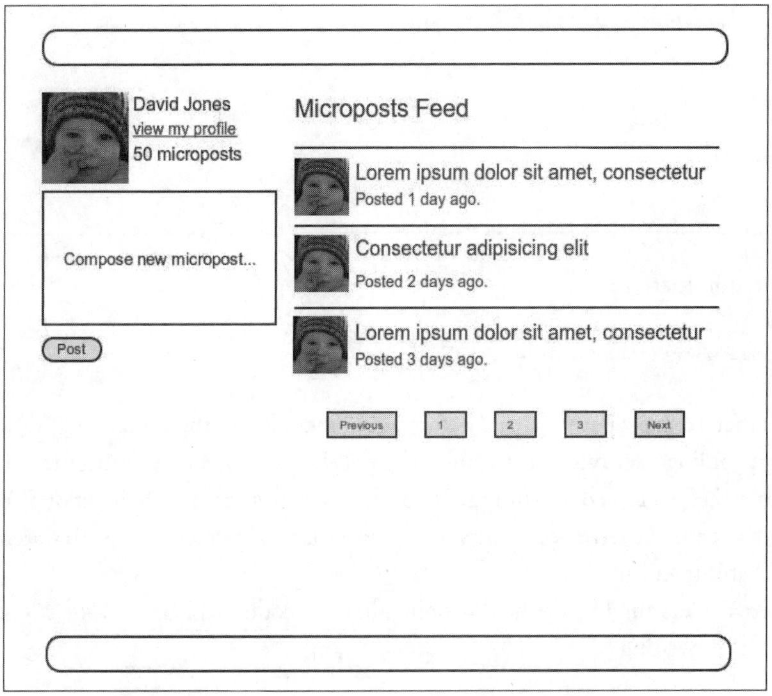

Figure 11.13 A mockup of the Home page with a proto-feed.

current user. We'll accomplish this using the **where** method on the **Micropost** model (seen briefly in Section 10.5), as shown in Listing 11.44.[10]

Listing 11.44 A preliminary implementation for the micropost status feed.
app/models/user.rb

```
class User < ActiveRecord::Base
  .
  .
  .
  # Defines a proto-feed.
  # See "Following users" for the full implementation.
  def feed
```

---

10. See the Rails Guide on the Active Record Query Interface for more on **where** and related methods.

```
    Micropost.where("user_id = ?", id)
  end

    private
    .
    .
    .

end
```

The question mark in

```
Micropost.where("user_id = ?", id)
```

ensures that **id** is properly *escaped* before being included in the underlying SQL query, thereby avoiding a serious security hole called *SQL injection*. The **id** attribute here is just an integer (i.e., **self.id**, the unique ID of the user), so there is no danger of SQL injection in this case. Nevertheless, *always* escaping variables injected into SQL statements is a good habit to cultivate.

Alert readers might note at this point that the code in Listing 11.44 is essentially equivalent to writing

```
def feed
  microposts
end
```

We've used the code in Listing 11.44 instead because it generalizes much more naturally to the full status feed needed in Chapter 12.

To use the feed in the sample application, we add an **@feed_items** instance variable for the current user's (paginated) feed, as in Listing 11.45, and then add a status feed partial (Listing 11.46) to the Home page (Listing 11.47).

Listing 11.45 Adding a feed instance variable to the **home** action.
app/controllers/static_pages_controller.rb

```
class StaticPagesController < ApplicationController

  def home
```

```
   if logged_in?
     @micropost  = current_user.microposts.build
     @feed_items = current_user.feed.paginate(page: params[:page])
   end
 end

 def help
 end

 def about
 end

 def contact
 end
end
```

Listing 11.46 The status feed partial.

app/views/shared/_feed.html.erb

```
<% if @feed_items.any? %>
  <ol class="microposts">
    <%= render @feed_items %>
  </ol>
  <%= will_paginate @feed_items %>
<% end %>
```

The status feed partial defers the rendering to the micropost partial defined in Listing 11.21:

```
<%= render @feed_items %>
```

Here Rails knows to call the micropost partial because each element of `@feed_items` has class `Micropost`. This causes Rails to look for a partial with the corresponding name in the views directory of the given resource:

```
app/views/microposts/_micropost.html.erb
```

We can add the feed to the Home page by rendering the feed partial as usual (Listing 11.47). The result is a display of the feed on the Home page, as required (Figure 11.14).

Listing 11.47 Adding a status feed to the Home page.

app/views/static_pages/home.html.erb

```
<% if logged_in? %>
  <div class="row">
    <aside class="col-md-4">
      <section class="user_info">
        <%= render 'shared/user_info' %>
      </section>
      <section class="micropost_form">
        <%= render 'shared/micropost_form' %>
      </section>
    </aside>
    <div class="col-md-8">
      <h3>Micropost Feed</h3>
      <%= render 'shared/feed' %>
    </div>
  </div>
<% else %>
  .
  .
  .
<% end %>
```

At this point, creating a new micropost works as expected, as seen in Figure 11.15. There is one subtlety, though: On *failed* micropost submission, the Home page expects an `@feed_items` instance variable, so failed submissions currently break. The easiest solution is to suppress the feed entirely by assigning it an empty array, as shown in Listing 11.48.

Listing 11.48 Adding an (empty) `@feed_items` instance variable to the **create** action.

app/controllers/microposts_controller.rb

```
class MicropostsController < ApplicationController
  before_action :logged_in_user, only: [:create, :destroy]

  def create
    @micropost = current_user.microposts.build(micropost_params)
    if @micropost.save
      flash[:success] = "Micropost created!"
      redirect_to root_url
    else
      @feed_items = []
```

```
      render 'static_pages/home'
    end
  end

  def destroy
  end

  private

    def micropost_params
      params.require(:micropost).permit(:content)
    end
end
```

Unfortunately, returning a paginated feed doesn't work in this case. Implement it and click on a pagination link to see why.

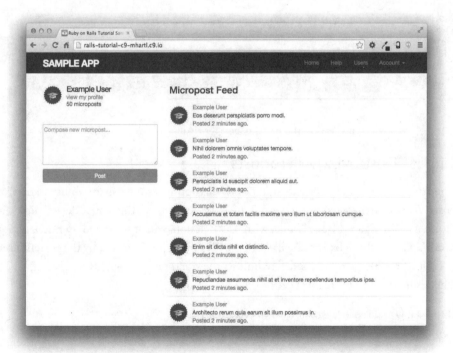

Figure 11.14 The Home page with a proto-feed.

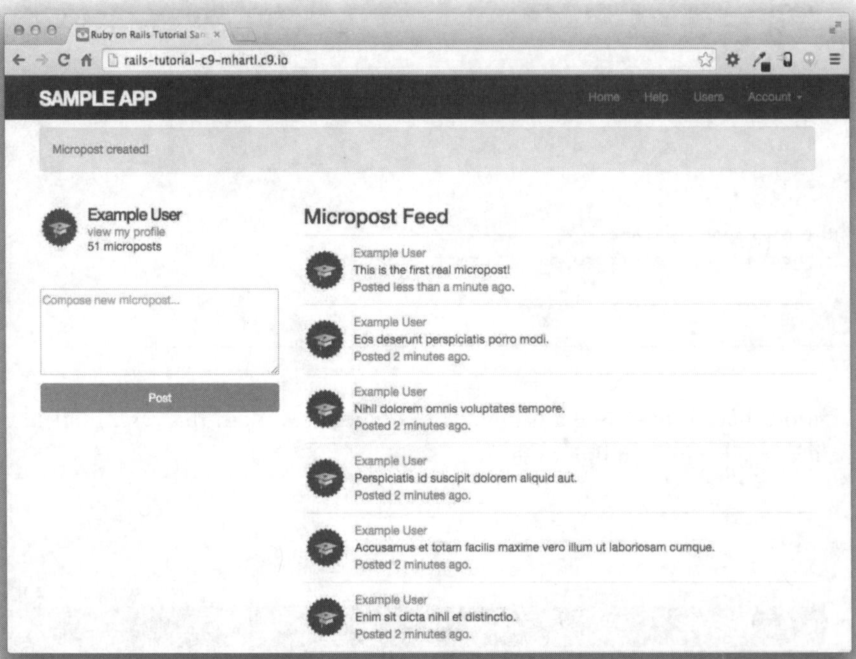

Figure 11.15 The Home page after creating a new micropost.

11.3.4 Destroying Microposts

The last piece of functionality to add to the Microposts resource is the ability to destroy posts. As with user deletion (Section 9.4.2), we accomplish this with "delete" links, as mocked up in Figure 11.16. Unlike with user deletion, which restricted user destruction to admin users, the delete links will work only for microposts created by the current user.

Our first step is to add a delete link to the micropost partial, as in Listing 11.21. The result appears in Listing 11.49.

Listing 11.49 Adding a delete link to the micropost partial.
app/views/microposts/_micropost.html.erb

```
<li id="<%= micropost.id %>">
  <%= link_to gravatar_for(micropost.user, size: 50), micropost.user %>
  <span class="user"><%= link_to micropost.user.name, micropost.user %></span>
  <span class="content"><%= micropost.content %></span>
```

```
<span class="timestamp">
  Posted <%= time_ago_in_words(micropost.created_at) %> ago.
  <% if current_user?(micropost.user) %>
    <%= link_to "delete", micropost, method: :delete,
                              data: { confirm: "You sure?" } %>
  <% end %>
</span>
</li>
```

The next step is to define a **destroy** action in the Microposts controller, which is analogous to the user case in Listing 9.54. The main difference is that, rather than using an **@user** variable with an **admin_user** before filter, we'll find the micropost through the association, which will automatically fail if a user tries to delete another user's micropost. We'll put the resulting **find** inside a **correct_user** before filter, which checks that the current user actually has a micropost with the given ID. The result appears in Listing 11.50.

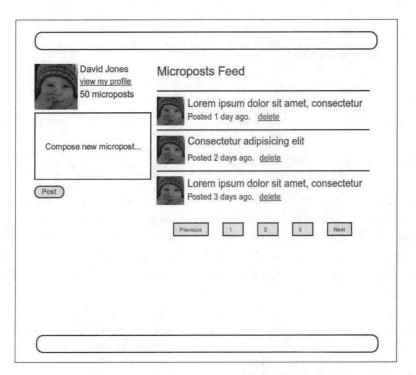

Figure 11.16 A mockup of the proto-feed with micropost delete links.

Listing 11.50 The Microposts controller **destroy** action.

app/controllers/microposts_controller.rb

```
class MicropostsController < ApplicationController
  before_action :logged_in_user, only: [:create, :destroy]
  before_action :correct_user,   only: :destroy
  .
  .
  .
  def destroy
    @micropost.destroy
    flash[:success] = "Micropost deleted"
    redirect_to request.referrer || root_url
  end

  private

    def micropost_params
      params.require(:micropost).permit(:content)
    end

    def correct_user
      @micropost = current_user.microposts.find_by(id: params[:id])
      redirect_to root_url if @micropost.nil?
    end
end
```

Note that the **destroy** method in Listing 11.50 redirects the user to the URL

```
request.referrer || root_url
```

This redirect action uses the **request.referrer** method,[11] which is closely related to the **request.url** variable used in friendly forwarding (Section 9.2.3), and is just the previous URL (in this case, the Home page).[12] It is a convenient choice because microposts appear on both the Home page and the user's profile page; thus, by using **request.referrer**, we arrange to redirect the user back to the page issuing the delete

---

11. This corresponds to HTTP_REFERER, as defined by the specification for HTTP. Note that "referer" is not a typo—the word is actually misspelled in the spec. Rails corrects this error by writing "referrer" instead.

12. I didn't remember offhand how to get this URL inside a Rails application, so I Googled "rails request previous url" and found a Stack Overflow thread with the answer.

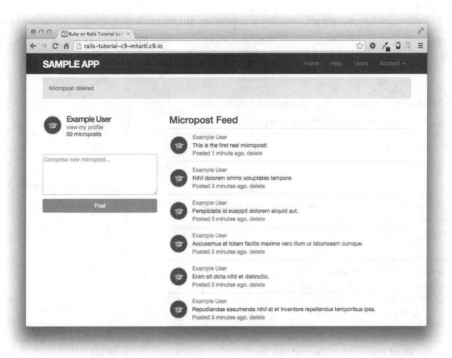

Figure 11.17 The Home page after deleting the second-most-recent micropost.

request in both cases. If the referring URL is `nil` (as is the case inside some tests), Listing 11.50 sets the `root_url` as the default using the || operator. (Compare this to the default options defined in Listing 8.50.)

With the code in Listing 11.50, the result of destroying the second-most-recent post appears in Figure 11.17.

11.3.5 Micropost Tests

With the code in Section 11.3.4, the Micropost model and interface are complete. All that's left is writing a short Microposts controller test to check authorization and a micropost integration test to tie it all together.

We'll start by adding a few microposts with different owners to the micropost fixtures, as shown in Listing 11.51. (We'll be using only one for now, but we've put in the others for future reference.)

Listing 11.51 Adding a micropost with a different owner.

test/fixtures/microposts.yml

```
  .
  .
  .
ants:
  content: "Oh, is that what you want? Because that's how you get ants!"
  created_at: <%= 2.years.ago %>
  user: archer

zone:
  content: "Danger zone!"
  created_at: <%= 3.days.ago %>
  user: archer

tone:
  content: "I'm sorry. Your words made sense, but your sarcastic tone did not."
  created_at: <%= 10.minutes.ago %>
  user: lana

van:
  content: "Dude, this van's, like, rolling probable cause."
  created_at: <%= 4.hours.ago %>
  user: lana
```

We next write a short test to make sure one user can't delete the microposts of a different user, and we also check for the proper redirect, as seen in Listing 11.52.

Listing 11.52 Testing micropost deletion with a user mismatch. **GREEN**

test/controllers/microposts_controller_test.rb

```
require 'test_helper'

class MicropostsControllerTest < ActionController::TestCase
```

```
def setup
  @micropost = microposts(:orange)
end

test "should redirect create when not logged in" do
  assert_no_difference 'Micropost.count' do
    post :create, micropost: { content: "Lorem ipsum" }
  end
  assert_redirected_to login_url
end

test "should redirect destroy when not logged in" do
  assert_no_difference 'Micropost.count' do
    delete :destroy, id: @micropost
  end
  assert_redirected_to login_url
end

test "should redirect destroy for wrong micropost" do
  log_in_as(users(:michael))
  micropost = microposts(:ants)
  assert_no_difference 'Micropost.count' do
    delete :destroy, id: micropost
  end
  assert_redirected_to root_url
end
end
```

Finally, we'll write an integration test to log in, check the micropost pagination, make an invalid submission, make a valid submission, delete a post, and then visit a second user's page to make sure there are no "delete" links. We start by generating a test as usual:

```
$ rails generate integration_test microposts_interface
     invoke  test_unit
     create    test/integration/microposts_interface_test.rb
```

The test appears in Listing 11.53. See if you can connect the lines in Listing 11.11 to the preceding steps. Listing 11.53 uses **post** followed by **follow_redirect!** in place of the equivalent **post_via_redirect** in anticipation of the image upload test in the exercises (Listing 11.68).

Listing 11.53 An integration test for the micropost interface. **GREEN**

test/integration/microposts_interface_test.rb

```ruby
require 'test_helper'

class MicropostsInterfaceTest < ActionDispatch::IntegrationTest

  def setup
    @user = users(:michael)
  end

  test "micropost interface" do
    log_in_as(@user)
    get root_path
    assert_select 'div.pagination'
    # Invalid submission
    assert_no_difference 'Micropost.count' do
      post microposts_path, micropost: { content: "" }
    end
    assert_select 'div#error_explanation'
    # Valid submission
    content = "This micropost really ties the room together"
    assert_difference 'Micropost.count', 1 do
      post microposts_path, micropost: { content: content }
    end
    assert_redirected_to root_url
    follow_redirect!
    assert_match content, response.body
    # Delete a post.
    assert_select 'a', text: 'delete'
    first_micropost = @user.microposts.paginate(page: 1).first
    assert_difference 'Micropost.count', -1 do
      delete micropost_path(first_micropost)
    end
    # Visit a different user.
    get user_path(users(:archer))
    assert_select 'a', text: 'delete', count: 0
  end
end
```

Because we wrote working application code first, the test suite should be **GREEN**:

Listing 11.54 GREEN

```
$ bundle exec rake test
```

11.4 Micropost Images

Now that we've added support for all relevant micropost actions, in this section we'll make it possible for microposts to include images as well as text. We'll start with a basic version good enough for development use, and then add a series of enhancements to make image upload production-ready.

Adding image upload involves two main visible elements: a form field for uploading an image and the micropost images themselves. A mockup of the resulting "Upload image" button and micropost photo appears in Figure 11.18.[13]

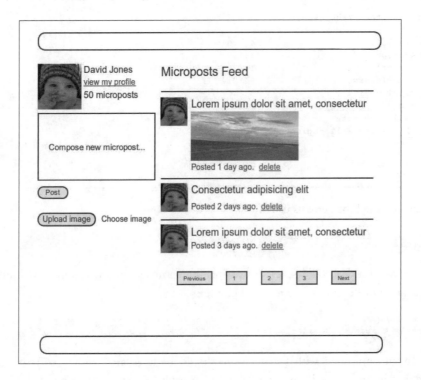

Figure 11.18 A mockup of micropost image upload (with an uploaded image).

---

13. Beach photo from https://www.flickr.com/photos/grungepunk/14026922186

11.4.1 Basic Image Upload

To handle an uploaded image and associate it with the Micropost model, we'll use the CarrierWave image uploader. To get started, we need to include the `carrier-wave` gem in the `Gemfile` (Listing 11.55). For completeness, Listing 11.55 also includes the `mini_magick` and `fog` gems needed for image resizing (Section 11.4.3) and image upload in production (Section 11.4.4).

Listing 11.55 Adding CarrierWave to the `Gemfile`.

```
source 'https://rubygems.org'

gem 'rails',                    '4.2.0'
gem 'bcrypt',                   '3.1.7'
gem 'faker',                    '1.4.2'
gem 'carrierwave',              '0.10.0'
gem 'mini_magick',              '3.8.0'
gem 'fog',                      '1.23.0'
gem 'will_paginate',            '3.0.7'
gem 'bootstrap-will_paginate', '0.0.10'
.
.
.
```

Then we install the gems as usual:

```
$ bundle install
```

CarrierWave adds a Rails generator for creating an image uploader, which we'll use to make an uploader for an image called `picture`:[14]

```
$ rails generate uploader Picture
```

Images uploaded with CarrierWave should be associated with a corresponding attribute in an Active Record model, which simply contains the name of the image file in a string field. The resulting augmented data model for microposts appears in Figure 11.19.

---

14. Initially, I called the new attribute `image`, but that name was so generic it ended up being confusing.

microposts	
`id`	integer
`content`	text
`user_id`	integer
`created_at`	datetime
`updated_at`	datetime
`picture`	string

Figure 11.19 The Micropost data model with a `picture` attribute.

To add the required `picture` attribute to the Micropost model, we generate a migration and migrate the development database:

```
$ rails generate migration add_picture_to_microposts picture:string
$ bundle exec rake db:migrate
```

To tell CarrierWave to associate the image with a model we use the `mount_uploader` method. It takes as arguments a symbol representing the attribute and the class name of the generated uploader:

```
mount_uploader :picture, PictureUploader
```

Here `PictureUploader` is defined in the file `picture_uploader.rb`, which we'll start editing in Section 11.4.2, but for now the generated default is fine.

Adding the uploader to the Micropost model gives the code shown in Listing 11.56.

Listing 11.56 Adding an image to the Micropost model.
app/models/micropost.rb

```
class Micropost < ActiveRecord::Base
  belongs_to :user
  default_scope -> { order(created_at: :desc) }
  mount_uploader :picture, PictureUploader
  validates :user_id, presence: true
  validates :content, presence: true, length: { maximum : 140 }
end
```

On some systems, you may need to restart the Rails server at this point to keep the test suite **GREEN**. (If you're using Guard as described in Section 3.7.3, you may need to restart that as well, and it may even be necessary to exit the terminal shell and re-run Guard in a new one.)

To include the uploader on the Home page as in Figure 11.18, we need to include a `file_field` tag in the micropost form, as shown in Listing 11.57.

Listing 11.57 Adding image upload to the micropost create form.
app/views/shared/_micropost_form.html.erb

```erb
<%= form_for(@micropost, html: { multipart: true }) do |f| %>
  <%= render 'shared/error_messages', object: f.object %>
  <div class="field">
    <%= f.text_area :content, placeholder: "Compose new micropost..." %>
  </div>
  <%= f.submit "Post", class: "btn btn-primary" %>
  <span class="picture">
    <%= f.file_field :picture %>
  </span>
<% end %>
```

Note the inclusion of

```
html: { multipart: true }
```

in the arguments to `form_for`, which is necessary for file uploads.

Finally, we need to add `picture` to the list of attributes permitted to be modified through the web. This involves editing the `micropost_params` method, as shown in Listing 11.58.

Listing 11.58 Adding `picture` to the list of permitted attributes.
app/controllers/microposts_controller.rb

```ruby
class MicropostsController < ApplicationController
  before_action :logged_in_user, only: [:create, :destroy]
  before_action :correct_user,   only: :destroy
  .
  .
  .
  private
```

```
    def micropost_params
      params.require(:micropost).permit(:content, :picture)
    end

    def correct_user
      @micropost = current_user.microposts.find_by(id: params[:id])
      redirect_to root_url if @micropost.nil?
    end
end
```

Once the image has been uploaded, we can render it using the `image_tag` helper in the micropost partial, as shown in Listing 11.59. Notice the use of the `picture?` boolean method to prevent displaying an image tag when there isn't an image. This method is created automatically by CarrierWave based on the name of the image attribute. The result of making a successful submission by hand appears in Figure 11.20. Writing an automated test for image upload is left as an exercise (Section 11.6).

Listing 11.59 Adding image display to microposts.

app/views/microposts/_micropost.html.erb

```
<li id="micropost-<%= micropost.id %>">
  <%= link_to gravatar_for(micropost.user, size: 50), micropost.user %>
  <span class="user"><%= link_to micropost.user.name, micropost.user %></span>
  <span class="content">
    <%= micropost.content %>
    <%= image_tag micropost.picture.url if micropost.picture? %>
  </span>
  <span class="timestamp">
    Posted <%= time_ago_in_words(micropost.created_at) %> ago.
    <% if current_user?(micropost.user) %>
      <%= link_to "delete", micropost, method: :delete,
                                        data: { confirm: "You sure?" } %>
    <% end %>
  </span>
</li>
```

11.4.2 Image Validation

The uploader in Section 11.4.1 is a good start, but it has significant limitations. In particular, it doesn't enforce any constraints on the uploaded file, which can cause problems if users try to upload large files of invalid file types. To remedy this defect, we'll add

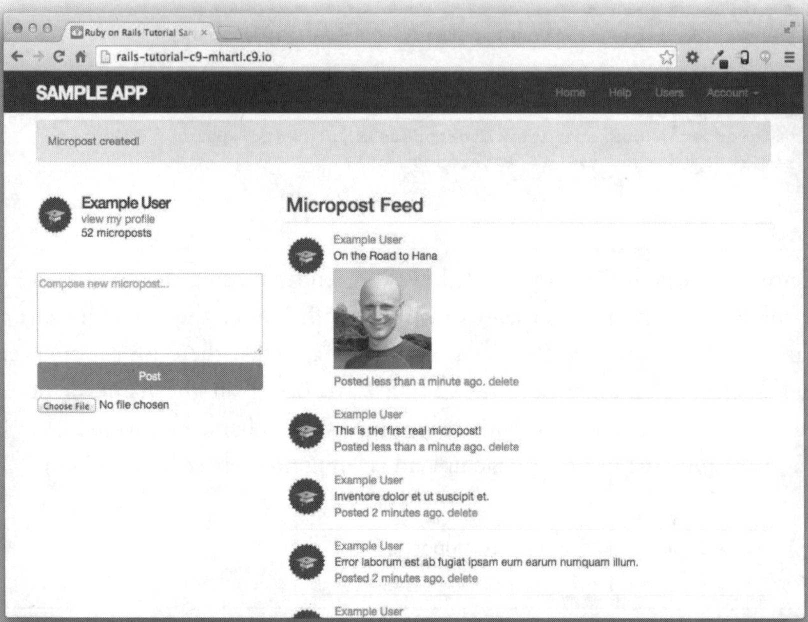

Figure 11.20 The result of submitting a micropost with an image.

validations for the image size and format, both on the server and on the client (i.e., in the browser).

The first image validation, which restricts uploads to valid image types, appears in the CarrierWave uploader itself. The resulting code (which appears as a commented-out suggestion in the generated uploader) verifies that the image filename ends with a valid image extension (PNG, GIF, or one of the variants of JPEG), as shown in Listing 11.60.

Listing 11.60 The picture format validation.
app/uploaders/picture_uploader.rb

```
class PictureUploader < CarrierWave::Uploader::Base
  storage :file

  # Override the directory where uploaded files will be stored.
  # This is a sensible default for uploaders that are meant to be mounted:
```

```
  def store_dir
    "uploads/#{model.class.to_s.underscore}/#{mounted_as}/#{model.id}"
  end

  # Add a white list of extensions which are allowed to be uploaded.
  def extension_white_list
    %w(jpg jpeg gif png)
  end
end
```

The second validation, which controls the size of the image, appears in the Micro-post model itself. In contrast to previous model validations, file size validation doesn't correspond to a built-in Rails validator. As a result, validating images requires defining a custom validation, which we'll call `picture_size` and define as shown in Listing 11.61. Note the use of **validate** (as opposed to **validates**) to call a custom validation.

Listing 11.61 Adding validations to images.
app/models/micropost.rb

```
class Micropost < ActiveRecord::Base
  belongs_to :user
  default_scope -> { order(created_at: :desc) }
  mount_uploader :picture, PictureUploader
  validates :user_id, presence: true
  validates :content, presence: true, length: { maximum: 140 }
  validate  :picture_size

  private

  # Validates the size of an uploaded picture.
  def picture_size
    if picture.size > 5.megabytes
      errors.add(:picture, "should be less than 5MB")
    end
  end
end
```

This custom validation arranges to call the method corresponding to the given symbol (:`picture_size`). In `picture_size` itself, we add a custom error message to the **errors** collection (seen before briefly in Section 6.2.2)—in this case, a limit of 5 megabytes (using a syntax seen before in Box 8.2).

To go along with the validations in Listing 11.60 and Listing 11.61, we'll add two client-side checks on the uploaded image. We'll first mirror the format validation by using the **accept** parameter in the **file_field** input tag:

```
<%= f.file_field :picture, accept: 'image/jpeg,image/gif,image/png' %>
```

The valid formats consist of the MIME types accepted by the validation in Listing 11.63.

Next, we'll include a little JavaScript (or, more specifically, jQuery) to issue an alert if a user tries to upload an image that's too big (which prevents accidental time-consuming uploads and lightens the load on the server):

```
$('#micropost_picture').bind('change', function() {
  size_in_megabytes = this.files[0].size/1024/1024;
  if (size_in_megabytes > 5) {
    alert('Maximum file size is 5MB. Please choose a smaller file.');
  }
});
```

Although jQuery isn't the focus of this book, you might be able to figure out that this code monitors the page element containing the CSS ID **micropost_picture** (as indicated by the hash mark #), which is the ID of the micropost form in Listing 11.57. (The way to figure this out is to Ctrl-click and use your browser's web inspector.) When the element with that CSS ID changes, the jQuery function fires and issues the **alert** method if the file is too big.[15]

The result of adding these additional checks appears in Listing 11.62.

Listing 11.62 Checking the file size with jQuery.
app/views/shared/_micropost_form.html.erb

```
<%= form_for(@micropost, html: { multipart: true }) do |f| %>
  <%= render 'shared/error_messages', object: f.object %>
  <div class="field">
    <%= f.text_area :content, placeholder: "Compose new micropost..." %>
  </div>
  <%= f.submit "Post", class: "btn btn-primary" %>
```

---

15. To learn how to do things like this, you can do what I did: Google for things like "javascript maximum file size" until you find something on Stack Overflow.

```
<span class="picture">
   <%= f.file_field :picture, accept: 'image/jpeg,image/gif,image/png' %>
</span>
<% end %>

<script type="text/javascript">
  $('#micropost_picture').bind('change', function() {
    size_in_megabytes = this.files[0].size/1024/1024;
    if (size_in_megabytes > 5) {
      alert('Maximum file size is 5MB. Please choose a smaller file.');
    }
  });
</script>
```

It's important to understand that code like that shown in Listing 11.62 can't actually prevent a user from trying to upload a file that's too big. Even if our code prevents the user from submitting the file through the web, that user could always edit the JavaScript with a web inspector or issue a direct POST request using, for example, `curl`. To prevent users from uploading arbitrarily large files, it is therefore essential to include a server-side validation, as in Listing 11.61.

11.4.3   Image Resizing

The image size validations in Section 11.4.2 are a good start, but they still allow the uploading of images large enough to break our site's layout, sometimes with frightening results (Figure 11.21). Thus, while it's convenient to allow users to select fairly large images from their local disk, it's also a good idea to resize the images before displaying them.[16]

We'll be resizing images using the image manipulation program ImageMagick, which we need to install in the development environment. (As we'll see in Section 11.4.4, when you're using Heroku for deployment, ImageMagick comes preinstalled in production.) On the cloud IDE, we can do this as follows:[17]

```
$ sudo apt-get update
$ sudo apt-get install imagemagick --fix-missing
```

---

16. It's possible to constrain the *display* size with CSS, but this doesn't change the image size. In particular, large images would still take a while to load. (You've probably visited websites where "small" images seemingly take forever to load—this is why.)

17. I got this from the official Ubuntu documentation. If you're not using the cloud IDE or an equivalent Linux system, do a Google search for "imagemagick <your platform>." On OS X, `brew install imagemagick` should work if you have Homebrew installed.

Figure 11.21 A frighteningly large uploaded image.

Next, we need to include CarrierWave's MiniMagick interface for ImageMagick, together with a resizing command. For the resizing command, several possibilities are listed in the MiniMagick documentation, but the one we want is `resize_to_limit: [400, 400]`, which resizes large images so that they aren't any bigger than 400 pixels in either dimension, while simultaneously leaving smaller images alone. (The other main possibilities listed in the CarrierWave documentation on MiniMagick *stretch* images if they're too small, which isn't what we want in this case.) With the code as shown in Listing 11.63, large images are now resized nicely (Figure 11.22).

Listing 11.63 Configuring the image uploader for image resizing.
app/uploaders/picture_uploader.rb

```
class PictureUploader < CarrierWave::Uploader::Base
  include CarrierWave::MiniMagick
  process resize_to_limit: [400, 400]

  storage :file
```

Figure 11.22 A nicely resized image.

```
# Override the directory where uploaded files will be stored.
# This is a sensible default for uploaders that are meant to be mounted:
def store_dir
  "uploads/#{model.class.to_s.underscore}/#{mounted_as}/#{model.id}"
end

# Add a white list of extensions which are allowed to be uploaded.
def extension_white_list
  %w(jpg jpeg gif png)
end
end
```

11.4.4 Image Upload in Production

The image uploader developed in Section 11.4.3 is good enough for development, but (as seen in the **storage :file** line in Listing 11.63) it uses the local filesystem for storing the images, which isn't a good practice in production.[18] Instead, we'll use a cloud storage service to store images separately from our application.[19]

To configure our application to rely on cloud storage in production, we'll use the `fog` gem, as shown in Listing 11.64.

Listing 11.64   Configuring the image uploader for production.
app/uploaders/picture_uploader.rb

```ruby
class PictureUploader < CarrierWave::Uploader::Base
  include CarrierWave::MiniMagick
  process resize_to_limit: [400, 400]

  if Rails.env.production?
    storage :fog
  else
    storage :file
  end

  # Override the directory where uploaded files will be stored.
  # This is a sensible default for uploaders that are meant to be mounted:
  def store_dir
    "uploads/#{model.class.to_s.underscore}/#{mounted_as}/#{model.id}"
  end

  # Add a white list of extensions which are allowed to be uploaded.
  def extension_white_list
    %w(jpg jpeg gif png)
  end
end
```

Listing 11.64 uses the **production?** boolean from Box 7.1 to switch the storage method based on the environment:

```ruby
if Rails.env.production?
  storage :fog
else
  storage :file
end
```

---

18. Among other things, file storage on Heroku is temporary, so uploaded images will be deleted every time you deploy your app.

19. This is a challenging section and can be skipped without loss of continuity.

There are many choices for cloud storage, but we'll use one of the most popular and well supported, Amazon.com's Simple Storage Service (S3).[20] Here are the essential steps to getting set up:

1. Sign up for an Amazon Web Services account.
2. Create a user via AWS Identity and Access Management (IAM) and record the access key and secret key.
3. Create an S3 bucket (with a name of your choice) using the AWS Console, and then grant read and write permission to the user created in the previous step.

For further details on these steps, consult the S3 documentation[21] (and, if necessary, Google or Stack Overflow).

Once you've created and configured your S3 account, you should create and fill the CarrierWave configuration file as shown in Listing 11.65.

Listing 11.65 Configuring CarrierWave to use S3.
config/initializers/carrier_wave.rb

```ruby
if Rails.env.production?
  CarrierWave.configure do |config|
    config.fog_credentials = {
      # Configuration for Amazon S3
      :provider              => 'AWS',
      :aws_access_key_id     => ENV['S3_ACCESS_KEY'],
      :aws_secret_access_key => ENV['S3_SECRET_KEY']
    }
    config.fog_directory     =  ENV['S3_BUCKET']
  end
end
```

As with production email configuration (Listing 10.55), Listing 11.65 uses Heroku **ENV** variables to avoid hard-coding sensitive information. In Section 10.3, these variables were defined automatically via the SendGrid add-on, but in this case we need to define them explicitly. We can accomplish this by using **heroku config:set** as follows:

---

20. S3 is a paid service, but the storage needed to set up and test the Rails Tutorial sample application costs less than 1 cent per month.

21. http://aws.amazon.com/documentation/s3/

```
$ heroku config:set S3_ACCESS_KEY=<access key>
$ heroku config:set S3_SECRET_KEY=<secret key>
$ heroku config:set S3_BUCKET=<bucket name>
```

With this configuration in place, we are ready to commit our changes and deploy. We start by committing the changes on our topic branch and merging back to **master**:

```
$ bundle exec rake test
$ git add -A
$ git commit -m "Add user microposts"
$ git checkout master
$ git merge user-microposts
$ git push
```

Then we deploy, reset the database, and reseed the sample data:

```
$ git push heroku
$ heroku pg:reset DATABASE
$ heroku run rake db:migrate
$ heroku run rake db:seed
```

Because Heroku comes with an installation of ImageMagick, the result is successful image resizing and upload in production, as seen in Figure 11.23.

11.5 Conclusion

With the addition of the Microposts resource, we are nearly finished with our sample application. All that remains is to add a social layer that lets users follow each other. We'll learn how to model such user relationships, and see the implications for the microposts feed, in Chapter 12.

If you skipped Section 11.4.4, be sure to commit and merge your changes:

```
$ bundle exec rake test
$ git add -A
$ git commit -m "Add user microposts"
$ git checkout master
$ git merge user-microposts
$ git push
```

Then deploy to production:

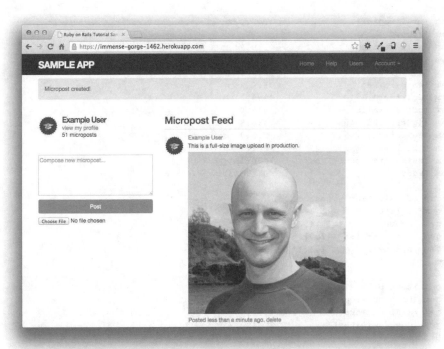

Figure 11.23 Image upload in production.

```
$ git push heroku
$ heroku pg:reset DATABASE
$ heroku run rake db:migrate
$ heroku run rake db:seed
```

It's worth noting that this chapter saw the last of the necessary gem installations. For reference, the final **Gemfile** is shown in Listing 11.66.

Listing 11.66 The final **Gemfile** for the sample application.

```
source 'https://rubygems.org'

gem 'rails',                    '4.2.0'
gem 'bcrypt',                   '3.1.7'
gem 'faker',                    '1.4.2'
gem 'carrierwave',              '0.10.0'
```

```
gem 'mini_magick',                '3.8.0'
gem 'fog',                        '1.23.0'
gem 'will_paginate',              '3.0.7'
gem 'bootstrap-will_paginate',    '0.0.10'
gem 'bootstrap-sass',             '3.2.0.0'
gem 'sass-rails',                 '5.0.1'
gem 'uglifier',                   '2.5.3'
gem 'coffee-rails',               '4.1.0'
gem 'jquery-rails',               '4.0.3'
gem 'turbolinks',                 '2.3.0'
gem 'jbuilder',                   '2.2.3'
gem 'rails-html-sanitizer',       '1.0.1'
gem 'sdoc',                       '0.4.0', group: :doc

group :development, :test do
  gem 'sqlite3',     '1.3.9'
  gem 'byebug',      '3.4.0'
  gem 'web-console', '2.0.0.beta3'
  gem 'spring',      '1.1.3'
end

group :test do
  gem 'minitest-reporters', '1.0.5'
  gem 'mini_backtrace',     '0.1.3'
  gem 'guard-minitest',     '2.3.1'
end

group :production do
  gem 'pg',            '0.17.1'
  gem 'rails_12factor', '0.0.2'
  gem 'puma',          '4.8.3'
end
```

11.5.1 What We Learned in This Chapter

- Microposts, like Users, are modeled as a resource backed by an Active Record model.

- Rails supports multiple-key indices.

- We can model a user having many microposts using the `has_many` and `belongs_to` methods in the User and Micropost models, respectively.

- The `has_many`/`belongs_to` combination gives rise to methods that work through the association.

- The code `user.microposts.build(...)` returns a new Micropost object automatically associated with the given user.

- Rails supports default ordering via `default_scope`.
- Scopes take anonymous functions as arguments.
- The `dependent: :destroy` option causes objects to be destroyed at the same time as associated objects.
- Pagination and object counts can both be performed through associations, leading to automatically efficient code.
- Fixtures support the creation of associations.
- It is possible to pass variables to Rails partials.
- The `where` method can be used to perform Active Record selections.
- We can enforce secure operations by always creating and destroying dependent objects through their associations.
- We can upload and resize images using CarrierWave.

11.6 Exercises

Note: To receive a copy of the *Solutions Manual for Exercises*, with solutions to every exercise in the *Ruby on Rails™ Tutorial*, visit www.railstutorial.org/<word>, where "<word>" is the last word of the Figure 3.9 caption.

For a suggestion on how to avoid conflicts between exercises and the main tutorial, see the note on exercise topic branches in Section 3.6.

1. Refactor the Home page to use separate partials for the two branches of the `if-else` statement.
2. Add tests for the sidebar micropost count (including proper pluralization). Listing 11.67 will help get you started.
3. By following the template in Listing 11.68, write a test of the image uploader in Section 11.4. As preparation, you should add an image to the fixtures directory (using, for example, `cp app/assets/images/rails.png test/fixtures/`). (If you're using Git, I also recommend updating your `.gitignore` file as shown in Listing 11.69.) To avoid a confusing error, you will need to configure CarrierWave to skip image resizing in tests by creating an initializer file as shown

in Listing 11.70. The additional assertions in Listing 11.68 check both for a file upload field on the Home page and for a valid image attribute on the micropost resulting from valid submission. Note the use of the special `fixture_file_upload` method for uploading files as fixtures inside tests.[22] *Hint*: To check for a valid `picture` attribute, use the `assigns` method mentioned in Section 10.1.4 to access the micropost in the `create` action after valid submission.

Listing 11.67 A template for the sidebar micropost count test.

test/integration/microposts_interface_test.rb

```
require 'test_helper'

class MicropostsInterfaceTest < ActionDispatch::IntegrationTest

  def setup
    @user = users(:michael)
  end
  .
  .
  .
  test "micropost sidebar count" do
    log_in_as(@user)
    get root_path
    assert_match "#{FILL_IN} microposts", response.body
    # User with zero microposts
    other_user = users(:mallory)
    log_in_as(other_user)
    get root_path
    assert_match "0 microposts", response.body
    other_user.microposts.create!(content: "A micropost")
    get root_path
    assert_match FILL_IN, response.body
  end
end
```

Listing 11.68 A template for testing image upload.

test/integration/microposts_interface_test.rb

```
require 'test_helper'

class MicropostInterfaceTest < ActionDispatch::IntegrationTest
```

---

22. Windows users should add a `:binary` parameter: `fixture_file_upload(file, type, :binary)`.

```
    def setup
      @user = users(:michael)
    end

    test "micropost interface" do
      log_in_as(@user)
      get root_path
      assert_select 'div.pagination'
      assert_select 'input[type=FILL_IN]'
      # Invalid submission
      post microposts_path, micropost: { content: "" }
      assert_select 'div#error_explanation'
      # Valid submission
      content = "This micropost really ties the room together"
      picture = fixture_file_upload('test/fixtures/rails.png', 'image/png')
      assert_difference 'Micropost.count', 1 do
        post microposts_path, micropost: { content: content, picture: FILL_IN }
      end
      assert FILL_IN.picture?
      follow_redirect!
      assert_match content, response.body
      # Delete a post.
      assert_select 'a', text: 'delete'
      first_micropost = @user.microposts.paginate(page: 1).first
      assert_difference 'Micropost.count', -1 do
        delete micropost_path(first_micropost)
      end
      # Visit a different user.
      get user_path(users(:archer))
      assert_select 'a', text: 'delete', count: 0
    end
    .
    .
    .
end
```

Listing 11.69 Adding the uploads directory to the `.gitignore` file.

```
# See https://help.github.com/articles/ignoring-files for more about ignoring
# files.
#
# If you find yourself ignoring temporary files generated by your text editor
# or operating system, you probably want to add a global ignore instead:
#   git config --global core.excludesfile '~/.gitignore_global'

# Ignore bundler config.
/.bundle

# Ignore the default SQLite database.
```

```
/db/*.sqlite3
/db/*.sqlite3-journal

# Ignore all logfiles and tempfiles.
/log/*.log
/tmp

# Ignore Spring files.
/spring/*.pid

# Ignore uploaded test images.
/public/uploads
```

Listing 11.70 An initializer to skip image resizing in tests.

config/initializers/skip_image_resizing.rb

```
if Rails.env.test?
  CarrierWave.configure do |config|
    config.enable_processing = false
  end
end
```

CHAPTER 12

Following Users

In this chapter, we will complete the sample application by adding a social layer that allows users to follow (and unfollow) other users, resulting in each user's Home page displaying a status feed of the followed users' microposts. We'll start by learning how to model relationships between users in Section 12.1, and we'll build the corresponding web interface in Section 12.2 (including an introduction to Ajax). We'll end by developing a fully functional status feed in Section 12.3.

This final chapter contains some of the most challenging material in the tutorial, including some Ruby/SQL trickery to make the status feed. Through these examples, you will see how Rails can handle even rather intricate data models, which should serve you well as you go on to develop your own applications with their own specific requirements. To help with the transition from tutorial to independent development, Section 12.4 offers some pointers to more advanced resources.

Because the material in this chapter is particularly challenging, before writing any code we'll pause for a moment and take a tour of the interface. As in previous chapters, at this early stage we'll represent pages using mockups.[1] The full page flow runs as follows: A user (John Calvin) starts at his profile page (Figure 12.1) and navigates to the Users page (Figure 12.2) to select a user to follow. Calvin navigates to the profile of a second user, Thomas Hobbes (Figure 12.3), clicking on the "Follow" button to follow that user. This changes the "Follow" button to "Unfollow" and increments Hobbes's "followers" count by one (Figure 12.4). Navigating to his home page, Calvin

---

1. The new photographs in the mockup tour are from http://www.flickr.com/photos/john_lustig/2518452221/ and https://www.flickr.com/photos/renemensen/9187111340.

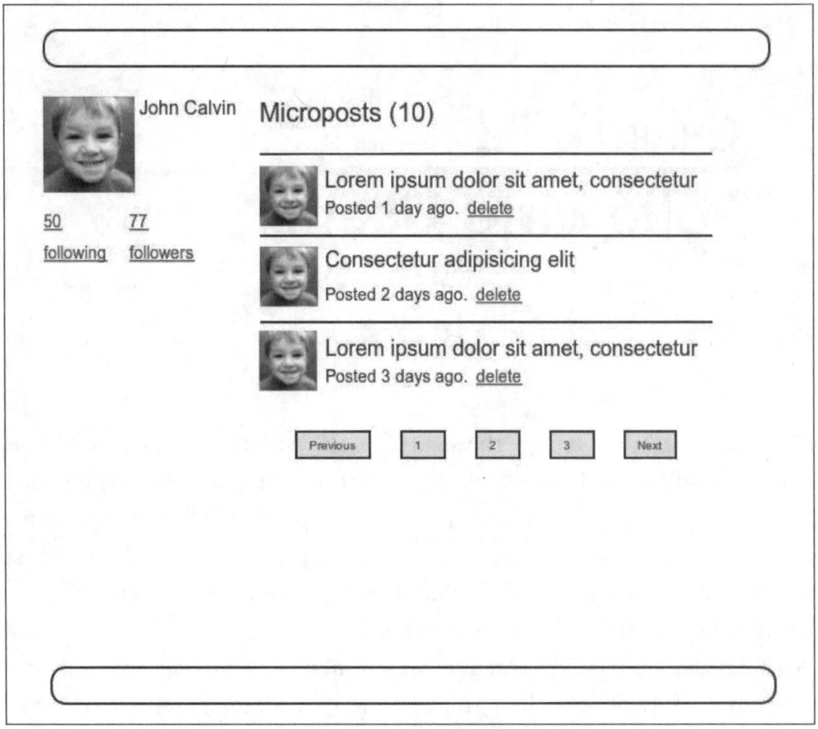

Figure 12.1 A current user's profile.

now sees an incremented "following" count and finds Hobbes's microposts in his status feed (Figure 12.5). The rest of this chapter is dedicated to making this page flow actually work.

12.1 The Relationship Model

Our first step in implementing following users is to construct a data model, which is not as straightforward as it seems. Naïvely, it might seem that a `has_many` relationship would do: A user `has_many` followed users and `has_many` followers. As we will see, there is a problem with this approach, and we'll learn how to fix it using `has_many :through`.

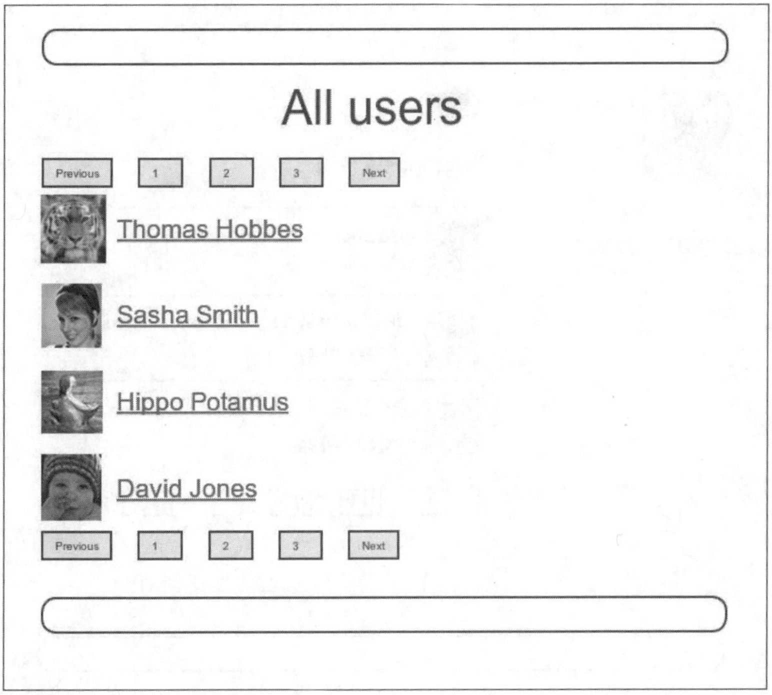

Figure 12.2 Finding a user to follow.

As usual, Git users should create a new topic branch:

```
$ git checkout master
$ git checkout -b following-users
```

12.1.1 A Problem with the Data Model (and a Solution)

As a first step toward constructing a data model for following users, let's examine a typical case. For instance, consider a user who follows a second user. We could say that, for example, Calvin is following Hobbes, and Hobbes is followed by Calvin, so that Calvin is the *follower* and Hobbes is *followed*. Using Rails' default pluralization convention, the set of all users following a given user is that user's *followers*, and `hobbes.followers` is an array of those users. Unfortunately, the reverse doesn't work: By default, the set of all

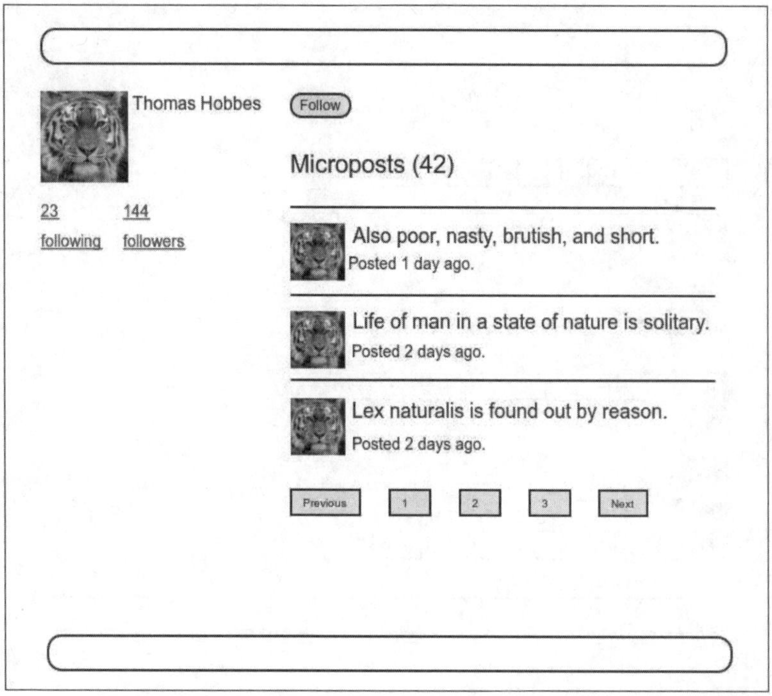

Figure 12.3 The profile of a user to follow, with a follow button.

followed users would be called the *followeds*, which is ungrammatical and clumsy. We'll adopt Twitter's convention and call them *following* (as in "50 following, 75 followers"), with a corresponding `calvin.following` array.

This discussion suggests modeling the followed users as in Figure 12.6, with a `following` table and a `has_many` association. Since `user.following` should be a collection of users, each row of the `following` table would need to be a user, as identified by the `followed_id`, together with the `follower_id` to establish the association.[2] In addition, because each row is a user, we would need to include the user's other attributes, including the name, email, password, and so on.

The problem with the data model in Figure 12.6 is that it is terribly redundant: Each row contains not only each followed user's ID, but also all of that user's other

---

2. For simplicity, Figure 12.6 omits the `following` table's `id` column.

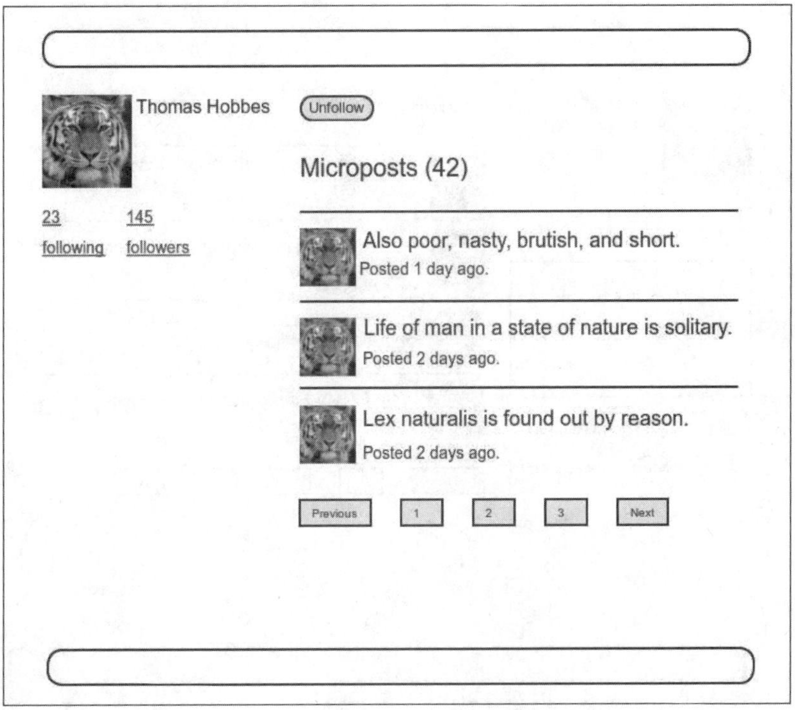

Figure 12.4 A profile with an unfollow button and incremented followers count.

information—all of which is *already* in the **users** table. Even worse, to model user *followers* we would need a separate, similarly redundant **followers** table. Finally, this data model is a maintainability nightmare: Each time a user changed (say) his or her name, we would need to update not just the user's record in the **users** table but also *every row containing that user* in both the **following** and **followers** tables.

The problem here is that we are missing an underlying abstraction. One way to find the proper model is to consider how we might implement the act of *following* in a web application. Recall from Section 7.1.2 that the REST architecture involves *resources* that are created and destroyed. This leads us to ask two questions: (1) When a user follows another user, what is being created? and (2) When a user *un*follows another user, what is being destroyed? Upon reflection, we see that in these cases the application should either create or destroy a *relationship* between two users. A user then has many relationships, and has many **following** (or **followers**) *through* these relationships.

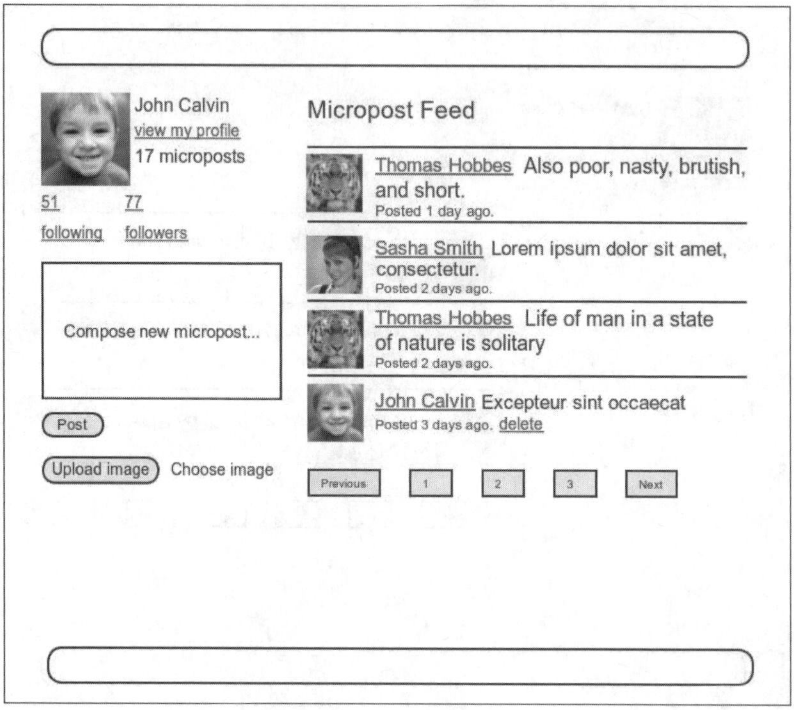

Figure 12.5 The Home page with status feed and incremented following count.

There's an additional detail we need to address regarding our application's data model: Unlike symmetric Facebook-style friendships, which are always reciprocal (at least at the data-model level), Twitter-style following relationships are potentially *asymmetric*—Calvin can follow Hobbes without Hobbes following Calvin. To distinguish between these two cases, we'll adopt the terminology of *active* and *passive* relationships: If Calvin is following Hobbes but not vice versa, Calvin has an active relationship with Hobbes and Hobbes has a passive relationship with Calvin.[3]

We'll focus now on using active relationships to generate a list of followed users, and consider the passive case in Section 12.1.5. Figure 12.6 suggests how to implement it: Given that each followed user is uniquely identified by `followed_id`, we could convert

---

3. Thanks to reader Paul Fioravanti for suggesting this terminology.

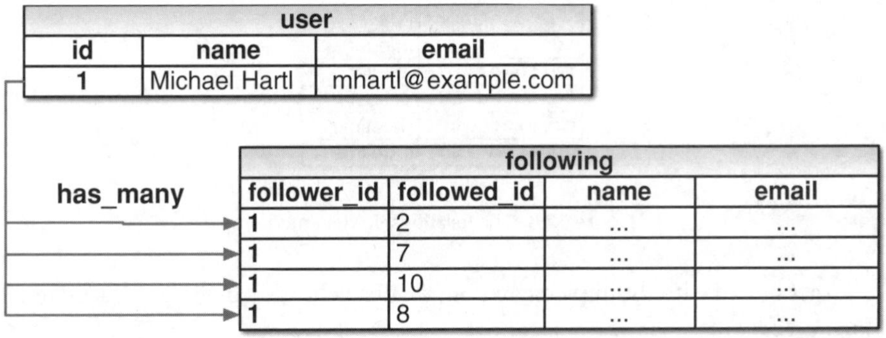

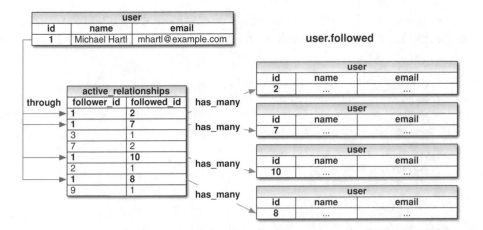

Figure 12.6 A naïve implementation of user following.

Figure 12.7 A model of followed users through active relationships.

`following` to an `active_relationships` table, omit the user details, and use `followed_id` to retrieve the followed user from the `users` table. A diagram of this data model appears in Figure 12.7.

Because we'll end up using the same database table for both active and passive relationships, we'll use the generic term *relationship* for the table name, with a corresponding Relationship model. The result is the Relationship data model shown in Figure 12.8. We'll see starting in Section 12.1.4 how to use the Relationship model to simulate both Active Relationship and Passive Relationship models.

relationships	
id	integer
follower_id	integer
followed_id	integer
created_at	datetime
updated_at	datetime

Figure 12.8 The Relationship data model.

To get started with the implementation, we first generate a migration corresponding to Figure 12.8:

```
$ rails generate model Relationship follower_id:integer followed_id:integer
```

Because we will be finding relationships by **follower_id** and by **followed_id**, we should add an index on each column for efficiency, as shown in Listing 12.1.

Listing 12.1 Adding indices for the **relationships** table.
db/migrate/[timestamp]_create_relationships.rb

```
class CreateRelationships < ActiveRecord::Migration
  def change
    create_table :relationships do |t|
      t.integer :follower_id
      t.integer :followed_id

      t.timestamps null: false
    end
    add_index :relationships, :follower_id
    add_index :relationships, :followed_id
    add_index :relationships, [:follower_id, :followed_id], unique: true
  end
end
```

Listing 12.1 also includes a multiple-key index that enforces uniqueness on (**follower_id**, **followed_id**) pairs, so that a user can't follow another user more than once. (Compare to the email uniqueness index from Listing 6.28 and the multiple-key index in Listing 11.1.) As we'll see starting in Section 12.1.4, our user interface won't allow this to happen, but adding a unique index arranges to raise an error if a user tries to create duplicate relationships anyway (e.g., by using a command-line tool such as **curl**).

To create the `relationships` table, we migrate the database as usual:

```
$ bundle exec rake db:migrate
```

12.1.2 User/Relationship Associations

Before implementing user following and followers, we first need to establish the association between users and relationships. A user `has_many` relationships, and—since relationships involve *two* users—a relationship `belongs_to` both a follower and a followed user.

As with microposts in Section 11.1.3, we will create new relationships using the user association, with code such as

```
user.active_relationships.build(followed_id: ...)
```

At this point, you might expect application code as in Section 11.1.3. While the code here is indeed similar, there are two key differences.

First, in the case of the user/micropost association, we could write

```
class User < ActiveRecord::Base
  has_many :microposts
  .
  .
  .
end
```

This works because by convention Rails looks for a Micropost model corresponding to the `:microposts` symbols.[4] In the present case, though, we want to write

```
has_many :active_relationships
```

even though the underlying model is called Relationship. We will thus have to tell Rails the model class name to look for.

Second, before we wrote

---

4. Technically, Rails converts the argument of `has_many` to a class name using the `classify` method, which converts `"foo_bars"` to `"FooBar"`.

```
class Micropost < ActiveRecord::Base
  belongs_to :user
  .
  .
  .
end
```

in the Micropost model. This works because the **microposts** table has a **user_id** attribute to identify the user (Section 11.1.1). An ID used in this manner to connect two database tables is known as a *foreign key*. When the foreign key for a User model object is **user_id**, Rails infers the association automatically: By default, Rails expects a foreign key of the form **<class>_id**, where **<class>** is the lowercase version of the class name.[5] In the present situation, although we are still dealing with users, the user following another user is now identified with the foreign key **follower_id**, so we need to inform Rails of that fact.

The result of this is the user/relationship association shown in Listing 12.2 and Listing 12.3.

Listing 12.2 Implementing the active relationships **has_many** association.
app/models/user.rb

```
class User < ActiveRecord::Base
  has_many :microposts, dependent: :destroy
  has_many :active_relationships, class_name:  "Relationship",
                                  foreign_key: "follower_id",
                                  dependent:   :destroy
  .
  .
  .
end
```

(Since destroying a user should also destroy that user's relationships, we've added **dependent: :destroy** to the association.)

---

5. Technically, Rails uses the **underscore** method to convert the class name to an ID. For example, **"FooBar".underscore** is **"foo_bar"**, so the foreign key for a **FooBar** object would be **foo_bar_id**.

Listing 12.3 Adding the follower `belongs_to` association to the Relationship model.
app/models/relationship.rb

```
class Relationship < ActiveRecord::Base
  belongs_to :follower, class_name: "User"
  belongs_to :followed, class_name: "User"
end
```

The `followed` association isn't actually needed until Section 12.1.5, but the parallel follower/followed structure is clearer if we implement them both at the same time. The relationships in Listing 12.2 and Listing 12.3 give rise to methods analogous to the ones we saw in Table 11.1, as shown in Table 12.1.

12.1.3 Relationship Validations

Before moving on, we'll add a couple of Relationship model validations for completeness. The tests (Listing 12.4) and application code (Listing 12.5) are straightforward. Like the generated user fixture (Listing 6.29), the generated relationship fixture violates the uniqueness constraint imposed by the corresponding migration (Listing 12.1). The solution—removing the fixture contents as in Listing 12.6—is also the same.

Table 12.1 A summary of user/active relationship association methods.

Method	Purpose
`active_relationship.follower`	returns the follower
`active_relationship.followed`	returns the followed user
`user.active_relationships.` `  create(followed_id: user.id)`	creates an active relationship associated with **user**

`user.active_relationships.`
`  create!(followed_id: user.id)`
	creates an active relationship
	  associated with **user**
	  (exception on failure)

`user.active_relationships.` `  build(followed_id: user.id)`	returns a new Relationship object associated with **user**

Listing 12.4 Testing the Relationship model validations.

test/models/relationship_test.rb

```ruby
require 'test_helper'

class RelationshipTest < ActiveSupport::TestCase

  def setup
    @relationship = Relationship.new(follower_id: 1, followed_id: 2)
  end

  test "should be valid" do
    assert @relationship.valid?
  end

  test "should require a follower_id" do
    @relationship.follower_id = nil
    assert_not @relationship.valid?
  end

  test "should require a followed_id" do
    @relationship.followed_id = nil
    assert_not @relationship.valid?
  end
end
```

Listing 12.5 Adding the Relationship model validations.

app/models/relationship.rb

```ruby
class Relationship < ActiveRecord::Base
  belongs_to :follower, class_name: "User"
  belongs_to :followed, class_name: "User"
  validates :follower_id, presence: true
  validates :followed_id, presence: true
end
```

Listing 12.6 Removing the contents of the relationship fixture.

test/fixtures/relationships.yml

```yaml
# empty
```

At this point, the tests should be **GREEN**:

Listing 12.7   GREEN

```
$ bundle exec rake test
```

12.1.4 Followed Users

We come now to the heart of the Relationship associations: `following` and `followers`. Here we will use `has_many :through` for the first time: A user has many following *through* relationships, as illustrated in Figure 12.7. By default, in a `has_many :through` association, Rails looks for a foreign key corresponding to the singular version of the association. In other words, with code like

```
has_many :followeds, through: :active_relationships
```

Rails would see "followeds" and use the singular "followed," assembling a collection using the `followed_id` in the `relationships` table. But, as noted in Section 12.1.1, `user.followeds` is rather awkward, so we'll write `user.following` instead. Naturally, Rails allows us to override the default, in this case using the `source` parameter (as shown in Listing 12.8), which explicitly tells Rails that the source of the `following` array is the set of `followed` IDs.

Listing 12.8   Adding the User model `following` association.
app/models/user.rb

```
class User < ActiveRecord::Base
  has_many :microposts, dependent: :destroy
  has_many :active_relationships, class_name:  "Relationship",
                                  foreign_key: "follower_id",
                                  dependent:   :destroy
  has_many :following, through: :active_relationships, source: :followed
  .
  .
  .
end
```

The association defined in Listing 12.8 leads to a powerful combination of Active Record and array-like behavior. For example, we can check whether the followed users collection includes another user with the **include?** method (Section 4.3.1), and we can find objects through the association:

```
user.following.include?(other_user)
user.following.find(other_user)
```

Although in many contexts we can effectively treat **following** as an array, Rails is smart about how it handles things under the hood. For example, code like

```
following.include?(other_user)
```

looks as if it might have to pull all the followed users out of the database to apply the **include?** method, but in fact for efficiency Rails arranges for the comparison to happen directly in the database. (Compare this approach to the code in Section 11.2.1, where we saw that

```
user.microposts.count
```

performs the count directly in the database.)

To manipulate following relationships, we'll introduce **follow** and **unfollow** utility methods so that we can write, for example, **user.follow(other_user)**. We'll also add an associated **following?** boolean method to test whether one user is following another.[6]

This is exactly the kind of situation where I like to write some tests first. The reason is that we are quite far from writing a working web interface for following users, but it's hard to proceed without some sort of *client* for the code we're developing. In this case, it's easy to write a short test for the User model, in which we use **following?** to make sure the user isn't following the other user, use **follow** to follow another user, use **following?** to verify that the operation succeeded, and finally **unfollow** and verify that it worked. The result appears in Listing 12.9.

---

6. Once you have a lot of experience modeling a particular domain, you can often guess such utility methods in advance; even when you can't, you'll often find yourself writing them to make the tests cleaner. In this case, it's OK if you wouldn't have guessed them. Software development is usually an iterative process—you write code until it starts getting ugly, and then you refactor it—but for brevity the tutorial presentation is streamlined a bit.

Listing 12.9 Tests for some "following" utility methods. **RED**

test/models/user_test.rb

```
require 'test_helper'

class UserTest < ActiveSupport::TestCase
  .
  .
  .
  test "should follow and unfollow a user" do
    michael = users(:michael)
    archer  = users(:archer)
    assert_not michael.following?(archer)
    michael.follow(archer)
    assert michael.following?(archer)
    michael.unfollow(archer)
    assert_not michael.following?(archer)
  end
end
```

By referring to the methods in Table 12.1, we can write the **follow**, **unfollow**, and **following?** methods using the association with **following**, as shown in Listing 12.10. (Note that we have omitted the user **self** variable whenever possible.)

Listing 12.10 Utility methods for following. **GREEN**

app/models/user.rb

```
class User < ActiveRecord::Base
  .
  .
  .
  def feed
    .
    .
    .
  end

  # Follows a user.
  def follow(other_user)
    active_relationships.create(followed_id: other_user.id)
  end

  # Unfollows a user.
```

```
  def unfollow(other_user)
    active_relationships.find_by(followed_id: other_user.id).destroy
  end

  # Returns true if the current user is following the other user.
  def following?(other_user)
    following.include?(other_user)
  end

  private
    .
    .
    .
end
```

With the code in Listing 12.10, the tests should be **GREEN**:

Listing 12.11 GREEN

```
$ bundle exec rake test
```

12.1.5 Followers

The final piece of the relationships puzzle is to add a `user.followers` method to go with `user.following`. You may have noticed from Figure 12.7 that all the information needed to extract an array of followers is already present in the `relationships` table (which we are treating as the `active_relationships` table via the code in Listing 12.2). Indeed, the technique is exactly the same as for followed users, with the roles of `follower_id` and `followed_id` reversed, and with `passive_relationships` in place of `active_relationships`. The data model then appears as in Figure 12.9.

The implementation of the data model in Figure 12.9 parallels Listing 12.8 exactly, as seen in Listing 12.12.

Listing 12.12 Implementing `user.followers` using passive relationships.
app/models/user.rb

```
class User < ActiveRecord::Base
  has_many :microposts, dependent: :destroy
  has_many :active_relationships,  class_name:  "Relationship",
                                   foreign_key: "follower_id",
```

```
                                        dependent:      :destroy
  has_many :passive_relationships, class_name:  "Relationship",
                                        foreign_key: "followed_id",
                                        dependent:      :destroy
  has_many :following, through: :active_relationships,  source: :followed
  has_many :followers, through: :passive_relationships, source: :follower
   .
   .
   .
end
```

In reality, we could omit the `:source` key for `followers` in Listing 12.12, using simply

```
has_many :followers, through: :passive_relationships
```

This is possible because, in the case of a `:followers` attribute, Rails will singularize "followers" and automatically look for the foreign key `follower_id` in this case. Listing 12.8 keeps the `:source` key to emphasize the parallel structure with the `has_many :following` association.

We can conveniently test our data model using the `followers.include?` method, as shown in Listing 12.13. (Listing 12.13 might have used a `followed_by?` method to complement the `following?` method, but it turns out we won't need it in our application.)

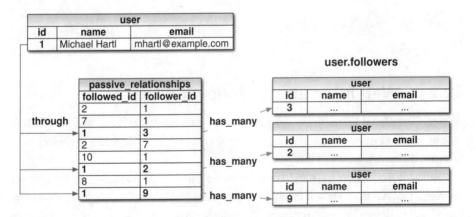

Figure 12.9 A model for user followers through passive relationships.

Listing 12.13 A test for `followers`. **GREEN**

test/models/user_test.rb

```ruby
require 'test_helper'

class UserTest < ActiveSupport::TestCase
  .
  .
  .
  test "should follow and unfollow a user" do
    michael  = users(:michael)
    archer   = users(:archer)
    assert_not michael.following?(archer)
    michael.follow(archer)
    assert michael.following?(archer)
    assert archer.followers.include?(michael)
    michael.unfollow(archer)
    assert_not michael.following?(archer)
  end
end
```

Listing 12.13 adds only one line to the test from Listing 12.9, but so many things have to go right to get it to pass that it's a very sensitive test of the code in Listing 12.12.

At this point, the full test suite should be **GREEN**:

```
$ bundle exec rake test
```

12.2 A Web Interface for Following Users

Section 12.1 placed rather heavy demands on our data modeling skills, and it's fine if its lessons take a while to soak in. In fact, one of the best ways to understand the associations is to use them in the web interface.

In the introduction to this chapter, we saw a preview of the page flow for user following. In this section, we will implement the basic interface and following/unfollowing functionality shown in those mockups. We will also make separate pages to show the user following and followers arrays. In Section 12.3, we'll complete our sample application by adding the user's status feed.

12.2.1 Sample Following Data

As in previous chapters, we will find it convenient to use the seed data Rake task to fill the database with sample relationships. This will allow us to design the look and feel of the web pages first, deferring the back-end functionality until later in this section.

The code to seed the following relationships appears in Listing 12.14. Here we somewhat arbitrarily arrange for the first user to follow users 3 through 51, and then have users 4 through 41 follow that user back. The resulting relationships will be sufficient for developing the application interface.

Listing 12.14 Adding following/follower relationships to the sample data.
db/seeds.rb

```
# Users
User.create!(name:  "Example User",
             email: "example@railstutorial.org",
             password:              "foobar",
             password_confirmation: "foobar",
             admin:     true,
             activated: true,
             activated_at: Time.zone.now)

99.times do |n|
  name  = Faker::Name.name
  email = "example-#{n+1}@railstutorial.org"
  password = "password"
  User.create!(name: name,
               email: email,
               password:              password,
               password_confirmation: password,
               activated: true,
               activated_at: Time.zone.now)
end

# Microposts
user = Users.order(:created_at).take(6)
50.times do
    content = Faker::Lorem.sentence(5)
    user.each  { |user| user.microposts.create!(content: content) }
end

# Following relationships
```

```
users = User.all
user  = users.first
following = users[2..50]
followers = users[3..40]
following.each { |followed| user.follow(followed) }
followers.each { |follower| follower.follow(user) }
```

To execute the code in Listing 12.14, we reseed the database as usual:

```
$ bundle exec rake db:migrate:reset
$ bundle exec rake db:seed
```

12.2.2 Stats and a Follow Form

Now that our sample users have both followed users and followers, we need to update the profile page and Home page to reflect these relationships. We'll start by developing a partial to display the following and follower statistics on the profile and home pages. We'll next add a follow/unfollow form, and then make dedicated pages for showing "following" (followed users) and "followers."

As noted in Section 12.1.1, we'll adopt Twitter's convention of using "following" as a label for followed users, as in "50 following". This usage is reflected in the mockup sequence starting in Figure 12.1 and shown in close-up in Figure 12.10.

The statistics in Figure 12.10 consist of the number of users the current user is following and the number of followers, each of which should be a link to its respective dedicated display page. In Chapter 5, we stubbed out such links with the dummy text `"#"`, but that was before we had much experience with routes. This time, although we'll defer construction of the the actual pages to Section 12.2.3, we'll make the routes now, as seen in Listing 12.15. This code uses the `:member` method inside a `resources` *block*, which we haven't seen before. Can you can guess what it does?

Figure 12.10 A mockup of the stats partial.

Listing 12.15 Adding **following** and **followers** actions to the Users controller.
config/routes.rb

```
Rails.application.routes.draw do
  root                   'static_pages#home'
  get     'help'     => 'static_pages#help'
  get     'about'    => 'static_pages#about'
  get     'contact'  => 'static_pages#contact'
  get     'signup'   => 'users#new'
  get     'login'    => 'sessions#new'
  post    'login'    => 'sessions#create'
  delete 'logout'    => 'sessions#destroy'
  resources :users do
    member do
      get :following, :followers
    end
  end
  resources :account_activations, only: [:edit]
  resources :password_resets,     only: [:new, :create, :edit, :update]
  resources :microposts,          only: [:create, :destroy]
end
```

You might suspect that the URLs for following and followers will look like
/users/1/following and /users/1/followers, and that is exactly what the code in Listing 12.15 arranges. Since both pages will be *showing* data, the proper HTTP verb is
a GET request; thus we use the **get** method to arrange for the URLs to respond appropriately. Meanwhile, the **member** method arranges for the routes to respond to URLs
containing the user ID. The other possibility, **collection**, works without the ID, so
that

```
resources :users do
  collection do
    get :tigers
  end
end
```

would respond to the URL /users/tigers (presumably to display all the tigers in our
application).[7]

---

7. For more details on such routing options, see the Rails Guides article on "Rails Routing from the Outside In."

Table 12.2 RESTful routes provided by the custom rules in Listing 12.15.

HTTP request	URL	Action	Named route
GET	/users/1/following	`following`	`following_user_path(1)`
GET	/users/1/followers	`followers`	`followers_user_path(1)`

A table of the routes generated by Listing 12.15 appears in Table 12.2. Note the named routes for the followed user and followers pages, which we'll put to use shortly.

With the routes defined, we are now in a position to define the stats partial, which involves a couple of links inside a div, as shown in Listing 12.16.

Listing 12.16 A partial for displaying follower statistics.
app/views/shared/_stats.html.erb

```erb
<% @user ||= current_user %>
<div class="stats">
  <a href="<%= following_user_path(@user) %>">
    <strong id="following" class="stat">
      <%= @user.following.count %>
    </strong>
    following
  </a>
  <a href="<%= followers_user_path(@user) %>">
    <strong id="followers" class="stat">
      <%= @user.followers.count %>
    </strong>
    followers
  </a>
</div>
```

Since we will be including the statistics on both the user show pages and the home page, the first line of Listing 12.16 picks the right one using

```erb
<% @user ||= current_user %>
```

As discussed in Box 8.1, this code does nothing when **@user** is not **nil** (as on a profile page), but when **@user** is **nil** (as on the Home page) it sets **@user** to the current user. Note also that the following/follower counts are calculated through the associations using

```
@user.following.count
```

and

```
@user.followers.count
```

Compare these to the microposts count from Listing 11.23, where we wrote

```
@user.microposts.count
```

to count the microposts. As in that case, Rails calculates the count directly in the database for efficiency.

One final detail worth noting is the presence of CSS IDs on some elements, as in

```
<strong id="following" class="stat">
...
</strong>
```

They are provided for the benefit of the Ajax implementation in Section 12.2.5, which accesses elements on the page using their unique IDs.

With the partial in hand, including the statistics on the Home page is easy, as shown in Listing 12.17.

Listing 12.17 Adding follower statistics to the Home page.
app/views/static_pages/home.html.erb

```erb
<% if logged_in? %>
  <div class="row">
    <aside class="col-md-4">
      <section class="user_info">
        <%= render 'shared/user_info' %>
      </section>
      <section class="stats">
        <%= render 'shared/stats' %>
      </section>
      <section class="micropost_form">
        <%= render 'shared/micropost_form' %>
      </section>
    </aside>
    <div class="col-md-8">
      <h3>Micropost Feed</h3>
```

```
      <%= render 'shared/feed' %>
    </div>
  </div>
<% else %>
  .
  .
  .
<% end %>
```

To style the statistics, we'll add some SCSS, as shown in Listing 12.18 (which contains all the style sheet code needed in this chapter). The resulting Home page appears in Figure 12.11.

Listing 12.18 SCSS for the Home page sidebar.

app/assets/stylesheets/custom.css.scss

```scss
.
.
.
/* sidebar */
.
.
.
.gravatar {
  float: left;
  margin-right: 10px;
}

.gravatar_edit {
  margin-top: 15px;
}

.stats {
  overflow: auto;
  margin-top: 0;
  padding: 0;
  a {
    float: left;
    padding: 0 10px;
    border-left: 1px solid $gray-lighter;
    color: gray;
    &:first-child {
      padding-left: 0;
      border: 0;
    }
```

```
      &:hover {
        text-decoration: none;
        color: blue;
      }
    }
    strong {
      display: block;
    }
}

.user_avatars {
  overflow: auto;
  margin-top: 10px;
  .gravatar {
    margin: 1px 1px;
  }
  a {
    padding: 0;
  }
}

.users.follow {
  padding: 0;
}

/* forms */
    .
    .
    .
```

We'll render the stats partial on the profile page in a moment, but first let's make a partial for the follow/unfollow button, as shown in Listing 12.19.

Listing 12.19 A partial for a follow/unfollow form.
`app/views/users/_follow_form.html.erb`

```erb
<% unless current_user?(@user) %>
  <div id="follow_form">
  <% if current_user.following?(@user) %>
    <%= render 'unfollow' %>
  <% else %>
    <%= render 'follow' %>
  <% end %>
  </div>
<% end %>
```

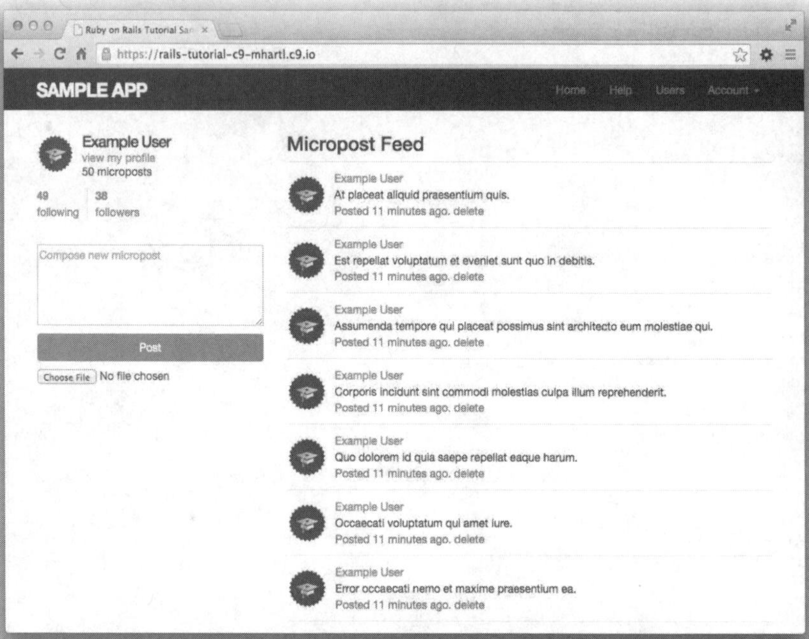

Figure 12.11   The Home page with follow statistics.

This code does nothing but defer the real work to the **follow** and **unfollow** partials, which need new routes for the Relationships resource, which follows the Microposts resource example (Listing 11.29), as seen in Listing 12.20.

Listing 12.20   Adding the routes for user relationships.
config/routes.rb

```
Rails.application.routes.draw do
  root                   'static_pages#home'
  get     'help'     => 'static_pages#help'
  get     'about'    => 'static_pages#about'
  get     'contact'  => 'static_pages#contact'
  get     'signup'   => 'users#new'
  get     'login'    => 'sessions#new'
```

```
post   'login'  => 'sessions#create'
delete 'logout' => 'sessions#destroy'
resources :users do
  member do
    get :following, :followers
  end
end
resources :account_activations, only: [:edit]
resources :password_resets,     only: [:new, :create, :edit, :update]
resources :microposts,          only: [:create, :destroy]
resources :relationships,       only: [:create, :destroy]
end
```

The follow/unfollow partials themselves are shown in Listing 12.21 and Listing 12.22.

Listing 12.21   A form for following a user.

app/views/users/_follow.html.erb

```
<%= form_for(current_user.active_relationships.build) do |f| %>
  <div><%= hidden_field_tag :followed_id, @user.id %></div>
  <%= f.submit "Follow", class: "btn btn-primary" %>
<% end %>
```

Listing 12.22   A form for unfollowing a user.

app/views/users/_unfollow.html.erb

```
<%= form_for(current_user.active_relationships.find_by(followed_id: @user.id),
             html: { method: :delete }) do |f| %>
  <%= f.submit "Unfollow", class: "btn" %>
<% end %>
```

Both of these forms use **form_for** to manipulate a Relationship model object; the main difference between the two is that Listing 12.21 builds a *new* relationship, whereas Listing 12.22 finds the existing relationship. Naturally, the former sends a POST request to the Relationships controller to **create** a relationship, while the latter sends a DELETE request to **destroy** a relationship. (We'll write these actions in Section 12.2.4.) Finally, note that the follow form doesn't have any content other than the button, but it still needs to send the **followed_id** to the controller. We accomplish this with the **hidden_field_tag** method in Listing 12.21, which produces HTML of the form

```
<input id="followed_id" name="followed_id" type="hidden" value="3" />
```

As we saw in Section 10.2.4 (Listing 10.49), the hidden **input** tag puts the relevant information on the page without displaying it in the browser.

   We can now include the follow form and the following statistics on the user profile page simply by rendering the partials, as shown in Listing 12.23. Profiles with follow and unfollow buttons, respectively, appear in Figure 12.12 and Figure 12.13.

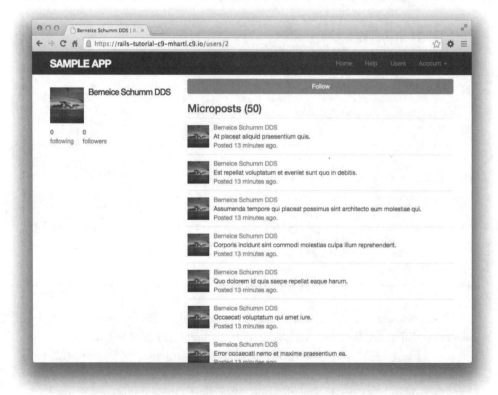

Figure 12.12 A user profile with a follow button (/users/2).

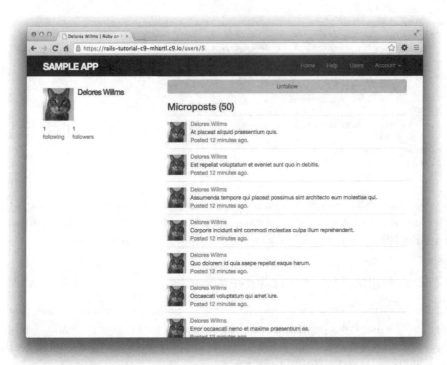

Figure 12.13 A user profile with an unfollow button (/users/5).

Listing 12.23 Adding the follow form and follower statistics to the user profile page.
app/views/users/show.html.erb

```
<% provide(:title, @user.name) %>
<div class="row">
  <aside class="col-md-4">
    <section>
      <h1>
        <%= gravatar_for @user %>
        <%= @user.name %>
      </h1>
    </section>
    <section class="stats">
      <%= render 'shared/stats' %>
    </section>
```

```
    </aside>
    <div class="col-md-8">
      <%= render 'follow_form' if logged_in? %>
      <% if @user.microposts.any? %>
        <h3>Microposts (<%= @user.microposts.count %>)</h3>
        <ol class="microposts">
          <%= render @microposts %>
        </ol>
        <%= will_paginate @microposts %>
      <% end %>
    </div>
</div>
```

We'll get these buttons working soon enough—in fact, we'll do it two ways, the standard way (Section 12.2.4) and using Ajax (Section 12.2.5). First, however, we'll finish the HTML interface by making the following and followers pages.

12.2.3 Following and Followers Pages

Pages to display followed users and followers will resemble a hybrid of the user profile page and the user index page (Section 9.3.1), with a sidebar of user information (including the following statistics) and a list of users. In addition, we'll include a raster of smaller user profile image links in the sidebar. Mockups matching these requirements appear in Figure 12.14 (following) and Figure 12.15 (followers).

Our first step is to get the following and followers links to work. We'll follow Twitter's lead and have both pages require user login. As with most previous examples of access control, we'll write the tests first, as shown in Listing 12.24.

Listing 12.24 Tests for the authorization of the following and followers pages. **RED**

test/controllers/users_controller_test.rb

```
require 'test_helper'

class UsersControllerTest < ActionController::TestCase

  def setup
    @user = users(:michael)
    @other_user = users(:archer)
  end
  .
  .
  .
```

```
test "should redirect following when not logged in" do
  get :following, id: @user
  assert_redirected_to login_url
end

test "should redirect followers when not logged in" do
  get :followers, id: @user
  assert_redirected_to login_url
end
end
```

The only tricky part of the implementation is realizing that we need to add two new actions to the Users controller. Based on the routes defined in Listing 12.15, we need to call them **following** and **followers**. Each action needs to set a title, find the user, retrieve either **@user.following** or **@user.followers** (in paginated form), and then render the page. The result appears in Listing 12.25.

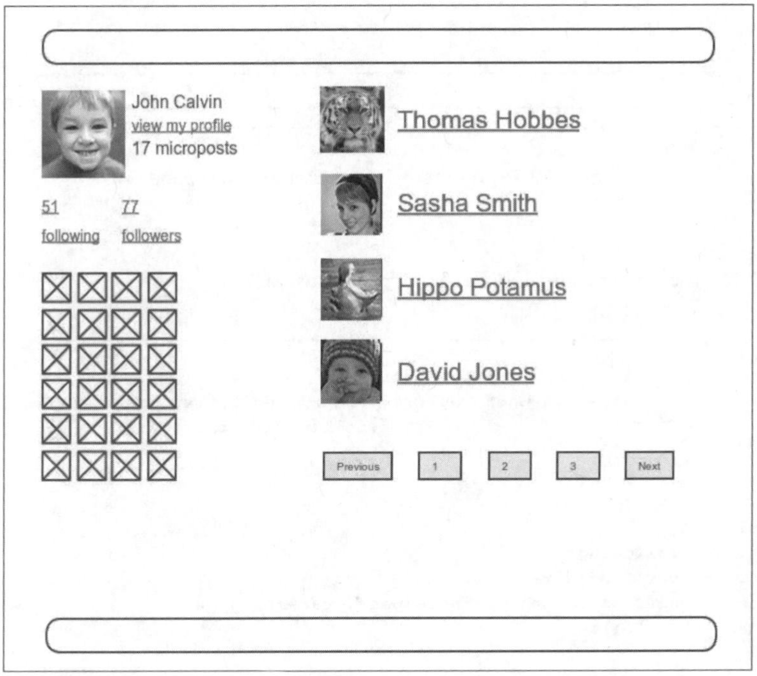

Figure 12.14 A mockup of the user following page.

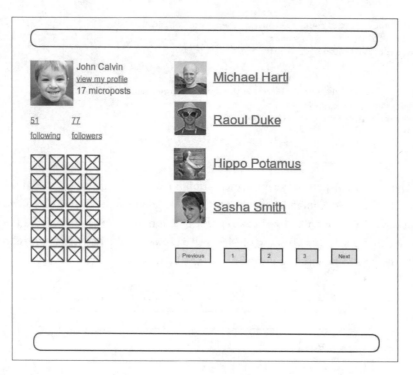

Figure 12.15 A mockup of the user followers page.

Listing 12.25 The **following** and **followers** actions. **RED**

app/controllers/users_controller.rb

```
class UsersController < ApplicationController
  before_action :logged_in_user, only: [:index, :edit, :update, :destroy,
                                        :following, :followers]
  .
  .
  .
  def following
    @title = "Following"
    @user  = User.find(params[:id])
    @users = @user.following.paginate(page: params[:page])
    render 'show_follow'
  end

  def followers
    @title = "Followers"
```

```
  @user  = User.find(params[:id])
  @users = @user.followers.paginate(page: params[:page])
  render 'show_follow'
end

private
  .
  .
  .
end
```

As we've seen throughout this tutorial, the usual Rails convention is to implicitly render the template corresponding to an action, such as rendering **show.html.erb** at the end of the **show** action. In contrast, both actions in Listing 12.25 make an *explicit* call to **render**—in this case, rendering a view called **show_follow**, which we must create. The reason for the common view is that the ERb is nearly identical for the two cases, and Listing 12.26 covers them both.

Listing 12.26   The **show_follow** view used to render following and followers. **GREEN**
app/views/users/show_follow.html.erb

```erb
<% provide(:title, @title) %>
<div class="row">
  <aside class="col-md-4">
    <section class="user_info">
      <%= gravatar_for @user %>
      <h1><%= @user.name %></h1>
      <span><%= link_to "view my profile", @user %></span>
      <span><b>Microposts:</b> <%= @user.microposts.count %></span>
    </section>
    <section class="stats">
      <%= render 'shared/stats' %>
      <% if @users.any? %>
        <div class="user_avatars">
          <% @users.each do |user| %>
            <%= link_to gravatar_for(user, size: 30), user %>
          <% end %>
        </div>
      <% end %>
    </section>
  </aside>
  <div class="col-md-8">
    <h3><%= @title %></h3>
    <% if @users.any? %>
```

```
    <ul class="users follow">
      <%= render @users %>
    </ul>
    <%= will_paginate %>
  <% end %>
  </div>
</div>
```

The actions in Listing 12.25 render the view from Listing 12.26 in two contexts, "following" and "followers," with the results shown in Figure 12.16 and Figure 12.17, respectively. Nothing in this code relies on the current user, however, so the same links work for other users, as shown in Figure 12.18.

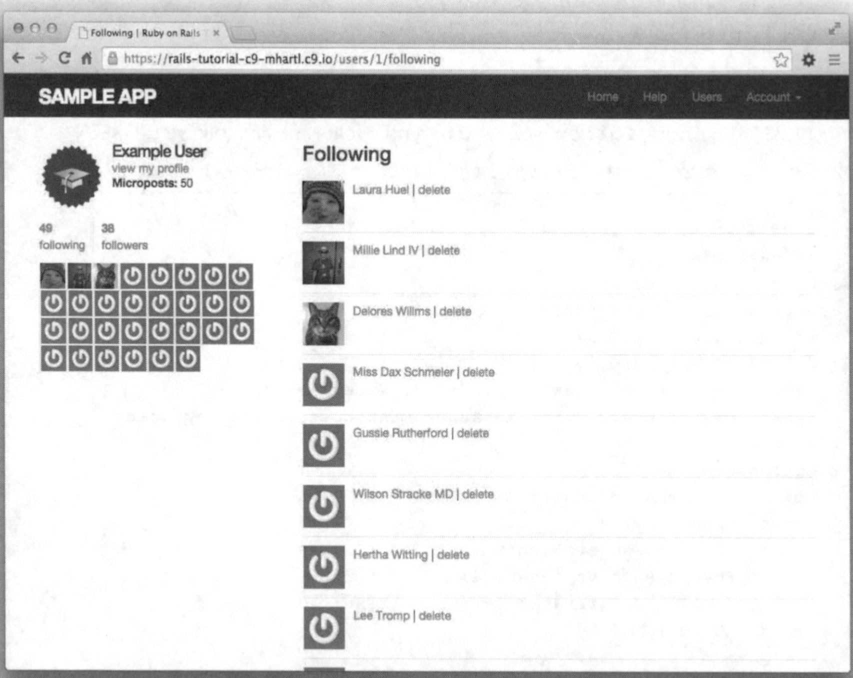

Figure 12.16 Showing the users the given user is following.

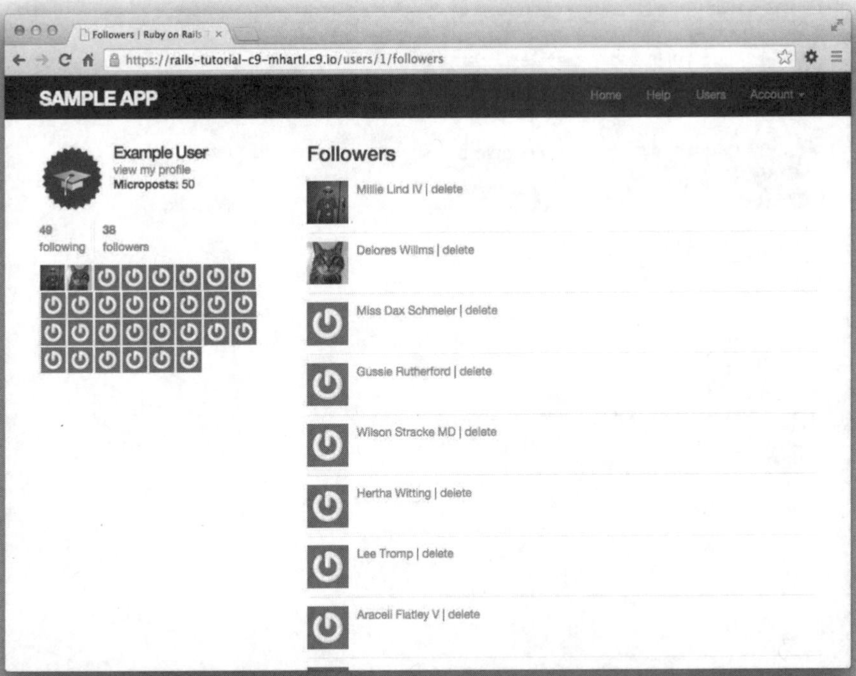

Figure 12.17 Showing the given user's followers.

Now that we have working following and followers pages, we'll write a couple of short integration tests to verify their behavior. They are designed to act as a sanity check, not to be comprehensive. Indeed, as noted in Section 5.3.4, comprehensive tests of things like HTML structure are likely to be brittle and thus counterproductive. Our plan in the case of following/followers pages is to check that the number is correctly displayed and that links with the right URLs appear on the page.

To get started, we'll generate an integration test as usual:

```
$ rails generate integration_test following
    invoke  test_unit
    create    test/integration/following_test.rb
```

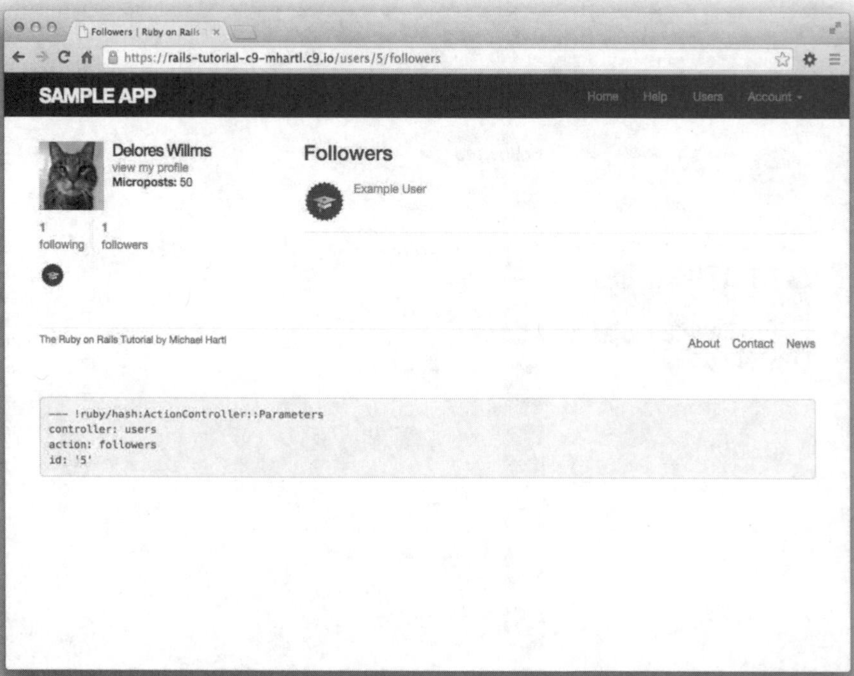

Figure 12.18 Showing a different user's followers.

Next, we need to assemble some test data, which we can do by adding some relationships fixtures to create following/follower relationships. Recall from Section 11.2.3 that we can use code like

```
orange:
  content: "I just ate an orange!"
  created_at: <%= 10.minutes.ago %>
  user: michael
```

to associate a micropost with a given user. In particular, we can write

```
user: michael
```

instead of

```
user_id: 1
```

Applying this idea to the relationships fixtures gives the associations in Listing 12.27.

Listing 12.27 Relationships fixtures for use in following/follower tests.
test/fixtures/relationships.yml

```
one:
  follower: michael
  followed: lana

two:
  follower: michael
  followed: mallory

three:
  follower: lana
  followed: michael

four:
  follower: archer
  followed: michael
```

The fixtures in Listing 12.27 first arrange for Michael to follow Lana and Mallory, and then arrange for Michael to be followed by Lana and Archer. To test for the right count, we can use the same **assert_match** method we used in Listing 11.27 to test for the display of the number of microposts on the user profile page. Adding in assertions for the right links yields the tests shown in Listing 12.28.

Listing 12.28 Tests for following/follower pages. **GREEN**
test/integration/following_test.rb

```
require 'test_helper'

class FollowingTest < ActionDispatch::IntegrationTest

  def setup
    @user = users(:michael)
```

```
    log_in_as(@user)
  end

  test "following page" do
    get following_user_path(@user)
    assert_not @user.following.empty?
    assert_match @user.following.count.to_s, response.body
    @user.following.each do |user|
      assert_select "a[href=?]", user_path(user)
    end
  end

  test "followers page" do
    get followers_user_path(@user)
    assert_not @user.followers.empty?
    assert_match @user.followers.count.to_s, response.body
    @user.followers.each do |user|
      assert_select "a[href=?]", user_path(user)
    end
  end
end
```

In Listing 12.28, note that we include the assertion

```
assert_not @user.following.empty?
```

which is included to make sure that

```
@user.following.each do |user|
  assert_select "a[href=?]", user_path(user)
end
```

isn't vacuously true (and similarly for followers).

The test suite should now be **GREEN**:

Listing 12.29 GREEN

```
$ bundle exec rake test
```

12.2.4   A Working Follow Button the Standard Way

Now that our views are in order, it's time to get the follow/unfollow buttons working. Because following and unfollowing involve creating and destroying relationships, we need a Relationships controller, which we generate as usual:

```
$ rails generate controller Relationships
```

As we'll see in Listing 12.31, enforcing access control on the Relationships controller actions won't much matter, but we'll still maintain our previous practice of enforcing the security model as early as possible. In particular, we'll check that attempts to access actions in the Relationships controller require a logged-in user (and thus get redirected to the login page), while also not changing the Relationship count, as shown in Listing 12.30.

Listing 12.30 Basic access control tests for relationships. **RED**
test/controllers/relationships_controller_test.rb

```
require 'test_helper'

class RelationshipsControllerTest < ActionController::TestCase

  test "create should require logged-in user" do
    assert_no_difference 'Relationship.count' do
      post :create
    end
    assert_redirected_to login_url
  end

  test "destroy should require logged-in user" do
    assert_no_difference 'Relationship.count' do
      delete :destroy, id: relationships(:one)
    end
    assert_redirected_to login_url
  end
end
```

We can get the tests in Listing 12.30 to pass by adding the `logged_in_user` before filter (Listing 12.31).

Listing 12.31 Access control for relationships. **GREEN**

app/controllers/relationships_controller.rb

```ruby
class RelationshipsController < ApplicationController
  before_action :logged_in_user

  def create
  end

  def destroy
  end
end
```

To get the follow and unfollow buttons to work, all we need to do is find the user associated with the **followed_id** in the corresponding form (i.e., Listing 12.21 or Listing 12.22), and then use the appropriate **follow** or **unfollow** method from Listing 12.10. The full implementation appears in Listing 12.32.

Listing 12.32 The Relationships controller.

app/controllers/relationships_controller.rb

```ruby
class RelationshipsController < ApplicationController
  before_action :logged_in_user

  def create
    user = User.find(params[:followed_id])
    current_user.follow(user)
    redirect_to user
  end

  def destroy
    user = Relationship.find(params[:id]).followed
    current_user.unfollow(user)
    redirect_to user
  end
end
```

We can see from Listing 12.32 why the security issue mentioned earlier is a minor one: If an unlogged-in user were to hit either action directly (e.g., using a command-line tool like **curl**), **current_user** would be **nil**. In both cases the action's second line would

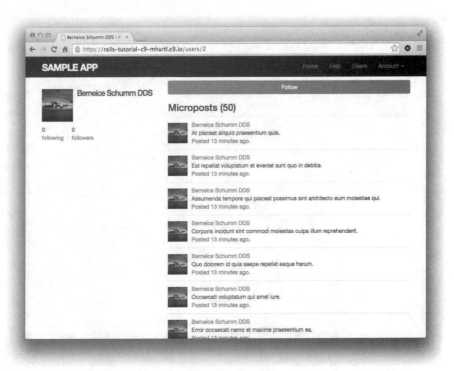

Figure 12.19   An unfollowed user.

raise an exception, resulting in an error but no harm to the application or its data. It's best not to rely on that behavior, though, so we've taken the extra step and added an extra layer of security.

With that, the core follow/unfollow functionality is complete, and any user can follow or unfollow any other user, as you can verify by clicking the corresponding buttons in your browser. (We'll write integration tests to verify this behavior in Section 12.2.6.) The result of following user #2 is shown in Figure 12.19 and Figure 12.20.

12.2.5 A Working Follow Button Created with Ajax

Although our user following implementation is complete as it stands, we have one bit of polish left to add before starting work on the status feed. You may have noticed in Section 12.2.4 that the `create` and `destroy` actions in the Relationships controller

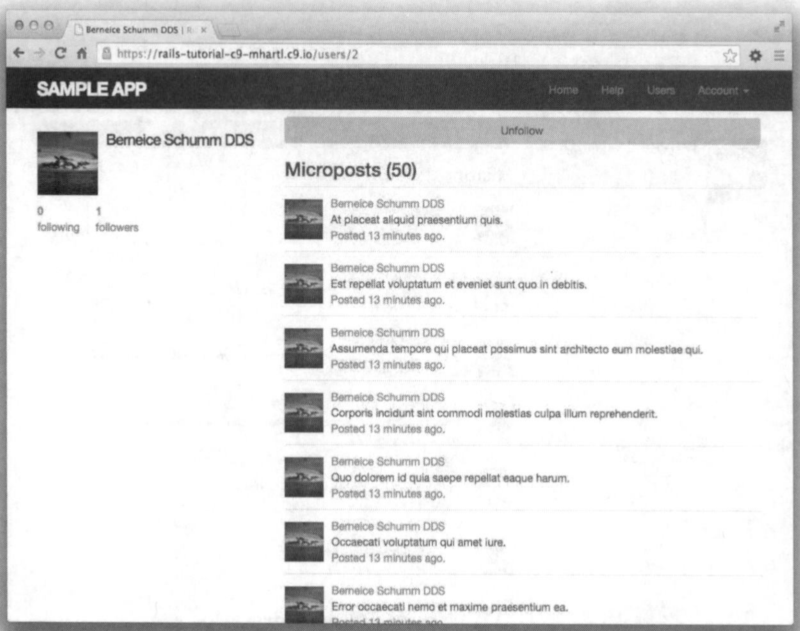

Figure 12.20 The result of following an unfollowed user.

simply redirect the user *back* to the original profile. In other words, a user starts on another user's profile page, follows the other user, and is immediately redirected back to the original page. It is reasonable to ask why the user needs to leave that page at all.

This is exactly the problem solved by *Ajax*, which allows web pages to send requests asynchronously to the server without leaving the page.[8] Because adding Ajax to web forms is a common practice, Rails makes Ajax easy to implement. Indeed, updating the follow/unfollow form partials is trivial: Just change

```
form_for
```

to

---

8. Because it is nominally an acronym for *asynchronous JavaScript and XML*, Ajax is sometimes misspelled "AJAX," even though the original Ajax article spells it as "Ajax" throughout.

```
form_for ..., remote: true
```

and Rails automagically uses Ajax. The updated partials appear in Listing 12.33 and Listing 12.34.

Listing 12.33   A form for following a user using Ajax.
app/views/users/_follow.html.erb

```
<%= form_for(current_user.active_relationships.build, remote: true) do |f| %>
  <div><%= hidden_field_tag :followed_id, @user.id %></div>
  <%= f.submit "Follow", class: "btn btn-primary" %>
<% end %>
```

Listing 12.34   A form for unfollowing a user using Ajax.
app/views/users/_unfollow.html.erb

```
<%= form_for(current_user.active_relationships.find_by(followed_id: @user.id),
            html: { method: :delete },
            remote: true) do |f| %>
  <%= f.submit "Unfollow", class: "btn" %>
<% end %>
```

The actual HTML generated by this ERb isn't particularly relevant. You might be curious, though, so here's a peek at a schematic view (details may differ):

```
<form action="/relationships/117" class="edit_relationship" data-remote="true"
    id="edit_relationship_117" method="post">
  .
  .
  .
</form>
```

This code sets the variable **data-remote="true"** inside the form tag, which tells Rails to allow the form to be handled by JavaScript. By using a simple HTML property instead of inserting the full JavaScript code (as in previous versions of Rails), Rails follows the philosophy of *unobtrusive JavaScript*.

Having updated the form, we now need to arrange for the Relationships controller to respond to Ajax requests. We can do this by using the **respond_to** method, responding appropriately depending on the type of request. The general pattern looks like this:

```
respond_to do |format|
  format.html { redirect_to user }
  format.js
end
```

The syntax is potentially confusing, and it's important to understand that in this code only *one* of the lines gets executed. (In this sense, `respond_to` is more like an `if-then-else` statement than a series of sequential lines.) Adapting the Relationships controller to respond to Ajax involves adding `respond_to` to the `create` and `destroy` actions from Listing 12.32. The result appears as in Listing 12.35. Notice the change from the local variable `user` to the instance variable `@user`; in Listing 12.32 there was no need for an instance variable, but now such a variable is necessary for use in Listing 12.33 and Listing 12.34.

Listing 12.35   Responding to Ajax requests in the Relationships controller.
app/controllers/relationships_controller.rb

```
class RelationshipsController < ApplicationController
  before_action :logged_in_user

  def create
    @user = User.find(params[:followed_id])
    current_user.follow(@user)
    respond_to do |format|
      format.html { redirect_to @user }
      format.js
    end
  end

  def destroy
    @user = Relationship.find(params[:id]).followed
    current_user.unfollow(@user)
    respond_to do |format|
      format.html { redirect_to @user }
      format.js
    end
  end
end
```

The actions in Listing 12.35 degrade gracefully, which means that they work fine in browsers that have JavaScript disabled (although a small amount of configuration is necessary, as shown in Listing 12.36).

Listing 12.36 Configuration needed for graceful degradation of form submission.
config/application.rb

```
require File.expand_path('../boot', __FILE__)
  .
  .
  .
module SampleApp
  class Application < Rails::Application
    .
    .
    .
    # Include the authenticity token in remote forms.
    config.action_view.embed_authenticity_token_in_remote_forms = true
  end
end
```

On the other hand, we have yet to respond properly when JavaScript is enabled. In the case of an Ajax request, Rails automatically calls a *JavaScript embedded Ruby* (`.js.erb`) file with the same name as the action (i.e., `create.js.erb` or `destroy.js.erb`). As you might guess, such files allow us to mix JavaScript and embedded Ruby to perform actions on the current page. It is these files that we need to create and edit in order to update the user profile page upon being followed or unfollowed.

Inside a JS-ERb file, Rails automatically provides the jQuery JavaScript helpers to manipulate the page using the Document Object Model (DOM). The jQuery library (which we saw briefly in Section 11.4.2) provides a large number of methods for manipulating the DOM, but here we will need only two. First, we will need to know about the dollar-sign syntax to access a DOM element based on its unique CSS ID. For example, to manipulate the `follow_form` element, we will use the syntax

```
$("#follow_form")
```

(Recall from Listing 12.19 that this is a `div` that wraps the form, not the form itself.) This syntax, inspired by CSS, uses the `#` symbol to indicate a CSS ID. As you might guess, jQuery, like CSS, uses a dot `.` to manipulate CSS classes.

The second method we'll need is **html**, which updates the HTML inside the relevant element with the contents of its argument. For example, to replace the entire follow form with the string **"foobar"**, we would write

```
$("#follow_form").html("foobar")
```

Unlike plain JavaScript files, JS-ERb files allow the use of embedded Ruby, which we apply in the **create.js.erb** file to update the follow form with the **unfollow** partial (which is what should be displayed after a successful following) and update the follower count. The result is shown in Listing 12.37. This uses the **escape_javascript** method, which is needed to escape out the result when inserting HTML in a JavaScript file.

Listing 12.37 The JavaScript embedded Ruby to create a following relationship.
app/views/relationships/create.js.erb

```
$("#follow_form").html("<%= escape_javascript(render('users/unfollow')) %>")
$("#followers").html('<%= @user.followers.count %>')
```

The **destroy.js.erb** file is analogous (Listing 12.38).

Listing 12.38 The Ruby JavaScript (RJS) to destroy a following relationship.
app/views/relationships/destroy.js.erb

```
$("#follow_form").html("<%= escape_javascript(render('users/follow')) %>")
$("#followers").html('<%= @user.followers.count %>')
```

With that, you should navigate to a user profile page and verify that you can follow and unfollow without a page refresh.

12.2.6 Following Tests

Now that the follow buttons are working, we'll write some simple tests to prevent regressions. To follow a user, we post to the relationships path and verify that the number of followed users increases by 1:

```
assert_difference '@user.following.count', 1 do
  post relationships_path, followed_id: @other.id
end
```

This tests the standard implementation, but testing the Ajax version is almost the same, with **xhr :post** in place of plain **post**:

```
assert_difference '@user.following.count', 1 do
  xhr :post, relationships_path, followed_id: @other.id
end
```

This uses the **xhr** method (for XmlHttpRequest) to issue an Ajax request, which causes the **respond_to** block in Listing 12.35 to execute the proper JavaScript method.

The same parallel structure applies to deleting users, with **delete** instead of **post**. Here we check that the followed user count goes down by 1 and include the relationship and the followed user's ID:

```
assert_difference '@user.following.count', -1 do
  delete relationship_path(relationship),
         relationship: relationship.id
end
```

and

```
assert_difference '@user.following.count', -1 do
  xhr :delete, relationship_path(relationship),
               relationship: relationship.id
end
```

Putting the two cases together gives the tests in Listing 12.39.

Listing 12.39   Tests for the follow and unfollow buttons. **GREEN**
test/integration/following_test.rb

```
require 'test_helper'

class FollowingTest < ActionDispatch::IntegrationTest
```

```
def setup
  @user  = users(:michael)
  @other = users(:archer)
  log_in_as(@user)
end
  .
  .
  .
test "should follow a user the standard way" do
  assert_difference '@user.following.count', 1 do
    post relationships_path, followed_id: @other.id
  end
end

test "should follow a user with Ajax" do
  assert_difference '@user.following.count', 1 do
    xhr :post, relationships_path, followed_id: @other.id
  end
end

test "should unfollow a user the standard way" do
  @user.follow(@other)
  relationship = @user.active_relationships.find_by(followed_id: @other.id)
  assert_difference '@user.following.count', -1 do
    delete relationship_path(relationship)
  end
end

test "should unfollow a user with Ajax" do
  @user.follow(@other)
  relationship = @user.active_relationships.find_by(followed_id: @other.id)
  assert_difference '@user.following.count', -1 do
    xhr :delete, relationship_path(relationship)
  end
end
end
```

At this point, the tests should be **GREEN**:

Listing 12.40 GREEN

```
$ bundle exec rake test
```

12.3 The Status Feed

We come now to the pinnacle of our sample application: the status feed of microposts. Appropriately, this section contains some of the most advanced material in the entire tutorial. The full status feed builds on the proto-feed from Section 11.3.3 by assembling an array of the microposts from the users being followed by the current user, along with the current user's own microposts. Throughout this section, we'll proceed through a series of feed implementations of increasing sophistication. To accomplish this, we will need some fairly advanced Rails, Ruby, and even SQL programming techniques.

Because of the heavy lifting ahead, it's especially important to review where we're going. A recap of the final status feed, shown in Figure 12.5, appears in Figure 12.21.

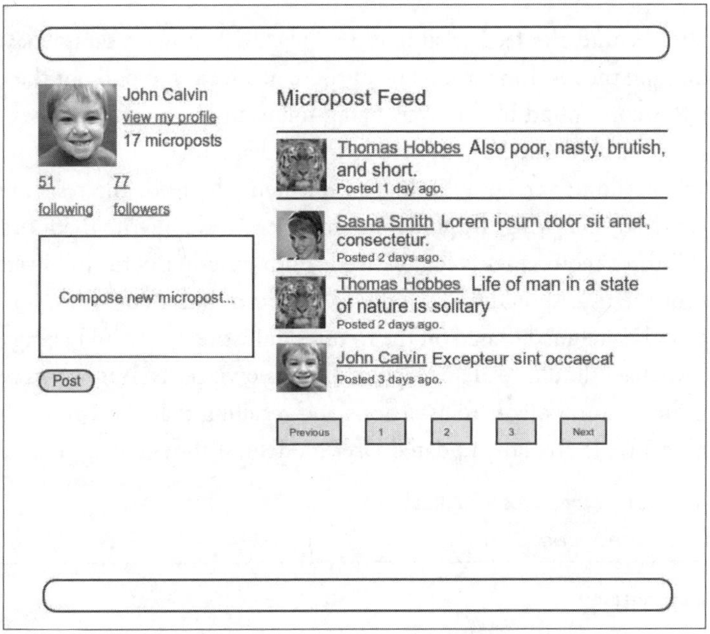

Figure 12.21 A mockup of a user's Home page with a status feed.

microposts		
id	content	user_id
1	...	1
2	...	2
3	...	4
4	...	7
5	...	1
6	...	18
7	...	8
8	...	9
9	...	10
10	...	2

user.feed

1	...	1
2	...	2
4	...	7
5	...	1
7	...	8
9	...	10
10	...	2

Figure 12.22 The feed for a user (ID 1) following users with IDs 2, 7, 8, and 10.

12.3.1 Motivation and Strategy

The basic idea behind the feed is simple. Figure 12.22 shows a sample `microposts` database table and the resulting feed. The purpose of a feed is to pull out the microposts whose user IDs correspond to the users being followed by the current user (as well as the current user), as indicated by the arrows in the diagram.

Although we don't yet know how to implement the feed, the tests are relatively straightforward, so (following the guidelines in Box 3.3) we'll write them first. The key is to check all three requirements for the feed: Both microposts for followed users and microposts for the user should be included in the feed, but a post from an *unfollowed* user should not be included. Based on the fixtures in Listing 9.43 and Listing 11.51, this means that Michael should see Lana's posts and his own posts, but not Archer's posts. Converting these requirements to assertions and recalling that the `feed` is in the User model (Listing 11.44) gives the updated User model test shown in Listing 12.41.

Listing 12.41 A test for the status feed. **RED**

test/models/user_test.rb

```
require 'test_helper'

class UserTest < ActiveSupport::TestCase
    .
    .
    .
  test "feed should have the right posts" do
    michael = users(:michael)
    archer  = users(:archer)
    lana    = users(:lana)
```

```
  # Posts from followed user
  lana.microposts.each do |post_following|
    assert michael.feed.include?(post_following)
  end
  # Posts from self
  michael.microposts.each do |post_self|
    assert michael.feed.include?(post_self)
  end
  # Posts from unfollowed user
  archer.microposts.each do |post_unfollowed|
    assert_not michael.feed.include?(post_unfollowed)
  end
 end
end
```

Of course, the current implementation is just a proto-feed, so the new test is initially **RED**:

Listing 12.42   RED

```
$ bundle exec rake test
```

12.3.2   A First Feed Implementation

With the status feed design requirements captured in the test from Listing 12.41, we're ready to start writing the feed. Since the final feed implementation is rather intricate, we'll build up to it by introducing one piece at a time. The first step is to think of the kind of query we'll need. We need to select all the microposts from the **microposts** table with IDs corresponding to the users being followed by a given user (or the user itself). We might write this schematically as follows:

```
SELECT * FROM microposts
WHERE user_id IN (<list of ids>) OR user_id = <user id>
```

In writing this code, we've guessed that SQL supports an **IN** keyword that allows us to test for set inclusion. (Happily, it does.)

Recall from the proto-feed in Section 11.3.3 that Active Record uses the **where** method to accomplish the kind of select shown here, as illustrated in Listing 11.44.

There, our select was very simple—we just picked out all the microposts with a user ID corresponding to the current user:

```
Micropost.where("user_id = ?", id)
```

Here, we expect the select to be more complicated, something like this:

```
Micropost.where("user_id IN (?) OR user_id = ?", following_ids, id)
```

We see from these conditions that we'll need an array of IDs corresponding to the users being followed. One way to do this is to use Ruby's **map** method, available on any "enumerable" object—that is, any object (such as an Array or a Hash) that consists of a collection of elements.[9] We saw an example of this method in Section 4.3.2. As another example, we'll use **map** to convert an array of integers to an array of strings:

```
$ rails console
>> [1, 2, 3, 4].map { |i| i.to_s }
=> ["1", "2", "3", "4"]
```

Situations like this one, illustrated above, where the same method gets called on each element in the collection, are common enough that there's a shorthand notation for it (seen briefly in Section 4.3.2) that uses an *ampersand* **&** and a symbol corresponding to the method:

```
>> [1, 2, 3, 4].map(&:to_s)
=> ["1", "2", "3", "4"]
```

Using the **join** method (Section 4.3.1), we can create a string composed of the IDs by joining them with a comma and space:

```
>> [1, 2, 3, 4].map(&:to_s).join(', ')
=> "1, 2, 3, 4"
```

---

9. The main requirement is that enumerable objects must implement an **each** method to iterate through the collection.

We can use this method to construct the necessary array of followed user IDs by calling `id` on each element in `user.following`. For example, for the first user in the database, this array appears as follows:

```
>> User.first.following.map(&:id)
=> [4, 5, 6, 7, 8, 9, 10, 11, 12, 13, 14, 15, 16, 17, 18, 19, 20, 21, 22, 23,
24, 25, 26, 27, 28, 29, 30, 31, 32, 33, 34, 35, 36, 37, 38, 39, 40, 41, 42,
43, 44, 45, 46, 47, 48, 49, 50, 51]
```

In fact, because this sort of construction is so useful, Active Record provides it by default:

```
>> User.first.following_ids
=> [4, 5, 6, 7, 8, 9, 10, 11, 12, 13, 14, 15, 16, 17, 18, 19, 20, 21, 22, 23,
24, 25, 26, 27, 28, 29, 30, 31, 32, 33, 34, 35, 36, 37, 38, 39, 40, 41, 42,
43, 44, 45, 46, 47, 48, 49, 50, 51]
```

Here the `following_ids` method is synthesized by Active Record based on the `has_many :following` association (Listing 12.8); the result is that we need only append `_ids` to the association name to get the IDs corresponding to the `user.following` collection. A string of followed user IDs then appears as follows:

```
>> User.first.following_ids.join(', ')
=> "4, 5, 6, 7, 8, 9, 10, 11, 12, 13, 14, 15, 16, 17, 18, 19, 20, 21, 22, 23,
24, 25, 26, 27, 28, 29, 30, 31, 32, 33, 34, 35, 36, 37, 38, 39, 40, 41, 42,
43, 44, 45, 46, 47, 48, 49, 50, 51"
```

When inserting into an SQL string, though, you don't need to do this. Instead, the `?` interpolation takes care of it for you (and, in fact, eliminates some database-dependent incompatibilities). This means we can use `following_ids` by itself.

As a result, the initial guess of

```
Micropost.where("user_id IN (?) OR user_id = ?", following_ids, id)
```

actually works! The result appears in Listing 12.43.

Listing 12.43 The initial working feed. **GREEN**

app/models/user.rb

```
class User < ActiveRecord::Base
  .
  .
  .
  # Returns true if a password reset has expired.
  def password_reset_expired?
    reset_sent_at < 2.hours.ago
  end

  # Returns a user's status feed.
  def feed
    Micropost.where("user_id IN (?) OR user_id = ?", following_ids, id)
  end

  # Follows a user.
  def follow(other_user)
    active_relationships.create(followed_id: other_user.id)
  end
  .
  .
  .
end
```

The test suite should be **GREEN**:

Listing 12.44 GREEN

```
$ bundle exec rake test
```

In some applications, this initial implementation might be good enough for most practical purposes, but Listing 12.43 isn't the final implementation. See if you can guess why not before moving on to the next section. (*Hint*: What if a user is following 5000 other users?)

12.3.3 Subselects

As hinted at in the last section, the feed implementation in Section 12.3.2 doesn't scale well when the number of microposts in the feed is large, as would likely happen if a user were following, say, 5000 other users. In this section, we'll reimplement the status feed in a way that scales better with the number of followed users.

The problem with the code in Section 12.3.2 is that `following_ids` pulls *all* of the followed users' IDs into memory, and creates an array the full length of the followed users array. Because the condition in Listing 12.43 actually just checks inclusion in a set, there must be a more efficient way to do this—and indeed SQL is optimized for just such set operations. The solution involves pushing the finding of followed user IDs into the database using a *subselect*.

We'll start by refactoring the feed with the slightly modified code in Listing 12.45.

Listing 12.45 Using key-value pairs in the feed's **where** method. **GREEN**
app/models/user.rb

```
class User < ActiveRecord::Base
  .
  .
  .
  # Returns a user's status feed.
  def feed
    Micropost.where("user_id IN (:following_ids) OR user_id = :user_id",
                    following_ids: following_ids, user_id: id)
  end
  .
  .
  .
end
```

As preparation for the next step, we have replaced

```
Micropost.where("user_id IN (?) OR user_id = ?", following_ids, id)
```

with the equivalent

```
Micropost.where("user_id IN (:following_ids) OR user_id = :user_id",
                following_ids: following_ids, user_id: id)
```

The question mark syntax is fine, but when we want the *same* variable inserted in more than one place, the second syntax is more convenient.

The preceding discussion implies that we will be adding a *second* occurrence of **user_id** in the SQL query. In particular, we can replace the Ruby code

```
following_ids
```

with the SQL snippet

```
following_ids = "SELECT followed_id FROM relationships
                 WHERE  follower_id = :user_id"
```

This code contains an SQL subselect, and internally the entire select for user 1 would look something like this:

```
SELECT * FROM microposts
WHERE user_id IN (SELECT followed_id FROM relationships
                  WHERE  follower_id = 1)
    OR user_id = 1
```

This subselect arranges for all the set logic to be pushed into the database, which is more efficient.

With this foundation, we are ready for a more efficient feed implementation, as seen in Listing 12.46. Note that, because it is now raw SQL, **following_ids** string is *interpolated*, not escaped.

Listing 12.46 The final implementation of the feed. **GREEN**
app/models/user.rb

```
class User < ActiveRecord::Base
  .
  .
  .
  # Returns a user's status feed.
  def feed
    following_ids = "SELECT followed_id FROM relationships
                     WHERE  follower_id = :user_id"
    Micropost.where("user_id IN (#{following_ids})
                     OR user_id = :user_id", user_id: id)
  end
```

```
   .
   .
   .
end
```

This code has a formidable combination of Rails, Ruby, and SQL, but it does the job, and does it well:

Listing 12.47 GREEN

```
$ bundle exec rake test
```

Of course, even the subselect won't scale forever. For bigger sites, you would probably need to generate the feed asynchronously using a background job, but such scaling subtleties are beyond the scope of this tutorial.

With the code in Listing 12.46, our status feed is now complete. Recall from Section 11.3.3 that the Home page already includes the feed; as a reminder, the **home** action appears again in Listing 12.48. In Chapter 11, the result was only a proto-feed (Figure 11.14), but with the implementation in Listing 12.46 as seen in Figure 12.23 the Home page now shows the full feed.

Listing 12.48 The **home** action with a paginated feed.
app/controllers/static_pages_controller.rb

```
class StaticPagesController < ApplicationController

  def home
    if logged_in?
      @micropost  = current_user.microposts.build
      @feed_items = current_user.feed.paginate(page: params[:page])
    end
  end
   .
   .
   .
end
```

At this point, we're ready to merge our changes into the master branch:

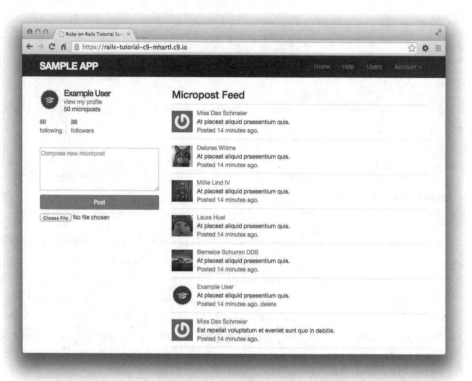

Figure 12.23 The Home page with a working status feed.

```
$ bundle exec rake test
$ git add -A
$ git commit -m "Add user following"
$ git checkout master
$ git merge following-users
```

We can then push the code to the remote repository and deploy the application to production:

```
$ git push
$ git push heroku
$ heroku pg:reset DATABASE
$ heroku run rake db:migrate
$ heroku run rake db:seed
```

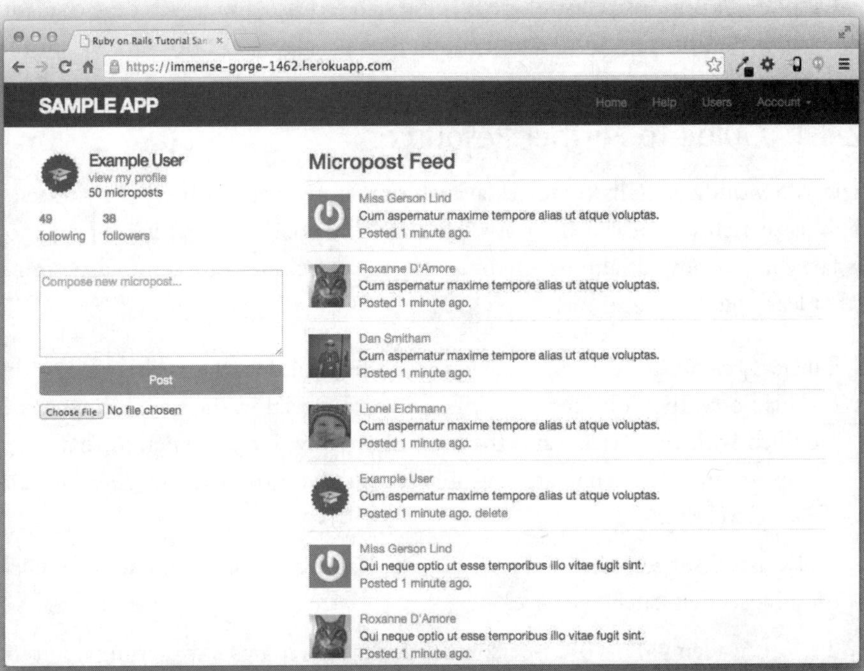

Figure 12.24 A working status feed on the live web.

The result is a working status feed on the live web (Figure 12.24).

12.4 Conclusion

With the addition of the status feed, we've finished the sample application for the *Ruby on Rails*™ *Tutorial*. This application includes examples of all the major features of Rails, including models, views, controllers, templates, partials, filters, validations, callbacks, `has_many`/`belongs_to` and `has_many :through` associations, security, testing, and deployment.

Despite this impressive list, there is still much to learn about web development. As a first step in this process, this section contains some suggestions for further learning.

12.4.1 Guide to Further Resources

There is a wealth of Rails resources available in stores and on the web—indeed, the supply is so rich that it can be overwhelming. The good news is that, having gotten this far, you're ready for almost anything else out there. Here are some suggestions for further learning:

- The *Ruby on Rails*™ *Tutorial* screencasts: I offer a full-length screencast course based on this book. In addition to covering all the material in the book, the screencasts are filled with tips, tricks, and the kind of see-how-it's-done demos that are hard to capture in print. They are available for purchase through the *Ruby on Rails*™ *Tutorial* website.

- RailsCasts: I suggest starting by visiting the RailsCasts episode archive and clicking on subjects that catch your eye.

- Tealeaf Academy: Lots of in-person developer bootcamps have sprung up in recent years, and I recommend looking for one in your area. Tealeaf Academy is available online, however, so it can be accessed from anywhere. Tealeaf is an especially good choice if you want instructor feedback within the context of a structured curriculum.

- The Turing School of Software Design: A full-time, 27-week Ruby/Rails/JavaScript training program in Denver, Colorado. Most of their students start with limited programming experience but have the determination and drive needed to pick it up quickly. Turing guarantees its students will find a job after graduating or they'll refund the cost of tuition. Rails Tutorial readers can get a $500 discount using the code RAILSTUTORIAL500.

- Thinkful: An online class that pairs you with a professional engineer as you work through a project-based curriculum. Subjects include Ruby on Rails, front-end development, web design, and data science.

- Pragmatic Studio: Online Ruby and Rails courses from Mike and Nicole Clark.

- RailsApps: Instructive sample Rails apps.

- Code School: A large variety of interactive programming courses.

- Bala Paranj's Test Driven Development in Ruby: A more advanced online course focusing on TDD in pure Ruby.

- Ruby and Rails books: For further Ruby learning, I recommend *Beginning Ruby* by Peter Cooper, *The Well-Grounded Rubyist* by David A. Black, *Eloquent Ruby* by Russ Olsen, and *The Ruby Way* by Hal Fulton. For further Rails learning, I recommend *Agile Web Development with Rails* by Sam Ruby, Dave Thomas, and David Heinemeier Hansson; *The Rails 4 Way* by Obie Fernandez and Kevin Faustino; and *Rails 4 in Action* by Ryan Bigg and Yehuda Katz.

12.4.2 What We Learned in This Chapter

- Rails' `has_many :through` allows the modeling of complicated data relationships.

- The `has_many` method takes several optional arguments, including the object class name and the foreign key.

- Using `has_many` and `has_many :through` with properly chosen class names and foreign keys, we can model both active (following) and passive (being followed) relationships.

- Rails routing supports nested routes.

- The `where` method is a flexible and powerful way to create database queries.

- Rails supports issuing lower-level SQL queries if needed.

- By putting together everything we've learned in this book, we've successfully implemented user following with a status feed of microposts from followed users.

12.5 Exercises

Note: To receive a copy of the *Solutions Manual for Exercises*, with solutions to every exercise in the *Ruby on Rails*™ *Tutorial*, visit www.railstutorial.org/<word>, where "<word>" is the last word of the Figure 3.9 caption.

For a suggestion on how to avoid conflicts between exercises and the main tutorial, see the note on exercise topic branches in Section 3.6.

1. Write tests for the statistics on the Home and profile pages. *Hint*: Add to the test in Listing 11.27. (Why don't we have to test the statistics on the Home page separately?)

2. Write a test to verify that the first page of the feed appears on the Home page as required. A template appears in Listing 12.49. Note the use of HTML escaping via `CGI.escapeHTML`; see if you can figure out why this is necessary. (Try removing the escaping and carefully inspect the page source for the micropost content that doesn't match.)

Listing 12.49   Testing the feed HTML. **GREEN**

test/integration/following_test.rb

```
require 'test_helper'

class FollowingTest < ActionDispatch::IntegrationTest

  def setup
    @user = users(:michael)
    log_in_as(@user)
  end
  .
  .
  .
  test "feed on Home page" do
    get root_path
    @user.feed.paginate(page: 1).each do |micropost|
      assert_match CGI.escapeHTML(FILL_IN), FILL_IN
    end
  end
end
```

Index

Note: Page numbers in *italics* indicate figures, those with *t* indicate tables, and those with n indicate footnotes.

inform**IT**.com

Learn**IT** at Inform**IT**

Looking for a book, eBook, or training video on a new technology? Seeking timely and relevant information and tutorials. Looking for expert opinions, advice, and tips? **InformIT has a solution**.

- Learn about new releases and special promotions by subscribing to a wide variety of monthly newsletters. Visit **informit.com/newsletters**.

- FREE Podcasts from experts at **informit.com/podcasts**.

- Read the latest author articles and sample chapters at **informit.com/articles**.

- Access thousands of books and videos in the Safari Books Online digital library. **safari.informit.com**.

- Get Advice and tips from expert blogs at **informit.com/blogs**.

Visit **informit.com** to find out all the ways you can access the hottest technology content.

Are you part of the **IT** crowd?

Connect with Pearson authors and editors via RSS feeds, Facebook, Twitter, YouTube and more! Visit **informit.com/socialconnect**.